*Major Problems
in the History
of the American West*

MAJOR PROBLEMS IN AMERICAN HISTORY SERIES

GENERAL EDITOR

THOMAS G. PATERSON

Major Problems
in the History
of the American West

DOCUMENTS AND ESSAYS

SECOND EDITION

EDITED BY

CLYDE A. MILNER II
UTAH STATE UNIVERSITY

ANNE M. BUTLER
UTAH STATE UNIVERSITY

DAVID RICH LEWIS
UTAH STATE UNIVERSITY

HOUGHTON MIFFLIN COMPANY   Boston   New York

Address editorial correspondence to:

Houghton Mifflin Company
College Division
222 Berkeley Street
Boston, MA 02116-3764

Editor-in-Chief: Jean L. Woy
Senior Associate Editor: Frances Gay
Associate Project Editor: Magdalena Hernandez
Associate Production/Design Coordinator: Deborah Frydman
Electronic Production Supervisor: Irene V. Cinelli
Director of Manufacturing: Michael O'Dea

Cover design: Alwyn Velásquez, Lapis Design.
Cover art: Thomas Hart Benton, *Boom Town,* Memorial Art Gallery of the University
of Rochester, Marion Stratton Gould Fund.

Printed in the U.S.A.

Library of Congress Catalog Card Number: 96-77445

ISBN: 0-669-41580-4

6 7 8 9-MP-08 07 06 05 04

To our friends and mentors in western history
Allan G. Bogue
Howard R. Lamar
Douglas D. Martin
Floyd A. O'Neil
Charles S. Peterson
and
Glenda Riley

Preface

In recent years, new scholarship and energetic debates have become hall-marks of writing about the American West. So much interesting work has appeared that the first edition of *Major Problems in the History of the American West,* published in 1989, already seems the product of an earlier era, before the boom times started. We remain fondly attached to the selections published in the first edition, but we are pleased to be able to incorporate a good sampling of the new scholarship and current debates in this second edition. Despite the positive reception for the first edition, we also learned from many instructors that it was too long, especially for a one-quarter or even a one-semester course. Therefore, we faced the task of reducing the number of pages significantly, while at the same time adding more entries for the twentieth century and including new research into other topics in western history.

Our approach to this challenge involved both structural and conceptual adjustments. We conceived of the second edition as a volume that could expand on themes stressed in some of the newer studies of the West. In this way, we see our collection as truly *supplementary* reading for students. We know that some topics are so well established that they must be examined even if they do not appear in a book such as ours. For example, the impact of the California Gold Rush, the development of the cattle industry, the era of territorial politics, and the significance of World War II are all core stories in the history of the American West. References to these and other vital topics are not absent from our volume, but they are not given the full examination that we know occurs in many courses. We also changed the structure for this edition by limiting each chapter to only two essays. In many ways this limitation was as difficult as the conceptual decision about topical coverage. So much excellent scholarship has appeared in recent years that a book which reprints only thirty essays is a brief sampling of the riches available to readers. Fortunately, our updated suggested readings at the end of each chapter are good guides to recent scholarship as well as to some classic studies.

An examination of the table of contents for the second edition shows the topics, essays, and documents that we added to the collection. Twenty-seven of the thirty essays and sixty-nine of the one hundred documents did not appear in the first edition. With so much new material in this volume, the themes for the chapters also are significantly modified. We've expanded the consideration of environmental topics and of social history. Gender and labor issues are highlighted in several chapters. The significance of the West's diverse population becomes evident in many of the documents and essays; Native Americans, African Americans, Mexican Americans, and immigrants from Asia and Europe have played vital roles in aspects of the region's history. Other chapters demonstrate the importance of the actions and policies of the federal government in both the nineteenth and twentieth centuries.

Our book begins with the disparate, sometimes heated, attempts by historians to define the West and its history. The chapters then follow a chronological path from the era of Spanish colonial settlement to recent political debates over federal control of public lands. Our final chapter traces the impact of popular culture and how it has presented the West to a worldwide audience.

Like other volumes in this series, *Major Problems in the History of the American West* presents two key sources for historical understanding—primary documents and the writings of scholars. Readers are invited to consider diverse viewpoints in the primary sources and different interpretations by scholars. The selected documents and essays are meant to stimulate independent thinking about historical topics. We chose some essays because of their provocative insights, which we hope will stimulate discussion and further reading. We also selected some documents that present firsthand the kind of evidence that can lead to a different assessment than what appears in the accompanying essays. Chapter introductions and headnotes for the documents and essays place the readings in historical context and pose questions for further consideration. After studying the full contents of this collection, we hope our readers will see that the history of the American West, like the region itself, is big, important, and complex. The West, its people, and their histories deserve extended study.

We are pleased that the first edition, edited by Clyde Milner alone, has been so well received. For the second edition, he has been joined by two co-editors who are not only colleagues in the history department at Utah State University but also fellow editors at the *Western Historical Quarterly*. Anne Butler and David Lewis have brought fresh perspectives to the collaboration, and the quality of their contributions is evident in this second edition. Each editor took the lead in selecting the documents and essays and in writing the introduction for a set of five chapters. Clyde Milner was responsible for Chapters 1, 2, 4, 5, and 6. David Lewis oversaw Chapters 3, 10, 11, 12, and 14. Anne Butler organized Chapters 7, 8, 9, 13, and 15.

Barbara Stewart, the executive manager of the *Western Historical Quarterly,* coordinated mailings and other communications. Ona Siporin, the *Quarterly*'s assistant editor, tried to improve our writing. Todd Anderson, Jared Farmer, and Heather Kellogg, all students at Utah State University, assisted our efforts by finding the exact photographs, documents, and essays that we wished to examine. They also compiled an extensive list of titles for our suggested readings. Kevin Hatfield, James Feldman, and Kelly May, all graduates of our master's program in history, provided important materials for the document sections.

Our colleagues in history departments across the country have suggested improvements regularly since the first edition appeared. Special thanks are owed to Gary Okihiro at Cornell, Donald Fixico at Western

Michigan, Paul Hutton at the University of New Mexico, John Findlay at the University of Washington, Stephen Aron at UCLA, William Robbins at Oregon State, Mary Murphy at Montana State, William Cronon at the University of Wisconsin, Michael Tate at the University of Nebraska at Omaha, and David Gutiérrez at the University of California, San Diego.

Detailed and extremely helpful written reviews of draft tables of contents were also provided by John Findlay, University of Washington; Donald Fixico, Western Michigan University; Robert Goldberg, University of Utah; Emily Greenwald, University of Nebraska, Lincoln; Mark Harvey, North Dakota State University; Darlis Miller, New Mexico State University; Mary Murphy, Montana State University; Gary Okihiro, Cornell University; William Robbins, Oregon State University; James Sherow, Kansas State University; Sherry Smith, University of Texas at El Paso; Michael Tate, University of Nebraska at Omaha; David Walker, University of Northern Iowa; and Elliott West, University of Arkansas.

Initially we began the second edition in collaboration with editors at D.C. Heath—Sylvia Mallory, Pat Wakeley, and James Miller. Since the purchase of D.C. Heath by Houghton Mifflin, our editors have been Jean L. Woy, Frances Gay, and Magdalena Hernandez. We thank each of these editors for their help, and we also wish to thank Craig Mertens for securing permission to republish materials and Po-Yee McKenna for assisting us with the book's photographs.

Finally, we have dedicated this edition to six individuals who have been our special friends and mentors. These six names represent the many people who love the West and its history and who make our work in this field so wonderfully worthwhile.

C.A.M. II
A.M.B.
D.R.L.

Contents

CHAPTER 6
Cowboys, Outlaws, and Violence
Page 195

CHAPTER 7
Children, Marriage, and Families
Page 238

CHAPTER 10
Living on the Land, Leaving the Land
Page 341

CHAPTER 11
Dam Water, Damn Dust
Page 379

CHAPTER 12
The Other Western Homefront
Page 416

C H A P T E R   1 3
New Cities, New Lives
Page 454

C H A P T E R   1 4
Owning the West
Page 485

The West: A Reference Map

Legend:
- Lewis and Clark, 1804–1805
- California Trail
- Oregon Trail
- Santa Fe Trail

CANADA

ATLANTIC OCEAN

PACIFIC OCEAN

MEXICO

HAWAII

ALASKA

APPALACHIAN MOUNTAINS

ROCKY MOUNTAINS

St. Lawrence · L. Ontario · Lake Erie · Lake Huron · Lake Michigan · Lake Superior

Wisconsin · Illinois · Ohio · Wabash · Tennessee · Alabama · Mississippi

Missouri · Platte · Yellowstone · Arkansas · Red · Brazos · Rio Grande · Colorado · Gila · Snake · Columbia · Sacramento · San Joaquin

St. Louis · Independence · Dodge City · Sand Creek · Santa Fe · The Alamo

Fort Clark · Battle of Little Bighorn · Great Falls of the Missouri · Butte · South Pass · Rock Springs · Salt Lake City · Uintah Ouray Reservation · Fort Hall · Bingham · Topaz · Great Salt Lake · Hoover Dam · Mission San Diego · Santa Clara Mission · Sutter's Fort · Donner Pass · Seattle

Nome · Yukon · Kodiak Island

Defining the West
and Its History

Y

More than a century after its first public presentation, Frederick Jackson Turner's theory of the frontier still seems indelibly linked to the study of the American West. In 1893, at age thrity-two, Turner first composed his essay, "The Significance of the Frontier in American History." In his thesis, this young assistant professor at the University of Wisconsin disputed the significance of the "germ theory," which insisted that American institutions and values had originated from distinctive elements, or "germs," in European history. Instead, he emphasized the "germ" of the frontier experience as the critical influence on the shaping of the American character and commitment to democracy. Turner's ideas had a clear nationalistic tone that impressed many of his contemporaries. In 1910, he moved to Harvard University and became the scholarly mentor, directly or indirectly, for several generations of American historians. Turner's frontier thesis has been the subject of revision, rejection, and seemingly constant dispute. Turner himself refined, adjusted, and expanded his ideas in later essays and books. Today most historians do not consider the frontier to be the crucial, definitive element for all of American history. Since the mid-1980s, historians of the American West have hotly debated the relevance of Turner's frontier thesis in regard to the creation of a new western history. Prominent individuals identified as New Western Historians, such as Patricia Nelson Limerick and Richard White, have advocated the writing of western history with no reference to the term "frontier." Other prominent historians, such as Martin Ridge and William Cronon, have defended the significance of Turner's intellectual legacy in western history. This debate may never be fully resolved, but it does reveal the passion of historians who attempt to define the West and its history.

Y *S T A T E M E N T S*

This chapter begins not with documents, as such, but with statements by historians. Appropriately, Frederick Jackson Turner speaks first. The introduction to his famous essay, "The Significance of the Frontier in American History," explained *"the process of evolution in each western area"* (Turner's italics) where "American social development has been continually beginning over again on the frontier." Turner asked the rhetorical question, "What is the frontier?" but he did not give a specific definition. In the second statement, from his 1896 essay "The Problem of the West," Turner asked, "What is the West?" He believed that it was "a form of society, rather than an area." Did Turner put social development—a historical process—ahead of geographic location in defining the West? Thirty-five years later in 1931, Walter Prescott Webb, a historian at the University of Texas, wrote of place as the significant factor in shaping social development. As shown in the third statement, from his book *The Great Plains,* Webb did not contradict Turner's ideas but he did stress geographic location and environmental factors. Webb contrasted life on eastern frontiers with the struggles of pioneers on the arid plains. In her 1987 book *The Legacy of Conquest,* Patricia Nelson Limerick of the University of Colorado firmly advocated the primacy of place over process in understanding the history of the American West. In the fourth statement included here, Limerick rejects Turner's frontier thesis. Public recognition of her ideas brought attention to other scholars who were shaping what the media termed a "New Western History." The fifth statement is Limerick's informal definition of this new way to examine the western past which appeared in the 1991 collection *Trails: Toward a New Western History.* Other prominent scholars, however, continued to value the relevance of earlier historians as shown in the final two statements. In his 1987 essay, William Cronon of the University of Wisconsin argued for the relevance of some of Frederick Jackson Turner's ideas in environmental history and western history. Lastly, in an essay also published in 1987, Donald Worster of the University of Kansas, admonished western historians desiring to create a new regional history to follow the path blazed by Walter Prescott Webb. Where do Cronon and Worster stand in the debate over process and place in defining western history?

The Significance of the Frontier in American History

FREDERICK JACKSON TURNER

In a recent bulletin of the superintendent of the census for 1890 appear these significant words: "Up to and including 1880 the country had a frontier of settlement, but at present the unsettled area has been so broken into by isolated bodies of settlement that there can hardly be said to be a frontier line. In the discussion of its extent, its westward movement, etc., it cannot, therefore, any longer have a place in the census reports." This brief official statement marks the closing of a great historic movement. Up to our own day American history has been in a large degree the history of the col-

Frederick Jackson Turner, "The Significance of the Frontier in American History," *Proceedings of the Forty-First Annual Meeting of the State Historical Society of Wisconsin* (Madison, Wis., 1894), 79–112.

onization of the Great West. The existence of an area of free land, its continuous recession, and the advance of American settlement westward,
explain American development. Behind institutions, behind constitutional
forms and modifications, lie the vital forces that call these organs into life,
and shape them to meet changing conditions. Now, the peculiarity of American institutions is, the fact that they have been compelled to adapt themselves to the changes of an expanding people—to the changes involved in
crossing a continent, in winning a wilderness, and in developing at each
area of this progress out of the primitive economic and political conditions
of the frontier into the complexity of city life. Said [John C.] Calhoun in
1817, "We are great, and rapidly—I was about to say fearfully—growing!"
So saying, he touched the distinguishing feature of American life. All peoples show development: the germ theory of politics has been sufficiently
emphasized. In the case of most nations, however, the development has
occurred in a limited area; and if the nation has expanded, it has met other
growing peoples whom it has conquered. But in the case of the United
States we have a different phenomenon. Limiting our attention to the
Atlantic coast, we have the familiar phenomenon of the evolution of institutions in a limited area, such as the rise of representative government; the
differentiation of simple colonial governments into complex organs; the
progress from primitive industrial society, without division of labor, up to
manufacturing civilization. But we have in addition to this *a recurrence of
the process of evolution in each western area reached in the process of
expansion.* Thus American development has exhibited not merely advance
along a single line, but a return to primitive conditions on a continually
advancing frontier line, and a new development for that area. American
social development has been continually beginning over again on the frontier. This perennial rebirth, this fluidity of American life, this expansion
westward with its new opportunities, its continuous touch with the simplicity of primitive society, furnish the forces dominating American character. The true point of view in the history of this nation is not the Atlantic
coast, it is the Great West. Even the slavery struggle, which is made so
exclusive an object of attention by writers like Professor [Hermann E.] von
Holst, occupies its important place in American history because of its relation to westward expansion.

   In this advance, the frontier is the outer edge of the wave—the meeting
point between savagery and civilization. Much has been written about the
frontier from the point of view of border warfare and the chase, but as a
field for the serious study of the economist and the historian it has been
neglected.

   What is the frontier? It is not the European frontier—a fortified boundary line running through dense populations. The most significant thing
about it is, that it lies at the hither edge of free land. In the census reports
it is treated as the margin of that settlement which has a density of two or
more to the square mile. The term is an elastic one, and for our purpose
does not need sharp definition. We shall consider the whole frontier belt,
including the Indian country and the outer margin of the "settled area" of

the census reports. This paper will make no attempt to treat the subject exhaustively; its aim is simply to call attention to the frontier as a fertile field for investigation, and to suggest some of the problems which arise in connection with it.

In the settlement of America we have to observe how European life entered the continent, and how America modified and developed that life, and reacted on Europe. Our early history is the study of European germs developing in an American environment. Too exclusive attention has been paid by institutional students to the Germanic origins, too little to the American factors. Now, the frontier is the line of most rapid and effective Americanization. The wilderness masters the colonist. It finds him a European in dress, industries, tools, modes of travel, and thought. It takes him from the railroad car and puts him in the birch canoe. It strips off the garments of civilization, and arrays him in the hunting shirt and the moccasin. It puts him in the log cabin of the Cherokee and the Iroquois, and runs an Indian palisade around him. Before long he has gone to planting Indian corn and plowing with a sharp stick; he shouts the war cry and takes the scalp in orthodox Indian fashion. In short, at the frontier the environment is at first too strong for the man. He must accept the conditions which it furnishes, or perish, and so he fits himself into the Indian clearings and follows the Indian trails. Little by little he transforms the wilderness, but the outcome is not the old Europe, not simply the development of Germanic germs, any more than the first phenomenon was a case of reversion to the Germanic mark. The fact is, that here is a new product that is American. At first, the frontier was the Atlantic coast. It was the frontier of Europe in a very real sense. Moving westward, the frontier became more and more American. *As successive terminal moraines result from successive glaciations, so each frontier leaves its traces behind it, and when it becomes a settled area the region still partakes of the frontier characteristics.* Thus the advance of the frontier has meant a steady movement away from the influence of Europe, a steady growth of independence on American lines. And to study this advance, the men who grew up under these conditions, and the political, economic and social results of it, is to study the really American part of our history.

The Problem of the West

FREDERICK JACKSON TURNER

The problem of the West is nothing less than the problem of American development. A glance at the map of the United States reveals the truth. To write of a "Western sectionalism," bounded on the east by the Alleghanies, is, in itself, to proclaim the writer a provincial. What is the West? What has it been in American life? To have the answers to these questions is to understand the most significant features of the United States of to-day.

Frederick Jackson Turner, "The Problem of the West." *Atlantic Monthly* 77, September 1896.

The West, at bottom, is a form of society, rather than an area. It is the term applied to the region whose social conditions result from the application of older institutions and ideas to the transforming influences of free land. By this application, a new environment is suddenly entered, freedom of opportunity is opened, the cake of custom is broken, and new activities, new lines of growth, new institutions and new ideals, are brought into existence. The wilderness disappears, the "West" proper passes on to a new frontier, and in the former area, a new society has emerged from its contact with the backwoods. Gradually this society loses its primitive conditions, and assimilates itself to the type of the older social conditions of the East; but it bears within it enduring and distinguishing survivals of its frontier experience. Decade after decade, West after West, this rebirth of American society has gone on, has left its traces behind it, and has reacted on the East. The history of our political institutions, our democracy, is not a history of imitation, of simple borrowing; it is a history of the evolution and adaptation of organs in response to changed environment, a history of the origin of new political species. In this sense, therefore, the West has been a constructive force of the highest significance in our life. To use the words of that acute and widely informed observer, Mr. [Lord James] Bryce, "The West is the most American part of America. . . . What Europe is to Asia, what America is to England, that the Western States and Territories are to the Atlantic States."

The Great Plains

WALTER PRESCOTT WEBB

The Great Plains offered such a contrast to the region east of the ninety-eighth meridian, the region with which American civilization had been familiar until about 1840, as to bring about a marked change in the ways of pioneering and living. For two centuries American pioneers had been working out a technique for the utilization of the humid regions east of the Mississippi River. They had found solutions for their problems and were conquering the frontier at a steadily accelerating rate. Then in the early nineteenth century they crossed the Mississippi and came out on the Great Plains, an environment with which they had had no experience. The result was a complete though temporary breakdown of the machinery and ways of pioneering. They began to make adjustments. . . .

As one contrasts the civilization of the Great Plains with that of the eastern timberland, one sees what may be called an institutional *fault* (comparable to a geological fault) running from the middle Texas to Illinois or Dakota, roughly following the ninety-eighth meridian. At this *fault* the ways of life and of living changed. Practically every institution that was carried across it was either broken and remade or else greatly altered. The

Walter Prescott Webb, *The Great Plains* (New York: Grosset & Dunlap, 1931). Copyright 1931 by Walter Prescott Webb, copyright © 1959 by Walter Prescott Webb. Published by Ginn and Company. Used by permission of Silver Burdett Ginn, Inc.

ways of travel, the weapons, the method of tilling the soil, the plows and other agricultural implements, and even the laws themselves were modified. When people first crossed this line they did not immediately realize the imperceptible change that had taken place in their environment, nor, more is the tragedy, did they foresee the full consequences which that change was to bring in their own characters and in their modes of life. In the new region—level, timberless, and semi-arid—they were thrown by Mother Necessity into the clutch of new circumstances. Their plight has been stated in this way: east of the Mississippi civilization stood on three legs—land, water, and timber; west of the Mississippi not one but two of these legs were withdrawn,—water and timber,—and civilization was left on one leg—land. It is small wonder that it toppled over in temporary failure. . . .

. . . It has been pointed out that the ninety-eighth meridian separates the United States into two equal parts, that the Anglo-Americans who approached the Great Plains from the east came with an experience of more than two centuries of pioneering in the woodland environment, and that when they crossed over into the Plains their technique of pioneering broke down and they were compelled to make a radical readjustment in their way of life. The key to an understanding of the history of the West must be sought, therefore, in a comparative study of what *was* in the East and what *came to be* in the West. The salient truth, the essential truth, is that the West cannot be understood as a mere extension of things Eastern. Though "the roots of the present lie deep in the past," it does not follow that the fruits of the present are the same or that the fruits of the West are identical with those of the East. Such a formula would destroy the variable quality in history and make of it an exact science. In history the differences are more important than the similarities. When one makes a comparative study of the sections, the dominant truth which emerges is expressed in the word *contrast.*

The contrast begins in geology and topography and is continued in climate, reflected in vegetation, apparent in wild animal life, obvious in anthropology, and not undiscernible in history. To the white man, with his forest culture, the Plains presented themselves as an obstacle, one which served to exercise and often defeat his ingenuity, to upset his calculations, to hinder his settlement, and to alter his weapons, tools, institutions, and social attitudes; in short, to throw his whole way of life out of gear. The history of the white man in the Great Plains is the history of adjustments and modifications, of giving up old things that would no longer function for new things that would, of giving up an old way of life for a new way in order that there might be *a* way. Here one must view the white man and his culture as a dynamic thing, moving from the forest-clad land into the treeless plain.

History may take another view of the Great Plains which we may call the static view—a still picture which will show the results of man's efforts at a given time. Such a picture reveals the Great Plains as a land of survival where nature has most stubbornly resisted the efforts of man. Nature's very stubbornness has driven man to the innovations which he has made; but above the level of his efforts and beyond his achievements stand the fragments and survivals of the ancient order. The new and the old, innovation and survival, dwell there side by side, the obverse and the converse of the struggle between man and nature.

The land itself is a survival. The High Plains are, according to [Willard D.] Johnson, but fragments of the old plains built up through countless ages by the aggrading rivers swinging down from the desert mountains across the eastward-tilted marine rock sheet. But we are concerned here with a much more recent period—that of the white man's entrance.

The Plains Indians were survivals of savagery, even when compared with the Indians to the east and to the west. They lagged in the nomadic state when practically all other tribes in America had progressed to some form of agriculture and settled village life; they were designated as "wild" Indians, to distinguish them from the more docile tribes of the timberland.

It is today, however, that the Plains present the Indians as survivals. Practically all Indians in the United States are found now in the West, most of them within or near the margins of the Plains. They were pushed in there from the east and from the west; and at a time when there was nowhere else to push them they were permitted to settle down on the reservations. The map of the reservations as looked at by a student a thousand years hence will present the Great Plains as the region of survival of the native races. . . .

It is in the West that rural life has remained dominant over urban life. The automobile has tended to obliterate the difference between rural and urban life, but before its coming rural ideals, virtues, and prejudices prevailed all over the Great Plains region. As yet the Great Plains have produced but few cities, and fewer that do not lie along the timber line. Minneapolis, Chicago, St. Louis, Kansas City, Fort Worth, and San Antonio mark the line that separates the East from the West. These cities owe much of their growth to the fact that they receive tribute from the Plains. Plains wheat made Minneapolis and St. Paul; Plains cattle helped to make Chicago, St. Louis, Kansas City, and Fort Worth. These were the railheads and distributing centers for the Great Plains. It is probable that a careful study of the rise of mail-order houses in Chicago and Kansas City can be shown to have had a very close relation to the business that came in from the isolated people of the Great Plains.

The public domain, or public land, has also proved to be a survival. It is only in the Western states that any considerable portion of public land remains in the hands of the government. A map of national parks and monuments will show that the West is the museum of natural wonders. The Westerner today resents the fact that the government withholds this land from development.

The Legacy of Conquest

PATRICIA NELSON LIMERICK

If we give up a preoccupation with the frontier and look instead at the continuous sweep of Western American history, new organizing ideas await our attention, but no simple, unitary model. Turner's frontier rested on a single point of view; it required that the observer stand in the East and look to the West. Now, like many scholars in other fields, Western historians have had to learn to live with relativism.

A deemphasis of the frontier opens the door to a different kind of intellectual stability. Turner's frontier was a process, not a place. When "civilization" had conquered "savagery" at any one location, the process—and the historian's attention—moved on. In rethinking Western history, we gain the freedom to think of the West as a place—as many complicated environments occupied by natives who considered their homelands to be the center, not the edge.

In choosing to stress place more than process, we cannot fix exact boundaries for the region, any more than we can draw precise lines around "the South," "the Midwest," or that most elusive of regions "the East." Allowing for a certain shifting of borders, the West in this book will generally mean the present-day states of California, Oregon, Washington, Idaho, Utah, Nevada, Arizona, New Mexico, Colorado, Kansas, Nebraska, Oklahoma, Texas, Montana, Wyoming, North Dakota, and South Dakota and, more changeably, Iowa, Missouri, Arkansas, and Louisiana. (Many patterns explored here apply also to Alaska, but limits of space and time have prohibited its full inclusion.) This certainly makes for a complicated package, but the West as place has a compensatory, down-to-earth clarity that the migratory, abstract frontier could never have.

Reorganized, the history of the West is a study of a place undergoing conquest and never fully escaping its consequences. In these terms, it has distinctive features as well as features it shares with the histories of other parts of the nation and the planet. Under the Turner thesis, Western history stood alone. An exciting trend in modern scholarship leads toward comparative history—toward Western American history as one chapter in the global story of Europe's expansion. Studies in "comparative conquests" promise to help knit the fragmented history of the planet back together. Western American history can be a prime contributor to that endeavor.

Deemphasize the frontier and its supposed end, conceive of the West as a place and not a process, and Western American history has a new look. First, the American West was an important meeting ground, the point where Indian America, Latin America, Anglo-America, Afro-America, and Asia intersected. In race relations, the West could make the turn-of-the-century Northeastern urban confrontation between European immigrants and American nativists look like a family reunion. Similarly, in the diversity of languages, religions, and cultures, it surpassed the South.

Second, the workings of conquest tied these diverse groups into the same story. Happily or not, minorities and majorities occupied a common ground. Conquest basically involved the drawing of lines on a map, the definition and allocation of ownership (personal, tribal, corporate, state, federal, and international), and the evolution of land from matter to property. The process had two stages: the initial drawing of the lines (which we have usually called the frontier stage) and the subsequent giving of meaning and power to those lines, which is still under way. Race relations parallel the distribution of property, the application of labor and capital to make the property productive, and the allocation of profit. Western history has been an ongoing competition for legitimacy—for the right to claim for oneself and sometimes for one's group the status of legitimate beneficiary of Western resources. This intersection of ethnic diversity with property allocation unifies Western history.

The contest for property and profit has been accompanied by a contest for cultural dominance. Conquest also involved a struggle over languages, cultures, and religions; the pursuit of legitimacy in property overlapped with the pursuit of legitimacy in way of life and point of view. In a variety of matters, but especially in the unsettled questions of Indian assimilation and in the disputes over bilingualism and immigration in the still semi-Hispanic Southwest, this contest for cultural dominance remains a primary unresolved issue of conquest. Reconceived as a running story, a fragmented and discontinuous past becomes whole again.

With its continuity restored, Western American history carries considerable significance for American history as a whole. Conquest forms the historical bedrock of the whole nation, and the American West is a preeminent case study in conquest and its consequences.

What on Earth Is the New Western History?

PATRICIA NELSON LIMERICK

What, then, is the essence of this emerging way of looking at the western past? Preparing for a symposium called "Trails: Toward a New Western History" (held in Santa Fe, New Mexico, in September 1989), one of the participants quite sensibly wrote me to ask what "New Western History" meant. In response, I wrote a summation, a one-page text that has had a prosperous career in copying machines and appears here in print for the first time:

> New Western Historians define "the West" primarily as a place—the
> trans-Mississippi region in the broadest terms, or the region west of the

From *Trails: Toward a New Western History,* edited by Patricia Limerick, Charles Rankin, and Clyde A. Milner II, © 1991 by the University Press of Kansas. Reprinted by permission of the publisher.

hundredth meridian. The boundaries are fuzzy because nearly all regional boundaries are.

New Western Historians do see a "process" at work in this region's history, a process that has affected other parts of the nation as well as other parts of the planet. But they reject the old term "frontier" for that process. When clearly and precisely defined, the term "frontier" is nationalistic and often racist (in essence, the area where white people get scarce); when cleared of its ethnocentrism, the term loses an exact definition.

To characterize the process that shaped the region, New Western Historians have available a number of terms—invasion, conquest, colonization, exploitation, development, expansion of the world market. In the broadest picture, the process involves the convergence of diverse people—women as well as men, Indians, Europeans, Latin Americans, Asians, Afro-Americans—in the region, and their encounters with each other and with the natural environment.

New Western Historians reject the notion of a clear cut "end to the frontier," in 1890, or in any other year. The story of the region's sometimes contested, sometimes cooperative, relations among its diverse cast of characters and the story of human efforts to "master" nature in the region are both ongoing stories, with their continuity unnecessarily ruptured by attempts to divide the "old West" from the "new West."

New Western Historians break free of the old model of "progress" and "improvement," and face up to the possibility that some roads of western development led directly to failure and to injury. This reappraisal is not meant to make white Americans "look bad." The intention is, on the contrary, simply to make it clear that in western American history, heroism and villainy, virtue and vice, and nobility and shoddiness appear in roughly the same proportions as they appear in any other subject of human history (and with the same relativity of definition and judgment). This is only disillusioning to those who have come to depend on illusions.

New Western Historians surrender the conventional, never-very-convincing claim of an omniscient, neutral objectivity. While making every effort to acknowledge and understand different points of view, New Western Historians admit that it is OK for scholars to care about their subjects, both in the past and the present, and to put that concern on record.

Does all this add up to a revolution that should alarm westerners outside the ivory towers? A grumpy columnist for the *Arizona Republic* (October 23, 1989, p. A10), responding to news of the "Trails" conference, seemed to think so: "Why can't the revisionists simply leave our myths alone?" Phil Sunkel wrote. "Westerners—and most other Americans, for that matter—are quite content with our storied past, even if it tends to fib a bit." To this writer and others of his persuasion, the western public is composed of cheerful fools, people happy to deny their own lived experiences out of a preference for appealing and colorful legends.

My own experience, speaking to diverse public audiences around the West, leads to very different conclusions. Far from being a region filled with Hollywood's dupes and suckers, the American West in 1990 has a population well supplied with serious, concerned citizens, people doing the best they can to figure out where they are and who they are. These people are usually quick to accept the New Western History. It takes the region, its dilemmas and its charms, seriously; it restores full human dignity to westerners of the past and present; and by dissolving the great divide between the "Old West" and the "New West," it simply does a better job of explaining how we got where we are today. Many westerners realize that we cannot take ourselves and our present challenges seriously until we take our history seriously. We cannot live responsibly in the American West until we have made a responsible and thorough assessment of our common past.

Revisiting the Vanishing Frontier: The Legacy of Frederick Jackson Turner

WILLIAM CRONON

It is no accident that much of what we today call "environmental history" has been written in this country under the guise of *western* history. No other academic field, historical geography excluded, has proven to be a better home for those interested in studying human uses of the earth. This is Turner's doing. His initial frontier essay emphasized environment, but defined "free land" too narrowly in terms of unoccupied agricultural territory. Later in his life, he broadened this definition to include "the unpossessed resources of the nation." In so doing, he came close to anticipating the central thesis of David Potter's *People of Plenty,* a remarkable book that suggests at least one major linkage between Turner's work and a more general environmental history. For Potter, Turner's frontier was but a special case of the general abundance of natural resources that had made America exceptional from the start. "By failing to recognize that the frontier was only one form in which America offered abundance," Potter wrote, Turner "cut himself off from an insight into the fact that other forms of abundance had superseded the frontier even before the supply of free land had been exhausted. . . ." Potter's book has flaws that are akin to Turner's—he too chose to rest his argument on the fuzzy category of "national character"— but his central insight is surely a major key to the Turnerian riddle.

If the frontier represented only one kind of plenty, then it ought to be possible to rewrite western history—which in one rather Turnerian sense is actually the environmental history of North America—in terms of a transition not from free to occupied land, but from abundance to scarcity. Even that formulation is too sweepingly simple. . . . Neither abundance nor scarcity has ever been absolute. Instead, their definitions shift always according to natural and artificial constraints on systems of human activity,

"Revisiting the Vanishing Frontier: The Legacy of Frederick Jackson Turner," by William Cronon. *Western Historical Quarterly,* 18 (April 1987), pp. 157–176. Copyright by Western History Association. Reprinted by permission.

and according to people's *beliefs* about whether they are experiencing economic and environmental stasis, progress, or decline. Different forms of technology or social organization can produce entirely different levels of resource use, even when they exist on the same landscape; conversely, diminishing quantities of an essential resource, or newly discovered supplies of it, can produce drastic shifts in social organization and technology. People's notions of abundance and scarcity—of wealth and poverty—change accordingly, and so too does their political life. Communities that define abundance in one way all too easily come into conflict with those that define it otherwise. Much of regional history can be organized around these fundamental relationships. Western history, under this framework, can become what it has always been, the story of human beings working with changing tools to transform the resources of the land, struggling over how that land should be owned and understood, and defining their notions of political and cultural community, all within a context of shifting environmental and economic constraints. . . .

Among the deepest struggles in American western history have been those among peoples who have defined abundance—and the "good life"—in conflicting ways. Such struggles must fit into this story without oversimplifying the values embraced by opposing sides, for ultimately "abundance" was as culturally contested a terrain as "community." In the West, to occupy the natural landscape meant, simultaneously, to occupy a human community; those two acts of belonging are among the most fundamental that a historian of the region can trace. And here we may as well return to Turner's most important questions as well: what *is* the relation between abundance and American notions of liberal democracy? To what extent *has* the peculiar nature of American class consciousness and republican government been shaped by the shifting resource base of our economic and social life? How *do* nature and humanity transform each other?

None of these are dead or answered questions, and all are part of Turner's continuing legacy. Turner's notion of the "frontier" may be so muddled as to be useless, but if Turner's "free land" is a special case of Potter's American abundance, then the general direction of Turner's approach remains sound. In his commitment to ignoring the walls between disciplines, in his faith that history must in large measure be the story of ordinary people, in his emphasis on the importance of regional environments to our understanding the course of American history—in all these ways, he remains one of the pathfinders whose well-blazed trail we continue to follow. And whether or not we ultimately abandon the frontier thesis, we are unlikely ever to escape its narrative implications. In fashioning a rhetorical framework for telling the history of the first continental republic, Frederick Jackson Turner, almost in spite of himself, gave American history its central and most persistent story. However much we may modify the details and outline of that story, we are unlikely ever to break entirely free of it.

New West, True West: Interpreting the Region's History

DONALD WORSTER

Frederick Jackson Turner started historians down a muddy, slippery road that ultimately leads to a swamp. That destination was not apparent for a long while. The route signs Turner put up had a deceptively concrete promise to them. In a letter written in the 1920s, he pointed out that "the 'West' with which I dealt, was a *process* rather than a fixed geographical region." . . .

When you are lost, the most sensible strategy is to go back to the point of departure, back where Mr. Turner once stood pointing the way, and look for another road. Ignore the signs saying, "[t]his way to process," and look instead for the one reading, "[T]o a fixed geographical region." Or better yet, look for the specific processes that went on in the specific region. We may grope and argue a lot along that way too, but we won't end up back in Massachusetts befuddled by Puritan theology or back with the Crusaders defeated and dead.

My strategy of diverging from Turner and his frontier theme is hardly original. It was implicitly recommended almost thirty years ago, in a 1957 article published in *Harper's Magazine,* by a man then described as "the West's leading historian," Walter Prescott Webb. The article was entitled "The American West: Perpetual Mirage." Had it been taken more fully to heart, it might have started the field off in a more promising direction. There was absolutely nothing in it of Turner's vaporous notion of the West as frontier advance. On the contrary, Webb gave the West a set of firm coordinates on the North American landscape. In his second paragraph he declared.

> Fortunately, the West is no longer a shifting frontier, but a region that can be marked off on a map, traveled to, and seen. Everybody knows when he gets there. It starts in the second tier of states west of the Big River.

The West, in other words, begins with the Dakotas, Nebraska, Kansas, Oklahoma, and Texas. So defined, the West would become, along with the North and South, one of the three great geographical regions of the coterminous United States.

In Webb's view, what sets this western region off from the other two major regions is the lack of enough rainfall to sustain traditional, European-derived agriculture. In that second tier of states the average yearly precipitation falls below the twenty-inch minimum needed to grow crops in the accustomed way. From there to the California coast the region is mainly dry: in its extremes it is a desert, elsewhere it is a subhumid environment. Admittedly, within it are some anomalies and further diversities—the Pacific northwest coast outstanding among them—which, for the sake of

"New West, True West: Interpreting the Region's History," by Donald Worster, *Western Historical Quarterly,* 18 (April 1987), pp. 141–156. Copyright by Western History Association. Reprinted by permission."

analysis, Webb had to ignore. Every region is, after all, only a genralization and is subject to exceptions.

This more mappable West, as everyone in the field knows, was an idea Webb took from the nineteenth-century explorer John Wesley Powell, whose *Report on the Lands of the Arid Region of the United States,* published in 1878 as a House of Representatives document, identified the 100th meridian as the line roughly dividing a humid from a subhumid America. Webb nudged the line eastward a couple of degrees so it lay right outside Austin, Texas, where he lived. And he boldly declared that Powell's arid region was one and the same as the American West. For the post-World War Two generation, he sensed, the two regions had merged completely, and historians had better acknowledge the fact and stop harking back to Turner.

I know in my bones, if not always through my education, that Webb was right. His notion of the West as the arid region of the country fits completely my own experience and understanding. Born eighty years to the day after Frederick Jackson Turner—on the 14th of November, 1941 (Turner was born on the 14th of November, 1861)—I have never been able to think of the West as Turner did, as some process in motion. Instead, I think of it as a distinct place inhabited by distinct people: people like my parents, driven out of western Kansas by dust storms to an even hotter, drier life in Needles, California, working along the way in flyblown cafes, fruit orchards, and on railroad gangs, always feeling dwarfed by the bigness of the land and by the economic power accumulated there. In my West, there are no coonskin caps, nor many river boats, axes, or log cabins. Those things all belong to another time, another place—to an eastern land where nature offered an abundance of survival resources near at hand. My West is, by contrast, the story of men and women trying to wrest a living from a condition of severe natural scarcity and, paradoxically, of trying to survive in the midst of entrenched wealth.

This picture of the West, I submit, is the closer to the one most western historians carry around in their heads today. When pushed hard to make a stand, we usually line up with Webb and Powell, not Turner. For instance, on the first page or so of the introduction to his book *Historians and the American West,* Michael Malone grants that he means by the West more or less what Webb meant: "the entire region lying west of the 98th meridian, the line of diminishing rainfall which runs from the eastern Dakotas on the north through central Texas on the south." But having admitted that much to ourselves, we often resist the logical implications in what we have done. We still feel obliged to keep feeding Turner's ghost at the table. We may accept the modern view that the West is a settled region distinct unto itself, but we are not always steadfast, clear-minded regionalists in writing its history.

Υ *E S S A Y S*

Walter Nugent is Andrew V. Tackes Professor of History at the University of
Notre Dame. The author of numerous books on western and American history,
his most recent work has examined comparative frontier history in global
terms and the great transatlantic migrations of the late nineteenth and early
twentieth centuries. Like many teachers of western history, Nugent became
both bemused and perplexed by the numerous definitions of the American
West. He decided to survey western historians, writers, and journalists about
their answers to the question: "Where is the American West?" The results
appeared in his 1992 article. The diverse definitions that people expressed to
Nugent demonstrated how debates about the West and its history remain
vibrant, especially in regard to the issue of "place" versus "process." Clyde A.
Milner II, editor of the *Western Historical Quarterly* and professor of history
at Utah State University, faced a different challenge. As one of three editors
for the *Oxford History of the American West,* he needed to write an introduction to this large volume that captured the full complexity of western history,
including the most recent historical scholarship. Both the Nugent article and
the Milner essay confront the problem of definition. Ultimately, it is worth
considering whether the history of the American West is defined by what one
chooses to include or by what one chooses to exclude. Are only certain people
and certain places truly western? Is there only a certain time in the past that
truly represents western history?

Where Is the American West?
Report on a Survey

WALTER NUGENT

Disagreements about how to define "West" and "frontier" and how to distinguish the two terms are nothing new to historians of both. The urgency
of these problems has ebbed and flowed. Lately it has flooded like a spring
torrent, fed by the assertions of some "new western historians" that the
West is a place, not a Turnerian process. Before the day is done, the torrent
may further swell by the melting snowpack from "old western historians"
who think that process remains very much part of the story.

But new western historians have raised the place-versus-process issue,
and hence, questioned anew the definition of "the West." They have stated
their premises clearly in several recent publications. Among these premises
(though not every new western historian agrees on all of them) are these:
that western history hardly stopped in 1890 or 1893 or any other year; that
it has been marked less by "progress" than by "conquest" and conflict; that
the West is a place where this conquest has taken place, a definite place on
the map, rather than the process that Frederick Jackson Turner stated was
essential to the frontier idea. As Patricia Nelson Limerick wrote in *Legacy
of Conquest,* "De-emphasize the frontier and its supposed end, conceive of

Walter Nugent, "Where Is the American West: Report on a Survey," *Montana The Magazine of Western
History,* Vol. 42 (Spring 1992), pp. 2–23. Excerpted by permission of the Montana Historical Society.

the West as a place and not a process, and Western American history has a new look." Richard White, in his massive new history of the western region, avoids the term "frontier." In the set of essays edited by William Cronon, George Miles, and Jay Gitlin, Limerick explains that

> To Frederick Jackson Turner and his followers in conventional western history, the frontier (and, by extension, the West) was a process, not a place; a concept, not an actual geographical location. In this way of thinking, the West is wherever the American mind puts it—a pretty vague and ephemeral target for "image" analysis.

It seemed to me, since the new western history continued to gain attention and generate controversy, that it would be interesting and useful to know how widely the "place" versus "process" antinomy operates in people's minds, and where people believe the *true* West to be. That question leads, of course, to what the West signifies. Since the frontier idea, as William Goetzmann and others have said, has been our great American creation myth, the question touches not just on images of the West but on conceptions of the whole of America.

But does not the question of "where" the West is, also suggest "when" the West was? And this suggests yet another question—do frontiers end, do regions come and go, and if so how can we tell? That last question must wait for another occasion. It is enough for now to inquire of people seriously interested in the West, from different perspectives, how they feel about the place-versus-process argument. I have also been curious, long before the new western history appeared, in the simple question of where other people began to sense westernness as they traveled from east to west across the country (or where they no longer felt "western" if they were leaving the region). The answers should help define regionalism.

What interested parties think about place-versus-process and where one starts or stops feeling "western" are questions resolvable by a survey. Therefore, in the spring of 1991, I designed and mailed out nearly five hundred questionnaires to members of the Western History Association, a list of editors and publishers of newspapers and magazines from Colorado to California, and members of the Western Writers of America. The response was remarkable for size, vehemence, and content. The results appear below.

The Questions

The questionnaire consisted of three short questions: (1) "How would you describe the boundaries of 'the West' (on the east, south, north, and west)?"; (2) "Where are you now (i.e. in what section of the country), and where would you have to go to get to the edge of the West?"; (3) "What characteristics set apart the West, as you have defined it, from other regions?" Each person also received a personal data form so that answers could be linked to age, sex, place of residence, and occupation. The three questions are increasingly open-ended. The first asks for a specific geographic response; the second for a more personal but still presumably geographic response; while the third is almost completely open, and to it many people gave several answers—Wests of geography, climate, myth, history, imagination, and more.

The cover letter explained that various people have defined the West differently. Bernard DeVoto and Joan Didion said it starts where rainfall drops below twenty inches a year. But that excludes San Francisco and the coast north of it. An "eminent historian of the West who lives in New England" felt "western," so he once told me, when he crossed Indiana. The columnist Richard Reeves said he "got the notion that Chillicothe, Ohio, was where the West really began."

On the back of the data sheet was a map, and it contained one of the two major biases in the questionnaire—both unavoidable but also not without malice aforethought. The map was of the continental United States, with insets of Hawaii, Alaska, and Puerto Rico. State boundaries were indicated but rivers and other natural features were not, nor were Canada or Mexico. The map was therefore skewed toward a political response and against including Canada or Mexico. My alternative was to provide a map of North America, but that, I thought, would have introduced an even stronger bias toward including Canada and Mexico. Secondly, the very presence of a map invited responses that were geographical and also presentist. It discouraged responses that located or defined the West as it may have been at any past time, or as it may now exist in people's minds.

Despite these biases, many respondents insisted on including Canada and/or Mexico; many insisted that the "West" must be defined not only by "where," but also by "when"; and many pronounced it not a geographical entity at all, but a cultural one. Many insisted, explicitly, on the West as process rather than just as place. One respondent, in a personal letter, upbraided me for the questionnaire's "refusal to situate itself in time," but concluded, "My suspicion is that you probably share a number of the reservations [about defining the West exclusively as place] I've expressed . . . [and] your strategy in framing the questions as you have is no doubt cleverer and sneakier than I've realized." True. Also, given the geographic and presentist bias of the questionnaire, we can assume that historical and cultural definitions are even stronger in the respondents' minds than the numerical results indicate.

The Questionnaire

The questionnaire went to three groups of people. The first and largest was a roughly one-fifth sample, basically random, of the members of the Western History Association (WHA)—307 people. The second was a group of 97 editors and publishers ranging from metropolitan dailies to special-interest magazines. The third was a roughly one-fifth sample, 76 people, of the Western Writers of America (WWA). These 480 questionnaires were mailed in March and April 1991.

The Responses

By the end of June we received 251 responses: 188 from WHA members (61 percent); 25 from journalists (26 percent); and 38 from WWA members (50 percent). The WHA response was especially gratifying. Reading them was like arriving at a WHA meeting on an October Thursday and actually having time to talk with almost two hundred friends and colleagues about an ostensibly casual but really quite complex question. Clearly the great majority of respondents regard these as serious questions. The respondents had lived, on average, nineteen years in their state of present residence, and divided about equally among large, medium, and small cities, and rural places. The WWA people were more reclusive—fully a quarter of them live on farms, ranches, and in villages, compared to only 4 percent of historians and none of the journalists. Two-thirds were between thirty and sixty years old, most of the rest were over sixty, and only 2 percent were under thirty. Of the WWA group, 43 percent were female compared to 19 percent of the WHA group and 20 percent of the journalists. Only 8 percent of the WHA and WWA respondents—but 21 percent of the journalists!—asked not to be quoted.

The personal data sheets were not dry profiles. To the question, "how long have you lived in your present state of residence" and how long else-where, Michael Harrison answered, "57 years in California (present), plus 10 in Arizona, 3 in New Mexico, and 25 in New Jersey; total 95." A WWA member from Buena Vista, Colorado, replied that "I've lived here as a child, student, teacher, wife, widow, mother, journalist, writer, camper, rockhound;" and another, from Santa Fe, wrote, "I write under a man's name. Please don't use my real name. Ladies don't sell westerns." One WWA member, Lauran Paine of Siskiyou County, California, wrote,

> I have worked and lived in most Far Western and Southwestern states. Cattle ranching, wild horse trapping, blacksmithing, even sank so low as to become a motion picture rider, and upon discovering that none of these vocations would provide the income I aspired to . . . I began writing. Total published books to date 912 of which 714 Westerns have been for one publisher.

But now for the meat and potatoes. Where do these people think the West is, and why?

Question 1: Where are the West's Boundaries?

The answers may be summed up in these ten points:

1. Respondents focused much more on the eastern boundary than the other three. Everyone made a choice, and only about 5 percent were unclear (10/211). Regarding the western boundary, again only 5 percent were unclear, but 22 percent gave no response.

2. Respondents were much more indecisive, or just inattentive, about the northern and southern boundaries. Many probably took the Canadian and Mexican borders for granted. In both cases 5 percent answered

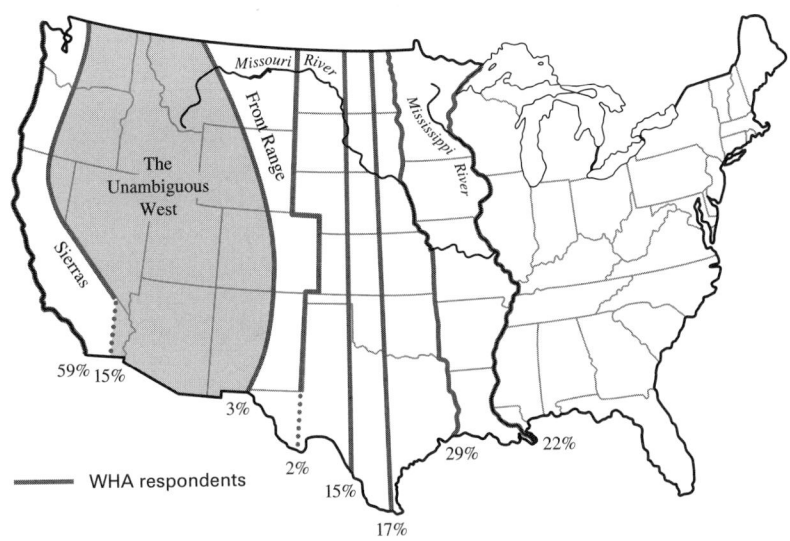

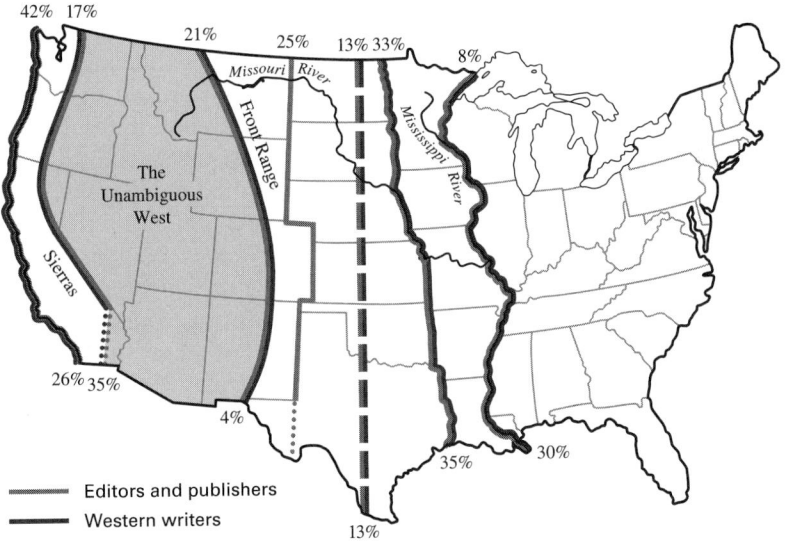

unclearly; and 25 percent simply did not state a northern boundary and 27 percent did not state a southern one. Differences were not great among the three groups (WHA, journalists, WWA).

3. A number of people identified only an eastern boundary, perhaps having mentally exhausted themselves in so doing. And a few who were reluctant to set any geographical boundaries said, well, if you insist, I'd place the eastern one at X or Y, then left it at that.

4. About one out of 6 (40/251 = 15.9%) refused to name any geographical boundaries. Instead, they said the West is a "state of mind," an "idea," "myth," or "mental construct," or something similar. Of the three groups, about one-eight of the WHA members took this position (23/187 = 12.3%), only one of the editors did so (1/25 = 4%), but nearly half of the western writers (16/39 = 41%). The writers, or many of them, believe the West is myth, and they write about and perpetuate the myth.

Many of them are genre writers and adamantly oppose the whole idea of demythologizing. Many in this group also reject the idea that the West is a contemporary, twentieth-century matter. I can think of other fiction writers who would scarcely agree—Ivan Doig and Tom King, for example, whose material is twentieth-century. But the Western Writers of America largely work with material from, or redolent of, the past. Their livelihood depends on the myths. It's not that they are necessarily more romantic about the West (though some are deeply attached to it) but that they write and sell what is romantic to many readers.

5. Regarding the eastern boundary, geographical responses were as follows. WHA members chose the Mississippi River in 22 percent of the cases, sometimes reluctantly but because that is where many begin the courses they teach. The largest group, 29 percent, picked the north-south line of the Red, Missouri, and Sabine rivers. But combining the 16.5 percent who chose the 98th meridian and the 15 percent who chose the 100th, fully 31 percent locate it at the eastern edge of the Great Plains, often with a verbal bow to Walter Prescott Webb. Only 5 percent chose the Rockies or close by, with 13 percent giving unclear or other responses, from the Atlantic Coast to eastern Idaho.

The editors, all from Colorado to California, opted strongly—46 percent—for the Rockies or the eastern borders of states in the front range of the Rockies (Montana, Wyoming, Colorado, New Mexico), with only 8 percent choosing the Mississippi River.

The writers—the slight majority who gave geographical responses—stuck to the traditional Mississippi River or Missouri River two-thirds of the time (65 percent).

6. Regarding the western boundary, most of the historians and journalists clearly opted for the Pacific Coast, but a minority of about one in six excluded all or parts of California, Oregon, and Washington. The writers were again more traditional; 40 percent of them excluded all or parts of the coastal states, and several refused to include any large cities, or what one called "plastic places" such as Vail, Aspen, and Las Vegas.

The exclusion of the coastal states, coastal strip, or cities, is a minority view but a significant one. Interestingly, most of those who hold it do not live in those areas. People who do live there, quite definitely those who live in Los Angeles, regard themselves as being not only in the West but in the center of the West.

7. As to whether Alaska and Hawaii are western: both appeared on the map circulated with the questionnaire, so it was hard to ignore them. Yet many did. Of the 70 (27.8 percent) who did refer to Alaska, 83 percent think it is indeed part of the West, wherever else they place the western or northern boundaries of the region. Of the 47 (18.7 percent) referring to Hawaii, the split was close—49 percent including it, 51 percent saying it is not western. The divisions on Alaska and Hawaii were nearly the same among all three respondent groups, except that the writers (WWA) were less inclined than the historians (WHA) to include Alaska.

8. Regarding the northern boundary, many took it for granted. The map I provided showed the United States only, so a respondent had to go slightly against the grain to include Canada. But many did. More historians (62) said, "include some parts of it," than said, "stop at the border" (57). The writers split about evenly. The journalists strongly (13 to 1) preferred to use the United States border than to include any part of Canada. Had I circulated a map of North America rather than of the United States, I suspect more would have included Canada. The tilt of the historians may indicate—so their comments often suggest—that, influenced by Webb, James Malin, and perhaps Turner, they think more in terms of environment and physiography than the other groups do, and more in terms of prairie settlement patterns than they think of political boundaries.

9. The southern boundary brought more non-responses than the other three. Many probably take the Rio Grande and the line across the Sonoran desert as a given. Some of the historians, especially those living in Arizona or New Mexico or who specialize in borderlands history, pointed out that the border arbitrarily divides people and geography that are better thought of as a unit. Thus 24 percent of the historians, 26 percent of the writers, and only 8 percent of the editors consider parts of northern Mexico as being in the West.

10. A consensus? Not quite. On the east, about half see the West as beginning at the Mississippi River or Missouri River, the other half at the eastern edge of the Great Plains or in a few cases the Rockies' front range. On the west, most stop at the Pacific Ocean but a sizeable minority say, leave out the coast and its cities. On the north, historians divide, slightly in favor of including western Canada, the rest stopping at the border. On the south, most of those saying anything at all stop at the border, though a goodly minority of historians would include parts of northern Mexico, especially the desert. But, to repeat, fully one-sixth (and nearly half of the writers) refused to identify any geographical boundaries at all, and many others stated them under protest. These people remain convinced that "West" and "frontier" are not that separable, and that process remains more important than present place.

Responses to question 1 ("How would you describe the boundaries of the West?")

Who responded?	WHA	PRESS	WWA	TOTAL
Total, each group	187	25	39	251
Gave non-geographical response	23	1	16	40
Geographical responses	164	24	23	211
Place the Eastern boundary at:				
Mississippi River	36	2	7	45
Red-Missouri-Sabine Rrs.	40	8	6	54
Same, but exclude east Texas or other small area	7	0	2	9
98th meridian	27	2	1	30
100th meridian	24	1	2	27
Eastern borders of MT-NM	4	6	0	10
Rockies (east face)	5	5	1	11
Other (often includes Old Northwest, or "between" Miss. & Mo., 98th & 100th)	15	0	0	15
Unclear	6	0	4	10
Blank	0	0	0	0
Northern boundary:				
Border, 49th parallel	57	13	6	76
Include parts of Canada	54	1	6	61
Arctic Circle or Ocean	8	0	1	9
Other	1	0	0	1
Unclear	6	1	4	11
Blank	38	9	6	53
Include Alaska? (at northern or western boundary)				
Yes	52	2	4	58
No	10	0	2	12
Include Hawaii?				
Yes	20	1	2	23
No	22	0	2	24
Southern boundary:				
Border or "Gulf"	75	11	7	93
Include parts of Mexico	40	2	6	48
Other	1	1	0	2
Unclear	6	1	4	11
Blank	42	9	6	57
Western boundary:				
Pacific Ocean	97	10	6	113
Pacific, with exclusions	12	1	3	16
(Exclude large cities:	3	0	1	4)
southern Calif.,	0	0	1	1)
all of Calif.	3	1	0	4)
Pacific N.W.	3	0	0	3)
"coastal strip"	3	0	1	4)
Cascades-Sierras	9	3	5	17
Exclude Calif.-Ore.-Wash.	4	0	0	4
Other	3	1	0	4
Unclear	6	1	4	11
Blank	33	8	5	46

Question 2: Where do *you* have to go to get to the West?

Replies to this question were not always consistent with replies to question 1. Here, respondents often placed the eastern edge farther west. Many seem to have answered #1 mindful of how they teach, but #2 in more personal terms. For example, the same person might say "Mississippi River" to #1, but "Grand Island, Nebraska" to #2.

Unanimously, everyone east of the plains states, when asked about the edge, identified an eastern edge. So did most of the Texans, but two of them and one Kansan referred only to a western edge (the Pacific). The farther west the respondent's residence, the more often she or he mentioned the Pacific or some other western border, rather than an eastern border. A few in the Southwest, assuming they should choose the closest edge, mentioned "somewhere in Mexico" or, specifically, Nogales (either Arizona or Sonora).

A few non-Californians put the edge at the California-Nevada line—that is, west of that is no longer "the West," but only 4 of the 37 Californians (WHA) did so. The other 33 Californians in the WHA group regarded themselves as inside the West; 8 expressly said, "I'm at the edge of the West." Thus, although some (especially among the writers) wanted California declared outside the region, the Californians nearly all dealt themselves in. One wrote that, being in Los Angeles, she was at the edge and the center simultaneously.

Everybody in the WHA living east of the Missouri River regard themselves as outside the West. (This is despite the fact that 34 respondents, from all over, placed the eastern edge at the Mississippi, not the Missouri; but nobody actually living between the Mississippi and Missouri rivers—in Minnesota, Iowa, Missouri, Arkansas, and Louisiana—claimed to be within the West.) On the other hand, respondents from Oklahoma, Texas, Colorado, Wyoming, Montana, and everywhere farther west said they were inside, except one Texan and six Californians.

The states whose respondents split over whether their state was part of the West—and most of them said the boundary was somewhere within their own state—were Kansas, Nebraska, and South Dakota. The Kansans split, five thinking themselves inside, two outside, with three ambiguous. The "outsiders" live in Lawrence and Topeka and said the edge was at Dodge City, or west of Salina and Wichita; two said they were half in, half out (Emporia and the Flint Hills); six said they were inside (they live in Lawrence, Topeka, Manhattan, Wichita, and Dodge City) and would have to go to the Pacific, to Ohio, to St. Louis, or to Micronesia to get to the edge. The respondent from Dodge City, Betty Braddock, who manages a cultural resource center there, wrote that the edge of the West is "In Dodge City—on the 100th meridian."

As for the ten Nebraskans and South Dakotans, all but one placed the edge somewhere within their states. Two wrote "I'm there"; they live in Lincoln. Another Lincolnian said he was right on the edge. Two others (from Lincoln or Omaha) said the edge was 90 or 100 miles west of Omaha;

one named Grand Island, another North Platte. The two South Dakotans both named the 100th meridian; one lives on it, the other a bit east and hence declared himself outside. The sole North Dakotan also named the 100th meridian. So, as identified by those closest to it and most conscious of it, the eastern edge of the West consists of the eastern borders of Texas and Oklahoma, and it either continues straight north along the Missouri and Red rivers or jumps somewhere to a north-south line through the middle of Kansas, Nebraska, and the Dakotas.

The replies to question 2 were more personal, less cerebral, less insistent that the West cannot be identified geographically. Thus, question 2 (rather unintentionally—I sought primarily a personal feeling of when one gets there or gets out of it) served as a validity check on question 1.

A few places received several mentions. St. Louis was often claimed to be the western edge, East St. Louis as just outside; others drew lines between Kansas City, Missouri, and Kansas City, Kansas; Omaha and Council Bluffs; and Dallas and Fort Worth (five respondents) in the same way. Kearney and North Platte, Nebraska, and Topeka, Kansas, each got two votes. Five chose Grand Island, Nebraska, and five others Fort Smith, Arkansas.

The more imperialistic (or cosmopolitan) respondents placed the western and northern edges (one vote each) at Kamchatka, Attu Island, Japan, Micronesia, the North Pole, or the Arctic Ocean. The farthest eastward placement of the eastern boundary was western New England.

Does residence or previous experience have much to do with where people put the boundaries? Initially I suspected so but it seems to have minimal influence except in a couple of ways. I had expected that people in, say, New York would say Chicago is West (as people did when I was a child in northern New York) and that people on the plains would consider Chicago and Indiana as East (as my wife's graduate-school roommate, a South Dakotan, did). But not many did so. It is true that eastern people picked the Mississippi River or St. Louis more often than did people living in the middle of the country (in Kansas, for example), but so did Californians, looking from the other direction. Haziness about distant geography played some role—Californians were happy with any place from the Missouri River to Ohio, while some easterners think that not much separates the Rockies from the Sierras or the Pacific. That aside, there were few differences that seem based solely on residential experience.

Question 3: What are the West's Characteristics?

This was the most open-ended of the three questions. Question 1 directed the reply toward four compass directions; question 2 asked for specific locations on the "edge" of the West. But question 3 did not limit responses. The result was that many people gave more than one defining characteristic. They fall into two broad categories: geographical definitions such as aridity, scenery, open space, lack of population density, or environment;

and cultural definitions such as openness, friendliness, or other attitudes; a common and recent frontier history; or that the West is a myth or state of mind. Clearly, here as in the replies to the other two questions, historians were more geographically minded; editors and, above all, writers more culturally minded. While 61 percent of the WHA group mentioned cultural definitions, virtually all of the writers did so. The historians often said that a definition of the West depends on *when* one is talking about—the term means nothing without a time frame. The writers often said that the West exists in the past, and in the mind; very few of them seem to think that there is such a thing as a twentieth-century West, while few historians would now wish to conclude western history at 1890 or 1920. Again the separation of historians (seeking verifiable truths) from the writers (seeking to explain, extol, and extend the myth) is very sharp.

Besides the geographical and cultural definitions, a few others appeared. Thirty historians (but only two editors and two writers) found the West distinctive as the place of greatest ethnic and racial mixing, the most varied multicultural region. Seventeen historians (but no editors or writers) found the presence of Indians a distinguishing feature. Twenty-eight historians (only two editors and two writers) noted the unusually extraction-oriented economy, and fourteen cited environmental attitudes and practices (reckless or careful) as western traits. Four historians believe the West is distinctive because slavery never flourished there. Nine historians said that the West cannot be defined; they see no distinguishing features that are not so riddled by exceptions as to make the regional concept useless.

These responses are so rich and nuanced that I would be editorializing if I attempted to summarize them further. Look instead at the next article, where many of them appear verbatim.

A few replies could not easily be categorized. The West is defined, said one historian, by its lack of a distinct accent; another said it keeps shrinking; another said it is defined only by simple latitude and longitude; another by the use of six- and eight-man high school football teams. Among the writers, one said westerners are distinct because they *do* have a distinct accent; another cited "reading habits" (but didn't say what they are). One of the editors said the West simply has "fewer asses."

It seems clear that the idea of the West solely as place—where it now is—has some way to go. The majority of WHA members, and larger proportions of western fiction writers and the editors and publishers of newspapers and magazines in the West, do not agree—not yet, anyway—that the West is limited to the present western half of the country, or that "frontier" is a dirty word, or that history began in 1850. The "new" and "old" western histories each claim many adherents. To judge by the results of this survey, they will be arguing the place-versus-process question for a long time.

What the Respondents Wrote

When you put a few questions concerning something they really care about to a few hundred historians, journalists, and creative writers, you can expect to get some interesting answers. What follows is a sampling. In many cases, quotations are only parts of responses sent. Western Writers of America members are identified as "WWA"; editors and publishers are so indicated; otherwise respondents are members of the Western History Association.

Because it touches on many points, we begin with a letter from Charles S. Peterson, former editor of the *Western Historical Quarterly,* writing from St. George, Utah:

> What a heck of a thing to do to people! How should I know where the West is? Having grown up in its heartland and spent my life thinking about where it is and associating with its historians I tend to be expansive about what Western history is, claiming to Columbus in point of time and sprawling through place, process, and topic to find it wherever my interests and state of mind take me. To paraphrase Mark Twain's happy phrase, "Wheresoever Eve was, there was Eden" . . . , wheresoever I am (in scholarly need and inner pleasure, as well as physical being), there is West. It doesn't make much sense and probably can't be applied to any form of analysis but [the West] has made for a good life. . . . Its role as the last West . . . of the great era of world imperial/Manifest Destiny expansion and as last tip of a romantic/simpler world gives it extraordinary nostalgic force or imaginative appeal as does . . . its utility as a comparative tool as "new frontiers" are . . . contemplated. [Also,] the way its past cuts across other regional and national histories fuzzes its dimensions, complicates its definition, makes it the country cousin of American history, but gives it continuing relevance. [Richard] Hofstadter talks of Turner's continuing relevance to four generations of historians, and by now he is relevant to yet another. While he won't condescend to say it Hofstadter implies that it is in defining West as process Turner continually reflects the West's essential tie on the American mind and its past. . . .

Responses to the question involving the boundaries of the West ranged from extremely detailed and specific to quite broad. Among them:

Merle Wells, Idaho State Historical Society:

> East . . . from a point just west of Mackenzie river delta, proceed along Yukon's district boundary and an irregular line past Fort McMurray, Saskatoon, Regina, Williston, Rapid City, Chadron, Scotts Bluff, Sterling, Clovis, Fort Stockton, and a point directly south (approximately 80 miles into Coahuila); South: through Coahuila and Chihuahua to a point south of Colonia Juarez; continue northwest across Sonora below Oaxaca to a Pacific coast terminal west of Ensenada. West: a Pacific coastal boundary (including islands) along California as far as all of Alaska. North: along Alaska's coast past Port Hope almost to Mackenzie delta.

Maxine Benson, Denver:

> The Mountain and Pacific Time zones—no place in the Central time zone seems really "western" to me.

A well-known writer and historian who wishes anonymity here:

As I drive West fron the East, whenever my discomfort from humidity ends, that's where the West begins. On I-80, it happens at Kearney, Nebraska—zingo! without fail.

Richard Maxwell Brown, University of Oregon:

Those who desire inflexible scholarly certitude will not be comfortable with regionalism.

Elliott West, University of Arkansas:

Bob Athearn used to say: "I wouldn't let California into the West with a search warrant," and with some exceptions I tend to agree.

Robert Gunderson, Indiana University and Huntington Library:

When I got back to Indiana from Pasadena, I saw a pickup with a bumper sticker: "Eat more Possum"—I realized I was a long way from L.A. where bumper stickers advised me to "ski naked"—Both places, however, for some strange geographical reason, belong in the *West*.

Clayton Fox (WWA), Olympia, Washington:

The "West" started just west of Tidewater and was pushed by succeeding waves all the way to the Parker Ranch in Hawaii and the tundra at Nome.

Some respondents stressed the multicultural character of the West. Richard White of the University of Washington:

The American West is a product of conquest and of the mixing of diverse groups of peoples. The West began when Europeans sought to conquer various areas of the continent and when people of Indian, European, Asian, and African ancestry began to meet within the territories west of the Missouri that would later be part of the United States. The West did not suddenly emerge; rather, it was gradually created.

Kathleen Underwood, University of Texas–Arlington:

I think "the West" is much more complex than we who study it would like it to be—I contemplate the multicultural past in this region and find trouble labeling it.

Gunther Barth, University of California–Berkeley:

The persistent struggle to subjugate the previous occupants of any newly emerging West.

Robert Maynard, Publisher, *Oakland Tribune:*

It's younger, newer, and less traditional than the East or Midwest. It is also much more diverse and less rigid about race.

Lawrence C. Kelly, Denton, Texas:

Historically, my West is . . . separated from the rest of the nation by its for-
tuitous escape (for the most part) from the debilitating baggage of slavery,
a factor that enabled Westerners to go their way without expending psychic energy on this destructive inheritance from the past.

Cynthia Sturgis, San Diego:

There's a psychic or spiritual West, that is unfettered, outrageous, simple,
strong, blunt, even impolite but fundamentally decent (which is not the
same thing as kind). To those who came first, tens of thousands of years
ago, it was just "home." So the EuroAmerican concept of Indians as a part
of the landscape is, however condescending, in some sense right and correct. We may have abused that hospitality, as we did that of the land and
the animals, but our recognition that Indians belonged in a special sort of
a way, were a part of and not apart from, was searingly accurate. . . . The
West is a state of mind . . . a dream. That's why "gone west" is a euphemism for dying—and being reborn.

Question 3, asking *why* respondents named the boundaries as they did,
that is, what characteristics set apart the West, elicited more cultural than
geographical answers. They fall into several categories: general answers;
the West is a "state of mind"; in the West live good people (positive stereotypes); in the West live not-so-good people (negative or shaded stereotypes); cultural definitions; environmental definitions; the West as myth;
and finally, process-versus-place.

General, varied answers include the following:

Richard A. Bartlett, Tallahassee, Florida:

I consider the most un-West part of the West its teeming cities. Increasingly they are more similar than dissimilar to eastern cities; and their
inhabitants, increasingly, share the same thoughts and mind-sets of their
eastern compatriots.

Bruce Walton, Pasadena, California:

It is so difficult to categorize "the West" because it is so diversified from
locale to locale. *Elevation:* the highest and the lowest. *Rainfall:* the most
and the least. The distances are longer from place to place. Our clocks are
behind all the other sections. We have the most and best of earthquakes,
etc. But all this is *today.* To me *History* stops in 1915; since that date, all
is *modern.*

Carl Abbott, Portland, Oregon:

The search for a "real West" . . . [explicitly assumes] the historical West
was a low-density farming and mining frontier. I could certainly counter
that the historical West was urban first and rural second, from the early
Spanish and Russian settlements through gold rush San Francisco, silver
rush Denver, railroad boom Bismarck, health boom Pasadena, oil boom

Midland, and defense boom San Diego. If there *is* one thing that sets apart the western half of the nation (and continent), it is space or elbow room as a neutral category. The West has longer distances and higher mountains. What makes "space" less than satisfying as a defining concept is its relativity. Dry is dry, and can be defined absolutely. "High, wide, and handsome" has meaning only in comparative terms when juxtaposed against a "low, narrow, and ugly" East or Europe. Nevertheless, I don't see any other single factor that will come as close.

Tom Bryant (WWA), Corvallis, Montana:

Sheer space is the main characteristic of the West. The expanse of unpopulated areas, that's the real West. We've still got some counties in Montana that have less than 1,500 people living there and neighbors are miles and miles apart. That's the definition of the west and also the attraction. The open plains, the shining mountains and the clear streams—the Big Sky.

Bill Crider (WWA), Alvin, Texas:

You asked where it is that I have to go to get into the West. Well, for me the answer is that I have to go into a book [and he cites *Deerslayer, Giants in the Earth,* and *The Big Sky* as examples. But on a map:] Ft. Worth is "where the West begins." But to tell the truth, the West for me is associated with the frontier that's long gone. The West is a part of my imagination much more than it's a part of my reality.

Janet R. Fireman, Los Angeles Museum of Natural History:

The West is distinguished from other regions by its extraordinarily strong sense of place, which is retained along with and despite all else.

Roberta McGowen (WWA), Ulysses, Nebraska:

The ethic of the true West is the ethic of the cattleman: Not the cattle feeder, not the horse breeder, but the cow/calf man, the old, hard bitten, dedicated, "stay with it come hell or high water stockman." Anything else is just scenery.

Dee Brown (WWA), Little Rock:

The old West was set apart by its vast distances, plains, mountains and forests. Except for native tribes, the inhabitants were from somewhere else. They were more venturesome than most, friendlier, crueler, more generous, greedier, more intensely independent, more exploitive of natural resources. Today such differences are rapidly disappearing into homogeneity.

To some, the West is "a state of mind":

Donald C. Cutter, Albuquerque:

The boundaries are more psychological than geographical. [T]he bottom line [is] "whatever the Western historian wishes it to be."

Lawrence Jelinek, Los Angeles:

The Historic West began at the Fall Line on the Piedmont Plateau and extended to the offshore islands of the Pacific. . . .

The Contemporary American West begins where the woodlands give way to the tall grass prairies. . . .

The West of the Imagination begins in the minds and dreams of the immigrants and emigrants. It lives on in the thoughts, dreams, and art of the West's residents, immigrants, and migrants of the day, as well as within those nonwesterners, worldwide, who ponder the West at any moment for any span of time for any purpose.

The West of myth knows no boundaries short of the limits of the mind and spirit, and the ability to communicate.

A number of respondents spoke of—or manifested—stereotypes about the West. Some are favorable, some unfavorable, some mixed:

Sam Arnold, Denver:

Westerners teach their children two values: (1) Close the gate! (responsibility) (2) Keep yer word *good*! (truth & honesty).

Jerry Glenn, Rexburg, Idaho:

Independent enough to leave surveys to Eastern folks.

Elmer Kelton (WWA), San Angelo, Texas:

What sets the West apart is an attitude of openness, friendliness and self-reliance inherited from pioneer ancestors whose neighbors were few and therefore treasured, and whose independence and self-reliance were necessary for survival. The West tends to distrust unsolicited advice, much less orders from people two thousand miles to the east whose motives and capabilities are subject to question. It resents the attitude that it is somehow still a colony, needing guidance from its betters.

Richard Cheverton, *Orange County Register,* California:

It's a state of mind, really—a metaphor for the freedom to work our will on the real world—West is anyplace in America where you sense new beginnings. [Its characteristics are] openness—a certain ruthlessness—optimism—brutality, sometimes, but not as mindless as in "the East"—a focus on self-realization—identification with/control of the environment.

Paula Petrik, Orono, Maine:

The mixture of cultures; the isolation of one community from another . . . the geography both physical and demographic; and . . . the longer I live in New England, the more convinced I am that westerners are, in fact, more friendly and outgoing.

Elliott West, University of Arkansas:

A genuine openness to strangers and a directness of expression and opinion. That peculiar blend of get-your-back-up individualism and close reliance on neighbors. It also can be silly posturing and truly unpleasant behavior. (It occurs to me that in question #1 we might set one point of the eastern boundary of the West along a stretch of the old Jacksboro Highway—Texas 199—west of Fort Worth, a line of low groggeries and whiskey holes where it was hard to drink a glass of beer without some lout in a big hat offering to break a bottle over your head because you were wearing those sissy Wrangler jeans instead of Levis.) Anyway, . . . to a point the West is the West because its people say it is, or act it out. Myth, place, and identity . . . are inexplicably intertwined. Trying to unravel them is impossible; more than that, it also misses the point.

Sandra Schackel, Boise:

Sense of space. Somewhat slower pace of life. Sense of well-being that comes from the climate and geography. Less pretentious. Conservative. Arid.

Zeese Papanikolas, Oakland:

A higher degree of willful self-delusion than any other region except perhaps the white south before *Brown vs. Board of Education.* Westerners (myself included) continue to think of themselves as independent, free-spirited, culturally unique, when in fact their land and their jobs, the TV programs they watch and the politicians they vote for are owned by the same corporations that own everything else.

Others stressed environment:

Frederick C. Luebke, University of Nebraska:

No one quality defines the West and no one part of the West need display all of the characteristics of the West. It is spacious, open, and perhaps less friendly in fact than its reputation would have it. Most of the people have come from somewhere else (which paradoxically can even be said of many people born there). Its culture is highly varied, derivative, and therefore superficial. It is an exploited, colonial area with an environment far more fragile than many of its inhabitants seem to realize, even though environmental forces are obviously powerful.

Gerald Warren, San Diego *Union:*

We are more mobile, tend to look toward the Pacific basin as well as Europe and share an interest in Latin America with Texas. We inherit from the Old West our concern about the land and water. The Federal Government affects us greatly but we tend to look to municipal and state governments for results.

William Lang, Hood River, Oregon:

The most important characteristic is the dominant role of the environment on the people who have chosen to live in the region. Weather and landforms are similarly dramatic and domineering elsewhere—Australia, Siberia, Tibet—but the essence of the American West is the interface

between human community and the environment. It is a love-hate &
despoil-protect relationship that defines the West for me.

Florence Williams, *High Country News,* Paonia, Colorado:

[The West's characteristics include] trout, grizzlies, granite, canyons of
sand. Country music, drive-ins. Logging, grazing, federal land agencies.
Poor Mexican food. Really old Ford trucks with no emission controls.

A few underscored the West as *myth*—in very different ways:

William H. Goetzmann, University of Texas, Austin:

It is the creation myth of the United States. It is the area populated by the
major figures and characteristic landscapes, both urban and rural, of the
creation myth.

John Opie, New Jersey Institute of Technology, Newark:

The West is America's mythic region, containing rites of passage, archetypal heroes, containing models of human behavior, and giving meaning
and value to life. History of the West is sacred history that tells of entry
into superpowerful places by extraordinary beings, living a fateful
sequence of events. . . . It is sacred because it is saturated with power and
being. It is a history because it relates how a people came into being.

Robert Smith, Eastern Montana College, Billings:

"The West" has no boundaries. It is a direction and as such it has great
meaning. It is the direction in which the sun sets and therefore has some
very important psychological implications. The sun has long been associated with Apollo the Lightbringer, with consciousness and knowledge. As
the sun sets in "the west" a symbolic extinguishing of the consciousness
takes place. With the end of consciousness begins a journey through the
underworld fraught with danger and uncertainty. Historians, particularly
professional historians who emerged in the late nineteenth century and
their intellectual descendants, have confused this metaphysical aspect of
"the West" with a physical place, largely due to a material bias which lies
at the very foundations of objective history, a product of nineteenth-
century positivism. . . . "The West" is the direction of paradox. It leads to
the place where souls are extinguished and reborn. It is the most fearful
place and at the same time the place of hope. . . .

Shirl Henke (WWA), Youngstown, Ohio:

Bernard DeVoto perhaps defined the West better than anyone. "Eastward
Thoreau went only by force, but westward, ever since Columbus dared the
Ocean Sea, westward he had gone free. The lodestone of the West tugged
deep in the blood. . . . And if either Freud or the Navajo speak true, westward we shall find the hole in the earth through which the soul may plunge
to peace." The West is a dream, the freedom to begin again. As such it is
the stuff of primal myth and will never be defined absolutely. I do not
believe it accidental that Star Trek has become a classic. Its opening line
says it all: "Space, the final Frontier. . . ."

We began this discussion with the mention of the controversy about the West as process, and the West as place. Robert Utley spoke to this:

> There are two Wests, in my conception: the chronological West and the geographic West. The chronological West is everything west of the north-south frontier line at any point in history. The east-west frontier of the Spanish borderlands does not figure into this conception. . . . My geographical West is only partly defined by such precise measures as rainfall, topography, and vegetation. As shown on the map, it is everything west of the eastern boundaries of the Dakotas, Nebraska, Kansas, and Oklahoma, with a line through Texas roughly represented by the Balcones Escarpment. This West extends all the way to the Pacific shore, with no exclusions. It includes Alaska but not Hawaii. It includes Canada to the Arctic and the North Mexican states. One big caveat: when the frontier of the chronological West crosses the eastern border of the geographic West, the two merge and the frontier loses its significance as a definition of the West. In essence, this means that for me the geographic West has been *the* West from that day to this. . . . For both chronological and geographical West, historical experience is the prime determinant in my mind—every element of what we term the westward movement. This, of course, is the Anglo-Saxon westward movement the "new" historians decry. The geographical West—the "Old West" of the imagination as well as reality—is characterized in addition by the usual Webb measures of aridity, topography, etc., but as modified or even eliminated by historical experience in non-Webbian places like the Pacific Northwest or California's Central Valley. Such precision as this definition lacks does not trouble me, for my definition of the West is personal, drawn not only from formal study but from feelings shaped by forty years of intellectual, physical, and emotional experience.

America Only More So

CLYDE A. MILNER II

Often a dream, sometimes a metaphor, the American West is a place that millions of people can visualize. Certain landscapes of mountain and desert are instantly recognizable. So are certain residents, if they ride horses and wear broad hats or feathered headbands. In these nearly universal images, the West seems grandly conceived and easily explained. It is the West that serves as popular myth and national symbol.

The American West of historical interpretation is much more complex. The people of the West are not readily stereotyped. Lakotas, Navajos, and other Native Americans retain distinct cultural identities, as do a cornucopia of immigrants whose cultural heritages may be traced to Europe, Africa, or Asia but who sometimes arrived from farther north via Canada, from farther west via the Pacific Islands, or from farther south via Mexico and Latin America.

Like its residents, the location of the American West has changed over time. One generation's West became another generation's Midwest or Upper South. Such was the case for Andrew Jackson, who served as president of the United States from 1829 to 1837. In the late 1780s, after two years of studying law in Salisbury, North Carolina, while still in his early twenties, Jackson moved first to Martinsville in North Carolina and then to Jonesboro across the Appalachian Mountains in what would become the state of Tennessee. By the fall of 1788, he had arrived in the log-cabin village of Nashville, where he made his home and established his political career. Throughout his adult life, Jackson called himself a "westerner," and his avid supporters reveled in "Old Hickory's" regional identity.

By the late decades of the twentieth century, a western president could no longer hale from Tennessee, and his western identity needed to relate to cowboys of the open range rather than pioneers of the backwoods. Ronald Reagan fit both the image and the location. He owned a ranch, rode a horse, and wore cowboy boots. Reagan grew up in Illinois, but he found personal and political success in California. In his career as an actor, he spent four years on screen in western clothes as the announcer for the television series *Death Valley Days*. He became governor of California, which made him an important political figure. California had not been part of the United States during Jackson's lifetime, but even before Reagan's presidency (1981–89), it had the largest population of all the states, not only in the West but also in the nation.

Historical study recognizes the significance of change over time. One story of change explains how the West of the nation's political map once included Tennessee but not California and then at a later time included California but not Tennessee. This story of change emphasizes the nation's expansion westward. But there is another way to tell the historical story of the West. This story forms around the idea of place—a West firmly located beyond the Mississippi River. In this trans-Mississippi West, various historical factors, including the expansion of the United States, have shaped the story.

Beyond the Mississippi, the American West became a distinct place whose historical interpretation follows no one master narrative and no single factor of plot. Instead many narratives, themes, and ideas, like the many peoples of the region, are brought together. In other words, the large and complex story of the West stretches across a shared historical terrain. It is a terrain containing many discrete locations, separate voices, and diverse ideas. For example, the West's story has many beginnings—first in the different origin tales of the region's native peoples and then in the tales of exploration created by the new peoples from Europe. The West's geographic boundaries are also variable. The *eastern* boundary takes form beyond the Mississippi River where the aridity of the Great Plains is clearly established, such as along the ninety-eighth meridian, which roughly coincides with the isohyetal line of less than twenty inches annual rainfall. The *western* boundary extends beyond the coast of the Pacific Ocean to the Aleutian Islands of Alaska and to the chain of islands, atolls, and reefs that make up the state of Hawai`i.

Alaska and Hawai`i represent a greater West that connects to the history of the United States in both the nineteenth and twentieth centuries. Their inclusion also recognizes the grand geographic diversity of the American West. Just as the West has no fixed set of external boundaries, it has no fixed goegraphic or cultural unity. Crosscut with various subregions, disparate states, and distinct peoples, the West demonstrates an intentional oxymoron, what the historian Richard Etulain has called a "fragmented unity."

In this complex and puzzling place, in this "fragmented unity" that is the West, the clearest boundaries may be those delineated by the people within the region. The historian Martin Ridge has stated: "There is a location on the plains of the West where, for some undetermined reason, people think of themselves as being westerners. . . . There is a psychological fault line that separates regions. As these people see it, they are not from the South but from the Southwest; not from the Middle West but from the West." Travelers sense this same fault line. Somewhere beyond the Mississippi, the horizon is more distant, the land more open, and the sky much larger. Well before they reach the Rocky Mountains, they know they have reached the West.

Archaeologists and historians know that crossing the plains was not the only way to reach the West. The first major migrations by native peoples came from the north, whereas the first major incursion by Europeans came from the south. These Spanish expeditions arrived in the homelands of well-established settlers. Did either group know that they were *in* the West? Of course not.

The American West is an idea that became a place. This transformation did not occur quickly. The idea developed from distinctly European origins into an American nationalistic conception. The western edge of several European empires, especially the British, moved into the hinterlands of North America. The United States inherited this westward edginess and made it the main directional thrust of its own empire. Once across the Mississippi, these American lands did not fill up with a steady progression of settlers. Overlanders and gold seekers pushed ahead to Oregon and California. The mountains, plains, and deserts would be filled in later, if at all. Throughout the nineteenth century, the United States laid claim to more and more of its West, culminating in 1898 with the annexation of Hawai`i. All of this occurred because a nation established mainly by African and European peoples created a region that replaced a world—a homeland once defined exclusively by native peoples.

Throughout the twentieth century, the West became a very American place with an increasingly diverse population. To expand on a statement about California, attributed to the writer Wallace Stegner, the West is America *only more so.* In this light, the culmination of America's history occurs in the West in the last half of the twentieth century. Writing the history of the West becomes, therefore, a vital aspect of understanding the history of the United States. Such a perspective is hardly new, but it should be carefully considered. The important distinction is whether the West is created and shaped primarily by the forces of American history both from within the region and from without, or whether the history of the West is what shaped the history of the United States. The latter proposition, in somewhat different formulation, has generated an astoundingly long-lived scholarly debate.

For several intellectual generations, a dispute has raged over the concept of the "frontier" as articulated by Frederick Jackson Turner in his 1893 essay "The Significance of the Frontier in American History." Turner first presented his famous frontier thesis on an especially warm July evening in 1893, when as a young, thirty-two-year-old historian from the University of Wisconsin, he gave the final talk at the last session on the second day of the World's Congress of Historians and Historical Students organized as part of the Columbian Exposition in Chicago. His audience did not respond with any enthusiasm, but four other speakers had preceded him. So it was a long meeting after a very hot day, yet Turner's essay would not be forgotten.

Turner's published version of his talk began with a quotation from the 1890 bulletin of the superintendent of the census. "Up to and including 1880 the country had a frontier of settlement, but at present the unsettled area has been so broken into by isolated bodies of settlement that there can hardly be said to be a frontier line." The census bureau defined the frontier as the outer margin of non-Indian settlement with a density of two persons per square mile. Turner made more of the frontier than just a line of population scarcity. He told his readers: "Up to our own day American history has been in a large degree the history of the colonization of the Great West. The existence of an area of free land, its continuous recession, and the advance of American settlement westward, explain American development." Turner went on to claim that the frontier also explained American democracy and American character. The challenges of the wild land forged the values of the American citizen. If nothing else, Turner's thesis expressed a vital moment in the conception of the nation's history.

More than a century after its presentation, Turner's frontier and its scholarly significance have undergone extensive revision—at times to praise his ideas and at other times, such as in recent years, to bury them. Even his advocates are aware that Turner's words occasionally exhibit the ethnocentric perspective of a bygone era. Early in his essay, he refers to the frontier as "the meeting point between savagery and civilization." Of course, anthropology and ethnohistory now recognize the complexity of native life that seems more "civilized" in many locations than the behavior of the invading nonnative peoples. Other critics remain frustrated by the vague use of the term *frontier* itself. In this case, Turner candidly admitted, "The term is an elastic one, and for our purpose does not need sharp definition."

Turner ended his essay on a grandly apprehensive note by asserting, "The frontier has gone, and with its going has closed the first period of American history." He did not apply his "elastic" term into the next century, although others have done so. . . . Many historians have disputed Turner's ideas, and many of these arguments have proposed new ways to understand the significance of the history of the American West. This search for a new significance is also an attempt to free the history of the American West from what could be termed "the Mount Rushmore dilemma."

The four gigantic presidential heads carved into the granite of a prominent mountain in the Black Hills of South Dakota represent American nationalism in its most artificially monumental form. George Washington's nose alone is longer than the entire head, from the chin upward, of the Great Sphinx at Giza. Three of the four historical figures seem out of context for such a distinctly western setting: Washington, Thomas Jefferson, and Abraham Lincoln never visited the area. Theodore Roosevelt spent three years, from 1884 to 1886, ranching in the Badlands of the Dakota Territory. But Roosevelt was not chosen because of his sojourn in the West. According to Lincoln Borglum, the son of Gutzon Borglum, who designed the monument, then-president Calvin Coolidge made the decisive argument. Coolidge admired Roosevelt on the questionable assessment that he was a president who had protected the rights of working men.

In 1923 and 1924, Doane Robinson, the state historian of South Dakota, conceived the idea of a monument that depicted the great heroes of western history such as Lewis and Clark, John C. Frémont, and Red Cloud. Borglum accepted the challenge to find the appropriate mountain, but as his son reported, "He had become convinced that the proposed theme—heroes of western history—was too regionally circumscribed, too insignificant nationally." In effect, Borglum had decided that the West did not have historical figures grand enough to match its own mountains. Both Robinson and Borglum thought of heroic men and considered no representation of women. The elimination of Red Cloud only increased the irony that surrounds this monument, since his people, the Oglala Lakota Sioux, consider the Black Hills to be sacred land.

The dilemma of the Mount Rushmore monument is that it presents a visual argument for the *in*significance of western history, whereas the dilemma of Frederick Jackson Turner's frontier thesis is that it presents a scholarly argument for too much significance. No one monument and no single theory can either eradicate or explain the history of the American West. Instead, during what is now at least four decades of revitalized study, a set of significant themes has emerged. Four are worthy of some consideration here; but they are not an exclusive list.

The Non-Vanishing Native Americans. The persistence of native peoples today would startle visitors from the nineteenth century. Even the best "friends" of the Indians assumed that Native Americans would die out, culturally if not physically. Native population reached its nadir in the 1890s at approximately 250,000. In the same decade, the non-Indian population of the United States grew to over 75 million. These original residents had not lived solely in what the United States considered its West. But governmental efforts in the first half of the nineteenth century attempted to relocate all Indians to lands beyond the Mississippi. The removal policy did not eliminate eastern Indians, but it did concentrate even more native peoples in the West, especially in the Indian Territory, which eventually became the state of Oklahoma.

A hundred years after its nadir, federally recognized Native American population is approaching 2 million. These native peoples exist in greater numbers and have greater landholdings in the American West than in any other region of the nation. Native peoples, their cultures and histories, have not been eradicated. They are living proof of the centuries of human history connected to what is now the American West.

The Impact of the Federal Government. In a region supposedly characterized by personal freedom and rugged individualism, the federal government has played an astonishingly large role. In political terms, the federal government created the territories and states of the trans-Mississippi, and it has not left them alone. From the explorations of Meriwether Lewis and William Clark in 1804–6 to the atmospheric testing of nuclear bombs in southern Nevada from 1951 to 1958, projects funded by Congress and administered by federal agencies have affected life in the West. Federal land grants underwrote the establishment of four transcontinental railroads after the Civil War, and military spending transformed the West's economy during and after World War II.

The federal government remains the greatest single landholder in the West. National parks and national forests are only two examples. In 1944, the federal government controlled 99 percent of the land in Alaska and 87 percent of the land in Nevada. Currently, the average for all twelve states from the Rocky Mountains westward, excluding Hawai`i, is over 50 percent. Not surprisingly, water, forest, and land-management programs continue to shape the West through the sometimes heavy-handed implementation of national policy.

The Exploitation of a Golden Land. The West's majestically scenic landscape has inspired not only artists but also entrepreneurs. Many of the latter sought wealth, not only on the western land but also beneath it in the mining of gold and silver and then of copper, coal, and uranium. Only a few made their fortunes. Many more toiled for little gain and often greater loss. Oil, especially in Texas, Oklahoma, and California, developed a similar story of boom and bust. Even wheat farming in the Red River valley of North Dakota had a bonanza era in the late 1870s and early 1880s.

For regional, national, and global markets, the economic development of the West has exploited a cornucopia of resources from timber in the Northwest to hydroelectric power on the Colorado River. Yet, in a term coined in the 1960s by Arizona's Stewart Udall, the "myth of super-abundance" has obscured a troubled and fragile natural environment. Water is an especially problematic resource in a predominantly arid West. The large-scale environmental cost of economic development began in the nineteenth century but became a major public issue only in the final decades of the twentieth century.

The Global Population of an International Borderland. The grand American story of mobility and immigration culminates in the American West. To some excited observers, it seemed nearly the entire world rushed toward California after 1848 to pan for gold. The influx of diverse peoples has continued to the present day, especially along the Pacific coast and in Hawai`i. The American West began as an international borderland between native peoples, the Spanish, Russians, French, and British. Today the international borderlands are even more significant with connections directly to Canada in the north, Mexico to the south, and numerous Asian nations via the Pacific. Immigrant groups who first arrived on America's east coast have representative populations in the West, as do peoples from Latin America, Asia, Australia, and the Pacific Islands. Just as the West's economy since the nineteenth century has increasingly connected to world markets, its population has increased its connections to the world's peoples.

Ultimately, the case for the significance of the history of the American West moves beyond the national context to the world's stage. The world knows the American West through mass media images and occasional tourist visits. It also knows the West in the nationalistic rhetoric of journalists and politicians. The West has been oversold and oversimplified as a vast vista of mountain, plain, and desert occupied by heroic, often male, archetypes noted for their violent actions. Through these misrepresentations, the world's peoples, and even the people of the United States, have little knowledge of western history. Responsible scholarship and thoughtful analysis need to supplant widespread distortions and easy assumptions. The West deserves a history that enfolds the complex landscape and the diverse peoples of this distinctively American region.

Y *FURTHER READING*

Ray Allen Billington, *America's Frontier Heritage* (1966)
——, *Frederick Jackson Turner* (1973)
Ray Allen Billington and Martin Ridge, *Westward Expansion: A History of the American Frontier,* 5th ed. (1982)
William Cronon, George Miles, and Jay Gitlin, eds., *Under an Open Sky: Rethinking America's Western Past* (1992)

Stanley Elkins and Eric McKitrick, "A Meaning for Turner's Frontier," *Political Science Quarterly* 69 (1954): 321–53, 562–602.

David M. Emmons, "Constructed Province: History and the Making of the Last American West," *Western Historical Quarterly* 25 (1994): 437–59

Richard Etulain, ed., *Writing Western History: Essays on Major Western Historians* (1991)

Gene M. Gressley, "The West: Past, Present, and Future," *Western Historical Quarterly* 17 (1986): 5–23

Richard Hofstadter and Seymour Martin Lipset, eds., *Turner and the Sociology of the Frontier* (1968)

Wilbur Jacobs, *On Turner's Trail: 100 Years of Writing Western History* (1994)

——, ed., *The Historical World of Frederick Jackson Turner* (1968)

Richard Jensen, "On Modernizing Frederick Jackson Turner: The Historiography of Regionalism," *Western Historical Quarterly* 11 (1980): 307–22

Howard Lamar, "Persistent Frontier: The West in the Twentieth Century," *Western Historical Quarterly* 4 (1973): 5–25

Howard Lamar and Leonard Thompson, eds., *The Frontier in History: North America and Southern Africa Compared* (1981)

Robert E. Lang, Deborah Epstein Popper, and Frank J. Popper, "Progress of the Nation: The Settlement History of the Enduring American Frontier," *Western Historical Quarterly* 26 (1995): 289–307

Patricia Nelson Limerick, Clyde A. Milner II, and Charles E. Rankin, eds., *Trails: Toward a New Western History* (1991)

Frederick Merk, *History of the Westward Movement* (1978)

Clyde A. Milner II, ed., *A New Significance: Re-envisioning the History of the American West* (1996)

Gerald Nash, *Creating the West: Historical Interpretations, 1890–1990* (1991)

Walter Nugent, "Comparing Wests and Frontiers." In *The Oxford History of the American West.* Eds. Clyde A. Milner II, Carol A. O'Connor, and Martha A. Sandweiss (1994)

Rodman W. Paul and Michael P. Malone, "Tradition and Challenge in Western Historiography," *Western Historical Quarterly* 16 (1985): 27–53

Earl Pomeroy, "Toward a Reorientation on Western History: Continuity and Environment," *Mississippi Valley Historical Review* 41 (1955): 579–600

Frank J. Popper, "The Strange Case of the Contemporary American Frontier," *Yale Review* 76 (Autumn 1976): 101–121

Jackson K. Putnam, "The Turner Thesis and the Westward Movement: A Reappraisal," *Western Historical Quarterly* 7 (1976): 377–404

Martin Ridge, "Frederick Jackson Turner, Ray Allen Billington, and American Frontier History," *Western Historical Quarterly* 19 (1988): 5–20

——, "The American West: From Frontier to Region," *New Mexico Historical Quarterly* 64 (April 1989): 125–141

Walter Rundell, Jr., "Concepts of the 'Frontier' and the 'West'," *Arizona and the West* 1 (1959): 13–41

Jerome O. Steffen, *Comparative Frontiers: A Proposal for Studying the American West* (1980)

Michael Steiner, "From Frontier to Region: Frederick Jackson Turner and the New Western History," *Pacific Historical Review* 64 (1995): 479–501

Walter Prescott Webb, *The Great Frontier* (1952)

David J. Weber, "Turner, the Boltonians, and the Borderlands," *American Historical Review* 91 (1986): 66–81

Richard White, *"It's Your Misfortune and None of My Own": A History of the American West* (1991)

Richard White and Patricia Nelson Limerick, *The Frontier in American Culture* (1994)

David M. Wrobel, *The End of American Exceptionalism: Frontier Anxiety from the Old West to the New Deal* (1993)
John R. Wunder, ed., *Historians of the American Frontier: A Bio-Bibliographic Sourcebook* (1988)

Spanish Borderlands and

Native Homelands

Y

*For the native peoples of North America, this continent has been a home-
land for thousands of years. Misnamed "Indians" by the European newcomers, these original Americans had established an "old world" of their
own long before 1492. In the areas that became known as California and
New Mexico, Spanish newcomers in the 1600s found themselves on the far
northern rim of their nation's empire. In fact, they were attempting to make
a new life in the midst of well-established native peoples. How these Spanish
settlers organized their communities and how they tried to organize their
relations with their "Indian" neighbors is one of the first major stories of
American and western history. The social interactions were complex and
troubling. Within the Spanish communities, a form of hierarchy evolved
based on economic status, racial heritage, and gendered relations. Treatment
of native peoples could be violent as well as benevolent, and Native Americans responded in kind. For example, uprisings against Catholic missions
occurred in New Mexico and California. These events raise the question
whether native converts were valued more for their labor than for their
souls. The role of women in this society is worth examination as well.
Women could be Spanish, native, or of mixed heritage. Where did they fit in
a "new world" that Spanish men attempted to dominate militarily, reli-
giously, economically, and politically?*

Y *DOCUMENTS*

The first two documents compare the personal property of two Spanish soldiers. Captain Don Luís de Velasco accompanied Don Juan de Oñate in his
colonizing expedition to the area that was to become New Mexico. His manifest of 1597 shows that the captain was a wealthy man who, one may assume,
anticipated acquiring even more wealth in New Mexico. In the second document, dated 1663, Nicolás de Aguilar appears less fortunate in two ways. First,

he has been excommunicated from the Catholic church, arrested by the Inquisition, and taken to Mexico City because he accused New Mexican clerics of fathering children by Indian women under their care. Second, his worldly goods, as recorded by the religious court, are far more modest than those of Captain de Velasco. What items on the 1597 manifest seem essential for life on New Spain's far northern frontier? What equally essential items seem to be missing from the manifest of 1663? What do the recorded possessions of Nicolás de Aguilar reveal about living conditions for some residents of colonial New Mexico?

Documents three and four are accounts of the Pueblo revolt of 1680. The recently arrived viceroy of New Spain, the count of Paredes, reports to the king of Spain in document three. The count has already learned of a rebellion on the northern frontier before reaching Mexico City to take up his new post. Document four is the testimony before the Spanish inquisitors of Pedro Naranjo, an imprisoned Pueblo Indian. Naranjo indicated how one native leader affirming traditional religious beliefs helped launch the revolt. The revolt of 1680 remains a vivid memory in the minds of present-day Pueblo Indians—as significant to them as the American Revolution is to Anglo-Americans. Although New Mexico was reconquered after the revolt, Spanish domination was never as intense as before 1680.

The final two documents from the 1700s report on two towns in northern New Mexico and on the burning of a mission in California. In the mid-1700s, Dr. Pedro Tamarón y Romeral, the sixteenth bishop of Durango, had official ecclesiastical reasons for touring the New Mexican part of his vast diocese. His description of Santa Fe and Taos revealed a constant fear of raids by Comanches and the selling of captives at trading fairs. In 1775, Father Junípero Serra described the burning of the Catholic mission in San Diego when several hundred nonmission Indians attacked and killed the resident priest. Serra requested that soldiers be stationed at the missions but that the military not retaliate. Based on information from these two documents, how effective was Spanish control over its far northern frontier—even by the late 1700s?

Don Luís de Velasco's Extensive Manifest of Personal Property, 1597

Manifest made by Captain Don Luís de Velasco of the goods, arms, and horses which he is taking to serve his Majesty in the expedition to New Mexico, of which Don Juan de Oñate goes as governor and captain-general.

Being at the mines of Casco, where is encamped the army of his Majesty, which is going to the conquest and pacification of the provinces of New Mexico, on the nineteenth day of May, 1597, before Señor Don Juan de Oñate, governor and captain-general of the provinces of New Mexico and

From *Historical Documents Relating to New Mexico, Nueva Vizcaya, and Approaches Thereto, to 1773*, Volume I. Collected by Adolph F. A. Bandelier and Fanny R. Bandelier. Edited with introduction and annotations by Charles Wilson Hackett (Washington, D.C.: Carnegie Institution of Washington, 1923), pp. 429–33.

its kingdoms and the adjacent territories for the king, our Lord, and before me, Juan Pérez de Donis, clerk of his royal Majesty and secretary of the said expedition, appeared Captain Don Luís de Velasco, whom I swear that I know. He declared that in fulfillment of what some captains and officers of the royal army have petitioned before his lordship, he wished to make a manifest of the goods that he is taking; and, so doing, he exhibited and brought into the presence of the señor governor and myself, to which I swear, the following things:

First, he exhibited and brought before his lordship a standard of figured white Castilian silk, with fringes and trimmings of gold and crimson silk, which has stamped on one side the pictures of Our Lady and Saint John the Baptist. Encircling these two figures is painted the rosary of Our Lady with large gold beads, and at their feet the escutcheon and arms of the governor. On the other side it has the figure of the lord Saint James, with an inscription encircling it which says *Sic ut sanguino centa,* and at the feet of the horse of the lord Saint James the escutcheon and arms of the Velascos, with large tassels trimmed with gold and crimson silk.

Item: A silver lance, in its handle, for the exercise of his office as captain, with tassels of gold and yellow and purple silk.

Item: For the said purpose three complete suits of armor, to arm himself and two other soldiers in coat of mail, with thigh piece, beaver, and helmet, all complete, and with nothing lacking.

Item: Three calivers, with their large and small powder horns, firelocks, bullet screws, moulds, and all the rest that pertains to each one.

Item: Three sets of horse armor of buckskin, lined with undressed leather, for the flanks, foreheads, breasts, necks—all, without anything lacking.

Item: A halberd, garnished with yellow velvet and purple tassels, and all studded with nails, which he bought for his sergeant to carry.

Item: Thirty war-horses of different brands and marks, marked with his brand, which is in the margin.

Item: Two saddle mules to take on the said expedition and two pack mules.

Item: A sword and a gilded dagger with their waist belts stitched with purple, yellow, and white silk.

Item: One broadsword with shoulder belt, and two shields for defense against arrows.

Item: Two trooper saddles of Cordovan leather, with housings of blue flowered Spanish cloth bound with Cordovan leather, all complete and with loose stirrups.

Item: Two *estradiotas* [light cavalry] saddles of Cordovan leather, with the stirrups, bridles, girths, halters, and reins that go with them, one *estradiote* and two troopers' bridles.

Item: One bed with two mattresses, a coverlet, sheets, pillow-cases, pillows, and a canvas mattress-bag bound with sole leather.

Item: He is taking in his service two Spanish servants, from eighteen to twenty years old, to serve his Majesty on the expedition, to each of whom he has given four horses and complete equipment of armor for themselves and their horses.

Item: One suit of blue Italian velvet trimmed with wide gold passementerie, consisting of doublet, breeches, and green silk stockings with blue garters with points of gold lace.

Item: Another suit of rose-colored lustrous Castilian satin, consisting of a Walloon doublet, trimmed with narrow gold passementerie and a short cloak of gray cloth trimmed with wide gold and silver fringe, rose-colored silk stockings, and garters of striped rose-colored taffeta.

Item: Another suit of straw-colored Castilian satin, slashed with wide slashes and trimmed with interlinings of crimson Castilian taffeta, consisting of breeches, doublet, stockings of straw-colored silk and garters of purple taffeta with points.

Item: Another suit of purple Castilian cloth, consisting of Walloon breeches and doublet, trimmed with narrow gold passementerie, a cape with a wide gold fringe and ruffles of purple taffeta, purple silk stockings and garters of purple taffeta with points of gold lace.

Item: Another suit of chestnut-colored London cloth in the Walloon style, doublet and short cloak all trimmed with silver passementerie embroidery.

Item: Another suit of Chinese flowered silk, tan and green, trimmed with very narrow gold passementerie, consisting of breeches, doublet, and a jacket of ordinary cloth.

Item: Two doublets of kid dressed in Castile, one from the royal city being trimmed with gold and purple silk passementerie, and the other with wide silver passementerie.

Item: Another doublet of royal lion skin trimmed with gold and purple passementerie, with buttons of the same.

Item: One rain-cloak of gray cloth of the country.

Item: Two Rouen linen shirts with collars and cuffs of Holland cambric.

Item: Six handkerchiefs of Rouen linen and eight pairs of linen breeches with their socks.

Item: Six pairs of trimmed Rouen linen breeches.

Item: Eight pairs Cordovan leather boots, six white pairs and four black, and four pairs of laced gaiters.

Item: Fourteen pairs of Cordovan leather shoes, white and black, and four pairs of boots of sole leather and buckskin.

Item: Two hats, one black, trimmed around the crown with a silver cord, with black, purple, and white feathers, and the other gray, with yellow and purple feathers.

Item: Another hat of purple taffeta with blue, purple, and yellow feathers, and trimmed with a band of gold and silver passementerie.

Item: Four pairs of spurs for long stirrups, two for short stirrups, and some Moorish spurs with tassels and cords of silk.

Item: Fifty yards of striped canvas of Michoacan bindweed for a tent, with all the appurtenances necessary for setting it up with forked stakes, and everything else belonging to it.

The said goods having been thus declared, Captain Don Luís de Velasco begged his lordship to declare them manifested. Besides the aforesaid—as his lordship is aware, and, as is well known—some of his officers and soldiers are in debt to him for a large quantity of goods which they carried off when they absconded because of the delay in the expedition. With all this he came to serve his Majesty, and he will also give a report separately, presenting a petition that it be received. With this declaration he said that at present he has nothing more to manifest.

Nicolás de Aguilar's Few Worldly Goods, 1663

First Hearing and Deposition of Nicolás de Aguilar, April 12 and May 8, 1663

Nicolás de Aguilar, [a native of the pueblo of Yorerapudaro, Michoacán,] and a resident of Las Salinas in New Mexico, thirty-six years of age; his occupation, past and present, is that of a soldier in those provinces of New Mexico, having served the king, our lord, since he was ten years old. He has been sergeant and aide in the villa of Santa Fé, and *visitador* [wagonmaster] of the wagons of Andrés de Gracias, which went to the provinces of New Mexico; he has also twice been field captain of New Mexico and *alcalde mayor* [principal town clerk] of the jurisdiction of Las Salinas. One year and six days ago he was made prisoner in the pueblo of La Isleta in that kingdom by order of this Holy Office; he was brought here and entered the secret prisons, where he now is. . . .

He is a man of large body, coarse, and somewhat brown; . . . He wears a gabardine of buff and black wool, adorned with very small points of black wool [lace], a doublet of white cloth embroidered with blue wool, trousers of dark red flannel with small points of black wool lace, blue woolen stockings, a cotton neckcloth adorned with drawn work, and shoes of buckskin from New Mexico. Apparently he brought nothing else with him. In a [1] white wooden box, the [2] key of which he handed over, there were also found:

    3. A doublet of buff and black wool, badly worn, with cotton sleeves embroidered with blue wool.

    4. Another doublet of buff and black woolen cloth, with the same sort of sleeves.

    5. Item. An old cotton shirt, adorned with drawn work.

    6. Item. Another cloth shirt, worn out.

    7. Item. A shirt of ordinary Rouen linen.

    8. A cotton shirt, embroidered with dark red wool.

    9. A short jacket of dark red flannel, decorated with black wool.

From *Historical Documents Relating to New Mexico, Nueva Vizcaya, and Approaches Thereto, to 1773,* Volume III. Collected by Adolph F. A. Bandelier and Fanny R. Bandelier. Edited with introduction and annotations by Charles Wilson Hackett (Washington, D.C.: Carnegie Institution of Washington, 1937), pp. 139–140, 169.

10. Two pairs of woollen stockings, one pair red and the other buff-colored.

11. One pair of white cotton stockings.

12. One pair of shoes of Córdovan leather, worn out.

13. A book, entitled, "Catechism in the Castilian and Timuquana languages." Inside of this was another very small book, entitled, "Instructions for examining the conscience."

14. A bar of soap and a little *alucema* [polishing brush] wrapped in an old black rag.

15. An antelope skin muffler lined with yellow linen.

16. A cloth containing, apparently, roots of dry grass, which he said they call bear grass in New Mexico, used for curing fevers.

17. Three small pieces of dried grass roots, which he said is called *manso* grass, and is good for healing wounds.

18. A fair-sized bag of relics, inside of which was another bag containing a paper telling of the restitution which must be made. It covers about half of a half-sheet of paper.

19. A little printed copy of the four Gospels.

20. A quantity of folded papers, which he said were relics.

21. A rosary strung on *coyole* wire, having large beads, and a little silver cross.

22. A small and very old book bound with small black boards, which had no title at the beginning, and seems to consist, in the middle, of exercises and reflections.

23. A very old cloak of olive-colored cloth.

24. A very old black hat.

25. A buckskin bag within which is a cotton pillow filled with sheep's wool.

26. A mattress of coarse black and white stuff, filled with sheep's wool.

27. Two black woollen blankets.

28. Two woollen sheets.

29. A large buckskin into which the leather bag goes. He has apparently nothing else.

The Count of Paredes' Report on the Pueblo Indians' Revolt, 1681

Before entering upon this government I received information (while on the road from Vera Cruz to the city of Mexico, and more fully as soon as I entered the latter city, from the letters and certified documents which the archbishop viceroy, my predecessor, delivered to me) of the general uprising of the Indians of the provinces of New Mexico. According to the *autos*, reports, and documents which were remitted to this government, on the

From *Revolt of the Pueblo Indians of New Mexico and Otermin's Attempted Reconquest 1680–1682* translations by Charmion Clair Shelby. Introduction and annotations by Charles Wilson Hackett (Albuquerque: University of New Mexico Press, 1942), pp. 3–4.

thirteenth day of August of the past year 1680 the rebellious Indians, by prearranged conspiracy, fell upon all the pueblos and farms at the same time with such vigor and cruelty that they killed twenty-one missionary religious—nineteen priests and two lay brothers—and more than three hundred and eighty Spaniards, not sparing the defenselessness of the women and children. They set fire to the temples, seizing the images of the saints and profaning the holy vessels with such shocking desecrations and insolences that it is indecent to mention them. They left thirty-four pueblos totally desolated and destroyed, not counting many other farms and haciendas at a distance from them. . . .

The ferocity of these Indians met with no resistance except in the villa and capital of Santa Fe, where the governor resides, who was, and is, Don Antonio de Otermín. He defended himself in the casas reales [royal mansions] where he was besieged for nine days, having gathered therein all the people and cattle that he could. Realizing that they had cut off his water supply, that provisions were becoming scarce, and that the number of the enemy who were arriving from other pueblos and nations was increasing, and that such were their boldness and fury that they had set fire to the houses and the temples, attempting also to fire the casas reales, and considering that no help could reach him from any direction, alike because of the multitude of the barbarians who had taken all the passes, and because of the information that he had received from some of them whom our people captured and from others who fled from the enemy, that all the religious and the Spaniards from the surrounding pueblos had been killed, the governor resolved, in accordance with the opinion of a junta of the besieged, seeing the imminent danger of starvation or death at the hands of the Indians, to go out to attack them and retreat as well as he could. This he did, breaking through the chief division of the barbarians with the loss of one Spaniard [killed] and many wounded, the governor himself receiving two wounds in the face and a gunshot in the breast. This movement having put the barbarians to flight, our people turned quickly upon some houses where forty-seven Indians were fortified, whom they shot with harquebuses after they had declared that the uprising had been deliberated upon for a long time, at the instance of the Teguas Indians of the pueblo of Tesuque.

Notwithstanding that more than three hundred Indians had been killed in the affray, fearing that they would be joined by those from other pueblos and that all the heathen nations would be convoked, [the Spaniards] resolved to withdraw from the villa, taking all the provisions they could and the few cattle that remained to them.

The Testimony of Pedro Naranjo, a Pueblo Indian, 1681

Declaration of Pedro Naranjo of the Queres Nation. [Place of the Río del Norte, December 19, 1681.]

In the said plaza de armas on the said day, month, and year, for the prosecution of the judicial proceedings of this case his lordship caused to appear before him an Indian prisoner named Pedro Naranjo, a native of the pueblo of San Felipe, of the Queres nation, who was captured in the advance and attack upon the pueblo of La Isleta. He makes himself understood very well in the Castilian language and speaks his mother tongue and the Tegua. He took the oath in due legal form in the name of God, our Lord, and a sign of the cross, under charge of which he promised to tell the truth concerning what he knows and as he might be questioned, and having understood the seriousness of the oath and so signified through the interpreters, he spoke.

Asked whether he knows the reason or motives which the Indians of this kingdom had for rebelling, forsaking the law of God and obedience to his Majesty, and committing such grave and atrocious crimes, and who were the leaders and principal movers, and by whom and how it was ordered; and why they burned the images, temples, crosses, rosaries, and things of divine worship, committing such atrocities as killing priests, Spaniards, women, and children, and the rest that he might know touching the question, he said that since the government of Señor General Hernando Ugarte y la Concha they have planned to rebel on various occasions through conspiracies of the Indian sorcerers, and that although in some pueblos the messages were accepted, in other parts they would not agree to it; and that it is true that during the government of the said señor general seven or eight Indians were hanged for this same cause, whereupon the unrest subsided. Some time thereafter they [the conspirators] sent from the pueblo of Los Taos through the pueblos of the custodia two deerskins with some pictures on them signifying conspiracy after their manner, in order to convoke the people to a new rebellion, and the said deerskins passed to the province of Moqui, where they refused to accept them. The pact which they had been forming ceased for the time being, but they always kept in their hearts the desire to carry it out, so as to live as they are living to-day. Finally, in the past years, at the summons of an Indian named Popé who is said to have communication with the devil, it happened that in an estufa* of the pueblo of Los Taos there appeared to the said Popé three figures of Indians who never came out of the estufa. They gave the said Popé to understand that they were going underground to the lake of Copala. He saw these figures emit fire from all the extremities of their bodies. . . . They told

---

From *Revolt of the Pueblo Indians of New Mexico and Otermín's Attempted Reconquest 1680–1682* translations by Charmion Clair Shelby. Introduction and annotations by Charles Wilson Hackett (Albuquerque: University of New Mexico Press, 1942), pp. 245–249.

* ceremonial chamber, often called a "kiva."

him to make a cord of maguey fiber and tie some knots in it which would signify the number of days that they must wait before the rebellion. He said that the cord was passed through all the pueblos of the kingdom so that the ones which agreed to it [the rebellion] might untie one knot in sign of obedience, and by the other knots they would know the days which were lacking; and this was to be done on pain of death to those who refused to agree to it. As a sign of agreement and notice of having concurred in the treason and perfidy they were to send up smoke signals to that effect in each one of the pueblos singly. The said cord was taken from pueblo to pueblo by the swiftest youths under the penalty of death if they revealed the secret. Everything being thus arranged, two days before the time set for its execution, because his lordship had learned of it and had imprisoned two Indian accomplices from the pueblo of Tesuque, it was carried out prematurely that night, because it seemed to them that they were now discovered; and they killed religious, Spaniards, women, and children. This being done, it was proclaimed in all the pueblos that everyone in common should obey the commands of their father whom they did not know, which would be given through El Caydi or El Popé. This was heard by Alonso Catití, who came to the pueblo of this declarant to say that everyone must unite to go to the villa to kill the governor and the Spaniards who had remained with him, and that he who did not obey would, on their return, be beheaded; and in fear of this they agreed to it. Finally the señor governor and those who were with him escaped from the siege, and later this declarant saw that as soon as the Spaniards had left the kingdom an order came from the said Indian, Popé, in which he commanded all the Indians to break the lands and enlarge their cultivated fields, saying that now they were as they had been in ancient times, free from the labor they had performed for the religious and the Spaniards, who could not now be alive. He said that this is the legitimate cause and the reason they had for rebelling, because they had always desired to live as they had when they came out of the lake of Copala. . . .

Asked for what reason they so blindly burned the images, temples, crosses, and other things of divine worship, he stated that the said Indian, Popé, came down in person, and with him El Saca and El Chato from the pueblo of Los Taos, and other captains and leaders and many people who were in his train, and he ordered in all the pueblos through which he passed that they instantly break up and burn the images of the holy Christ, the Virgin Mary and the other saints, the crosses, and everything pertaining to Christianity, and that they burn the temples, break up the bells, and separate from the wives whom God had given them in marriage and take those whom they desired. In order to take away their baptismal names, the water, and the holy oils, they were to plunge into the rivers and wash themselves with amole, which is a root native to the country, washing even their clothing, with the understanding that there would thus be taken from them the character of the holy sacraments. They did this, and also many other things which he does not recall, given to understand that this mandate had come from the Caydi and the other two who emitted fire from their extremities in the said estufa of Taos, and that they thereby returned to the state of their antiquity, as when they came from the lake of Copala; that this was the better life and the one they desired, because the God of the Spaniards was worth nothing and theirs was very strong, the Spaniards's God being rotten wood. These things were observed and obeyed by all except some who, moved by the zeal of Christians, opposed it, and such persons the said Popé caused to be killed immediately. He saw to it that they at once erected and rebuilt their houses of idolatry which they call estufas, and made very ugly masks in imitation of the devil in order to dance the dance of the cacina;* and he said likewise that the devil had given them to understand that living thus in accordance with the law of their ancestors, they would harvest a great deal of maize, many beans, a great abundance of cotton, calabashes, and very large watermelons and cantaloupes; and that they could erect their houses and enjoy abundant health and leisure. As he has said, the people were very much pleased, living at their ease in this life of their antiquity, which was the chief cause of their falling into such laxity. . . .

Asked what arrangements and plans they had made for the contingency of the Spaniards' return, he said that what he knows concerning the question is that they were always saying they would have to fight to the death, for they do not wish to live in any other way than they are living at present; and the demons in the estufa of Taos had given them to understand that as soon as the Spaniards began to move toward this kingdom they would warn them so that they might unite, and none of them would be caught. . . . He greatly fears in his heart that he may have offended God, and that now having been absolved and returned to the fold of the church, he has spoken the truth in everything he has been asked. His declaration being read to him, he affirmed and ratified all of it. He declared himself to be eighty years of age, and he signed it with his lordship and the interpreters and assisting witnesses.

Bishop Tamarón Visits Santa Fe and Taos, 1760

Santa Fe

This villa of Santa Fe has 379 families of citizens of Spanish and mixed blood, with 1285 persons. Since I have confirmed 1532 persons in the said villa, I am convinced that the census they gave me is very much on the low side, and I do not doubt that the number of persons must be at least twice that given in the census.

In this villa I visited another church dedicated to the Archangel St. Michael. It is fairly decent; at that time they were repairing the roof.

In the plaza, a very fine church dedicated to the Most Holy Mother of

---

"Bishop Tamarón's Visitation of New Mexico, 1760," edited by Eleanor B. Adams, *New Mexico Historical Review* 28 (July, 1953), pp. 192–94, 204–6, 212–13, and 215–16.

Cacinas (now most commonly spelled *kachinas*) are powerful spirits impersonated by the dancers.

Light was being built. It is thirty varas long and nine wide, with a transept. Eight leagues from there a vein of very white stone had been discovered, and the amount necessary for an altar screen large enough to fill a third [of the wall] of the high altar was brought from this place. This was then almost carved. Later both it and the church were finished. The dedication of this church was also celebrated, and I was informed that it was all well adorned. The chief founder of this church was the governor himself, Don Francisco Marín del Valle, who simultaneously arranged for the founding of a confraternity which was established while I was there. I attended the first meeting and approved everything.

The buildings of this villa, both churches and houses, are all adobe. There is no fortress there, nor any formal presidio building. The garrison consists of 80 mounted soldiers in the pay of the King. In that villa, in Galisteo, and in Taos there was need of a stone fort in the vicinity of each. Santa Fe is a very open place; the houses are far apart; and therefore it does not have the least defence. If there had been a fort at the time of the uprising in the year 1680, the Indians would not have dared to do what they did.

This villa lies at the foot of a sierra, which is east of it and runs to the north. Water is scarce, because the river that traverses it dries up entirely in the months just before harvest, when only an inadequate small spring remains for drinking water, in addition to the wells. On May 25 it rained and hailed, and the sierra was covered with snow which soon melted. That people rejoiced, since they thought that such early precipitation augured a good winter. The villa of Santa Fe is located in latitude 37°28´, longitude 262°40´.

Since the two pueblos of Pecos and Galisteo are off the beaten track, the decision to break off the visitation of Santa Fe and to proceed to make that of the said two pueblos was taken. . . .

From Galisteo I returned to Santa Fe. I also experienced another alarm about the Comanches, the news of whose coming was given by the peaceful heathen Apaches. The governor took precautions, and the Comanches went in another direction. And the force marched on the day of Corpus, on which I celebrated a pontifical high mass and organized the procession with His Divine Majesty. The street through which the procession passed was decorated with branches and splendid altars; there were salvos by the military squadrons, and a large crowd was present. I consecrated six altar stones at Santa Fe.

Here I received a petition which I shall relate because of its unusual nature. A woman fifteen years of age, who had already been married for five years, presented herself, asking for the annulment of her marriage because she had been married at the age of ten. Then the husband, who was a soldier of the presidio, appeared. The fact that the marriage had taken place when she was ten years old was verified, but there was also proof that she immediately conceived and bore a son, and then another, and that she was already pregnant with the first child at the age of eleven. For this reason her petition was not valid, and the couple was ordered to continue in the state of matrimony. . . .

Taos

The titular patron of this Indian pueblo is San Jerónimo. To reach it we traveled through pine forests and mountains until we descended to the spacious and beautiful valley they call the valley of Taos. In this valley we kept finding encampments of peaceful infidel Apache Indians, who have sought the protection of the Spaniards so that they may defend them from the Comanches. Then we came to a river called Trampas, which carries enough water. The midday halt was made at the large house of a wealthy Taos Indian, very civilized and well-to-do. The said house is well walled in, with arms and towers for defense. In the afternoon the journey through that valley continued. Three rivers of similar current and water were crossed. The first one in particular provided abundant ditches for irrigation. They are about a league and a half from one another. And, crossing the last one, we entered the pueblo of Taos, where a Franciscan missionary parish priest resides.

. . . It is the last and most distant pueblo. . . . It lies at the foot of a very high sierra. . . . This pueblo has 159 families of Indians, with 505 persons. There are 36 families of Europeanized citizens, with 160 persons. There is a very decent and capacious church.

I also put forth every effort there to induce those best acquainted with Spanish to perform the act of contrition and confess. I therefore left this group until last, confirming the children first. And in fact some did confess, and, encouraged to contrition, were confirmed. But since they do not know the catechism except in Spanish, I did not feel as pleased and easy in my mind as I should have liked. Therefore I reprimanded the mission father and duly reminded him of his duty, ordering him to continue receiving their confessions.

This pueblo is divided into three many-storied tenements. It would have been better, as I told them, if they had been kept together, for one is on the other side of the river about two hundred varas away. There is a wooden bridge to cross the river. It freezes every year, and they told me that when it is thus covered with ice, the Indian women come with their naked little ones, break the ice with a stone, and bathe them in those waters, dipping them in and out. And they say it is for the purpose of making them tough and strong.

When I was in the pueblo two encampments of Ute Indians, who were friendly but infidels, had just arrived with a captive woman who had fled from the Comanches. They reported that the latter were at the Río de las Animas preparing buffalo meat in order to come to trade. They come every year to the trading, or fairs. The governor comes to those fairs, which they call *rescates* [barter, trade], every year with the majority of his garrison and people from all over the kingdom. They bring captives to sell, pieces of chamois, many buffalo skins, and, out of the plunder they have obtained elsewhere, horses, muskets, shotguns, munitions, knives, meat, and various other things. Money is not current at these fairs, but exchange of one thing for another, and so those people get provisions. I left Taos on June 12, and a few days later seventeen tents of Comanches arrived. They make these of buffalo hide, and they say that they are good and well suited for defense; and a family occupies each one. And at the end of the said month of June seventy of these field tents arrived. This was the great fair.

The character of these Comanches is such that while they are peacefully trading in Taos, others of their nation make warlike attacks on some distant pueblo. And the ones who are at peace, engaged in trade, are accustomed to say to the governor, "Don't be too trusting. Remember, there are rogues among us, just as there are among you. Hang any of them you catch."

Father Junípero Serra Asks Viceroy Antonio Bucareli for Leniency for the Indians, 1775

Monterey, December 15, 1775

✝

Hail Jesus, Mary, Joseph!

Most Excellent Lord.

My most revered and most excellent Sir:

As we are in the vale of tears, not all the news I have to relate can be pleasant. And so I make no excuses for announcing to Your Excellency the tragic news I have just received of the total destruction of the San Diego Mission, and of the death of the senior of its two religious ministers, called Father Fray Luis Jayme, at the hand of the rebellious gentiles and of the Christian neophytes. All this happened, November 5th, about one or two o'clock at night. The gentiles came together from forty rancherías, according to information given me, and set fire to the church, after sacking it. Then they went on to the storehouse, the house where the Fathers lived, the soldiers' barracks, and all the rest of the buildings.

They killed a carpenter from Guadalaxara and a blacksmith from Tepic. They wounded with their arrows the four soldiers, who alone were on guard at the said mission. Even though two of them were badly wounded, they have already recovered.

The other religious, whose name is Father Fray Vicente Fuster, over and above the fright he got, received no further injuries than a wound in the shoulder, caused by a stone. He suffered pain from it for several days. On the morning following that sad night, he withdrew, in company with the handful still surviving, to the presidio. They carried on the shoulders of those Christian Indians who had remained loyal the dead, and the badly wounded. From there he writes to me asking me to tell him what to do.

. . . On the subject of the loss of San Diego Mission, various thoughts have come to mind. But since complaining about the past remedies nothing,

From *The Writings of Junípero Serra,* edited by Antonine Tibesar, O. F. M. (Washington, D. C.: Academy of American Franciscan History, 1956).

I will change the subject. But, while I think of it, I might suggest again to Your Excellency what I proposed in one of my earlier letters: that in conquests of this kind the place where soldiers are most important is in the missions. The presidios, in many places, may be most suitable and very necessary; but for the situation here, I describe only what is before my eyes.

The San Diego Mission is about two leagues from the presidio, but it is in such a position that, throughout the day, they can see the mission from the presidio; and the gunshot that is fired each morning at dawn in the presidio, to change the watchword of the night guard, can generally be heard in the Mission. Yet while the mission was all on fire, the flames leaping up to a great height from one or two o'clock in the morning until dawn, and during all that time shooting was going on, they saw and heard nothing at the presidio; and the wind, they say, was favorable.

Although there were only two men who fired shots during all that time, many lives were saved which would have been lost without the said defense. And now, after the Father has been killed, the Mission burned, its many and valuable furnishings destroyed, together with the sacred vessels, its paintings, its baptismal, marriage and funeral records, and all the furnishings for the sacristy, the house, and the farm implements—now, the forces of both presidios come together to set things right.

While the circumstances leading up to the outbreak seem very much like the case of San Sabá Mission—which I was appointed to, and all in readiness to set out for, from our College, having been summoned in great haste for that purpose from the Sierra Gorda—may God not permit the results to be the same.

What happened was that before they set about re-establishing the Mission, they wanted to join the various presidios together, and lay hands on the guilty ones who were responsible for the burning of the Mission, and the death of the Fathers, and chastise them. The harassed Indians rebelled anew and became more enraged. I had to stay home and not set out for the Mission and I did not know whether, up to the present time, the Mission has been re-established or not.

And so the soldiers there are gathered together in the presidios, and the Indians in their state of heathenism.

Most Excellent Lord, one [of] the most important requests I made of the Most Illustrious Inspector General, at the beginning of these conquests was: if ever the Indians, whether they be gentile or Christian, killed me, they should be forgiven. The same request I make of Your Excellency. It has been my own fault I did not make this request before. To see a formal statement drawn up by Your Excellency to that effect, in so far as it concerns me, and the other religious who at present are subject to me or will be in the future, would be for me a special consolation during the time Our Lord God will be pleased to add to my advancing years.

While the missionary is alive, let the soldiers guard him, and watch over him, like the pupils of God's very eyes. That is as it should be. Nor do I disdain such a favor for myself. But after the missionary has been killed, what can be gained by campaigns?

Some will say to frighten them and prevent them from killing others.

What I say is that, in order to prevent them from killing others, keep better guard over them than they did over the one who has been killed; and, as to the murderer, let him live, in order that he should be saved—which is the very purpose of our coming here, and the reason which justifies it. Give him to understand, after a moderate amount of punishment, that he is being pardoned in accordance with our law, which commands us to forgive injuries; and let us prepare him, not for death, but for eternal life.

Most Excellent Lord, may Your Excellency pardon me for my interference, who knows for what result.

The details of all that has occurred, Your Excellency will see in the Officers' reports.

In the statements are suggested some discouraging news from the Colorado River. The fact is that Señor Anza has not yet put in his appearance, and we do not know what may have happened to him.

I have no time to say more, and I ask Your Excellency to overlook my deficiencies and indiscretions, because this letter has been written in great haste.

May God keep Your Excellency many years, and, in the interest of souls in these regions, may He extend the period in which you are to rule over these territories, as you now do with so much conscientious care, for the length of time I so devoutly wish. And may He ever keep you increasingly in His holy grace.

From this Mission, totally dependent on Your Excellency, of San Carlos de Monterey, December 15, 1775.

Most Excellent Lord,

Kissing the hand of Your Excellency,

Your most affectionate and devoted servant and chaplain, who holds you in the highest affection,

Fray Junípero Serra

Y ESSAYS

Ramón A. Gutiérrez, who teaches colonial Latin American and Chicano/a history at the University of California, San Diego, is the author of the multiple-prize-winning book *When Jesus Came, the Corn Mothers Went Away: Marriage, Sexuality, and Power in New Mexico, 1500–1846,* published in 1991. In the first essay, as a way to uncover patterns of race, class, and gender, he examines forms of marriage in colonial New Mexico. Albert L. Hurtado of Arizona State University is the author of another prize-winning book— *Indian Survival on the California Frontier,* published in 1988. In the second essay, Hurtado explores Spanish-Indian relations at a basic level of human existence—sexuality. The Franciscan missions in California tried to control Indian sexual relations with unintended consequences. Both Gutiérrez and Hurtado examine the problems of human choice and social control. The results are not what people at the time might have expected. Are human relationships, especially between distinctly different cultures, so complex that they result in only misunderstandings and tragedies?

Honor and Marriage in Colonial New Mexico

RAMÓN A. GUTIÉRREZ

The ways in which societies organize marriage provide us an important window into how economic and political arrangements are construed. When people marry, they forge affinal alliances, change residence, establish rights to sexual service, and exchange property. Besides being about the reproduction of class and power, however, marriage is about gender. The marital exchange of women gives men rights over women that women never gain over men. This feature of marriage provides a key to the political economy of sex, by which cultures organize "maleness" and "femaleness," sexual desire, fantasy, and concepts of childhood and adulthood.

With these theoretical moorings in mind, I present here an essay on the history of marriage in a colonial setting, New Mexico between 1690 and 1846, an environment in which class domination was culturally articulated and justified through hierarchies of status based on race, ethnicity, religion, and gender. My major concern will be to examine the key role that control over marriage choice played in the maintenance of social inequality, focusing on changes in the mode of marriage formation during the period under study—a decline in the incidence of parentally arranged nuptials and an increase in those freely contracted by adolescents on the basis of love and personal attraction. Rather than discussing the roots of these changes abstractly, I will explore how parents and children negotiated their behavior, the disparities of power that constrained their actions, and the ambiguities, tensions, and contradictions within the ideological superstructure that gave historical agency meaning.

Historical Setting

Once the ancient temples of Mexico City had been leveled and cities of gold had failed to materialize, the business of colonizing Mexico's central plateau began. The 1548 discovery of silver at Zacatecas quickly moved the frontier north and set the pace for the establishment of a rapid succession of towns: Guanajuato, Queretaro, San Luis Potosí, Durango. The far north, the areas we know today as New Mexico, California, and Texas, was

Ramón A. Gutiérrez, "Honor Ideology, Marriage Negotiation, and Class-Gender Domination in New Mexico, 1690–1846," *Latin American Perspectives,* 12 (Winter 1985), 81–93, 98–101. Reprinted by permission of Sage Publications.

explored in the first half of the sixteenth century by such men as Álvar
Núñez Cabeza de Vaca, Fray Marcos de Niza, and Francisco Vásquez de
Coronado. Nonetheless, it remained a fantasy of future enrichment in the
Spanish imagination until the end of the century. Then, in 1598, Don Juan
de Oñate, the son of one of Zacatecas's wealthiest silver miners, mustered
129 soldiers and together with their dependents ventured into the land of
the Chichimecas—the fierce nomadic Indian tribes that had effectively curtailed Spanish expansion north—to establish the Kingdom of New Mexico.

Arriving in August of 1598 armed with the cross of Christ and the
sword to impose it, the soldier-settlers and friars quickly set about the task
of "civilizing" the Indians through baptism, the introduction of European
seeds and livestock, and the imposition of Spanish mores of comportment
and dress. To ensure the presumed physical and spiritual well-being of New
Mexico's Pueblo Indians, they were divided into 41 *encomiendas* awarded
to notables of the conquest. For this "entrustment" to the protection and
spiritual care of the Spanish, the natives paid dearly in tribute, labor, and,
often, lives.

Though "savages" were all the Spaniards saw when they arrived in the
Rio Grande Valley, the word is hardly adequate to describe the Indians living there. Since the thirteenth century, the river basin had been occupied by
the compact agricultural villages of the Pueblo Indians. The 90 pueblos—
so named by the Spanish because their multistoried dwellings resembled
Aztec cities—were economically independent, politically autonomous, and
best described as city-states. In 1598 the Pueblo population totaled approximately 60,000. Though several nomadic Indian tribes, notably the Apache
and Navajo, hunted in the surrounding plains and mountains, their low
level of material culture and social organization spared them the yoke of
subjugation until the early 1700s.

The years 1598–1680 were brutal ones for the Pueblo peoples. Their
food reserves were depleted by the colonists; their lives were disrupted by
Spanish labor demands; their religious images were desecrated by the friars and their rituals suppressed. Many saw their kin driven to the point of
death; women were raped and children enslaved. In 1680 they formed a
confederation and routed the Spanish from the area, a feat that reverberated
throughout New Spain and spurred other Indians to similar action. When
the fury of the Pueblo Revolt was over, 21 out of 33 Franciscan friars were
dead and 380 settlers had lost their lives. The 2,300 white survivors fled
south to El Paso (Texas), where they regrouped and remained until 1693.

Don Diego de Vargas was charged with the reconquest of the territory
and in 1693 led 100 soldiers, 70 families, and 18 friars to reestablish Spanish presence in Santa Fe. A second Spanish town, Santa Cruz de la Cañada,
was founded in 1695, followed by Albuquerque in 1706. Colonists who did
not live in one of these three towns resided in small dispersed ranches or
hamlets situated along the banks of the Rio Grande. The white population
in 1700 was perhaps no more than 3,000. The Pueblo population by that
year had declined to 15,000.

The period following the reconquest saw a major readjustment in Indian-white relations. Faced with the realization that there was a limit to the exploitation the Pueblo would tolerate and that they would not be cowed into abandoning their native religious beliefs easily, the crown abolished the encomienda and replaced it with the *repartimiento,* a less onerous rotational labor levy. New Mexico's governors were ordered to observe Indian rights strictly, and the martyrdom of their brothers impressed on the friars that their evangelical zeal would have to be tempered.

But the problem of extracting labor and wealth from the native population in its various forms remained. The revolt had not altered the practice of using political office as a vehicle for personal enrichment. Someone still had to construct the imposing mission compounds that were to dot the landscape, and the aristocracy's sense of preeminence was still dependent on the labor of others. For these ends, then, a new enemy was necessary. The "Apaches"—as the Spanish called all the nomadic Indians whose hunting grounds bordered on the agricultural settlements of the river basin (Jicarilla, Mescalero, Navajo, Ute, and Comanche)—were quickly defined as Satan's minions; this status made them eligible for "just war." Scores of men, women, and particularly children were brought into Spanish villages enslaved as prisoners of war. Some *genízaros,* as these detribalized Indians became known, were retained in local households for the performance of domestic tasks while others were traded for luxury goods in the mining centers of northern New Spain. The growth of this commerce in captives during the eighteenth century was directly responsible for the constant warfare the kingdom's colonists were to experience.

In this environment, the Spanish colonists of the post-reconquest period fashioned a society that they perceived as ordered hierarchically by honor, a prestige system based on principles of inherent personal worth. Honor was a complex gradient of status that encompassed several other measures of social standing such as descent, ethnicity, religion, profession, and authority over land. The summation and ordering of these statuses and the pragmatic outcome of evaluations of honor resulted in the organization of society into three broadly defined groups: the nobility, the landed peasantry, and the genízaros.

The status hierarchy did not completely encompass class standing as structured by relations of production. The Pueblo Indians on whose labor and tribute the colonists so heavily relied fell outside the groups to whom honor mattered and refused to accept, cherish, and validate the ideals by which Spanish society organized its interactions. From the colonists' point of view, the physical tasks the Pueblo Indians performed were intrinsically dishonorable and conquest by a superior power itself dishonoring. Obviously, the Pueblo did not consciously share this view. In colonial New Mexico, honor and class were nevertheless interdependent. Social power ultimately gained its effectiveness from the combination of the two.

The nobility consisted of 15–20 families that intermarried to ensure their continued dominance. Their sense of aristocracy was rooted in the legally defined honor granted to the kingdom's colonizers by King Phillip II in their 1595 charter of incorporation. As the colony developed, nobility gained a broader social meaning and was claimed by individuals who acquired large amounts of land, by military officials, and by bureaucrats— wealth and power acting as the determinants of intragroup mobility. By comparison with the titled peerage of central Mexico, New Mexico's nobility at best enjoyed the life of a comfortable gentry. Yet, perhaps because of its isolation—and the attendant belief that it was a cultural oasis in a sea of barbarism—New Mexico's aristocracy considered itself second to none. Bearing Old Christian ancestry, harboring pretensions of purity of blood, and eschewing physical labor, it reveled in its rituals of precedence, in ostentatious display of lavish clothing and consumption of luxury goods, in respectful forms of address and titles. Needless to say, such habits were buttressed by force of arms, wealth, and a legal superstructure premised on the belief that the social order was divinely ordained.

Landed peasants who were primarily of mestizo origin but considered themselves "Spaniards" were next in the hierarchy of honor. They had been recruited for the colonization of New Mexico with promises of land, and in 1700 all enjoyed rights to *merced*, a communal land grant consisting of private irrigated farmlands, house plots, and commons for livestock grazing. By 1800, the progressive subdivision of private plots had resulted in parcels too small for subsistence. Under these circumstances, owners of morseled holdings increasingly turned to wage labor. Their ranks were swelled by persons who had not gained access to land as part of their patrimony. Though the land area of New Mexico may seem boundless, it was constrained by limited water sources, by the previous and competing water and land claims of the Pueblo Indians, and by the resistance to geographic expansion offered by hostile tribes.

Lowest in prestige, dishonored and infamous because of their slave status, were the genízaros, a diverse group of Indians who resided in Spanish towns and performed the community's most menial and degrading tasks. Between 1694 and 1849, 3,294 genízaros entered Hispanic households. Early in the seventeenth century, New Mexicans had been granted the privilege of warring against infidel Indians and retaining them in bondage for ten years as compensation for the costs of battle. Though many genízaros remained slaves much longer, they were customarily freed at marriage. Lack of access to land and the development of emotional dependencies on their masters, by whom in most cases they had been raised, meant that even after manumission genízaros had few options for social mobility. Remaining in the household and employment of their former owners was common.

Genízaros (from the Turkish *yeni,* "new," and *cheri,* "troops") were truly New Mexico's shock troops against the infidel. Stigmatized by their former slavery, lacking kinship ties to the European community, and deemed devious because of their lack of mastery of Spanish, the increasing numbers of free genízaros were segregated in special neighborhoods such as Santa Fe's Barrio de Analco or congregated in new settlements such as Belén (1740), Abiquiu (1754), Ojo Caliente (1754), and San Miguel del

Vado (1794). All of these genízaro communities—communities now of landed peasants of genízaro origin—were strategically established along the Indian raiding routes and were to serve Spanish settlements as buffers against attack.

The Ideology of Honor

Honor was a polysemic word embodying meanings at two different but fundamentally interrelated levels, one of status and one of virtue. Honor was first and foremost society's measure of social standing, ordering on a single vertical continuum those persons with much honor and differentiating them from those with little. Excellence manifested as territorial expansion of the realm was the monarchy's justification for the initial distribution of honor. Yet, "the claim to honor," as Julian Pitt-Rivers notes, "depends always in the last resort, upon the ability of the claimant to impose himself. Might is the basis of right to precedence, which goes to the man who is bold enough to enforce his claim." The children of the conquistadores gained their parents' honor through ascription and maintained and enhanced it through behavior deemed appropriate to a highly esteemed person.

The second dimension of honor was a constellation of virtue ideals. Dividing the community horizontally along prestige-group boundaries, honor-virtue established the status ordering among equals. Definitions of virtue were gender-specific. Males embodied honor (the sentiment of honor) when they acted *con hombría* (in a manly fashion), exercised authority over family and subordinates, and esteemed honesty and loyalty. Females possessed the moral and ethical equivalent of honor, *vergüenza* (shame), if they were timid, shy, feminine, virginal before marriage and afterwards faithful to their husbands, discreet in the presence of men, and concerned for their reputations. Infractions of the rules of conduct dishonored men and were a sign of shamelessness in women. Shamelessness accumulated around the male head of household and dishonored both the family as a corporate group and all its members.

The maintenance of social inequality was central to the way in which status and virtue were defined to interact, the aim being the perpetuation of the nobility's preeminence. An aristocrat of however low repute was always legally more honorable than the most virtuous peasant. Because precedence at the upper reaches of the social structure guaranteed more material and symbolic benefits, it was usually among the nobility and elites that the most intense conflicts over honor-virtue occurred. Family feuds and vendettas were frequently the way sullied reputations were avenged and claims to virtue upheld.

Consensus seems to have existed among New Mexicans of Hispanic origin regarding the behavior deemed virtuous and worthy of honor. Among the nobility and the peasantry alike, men concerned for their personal and familial repute, judged by how well they resolved the contradictory imperatives of domination (protection of one's womenfolk from assault) and conquest (prowess gained through sullying the purity of other men's women), hoped to minimize affronts to their virtue, thereby maintaining their status. Female seclusion and a high symbolic value placed on virginity and marital fidelity helped accomplish this aim.

Yet only in aristocratic households, where servants and retainers abounded, could resources be expended to ensure that females were being properly restrained and shameful. The maintenance of their virtue was +

Inequalities in power and status kept peasant men from honorably challenging aristocrats. Both because of this disparity in status and because of the excesses of the nobility in asserting their virility, ideals of female virtue were as intensely cherished by peasants. Manuel Alvarez, the United States consul in Sante Fe, alluded to this when he wrote in 1834: "the honorable man (if it is possible for a poor man to be honorable) has a jewel in having an honorable wife." Among the peasantry, gender prescriptions undoubtedly had to be reconciled with the exigencies of production and reproduction of material life. The required participation of all able household members in planting and the harvest meant that there were periods when constraints on females of this class were less rigorously enforced. Juana Carillo of Santa Fe admitted as much in 1712 when she confessed enjoying the affections of two men her father had hired for their spring planting. Again, in households where men were frequently absent, such as those of soldiers, muleteers, shepherds, and hunters, cultural ideals were less rigid. The fact that females supervised family and home for large parts of the year, staved off Indian attack, and cared for the group's public rights meant that it was difficult for them to lead sheltered and secluded lives. It was not uncommon for these women to lament that they had been assaulted, raped, or seduced while their husbands or fathers were away from home.

Honor and Marriage

Marriage was the most important ritual event in the life-course, and in it the honor of the family took precedence over all other considerations. The union of two properties, the joining of two households, the creation of a web of affinal relations, the perpetuation of a family's symbolic patrimony—its name and reputation—were transactions so important to the honor-status of the group that marriage was hardly a decision to be made by minors. The norm in New Mexico was for parents to arrange nuptials for their children with little or no consideration of their wishes. Filial piety required the acceptance of any union one's parents deemed appropriate or advantageous.

The 1786 marriage of Francisco Narpa and Juana Lorem in Sandia provides a glimpse of the familial motivations involved in an arranged union. Appearing before the provincial ecclesiastical judge to explain how he had married, Francisco reported: "Having agreed with Juana Lorem that we wished to marry, I asked her grandmother Tomasa Cibaa, and with her permission and that of her relatives, I married." Juana Lorem had a slightly different understanding of the events that led up to her marriage to Francisco.

She told the judge, "It is totally false that I agreed to marry the said Francisco. I never wanted to marry the said Francisco. But for fear of my grandmother Tomasa Cibaa I contracted the marriage." Finally, Tomasa Cibaa explained: "I ordered my granddaughter Juana to marry the said Francisco Narpa because he is moderately wealthy, and it is true that I pressured Juana to appear before the priest [for the matrimonial investigation] and say nothing that might provoke questioning." The details of this marriage surface as part of an ecclesiastical investigation into the allegation that the union was incestuous. Francisco had fathered a child by Maria Quieypas, Juana's mother, and therefore his marriage to Juana was invalid. The marriage was annulled, dotal and patrimonial property were confiscated, the three were publicly flogged, and Narpa was exiled from New Mexico.

Of course, I do not wish to suggest that arranged marriage was an inflexible rule. The extent to which parental preference for arranged marriage could be enforced was mediated both by the person's status and by each family's particular fertility history. The number of children in a family, their birth order, and their sex dictated the options available to parents to secure their son or daughter an acceptable or advantageous spouse. These and other variables also conditioned the range of filial responses possible—whether a son or daughter acted as if bound by duty or sentiment or resisted or attempted to manipulate the situation so as to appease everyone's concerns.

From a father's point of view, a round of poker is an excellent metaphor for the way in which limited resources (the patrimony) were manipulated to maximize the gains associated with marital alliance. Pierre Bourdieu has applied this metaphor to the marriage of a family's children. Success at enhancing and perpetuating the family's status is based not only on the hand one is dealt (whether the nuptial candidate is an only child, the eldest of several sons, or the youngest of many daughters) but also the skill with which one plays it (bids, bluffs, and displays). The patrimony was the material resource a father had to apportion among its claimants at strategic moments to maximize reproductive success. Although legally every legitimate child in New Mexico was entitled to an equal share of this wealth, practice varied by class. Aristocratic holders of large landed estates preferred male primogeniture as a way of keeping their property intact. The eldest son, as the heir to the household head's political rights over the group and the person responsible for the name and reputation of the family, was the individual to whom a disproportionate amount of parents' premortem resources was committed. As first in importance, even if preceded by older sisters, he could not suffer a misalliance without lowering the entire family's public rating and diminishing the possibilities of securing honorable partners for his unmarried brothers and sisters. Therefore, he was the child of whom parents expected the most and the child disciplined most severely to ensure obedience but allowed the greatest excesses in other matters. He was also perhaps the most predisposed to bow to duty.

If the eldest son had married well and the family's position had thus been attended to, filial participation in the marriage process was tolerated in subsequent cases. Because younger sons were unlikely to fare as well in the acquisition of marital property and could expect only enough money and movable goods to avoid misalliance, fathers might be more open to their suggestions regarding eligible brides.

Daughters of the nobility were a potential liability on the marriage market, dissipating the material and symbolic patrimony by having their dowries absorbed into their husbands' assets. Every attempt would be made to dispose of nubile females as quickly as possible and at minimal expense. If a daughter experienced a prenuptial dishonor, such as the loss of her virginity, additional resources would have to be committed to secure her an appropriate mate. Thus large amounts of time and energy were spent ensuring that a maiden's sexual shame was being maintained. Undoubtedly, the result was that a woman's freedom to object to a marriage, to express her desires in spouse selection, was more limited than that of her brothers.

Peasants enjoying rights to communal land grants practiced partible inheritance. Sons were given their share of the family's land when they took a bride and were assigned a certain number of *vigas* ("beams"—a way of dividing the space in a house) in the parental home. If space limitations prohibited such a move, assistance was given in the addition of rooms to the house or the construction of a separate edifice in the immediate vicinity. For females, premortem dowries usually consisted of household items and livestock. Daughters seldom received land rights at marriage because parents fully expected the husband's family to meet this need. The authority relations springing from this mode of property division meant that parental supervision over spouse selection and its timing was as rigidly exercised as among the nobility.

For landless freed genízaros, the institution of marriage itself was of no consequence. Many preferred concubinage, as they held no property to transmit and the alienation from their Indian kin that accompanied enslavement made the issue of perpetuation of family name irrelevant. Wage earners and landless peasants were in a similar situation with regard to marriage. Once children were old enough to leave the familial hearth in search of a livelihood, parental control over their behavior all but ceased. Their only concern in the timing of marriage, if in fact they chose matrimony for cultural reasons, was the necessity to accumulate a nest egg with which to establish a conjugal residence.

Marriage and the Church

The settlement of the Kingdom of New Mexico was a joint venture of church and state. In all the remote areas of the Spanish empire in which civilization was to be brought to the Indians, it was by the religious orders, through the institution of missions, that the task was accomplished. Acting as defenders of the Indians, as guardians of community piety and morality, and as a counterpoint to the power of the state, the church at one and the same time legitimated and buttressed the colonial system and challenged certain tenets of its rule. Nowhere was this tension among the authorities of

God, of the family head, and of the state clearer than on the issue of marriage.

Until 1776, the Catholic church enjoyed exclusive jurisdiction over the ritual, sacramental, and contractual aspects of matrimony. Ecclesiastical law, articulated as a theory of impediments to marriage, was dominated by two concerns: the prohibition of incest and the determination of the exercise of free will. The latter principle drew on the Roman legal tradition that a nuptial contract was valid only if the parties had given free and absolute consent. The use of persuasion and coercion to arrange marriages of children could place patriarchs in direct confrontation with the church and its clerics.

Arranged marriage was a complex issue for the church. Scripture and canon law were fraught with ambiguities and contradictions on the matter. Christian ideology reinforced the honor code regarding the obedience and personal subordination children owed their parents. "Honor your father and mother," ordered the fourth commandment. "Children, obey your parents in the Lord," enjoined St. Paul in his Epistle to the Ephesians (5:22). The church maintained that the law of nature bound parents and children in a relationship that entailed reciprocal rights and obligations. The authority of man over his wife, children, and servants emanated from God's power over creation, and therefore his was the right to guide and discipline children as necessary. Filial submission, St. Paul promised, would be reciprocated with paternal love, protection, and guidance.

But the vexing question clerics were obliged to ask, in the case of marriage, was when paternal guidance and filial obedience simply became coercion. The issue was of some importance because forced marriages, or those contracted under duress, were invalid. Matrimony was the sacramental union of free will based on mutual consent. Ideally it was the work of God, and "what God has joined together, let no man separate."

The autonomy of individual will, responsibility, and conscience in undertaking marriage was central to Catholic thought. In arranged marriages, in which conflicts between obedience to parents and obedience to one's conscience existed, the will of the individual was to take precedence. The scriptural basis for limits on the authority of the father and the freedom of Christ's message rested in the following: "Call no man your father upon the earth: for One is your Father, which is in heaven" (Matthew 23:9). And again (Matthew 10:34–37):

> Think not that I am come to send peace on earth: I came not to send peace, but a sword. For I am come to set a man at variance against his father, and the daughter against her mother, and the daughter-in-law against her mother-in-law. And a man's foes shall be they of his own household. He that loveth father or mother more than me is not worthy of me: and he that loveth son or daughter more than me is not worthy of me.

A mechanism for the determination that a person was marrying freely existed in canon law. If the slightest hint of coercion surfaced, the local priest had the power to remove the candidate from his/her home for isolation from parental pressures. Once the person's wishes became known, the priest was legally bound either to marry the person, even against parental wishes, or to prohibit a forced union. Don Salvador Martínez of Albuquerque, for example, availed himself of ecclesiastical intervention when he sought Vicar Fray Manuel Roxo's help in his 1761 matrimonial bid for Doña Simona Baldes. Though Martínez had twice asked for Doña Simona's hand in marriage, his proposals had been ignored. Moved by the evidence, the vicar sequestered Doña Simona, who admitted she wanted to be Martínez's bride. The marriage occurred despite parental objections, which may have been due to a gross age difference. Don Salvador was a 62-year-old widower; Doña Simona was only 19.

The freedom that the Catholic church might grant the sexes in the selection of conjugal mates formed the legal foundation for the subversion of parental authority, but, as the experience of all areas of the Spanish colonial empire testifies, the law and its execution were two very different matters. It was not uncommon for clerics charged with the interpretation and execution of canon law to enforce it selectively or to bend its dictates to avoid misalliances or subversion of the social order. If a friar believed an arranged marriage was a good match, he might uphold parental prerogatives and rationalize that the natural authority of a father over his children was in full accord with the will of God.

A variant of such an alliance between priest and parents occurred in Santa Fe in 1710. María Belasquez and Joseph Armijo appeared before Fray Lucas Arebalo that year claiming that her parents would not allow her to marry Joseph. They asked the friar to take María into his custody so that she could express her "true" wishes. María was sequestered but was returned to her father shortly after Joseph left the rectory. Joseph immediately appealed to the provincial ecclesiastical judge, who agreed that Fray Lucas had not upheld the marriage canons of the Council of Trent. The two were sequestered anew and were finally joined in wedlock after affirming their desire to be husband and wife.

From the evidence in the ecclesiastical archives, "absolute" legal liberty to choose a spouse meant, in fact, freedom to select a mate from *within* one's class and ethnic group. No examples exist in the Archives of the Archdiocese of Santa Fe of clerics' sanctioning a cross-class marriage over parental objections. The church might subvert the particular authority of parents, but it would not subvert the social order at large. . . .

Social Change

From the years following the reconquest to the early 1770s, the Kingdom of New Mexico was peripheral to the empire. Isolated on the northern margins of New Spain, the colony's only link to "civilization" was a yearly mule train to Mexico City, which traveled over several thousand miles of territory inhabited by hostile Indians. New Mexico contained no significant mineral deposits, its population's material culture was rudimentary, and its cash-crop production (wheat, cotton, corn, pine nuts) was insignificant. In fact, had the Franciscan order not pleaded passionately before the crown for the privilege of converting New Mexico's Indians, colonists might never have been sent there in the first place.

The isolation of the province slowly began to crumble in the 1760s. Frightened by the increasing levels of Russian, Anglo-American, and French encroachment into Texas, New Mexico, and California, King Charles III ordered a series of economic, military, and administrative reforms, commonly known as the Bourbon reforms, to safeguard the territory.

The reform project began in 1765 when the Spanish Royal Corps of Engineers was sent to the northern frontier of New Spain to map the area thoroughly, to identify its mineral and hydraulic resources, to assess the feasibility of textile production, to propose methods for increasing agricultural production, and to outline the military changes necessary to fortify the frontier. On the basis of the expedition's recommendations, northern New Spain was reorganized in 1776 into one military and administrative unit called the Internal Provinces. New presidios were constructed to ward off foreign attack, and vigorous campaigns were staged to subdue the "Apaches," who made trade and communication difficult. It was precisely in this period that permanent settlements were finally established in California, the first mission being built in 1769 at San Diego.

The crown believed that New Mexico could be retained as part of the empire only through fuller integration into the market economy centered in Chihuahua. To achieve this aim, trade and travel restrictions were abolished, New Mexican products were given sales tax exemptions, and agricultural specialists, veterinarians, and master weavers were sent to the area to upgrade local production and improve the competitive position of the kingdom's products. Within a few years the frequency of mule trains to and from Chihuahua increased, money began to circulate more widely, and new colonists from north-central Mexico migrated into the area.

Imperial economic reforms coincided with a period of demographic growth in New Mexico, which resulted in intense land pressure. Between 1760 and 1820, the Spanish and mixed-blood population of New Mexico grew from 7,666 to 28,436. By the 1780s, many of the land grants to the initial colonists were insufficient for subsistence. A few new *mercedes* were conceded in the late 1780s, but not enough to meet the population's needs. Governor Fernando de la Concha noted this in his 1796 report to the commandant of the Internal Provinces and estimated that there were 1,500 individuals without land to till. The inevitable upshot of this situation was the expansion of wage labor. A comparison of the occupational structures of the kingdom in 1790 and 1827 reflects this expansion of wage laborers. In 1790, Albuquerque had an adult working population of 601. Farmers constituted 65 percent (391), 25 percent (151) were craftsmen, and 10 percent (58) were day laborers. By 1827, 610 persons were listed as full-time workers: 66 percent (397) were farmers, 14 percent (85) craftsmen, and 19 percent (113) day laborers. The 1790 census of Santa Fe listed 413 individuals with occupations. Farmers represented 85 percent (350), craftsmen 7 per-

cent (28), and day laborers 8 percent (34). By 1827, of 846 workers, 55 percent (467) were farmers, 12 percent (101) craftsmen, and 31 percent (264)
day laborers. An expansion of the day-laborer category in both size and
proportion also occurred in Santa Cruz during this period. The end result of
the Bourbon reforms and the land pressure that accompanied them was the
expansion of socially autonomous forms of labor and increased mobility
for a significant portion of the population.

To complete the picture of changes that occurred in the last quarter of
the eighteenth century, we must also examine church-state relations as they
affected New Mexico. During the reign of Charles III many of the formal
aspects of the Patronato Real, the partnership between church and state that
had been so effective in the colonization of the Americas, were abolished.
The religious orders, perceived as independent and powerful because of
their relationship to the indigenous population, were first to lose their privileged status. In New Mexico, where the Franciscan friars and the area's
governors had battled incessantly since the 1600s over the extent to which
each could exploit Indian land and labor, the Bourbon attack on clerical
rights put an end to the feud. The missions were gradually secularized;
where 30 friars had administered the sacraments in 1760, by 1834 none
remained.

The loosening of the Franciscans' grip on the population of New Mexico, part and parcel of the growth of secularism and the diffusion of ratio-
nalism throughout Europe and its colonies, bred an indifference toward
moral theology, the scriptures, and the authority of priests. One of the first
changes one notes in this increasingly secular society is a linguistic change
in the ecclesiastical marriage records. Whereas between 1690 and 1790
most individuals married ostensibly "to save my soul," "to serve God and
no other reason," or motivated by similar religious convictions, after 1790
nuptial candidates are moved by "the growing desire we mutually have"
and by "the urges of the flesh, human wretchedness and the great love we
have for each other." Increasingly, individuals mention personal desires
such as love as the reason for marriage.

The Bourbon reforms and the growth of a landless population dependent on wage labor for its reproduction had increased social differentiation.
This in turn brought into open question the ideological consensus that had
formerly existed between the nobility and the landed peasants regarding
ascribed honor as a sign of social status premised on family origin and control over means and instruments of production. For free genízaros, mestizos
who could not boast of "Spanish" origin, and landless peasants, honor was
of little material consequence. Their social status was obtained primarily
through individual achievement; under such circumstances patriarchal control over marriage formation was of no functional significance. After all,
parental sanction for arranged marriage was effective because familial
honor carried with it property and social privileges. Once children were
""'h their own wages to accumulate the necessary resources to estab-
/usehold, and could not in any way count on significant inheritance
erty, generational relations were placed on a new footing.

Examining the period from 1690 to 1848, the major change that occurred in marriage formation was an increased preference for unions based explicitly on romantic love over those arranged by parents pursuing economic considerations. This change was not sudden; it was an ongoing process. Love matches were possible from the earliest days of Spanish settlement but occurred infrequently among the landed classes concerned for the perpetuation of their patrimonies. Children had plenty of parental counsels, ballads, folktales, laws, and sermons to make them realize the disastrous consequences of placing desires over reason.

The history of marriage in a colonial social formation such as New Mexico reveals the centrality of patriarchal control for generational, gender, and class forms of domination. Arranged marriages that enhanced honor provided the nobility and the landed peasantry with a tool by which to protect their status in an unequal society. The various ideologies by which gender and class hierarchies were comprehended and legitimated, however, were not monolithic and static. The partnership between the church and state so instrumental in the conquest of Latin America created distinct views on the meaning of marriage. Though the positions of church and state frequently converged, differences between them enabled children to challenge parental authority without danger to the social order. Similarly, the meanings attached to the system of status and prestige varied by class and changed in response to larger economic forces that themselves transformed relations of production and the power relations between church and state. By the 1800s, the material underpinnings of the honor code had been eroded, creating the conditions that allowed individual urges such as romantic love to exert greater influence on marriage formation.

Sexuality in Early California's Franciscan Missions: Cultural Perceptions and Sad Realities

ALBERT L. HURTADO

For a long time now, the Franciscan missions have figured prominently in the popular history of California and in the palmy brochures of the tourist industry. In the twentieth century, there has grown a powerful myth that is known to every school child and traveler in the Golden State: In 1769, good Father Junípero Serra led to California a band of pious missionaries who Christianized the awed Indians, peacefully recruited them to the missions, and made the grateful neophytes into useful citizens of the Spanish empire. The kindly friars worked selflessly to make life—and afterlife— better for the Indians. When Mexico broke from Spain and took over California, jealous private citizens broke up the missions, took the land, and abused the mission Indians, thus undoing the religious work of half a century. The mis-

Excerpted from Albert L. Hurtado, "Sexuality in California's Franciscan Missions: Cultural Perceptions and Sad Realities," *California History,* 71 (Fall 1992), 371–385. Reprinted with permission of the author and the California Historical Society.

sion ruins remained, the story concludes, as crumbling and quaint reminders of California's humane and idealistic beginnings.

Like all good myths, there is some truth in this tale. Its main short-coming, however, is that it pays so little attention to the Indians who were the objects of the missionaries' attention. Few historians have looked care-fully at the impact of the missions on the native people. Fewer still have examined the motives and responses of Indians who chose to enter or remain outside the mission. These scholars have, however, unearthed the alarming population history of the missions that challenges the California mission myth. In 1769, there were about three hundred thousand Indians in California, with perhaps sixty thousand living between San Francisco Bay and San Diego, where the missions were located. By the end of the mission era in the 1830s, there were perhaps one hundred fifty thousand Indians left in the entire state. Disease was the principal cause of this appalling destruc-tion, for Indians had little resistance to the maladies that Spaniards brought to California. Evidently the missions facilitated the spread of illnesses because they concentrated native populations that had formerly been dis-persed. This tragic outcome, of course, was not what the fathers had intended. Nevertheless, missions became agencies of native destruction, even as they held out the promise of eternal salvation.

This essay will examine an aspect of the mission experience that has not received much attention—Indian sexuality and Franciscans' attempts to control it. Sexuality is only one aspect of Spanish-Indian relations, but it is important for several reasons. First, sexual relations are a universal feature of human existence that not only replicate life, but society as well. Second, anything that affects fertility is of particular importance in the study of a population like the California Indians, who were in rapid, prolonged decline. Third, because sexual relations are intensely human experiences, knowledge of sexuality provides insight into the historical life of the indi-vidual. Finally, an analysis of this one aspect of Spanish-Indian interaction provides a way to better understand population dynamics that advance beyond ungovernable environmental factors—such as disease—and delves into the realm of human choice.

Before Father Junípero Serra founded California's Franciscan mis-sions, he led a religious revival in Mexico's Oaxaca region. Francisco Palóu, Serra's companion and biographer, approvingly reported that Serra's religious work produced concrete results. He reformed an adultress who at the tender age of fourteen had begun to cohabit with a married man whose wife lived in Spain. This sinful arrangement had lasted for fourteen years, but upon Serra's order the woman left the house of her lover. The man was desolate. He threatened and begged her to return, but to no avail. Then "one night in desperation," Palóu related, "he got a halter, took it with him to the house where she was staying, and hung himself on an iron gate, giving over his soul to the demons." At the same moment a great earthquake shook the town whose inhabitants trembled with fear. Thereafter, the woman donned haircloth and penitential garb and walked the streets begging forgiveness for her shameful past. "All were edified and touched at seeing such an unusual conversion and subsequent penance," the friar wrote. "Nor were they less fearful of divine Justice," he added, "recalling the chastisement of that unfortunate man." Thus, Palóu believed, the tragedy brought "innumerable conversions . . . and great spiritual fruit" to Serra's Oaxaca mission.

This story was a kind of parable that prefaced Palóu's glowing account of Serra's missionary work in California. It demonstrated not only the presence of sexual sin in Spain's American colonies—which is not especially surprising—but that priestly intervention could break perverse habits, and that public exposure and sincere repentance could save souls. This incident is especially important to us because, on the eve of his expedition to California, Palóu linked Serra's Mexican missionary triumph with the rectification of sexual behavior. Thus, a discussion of sexuality in the California missions is not merely a prurient exercise, but goes to the heart of the missionaries' intentions. While errant sexuality was not the only concern of priests, the reformation of Indian sexual behavior was an important part of their endeavor to Christianize and Hispanicize native Californians. Their task was fraught with difficulty, peril, and tragedy for Indians and Spaniards alike.

Changing Indian behavior was difficult because native people already behaved according to sexual norms that, from their point of view, worked perfectly well. From north of San Francisco Bay to the present Mexican border, tribespeople regulated sexual life so as to promote productive family relationships that varied by tribe and locality. Everywhere, the conjugal couple and their children formed the basic household unit, which was sometimes augmented by aged relatives and unmarried siblings. Indian families, however, were not merely a series of nuclear units, but were knit into a complex set of associations that comprised native society. Kinship defined the individual's place within the cultural community, and family associations suffused every aspect of life. . . .

Recreating the sexual behavior of any historic people is difficult, but it is especially difficult in societies that lacked a written record. Still, modern anthropology and historical testimony make a plausible—if partial—reconstruction of intimate native life. California Indians regulated sexual behavior both in and out of marriage. Premarital sex does not seem to have been regarded with disapproval, so virginity was not a precondition for selecting a respectable mate. After marriage, spouses expected fidelity from their husbands and wives, possibly because of the importance of status inheritance. Consequently, adultery was a legitimate cause for divorce, and husbands could sometimes exact other punishments for sexual misbehavior by their wives. Chumash husbands sometimes whipped errant wives. An Esselin man could repudiate his wandering wife, or turn her over to her new lover, who had to pay the cuckold an indemnity, usually the cost of acquiring a new bride. A wronged Gabrielino husband could retaliate by claiming the wife of his wife's lover, and could even go so far as to kill an adulterous spouse, but such executions were probably rare.

Women were not altogether at the mercy of jealous and sadistic hus-

bands, for they could divorce husbands who mistreated them, a circumstance that probably meant they could leave if their husbands committed
sexual indiscretions. Chumash oral narratives reveal that women often initiated sex and ridiculed inadequate partners. When it suited them, some
women killed their husbands. It is impossible to know how frequently adulterous liaisons and subsequent divorces took place, but anthropologists
characterize the common Gabrielino marital pattern as serial monogamy
with occasional polygyny, indicating that separations were common. It is
not unreasonable to suppose that, because so many marriages were
arranged in youth, some California Indians subsequently took lovers after
meeting someone who struck deeper emotional chords than their initial
partners had. Nor is it implausible to speculate that some grievances were
overlooked completely in the interest of maintaining family harmony and to
keep intact the economic and diplomatic advantages that marriage ties were
meant to bind. Prostitution was extremely rare in California, and before the
arrival of the Spaniards, was noted only among the Salinan Indians. This
lack of a flesh trade may indicate that such outlets were simply not needed
because marriage, premarital, and extramarital associations provided sufficient sexual opportunities.

Another sexual practice recorded among a few California Indian groups
was male homosexual transvestism, or the so-called berdache tradition,
which was evident in some other North American tribes. The berdache
dressed like women and generally assumed many female gender roles, but
they were not thought of as homosexuals. Instead, it appears that some
Indian groups believed that they belonged to a third gender that combined
both male and female aspects. In sex, they took the female role, and they
often married men who were regarded as heterosexual males. Sometimes a
chief took a berdache for a "second wife" because it was believed that such
a person worked harder.

Horrified by existing social and marital patterns among the Indians
they encountered, Serra and the secular colonizers of Spain's northern frontier narrowly based their familial concepts on a Spanish model that was in
some respects internally contradictory. The state regarded marriage as a
contract that—among other things—transferred property and guaranteed
rights to sexual service. On the other hand, the Church regarded marriage
as a sacrament before God and sought to regulate alliances according to
religious principles.

In theory, if not always in practice, Spanish society forbade premarital
sex and required marital fidelity. Marriages were monogamous and lasted
for life; the Church granted divorces only in the most extraordinary cases,
although remarriage of widows and widowers was permitted. The Church
regarded all sexual transgressions with a jaundiced eye, but held some acts
in special horror. By medieval times Christian theologians had worked out
a scheme of acceptable sexual behavior that also reflected their abhorrence
of certain practices. Of course, fornication, adultery, incest, seduction,
rape, and polygamy were sins, but far worse than any of these were the exe-
crable "sins against nature," which included masturbation, bestiality, and

homosexual copulation. The Church allowed married intercourse only in the missionary position; other postures were unnatural because they made the woman superior to her husband, thus thwarting God's universal plan. Procreation, not pleasure, was God's purpose in creating the human sexual apparatus in the first place. Therefore, to misuse the instruments of man's procreative destiny was to thwart the will of God. Medieval constraints on intimate behavior began to erode in the early modern period, but Catholic proscriptions against "unnatural" sexual behavior remained a part of canon law when Spain occupied California.

Such was the *formal* sexual ideology that Franciscans, soldiers, and *pobladores* brought to California. All unapproved sexual practices were considered sinful lust. Maintaining sexual orthodoxy in the remotest reaches of the empire, however, proved to be a greater task than Franciscan missionaries and secular officials could accomplish. Part of the problem was that Spaniards also brought to California an *informal* sexual ideology rooted in Mediterranean folkways that often ran counter to the teachings of the Church. In this informal scheme, honor was an important element in determining family and individual social ranking, and male status was linked to sexual prowess. To seduce a woman was to shame her and to dishonor her family, while it conferred honor on her consort and asserted his dominant place in the social hierarchy. This double standard arose, in part, because men viewed women as sexually powerful creatures who could lead them astray, and more importantly, dishonor their families. Spanish society controlled female sexual power by segregating women, sometimes going so far as to sequester them behind locked doors, to assure that they would not sully the family escutcheon with lewd conduct. Thus, Catholic priests labored to restrict sexual activity in a world of philanderers, concubines, prostitutes, lovers, and lawful spouses.

California's Spanish colonizers brought with them these formal and informal ideas about sexuality that were riven with contradictions. The conquest of the New World and its existing alien sexual conventions made matters even more complicated but did not keep Spaniards from intimate encounters with native women. From the time of Cortéz, the Crown and the Church encouraged intermarriage with native people, and informal sexual amalgamation occurred with great regularity. Throughout the Spanish empire, interracial sex resulted in a large mixed-race (*mestizo*) population. Ordinarily, the progeny of these meetings attached themselves firmly to the religion and society of their Spanish fathers. Thus, sexual amalgamation was an integral part of the Spanish colonial experience that served to disable native society and strengthen the Hispanic population, as it drew Indians and their mixed-race children into the colonial orbit. This was the world that Serra had tried to reform in Oaxaca; yet it was a world that he and fellow Spaniards would unwittingly replicate in California.

In 1775 Father Serra wrote thoughtfully to the Viceroy of New Spain about interracial marriages. Three Catalan soldiers had already married neophyte women, and three more were "making up their minds to marry soon." Serra approved of new Spanish regulations that subsidized such marriages with a seaman's salary for two years and provided rations for the mixed-race couple for five years. Such families, it was agreed, should be attached permanently to the wife's mission and receive some livestock and a piece of land from the royal patrimony, provided the husband had "nothing else to fall back upon." To Father Serra these marriages symbolized the foundation of Spanish society. The new families formed "the beginnings of a town," because all the families lived in houses so placed as to form two streets. The little town of Monterey, Serra observed, also included the mission buildings, and "all together make up a square of their own, in front of our little residence and church." They noted happily that children were already beginning to appear in the little town, thus assuring that the community would have a future. Serra's idealistic vision of colonization incorporated Spanish town building and Catholic marriages that tamed the sinful natures of Spaniards and Indians and harnessed them to Spanish imperial goals. If Serra had had his way, however, the only sexual activity in California would have occurred in the few sanctified marriage beds that were under the watchful eye of the friars.

But that was not to be. Serra recognized that Spanish and Indian sexual transgressions occurred, and they troubled him. Common Indian sexual behavior, viewed in light of Catholic mores, amounted to serious sins that merited the friars' solemn condemnation. Perhaps the worse cases were the berdache, who seemed to be ubiquitous in some parts of California. Their so-called "sins against nature" challenged religious and military leaders alike. While Serra extolled the virtues of marriage, Captain Pedro Fages in 1775 reported that Chumash Indians were "addicted to the unspeakable vice of sinning against nature," and that each *ranchería* had a transvestite "for common use." Fages, reflecting common Spanish and Catholic values, apologized for even mentioning homosexuality, because it was "an excess so criminal that it seems even forbidden to speak its name." Similarly, the missionary Pedro Font observed "sodomites addicted to nefarious practices" among the Yuma and concluded that "there will be much to do when the Holy Faith and the Christian religion are established among them."

Civil and Church officials agreed on the need to eradicate homosexuality as an affront to God and Spanish men alike. At Mission Santa Clara, the fathers noticed an unconverted Indian who, though dressed like a woman and working among women, seemed to have undeveloped breasts, an observation easily made because Indian women traditionally wore only necklaces above the waist. The curious friars conspired with the corporal of the guard to take this questionable person into custody, where he was completely disrobed, confirming that he was indeed a man. The poor fellow was "more embarrassed than if he had been a woman," said one friar. For three days the soldiers kept him nude—stripped of his gender identity—and made him sweep the plaza near the guard house. He remained "sad and ashamed" until he was released under orders to abjure feminine clothes and stay out of women's company. Instead, he fled from the mission and reestablished a berdache identity among gentiles.

The Spanish soldiers thoroughly misconstrued what they were seeing and what they had done. The soldiers no doubt thought they had exposed an impostor who was embarrassed because his ruse had been discovered. They did not realize that their captive himself—and his people— regarded him as a woman, and he reacted accordingly when stripped and tormented by men. Humiliated beyond endurance and required to renounce a sexual preference that had never raised an eyebrow in Indian society, the Santa Clara transvestite was forced to flee, but perhaps he was more fortunate than he knew. Father Francisco Palóu reported a similar incident at the Mission San Antonio, where a berdache and another man were discovered "in an unspeakably sinful act." A priest, a corporal, and a soldier "punished them," Palóu revealed, "although not as much as they deserved." When the horrified priest tried to explain how terrible this sin was, the puzzled Indians told him that it was all right because they were married. Palóu's reaction to this news is not recorded, but it is doubtful that he accepted it with equanimity. After receiving a severe scolding, the homosexual couple left the mission vicinity. Palóu hoped that "these accursed persons will decrease, and such an abominable vice will be eradicated," as the Catholic faith increased "for the greater Glory of God and the good of those pitiful, ignorant people."

The revulsion and violence that ordinary Indian sexual relations inspired in the newcomers must have puzzled and frightened the native people. Formerly accepted by some Indian groups as an unremarkable part of social life, berdache faced persecution at the hands of friars and soldiers. To the Spaniards, homosexual behavior was loathsome, one of the many traits that marked California Indians as a backward race. In a word, they were "incomprehensible" to Father Geronimo Boscana. The "affirmative with them, is negative," he thought, "and the negative, the affirmative," a perversity that was clearly reflected in the open Indian practice of homosexuality. In frustration, Boscana compared the California Indians "to a species of monkey."

For Spaniards and California Indians alike, the early days of colonization created a confused sexual landscape, but Spanish intolerance of homosexuality was not the only cause of this. In order to convert the Indians, the Franciscans had to uproot other aspects of the normative social system that regulated Indian sexuality and marriage. At the very least, the missionaries meant to restructure Indian marriage to conform to orthodox Catholic standards of monogamy, permanence, and fidelity, changes in intimate conduct that engendered conflict in the California frontier.

At the outset, friars had to decide what to do about married Indians who became mission neophytes. Even the acerbic Father Boscana believed that monogamous Indian marriages were lawful and should be permanently binding on neophytes, except for couples who were united against their will. But what about marriages where one partner became a Christian while the other remained a heathen? And what should be done about polygynous unions? Missionaries worked out the answers according to canon law and its application to Indian converts in Mexico. Neophyte couples remarried in the Catholic Church, and when indigenous marriages were divided by religious beliefs, the Christian partner was permitted to take a new Christian spouse. . . .

Christian ceremonies did not automatically eliminate older cultural meanings of Indian marriage, nor did they necessarily engender Catholic values in the Indian participants. Dissident neophyte runaways sometimes abandoned their old wives and took new ones according to tribal custom. When fathers forbade specific neophyte marriages, unhappy Indians found ways to insist on having the relationship that they preferred. In 1816, for example, an Indian man, probably Chumash, left Mission San Buenaventura to be with the woman he wanted at Santa Barbara. "This happens," Father José Señan revealed, "every time his shackles are removed." It is not clear if the missionaries had shackled the man for previously running off to his lover or for some other offense, but Señan allowed that it would be best to permit the couple to wed quietly. If, however, the Indian made mischief, "send him back to us." . . .

Neophytes who failed to live up to Catholic standards ran afoul of the missionaries, who imposed corporal punishment. When, for example, Chumash neophytes at Mission Santa Barbara reverted to polygyny—which the friars evidently regarded as concubinage after Christian conversion—Father Esteban Tapis first admonished the offenders. On the second offense, Tapis laid on the whip, and when this did not convince the Indians of the error of their ways, he put them in shackles.

Franciscans believed they had a right to use corporal punishment to correct unruly Indians. Indeed, the lash was used as an instrument of discipline throughout Spanish society. Eighteenth-century Spanish parents whipped children; teachers whipped pupils; magistrates whipped civil offenders; pious Catholics whipped themselves as penance. Although many Indians appeared to have deeply resented corporal punishment, some neophytes accepted the lash as a fact of mission life when their sexual transgressions caught the watchful eyes of the friars, but the Spanish and Catholic understanding of the whip as an instrument of correction, teaching, mortification, and purification no doubt eluded them. In Indian society corporal punishment as a means of social control was rare. Some tribes permitted husbands to physically punish adulterous wives, who were judged not only to have violated moral codes but to have threatened the economic and diplomatic role of the family.

Indian sexuality was not the only carnal problem that the fathers had to contend with in California. Civilians and soldiers brought to California sexual attitudes and behavior that were at odds with both Catholic and Indian values. Rape was a special concern of friars, who persistently condemned Spanish deviant sexual behavior in California. As early as 1772, Father Luís Jayme complained about some of the soldiers, who deserved to be hanged for "continuous outrages" on the Kumeyaay women near Mission San Diego. "Many times," he asserted, the Indians were on the verge of attacking the mission because "some soldiers went there and raped their women." The situation was so bad that the Indians fled from the priests, even risking hunger "so the soldiers will not rape their women as they have already done so many times in the past."

Father Jayme thought Spaniards' assaults were all the worse because the Kumeyaay Indians had become Christians and had presumably given up polygyny. According to Jayme, married neophytes did not commit adultery, and bachelors were celibate. "If a man plays with a woman who is not his wife," Jayme explained, "he is scolded and punished by his captains." Kumeyaay sexual behavior was not only the result of the missionaries' teachings, but a reflection of their traditional belief that adultery was bad. An unconverted Indian told Jayme that "although we did not know that God would punish us in Hell, [we] considered [adultery] to be very bad, and we did not do it, and even less now that we know that God will punish us if we do so." When the missionary heard this, he "burst into tears to see how these gentiles were setting an example for us Christians."

Jayme's version of the Kumeyaay statement seems to confuse rape and adultery, a problem that may have stemmed from linguistic and cultural misunderstanding. In any case, Jayme described two rapes and their consequences. In one instance three soldiers raped an unmarried woman who became pregnant. She was ashamed of her condition and ultimately killed the newborn infant, an act that horrified and saddened Father Jayme. The second incident occurred when four soldiers and a sailor went to a *ranchería* and dragged off two women. The sailor refused to take part and left the four to complete the assault. Afterwards, the soldiers tried to convert the act from rape to prostitution by paying the women with some ribbon and a few tortillas. They also paid a neophyte man who had witnessed the assault and warned him not to divulge the incident. Insulted and angry, the Indians were not overawed by the rapists' threats. They told Jayme. In retaliation the soldiers locked the neophyte man in the stocks, an injustice that outraged Jayme, who personally released him.

The situation at San Diego was not unique. "There is not a single mission where all the gentiles have not been scandalized," Jayme wrote, "and even on the road, so I have been told." The Spaniards' sexual behavior also did not escape the eye of Father Serra, who asserted that "a plague of immorality had broken out." He had heard the bitter complaints of the friars who wrote to him of disorders at all the missions. Serra worried especially about the muleteers who traversed the vast distances between missions with their pack trains. Serra feared the consequences of allowing these unbridled characters among the Indians. There were so many Indian women on the road that Serra expected sexual transgressions, for "it would be a great miracle, yes, a whole series of miracles, if it did not provoke men of such low character to disorders which we have to lament in all our missions; they occur every day." Serra came perilously close to blaming the women for the sexual assaults they suffered. Nevertheless, he believed rapes could imperil the entire mission enterprise by alienating the Indians, who would "turn on us like tigers."

Serra was right. In 1775 some eight hundred neophyte and non-Christian Kumeyaays, fed up with sexual assaults and chafing under missionary supervision, attacked Mission San Diego. They burned the mission and killed three Spaniards, including Father Jayme, beating his face beyond recognition. As Jayme and Serra predicted, sexual abuse against Indians made California a perilous place. Still, the revolt did not dissuade some Spaniards from sexual involvement with Indian women. In 1779, Serra was still criticizing the government for "unconcern in the matter of shameful conduct between the soldiers and Indian women," a complaint that may have been directed at mutual as well as rapacious liaisons.

Serra's argument implied that without supervision, some Spaniards acted without sexual restraint. As we have seen, Spaniards believed in a code of honor that rewarded sexual conquest. Soldiers may have asserted their ideas about honor and status by seducing California Indian women, but there was no honor in rape. Honorable sexual conquest required a willing partner who was overcome by the man's sensuality, masculinity, and magnetism, not merely his brute ability to overpower her. Recall the San Diego rapists, who tried to mitigate their actions by making a payment to their victim. Serra argued that these were men of bad character who could not control their urges.

Rape, however, is a violent, complex act that requires more than opportunity and a supposed super-heightened state of sexual tension. Recent research shows that rape is an act of domination carried out by men who despise their victims, in this case because of their race, as well as their gender. Stress, anger, and fear also motivate some rapists.

It should not be forgotten that Spaniards were fearful of California Indians. The soldiers were outnumbered and surrounded by Indians who seemed capable of overwhelming them at any moment. Frequent minor skirmishes, livestock thefts, and occasional murders reinforced the Spanish conception of the Indian enemy. As late as 1822 one missionary thought it was impossible to know how many troops were necessary to defend the Mission San Buenaventura because there were so many unchristianized Indians in the interior. "May God keep our neophytes peaceful and submissive," he wrote "for they would not want for allies if they should rise against our Saint and our charity!" It is not difficult to imagine that some men, sent to a dangerous frontier outpost, violently used Indian women as objects to ward off fear and to express their domination over the numerous native people that the Spanish Crown and Catholic Church sought to subdue, colonize, and convert.

Sexuality, unsanctioned and perversely construed as a way to control native people, actually threatened Spain's weak hold on California by angering the Indians and insulting their ideas about sexuality, rectitude, and justice. It is impossible to know how many rapes occurred in Spanish California, but sexual assaults affected Indian society beyond their absolute numbers. Moreover, Indian rape victims likely displayed some of the somatic and emotional symptoms of rape trauma syndrome, including physical wounds, tension, sleeplessness, gastrointestinal irritations, and genitourinary disturbances. In our own time, rape victims are often stricken

with fear, guilt, anger, and humiliation, and some women who have suffered rape develop a fear of normal sexual activity. There is no reason to
believe that Indian women did not react to rape in similar ways. Fear of
assault may also have affected many women who were not themselves victims, but who tried to help friends and relatives cope with the consequences
of rape. Sexual assaults echoed in the Indian social world, even as they
frightened friars who feared the consequences of an outraged Indian population.

It is impossible to know how many free-will assignations occurred in
California during the mission period, but it is safe to assume that such
cross-cultural trysts were fraught with misunderstanding. Indian women,
accustomed to looking outside their communities for husbands, likely
viewed Spaniards as potential mates who could bring them and their families increased power, wealth, and status. Some women may have hoped that
sex would lead to marriage, but it seldom did.

Indians responded to Spanish sexual importunities in several ways.
Physical resistance to missionization, as happened at San Diego and on the
Colorado River, was one way to deal with rapists and other unwanted
intruders. Marriage to a Spaniard was another strategy that could protect
women, but evidently only some Indians, a small minority, were able to use
this tactic. Other Indians withdrew from Spanish-controlled areas to avoid
any infringement on their social life and values. On the other hand, some
women might have entered the missions for the protection from sexual
abuse that the mission setting provided.

There is also reason to believe that Indians altered their sexual practices as a result of meeting the Spanish. Prostitution, which had been rare
among the Indians, became common. In 1780, Father Serra complained
about Nicolas, a neophyte who procured women for the soldiers at San
Gabriel. A few years later, a Spanish naturalist observed that the Chumash
men had "become pimps, even for their own wives, for any miserable
profit."

Nicolas and other Indians had several reasons to resort to prostitution.
Spanish men seduced and raped their female kinfolk, but did not marry
them. Perhaps Indians were recovering lost bride prices through prostitution. Perhaps, since some Hispanic men were willing to pay for sex, prostitution seemed a logical way to enhance the economic value of wives and
daughters, who were expected to be productive. Perhaps, prostitution was
simply a means of economic survival, taken out of desperation. How
women felt about being so used is not known, but the missions would have
been one avenue of escape for those who were unhappy with these new
conditions. In the early years of colonization, Indian women outnumbered
male neophytes, indicating that females found the mission especially
attractive in a rapidly changing world.

Another California Indian reaction to a new sexual world was physiological: they contracted syphilis and other venereal diseases, maladies they
had not previously been exposed to. So rapidly did syphilis spread among
Indians that in 1792 a Spanish naturalist traveling in California believed the

disease was endemic among the Chumash. Twenty years later, the friars recorded it as the most prevalent and destructive disease in the missions. Syphilis was particularly deadly among the Indians because its weakened victims became easy prey for other epidemic diseases that periodically swept the missions. In addition, stillbirths increased, and syphilitic women died more frequently in childbirth. If the women bore live children, the infants were likely to have congenital syphilis. . . .

The combination of virulent endemic syphilis and sexual promiscuity created a fatal environment that killed thousands of mission Indians and inhibited the ability of survivors to recover population losses through reproduction. Franciscans—and some of their critics—believed that the carnal disintegration of the California missions occurred because the Indians simply continued to observe the sexual customs of their native society. According to the missionaries, the Indians were unrestrained libertines who had learned nothing of Catholic moral behavior in the missions, and were incapable of realizing that syphilis was killing them. This view is incomplete because it assumes that sexual behavior was unregulated in native society and that Indian sexual behavior was unchanged during sixty-five years of mission experience.

Perhaps mission Indian sexuality was a response to new conditions. Who would have understood disparate demographic conditions at the missions better than the neophytes themselves? Locked into a system that seemed to assure their ultimate destruction, dying rapidly from unheard-of diseases, perhaps neophytes chose procreation as a means of group survival. Sadly, they failed, but it was not for want of trying. . . .

Whatever the causes of mission sexuality, neophytes relied on old ways and new ones to solve difficult problems in a new setting. In the end, efficacious solutions eluded them, but it is not accurate to say that Indians were immoral, amoral, or incapable of assimilating the message that the missionaries brought them. The mission experience demonstrates that Indians were simultaneously resolute and unsure, conservative and radical, forward looking and bound to tradition. They exemplified, in other words, the human condition.

Ultimately, the history of California's missions is a sad story of human misunderstandings and failures and terrible unintended consequences. That Spaniards and Indians were often incapable of comprehending each other should hardly be surprising, because they came from radically different cultures. As was so often the case in the history of the Western Hemisphere, Indians and newcomers talked past each other, not with each other. This was true even of their most personal contacts in California. Sacred and profane, intimate, carnal, spiritual, ecstatic, bringing life and death—Indian and Spanish sexuality embodied the identity and paradox of their all-too-human encounter.

Y *FURTHER READING*

Robert Archibald, *Economic Aspects of the California Missions* (1978)

John Francis Bannon, *The Spanish Borderlands Frontier, 1513–1821* (1970)

Herbert E. Bolton, *Rim of Christendom* (1936)

——, *The Spanish Borderlands* (1921)

Donald E. Chipman, *Spanish Texas, 1519–1821* (1992)

Warren L. Cook, *Flood Tide of Empire: Spain and the Pacific Northwest, 1543–1819* (1973)

Arnoldo De León, *Mexican Americans in Texas: A Brief History* (1993)

Peter Gerhard, *The North Frontier of New Spain* (1982)

Charles Gibson, *Spain in America* (1966)

Ramón Gutiérrez, *When Jesus Came, the Corn Mothers Went Away: Marriage, Sexuality, and Power in New Mexico, 1500–1846* (1991)

Thomas D. Hall, *Social Change in the Southwest, 1350–1880* (1989)

Evelyn Hu-DeHart, *Missionaries, Miner and Indians: Spanish Contact with the Yaqui Nation of Northwestern New Spain, 1533–1820* (1981)

Elizabeth A. H. John, *Storms Brewed in Other Men's Worlds: The Confrontations of Indians, Spanish, and French in the Southwest, 1540–1795* (1975)

Oakah L. Jones, Jr., *Los Paisanos: Spanish Settlers on the Northern Frontier of New Spain* (1979)

John L. Kessell, *Friars, Soldiers, and Reformers: Hispanic Arizona and the Sonora Mission Frontier, 1767–1856* (1976)

——, *Kiva, Cross, and Crown: The Pecos Indians and New Mexico, 1540–1840* (1979)

Michael C. Meyer, *Water in the Hispanic Southwest: A Social and Legal History, 1550–1850* (1984)

Douglas Monroy, *Thrown Among Strangers: The Making of Mexican Culture in Frontier California* (1990)

Max L. Moorhead, *The Presidio: Bastion of the Spanish Borderlands* (1975)

James E. Officer, *Hispanic Arizona, 1536–1856* (1987)

Marc Simmons, *The Last Conquistador: Juan de Oñate and the Settling of the Far Southwest* (1991)

Edward H. Spicer, *Cycles of Conquest: The Impact of Spain, Mexico, and the United States on the Indians of the Southwest, 1533–1960* (1962)

David J. Weber, *The Mexican Frontier, 1821–1846: The American Southwest Under Mexico* (1982)

——, *Myth and the History of the Hispanic Southwest* (1988)

——, ed. *New Spain's Far Northern Frontier: Essays on Spain in the American West, 1540–1821* (1979)

——, *The Spanish Frontier in North America* (1992)

CHAPTER
3

Cultural Contacts and
Contracts

Y

Before contact with Europeans, hundreds of thousands of Native Americans lived in the Mountain West and Prairie-Plains regions of what became Canada and the United States. They had already shaped the land to fit their material needs and cultural desires, giving it meaning and making it home long before American and Canadian loggers, farmers, and ranchers remade it into "Home on the Range." French, British, Russian, Spanish, Mexican, and American fur trappers, traders, and missionaries initiated the contracts that tied native peoples and their lands to an expanding world system. These new peoples introduced horses, trade goods, firearms, and alcohol. They also brought epidemic diseases like smallpox and measles that devastated native populations. In return the Indians helped them understand the land and its resources. Native peoples took them into their villages and families, and expected them to be allies in existing intertribal struggles over hunting lands and trade routes. This form of reciprocal exchange functioned on multiple levels—economic, social, political, and biological—with multiple layers of meanings for both sides. Today, historians are charting this "middle ground" of contact and contracts, demonstrating that Indian peoples participated actively in events and were not passive victims of conquest. The reassessment of the role of native peoples in the fur trade brings to light a more complete story of the relationships between humans, animals, markets, and environments.

How did Indian peoples understand this contact situation? Why did they enter into contracts with Euro-Americans and how did they view that exchange? What roles did they play in this economic, political, and social relationship, and what kind of control or influence did they exercise?

Y *DOCUMENTS*

All peoples have their own explanations about who they are, where they came from, and where they are going. Culturally these oral traditions make perfect sense. They are a way of situating people in time and space, connecting them with past and future, and explaining "others" as they appear with their own different but culturally consistent set of explanations. The first three documents in this chapter describe the process of creation, contact, and the arrival of horses from a Southern Ute, Chippewa, and Piegan perspective. Although these narratives were recorded by white settlers long after the events described, they offer us a glimpse of how native peoples perceive and explain the process of culture contact.

The final two documents describe different aspects of the fur trade in the West after contact and contracts were well-established. The first account is from the 1837 journal of Francis Chandon, a trader at Fort Clark, located on the Missouri River some fifty-five miles above present-day Bismarck, North Dakota. His description of the impact of introduced epidemic diseases among the Arikiras, Mandans, Hidatsas, Assiniboins, and Blackfeet of the northern plains stands as understated testimony to the deadliness of the biological invasion of North America. The second document is English traveler George Frederick Ruxton's colorful and romantic account of his experiences among the mountain men. He records details of their work and appearance, their language, and their attitudes toward women.

Buckskin Charlie Recounts Southern Ute Creation, Recorded 1912

Sünä'wavi [Wolf, the Ute culture hero/creator] and Coyote were brothers. . . .

There were no people in any part of the world. [One] day Sünä'wavi made his knife very sharp but did not tell his brother the reason. He went off to the hills to a tü'av [service berry] brush, cut some nice straight bushes and brought several bundles to these sticks. He returned in the afternoon, cut them all up into pieces of about the same size, put them into a big sack and tied it up. The same evening he sharpened his knife again, went out and returned with the same kind of bundles, again cutting the sticks into pieces and tying them up in the sack. The next morning he started again, got bundles and put the cut sticks into the sack. He did this a fourth time, nearly filling the sack. He went a fifth time and then it was very nearly full. Coyote asked, "What is he going to do?"—"I am going out once more." He tied up his bag well. Coyote was curious to see the inside. It was a great big sack lying towards the east. After his brother had gone off, Coyote thought, "I don't know what he is going to do, I'll untie the bag and see what is in it." He untied it and looked in. Then people came out shouting. Coyote fell back and ran off for fear. Plenty of people came running out, speaking dif-

Robert H. Lowie, "Shoshonean Tales," *Journal of American Folklore* vol. 37 no. 143–144 (January–June, 1924), 2–4. Reproduced by permission of the American Folklore Society from *Journal of American Folklore*, Vol. 37, No. 143–144 (1924). Not for further reproduction.

ferent languages. Sünä'wavi came back. The country was covered with dust from so many people who had come out of the sack. Sünä'wavi cursed at his brother, for there were very few left, the rest having scattered in all directions. He said, "You always do things the wrong way, I always want to do things well." Coyote asked, "What is the matter?"—"Why did you open it?"—"I wanted to know what was inside."—"It was none of your business. You spoil everything. I was going to divide them and give them each a different place to live. Those who came out first and went east are Whites. The rest, who went north and south, are Indians." He counted those who were left, there were ten. He said to one group, "You shall be Apache and live to the west." Similarly he spoke to the Pueblo Indians, the Mescalero, the Ute, Navaho, and Paiute. "I was going to divide all by hundreds, but most of them are gone. This small tribe shall be Ute, but they will be very brave and able to defeat the rest." To Coyote he said, "You spoiled it, now the other Indians are going to attack us. You must look out carefully now. Those who speak different languages will be our enemies; they will fight and kill us and one another."

Chippewa Contact Narrative, Recorded 1855

For a long time before this story began, my people had lived on a small promontory on Lake Superior. It is called the Point of the Old Village.

One night one of my grandfathers, a prophet of the tribe, had a dream which had a strange effect on him. For days he busied himself very earnestly, as a result of this dream. He fasted, he took sweat baths every day, he shut himself alone in his prophet lodge.

His penance was so thorough, so unusual, that the people of the village were curious. What was about to happen? Was there to be a great famine or an unusually successful hunting season? Was there to be a serious war with the Sioux? Or was something else of equal importance about to take place?

At last when the prophet had considered everything carefully, and after he had the whole story of his dream clear in his mind, he called together the other prophets and the chiefs of his people. He had astonishing news for them.

"Men of strange appearance have come across the great water," he told them. "They have landed on our island. Their skins are white like snow, and on their faces long hair grows. These people have come across the great water in wonderfully large canoes which have great white wings like those of a giant bird. The men have long and sharp knives, and they have long black tubes which they point at birds and animals. The tubes make a smoke that rises into the air just like the smoke from our pipes. From them come fire and such terrific noise that I was frightened, even in my dream."

Half a day it took the prophet to tell his dream. He described the sails and the masts of the ships, the iron corslets, the guns and cannon. The other

---

From *Indian Legends of Canada,* 150–151, by Ella Elizabeth Clark, published by McClelland and Stewart Limited.

prophets and the chiefs listened in amazement. When he finished speaking, all agreed at once that they should prepare a fleet of several canoes and send it eastward along the Great Lakes and the great river. There at the big water, their messengers should find out about these strange people and, on their return home, should make a report to the tribe.

Canoes were made ready for the long journey, and trusted men were selected. For many suns and several moons they travelled over the waters of the lakes and down the great river, through the lands of friendly tribes. These people knew nothing yet of the white strangers, for they had no gifted dreamer and prophet among them.

At last the travellers from the Point of the Old Village came to the lower part of the great river. One evening they found a clearing in the forest, where even the largest trees had been cut down quite smoothly. The Indians camped there and examined the stumps closely. Giant beavers with huge, sharp teeth had done the cutting, the men thought.

"No," said the prophet. "These trees were probably cut by the long knives I saw in my dream. The white strangers must have camped here."

His companions were filled with awe, and with terror also. Using their own stone-headed axes, they could not cut down such large trees or cut anything so smoothly. Then they found some long, rolled-up shavings that puzzled them, and also some pieces of bright-coloured cloth. The shavings they stuck in their hair and in their ears; the cloth they wound around their heads.

Wearing these decorations, the travellers went on. Soon they came to the camp of the strangers. The men had white faces and bushy beards, just as the prophet had said. They had long knives, thundering fire-tubes, and giant canoes with white wings, just as the prophet had said. Now we know that these first white men were Frenchmen.

When the travellers had finished their visit, they made the long journey back to their home on Lake Superior and reported what they had seen. They were excited, and their story excited all the village. Everyone crowded round, to see the things the men had brought back: the shavings, the pieces of wood cut with sharp tools, the gaily-coloured cloth. This cloth was torn into small pieces, so that each person might have one.

To impress other chiefs and other tribes, the Chippewas followed an old custom. In former days they had bound the scalps of their enemies on long poles and sent them from one tribe to another; now they fastened splinters of wood and strips of calico to poles and sent them with special messengers.

And so these strange articles were passed from hand to hand around the whole lake. In this way the people of Lake Superior gained their first knowledge of the white men from Europe.

Wolf Calf (Piegan) Describes the Arrival of Horses, Recorded 1895

The first horses we ever saw came from west of the mountains. A band of the Piegans were camped on Belly River, at a place that we call "Smash the Heads," where we jumped buffalo. They had been driving buffalo over the cliff here, so that they had plenty of meat.

There had come over the mountains to hunt buffalo a Kutenai who had some horses, and he was running buffalo; but for some reason he had no luck. He could kill nothing. He had seen from far off the Piegan camp, but he did not go near it, for the Piegans and the Kutenais were enemies.

This Kutenai could not kill anything, and he and his family had nothing to eat and were starving. At last he made up his mind that he would go into the camp of his enemies and give himself up, for he said, "I might as well be killed at once as die of hunger." So with his wife and children he rode away from his camp up in the mountains, leaving his lodge standing and his horses feeding about it, all except those which his woman and his three children were riding, and started for the camp of the Piegans.

They had just made a big drive, and had run a great lot of buffalo over the cliff. There were many dead in the pískun [corral] and the men were killing those that were left alive, when suddenly the Kutenai, on his horse, followed by his wife and children on theirs, rode over a hill nearby. When they saw him, all the Piegans were astonished and wondered what this could be. None of them had ever seen anything like it, and they were afraid. They thought it was something mysterious. The chief of the Piegans called out to his people: "This is something very strange. I have heard of wonderful things that have happened from the earliest times until now, but I never heard of anything like this. This thing must have come from above (i.e., from the sun), or else it must have come out of the hill (i.e., from the earth). Do not do anything to it; be still and wait. If we try to hurt it, may be it will ride into that hill again, or may be something bad will happen. Let us wait."

As it drew nearer, they could see that it was a man coming, and that he was on some strange animal. The Piegans wanted their chief to go toward him and speak to him. The chief did not wish to do this; he was afraid; but at last he started to go to meet the Kutenai, who was coming. When he got near to him, the Kutenai made signs that he was friendly, and patted his horse on his neck and made signs to the chief. "I give you this animal." The chief made signs that he was friendly, and the Kutenai rode into the camp and were received as friends, and food was given them and they ate, and their hunger was satisfied.

The Kutenai stayed with these Piegans for some time, and the Kutenai man told the chief that he had more horses at his camp up in the mountains, and that beyond the mountains there were plenty of horses. The Piegan said, "I have never heard of a man riding an animal like this." He asked the

George Bird Grinnell, *Story of the Indian* (New York: Appleton Publishing Co., 1895).

Kutenai to bring in the rest of his horses; and one night he started out, and the next day came back driving all his horses before him, and they came to the camp, and all the people saw them and looked at them and wondered. . . .

This young man . . . finally became head chief of the Piegans. His name at first was Dog, and afterward Sits-in-the-Middle, and at last Many Horses. He had so many horses he could not keep track of them all. After he had so many horses, he would select ten boys out of each band of the Piegans to care for his horses. Many Horses had more horses than all the rest of the tribe. Many Horses died a good many years ago. These were the first horses the Piegans saw.

When they first got horses, the people did not know what they fed on. They would offer the animals pieces of dried meat, or would take a piece of backfat and rub their noses with it, to try to get them to eat it. Then the horses would turn away and put down their heads, and begin to eat the grass of the prairie. . . .

White people had begun to come into this country, and Many Horses' young men wanted ropes and iron arrowpoints and saddle blankets, and the people were beginning to kill furs and skins to trade. Many Horses began to trade with his own people for these things. He would ask the young men of the tribe to kill skins for him, and they would bring them to him and he would give them a horse or two in exchange. Then he would send his relations into the Hudson's Bay post to trade, but he would never go himself. The white men wanted to see him, and sent word to him to come in, but he would never do so.

At length, one winter, these white men packed their dog sledges with goods and started to see Many Horses. They took with them guns. The Pigeans heard that the whites were coming, and Many Horses sent word to all the people to come together and meet him at a certain place, where the whites were coming. When these came to the camp, they asked where Many Horses' lodge was, and the people pointed out to them the Crow painted lodge. The whites went to this lodge and began to unpack their things— guns, clothing, knives, and goods of all kinds.

Many Horses sent two men to go in different directions through the camp and ask all the principal men, young and old, to come together to his lodge. They all came. Some went in and some sat outside. Then these white men began to distribute the guns, and with each gun they gave a bundle of powder and ball. At this same time, the young men received white blankets and the old men black coats. Then we first got knives, and the white men showed us how to use knives; to split down the legs and rip up the belly— to skin for trade.

Francis Chardon Laments the Destruction
of the Arikaras and Mandans by Smallpox, 1837

[*July*] *Wednesday 26,*   The Rees [Arikaras] And Mandans all arrived to Day Well loaded With Meat, Mitchel also arrived with 15 pieces, The 4 Bears (Mandan) has caught the small pox, and got crazy, and has disappeared from camp—he arrived here in the afternoon—The Indians of the Little Village all arrived in the evening Well loaded—With dried Meat—the small Pox has broke Out among them, several has died,

Thursday 27,   Indians all Out after berries, No News from Any quarter, the small pox is Killing them of at the Village, four died to day—

Friday 28,   Rain in the Morning—This day was very Near being my last—a young Mandan came to the Fort with his gun cocked, And secreted under his robe, With the intention of Killing Me, after hunting Me in 3 or 4 of the houses he at last found Me, the door being shut, he waited some time for Me to come Out, just as I Was in the Act of going Out, Mitchel caught him, and gave him in the hands of two Indians Who Conducted him to the Village, had Not Mitchel perceived him the instant he did, I would Not be at the trouble of Makeing this statement—I am upon my guard, the Rees are Out rageous against the Mandans, they say that the first Mandan that Kills a White, they Will exterminate the whole race, I have got 100 Guns ready And 1000 Powder, ready to hand Out to them when the fun Commences—The War Party of Rees that left here the 7th inst came back to day—With five horses, that they stole from the Sioux—a lodge that was encamped at the Little Miss^r they attacked it in the Night, after fireing several shots they departed takeing with them all the Horses they think to have Killed 3 or 4 in the lodge—The Mandans & Rees gave us two splendid dances, they say they dance, on account of their Not haveing a long time to live, as they expect to all die of the Small Pox—and as long as they Are alive, They Will take it Out in danceing.

Saturday 29,   Several More Mandans died last night. Two GrosVentres arrived from their dried Meat camp, it appears that it has Not broke Out Among them as yet—

Sunday 30,   An other report from the GrosVentres to day say, they are Arrived at their Village, and that 10 or 15 of them have died, two big fish Among them, they threaten Death And Distruction to us all at this Place, saying that I was the Cause of the small pox Makeing its appearance in this Country—One of Our best friends of the Village (The Four Bears) died today, regretted by all Who Knew him,

Monday 31,   Mandans are getting worse Nothing Will do them except revenge. Three of the War party that left here the 26th of last Month Arrived to day. With each of them One horse, that they stole from the Yanctons on White River,

Killed 61 Rats this Month—total 1778

From *Mississippi Valley Historical Review* XVII (September 1930), 283–285, 289–291, 299.

August 31 Days—1837

Tuesday 1st,   The three horses that the war party brought in yesterday they say that they belong to the Compy that they were stole on the Island below the Little Missr the Soldiers was takeing them from them, but I told them to Waite untill the Arrival of Lachapelle Who I expect to Arrive in 4 or 5 days—

The Mandans Are Makeing their Medicine for rain, As their Corn is all drying up—to day we had several light showers—

Wednesday 2nd,   Yesterday an Indian that was Out after berris discovered a band of Cows, all hands Out to run them, they all Arrived in the Afternoon Well laden With fresh meat haveing ran three Bands—

Thursday 3rd,   All quiet, No News from Any quarter the GrosVentres Not yet Arrived from their Dried Meat excursion—

Friday 4th,   Same As Yesterday—Nothing New, Only two deaths today—sprinkled with rain in the Morning—

Saturday 5th,   Portrá a half breed from the North started to day—alone, for Red River, Indians Out after berries, others Out After Meat—News from the GrosVentres, they say that they are encamped this side of Turtle Mountain, And that a great Many of them have died of the Small Pox—several chiefs Among them, they swear vengence Against all the Whites, As they say the small Pox Was brought here by the S. B. [Steamboat].

Sunday 6,   One More Ree died last Night—To day we had a tremendous storm of rain, hale, And Wind, which Continued for $\frac{1}{2}$ hour With great Violence, the Fort came very Near blowing down, 40 or 50 Loads of hay that I have Out is Much damaged

Monday 7,   Six More died to day—several Rees left the Mandan Village and pitched their Lodges Out in the Prairies—rain all day—report from the GrosVentres say they will be at their Village tomorrow—

Tuesday 8,   Four More died to day—the two thirds of the Village are sick, to day I gave six pounds of Epsom salts in doses to Men, Women, and children   the small Pox has broke Out at the Little Mandan Village. three died yesterday, two chiefs—

Wednesday 9,   Seven More died to day—the Men came back from the hay at full speed haveing saw enemies, all hands out for the fight, False alarm,

Thursday 10,   All the Rees that were encamped in the Mandan lodges, except a few that are sick, Moved down to the Island hoping to get rid of the small Pox—the Mandans talk of Moveing to the other side of the river, 12 or 15 died to day—

Friday 11,   Sent old Charboneau up to the GrosVentres with some tobacco; and a bag full of good talk, as yesterday they sent a very severe threat to Me, Mandans all crossed to the other Side of the river to encamp—leaveing all that were sick in the Village, I Keep No A/c of the dead, as they die so fast that it is impossible—

Saturday 12,   Cool And pleasant Weather, one of My best friends of the Little Village died to day—(Le Fort)—News of a War party of GrosVentres And Rees (70) being used up by the Saons [Sioux], quicker Work than the small Pox.

Sunday 13,   Several reports from the GrosVentres that they are bent on the distruction of us all, As yet I do Not place Much confidence in what report says, Charboneau Will bring us the strait News—The Mandan are dying 8 and 10 every day—an Old fellow who has lost the whole of his family to the Number of 14, harrangued to day, that it was time to begin to Kill the Whites, as it was them that brought the small Pox in the Country—

Tuesday 22,   Cool pleasant Weather, The disease still Keeps ahead 8 and 10 die off daily, thirty five Mandans (Men) have died, the Women and Children I keep No Account of—Several Mandans have come back to remain in the Village, One of My Soldiers a (Ree) died to day—Two Young Mandans shot themselves this Morning—News from the Little Village, that the disease is getting worse and worse every day. it is now two months that it broke Out—A Ree that has the small Pox, And thinking that he was going to die, approached Near his Wife, a Young Woman of 19—And struck her in the head With his tommahawk, With the intent to Kill her, that she Might go With him in the Other World—she is badly Wounded   a few Minutes after he cut his throat, a report is in Circulation, that they intend to fire the Fort, Stationed guards in the Bastion

Wednesday 23,   May and Charboneau arrived late last night from the GrosVentres   all appears to be quiet in that quarter. The little Sioux a *Mandan* died last night, We had three allerts to day—all hands under Arms, all false reports   Several Rees Arrived from their camp at the GrosVentres

Thursday 24,   Seven More died at the Village last Night, and Many More at the Ree camp at the point of Woolds below   The fellow that we Killed on the 17th all his band Came to day to smoke With us and Make Peace, how long it will last I Cannot tell, however We Must put up With it, good or bad—

Friday 25,   May And Charboneau started last Night for the GrosVentres sent a few pounds of powder & Ball to the GrosVentres And Rees—An other Mandan chief died to day—(The long fingers)   total Number of Men that has died—50, I have turned Out to be a first rate doctor St Grado, an Indian that has been bleeding at the Nose all day, I gave him a decoction of all sorts of ingredients Mixed together, enough to Kill a Buffaloe Bull of the largest size, and stopped the effusion of Blood, the decoction of Medicine, Was, a little Magnisia, peppermint, sugar lead, all Mixed together in a phial, filled With Indian grog—and the Patient snuffing up his nose three or four times—I done it out of experiment And Am Content to say, that it proved effectual, the Confidence that an Indian has in the Medicine of the whites, is half the Cure,

Saturday 26,   The Indians all started Out on the North side in quest of Buffaloe, As they have Nothing to eat A Young Ree, the Nephew of Garreau, died at the Village last Night, Much regretted by us all, As he was one of the foresmost in aideing to Kill the dog on the 17th inst & A Mandan of the Little Village Came to the Fort to day to Sing his Medicine Song, got paid for his trouble, and Went off—glad to get clear of him—A young Ree that has the Small Pox, told his Mother to go and dig his grave, she accordingly did so—after the grave Was dug, he walked With the help of his Father to the Grave, I Went Out With the Interpreter to try to pursuade him to return back to the village—but he would not, Saying for the reason that all his young friends Were gone, And that he wished to follow them, torwards evening he died—

Sunday 27, Strong east Wind, rain in the Morning, The Indians Came back from the *Cerne* Well loaded With fresh Meat, report Cattle in abundance 20 Miles off—News from the GrosVentres of the disease breaking Out amongst them,

Monday 28, Wind from the North, rain, disagreeable Weather, several More Indians Arrived With fresh Meat—from the North Side gave us a small quantity which we found very good—Three More fell sick in the Fort to day—My interpreter for one, if I loose him I shall be badly off, the bad Weather continued all day—and no Prospects of Clearing off—

Tuesday 29, Last Night I Was taken Very Sick With the Fever, there is Six of us in the Fort that has the Fever, and One the Small Pox—An Indian Vacinated his child, by Cutting two small pieces of flesh Out of her Arms, and two on the belly—and then takeing a Scab from One, that Was getting Well of the disease, and rubbing it on the Wounded part, three days after, it took effect, and the child is perfectly Well—

Wednesday 30, All those that I thought had the small Pox turned out to be true, the fever left them yesterday, and the disease showed itself, I Am perfectly Well, as last Night, I took a hot Whiskey Punch, Which Made Me sweat all last Night, this Morning I took My daily Bitters as usual, Indians Arrived with fresh Meat, report Cattle in abundance opposite the Little Lake below—

Thursday 31, A Young Mandan that died 4 days ago, his Wife haveing the disease also Killed her two Children. one a fine Boy of eight years, and the other six, to complete the affair she hung herself.

Month of August I bid you farewell With all My heart, after running twenty hair breadth escapes, threatened every instant to be all Murdered, however it is the Wish of [your] humble Servant that the Month of September Will be More Favorable. the Number of Deaths up to the present is Very Near five hundred   The Mandans are all Cut off except 23 young and Old Men

Killed 89 Rats this Month   Total 1867—

September 30 Days—1837

Friday 1, This Morning two dead bodies wrapped in a White skin, and laid on a raft passed by the Forks on their way to the regions below. May success attend them. The Rees that are encamped in the Point of Woods below, Are Moveing up to encamp at the Mandans Corn fields No doubt with the intention of takeing all from them, as what few Mandans are left are Not able to Contend with the Rees—Mitchels squaw fell to day.

Saturday 2, Being Out of wood, risqued the Men—to the point of

Woods below   hauled eight loads. Several Indians Arrived With fresh
Meat, out 2 days, but one death to day, although several are sick, those that
catch the disease at Present, seldom die. One Fellow I saw on horseback to
day— he looked More like a gohst than a [human] being—

Sunday 3,   A Young Mandan came to pay us a Visit from the Little Village, he informes us, that they are all Most all used up, and that it is his
opinion that before the disease stops, that there will not One be left, except
8 or 10 that has Weathered Out the Sickness—. . . .

[*December*] *Sunday 31,*   Sent a Man down to the Ree camp to collect
some News—Caught three foxes last Night—Charboneau Arrived from the
GrosVentre camp. he was accompanied by 2 Mandan and one GrosVentre,
he is encamped with only Ten Lodges, the rest of the Lodges are scattered,
on the Little Misso he has had No News of them, for two Months, in all
Probability they Are all Dead, the last News that he had from them was, that
117 had died, and the disease was still rageing—

Killed 85 Rats this Month—   total 2294

Speech of the 4 Bears a Mandan Warrior to the Arricarees and Mandan—30th July 1837

My Friends one And all, Listen to what I have to say—Ever since I Can
remember, I have loved the Whites, I have lived With them ever since I was
a Boy, and to the best of My Knoweledge, I have Never Wronged a White
Man, on the Contrary, I have always Protected them from the insults of others, Which they Cannot deny, The 4 Bears Never saw a White Man hungry,
but what he gave him to eat, Drink, and a Buffaloe skin to sleep on, in time
of Need, I was always ready to die for them, Which they Cannot deny. I
have done every thing that a red Skin could do for them, And how have they
repaid it! With ingratitude! I have Never Called a White Man a Dog, but to
day, I do Pronounce them to be a set of Black harted Dogs, they have
deceived Me, them that I Always Considered as Brothers, has turned Out to
be My Worst enemies, I have been in Many Battles, and often wounded, but
the Wounds of My enemies, I exhalt in, but to day I am Wounded, And by
Whom, by those same White Dogs that I have Always Considered, and
Treated as Brothers, I do Not fear Death My friends, You Know it, but to
die With My face rotton, that even the Wolves will shrink With horror at
seeing Me, And say to themselves, that is the 4 Bears the Friend of the
Whites—Listen well what I have to say, as it will be the last time you will
hear Me. think of your Wives, children, Brothers, Sisters, Friends, and in
fact all that you hold dear, are all Dead, or Dying, with their faces all
rotton, caused by those dogs the whites, think of all that My friends, and
rise all together and Not leave one of them Alive, The 4 Bears Will act his
part. . . . [Four Bears died the same day.]

George Ruxton Depicts Life Among the Trappers, and the Trappers' View of Women, 1847–1849

The trappers of the Rocky Mountains belong to a "genus" more approximating to the primitive savage than perhaps any other class of civilized man. Their lives being spent in the remote wilderness of the mountains, with no other companion than Nature herself, their habits and character assume a most singular cast of simplicity mingled with ferocity, appearing to take their colouring from the scenes and objects which surround them. Knowing no wants save those of nature, their sole care is to procure sufficient food to support life, and the necessary clothing to protect them from the rigorous climate. This, with the assistance of their trusty rifles, they are generally able to effect, but sometimes at the expense of great peril and hardship. . . .

Keen observers of nature, they rival the beasts of prey in discovering the haunts and habits of game, and in their skill and cunning in capturing it. Constantly exposed to perils of all kinds, they become callous to any feeling of danger, and destroy human as well as animal life with as little scruple and as freely as they expose their own. . . . Not a hole or corner in the vast wilderness of the "Far West" but has been ransacked by these hardy men. From the Mississippi to the mouth of the Colorado of the West, from the frozen regions of the North to the Gila in Mexico, the beaver-hunter has set his traps in every creek and stream. All this vast country, but for the daring enterprise of these men, would be even now a *terra incognita* to geographers, as indeed a great portion still is; but there is not an acre that has not been passed and repassed by the trappers in their perilous excursions. The mountains and streams still retain the names assigned to them by the rude hunters; and these alone are the hardy pioneers who have paved the way for the settlement of the western country.

Trappers are of two kinds, the "hired hand" and the "free trapper:" the former hired for the hunt by the fur companies; the latter, supplied with animals and traps by the company, is paid a certain price for his furs and peltries.

There is also the trapper "on his own hook;" but this class is very small. He has his own animals and traps, hunts where he chooses, and sells his peltries to whom he pleases.

On starting for a hunt, the trapper fits himself out with the necessary equipment, either from the Indian trading-forts, or from some of the petty traders—coureurs des bois—who frequent the western country. This equipment consists usually of two or three horses or mules—one for saddle, the others for packs—and six traps, which are carried in a bag of leather called a *trap-sack*. Ammunition, a few pounds of tobacco, dressed deer-skins for mocassins, &c., are carried in a wallet of dressed buffalo-skin, called a

From *Adventures in Mexico and the Rocky Mountains*, 241–244, 245–246, by George F. Ruxton, published by the Rio Grande Press, Inc., 1973; and *Life in the Far West*, 57–59, 131–132, 265–267, by George F. Ruxton, published by William Blackwood and Sons, 1849.

possible-sack. His "possibles" and "trap-sack" are generally carried on the saddle-mule when hunting, the others being packed with the furs. The costume of the trapper is a hunting-shirt of dressed buckskin, ornamented with long fringes; pantaloons of the same material, and decorated with porcupine-quills and long fringes down the outside of the leg. A flexible felt hat and mocassins clothe his extremities. Over his left shoulder and under his right arm hang his powder-horn and bullet-pouch, in which he carries his balls, flint and steel, and odds and ends of all kinds. Round the waist is a belt, in which is stuck a large butcher-knife in a sheath of buffalo-hide, made fast to the belt by a chain or guard of steel; which also supports a little buckskin case containing a whetstone. A tomahawk is also often added; and, of course, a long heavy rifle is part and parcel of his equipment. I had nearly forgotten the pipe-holder, which hangs round his neck, and is generally a gage d'amour, and a triumph of squaw workmanship, in shape of a heart, garnished with beads and porcupine-quills.

Thus provided, and having determined the locality of his trapping-ground, he starts to the mountains, sometimes alone, sometimes with three or four in company, as soon as the breaking up of the ice allows him to commence operations. Arrived on his hunting-grounds, he follows the creeks and streams, keeping a sharp look-out for "sign." If he sees a prostrate cotton-wood tree, he examines it to discover if it be the work of beaver—whether "thrown" for the purpose of food, or to dam the stream. The track of the beaver on the mud or sand under the bank is also examined; and if the "sign" be fresh, he sets his trap in the run of the animal, hiding it under water, and attaching it by a stout chain to a picket driven in the bank, or to a bush or tree. A "float-stick" is made fast to the trap by a cord a few feet long, which, if the animal carry away the trap, floats on the water and points out its position. The trap is baited with the "medicine," an oily substance obtained from a gland in the scrotum of the beaver, but distinct from the testes. A stick is dipped into this and planted over the trap; and the beaver, attracted by the smell, and wishing a close inspection, very foolishly puts his leg into the trap, and is a "gone beaver."

When a lodge is discovered, the trap is set at the edge of the dam, at the point where the animal passes from deep to shoal water, and always under water. Early in the morning the hunter mounts his mule and examines the traps. The captured animals are skinned, and the tails, which are a great dainty, carefully packed into camp. The skin is then stretched over a hoop or framework of osier-twigs, and is allowed to dry, the flesh and fatty substance being carefully scraped (grained). When dry, it is folded into a square sheet, the fur turned inwards, and the bundle, containing about ten to twenty skins, tightly pressed and corded, and is ready for transportation. . . .

At a certain time, when the hunt is over, or they have loaded their pack animals, the trappers proceed to the "rendezvous," the locality of which has been previously agreed upon; and here the traders and agents of the fur companies await them, with such assortment of goods as their hardy customers may require, including generally a fair supply of alcohol. The trappers drop in singly and in small bands, bringing their packs of beaver to this mountain market, not unfrequently to the value of a thousand dollars each, the produce of one hunt. The dissipation of the "rendezvous," however, soon turns the trapper's pocket inside out. The goods brought by the traders, although of the most inferior quality, are sold at enormous prices:—Coffee, twenty and thirty shillings a pint-cup, which is the usual measure; tobacco fetches ten and fifteen shillings a plug; alcohol, from twenty to fifty shillings a pint; gunpowder, sixteen shillings a pint-cup; and all other articles at proportionably exorbitant prices.

The "beaver" is purchased at from two to eight dollars per pound; the Hudson's Bay Company alone buying it by the pluie, or "plew," that is, the whole skin, giving a certain price for skins, whether of old beaver or "kittens."

The rendezvous is one continued scene of drunkenness, gambling, and brawling and fighting, as long as the money and credit of the trappers last. Seated, Indian fashion, round the fires, with a blanket spread before them, groups are seen with their "decks" of cards, playing at "euker," "poker," and "seven-up," the regular mountain-games. The stakes are "beaver," which here is current coin; and when the fur is gone, their horses, mules, rifles, and shirts, hunting-packs, and *breeches,* are staked. Daring gamblers make the rounds of the camp, challenging each other to play for the trapper's highest stake,—his horse, his squaw (if he have one), and, as once happened, his scalp. There goes "hos and beaver!" is the mountain expression when any great loss is sustained; and, sooner or later, "hos and beaver" invariably find their way into the insatiable pockets of the traders. A trapper often squanders the produce of his hunt, amounting to hundreds of dollars, in a couple of hours; and, supplied on credit with another equipment, leaves the rendezvous for another expedition, which has the same result time after time; although one tolerably successful hunt would enable him to return to the settlements and civilised life, with an ample sum to purchase and stock a farm, and enjoy himself in ease and comfort the remainder of his days. . . .

The Indian women who follow the fortunes of the white hunters are remarkable for their affection and fidelity to their husbands, the which virtues, it must be remarked, are all on their own side; for, with very few exceptions, the mountaineers seldom scruple to abandon their Indian wives, whenever the fancy takes them to change their harems; and on such occasions the squaws, thus cast aside, wild with jealousy and despair, have been not unfrequently known to take signal vengeance both on their faithless husbands and on the successful beauties who have supplanted them in their affections. There are some honourable exceptions, however, to such cruelty, and many of the mountaineers stick to their red-skinned wives for better and for worse, often suffering them to gain the upper hand in the domestic economy of the lodges, and being ruled by their better halves in all things pertaining to family affairs; and it may be remarked, that, when once the lady dons the unmentionables, she becomes the veriest termagant that ever henpecked an unfortunate husband.

Your refined trappers, however, who, after many years of bachelor life, incline to take to themselves a better half, often undertake an expedition into the settlements of New Mexico, where not unfrequently they adopt a very "Young Lochinvar" system in procuring the required rib; and have been known to carry off, *vi et armis,* from the midst of a fandango in Fernandez, or El Rancho of Taos, some dark-skinned beauty—with or without her own consent is a matter of unconcern—and bear the ravished fair one across the mountains, where she soon becomes inured to the free and roving life fate has assigned her.

American women are valued at a low figure in the mountains. They are too fine and "fofarraw [fancy]." Neither can they make moccasins, or dress skins; nor are they so schooled to perfect obedience to their lords and masters as to stand a "lodge-poleing [sound thrashing]," which the western lords of the creation not unfrequently deem it their bounden duty to inflict upon their squaws for some dereliction of domestic duty. . . .

Y *E S S A Y S*

Sylvia Van Kirk, associate professor of history at the University of Toronto, explores more fully the role of Indian women in the fur trade in western Canada. Recognizing the mutual dependence of Indians and whites, men and women in the fur trade, she describes the social and economic significance of interracial marriage *à la façon du pays,* "after the custom of the country." Dan Flores, professor of history at the University of Montana, draws our attention to the hide trade of the southern plains. In a detailed environmental analysis of the relationships between humans and animals, Flores reveals the role Indians played in the devastation of their greatest resource. Consider what Van Kirk tells us about the lives of Indian women and mixed blood families. How does that differ from Ruxton's depiction of the fur trade? What was the impact of disease and the fur trade on Indians and their worlds? What were the relationships between Indian cultural preferences or motivations, their environments, and an expanding market economy?

Native Women in Canadian Fur Trade Society

SYLVIA VAN KIRK

In essence the history of the early Canadian West is the history of the fur trade. For nearly 200 years, from the founding of the Hudson's Bay Company in 1670 until the transfer of Rupert's Land to the newly created dominion of Canada in 1870, the fur trade was the dominant force in shaping the history of what are today Canada's four western provinces.

This long and unified experience gave rise in western Canada to a frontier society that seems to me to be unique in the realm of interracial con-

Sylvia Van Kirk, "The Role of Native Women in the Fur Trade Society of Western Canada, 1670–1830," *Frontiers* 7, No. 3 (1984), 9–13. Copyright © 1984, *Frontiers* Editorial Collective. Reprinted by permission.

tact. Canada's western history has been characterized by relatively little violent conflict between Indian and white. I would like to suggest that there were two major reasons why this was so. First, by its very nature the Canadian fur trade was predicated on a mutual exchange and dependency between Indian and white. "The only good Indian" was certainly not "a dead Indian," for it was the Indian who provided both the fur pelts and the market for European goods. New research has revealed that not just Indian men but also Indian women played an active role in promoting the fur trade. Although the men were the hunters of beaver and large game animals, the women were responsible for trapping smaller fur-bearing animals, especially the marten whose pelt was highly prized. The notable cases of Indian women emerging as diplomats and peacemakers also indicate that they were anxious to maintain the flow of European goods, such as kettles, cloth, knives, needles, and axes, that helped to alleviate their onerous work role.

The second factor in promoting harmonious relations was the remarkably wide extent of intermarriage between incoming traders and Indian women, especially among the Cree, the Ojibwa, and the Chipewyan. Indian wives proved indispensable helpmates to the officers and men of both the British-based Hudson's Bay Company and its Canadian rival, the North West Company. Such interracial unions were, in fact, the basis for a fur trade society and were sanctioned by an indigenous rite known as marriage *à la façon du pays*.

The development of marriage *à la façon du pays* underscores the complex and changing interaction between the traders and the host Indian societies. In the initial phase of contact, many Indian bands actively encouraged the formation of marital alliances between their women and the traders. The Indians viewed marriage in an integrated social and economic context: marital alliances created reciprocal social ties that served to consolidate their economic relationships with the incoming strangers. Thus, through marriage, many a trader was drawn into the Indian kinship circle. In return for giving the traders sexual and domestic rights to their women, the Indians expected reciprocal privileges such as free access to the posts and provisions.

The Indian attitude soon impressed upon the traders that marriage alliances were an important means of ensuring good will and cementing trade relations with new bands or tribes. The North West Company, a conglomerate of partnerships that began extensive trading into the West in the 1770s, had learned from its French predecessors of the benefits to be gained from intermarriage, and it officially sanctioned such unions for all ranks, from *bourgeois* (officer) down to *engagé* (laborer). The Hudson's Bay Company, on the other hand, was much slower to appreciate the realities of life in Rupert's Land (the name given to the chartered territory of the Hudson's Bay Company encompassing the vast drainage basin of Hudson Bay). Official policy formulated in faraway London forbade any intimacy with the Indians, but officers in the field early began to break the rules. They took the lead in forming unions with women related to prominent Indian

leaders, although there was great variation in the extent to which their servants were allowed to form connections with native women.

Apart from the public social benefits, the traders' desire to form unions
with Indian women was increased by the absence of white women.
Although they did not come as settlers, many of the fur traders spent the
better part of their lives in Rupert's Land, and it is a singular fact that in the
social development of the Canadian West that for well over a century there
were no white women. The stability of many of the interracial unions
formed in the Indian Country stemmed partly from the fact that an Indian
woman provided the only opportunity for a trader to replicate a domestic
life with women and children. Furthermore, although Indian mores differed
from those of whites, the traders learned that they trifled with Indian
women at their peril. As one old *voyageur* (canoeman) explained, a man
could not just dally with any native woman who struck his fancy. There was
a great danger of getting his head broken if he attempted to take an Indian
girl without her parents' consent.

It is significant that, just as in the trade ceremony, the rituals of marriage *à la façon du pays* conformed more to Indian custom than to European. There were two basic aspects to forming such a union. The first step
was to secure the consent of the woman's relations; it also appears that the
wishes of the woman herself were respected, for there is ample evidence
that Indian women actively sought fur trade husbands. Once consent was
secured, a bride price had then to be decided; thought it varied considerably
among the tribes, it could amount to several hundred dollars' worth of trade
goods. After these transactions, the couple were usually ceremoniously
conducted to the fort where they were duly recognized as man and wife. In
the Canadian West marriage *à la façon du pays* became the norm for
Indian-white unions, which were reinforced by mutual interest, tradition,
and peer group pressure. Although ultimately "the custom of the country"
was to be strongly denounced by the missionaries, it is significant that in
1867, when the legitimacy of the union between Chief Factor William Con-
nolly and his Cree wife was tried before a Canadian court, the judge
declared the marriage valid because the wife had been married according to
the customs and usages of her own people and because the consent of both
parties, the essential element of civilized marriage, had been proved by
twenty-eight years of repute, public acknowledgment, and cohabitation as
man and wife.

If intermarriage brought the trader commercial and personal benefit, it
also provided him with a remarkable economic partner. The Indian wife
was possessed of a range of skills and wilderness know-how that would
have been quite foreign to a white wife. Although the burdensome work
role of the nomadic Indian woman was somewhat alleviated by the move to
the fur trade post, the extent to which the traders relied upon native technology kept the women busy.

Perhaps the most important domestic task performed by the women at
the fur trade posts was to provide the men with a steady supply of "Indian
shoes" or moccasins. The men of both companies generally did not dress in

Indian style (the buckskinned mountain man was not part of the Canadian scene), but they universally adopted the moccasin as the most practical footwear for the wilderness. One wonders, for example, how the famed 1789 expedition of Alexander Mackenzie would have fared without the work of the wives of his two French-Canadian *voyageurs*. The women scarcely ever left the canoes, being "continually employ'd making shoes of moose skin as a pair does not last us above one Day." Closely related to her manufacture of moccasins was the Indian woman's role in making snow-shoes, without which winter travel was impossible. Although the men usu-ally made the frames, the women prepared the sinews and netted the intricate webbing that provided support.

Indian women also make a vital contribution in the preservation of food, especially in the manufacture of the all-important pemmican, the nutritious staple of the North West Company's canoe brigades. At the posts on the plains, buffalo hunting and pemmican making were an essential part of the yearly routine, each post being required to furnish an annual quota. In accordance with Indian custom, once the hunt was over, the women's work began. The women skinned the animals and cut the meat up into thin strips to be dried in the sun or over a slow fire. When the meat was dry, the women pounded it into a flaky mass, which was then mixed with melted buffalo fat. This pemmican would keep very well when packed into ninety-pound buffalo-hide sacks, which had been made by the women during the winter. But pemmican was too precious a commodity to form the basic food at the posts themselves. At the more northerly posts the people subsisted mainly on fish, vast quantities of which were split and dried by the women to provide food for the winter. Maintaining adequate food supplies for a post for the winter was a precarious business, and numerous instances can be cited of Indian wives keeping the fur traders alive by their ability to snare small game such as rabbits and partridges. In 1815, for example, the young Nor'Wester George Nelson would probably have starved to death when provisions ran out at his small outpost north of Lake Superior had it not been for the resourcefulness of his Ojibwa wife who during the month of February brought in fifty-eight rabbits and thirty-four partridges. Indian women also added to the diet by collecting berries and wild rice and mak-ing maple sugar. The spring trip to the sugar bush provided a welcome release from the monotony of the winter routine, and the men with their families and Indian relatives all enjoyed this annual event.

As in other preindustrial societies, the Indian women's role also extended well beyond domestic maintenance as they assisted in specific fur trade operations. With the adoption of the birchbark canoe, especially by the North West Company, Indian women continued in their traditional role of helping in its manufacture. It was the women's job to collect annual quo-tas of spruce roots, which were split fine to sew the seams of the canoes, and also to collect the spruce gum that was used for caulking the seams. The inexperienced and understaffed Hudson's Bay Company also found itself calling upon the labor power of Indian women, who were adept at paddling and steering canoes. Indeed, although the inland explorations of various Hudson's Bay Company men such as Anthony Henday and Samuel Hearne have been glorified as individual exploits, they were, in fact, entirely dependent upon the Indians with whom they traveled, being especially aided by Indian women. "Women," marveled one inlander, "were as useful as men upon Journeys." Henday's journey to the plains in 1754, for example, owed much of its success to his Cree female companion, who not only provided him with a warm winter suit of furs, but also with much timely advice about the plans of the Indians. The Hudson's Bay Company men emphasized to their London superiors that the Indian women's skill at working with fur pelts was also very valuable. In short, they argued that Indian women performed such important economic services at the fur trade posts that they should be considered as "Your Honours Servants." Indian women were indeed an integral part of the fur trade labor force, although, like most women, because their labor was largely unpaid, their contribution has been ignored.

The reliance on native women's skills remained an important aspect of fur trade life, even though by the early nineteenth century there was a notable shift in the social dynamic of fur trade society. By this time, partly because of the destructive competition between rival companies that had flooded the Indian country with alcohol, relations between many Indian bands and the traders deteriorated. In some well-established areas, traders sometimes resorted to coercive measures, and there were cases where their abuse of Indian women became a source of conflict. In this context, except in new areas such as the Pacific Slope, marriage alliances ceased to play the important function they once had. The decline of Indian-white marriages was also hastened by the fact that fur trade society itself was producing a new pool of marriageable women—the mixed-blood "daughters of the country." With her dual heritage, the mixed-blood woman possessed the ideal qualifications for a fur trader's wife: acclimatized to life in the West and familiar with Indian ways, she could also make a successful adaptation to white culture.

From their Indian mothers, mixed-blood girls learned the native skills so necessary to the functioning of the trade. As Governor Simpson of the Hudson's Bay Company emphasized in the 1820's, "It is the duty of the Women at the different Posts to do all that is necessary in regard to Needle Work," and the mixed-blood women's beautiful bead work was highly prized. In addition to performing traditional Indian tasks, the women's range of domestic work increased in more European ways. They were responsible for the fort's washing and cleaning; "the Dames" at York Factory, for example, were kept "in Suds, Scrubbing, and Scouring," according to one account. As subsistence agriculture was developed around many of the posts, the native women took an active role in planting and harvesting. Chief Factor John Rowand of Fort Edmonton succinctly summarized the economic role of native women in the fur trade when he wrote in the mid-nineteenth century, "The women here work very hard, if it was not so, I do not know how we would get on with the Company work." With her ties to the Indians and familiarity with native customs and language, the mixed-blood wife was also in a position to take over the role of intermediary or liaison previously played by the Indian wife. The daughters of the French-Canadian *voyageurs* were often excellent interpreters; some could speak several Indian languages. The timely intervention of more than one mixed-blood wife was known to have saved the life of a husband who had aroused Indian hostility. Indeed, in his account of fur trade life during the Hudson's Bay Company's monopoly after 1821, Isaac Cowie declared that many of the company's officers owed much of their success in overcoming difficulties and maintaining the Company's influence over the natives to "the wisdom and good counsel of their wives."

In spite of the importance of native connections, many fur trade fathers were most concerned to introduce their mixed-blood daughters to the rudiments of European culture. Since the place of home and work coincided, especially in the long winter months, the traders were able to take an active role in their children's upbringing, and they were encouraged to do so. When the beginnings of formal schooling were introduced at the posts on the Bay in the early 1800's, it was partly because it was felt to be essential that girls, who were very seldom sent overseas, should be given a basic education that would inculcate Christian virtue in them. Increasingly fathers also began to play an instrumental role in promoting the marriage of their daughters to incoming traders as the means to securing their place in fur trade society. In a significant change of policy in 1806, the North West Company acknowledged some responsibility for the fate of its "daughters" when it sanctioned marriage *à la façon du pays* with daughters of white men, but now prohibited it with full-blooded Indian women.

As mixed-blood wives became "the vogue" (to quote a contemporary), it is notable that "the custom of the country" began to evolve more toward European concepts of marriage. Most importantly, such unions were definitely coming to be regarded as unions for life. When Hudson's Bay Company officer J. E. Harriott espoused Elizabeth Pruden, for example, he promised her father, a senior officer, that he would "live with her and treat her as my wife as long as we both lived." It became customary for a couple to exchange brief vows before the officer in charge of the post, and the match was further celebrated by a dram to all hands and a wedding dance. The bride price was replaced by the opposite payment of a dowry, and many fur trade officers were able to dower their daughters quite handsomely. Marriage *à la facon du pays* was further regulated by the Hudson's Bay Company after 1821 with the introduction of marriage contracts, which emphasized the husband's financial obligations and the status of the woman as a legitimate wife.

The social role of the mixed-blood wife, unlike that of the Indian wife, served to cement ties within fur trade society itself. Significantly, in the North West Company there were many marriages that cut across class lines as numerous Scottish *bourgeois* chose their wives from the French-Canadian *engagés* who had married extensively among the native people. Among the Hudson's Bay Company men, it was appreciated that a useful way to enhance one's career was to marry the daughter of a senior officer.

Whatever a man's initial motivation, the substantial private fur trade correspondence that has survived from the nineteenth century reveals that many fur traders became devoted family men. Family could be a particular source of interest and consolation in a life that was often hard and monotonous. As Chief Factor James Douglas pointedly summed it up, "There is indeed no living with comfort in this country until a person has forgot the great world and has his tastes and character formed on the current standard of the stage . . . habit makes it familiar to us, softened as it is by the many tender ties which find a way to the heart."

However, the founding of the Selkirk Colony in 1811, the first agrarian settlement in western Canada, was to introduce new elements of white civilization that hastened the decline of an indigenous fur trade society. The chief agents of these changes were the missionaries and the white women. The missionaries, especially the Anglicans who arrived under the auspices of the Hudson's Bay Company in 1820, roundly denounced marriage *à la façon du pays* as immoral and debased. But while they exerted considerable pressure on long cohabiting couples to accept a church marriage, they were not in any way champions of miscegenation. In fact, this attack upon fur trade custom had a detrimental effect upon the position of native women. Incoming traders, now feeling free to ignore the marital obligations implicit in "the custom of the country," increasingly looked upon native women as objects for temporary sexual gratification. The women, on the other hand, found themselves being judged according to strict British standards of female propriety. It was they, not the white men, who were to be held responsible for the perpetuation of immorality because of their supposedly promiscuous Indian heritage. The double standard tinged with racism had arrived with a vengeance.

Both racial prejudice and class distinctions were augmented by the arrival of British women in Rupert's Land. The old fabric of fur trade society was severely rent in 1830 when Governor Simpson and another prominent Hudson's Bay Company officer returned from furlough, having wed genteel British ladies. The appearance of such "flowers of civilization" provoked unflattering comparisons with native women; as one officer observed, "This influx of white faces has cast a still deeper shade over the faces of our Brunettes in the eyes of many." In Red River especially, a white wife became a status symbol; witness the speed with which several retired Hudson's Bay Company factors married English schoolmistresses after the demise of their native wives. To their credit, many Company officers remained loyal to their native families, but they became painfully anxious to turn their daughters into young Victorian ladies, hoping that with accomplishments and connections the stigma of their mixed blood would not prevent them from remaining among the social elite. Thus, in the 1830s a boarding school was established in Red River for the children of Company officers; the girls' education was supervised by the missionary's wife, and more than one graduate was praised for being "quite English in her Manner." In numerous cases, these highly acculturated young women were able to secure advantageous matches with incoming white men, but to some extent only because white ladies did not in fact adapt successfully to fur trade life. It had been predicted that "the lovely, tender exotics" (as they were dubbed) would languish in the harsh fur trade environment, and indeed they did, partly because they had no useful social or economic role to play. As a result, mixed marriages continued to be a feature of western Canadian society until well into the mid-nineteenth century, but it was not an enduring legacy. Indian and mixed-blood women, like their male counterparts, were quickly shunted aside with the development of the agrarian frontier after 1870. The vital role native women had played in the opening of the Canadian West was either demeaned or forgotten.

Bison Ecology and Bison Diplomacy on the Southern Plains

DAN FLORES

Environmental historians and ethnohistorians whose interests have been environmental topics have in the two past decades been responsible for many of our most valuable recent insights into the history of native Americans since their contact with Euro-Americans. Thus far, however, modern scholarship has not reevaluated the most visible historic interaction, the set piece if you will, of native American environmental history. On the Great Plains of the American West during the two centuries from 1680 to 1880, almost three-dozen native American groups adopted horse-propelled, bison-hunting cultures that defined "Indianness" for white Americans and most of the world. It is the end of this process that has most captured the popular imagination: the military campaigns against and the brutal incarceration of the horse Indians, accompanied by the astonishingly rapid elimination of bison, and of an old ecology that dated back ten thousand years, at the hands of commercial hide hunters. That dramatic end, which occurred in less than fifteen years following the end of the Civil War, has by now entered American mythology. Yet our focus on the finale has obscured an examination of earlier phases that might shed new light on the historical and environmental interaction of the horse Indians and bison herds on the Plains.

In the nineteenth-century history of the Central and Southern Plains, there have long been perplexing questions that environmental history seems well suited to answer. Why were the Comanches able to replace the Apaches on the bison-rich Southern Plains? Why did the Kiowas, Cheyennes, and Arapahoes gradually shift southward into the Southern Plains between 1800 and 1825? And why, after fighting each other for two decades, did these Southern Plains people effect a rapprochement and alliance in the 1840s? What factors brought on such an escalation of Indian

Dan Flores, "Bison Ecology and Bison Diplomacy: The Southern Plains from 1800 to 1850," *Journal of American History,* 78 (September 1991), 465–485. Copyright © 1991, *Journal of American History.* Excerpted by permission of the author and the *Journal of American History.*

raids into Mexico and Texas in the late 1840s that the subject assumed critical importance in the Treaty of Guadalupe-Hidalgo? If the bison herds were so vast in the years before the commercial hide hunters, why were there so many reports of starving Indians on the Plains by 1850? And finally, given our standard estimates of bison numbers, why is it that the hide hunters are credited with bringing to market only some 10 million hides, including no more than 3.5 million from the Southern Plains, in the 1870s?

Apposite to all of these questions is a central issue: How successful were the horse Indians in creating a dynamic ecological equilibrium between themselves and the vast bison herds that grazed the Plains? That is, had they developed sustainable hunting practices that would maintain the herds and so permit future generations of hunters to follow the same way of life? This is not to pose the "anachronistic question" (the term is Richard White's) of whether Indians were ecologists. But how a society or a group of peoples with a shared culture makes adjustments to live within the carrying capacity of its habitat is not only a valid historical question, it may be one of the most salient questions to ask about any culture. . . . The answers are complex and offer a revision of both Plains history and western Indian ecological history.

Working our way through to them requires some digression into the large historical forces that shaped the Southern Plains over the last hundred centuries. The perspective of the *longue durée* is essential to environmental history. What transpired on the Great Plains from 1800 to 1850 is not comprehensible without taking into account the effect of the Pleistocene extinctions of ten thousand years ago, or the cycle of droughts that determined the carrying capacity for animals on the grasslands. Shallower in time than these forces but just as important to the problem are factors that stemmed from the arrival of Europeans in the New World. Trade was an ancient part of the cultural landscape of America, but the Europeans altered the patterns, the goods, and the intensity of trade. And the introduction of horses and horse culture accomplished a technological revolution for the Great Plains. The horse was the chief catalyst of an ongoing remaking of the tribal map of western America, as native American groups moved onto the Plains and incessantly shifted their ranges and alliances in response to a world where accelerating change seemed almost the only constant.

At the beginning of the nineteenth century, the dominant groups on the Southern Plains were the two major divisions of the Comanches: the Texas Comanches, primarily Kotsotekas, and the great New Mexico division, spread across the country from the Llano Estacado Escarpment west to the foothills of the Sangre de Cristo Mountains, and composed of Yamparika and Jupe bands that only recently had replaced the Apaches on the High Plains. The Comanches' drive to the south from their original homelands in what is now southwestern Wyoming and northwestern Colorado was a part of the original tribal adjustments to the coming of horse technology to the Great Plains. There is reason to believe that the Eastern Shoshones, from whom the Comanches were derived before achieving a different identity on the Southern Plains, were one of the first intermountain tribes of historic times to push onto the Plains. Perhaps as early as 1500 the proto-Comanches were hunting bison and using dog power to haul their mountain-adapted four-pole tipis east of the Laramie Mountains. . . .

These early Shoshonean hunters may not have spent more than three or four generations among the thronging Plains bison herds, for by the late seventeenth century they had been pushed back into the mountains and the sagebrush deserts by tribes newly armed with European guns moving westward from the region around the Great Lakes. If so, they were among a complex of tribes southwest of the lakes that over the next two centuries would be displaced by a massive Siouan drive to the west, an imperial expansion for domination of the prize buffalo range of the Northern Plains, and a wedge that sent ripples of tribal displacement across the Plains.

. . . Pressed back toward the mountains as Shoshones, they thus turned in a different direction and emerged from the passes through the Front Range as the same people but bearing a new name given them by the Utes: Komantcia. They still lacked guns but now began their intimate association with the one animal, aside from the bison, inextricably linked with Plains life. The Comanches began acquiring horses from the Utes within a decade or so after the Pueblo Revolt of 1680 sent horses and horse culture diffusing in all directions from New Mexico. Thus were born the "hyper-Indians," as William Brandon has called the Plains people.

The Comanches became, along with the Sioux, the most populous and widespread of all the peoples who now began to ride onto the vast sweep of grassland to participate in the hunter's life. They began to take possession of the Southern Plains by the early 1700s. By 1800 they were in full control of all the country east of the Southern Rocky Mountains and south of the Arkansas River clear to the Texas Hill Country. . . .

To the Comanches, the Southern Plains must have seemed an earthly paradise. The Pleistocene extinctions ten thousand years earlier had left dozens of grazing niches vacant on the American Great Plains. A dwarf species of bison with a higher reproductive capacity than any of its ancestors evolved to flood most of those vacant niches with an enormous biomass of one grazer. In an ecological sense, bison were a weed species that had proliferated as a result of a major disturbance. . . .

The dimensions of the wild bison resource on the Southern Plains, and the Great Plains in general, have been much overstated in popular literature. For one thing, pollen analysis and archaeological data indicate that for the Southern Plains there were intervals, some spanning centuries, others decades, when bison must have been almost absent. Two major times of absence occurred between 5000 and 2500 B.C. and between A.D. 500 and 1300. The archaeological levels that lack bison bones correspond to pollen data indicating droughts. The severe southwestern drought that ended early in the fourteenth century was replaced by a five hundred–year cycle of wetter and cooler conditions, and a return of bison in large numbers to the Southern Plains from their drought refugia to the east and west. . . .

More important, our popular perception of bison numbers—based on the estimates of awed nineteenth-century observers—probably sets them too high. There were very likely never 100 million or even 60 million bison on the Plains during the present climate regime because the carrying capacity of the grasslands was not so high. The best technique for determining bison carrying capacity on the Southern Plains is to extrapolate from United States census data for livestock, and the best census extrapolation is that of 1910, after the beef industry crashes of the 1880s had reduced animal numbers, but before the breakup of ranches and the Enlarged Homestead Act of 1909 resulted in considerable sections of the Southern Plains being broken out by farmers. Additionally, dendrochronological data seem to show that at the turn of the century rainfall on the Southern Plains was at median, between-droughts levels, rendering the census of 1910 particularly suitable as a base line for carrying capacity and animal populations.

The 1910 agricultural census indicates that in the 201 counties on the Southern Plains (which covered 240,000 square miles), the nineteenth-century carrying capacity during periods of median rainfall was about 7,000,000 cattle-equivalent grazers—specifically for 1910, about 5,150,000 cattle and 1,890,000 horses and mules. The bison population was almost certainly larger, since migratory grazing patterns and coevolution with the native grasses made bison as a wild species about 18 percent more efficient on the Great Plains than domestic cattle. And varying climate conditions during the nineteenth century, as I will demonstrate, noticeably affected grassland carrying capacity. The ecological reality was a dynamic cycle in which carrying capacity could swing considerably from decade to decade. But if the Great Plains bovine carrying capacity of 1910 expresses a median reality, then during prehorse times the Southern Plains might have supported an average of about 8.2 million bison, the entire Great Plains perhaps 28–30 million.

Although 8 million bison on the Southern Plains may not be so many as historians used to believe, to the Comanches the herds probably seemed limitless. Bison availability through horse culture caused a specialization that resulted in the loss of two-thirds of the Comanches' former plant lore and in a consequent loss of status for their women, an intriguing development that seems to have occurred to some extent among all the tribes that moved onto the Plains during the horse period. . . .

The Comanches were not the only people on the Southern Plains during the horse period. The New Mexicans, both Pueblo and Hispanic, continued to hunt on the wide-open Llanos, as did the prairie Caddoans, although the numbers of the latter were dwindling rapidly by 1825. The New Mexican peoples and the Caddoans of the middle Red and Brazos rivers played major trade roles for hunters on the Southern Plains, and the Comanches in particular. Although the Comanches engaged in the archetypal Plains exchange of bison products for horticultural produce and European trade goods and traded horses and mules with Anglo-American traders from Missouri, Arkansas, and Louisiana, they were not a high-volume trading people until relatively late in their history. Early experiences with American traders and disease led them to distrust trade with Euro-

Americans, and only once or twice did they allow short-lived posts to be established in their country. Instead, peace with the prairie Caddoans by the 1730s and with New Mexico in 1786 sent Comanche trade both east and west, but often through Indian middlemen.

In the classic, paradigmatic period between 1800 and 1850, the most interesting Southern Plains development was the cultural interaction between the Comanches and surrounding Plains Indians to the north. The Kiowas were the one of those groups most closely identified with the Comanches.

. . . The Kiowas believe that they started their journey to Rainy Mountain on the Oklahoma Plains from the north. And indeed, in the eighteenth century we find them on the Northern Plains, near the Black Hills. . . .

Displaced by the wars for the buffalo ranges in the north, the Kiowas began to drift southward again—or perhaps, since the supply of horses was in the Southwest, simply began to stay longer on the Southern Plains. Between 1790 and 1806, they developed a rapprochement with the Comanches. Thereafter they were so closely associated with the northern Comanches that they were regarded by some as merely a Comanche band, although in many cultural details the two groups were dissimilar. Spanish and American traders and explorers of the 1820s found them camped along the two forks of the Canadian River and on the various headwater streams of the Red River.

The other groups that increasingly began to interact with the Comanches during the 1820s and thereafter had also originated on the Northern Plains. These were the Arapahoes and the Cheyennes, who by 1825 were beginning to establish themselves on the Colorado buffalo plains from the North Platte River all the way down to the Arkansas River.

The Algonkian-speaking Arapahoes and Cheyennes had once been farmers living in earth lodges on the upper Mississippi. By the early 1700s both groups were in present North Dakota, occupying villages along the Red and Sheyenne rivers, where they first began to acquire horses, possibly from the Kiowas. Fur wars instigated by the Europeans drove them farther southwest and more and more into a Plains, bison-hunting culture, one that the women of these farming tribes probably resisted as long as possible. But by the second decade of the nineteenth century the Teton Sioux wedge had made nomads and hunters of the Arapahoes and Cheyennes.

Their search for prime buffalo grounds and for ever-larger horse herds, critical since both tribes had emerged as middlemen traders between the villagers of the Missouri and the horse reservoir to the south, first led the Cheyennes and Arapahoes west of the Black Hills, into Crow lands, and then increasingly southward along the mountain front. . . .

Three factors seem to have drawn the Arapahoes and the Cheyennes so far south. Unquestionably, one factor was the vast horse herds of the Comanches and Kiowas, an unending supply of horses for the trade, which by 1825 the Colorado tribes were seizing in daring raids. Another was the milder winters south of the Arkansas, which made horse pastoralism much easier. The third factor was the abnormally bountiful game of the early nineteenth-century Southern Plains, evidently the direct result of an extraordinary series of years between 1815 and 1846 when, with the exception of a minor drought in the late 1820s, rainfall south of the Arkansas was considerably above average. . . .

Thus, around 1825, the Comanches and Kiowas found themselves at war with the Cheyennes, Arapahoes, and other tribes on the north. Meanwhile, the Colorado tribes opened another front in a naked effort to seize the rich buffalo range of the upper Kansas and Republican rivers from the Pawnees. These wars produced an interesting type of ecological development that appeared repeatedly across most of the continent. At the boundaries where warring tribes met, they left buffer zones occupied by neither side and only lightly hunted. One such buffer zone on the Southern Plains was along the region's northern perimeter, between the Arkansas and North Canadian rivers. Another was in present-day western Kansas, between the Pawnees and the main range of the Colorado tribes, and a third seems to have stretched from the forks of the Platte to the mountains. The buffer zones were important because game within them was left relatively undisturbed; they allowed the buildup of herds that might later be exploited when tribal boundaries or agreements changed.

The appearance of American traders such as [Charles] Bent and [Ceran] St. Vrain marked the Southern Plains tribes' growing immersion in a market economy increasingly tied to worldwide trade networks dominated by Euro-Americans. Like all humans, Indians had always altered their environments. But as most modern historians of Plains Indians and the western fur trade have realized, during the nineteenth century not only had the western tribes become technologically capable of pressuring their resources, but year by year they were becoming less "ecosystem people," dependent on the products of their local regions for subsistence, and increasingly tied to biosphere trade networks. . . .

The crux of the problem in studying Southern Plains Indian ecology and bison is to determine whether the Plains tribes had established a society in ecological equilibrium, one whose population did not exceed the carrying capacity of its habitat and so maintained a healthy, functioning ecology that could be sustained over the long term. Answering that question involves an effort to come to grips with the factors affecting bison populations, the factors affecting Indian populations, and the cultural aspects of Plains Indians' utilization of bison. Each of the three aspects of the question presents puzzles difficult to resolve.

In modern, protected herds on the Plains, bison are a prolific species whose numbers increase by an average of 18 percent a year, assuming a normal sex ratio (51 males to 49 females) with breeding cows amounting to 35 percent of the total. In other words, if the Southern Plains supported 8.2 million bison in years of median rainfall, the herds would have produced about 1.4 million calves a year. To maintain an ecological equilibrium with the grasses, the Plains bison's natural mortality rate also had to approach 18 percent.

Today the several protected bison herds in the western United States have a natural mortality, without predation, ranging between 3 and 9 percent. The Wichita Mountains herd, the only large herd left on the Southern Plains, falls midway with a 6 percent mortality rate. Despite a search for it, no inherent naturally regulating mechanism has yet been found in bison populations; thus active culling programs are needed at all the Plains bison refuges. The starvation-induced population crashes that affect ungulates such as deer were seemingly mitigated on the wild, unfenced Plains by the bison's tendency—barring any major impediments—to shift their range great distances to better pasture.

Determining precisely how the remaining annual mortality in the wild herds was affected is not easy, because the wolf/bison relationship on the Plains has never been studied. Judging from dozens of historical documents attesting to wolf predation of bison calves, including accounts by the Indians, wolves apparently played a critical role in Plains bison population dynamics, and not just as culling agents of diseased and old animals.

Human hunters were the other source of mortality. For nine thousand years native Americans had hunted bison without exterminating them, perhaps building into their gene pool an adjustment to human predation (dwarfed size, earlier sexual maturity, and shorter gestation times, all serving to keep populations up). But there is archaeological evidence that beginning about A.D. 1450, with the advent of "mutualistic" trade between Puebloan communities recently forced by drought to relocate on the Rio Grande and a new wave of Plains hunters (probably the Athapaskan-speaking Apacheans), human pressures on the southern bison herd accelerated, evidently dramatically if the archaeological record in New Mexico is an accurate indication. That pressure would have been a function of both the size of the Indian population and the use of bison in Indian cultures. Because Plains Indians traded bison-derived goods for the produce of horticultural villages fringing the Plains, bison would be affected by changes in human population peripheral to the Great Plains as well as on them. . . .

The cultural utilization of bison by horse Indians has been studied by Bill Brown. Adapting a sophisticated formula worked out first for caribou hunters in the Yukon, Brown has estimated Indian subsistence (caloric requirements plus the number of robes and hides required for domestic use) at about 47 animals per lodge per year. At an average of 8 people per lodge, that works out to almost 6 bison per person over a year's time. Brown's article is not only highly useful in getting us closer to a historic Plains equation than ever before; it is also borne out by at least one historic account. In 1821 the trader Jacob Fowler camped for several weeks with 700 lodges of Southern Plains tribes on the Arkansas River. Fowler was no ecologist; in fact, he could hardly spell. But he was a careful observer, and he wrote that the big camp was using up 100 bison a day. In other words, 700 lodges were using bison at a rate of about 52 per lodge per year, or 6.5 animals per person. . . .

Estimates of the number of Indians on the Southern Plains during historic times are not difficult to find, but they tend to vary widely. . . . If the historic Southern Plains hunting population reached 30,000, then human hunters would have accounted for only 195,000 bison per year if we use the estimate of 6.5 animals per person.

But another factor must have played a significant role. While quadruped predators concentrated on calves and injured or feeble animals, human hunters had different criteria. Historical documents attest to the horse Indians' preference for and success in killing two- to five-year-old bison cows, which were preferred for their meat and for their thinner, more easily processed hides and the luxurious robes made from their pelts. Studies done on other large American ungulates indicate that removal of breeding females at a level that exceeds 7 percent of the total herd will initiate population decline. With 8.2 million bison on the Southern Plains, the critical upper figure for cow selectivity would have been about 574,000 animals. Reduce the total bison number to 6 million and the yearly calf crop to 1.08 million, probably more realistic median figures for the first half of the nineteenth century, and the critical mortality for breeding cows would still have been 420,000 animals. As mentioned, a horse-mounted, bison-hunting population of 30,000 would have harvested bison at a yearly rate of less than 200,000. Hence I would argue that, theoretically, on the Southern Plains the huge biomass of bison left from the Pleistocene extinctions would have supported the subsistence needs of more than 60,000 Plains hunters.

All of this raises some serious questions when we look at the historical evidence from the first half of the nineteenth century. By the end of that period, despite an effort at population growth by many Plains tribes, the population estimates for most of the Southern Plains tribes were down. And many of the bands seemed to be starving. . . . Bison were becoming less reliable, and the evolution toward an economy based on raiding and true horse pastoralism was well under way. Clearly, by 1850 something had altered the situation on the Southern Plains.

The "something" was, in fact, a whole host of ecological alterations that historians with a wide range of data at their disposal are only now, more than a century later, beginning to understand.

As early as 1850 the bison herds had been weakened in a number of ways. The effect of the horse on Indian culture has been much studied, but in working out a Southern Plains ecological model, it is important to note that horses also had a direct effect on bison numbers. By the second quarter of the nineteenth century the domesticated horse herds of the Southern Plains tribes must have ranged between .25 and .50 million animals (at an average of 10 to 15 horses per person). In addition, an estimated 2 million wild mustangs overspread the country between south Texas and the Arkansas River. That many animals of a species with an 80 percent dietary overlap with bovines and, perhaps more critically, with similar water requirements, must have had an adverse impact on bison carrying capacity, especially since Indian horse herds concentrated the tribes in the moist canyons and river valleys that bison also used for watering. Judging from the 1910 agricultural census, 2 million or more horses would have reduced the median grassland carrying capacity for the southern bison herd to under 6 million animals.

Another factor that may have started to diminish overall bison numbers was the effect of exotic bovine diseases. Anthrax, introduced into the herds from Louisiana around 1800, tuberculosis, and brucellosis, the latter brought to the Plains by feral and stolen Texas cattle and by stock on the overland trails, probably had considerable impact on the bison herds. All the bison that were saved in the late nineteenth century had high rates of infection with these diseases. Brucellosis plays havoc with reproduction in domestic cattle, causing cows to abort; it may have done so in wild bison, and butchering them probably infected Indian women with the disease.

Earlier I mentioned modern natural mortality figures for bison of 3 percent to 9 percent of herd totals. On the wilderness Plains, fires, floods, drowning, droughts, and strange die-offs may have upped this percentage considerably. But if we hold to a higher figure, then mortality might have taken an average of 50 percent of the annual bison increase of 18 percent. Thirty thousand subsistence hunters would have killed off only 18 percent of the bison's yearly increase (if the herd was 6 million). The long-wondered-at wolf predation was perhaps the most important of all the factors regulating bison populations, with a predation percentage of around 32% of the annual bison increase. (Interestingly, this dovetails closely with the Pawnee estimate that wolves got 3 to 4 of every 10 calves born.) Wolves and other canids are able to adjust their litter sizes to factors like mortality and resource abundance. Thus, mountain men and traders who poisoned wolves for their pelts may not have significantly reduced wolf populations. They may have inadvertently killed thousands of bison, however, for poisoned wolves drooled and vomited strychnine over the grass in their convulsions. Many Indians lost horses that ate such poisoned grass.

The climate cycle, strongly correlated with bison populations in the archaeological data for earlier periods, must have interacted with these other factors to produce a decline in bison numbers between 1840 and 1850. Except for a dry period in the mid- to late 1820s, the first four decades of the nineteenth century had been a time of above-normal rainfall on the Southern Plains. With the carrying capacity for bison and horses high, the country south of the Arkansas sucked tribes to it as into a vortex. But beginning in 1846, rainfall plunged as much as 30 percent below the median for nine of the next ten years. On the Central Plains, six years of that decade were dry. The growth of human populations and settlements in Texas, New Mexico, and the Indian Territory blocked the bison herds from migrating to their traditional drought refugia on the periphery of their range. Thus, a normal climate swing combined with unprecedented external pressures to produce an effect unusual in bison history—a core population, significantly reduced by competition with horses and by drought, that was quite susceptible to human hunting pressure.

Finally, alterations in the historical circumstances of the Southern Plains tribes from 1825 to 1850 had serious repercussions for Plains ecology. Some of those circumstances were indirect and beyond the tribes' abil-

ity to influence. Traders along the Santa Fe Trail shot into, chased, and disturbed the southern herds. New Mexican *Ciboleros* (bison hunters) continued to take fifteen to twenty-five thousand bison a year from the Llano
Estacado. And the United States government's removal of almost fifty thousand eastern Indians into Oklahoma increased the pressure on the bison
herds to a level impossible to estimate. . . .

Insofar as the Southern Plains tribes had an environmental policy, then,
it was to protect the bison herds from being hunted by outsiders. The
Comanches could not afford to emulate their Shoshone ancestors and limit
their own population. Beset by enemies and disease, they had to try to keep
their numbers high, even as their resource base diminished. For the historic
Plains tribes, warfare and stock raids addressed ecological needs created by
diminishing resources as well as the cultural impulse to enhance men's status, and they must have seemed far more logical solutions than consciously
reducing their own populations as the bison herds became less reliable.

For those very reasons, after more than a decade of warfare among the
buffalo tribes, in 1840 the Comanches and Kiowas adopted a strategy of
seeking peace and an alliance with the Cheyennes, Arapahoes, and Kiowa-
Apaches. From the Comanches' point of view, it brought them allies against
Texans and eastern Indians who were trespassing on the Plains. The
Cheyennes and the Arapahoes got what they most wanted: the chance to
hunt the grass- and bison-rich Southern Plains, horses and mules for trading, and access to the Spanish settlements via Comanche lands. But the
peace meant something else in ecological terms. Now all the tribes could
freely exploit the Arkansas Valley bison herds. This new exploitation of a
large, prime bison habitat that had been a boundary zone skirted by Indian
hunters may have been critical. . . .

One other advantage the Comanches and Kiowas derived from the
peace of 1840 was freedom to trade at Bent's Fort. Although the data to
prove it are fragmentary, this conversion of the largest body of Indians on
the Southern Plains from subsistence/ecosystem hunters to a people intertwined in the European market system probably added critical stress to a
bison herd already being eaten away. How serious the market incentive
could be is indicated by John Whitfield, agent at William Bent's second
Arkansas River fort in 1855, who wrote that 3,150 Cheyennes were killing
40,000 bison a year. That is about twice the number the Cheyennes would
have harvested through subsistence hunting alone. . . . Drought, Indian market hunting, and cow selectivity must stand as critical elements—albeit
augmented by minor factors such as white disturbance, new bovine diseases, and increasing grazing competition from horses—that brought on the
bison crisis of the midcentury Southern Plains. . . .

Did the Southern Plains Indians successfully work out a dynamic, ecological equilibrium with the bison herds? I would argue that the answer
remains ultimately elusive because the relationship was never allowed to
play itself out. The trends, however, suggest that a satisfactory solution was
improbable. One factor that worked against the horse tribes was their short
tenure. It may be that two centuries provided too brief a time for them to

create a workable system around horses, the swelling demand for bison robes generated by the Euro-American market, and the expansion of their own populations to hold their territories. Some of those forces, such as the tribes' need to expand their numbers and the advantages of participating in the robe trade, worked against their need to conserve the bison herds. Too, many of the forces that shaped their world were beyond the power of the Plains tribes to influence. And it is very clear that the ecology of the Southern Plains had become so complicated by mid-nineteenth century that neither the Indians nor the Euro-Americans of those years could have grasped how it all worked.

Finally and ironically, it seems that the Indian religions, so effective at calling forth awe and reverence for the natural world, may have inhibited the Plains Indians' understanding of bison ecology and their role in it. . . . This religious conception of the infinity of nature's abundance was poetic. On one level it was also empirical: Bison overwintered in large numbers in the protected canyons scored into the eastern escarpment of the Llano Estacado, and Indians had no doubt many times witnessed the herds emerging to overspread the high Plains in springtime. But such a conception did not aid the tribes in their efforts to work out an ecological balance amid the complexities of the nineteenth-century Plains.

In a real sense, then, the more familiar events of the 1870s only delivered the *coup de grace* to the free Indian life on the Great Plains. The slaughterhouse effects of European diseases and wars with the encroaching whites caused Indian numbers to dwindle after 1850 (no more than fourteen hundred Comanches were enrolled to receive federal benefits at Fort Sill, in present-day Oklahoma, in the 1880s). This combined with bison resiliency to preserve a good core of animals until the arrival of the white hide hunters, who nonetheless can be documented as taking only about 3.5 million animals from the Southern Plains.

But the great days of the Plains Indians, the primal poetry of humans and horses, bison and grass, sunlight and blue skies, and the sensuous satisfactions of a hunting life on the sweeping grasslands defined a meteoric time indeed. And the meteor was already fading in the sky a quarter century before the Big Fifties began to boom.

Y *FURTHER READING*

Gary C. Anderson, *Kinsmen of Another Kind: Dakota-White Relations in the Upper Mississippi Valley, 1650–1862* (1984)

Robert F. Berkhofer, Jr., *The White Man's Indian: Images of the American Indian from Columbus to the Present* (1978)

Jennifer S. H. Brown, *Strangers in Blood: Fur Trade Company Families in Indian Country* (1980)

——, "Women as Centre and Symbol in the Emergence of Metis Communities," *Canadian Journal of Native Studies,* 3 (1983), 39–46

Richmond Clow, "Bison Ecology, Brulé and Yankton Winter Hunting, and the Starving Winter of 1832–33," *Great Plains Quarterly,* 15 (Fall 1995), 259–70.

William Cronon, *Changes in the Land: Indians, Colonists, and the Ecology of New England* (1983)

Alfred Crosby, *The Columbian Exchange: Biological and Cultural Consequences of 1492* (1972)

Brian W. Dippie, *The Vanishing American: White Attitudes and U.S. Indian Policy* (1982)

R. David Edmunds, "Narrative Americans, New Voices: American Indian History, 1895–1995," *American Historical Review,* 100 (June 1995), 717–40

Daniel Francis and Toby Morantz, *Partners in Furs: A History of the Fur Trade in Eastern James Bay, 1600–1870* (1983)

James R. Gibson, *Otter Skins, Boston Ships, and China Goods: The Maritime Fur Trade of the Northwest Coast, 1785–1841* (1992)

Carolyn Gilman, *Where Two Worlds Meet: The Great Lakes Fur Trade* (1982)

LeRoy R. Hafen, ed., *The Mountain Men and the Fur Trade of the Far West* (1965–1972)

R. Douglas Hurt, *Indian Agriculture in America: Prehistory to the Present* (1987)

Peter Iverson, "Native Peoples and Native Histories," in *The Oxford History of the American West,* ed. Clyde A. Milner II, Carol A. O'Connor, and Martha A. Sandweiss (1994)

Alvin M. Josephy, Jr., ed., *America in 1492: The World of the Indian Peoples Before the Arrival of Columbus* (1991)

Alice B. Kehoe, *North American Indians: A Comprehensive Account* (1981)

Clyde A. Milner II and Floyd A. O'Neil, eds., *Churchmen and the Western Indians, 1820–1920* (1985)

Peter Nabokov, ed., *Native American Testimony: A Chronicle of Indian-White Relations from Prophesy to Present, 1492–1992* (1978; expanded 1991)

Jacqueline Peterson and J. S. H. Brown, eds., *The New Peoples: Being and Becoming Metis in North America* (1985)

Arthur J. Ray, *The Canadian Fur Trade in the Industrial Age* (1990)

——, *Indians in the Fur Trade: Their Role as Hunters, Trappers and Middlemen in the Lands Southwest of Hudson Bay, 1660–1870* (1974)

Lewis O. Saum, *The Fur Trader and the Indian* (1985)

William R. Swagerty, "Marriage and Settlement Patterns of Rocky Mountain Trappers and Traders," *Western Historical Quarterly,* 11 (April 1980), 159–80

Margaret Szasz, ed., *Between Indian and White Worlds: The Cultural Broker* (1994)

Russell Thornton, *American Indian Holocaust and Survival: A Population History Since 1492* (1987)

Sylvia Van Kirk, *"Many Tender Ties": Women in Fur-Trade Society in Western Canada, 1670–1870* (1980)

Richard White, *The Middle Ground: Indians, Empires, and Republics in the Great Lakes Region, 1650–1815* (1991)

——, *The Roots of Dependency: Subsistence, Environment, and Social Change among the Choctaws, Pawnees, and Navajos* (1983)

——, "The Winning of the West: The Expansion of the Western Sioux in the Eighteenth and Nineteenth Centuries," *Journal of American History,* 65 (September 1978), 319–43

David J. Wishart, *The Fur Trade of the American West, 1807–1840: A Geographical Synthesis* (1979)

W. Raymond Wood and Thomas D. Thiessen, *Early Fur Trade on the Northern Plains: Canadian Traders among the Mandan and Hidatsa Indians, 1738–1818* (1985)

CHAPTER
4

Federal Support of
Explorers and Emigrants

Y

Throughout the nineteenth century, the federal government acquired western lands. In tandem with these acquisitions, the government sponsored scientific exploration and then supported emigration and settlement. The Treaty of Paris in 1783, and the Louisiana Purchase only twenty years later, allowed the new United States of America to claim vast areas of land, first beyond the Appalachian Mountains and then beyond the Mississippi River. The second event can be considered the point at which the trans-Mississippi West entered United States history. Even as a U.S. delegation to Paris negotiated possible land purchases from France, President Thomas Jefferson initiated plans for an exploratory expedition to the Far West. Starting on May 14, 1804, Meriwether Lewis and William Clark led their "Corps of Discovery" up the Missouri River, across the Rocky Mountains, down the Clearwater, Snake, and Columbia rivers to the Pacific. On September 23, 1806, they returned to St. Louis. The Lewis and Clark expedition launched a century of western explorations that received national attention and created popular heroes like John Charles Frémont, Clarence King, and John Wesley Powell.

These government-sponsored explorations also demonstrated that the trans-Mississippi would be a region subject to the plans and policies of national officials typically located on the east coast in distant Washington, D.C. When large-scale emigration across the Great Plains to the Pacific coast began in the 1840s, the American overlanders expected help from their national government, especially in the form of military protection and emergency supplies. In effect, the trail west to Oregon and California became a site for government aid to private travelers. Ultimately, many of the overlanders stayed in the West, where they demanded control of the land and its resources. The formal role of the government in opening the way West was forgotten as self-proclaimed westerners asserted that individual initiative explained westward settlement.

115

DOCUMENTS

The first two documents present different expectations and perceptions in the act of exploration. Meriwether Lewis's entry in the expedition's journals for June 13, 1805, demonstrate his attempt to make the elaborate observations expected by President Thomas Jefferson. At the Great Falls of the Missouri River, near the present-day city of Great Falls, Montana, Lewis became frustrated in trying to convey the beauty of nature through the written word and scientific measurement. Major Stephen H. Long of the government's Topographical Engineers led an expedition west in the summer of 1820. Following the Platte River across present-day Nebraska and then proceeding along the south branch of that river into present-day Colorado, Long's party eventually reached Pike's Peak in mid-July before turning back. His report, reproduced as the second document, appeared under the authorship of Edwin James, the expedition's physician. The map that accompanied this account labeled the area east of the Rocky Mountains as the Great American Desert. Long and James seemed most interested in the agricultural usefulness of the land they explored. Given their expectations, might they have presented the Great Falls of the Missouri very differently than Meriwether Lewis?

Documents three and four describe overland travelers and conditions along the trail in 1849, the first full year of the California Gold Rush. Three years earlier, the U.S. Congress had authorized the establishment of military posts along the road to Oregon and had appropriated funds for a regiment of mounted riflemen. When news of gold in California swept across the country, George Gibbs, a lawyer in New York City, abandoned his practice and made his way to Fort Leavenworth in present-day Kansas, where he resumed his westward travels with the U.S. Army's Mounted Riflemen. A talented artist, Gibbs made drawings and kept a daily journal. The excerpts, reprinted here as the third document, recount his observations of overland wagon trains on the Great Plains and the work of the Mounted Riflemen in aiding these travelers.

Vincent Geiger and Wakeman Bryarly had fought in the Mexican War and after their military service had returned to the East where, infected with the California gold fever, they joined the Charlestown Company, an emigrant group which had been organized in Charlestown in what is now West Virginia. Each of the company's seventy-five members contributed $300 to a treasury from which was purchased the necessary wagons, mules, weapons, foodstuffs, and other supplies for the journey. A legally established enterprise, the Charlestown Company planned to divide equally profits from the gold diggings in California. In the fourth document, Bryarly and Geiger, during the trek west, noted the hospitality of government supply trains and their company's use of reports from government explorations, which, in the case of John Charles Frémont's writings, misrepresented the Sinks of the Humboldt River in present-day Nevada.

The final document, a set of three statistical tables, was compiled by the historian John D. Unruh, Jr. The first two tables present the total number of emigrants to Oregon, California, and Utah before the gold rush (Table 1) and after (Table 2). Table 4 shows how few emigrants were killed by Indians from 1840 to 1860. When one considers the stories about Indian attacks that overlanders told in their memoirs, and the high drama of circling the wagons, which Hollywood films later depicted, Unruh's statistics demonstrate a distinctly different experience. Was the overland journey so safe because of the military's efforts, or because many Native Americans tolerated wagon trains that were only "passing through" along well-known routes?

Meriwether Lewis Views the Great Falls of the Missouri, 1805

Thursday June 13th 1805.

This morning we set out about sunrise after taking breakfast off our venison and fish. we again ascended the hills of the river and gained the level country. the country through which we passed for the first six miles tho' more roling than that we had passed yesterday might still with propryety be deemed a level country; our course as yesterday was generally S W. the river from the place we left it appeared to make a considerable bend to the South. from the extremity of this roling country I overlooked a most beatifull and level plain of great extent or at least 50 or sixty miles; in this there were infinitely more buffaloe than I had ever before witnessed at a view. nearly in the direction I had been travling or S. W. two curious mountains presented themselves of square figures, the sides rising perpendicularly to the hight of 250 feet and appeared to be formed of yellow clay; their tops appeared to be level plains; these inaccessible hights appeared like the ramparts of immence fortifications; I have no doubt but with very little assistance from art they might be rendered impregnable. fearing that the river boar to the South and that I might pass the falls if they existed between this an the snowey mountains I altered my course nealy to the South leaving those insulated hills to my wright and proceeded through the plain; I sent Feels on my right and Drewyer and Gibson on my left with orders to kill some meat and join me at the river where I should halt for dinner. I had proceded on this course about two miles with Goodrich at some distance behind me whin my ears were saluted with the agreeable sound of a fall of water and advancing a little further I saw the spray arrise above the plain like a collumn of smoke which would frequently dispear again in an instant caused I presume by the wind which blew pretty hard from the S. W. I did not however loose my direction to this point which soon began to make a roaring too tremendious to be mistaken for any cause short of the great falls of the Missouri. here I arrived about 12 OClock having traveled by estimate about 15 Miles. I hurryed down the hill which was about 200 feet high and difficult of access, to gaze on this sublimely grand specticle. I took my position on the top of some rocks about 20 feet high opposite the center of the falls. this chain of rocks appear once to have formed a part of those over which the waters tumbled, but in the course of time has been seperated from it to the distance of 150 yards lying prarrallel to it and forming a butment against which the water after falling over the precipice beats with great fury; this barrier extends on the right to the perpendicular clift which

Reprinted from *The Journals of the Lewis and Clark Expedition,* Volume 4, 283–87, edited by Gary E. Moulton, by permission of University of Nebraska Press. Copyright 1987 by the University of Nebraska Press.

forms that board [bound? border?] of the river but to the distance of 120 yards next to the clift it is but a few feet above the level of the water, and here the water in very high tides appears to pass in a channel of 40 yds. next to the higher part of the ledg of rocks; on the left it extends within 80 or ninty yards of the lard. Clift which is also perpendicular; between this abrupt extremity of the ledge of rocks and the perpendicular bluff the whole body of water passes with incredible swiftness. immediately at the cascade the river is about 300 yds. wide; about ninty or a hundred yards of this next the Lard. bluff is a smoth even sheet of water falling over a precipice of at least eighty feet, the remaining part of about 200 yards on my right formes the grandest sight I ever beheld, the hight of the fall is the same of the other but the irregular and somewhat projecting rocks below receives the water in it's passage down and brakes it into a perfect white foam which assumes a thousand forms in a moment sometimes flying up in jets of sparkling foam to the hight of fifteen or twenty feet and are scarcely formed before large roling bodies of the same beaten and foaming water is thrown over and conceals them. in short the rocks seem to be most happily fixed to present a sheet of the whitest beaten froath for 200 yards in length and about 80 feet perpendicular. the water after decending strikes against the butment before mentioned or that on which I stand and seems to reverberate and being met by the more impetuous courant they role and swell into half formed billows of great hight which rise and again disappear in an instant. this butment of rock defends a handsom little bottom of about three acres which is deversified and agreeably shaded with some cottonwood trees; in the lower extremity of the bottom there is a very thick grove of the same kind of trees which are small, in this wood there are several Indian lodges formed of sticks. a few small cedar grow near the ledge of rocks where I rest. below the point of these rocks at a small distance the river is divided by a large rock which rises several feet above the water, and extends downwards with the stream for about 20 yards. about a mile before the water arrives at the pitch it decends very rappidly, and is confined on the Lard. side by a perpendicular clift of about 100 feet, on Stard. side it is also perpendicular for about three hundred yards above the pitch where it is then broken by the discharge of a small ravine, down which the buffaloe have a large beaten road to the water, for it is but in very few places that these anamals can obtain water near this place owing to the steep and inaccessible banks. I see several skelletons of the buffaloe lying in the edge of the water near the Stard. bluff which I presume have been swept down by the current and precipitated over this tremendious fall. about 300 yards below me there is another butment of solid rock with a perpendicular face and abot 60 feet high which projects from the Stard. side at right angles to the distance of 134 yds. and terminates the lower part nearly of the bottom before mentioned; there being a passage around the end of this butment between it and the river of about 20 yardes; here the river again assumes it's usual width soon spreading to near 300 yards but still continues it's rappidity. from the reflection of the sun on the spray or mist which arrises from these falls there is a beatifull rainbow produced which adds not a little to the

beauty of this majestically grand senery. after wrighting this imperfect dis-
cription I again viewed the falls and was so much disgusted with the imperfect idea which it conveyed of the scene that I determined to draw my pen
across it and begin agin, but then reflected that I could not perhaps succeed
better than pening the first impressions of the mind; I wished for the pencil
of Salvator Rosa or the pen of Thompson,* that I might be enabled to give
to the enlightened world some just idea of this truly magnificent and sublimely grand object, which has from the commencement of time been concealed from the view of civilized man; but this was fruitless and vain. I
most sincerely regreted that I had not brought a crimee obscura** with me
by the assistance of which even I could have hoped to have done better but
alas this was also out of my reach; I therefore with the assistance of my pen
only indeavoured to trace some of the stronger features of this seen by the
assistance of which and my recollection aided by some able pencil I hope
still to give to the world some faint idea of an object which at this moment
fills me with such pleasure and astonishment, and which of it's kind I will
venture to ascert is second to but one in the known world. I retired to the
shade of a tree where I determined to fix my camp for the present and dis-
patch a man in the morning to inform Capt. C. and the party of my success
in finding the falls and settle in their minds all further doubts as to the Missouri. the hunters now arrived loaded with excellent buffaloe meat and
informed me that they had killed three very fat cows about $^3/_4$ of a mile
hence. I directed them after they had refreshed themselves to go back and
butcher them and bring another load of meat each to our camp determining
to employ those who remained with me in drying meat for the party against
their arrival. in about 2 hours or at 4 OClock P. M. they set out on this duty,
and I walked down the river about three miles to discover if possible some
place to which the canoes might arrive or at which they might be drawn on
shore in order to be taken by land above the falls; but returned without
effecting either of these objects; the river was one continued sene of rap-
pids and cascades which I readily perceived could not be encountered with
our canoes, and the Clifts still retained their perpendicular structure and
were from 150 to 200 feet high; in short the river appears here to have
woarn a channel in the process of time through a solid rock. on my return I
found the party at camp; they had butchered the buffaloe and brought in
some more meat as I had directed. Goodrich had caught half a douzen very
fine trout and a number of both species of the white fish. these trout are
from sixteen to twenty three inches in length, precisely resemble our mountain or speckled trout in form and the position of their fins, but the specks
on these are of a deep black instead of the red or goald colour of those common to the U.' States. these are furnished long sharp teeth on the pallet and

---

*Salvator Rosa, a seventeenth-century Italian landscape painter, generally painted wild, desolate scenes.
James Thomson, an eighteenth-century Scottish poet, was a forerunner of the English Romantic movement; his best-known poem was "The Seasons."
**A camera obscura, basically a box with a lens mounted on the one wall; light entering through the lens
would project an image on the opposite wall of the dark box, which an artist could then trace, getting an
almost photographic image.

tongue and have generally a small dash of red on each side behind the front ventral fins; the flesh is of a pale yellowish red, or when in good order, of a rose red.—

I am induced to believe that the Brown, the white and the Grizly bear of this country are the same species only differing in colour from age or more probably from the same natural cause that many other anamals of the same family differ in colour. one of those which we killed yesterday was of a creemcoloured white while the other in company with it was of the common bey or rdish brown, which seems to be the most usual colour of them. the white one appeared from it's tallons and teath to be the youngest; it was smaller than the other, and although a monstrous beast we supposed that it had not yet attained it's growth and that it was a little upwards of two years old. the young cubs which we have killed have always been of a brownish white, but none of them as white as that we killed yesterday. one other that we killed sometime since which I mentioned sunk under some driftwood and was lost, had a white stripe or list of about eleven inches wide entirely arround his body just behind the shoalders, and was much darker than these bear usually are. the grizly bear we have never yet seen. I have seen their tallons in possession of the Indians and from their form I am perswaded if there is any difference between this species and the brown or white bear it is very inconsiderable. There is no such anamal as a black bear in this open country or of that species generally denominated the black bear

my fare is really sumptuous this evening; buffaloe's humps, tongues and marrowbones, fine trout parched meal peper and salt, and a good appetite; the last is not considered the least of the luxuries.

The Stephen Long Expedition's Report of a Frontier Barrier, 1821

Of the country situated between the meridian of the Council Bluff and the Rocky Mountains

We next proceed to a description of the country westward of the assumed meridian, and extending to the Rocky Mountains, which are its western boundary. This section embraces an extent of about four hundred miles square, lying between 96 and 105 degrees of west longitude, and between 35 and 42 degrees of north latitude.

Proceeding westwardly across the meridian above specified, the hilly country gradually subsides, giving place to a region of vast extent, spreading towards the north and south, and presenting an undulating surface, with nothing to limit the view or variegate the prospect, but here and there a hill, knob, or insulated tract of table-land. At length the Rocky Mountains break upon the view, towering abruptly from the plains, and mingling their snow-capped summits with the clouds.

Reuben Gold Thwaites, ed., *Early Western Travels 1748–1846,* Vol. XVII (Cleveland, OH: Arthur H. Clark Company, 1905), 132–135, 147–148.

On approaching the mountains, no other change is observable in the general aspect of the country, except that the isolated knobs and tablelands above alluded to become more frequent and more distinctly marked, the bluffs by which the valleys of watercourses are bounded present a greater abundance of rocks, stones lie in greater profusion upon the surface, and the soil becomes more sandy and sterile. If, to the characteristics above intimated, we add that of an almost complete destitution of woodland (for not more than one thousandth part of the section can be said to possess a timber-growth) we shall have a pretty correct idea of the general aspect of the whole country. . . .

Immediately at the base of the mountains, and also at those of some of the insular table-lands, are situated many remarkable ridges, rising in the form of parapets, to the height of between fifty and one hundred and fifty feet. These appear to have been attached to the neighbouring heights, of which they once constituted a part, but have, at some remote period, been cleft asunder from them by some extraordinary convulsion of nature, which has prostrated them in their present condition.

The rocky stratifications, of which these ridges are principally composed, and which are exactly similar to those of the insulated table-lands, are variously inclined, having various dips, from forty-five to eighty degrees.

Throughout this section of country the surface is occasionally characterized by water-worn pebbles, and gravel of granite, gneiss, and quartz, but the predominant characteristic is sand, which in many instances prevails almost to the entire exclusion of vegetable mould. Large tracts are often to be met with, exhibiting scarcely a trace of vegetation. The whole region, as before hinted, is almost entirely destitute of a timber-growth of any description. In some few instances, however, sandy knobs and ridges make their appearance, thickly covered with red cedars of a dwarfish growth. There are also some few tracts clad in a growth of pitch pine and scrubby oaks; but, in general, nothing of vegetation appears upon the uplands but withered grass of a stinted growth, no more than two or three inches high, prickly pears profusely covering extensive tracts, and weeds of a few varieties, which, like the prickly pear, seem to thrive best in the most arid and sterile soil. . . .

In regard to this extensive section of country, I do not hesitate in giving the opinion, that it is almost wholly unfit for cultivation, and of course uninhabitable by a people depending upon agriculture for their subsistence. Although tracts of fertile land considerably extensive are occasionally to be met with, yet the scarcity of wood and water, almost uniformly prevalent, will prove an insuperable obstacle in the way of settling the country. This objection rests not only against the section immediately under consideration, but applies with equal propriety to a much larger portion of the country. Agreeably to the best intelligence that can be had, concerning the country both northward and southward of the section, and especially to the inferences deducible from the account given by Lewis and Clarke of the country situated between the Missouri and the Rocky Mountains above the river Platte, the vast region commencing near the sources of the Sabine,

Trinity, Brases, and Colorado, and extending northwardly to the forty-ninth degree of north latitude, by which the United States' territory is limited in that direction, is throughout of a similar character. The whole of this region seems peculiarly adapted as a range for buffaloes, wild goats, and other wild game; incalculable multitudes of which find ample pasturage and subsistence upon it.

This region, however, viewed as a frontier, may prove of infinite importance to the United States, inasmuch as it is calculated to serve as a barrier to prevent too great an extension of our population westward, and secure us against the machinations or incursions of an enemy that might otherwise be disposed to annoy us in that part of our frontier.

George Gibbs with the Mounted Riflemen Observes Emigrants on the Overland Trails, 1849

Tuesday, May 15. . . . About three miles from Wolf creek the [Fort] Leavenworth [road] strikes into the great trail from St. Joseph, now the most traveled of all the routes. The town of St. Joseph, one of the principal outfitting towns in western Missouri, has been created entirely by the business of the emigrants and is of so late an origin that its very name is not given on the maps. We have begun to encounter the emigrant trains in numbers, winding slowly along with their white-topped wagons and trains of oxen and mules. In passing over this district, than which few can be more beautiful, the eye wanders in search of the familiar farmhouse and the barn, built upon some little knoll by the brookside, that greets the eye in our eastern landscape. I often found myself almost cheated into the belief that the canvas covers of some emigrant train, seen in the distance, were the fixed residence of the white man. But no smoke except that of the campfire rises here. The Indian himself is unseen, and so peaceful is all around, that the weapon which every man carries seemed a useless plaything.

Our route was intersected or joined by a number of smaller trails, some of them the perhaps immemorial war paths of Indians. Others [were] distinguished by their wheel marks as the roads made by emigrants from distant points on the Missouri. I noticed today, and frequently afterward, circular spots or rings on the prairie where the old grass remained unburnt in the midst of an extent of fresh verdure. These the guide explained as places where horses had been picketed the previous year, or where a corral had been formed. We found a good camping ground about a mile southeast from the road, some twelve miles from the Missouri, and fourteen or fifteen from our starting point. The descent into it [was] bad, [it] contained good water and [was] well protected. The evening was passed till a late hour round a campfire, and enlivened with merry chat and songs. . . .

Friday, May 18. Camp moved at six [o'clock], the regular hour for moving being resumed. I again went forward with the guide to select a

Reprinted by permission of the Publishers, The Arthur H. Clark Company, from *The March of the Mounted Riflemen,* ed. by Raymond W. Settle, Glendale, 1940.

position for the night. We passed a number of emigrant trains, some of which had now become old acquaintances. Two or three meetings constitute such on the prairie, and hearty salutations were exchanged as we went on. There are odd characters and odd vehicles among them too. Every profession and every class in society are represented, and every mode of conveyance from the Conestoga wagon and its lumbering oxen, and the light draft mule-team, to the saddle horse. We even saw a doctor's buggy with a bell-pull fastened to the hinder axle. The route today grows more monotonous, the divides longer, and the timbered streams more distant from the road and of less frequent occurrence. On either side we saw vestiges of campfires, but all [made by] whites, for the Indians are now mostly at their villages engaged in planting corn. A practiced eye readily distinguishes the fire made by an Indian from that of the emigrant or even the hunter. The white man lights his wood in the center of the sticks; the Indian always at the end, moving it up as it burns. The scarcity of wood in the prairie has taught him this lesson of economy. . . .

Saturday, May 19. A slight fall of rain occurred early this morning. Our course today lay nearly due west over the tops of long ridges. A heavy shower with hail fell about ten—the sky clearing off at noon and exhibiting the exquisite valley of the Great Nemaha. The approach to this stream on either side of the road is beautiful, the banks of the ravines being covered with wood. The river itself is small, notwithstanding its name, being at this time only some twenty feet wide and about a foot deep. The general course is here northwest, but its bed is very winding. The banks are high, disclosing horizontal strata of fossiliferous limestone, some of the inclosed shells preserving the nacre. I noticed also a number of recent shells in the mud of the bottom, but found no live specimens to preserve for identification. The pioneers had here constructed a tolerable road and we passed safely. The passage itself was highly picturesque, and I spent a pleasant hour or two in watering the teams and reading the various inscriptions which the Pilgrims of the West had left upon the trees announcing their arrival at this point of their long journey. Ascending the opposite bank we found a pretty and level plain, from which again arose the spurs of another dividing ridge. Here stood the newly-made grave of an emigrant marked by a rude headboard, with his name and the date of his death affixed on a scrap of paper. His search for the gold of the Sacramento had been soon ended. How will it be with the rest? . . .

Sunday, May 20. Again went in advance with our guide, leaving camp a little before six [o'clock]. About five miles out struck a branch of the Nemaha [river, where] there were two crossings that needed repair. It has been a matter of regret all along that the government did not send a body of pioneers a month previous to prepare the road between [Fort] Leavenworth and Fort Kearny by throwing bridges over the most difficult places, or marking out roads that might avoid them. The expense would have been trifling in comparison to the immense advantage both to the emigrants and ourselves. In most cases sufficient wood could be found for the purpose in the immediate neighborhood, and in others a few wagonloads of brush, easily procured within a mile or two or carried along from one place to another would have saved hours of delay and often the breakage of wagons. The crossings rarely need mending for more than twenty feet, and a number of the worst could have been turned by a circuitous march of a short distance. These we had of course no time to explore. As it is, we have been of great service to the emigrants who follow us. I could not but pity some whom we occasionally met on the road, with their wagons broken and no means of repairing them. The regiment was unprovided with materials beyond their own immediate wants, and though our forges have been kindly employed in many cases for their relief, our march is necessarily too hurried to delay a moment. It is, however, gratifying to observe that the emigrants are generally kind to one another, as well as that their conduct for the most part is exceedingly courteous and orderly. A few companies, we hear, have earned themselves bad names, but all that we have met have been as well behaved and well bred as [those] one would meet on a country road in the old states. Many are, in fact, led by men of high standing and composed of the most substantial class of the community. [It is a] pity that such should leave the comforts of civilized life to endure the sufferings that must await them before they reach the Utopia of the West.

This morning we again encountered heavy showers. The camp was selected to the right of the road, with good water, but wood scarce. This last item, the least important in our own calculations is, I observe, one of the most in that of the emigrants. "How far is it to timber?" is a question often asked of us as we return from our morning scout. . . .

Tuesday, May 22. [The] column moved this day only eight and a quarter miles by the viameter and camped a short distance to the right of the road, the mules needing rest. Grass excellent, the water [was] not so good, [but] enough however [was] found in pools. We now pass the graves of emigrants daily along the road, their inscriptions generally giving cholera or dysentery as the cause of their death, and on inquiring [we find that] almost every company has lost one or two members. [We] noticed cows frequently yoked in the teams with bulls and oxen. They are said to draw very well, but their milk must be unwholesome. The ox-teams keep very well up with the train, making fifteen miles on an average per day. In some respects they are preferable to mules, as they improve in condition so long as the grass holds good, and more easily tended, and less liable to escape. When, however, the grass is more exhausted I apprehend that they will suffer much. We are now on the war grounds, and although we have literally not seen an Indian since leaving Camp Sumner, greater precautions are deemed necessary, and for the first time we form a corral. This is made by enclosing a space within the wagons and tents, into which the animals are driven at night. The emigrants are nightly losing horses and mules, but whether from carelessness or theft it is difficult to tell. There is a report that buffalo have been seen today by one of the companies, but it is doubted. Our camp is called Camp Ann. During the night another shower fell. . . .

Tuesday, May 29. We are all too glad to rest ourselves to seek other amusement than sleep or lounging. I [here] take advantage of the time to transcribe the rough notes I have been able to make on the road, and to add something respecting the post itself. Fort Kearny, first called Fort Childs, was established under the act creating forts on the Oregon route in 1846–47. The first troops sent here were a battalion of mounted Missourians known as the Oregon battalion, who encamped at the place during the summer of 1847 and erected the walls of the long adobe building and the turf walls of a few others now used as officers quarters. The battalion was marched back in the fall and disbanded, and the post occupied in october by two companies of Mounted Riflemen under Captain, now Brevet-major [Charles F.] Ruff, who has since remained in command. The buildings, such as they are, were completed by the troops, and with a turf corral now constitute the "fort." The situation is on the low flat bottom, about a third of a mile from the Platte river, near the head of Grand island, and fifteen from where the trail enters the valley. A more unfortunate one in some respects could hardly have been chosen. Entirely unprotected by trees or high ground, its climate is excessively severe in winter and in the spring the plain is rendered a marsh by the heavy rains. Water can be obtained anywhere by digging to the depth of four or five feet. It is cold and palatable at first, but has a taste of sulphur after standing in the holes for some time. No wood is to be had except the soft cottonwood found on the islands of the Platte, which is brought up with difficulty and not fit for building when obtained. The original design was to form an inclosure of pickets, inclosing the building and an area of about four acres, with blockhouses on the diagonal corners containing each four guns. The number of these is however reduced to two each. The pickets and blockhouses are expected to be built of cottonwood, and the whole is to keep in awe a broken tribe of Pawnees, [which is] fast disappearing under their wars with the Sioux and whose nearest village is now one hundred twenty-five miles distant. The establishment, including the expenses of the Missouri battalion, cannot have cost less than half a million of dollars. The turf buildings are already so dilapidated as to be almost uninhabitable in wet weather. Were any substantial aid contemplated to the emigrants by retaining this post there might be wisdom in so doing, but so far as keeping the Indians in awe is concerned, a moving camp of dragoons during the summer months would be far more serviceable.

It is due the officers stationed here, and more particularly to Captain Van Vliet, the quartermaster, to say that every attention and kindness which they can personally afford the emigrants has been cheerfully rendered. The scene at the office during the time we have stopped here has been most amusing. Men are coming in at every moment bringing letters for the states, [which are] dispatched from here twice a month by a government express, making thousands of inquiries on every conceivable subject, offering to sell or to buy everything under the sun, and asking for every sort of assistance and information.

The condition of many of the emigrants already forbodes the disasters that await them. Numbers of them, finding their teams overloaded or insufficient, have thrown away portions of their provisions or used their bacon as fuel to cook with, [and] others have thrown out stools, stoves, etc. Some few have either abandoned their wagons or cut them up to make pack-saddles. Others, [being] wiser, have gone home again. It is amusing enough to see men carrying on their shoulders or their saddles, in a country where there is now neither game nor enemy, the long, heavy rifles of the west and their holsters filled with pistols—each one a marching ordnance department. We see them every day roaming about the country, miles to the right or left, looking, I presume, for buffalo or deer. The practice will probably be continued until a few are snapped [up] by some of the more western tribes. Government, I learn today, has with wise liberality directed that the commissary shall hold a surplus of provisions for the relief of emigrants broken down and returning to the states.

The number of wagons which have passed here up to tonight amounts to nearly four thousand. Allowing four persons to a team, which is less than the average, at least sixteen thousand men have already reached this point and probably half as many more are on their way. This does not include [trains] moving on the north side of the river from Council Bluffs. [These are] composed principally of Mormons, who may amount in all to ten thousand.

Impressions of the Overland Journey from Vincent Geiger and Wakeman Bryarly, 1849

Tuesday, June 12th. Four miles from Independence Rock [in Wyoming] we came to *"The Devil's Gate."** This is the most remarkable freak of nature I ever saw. It is the passing of the Sweet Water River through a mountain of solid rock. From the water below to the top of the rock is by measurement 400 ft., & being more than a hundred yds. wide. The rock presents the appearance of being split asunder, & this being the only outlet for the river it rushed through and went on its way to its mother home. The breadth across is 50 yds.

Four miles from "The Devils Gate" we nooned four hours, and started again and encamped at a bend of the river where the road leaves it for several miles. We had grass to the mules' knees, and they now seem to be improving fast.

We came up to a Government train bound for Bear River, to establish a garrison for the better protection of the emigrants to Oregon & California. They had 50 wagons under the command of Maj. Simonson. I joined the train after we had corralled & was delighted to meet some old friends, Lts. May, Addison, Irwin & Mr. Stevenson. We road together some 6 miles farther & came to the river again. On rising the hill, we saw for the first time

---

*A narrow gorge more than three hundred feet deep, by which the Sweetwater River passes through a range of hills which lies across its path in what is now Natrona County, Wyoming. This spectacular physical feature was another of the accepted landmarks of the trail.

the snow-capped Wind Mountain. We were attracted by a smoke up the mountain on our right side, and all had very considerable curiosity to know from whence it came. Maj. Simonson being something of a *"Tourist"* volunteered to go with anyone. Lt. Irwin offered to accompany him, & they started. They returned in the evening reporting the smoke to be from a large quantity of drift wood which was on fire, & which was found to have been set on fire by some of the deserters of the evening before. They found a pair of U.S. pantaloons, straps &c.

One mile farther the Government train halted & went into camp. I was the guest of Lt. May & [Mr.] Stevenson and was most hospitably received. We were fortunate enough to find some nice sprigs of mint upon the river, & soon were at work with our tools, knocking up one of those nectar drinks, a Julep. The invitation being extended to other officers of kindred spirits, after supper they assembled and with talking of friends at home, of days gone by, of hair-breadth escapes, of the journey over the plains, and with an occasional draw upon the blue pitcher, a bright fire, & that indispensable article, the life of a camp fire, "a Pipe," we whiled away some half dozen hours in almost complete forgetfulness of the many deprivations of the plains, & only broke up our levee when reminded we had but three hours to sleep before reveille. . . .

Saturday, August 11th. Twelve miles upon the old road brought us to the *Sink* [Humboldt Desert in Nevada], the disideratum of long hoped for weeks. "How far to the Sink?" has been a question *often* asked, & *often* answered, & *often* heard in the last month. This Sink extends over several miles & is generally grown up with rushes & grass. There is immense basins however on all sides, which, in high water, receive the back water. The road keeps in these basins, which extend over *miles* & *miles* without a vestige of vegetation, but so white & dazzling in the sun as scarcely to be looked at. We rolled by this, the water of which cannot be used by man or beast, [for] 4 miles, & came to some sulphur springs or rather wells. Here we encamped for the night. These wells were dug in a slough, & the water was very like many of our sulphur springs at home. The animals drank it freely & it seemed to do them no harm. In this slough just below the spring were a great number of cattle & mules, which had become mired & were not able to get out & were left. Some of them were still alive. The most obnoxious, hideous gases perfumed our camp all night, arising from the many dead animals around. In the morning some were found laying immediately by us & in the vicinity 30 [others] were adding their scents to the nauseous atmosphere. Our animals were turned to the grass we brought already dried, & they seemed [to] relish it much.

We were *past the Sink.* This is glory enough for one day. I would ask the learned & descriptive Mr. Frémont & the elegant & imaginative Mr. Bryant, where was the beautiful valley, the surpassing lovely valley of Humbolt?* Where was the country presenting the most splendid "agricul-

---

*John C. Frémont, *Report of the Exploring Expedition to the Rocky Mountains in the Year 1842, and to Oregon and Northern California in the Years 1843–'44* (Washington, 1845) and Edwin Bryant, *What I Saw in California* (New York, 1848).

tural features?" Where the splendid grazing, the cottonwood lining the banks of their *beautiful meandering stream,* & everything presenting the most interesting & picturesque appearance of any place they ever saw?

Perhaps Mr. Bryant was speaking ironically of all these most captivating things that he saw, or perhaps he thought it was "too far out" for anyone else but himself to see. If not, I have only to say, "Oh shame where is thy blush."

The Overland Trails: Three Tables of Statistics

Table 1   Overland Emigration to Oregon, California, Utah, 1840–48

Year	Oregon	California	Yearly West Coast Total	Cumulative West Coast Total	Utah	Cumulative Grand Total
1840	13	—	13	13	—	13
1841	24	34	58	71	—	71
1842	125	—	125	196	—	196
1843	875	38	913	1,109	—	1,109
1844	1,475	53	1,528	2,637	—	2,637
1845	2,500	260	2,760	5,397	—	5,397
1846	1,200	1,500	2,700	8,097	—	8,097
1847	4,000	450	4,450	12,547	2,200	14,747
1848	1,300	400	1,700	14,247	2,400	18,847
Pre-gold rush subtotals	11,512	2,735	14,247	14,247	4,600	18,847

Table 2   Overland Emigration to Oregon, California, Utah, 1849–60

Year	Oregon	California	Yearly West Coast Total	Cumulative West Coast Total	Utah	Cumulative Grand Total
1849	450	25,000	25,450	39,697	1,500	45,797
1850	6,000	44,000	50,000	89,697	2,500	98,297
1851	3,600	1,100	4,700	94,397	1,500	104,497
1852	10,000	50,000	60,000	154,397	10,000	174,497
1853	7,500	20,000	27,500	181,897	8,000	209,997
1854	6,000	12,000	18,000	199,897	3,167	231,164
1855	500	1,500	2,000	201,897	4,684	237,848
1856	1,000	8,000	9,000	210,897	2,400	249,248
1857	1,500	4,000	5,500	216,397	1,300	256,048
1858	1,500	6,000	7,500	223,897	150	263,698
1859	2,000	17,000	19,000	242,897	1,431	284,129
1860	1,500	9,000	10,500	253,397	1,630	296,259
Grand totals, 1840–60	53,062	200,335	253,397	253,397	42,862	296,259

Table 4   Estimated Overland Emigrants Killed by Indians, and Indians Killed by Overland Emigrants, 1840–60

YEAR	EMIGRANTS	INDIANS	YEAR	EMIGRANTS	INDIANS
1840	0	0	1851	60	70
1841	0	1	1852	45	70
1842	0	0	1853	7	9
1843	0	0	1854	35	40
1844	0	0	1855	6	10
1845	4	1	1856	20	15
1846	4	20	1857	17 (8)[a]	30
1847	24	2	1858	?	?
1848	2	2	1859	32 (13)[a]	10
1849	33	60	1860	25	10
1850	48	76	Totals	362	426

[a]Emigrants presumably killed by "white Indians"; these twenty-one deaths are not included in the yearly totals.

Y   *E S S A Y S*

William H. Goetzmann has been one of the most important historians of the American West over the past forty years. A professor of history and American studies at the University of Texas at Austin, Goetzmann received the Pulitzer Prize and the Parkman Award in 1967 for his book, *Exploration and Empire: The Role of the Explorer and Scientist in the Winning of the American West.* This volume was the second work in a trilogy of books on the history of exploration. The first essay is an excerpt from the third book of Goetzmann's trilogy, *New Lands, New Men: America and the Second Great Age of Discovery,* first published in 1986. The federal government appropriated considerable funds for the scientific exploration of the American West. This financial support included publishing the sometimes lavishly illustrated reports from these expeditions. Goetzmann demonstrates how science served the interest of the government in the era before the Civil War. The late John D. Unruh, Jr., was a professor of history at Bluffton College in Ohio before his untimely death in 1976. His monumental study of the overland trails experience, *The Plains Across,* was published posthumously in 1979. It won numerous prizes, including the Billington Award of the Organization of American Historians. The second essay presented here is an excerpt from Unruh's book which recounts the actions of the federal government in aiding travel along the overland trails to California, Utah, and Oregon. Both Goetzmann and Unruh permit readers to consider the benefits of national government as it supported the westward surge of the American people. Nonetheless, some westerners soon began to resent the power of this same government. Anger over federal "control" of the West persists to the present day. Are the continuing benefits of federal actions also as persistent?

From the Northwest Passage to the "Great Reconnaissance"

WILLIAM H. GOETZMANN

Thomas Jefferson was an avid reader of scientific treatises, a collector of Indian vocabularies, a geographer and surveyor, a romantic devotee of the great travel literature of the eighteenth century best typified by the reports of Captain Cook's magnificent voyages, and, perhaps most of all, a shrewd geopolitical thinker. Long before he became president, Jefferson was thinking in transcontinental terms. In 1786 he enthusiastically endorsed the visionary plan of one John Ledyard, a Connecticut Yankee who had sailed to the Northwest Coast with Captain Cook. At Secretary of State Jefferson's behest, and with support from Sir Joseph Banks of the Royal Society, Ledyard set out across Europe and the Empire of Russia in an effort to approach the Northwest Passage and the Northwest Coast, with its rich sea otter preserves, from the mysterious East via Siberia. Though for a time Russian authorities helped him—got him as a lone traveler all the way to Yakutsk in Siberia—they eventually recognized that he represented a potential Yankee threat to the exploitation by Russian companies of their private hunting grounds in Alaska. The Empress Catherine had him apprehended at Yakutsk, brought back across Russia, and deported. Ledyard never returned to the United States. Instead, on a mission for Sir Joseph Banks, he died on the Upper Nile trying to locate sub-Saharan passage to the Niger. Ledyard's career demonstrated in a dramatic way the ambivalence of the explorer in the Second Great Age of Discovery. He was first and foremost a man of science, an adventurer-explorer for whom climactic discoveries were more important than imperial or national interests. Thus he could change allegiances at will in the interests of discovery.

Something of this same spirit of ambivalence as to the interests of science versus national interests seems to have motivated Jefferson when he commissioned the French citizen André Michaux to journey via the Ohio and the Missouri to the Pacific in 1795. In many ways Michaux was an excellent choice for the mission. A dedicated naturalist, he had botanized in France as far south as the Pyrenees and had spent three years on similar activities in exotic Persia before he was sent by his government to America in 1785. Michaux's early years in North America rivaled in the breadth of his travels even the mighty John Bartram. Operating from a base in Charles Town, he virtually retraveled Bartram's route through the Carolina mountains and into Florida. He sailed to the Bahamas and in 1794 trekked through the vast wilderness west of Hudson Bay, where he learned of Mackenzie's recent transcontinental expedition. Upon his return he proposed that the American Philosophical Society support him in a venture that would duplicate Mackenzie's feat, only via the Ohio and Missouri rivers. With Jefferson's endorsement, he set out for the Ohio country, ostensibly on a nonpolitical scientific mission. But, unfortunately in his case, the

Reprinted from *New Lands, New Men* by William H. Goetzmann, courtesy of the Texas State Historical Association, Austin, Texas.

French ambassador, Edmond Genêt, persuaded him to act as an agent among the trans-Appalachian settlers in an effort to turn them against both Spanish America and the United States. Thus Michaux's mission was aborted in the wake of the Genêt affair. Something of the extent of his western travels is evident from the journal published by his son who accompanied him, *Travels to the West of the Allegheny Mountains in the States of Ohio, Kentucky, and Tennessee, and Back to Charleston by the Upper Carolinas . . . Undertaken in the Year 1802.*

Spurred on by his knowledge of Mackenzie's crossing, Gray's discovery of the Columbia, the increasingly accurate western data appearing on the English cartographer Aaron Arrowsmith's maps, and the almost daily news of Spanish-sponsored ventures up the Missouri, Jefferson determined at all costs to launch an American scientific expedition to the Pacific. For this mission he chose his own neighbor and personal secretary, Meriwether Lewis, who in turn chose as his partner the bluff frontier soldier William Clark, also of Virginia. In 1802, Jefferson presented his plan to Congress as a commercial venture. Congress approved an appropriation for this aim, since it was consistent with the views of the majority of its members, who considered the federal government's powers limited to those specifically enumerated in the Constitution. At the same time Jefferson presented the Lewis and Clark expedition to the Spanish minister Casa Yrujo as a "literary" or scientific mission. Clearly, Jefferson had multiple motives for the Lewis and Clark expedition. Indeed, the breadth of his objectives was to characterize almost all future American exploration, in contrast to the limited-objective expeditions of Britain and Spain in North America. Jefferson was after much more than trade in beaver skins, and much more than a defense of the holy faith and the mines of Mexico. He wished to project, through discovery, the future of the continent.

The extensive scientific training in all branches of knowledge given Meriwether Lewis by the members of the American Philosophical Society in Philadelphia attested to this. If that were not sufficient indication of the scope of his objectives, Jefferson's very detailed instructions, based on those given to the early western trader John Evans by a previous trader-explorer, James Mackay, when he ascended the Missouri River as far as the Mandan Indian villages in 1796, certainly were. Lewis and Clark were to explore the Missouri River, cross over the mountains to the Columbia, and thus locate "the most direct and practicable water communication across this continent for purposes of commerce." Jefferson meant not only commerce with far-off Canton, but also commerce with the Indians in the heart of the continent. Accordingly, he ordered Lewis and Clark to produce an accurate map of the country they traversed; they were to study the Indians carefully, especially their numbers and intertribal alliances and animosities, as well as their customs, their economies, and the possibilities of trade with them; they were, in addition, to note the "soil and face of the country," its vegetables, animals, minerals, volcanoes, and weather, and even its fossils. In short, they were to take note of everything that would be of use to future settlers, rather than simply fur traders. Moreover, their line of march and the influence that they might bring to bear on the Indians, whom they were enjoined to treat very well, would automatically form a kind of border or boundary between the United States and British Canada. Never mind that they would technically be in Spanish territory. The latter point was remedied, of course, by Spain's retrocession of Louisiana to France and Jefferson's purchase of Louisiana in 1803 just before Lewis and Clark got started on their epic trek.

From a scientific point of view, by the time they started up the Missouri on May 14, 1804, Lewis and Clark were exceedingly well informed. In addition to Lewis's scientific training in Philadelphia, they had access to Jefferson's own vast archive of information about the West, especially the latest maps. When they reached St. Louis, they could also study the Missouri River maps of the Spaniard Antoine Soulard, and those of John Evans and James Mackay. Not only had the latter two men been to the Mandan villages near present-day Bismarck, North Dakota, but Mackay, a former Northwester, had come down upon the Missouri from the north. Through the work of his former associate Antoine Larocque, he knew of the Yellowstone and its tributaries, the Big Horn and Powder rivers. So Lewis and Clark knew what to expect far above the great bend of the Missouri. Beyond that, the territory was completely unknown until they reached the Columbia River system.

There is no need here to trace their famous journey in detail. Day after day, they struggled up the broad reaches of the Missouri, sometimes sailing, sometimes pulling their heavy keelboat. They encountered surprisingly little trouble with the Indians, and they were almost daily dazzled by the teeming wildlife that abounded over the northern plains. On December 7, 1805, a bitter cold day, Sergeant Patrick Gass recorded in his journal, "Captain Lewis and eleven more of us went out . . . and saw the prairie covered with buffalo and the Indians on horseback killing them. They killed thirty or forty, and we killed eleven of them." Gass, who seems fixated on the plenitude of game, nearly every day recorded hunters returning with staggering loads of deer, elk, bear, buffalo, mountain sheep, wild turkeys, badger, beaver, and even porcupine. Fish, too, were abundant, as in one day the men netted over two hundred catfish.

The journey to the Mandan villages took seven months. There Lewis and Clark established quarters for the winter of 1804–1805 and sent a party back down the river with their preliminary reports in the early spring. The rest of the party continued upriver in homemade canoes. They made their way up around the Great Bend, past the Yellowstone and the Great Falls to the Three Forks, which mark the source of the Missouri. Then, with the help of Sacajawea, a Shoshone Indian woman who accompanied them, and a number of other Indians they met along the way, they found their way over the difficult mountains of Idaho via Lemhi Pass to the Salmon River and the Bitterroot Valley. From a point which they called Traveler's Rest, near present-day Missoula, Montana, they crossed, via Lolo Pass, over to the Clearwater, which flows into the Columbia. On November 7, 1805, they at last reached the shores of the Pacific. As a counter to Mackenzie's pointed message, far to the north on the Bella Coola, Clark carved on a tree near the mouth of the Columbia, "William Clark, December 3rd 1805. By Land from the U. States in 1804 and 1805." Despite Clark's scientific dedication, imperial rivalries were not far from his mind.

After wintering in a cluster of huts near the mouth of the Columbia, they returned home in two parties. Lewis led one group overland via Lolo Pass and the Sun River to the Great Falls, while Clark coursed southward along the outward route, then crossed over below the Great Falls to the Yellowstone River, where the two parties linked up again for the final voyage back down the Missouri. They arrived in St. Louis on September 26, 1806. A small group of citizens assembled on the bank to cheer them.

To the men of the West, Lewis and Clark's expedition had immense importance. It opened up the whole rich upper Missouri and Rocky Mountain country to fur traders and hunters. Before their main party even reached St. Louis, fur traders, hearing of their feat, had already launched expeditions up the Missouri and into the mountains. Some of these parties were aided by veterans of the expedition like George Drouillard and John Colter, who made spectacular explorations in their own right. And for the nation's future as a whole, the Lewis and Clark expedition had immense importance. They had measured the width of the continent and described its incredibly rich potential, and in their rugged journey they had laid out a crude Northwest Passage that underscored the importance of the Missouri and Columbia rivers, to which the United States now had the best claim. Most of all, they focused the attention of Americans upon the continent itself rather than the passage to India. With certain exceptions this was to preoccupy American explorers for much of the early nineteenth century. It certainly commanded a full measure of attention of her geopolitical thinkers, whose theories of Manifest Destiny were dimly foreshadowed by William Clark's bold mockery of the Canadian Alexander Mackenzie's vermilion paint message back on the Bella Coola too far to the north.

Significantly, the United States had launched its sweep to the west with a government-sponsored scientific expedition. Unlike the findings of the fur trade monopolists of Canada, or those of the secretive Spanish bureaucracy, Lewis and Clark's important and broad-ranging discoveries belonged to the people of the new democracy. In the first decades of the nineteenth century, with certain exceptions this became a conscious American policy. Jefferson, for example, understandably concerned with the boundaries of the Louisiana Purchase, was responsible for several federal expeditions to determine the southwest boundary of the new American domain. In these ventures he turned to men of science. In 1804, Dr. George Hunter and William Dunbar, lately of Philadelphia and friends of William Bartram, headed up the Red River, which was the assumed boundary of the Purchase. They were turned aside by Indians and explored the Ozark Plateau instead. Jefferson duly reported the results of their expedition to Congress, along with the preliminary information sent down from Fort Mandan by Lewis and Clark.

In the spring of 1805, Jefferson secured $5,000 from Congress to send

Captain Thomas Sparks and the naturalist Peter Custis up the Red River boundary. They marched nearly seven hundred miles upriver, conducting the first ecological survey of the southern reaches of the still-disputed Louisiana Territory. Intercepted by a detachment of belligerent Spanish cavalrymen, following Jefferson's instructions they meekly turned back downriver. Because it nearly precipitated a border war with Spain, this expedition was only casually mentioned in Jefferson's report to Congress, and its scientific results were never published. But as of 1806, the federal probes of the Louisiana frontier had produced nothing like a clear idea as to what President Jefferson and the American people had purchased. Regretting the permission granted to Lewis and Clark's "literary" venture, Spain had suddenly grown secretive and defensive.

This posture was not without cause. Michaux and the French had repeatedly intrigued against Spain's vulnerable northern provinces. And in 1796, General Collot had been allowed by Jefferson to make a meticulous survey of the Ohio and the Mississippi with an obvious eye to a campaign against New Spain. Already humiliated by the Nootka Sound incident and panicked over the possibility of losing New Orleans, St. Louis, the Mississippi, and the Californias, Spanish officials spent the first decades of the nineteenth century constantly on their guard.

In such an atmosphere of intrigue was conceived the prairie expedition of Lieutenant Zebulon Pike. Basically it was the brainchild of General James Wilkinson, the U.S. governor of Louisiana. Wilkinson, appointed in what must have been an oversight by Jefferson, was a master of intrigue. A friend of Aaron Burr, and a double agent in the pay of Spain, Wilkinson seems to have harbored thoughts of carving out a Louisiana empire for himself, or at least in partnership with Burr. Ruling this empire, as Burr put it in a coded letter to Wilkinson of July 29, 1806, "will be a host of choice spirits. Wilkinson shall be second to Burr only; Wilkinson shall dictate the rank and promotion of his officers. Burr will proceed westward never to return. . . ." But Wilkinson was even more devious than Burr. He managed to detach himself from that clumsy freebooter and, with Pike's scientific exploring expeditions, to gain credit for one of the most successful espionage operations in American history.

In the summer of 1806, Wilkinson ordered Pike to venture out across the prairies and locate the source of the Red River—a project which he knew to be dear to Jefferson's heart. At the same time he sent along Dr. John Robinson, who intended to collect a debt in Santa Fe, which was nowhere near the Red River. This clearly suggests that Pike's real mission was not the Red River but a Santa Fe spying venture. But then with incredible duplicity, Wilkinson warned the authorities in Santa Fe of Pike's mission and at the same time informed them of Burr's grandiose filibustering plan, possibly through Dr. Robinson, who also gained enough information about New Spain to compile his own important map of 1819.

How much Pike knew of this when he set out from Belle Fontaine, near St. Louis, on his prairied expedition perhaps no one will ever know. He seems everywhere to have done his duty with determination and coura-

geous devotion, even when he knew the Spanish cavalry, under Don Fal-
cundo Malgares, was pursuing him. Instead of being alarmed, he merely
used Malgares's trail as a road along the front range of the Rockies toward
Santa Fe. When he reached the Arkansas River, he sent his adjutant, Lieutenant James Wilkinson (the intriguer's son), downriver with maps and
reports for the general. Then he turned west toward the Rockies, which he
first sighted on November 15, 1806, "looking like a small blue cloud." For
the next two months he explored the southern Rockies, and climbed not
Pikes but Cheyenne Peak. From this vantage point he believed he could see
the whole of the Rockies. This led him into accepting Jonathan Carver's
erroneous belief that all the great rivers of the West had a single source. It
also ironically led him, in effect, to leave out Colorado on his map, since
he believed that just north of Cheyenne Peak lay the Yellowstone and other
tributaries of the upper Missouri. This was perhaps due to the fact that
when he drew his map of the western country back in Washington, Pike
copied Humboldt's map of New Spain, which the baron had recently presented to Jefferson. Thus, except for the Texas portion, Pike based the car-
tographical description of his expedition of the work of a savant who had
never seen the country at all.

Eventually, Pike took his men on a difficult winter climb over a pass in
the Sangre de Cristo mountains to a bleak encampment on the upper Rio
Grande. Though he declared he was lost, Pike certainly knew just where he
was, since Dr. Robinson had headed south to Santa Fe just a few days
before a detachment of Spanish soldiers arrived to arrest Pike and the
remaining men of his party. Pike's famous statement "What! Is this not the
Red River?" was disingenuous to say the least.

Pike's capture by the Spanish afforded him a chance to reconnoiter the
whole of New Mexico, much of Chihuahua, and the Camino Real across
Texas. The information, geographical, economic, and military, was thorough and comprehensive—ideal for anyone contemplating a venture
against Spain's northern provinces. That such a venture was not forthcoming might actually have been due to Pike's scientific reports. After traveling many days over the dry endless prairies, he concluded that the whole
high plains region was a "Great American Desert" where nothing but
nomads could live. In doing so, he stamped a geographical image upon the
minds of Americans that persisted for much of the nineteenth century and
greatly affected public policy.

But for all his efforts, neither Pike nor any other American had yet
traced out the course of the Red River boundary of Louisiana. This duty
was eventually assigned to another scientist-explorer, Major Stephen H.
Long. Long was a graduate of Dartmouth College and a member of the
newly created United States Army Corps of Topographical Engineers. By
the time he embarked on his Great Plains expedition, Long had already
served as terrain adviser to the Baltimore and Ohio Railroad and had traveled from Minnesota to Louisiana, locating sites for a ring of frontier forts.
His original mission in 1819 was to ascend the Missouri River as head of
the scientific contingent of General Henry Rice Atkinson's little army

designed to frighten the British fur traders entirely out of the Missouri River country. Atkinson's men all came down sick, however, near Council Bluffs, and Secretary of War John C. Calhoun changed Long's orders. At the head of a seasoned group of scientific naturalists and artists from Philadelphia, including Edwin James, Thomas Say, Samuel Seymour, and Titian Peale, he headed out across the prairies for the front range of the Rockies determined to located the source of the Red River. Long and his men made a careful survey of the high plains and Seymour made the first-known drawings of the Rockies, an accurate but hardly dramatic representation of that towering range.

Seymour, British-born but trained in Philadelphia, was essentially a topographical artist. Nothing in his previous experience, however, prepared him for the scenery of the vast western prairies and the dramatic front range of the Rockies. Thus his small, carefully made watercolors (painted over pencil sketches) hardly seem to do justice to the incredible country that he was paid to picture for the first time. Seymour was cautious. His two most dramatic paintings were *Distant View of the Rocky Mountains,* a panorama from about fifty miles out on the high plains, and *View of James* [Pikes] *Peak in the Rain.* These two works, though small, suggested something of the sweep and majesty of the country. Unfortunately, only one of them was printed as a plate in the Long expedition report. Seymour's other pictures were exact renditions of very specific places—sandstone formations at the foothills of the Rockies, the spot where the Platte entered the mountains, and a strange formation known as Elephant Rock. Seymour took his duty as a documentary artist very narrowly; consequently those Americans who viewed his lithographs in the Long expedition reports saw, as their first views of the Great West, only fragments of its sublime, endless immensity. Seymour's fellow artist Titian Peale likewise afforded little help to those curious about the West. Except for one striking watercolor of the fire-belching steamboat that took them up the Missouri to Fort Atkinson and a romantic view of a sunset on the river, Peale concentrated on making exact renditions of animals and plants. It was as if both artists, operating under military command, stuck to the exact letter of their instructions. In later years, Peale appears to have regretted doing so, because from the 1850s through the early 1870s he repeatedly repainted Seymour's landscapes in a more dramatic scale and fashion and populated them with groups of his animal drawings. And yet, just as one cannot dismiss the Long expedition for its faults and errors, one cannot dismiss these early works of Seymour and Peale. They represent the first visualization of the West—an important aspect of the scientific and imaginative understanding or lack of understanding of the still-to-be-discovered sweep of the continent. For almost ten years, between 1822 and 1832, these pictures, Long's map, and Dr. Edwin James's report on the expedition officially defined the West.

Long's men climbed Pikes Peak, measured its altitude above the plain, and in general conducted a significant reconnaissance of the whole plains and front range region. Then Long divided his party, sending Captain John

R. Bell down the Arkansas River, where his men deserted with most of the expedition's maps and notes to date. Major Long compounded the disaster when he mistook the Canadian for the Red River and sailed back down it to what he expected to be glory. Great was his mortification to find that he had chosen the wrong river and that the Red River still lay in unknown territory. His was an important oversight, because Secretary of State John Quincy Adams in 1819 had just concluded the Transcontinental Boundary Treaty with Spain, in which the elusive Red River figured most importantly.

Nonetheless, Long's expedition did produce, after Lewis and Clark's map of 1814, the most important and comprehensive view of the West. His map of 1821 remains a landmark of American cartography. So prominent was it that most geographers adopted it immediately and gave him instead of Pike the dubious honor of naming the Great Plains "the Great American Desert." Seymour's illustrations and the scientific descriptions in the report did little to dispel this impression. Captain Bell, Long's second-in-command, described the plains region as "a dusty plain of sand and gravel, barren as the deserts of Arabia." Edwin James, a chronicler of the expedition and its chief geologist, saw the western portion of the plains as an extension of "the Mexican Desert" and its eastern portion bore "a manifest resemblance to the deserts of Siberia." He apparently liked the Russian comparison because he elsewhere described the upper Canadian River region as "sandy wastes and inhospitable steppes."

But James's geological account of the plains and Rockies went far beyond mere descriptions of a desert region. He reconstructed the geological history of the region in a way that was both uncommonly perceptive and very daring for its time. Most significantly, in looking at the vast plains and Rockies region, James assumed it was formed over an exceedingly long span of time. He was not speaking of a few thousand years when he described the upthrusting of the Rocky Mountains, their gradual erosion, and the deposition of the various levels of strata that made up the Great Plains. He was thinking in terms of eons of time. In a striking passage he declared, "The sandstones being entirely mechanical aggregates, consisting of rounded fragments of rocks formerly constituting a part of the primitive mountains, would seem to have been deposited at a very remote period, when the waters of the primeval ocean covered the level of the great plain and the lower regions of the gigantic rocks." This vision was influenced by the great German geologist Abraham Gottlob Werner, who saw the entire earth as being the product of sediment formed from a primeval ocean. But James went beyond this, seeing a "primitive" layer of rocks beneath the surface sedimentary rocks, and more important, he grasped the fact that the Rockies were formed by a massive upthrust and the Great Plains themselves were also uplifted "by some cause equally unknown." As this happened, a great interior sea that covered the heart of the continent retreated toward the Gulf of Mexico. In an era that generally calculated the age of the earth biblically at 4004 years and that rejected the long time span needed to make the evolutionism of Erasmus Darwin and Robert Chambers plausible, Edwin James's dramatic reconstruction of the plains and Rockies geological history was indeed daring. This perhaps accounts for the neglect of his geological report on the part of contemporary reviewers.

Long's expedition, as its most recent historians have tried to point out, had a significant scientific impact, despite the fact that Long and his colleagues had to have their report privately printed by Carey, Lea and Carey of Philadelphia. John C. Calhoun, as Secretary of War, would only authorize the purchase of a few dozen copies, though the War Department paid for the printing of Long's important map. Despite the lack of federal support for its publication, the report of Long's expedition did appear in 1822 as a handsome work in two printed volumes and an atlas that included a small fraction of the artwork of Seymour and Peale. It was also reprinted in 1823 in an English edition of three volumes that did not include a separate atlas.

Long himself supervised the production of the report, though Edwin James, working along with Long and Thomas Say in an office in Philadelphia, appears to have done most of the writing, particularly the narrative and the long geological section. A number of Captain Bell's notebooks had been stolen on his trip down the Arkansas River, and James's notebook seems to have been the most extensive surviving account, so perhaps this is why he was selected as the expedition's chronicler. The report itself, however, contained much more than a narrative. There were extensive notes by Say, Peale, and Baldwin on the fauna and flora of the plains, and a number of animal species, such as the coyote, were named by their first scientific discoverer, Say. The plant specimens were used by John Torrey, America's foremost botanist, to work up a new "American System" of classification that was an attempt to replace that of Linnaeus. Museums and lyceums all up and down the East Coast of America benefited from the expedition—either through the reception of parts of its collections, or in hearing lectures delivered by members of the scientific corps.

Future explorers also were in Long's debt. They used his map and his personal advice, as well as that of members of his company, such as Titian Peale. But, in addition, they mined his work for specific information on the many plains Indian tribes that the expedition had encountered. And not the least useful appendix to Long's report was the first "dictionary" of trans-Mississippi Indian sign language—a seventeen-page treatise entitled *Indian Language of Signs.* This was the pioneer attempt at a systematic understanding of the universal plains language. It was not really replaced until the publication of Captain Garrick Mallory's work in the late nineteenth century.

Of all those who exploited Long's report, America's foremost novelist, James Fenimore Cooper, perhaps did so to the utmost. His elegiac Leatherstocking novel *The Prairie,* written in Paris and published in 1827, derives most of its details, if not its inspiration, from Long's report. In Cooper's novel the prairie itself becomes almost a character with its bleak wastelands and its gloomy landmarks like Scotts Bluff and Courthouse Rock. But just as later historians have impugned the Long expedition for falsely labeling the plains "the Great American Desert," later critics, like Mark Twain, failed to see the underlying geographical accuracy of Cooper's novel.

As for Pike and Long and those subsequent American explorers who followed them in labeling the plains a "Great American Desert," who is to say after the "Dust Bowl" of the 1930s that they were entirely wrong? Clearly given the pre-windmill, pre-artesian well, pre-dry-farming era in which they lived, no one possessed the technology to farm the plains successfully. Generations of discouraged sod-house pioneers could well attest to their wisdom.

These early military-scientific expeditions into the West, chiefly Jeffersonian in inspiration, were obviously important to the history of the United States and to science in general. Lewis and Clark spanned the continent, mapping the Missouri-Columbia routes remarkably well, given their crude instruments, while Pike and Long began another sort of venture into the interior and initiated more professional scientific mapping and analysis of the West. But their most important contributions were twofold. They turned the country's focus from the far Pacific to the West itself, and by the very Enlightenment-naturalist range of their inquiry they set the pattern for flexibility in American exploration. Their labors were meant to be the vanguard of the central adventure of nineteenth-century America: the settlement of the West. . . .

Throughout the 1840s and 1850s, Army explorers conducted what amounted to a "great reconnaissance" of the American West. In 1849, Lieutenant James Harvey Simpson led the first expedition since the days of the Spaniards into the Navajo stronghold at Canyon de Chelly. High up on the canyon walls he and his men discovered the lost cliff dwellings of the ancient Anasazi culture. In 1851, Captain Lorenzo Sitgreaves trekked across the Southwest just below the Grand Canyon in an early search for a wagon or railroad route. Both Simpson and Sitgreaves were accompanied by the artist Richard Kern, who visualized for the first time the vast Anasazi ruins at Chaco Canyon and Canyon de Chelly. He also recorded the first interior view of the mysterious, closely guarded pueblo kivas and the sacred dances at Zuñi. Six years later, aboard a prefabricated steamboat, Lieutenant Joseph Christmas Ives chugged up the Colorado River to the Grand Canyon at its juncture with Diamond Creek. He and his party were the first white men ever to reach the floor of the canyon. The artists of his party, Heinrich Balduin Möllhausen and F. W. von Egloffstein, were the first men to picture the stupendous canyon, which they did in highly dramatic views. Also along with this party was the geologist John Strong Newberry, who saw the possibilities of such a deep descent into the earth and traced out the first important stratigraphic column in the West. His description of the different layers of earth that he could observe from the canyon floor provided a measuring stick for all future geologists in the West. Ives's report on the expedition was a masterpiece in both literary and scientific terms. Not the least of its contributions, besides Newberry's column, was the first relief map of the West, drawn by the Prussian F. W. von Egloffstein. Hardly had Ives finished his expedition at the Hopi villages at Oraibi and Moenkopi when Captain John N. Macomb, also accompanied by the geologist Newberry, discovered and described the junction of the Green and the Grand rivers in western Colorado, thus fitting a key piece into the puzzle of western geography. Macomb and his men also saw abundant remains of the lost Anasazi civilization as they marched along the San Juan River, though they missed the grandest ruin of them all—Mesa Verde.

Farther north, Lieutenant Simpson crossed the Great Basin once again in search of a railroad route, while Lieutenant Governor Kemble Warren explored the Dakota Badlands and the upper Missouri. In 1859–60, Captain W. F. Raynolds explored the upper Missouri, the Big Horn Basin, and the Wind River Mountains, and marched all around but did not penetrate the Yellowstone Park region. Along with Raynolds were two paleontologists, Fielding Bradford Meek and Ferdinand V. Hayden. Together, and with data from the Warren expeditions as well, they worked out the cretaceous geological horizon of the Dakota country and a stratigraphic column for the upper Missouri region, and discovered great caches of extinct animal bones. When they brought their collections back to Philadelphia they provided Dr. Joseph Leidy with the material for the first accurate book on prehistoric American zoology, *The Ancient Fauna of Nebraska.* Leidy also found the remains of tiny primitive horses among the collections and published a paper showing how the horse evolved through time. This came out in 1859, just before Charles Darwin published his *On the Origin of Species.* And finally, as if to close out exploration in the continental United States, just on the eve of the Civil War, Lieutenant John G. Parke, working with the Royal Engineers, laid out the last boundary through the northwestern wilderness between the United States and Canada.

All of these expeditions were described in lavishly illustrated reports published by Congress. Taken together they represent the most conprehensive dissemination of scientific information about the West ever undertaken up to that time.

Between 1840 and 1860, Congress published in all some sixty works dealing with the exploration of the West. Many of these were lavishly printed series replete with esoteric reports by scientists who accompanied the expeditions and lithographs illustrating the virtually unknown western landscapes and aboriginal inhabitants. In a period usually decried as parsimonious with regard to the sciences and the arts this represented an incredible federal subsidy to these pursuits, which was critical in the professionalization of science in America and at the same time launched the careers of artists like Edward, Richard, and Benjamin Kern. It also made the mapmaking and printing as well as engraving and lithography industries for the first time independent of Europe. One must also add to these sixty subsidized western ventures in the period fifteen naval expeditions and their reports of activities around the globe, as well as the reports of the very large Coast and Geodetic Survey, the Naval Observatory, Schoolcraft's lavish six-volume *Historical and Statistical Information Respecting the History, Condition, and Prospects of the Indian Tribes of the United States* (1851–57), the reports of the Great Lakes Survey, Humphreys and Abbott's extensive studies of the Mississippi, and the *Annual Reports* of the Patent Office, which reported on scientific agriculture. And when one considers that the annual federal income fluctuated between a low of $8,302,702 in 1843 and $74,056,699 in 1856, this subsidy of the sciences and the arts (exclusive of federal buildings and the Smithsonian) must, at times, have represented perhaps one-quarter to one-third of the federal budget. At no time since in the history of the United States has anything like that ratio been reached.

The capstone of all the reports on Army exploring activity in the Era of the Great Reconnaissance was the extraordinary set of thirteen volumes generated by the Pacific Railroad Surveys. They represented "an encyclopedia of western science," and their publication cost amounted to over $1 million alone—almost twice as much as the actual surveys. In addition to the narrative accounts of the individual expeditions, the *Railroad Survey Reports* also included volumes on geology complete with geologic maps of vast regions and volumes on plants, animals, birds, and fishes as well as an ethnographic report that covered most of the Indian tribes of the West. Dozens of artists and scientific illustrators worked to enhance the large quarto volumes, presenting for the first time a comprehensive vision of the West to the public. In scientific terms the *Railroad Survey Reports* dramatically illustrated the advent of specialization and teamwork in the study of a region. In that they were also aimed at determining the possibilities of the whole West for settlement, they represented a very early ecological study, monumental in scope. And finally they represented a cartographic milestone. Each expedition leader had drawn a detailed map of the country he traversed. All these were published in the *Reports;* in addition, Lieutenant G. K. Warren compiled the data from these maps and those of all the other Army expeditions into the first scientifically accurate comprehensive map of the West. After the pioneering work of Lewis and Clark it was perhaps the most important map of the West ever drawn.

The era of Army exploration represented a strange phenomenon in a sense. As Professor Daniel Boorstin has put it, during this period part of the West was "settled before it was explored." But what this meant, of course, was that each age sought different things from the West, and the development of science and technology refined the questions that explorers sought to answer as each decade passed. Dramatically during the era of Army exploration, questions shifted from those of the fur trader and farmer to those of the gold seeker, townbuilder, and railroad entrepreneur as California suddenly filled with 300,000 people and Colorado threatened to do the same in 1859. The fact that the questions shifted and each age produced explorers bent on different missions merely underscores the fact that exploration is a social process of seeking—not necessarily and finally discovering.

The Federal Government's Aid to Overland Emigrants

JOHN D. UNRUH, JR.

The irascible editor of Portland's *Weekly Oregonian* charged in 1860 that Oregon was "cursed" by governmental policies of "imbecility and neglect" which stymied population growth and economic development by failing to furnish adequate protection to overland emigrants. For the previous two decades, newspapermen like Portland's T. J. Dryer, as well as presidents, secretaries of war, army officers, enlisted men, Indian commissioners, Indian agents, congressmen, and overland emigrants had been debating the proper role of the federal government in the westward migrations. Those debates, considering the federal funds ultimately authorized for emigrant-oriented policies and programs, had been decisively determined. For especially by the 1850s, the federal presence in the West was far more important to the success of the overland emigrations than Dryer acknowledged. Most pre–Civil War overlanders found the U.S. government, through its armed forces, military installations, Indian agents, explorers, surveyors, road builders, physicians, and mail carriers, to be an impressively potent and helpful force.

Statistically, frontier soldiers were the most significant dimension of the western federal presence. Throughout the 1850s up to 90 percent of the U.S. Army was deployed at the seventy-nine posts dotting the trans-Mississippi West. In 1860 this meant that 7,090 enlisted men and officers were stationed at the forts and camps of the four army departments whose geographic areas of responsibility incorporated the South Pass overland trails. Primarily, the army was so heavily concentrated in the West because of the "Indian problem"—the central facet of which was the threat to overland travel—and, following 1857, because of the Latter-Day Saints' challenge to national authority and union. And even though Indian agents were at least as influential in pacifying disgruntled and angry Indians, thereby preventing disastrous attacks upon emigrant caravans, overlanders persisted in regarding the frontier army as almost their sole guardian and protector.

Already in 1840, before any emigrant caravans had penetrated beyond the Missouri River, prospective overlanders had been entreating the Congress to provide military protection. The problem then, as in later years, was in agreeing on the kind of military protection that would be most effective. A group of 152 Missouri petitioners requested "the protection of the strong arm of the Government against Indian treachery" but were vague on what that might mean. The demand of twenty-seven Kentuckians had been more specific: that "small garrisons" for protective purposes be established along a federally built road to Oregon. Secretaries of War Joel R. Poinsett in 1840 and John C. Spencer in 1841 recommended that military posts be located along the trail to Oregon to protect overland travelers. Poinsett esti-

Excerpted from *The Plains Across: The Overland Emigrants and the Trans-Mississippi West* by John D. Unruh. Copyright © 1979 by the Board of Trustees of the University of Illinois Press. Used with permission of the author and the University of Illinois Press.

mated that three posts would suffice, while Spencer called for a "chain of posts." Presidents John Tyler and James K. Polk agreed and, beginning in 1841, used their annual messages to Congress for similar requests. Tyler emphasized that military posts along the overland route could serve as places of rest as well as security; Polk called not only for a "suitable number of stockades and blockhouse forts" but also for an "adequate force of mounted riflemen . . . to guard and protect them [the emigrants] on their journey." The House Committee on Military Affairs also strongly supported the fixed-post philosophy. Missouri's senators regularly introduced legislation to this effect, the prompt enactment of which was just as regularly demanded by newspaper editors across the nation.

Congress's reluctance to pass such legislation, however, revealed that not everyone was persuaded that permanent bastions of defense were particularly wise. Colonel Stephen W. Kearny, after an 1845 trip along the overland trail as far as South Pass, was confident that powerful military expeditions at periodic intervals would keep the Indians properly respectful of the rapid striking power which the United States could bring against them if depredations were committed. Kearny also prudently reminded his superior officers that such awe-inspiring military expeditions would be less expensive than the establishment and maintenance of a series of posts across the vast western spaces.

And so the issue was drawn: a series of permanent posts from the Missouri River to the Pacific Ocean or periodic campaigns along the trails to impress and, when necessary, chastise the Indians. Sending an occasional military expedition to cow the natives was not a new idea. . . .

Ultimately, governmental authorities resorted to a number of strategies, often simultaneously, in an attempt to neutralize the Indian threat to overland travel: treaties were negotiated, presents distributed, reservations established, awe-inspiring and/or punitive military expeditions dispatched, roving patrols instituted, military escorts provided. But initially, most persons concerned with this problem shared 1846 overlander Jessy Thornton's outlook that a series of permanent military forts was the best approach. In his book based upon a summer's overland trip to Oregon, Thornton helpfully listed potential fort sites, asserted that "the establishment of a cordon of military posts is important and necessary," and for good measure called for a graded wagon road with ferries and bridges at the major water crossings.

Thornton had barely pushed westward from Independence in 1846 when legislation authorizing the fixed-post concept finally cleared congressional hurdles. The May 19 act provided $76,500 for raising, mounting, and equipping one regiment of mounted riflemen, $3,000 for the establishment of each "military station" on the route to Oregon, and $2,000 to compensate the Indian tribes owning or possessing the land where each station was to be located. Although the act did not specify the exact function of the regiment, most contemporaries shared President Polk's understanding that the Mounted Riflemen were "intended to guard and protect our emigrants to Oregon." Noteworthy too was the nonrestrictive nature of the authorization: as many military posts as the President desired could be established. There would be no more turning back. The federal government had accepted responsibility for overland travel to the Pacific. . . .

Before the California gold rush . . . little had actually been accomplished. Two expeditions had been sent to overawe the Indians, one of which had escorted the 1845 emigration as far as South Pass. But no chain of army forts yet paved the way to the Pacific, although the second Fort Kearny marked a beginning. American regulars were still a novelty to both Indians and overlanders. After 1849 they were not. In that year the Mounted Riflemen marched the entire length of the trail, establishing additional military installations along the way. At last the long-cherished dream of overland travelers had reached fruition and a new phase in federal policy had been inaugurated—the permanent presence of the army in the West. . . .

The new decade thus dawned with the army firmly situated at three sites adjacent to the Oregon Trail—Forts Kearny, Laramie, and Drum—and in the process of abandoning the temporary Cantonment Loring. This permanent federal presence materially altered the pattern of overland travel during the remainder of the 1850s. Most obvious was a substantial increase in trail traffic, since vast quantities of supplies were constantly freighted to the various forts. Further, with reinforcements, troop rotation, and official inspections a part of the normal routine of military life, there was a great deal of military movement on the trails unrelated to escorts, patrols, or punitive campaigns. The need for swift and reliable communication between military posts virtually guaranteed that a more effective postal service would be forthcoming. Finally, the inevitable "supply" towns quickly appeared near the permanent forts, conveniently providing the soldiers— and all passing travelers—with opportunities to spend their money on such things as liquor, gambling, and carnal pleasures. Overland emigrants welcomed most of these developments, which seemed to imply that the trails would henceforth be safer.

During the 1850s additional military outposts were added to the nuclei of trail forts established by the Mounted Riflemen. Most were located where a skirmish or battle between troops and Indians had occurred or near where Indians were generally troublesome. Some were abandoned almost as quickly as they had appeared; others evolved into significant links in the trail's protective chain.

Perhaps the weakest link was Fort Grattan, a temporary mud fort about equidistant between Forts Kearny and Laramie. Located south of the Platte River on Ash Hollow's south bank, Fort Grattan was erected by General William S. Harney's troops immediately after their decisive triumph of September 3, 1855, over the Sioux Indians in the Battle of Ash Hollow. One company of infantry was left to man the fort and protect mail carriers and emigrant trains, but by mid-December of the same year Captain Wharton had abandoned the breastworks and taken his infantry company to Fort Kearny. Although the fort was never reconstituted, on occasion significant numbers of troops were placed at the Ash Hollow mail station to protect passing emigrants. Maria Norton, for example, found 200 soldiers "stationed" there on June 6 when she passed by en route to California. Somewhat analogous was the temporary installation at the bridge over the North Platte River some 130 miles west of Fort Laramie. Established by two companies of troops on July 29, 1858, and charged with maintaining communications with Salt Lake City, Fort Payne was operative at least until April 20 of the following year.

Fort Payne derived from the "Mormon War," an event which so accelerated the military presence in the West that thereafter sufficient troops were readily available for patrol and escort duty along the most treacherous portions of the overland trail west of South Pass. The Utah Expedition, an uncertain and poorly organized governmental response to presumed Mormon intransigence, left Fort Leavenworth in July of 1857, much too late for any kind of expedition to the Salt Lake Valley. Harassed by Mormon guerrilla raiders, impeded by initially ineffective leadership, and threatened by inclement weather, the troops wintered in bleak Camp Scott, a precarious encampment in and about Fort Bridger on Black's Fork. The Mormons had burned most of Jim Bridger's long-standing trading post prior to the arrival of the Gentile forces; rebuilt, the post served as a supply depot and protective bastion through the 1880s.

The major Utah installation, however, was located approximately forty miles south of Salt Lake City. Camp Floyd had been established by expedition commander Colonel Albert Sidney Johnston in June of 1858, after the "war" had been peacefully terminated. An average of 2,400 soldiers were stationed there until 1860, when the garrison's size was considerably reduced prior to its closing in 1861. During 1858 and 1859 more troops were concentrated at Camp Floyd than anywhere else in the United States. Although the post was not located precisely on the main overland trail, to knowledgeable overland emigrants it was easily the most important army establishment during the last years of the decade.

Meanwhile, considerable military activity was also under way in the Pacific Northwest. Following the Whitman massacre, Oregon endured more than a decade of Indian wars. As the various tribes were forced onto reservations, a number of army outposts—such as Forts Lane, Cascades, Yamhill, Hoskins, and Umpqua—were created to control the not yet tranquil Indians. These forts provided some protection, particularly for travelers on southern routes into Oregon. California-bound emigrants of 1860, especially those familiar with the bloody struggles known as the Pyramid Lake or Paiute Indian War occurring during the spring of that year, took comfort in the sight of Fort Churchill, established July 20 along the Carson River and garrisoned by two companies of infantry and one company of dragoons.

A review of developments during the 1850s reveals that the army's permanent western presence—a consequence of the trailside forts—had indeed launched a new era in both government-emigrant and government-Indian relationships. A wider range of responses was now possible, since protecting emigrants and punishing Indians were no longer dependent upon the slow process of troops being marched west from Fort Leavenworth. Overlanders and Indians saw a great many bluecoats during the 1850s; indeed, one calculation has it that between 1848 and 1861 there were 206 battles between soldiers and Indians. . . .

The foregoing summary makes clear the steady westward progression of army protective activity as well as the constantly increasing amount of that activity in behalf of the overland emigrants. Yet despite the establishment of the trailside forts, and the relief, punishment, patrol, and escort expeditions, many overlanders were not satisfied, particularly during the early 1850s. Some lamented the inadequate number and injudicious placement of the forts, others wanted more troops garrisoned at each outpost. More forts and more troops were also the incessant refrains of West Coast newspaper editors, who feared that the rising Indian threat during the mid-1850s would drastically curtail overland travel. Other emigrants desired fewer troops stationed at the forts in lieu of an escort squadron of troops every year. Still others stressed their ability to protect themselves and demanded not more military might but more governmental services: guidebooks based upon exhaustive route surveys, government workshops along the trail for wagon repairs, supply stations for provisions, governmental trains to pick up straggling and forsaken emigrants and transport them safely to their destination. All these requests—or demands—were based on the now-common conviction that the federal government carried a clear responsibility to insure safe overland travel.

Overlanders were generally unfamiliar with another important method by which the government endeavored to pacify Indians in the interests of safe plains travel—treaties and agreements negotiated by Indian agents and commissioners. By the time the overland caravans of the early 1840s suggested the nature of future problems, governmental treaty-making with Indian nations was a well-established practice. The Department of Indian Affairs provided the organizational framework within which agents and commissioners struggled with such perennial problems as controlling the Indian trade and stamping out the illicit liquor traffic.

The act organizing the department dated from 1834. Until 1849 the various superintendencies, agencies, and subagencies were located in the War Department, with the St. Louis Superintendency embracing virtually all the Indian tribes with whom overland emigrants came in contact. In 1849 responsibility for Indian affairs was transferred to the new Interior Department, in 1851 the St. Louis Superintendency was renamed the Central Superintendency, and by then there were also superintendencies in Oregon and Utah. Most matters of Indian-emigrant relationships were concentrated within these three areas. . . .

Within this milieu Indian agents and commissioners labored diligently to entice tribes away from the overland trails through treaties, annuities, and the establishment of reservations. Whether immediate treaty negotiations for the right of overland travel through the Indian country in 1841 or 1842 would have significantly altered the course of western Indian relationships is difficult to determine. It is clear, however, that by 1851, when the first meaningful efforts were made, Indian tribes had accumulated a

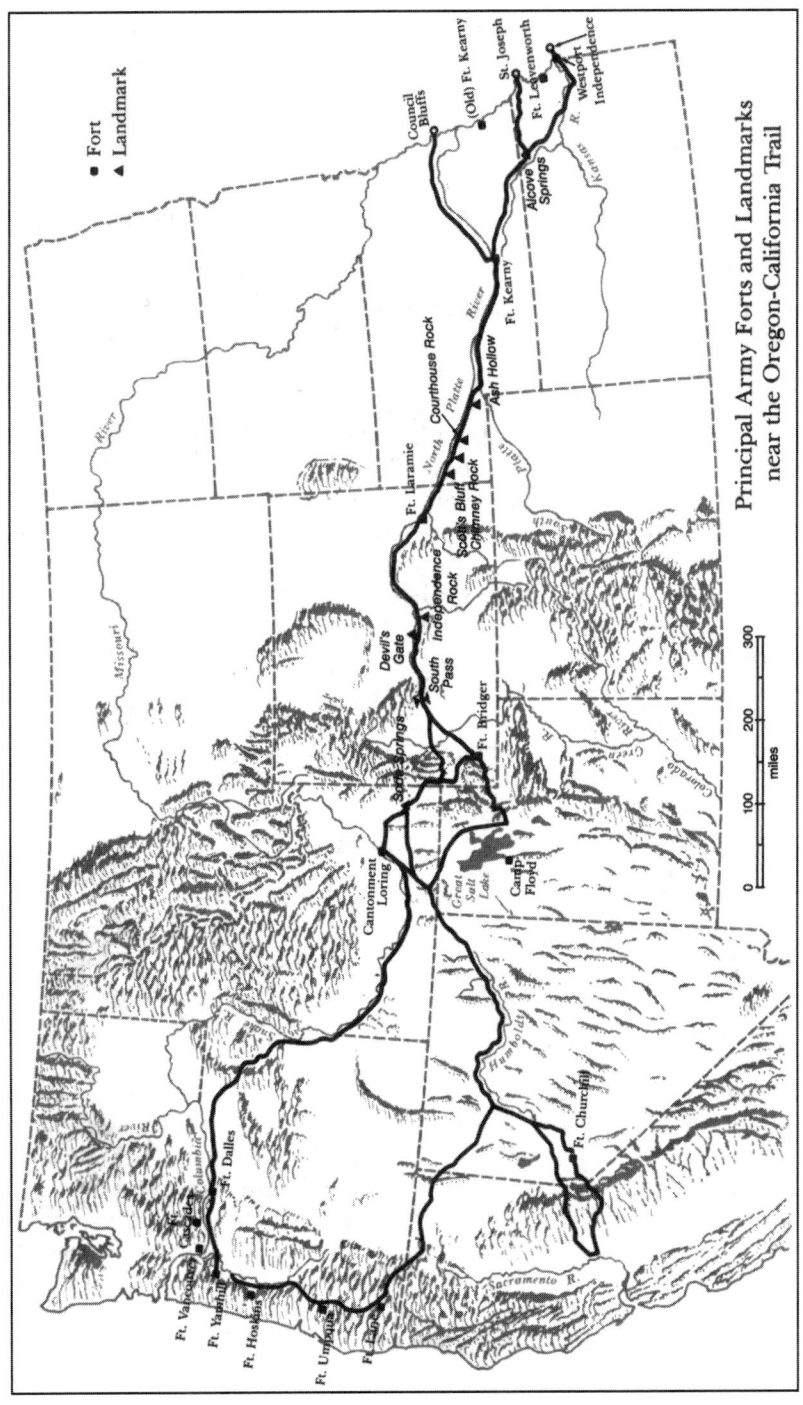

Principal Army Forts and Landmarks
near the Oregon-California Trail

decade of grievances. Emigrant-Indian and army-Indian skirmishes were increasingly the order of the day.

During the decade of the 1840s only minimal attempts had been made to satisfy accumulating Indian frustrations. To be sure, conventional wisdom recognized the importance of governmental representatives providing Indians with "presents" at every encounter. Senator Thomas H. Benton, for example, urged John C. Frémont to supply himself with ample quantities of suitable presents for his 1843 expedition, since "it is indispensable that the officer who carries the flag of the U. States into these remote regions, should carry presents. All savages expect them: they even demand them; and they feel contempt & resentment if disappointed." In the spring of 1848 Indian agent Thomas Fitzpatrick counseled peace to Arapaho and Sioux Indians along the Platte River, and the 1848 treaty by which the Pawnee Indians received $2,000 for 600 square miles around Grand Island had elicited Pawnee promises to refrain from molesting or injuring American travelers. In April, 1849, Governor Joseph Lane of Oregon Territory met with Cayuse and other Indians at The Dalles, gave them $200 in presents, and had them agree to meet oncoming overlanders in peace. Until 1851, however, this represented, in addition to the admonitions of army officers like Wharton and Kearny, the extent of governmental recognition of Indian distress at emigrant transit over their lands.

The 1850s, beginning with the Fort Laramie Treaty Council of 1851, were different. Agent Fitzpatrick, among others, had long encouraged a general treaty council with the plains tribes. In September Fitzpatrick and Superintendent David D. Mitchell of St. Louis met with over 10,000 Indians—the greatest gathering of plains tribes ever—at Horse Creek, some thirty-five miles east of Fort Laramie. The resultant treaty established tribal boundaries, specified peaceful relations among tribes, authorized the laying out of roads and construction of military posts in Indian territory, and provided for punishment and restitution of any depredations committed—by either Indian or white. For its part the United States promised an annuity of $50,000 of merchandise per year for fifty years. Soon after the signing ceremonies had been concluded, twenty-seven wagons rolled in direct from Fort Leavenworth with the first year's annuity. Additionally, Fitzpatrick escorted a delegation of Indian chiefs east to Washington, already a well-established tradition.

Although the treaty was initially regarded as successful, not all western tribes had been represented, and some that were eventually became troublesome. Therefore, beginning in 1852, Indian agents yearly traveled along the overland trails endeavoring to keep the peace, an activity of considerable importance in averting trail tragedies. Most of this trail peace-making took place west of South Pass—in the most dangerous travel locale— and among tribes which had not been represented at the 1851 Treaty Council. . . .

The desire for protection from marauding Indians prompted most emigrant requests for army troops and forts. Once military outposts had been established, however, it immediately became apparent that "protection" had many dimensions. In fact, for sizable numbers of overlanders the Indian fighting role of the frontier army was its *least* important function. To the chagrin of the commanding officers, emigrants came to depend upon the army outposts—particularly Forts Kearny and Laramie—for a host of services.

Not the least of these ancillary endeavors was dispensing information. Often doubting the accuracy of guidebooks or route information supplied by unknown persons met along the trails, overlanders were more inclined to trust their own government's army. An artist-naturalist who accompanied the Regiment of Mounted Riflemen to Oregon reported on the amusingly chaotic scene at Fort Kearny, where hordes of forty-niners made "thousands of inquiries on every conceivable subject." Troops encountered on the trails were plied with questions as zealously as were fort commanders, beginning with Kearny's dragoon march in 1845. Captain Philip Cooke noted that year that many overlanders "scarcely know where they are going; and these men eagerly question our guide—who has been in Oregon—on the simplest and best known points." In 1850 Major Chilton, Fort Kearny's commanding officer, dispatched an urgent message to all the major jumping-off towns that due to a late spring the prairie grasses were not yet able to support forage. In addition to advising overlanders to postpone their departure, Chilton cautioned them that no supplies or provisions would be available at any of the military forts that season.

Chilton's warning was sobering. Already in Kearny's and Laramie's first year many emigrants were in such dire need of food and other supplies, even though they had not yet traveled far from the jumping-off points, that post commanders and quartermasters felt compelled to assist hardship cases. At Fort Kearny provisions were kept in reserve for distribution to turn-around emigrants forced to forgo the trip and backtrack to their places of departure. Of course, Chilton's warning had fallen on deaf ears. Even though sutlers' stores were available at both forts from 1849 on, post commanders continued to be bombarded throughout the decade with urgent requests from emigrants who did not have the wherewithal to pay the sutlers' handsome prices. In 1850, at least at Fort Laramie, individuals without funds were generously given what they needed gratis. . . .

Considering the heavy armament favored by overlanders—fostered in part by the War Department's enticing 1849 offer to sell pistols, rifles, and ammunition at cost to California and Oregon emigrants—it was not surprising that a great many gunshot victims made their way to the fort hospitals. In mid-June, 1849, a passing overlander found four victims of accidental shootings under care at Fort Kearny, as well as a man whose arm had been amputated following a rattlesnake bite. Another four or five emigrant victims of firearm accidents were treated in the Fort Laramie hospital in July of 1849. Cholera also put many patients in fort hospitals and cemeteries, although resident troops remained surprisingly free of the disease. In June, 1850, alone, at least four overlanders died who had been left at Fort Laramie for treatment. In 1852 the hospitals at both Kearny and Laramie were filled with sick emigrants; at Kearny one observer reported the hospital so "crammed" that patients even occupied the soldiers' living quarters. Therefore it is probable that the sickly emigrant one company left in a makeshift tent near Fort Kearny with a fifteen-day supply of provisions because "they would not receive him at the Fort" was refused because the available facilities were so crowded. Doubtless the physician attended him in his tent, although the never-ending demands of diseased and injured overlanders did cause at least one army physician to lose his temper. This doctor, stationed at Fort Laramie, refused to treat some suffering overlanders, grumbling that neither he nor the fort had been placed there for the benefit of emigrants and that it made no difference to him whether the importuning overlanders lived or died. If true, this occurrence was an exception, for the overlanders almost uniformly agreed that the fort physicians were kind and generous. One even rode out from Kearny to administer to emigrants in surrounding camps. . . .

Matters of justice and law also occupied the attention of officers and men stationed at the forts, especially during the peak gold rush period. Since many bored, poorly paid soldiers were no more able to resist the lure of California gold than the thousands of their civilian countrymen thronging the routes west, desertions were common. Deserters often preyed upon the better-prepared emigrants. Four deserting Mounted Riflemen in 1849 robbed an emigrant of $200 and raped the man's wife. Although many soldiers deserted successfully, an army pursuit party caught these four near the Green River with some assistance from overlanders in the vicinity. The culprits were then marched back to Fort Laramie, on foot, to face charges.

Emigrant crime, while infrequent, periodically required the attention of Kearny and Laramie soldiers. Emigrants who stole horses from the army were energetically pursued. Troops were also apparently used to track down emigrants who had stolen possessions from other emigrants. There is fragmentary evidence that in 1849 army troops arrested up to forty emigrants for desecrating Indian graves and attempting to violate Indian women. As many as seven Indians may have been killed by the Pittsburgh emigrants allegedly involved. According to some accounts, the accused emigrants were being escorted to Fort Leavenworth to stand trial for murder. Finally, and certainly of considerable significance to the concerned parties, the Fort Laramie commanding officer adjudicated questions pertaining to traveling contracts. Explaining one such case in 1850, Dr. S. L. Grow commended the decision of an officer who fined and temporarily imprisoned a train captain who had refused to fulfill the terms of the contract he had made with one of his travelers. Grow approvingly concluded, "Good fellow Uncle Sam is." . . .

Federal assistance to overland emigrants was not limited to protection from Indians or ancillary benefits accruing from permanent trailside forts. Another substantial governmental contribution came through its exploration, survey, and road-building efforts. Although there were important developments during the 1840s—notably Frémont's reports of his explorations—once again it was not until the 1850s that governmental energies began to alter emigration patterns substantially. Those energies, channeled principally through the Army Corps of Topographical Engineers and the Interior Department's Pacific Wagon Road Office, had always been aimed at locating routes which would shorten and ease overland travel to Oregon and California.

Through 1855 the Corps of Topographical Engineers did the most significant work, and John Charles Frémont was by all odds their most illustrious explorer. Yet Frémont's relationship to overland travel is more intangible than that of some of his obscure colleagues. His real impact came not in the discovery of new and better trails, nor even the improvement of existing trails. Further, the intrepid Frémont had relatively little interaction with overlanders during his exploratory ventures. In 1842 his party traveled to the Rocky Mountains several weeks to the rear of the Oregon-bound emigrants; in 1843 there was only infrequent contact, as Frémont's party again spent much time off the main trail until late in the year. Rather, Frémont's importance came through publicity: the national publicity accorded his western heroics; the attention those activities centered on Oregon, enhancing American interest and commitment to that region; and the influence his well-written and generously distributed reports had on potential Oregon overlanders. Though technically a topographical engineer, Frémont always sought, in concert with his expansionist father-in-law, Senator Thomas Hart Benton of Missouri, to go beyond simple surveys or explorations. His expeditions invariably were aimed at the furtherance of broader national goals. For example, in the reports of 1842 and 1843–44 expeditions he carefully pointed out specific trail locations where American military posts could be situated to protect travelers to Oregon.

Thanks to Frémont's enthusiastic reports, many emigrants launched out for Oregon, and thanks to the excellent accompanying maps prepared by Charles Preuss they felt more comfortable in attempting the venture. Following Frémont's 1843–44 trip there was a hiatus in government activity, although Kearny's 1845 dragoon march had reconnaissance as a secondary objective. Also of momentary usefulness to overlanders were temporary bridges accruing from both Wharton's and Kearny's expeditions. . . .

In 1850 emigrants began using a new military road between Fort Leavenworth and the junction with the St. Joseph trace of the Oregon-California Trail. Laid out in April by Brevet Major Edmund A. Ogden, the road covered slightly more than 100 miles to its termination near the Big Blue River. Emigrants immediately praised the new trail, comparing it favorably with the older, longer, and more circuitous route.

For the next five years most reconnaissance missions pertained to the Pacific Railroad Surveys, an attempt to locate scientifically the best route for the transcontinental railroad. But with at least eight possible routes frequently advocated, and strong political and economic pressures involved, objectivity was hard to come by. The South Pass route, traversed yearly by thousands of overland emigrants, was neither included in the 1853–54 surveys nor given serious consideration. The only reconnaissance with potential relevance for travelers on the Oregon-California Trail was Frederick

Lander's essentially private survey from Puget Sound to Council Bluffs via South Pass in 1854—a route on which Lander reported favorably. . . .

By 1856 a great deal of western territory had been thoroughly surveyed, but no decision on a single Pacific railroad seemed imminent. Since only a few trail improvements had resulted despite all the reconnaissance activity, westerners began to petition Congress zealously for serviceable wagon roads. The Congress responded with a number of appropriations, several relating to the Oregon-California Trail. Thus, during the last four years of the decade the regular trail was markedly improved and several significant cutoffs were appended to it. . . .

At the heart of the demand for improved wagon roads was the fervent desire for quick and reliable communication between the fast-growing far western communities and the rest of the nation. The inconvenience of an irregular postal service was especially frustrating during the years of the gold rush, when family groups no longer were commonplace but males dominated both the trails and the California mining camps. Overlanders had been anxious for letters from loved ones by the time they reached the jumping-off points. Three or four months later, after a long and tedious overland journey, they were desperate for news of parents, wives, sweethearts, friends, and relatives. They queued up in front of post offices after every sea mail arrived—and sometimes even before. In hopes that letters would await them in California, overlanders instructed correspondents to write frequently. Henry Page directed his wife to adopt "write, write, write" as her motto. . . .

The initial beginnings were modest. Salt Lake City was the hub of the mail system, a government post office having been established there during the winter of 1849. A "monthly" mail between Independence and Salt Lake commenced on August 1 the following year, when Thomas D. Scroggins left Independence with mule-drawn light wagons to transport the mail. Scroggins was employed by James Brown and Samuel H. Woodson, who had received the government contract specifying departure from Independence and Salt Lake on the first day of every month with stops at Uniontown on the Kansas River and Forts Kearny, Laramie, and Bridger. Yearly remuneration for contractors Brown (who died in December of 1850) and Woodson was $19,500. Scroggins reached Salt Lake over a week late, on September 9, and returned to Independence over three weeks late, on October 24, thereby establishing what would be a recurring pattern. In 1851 Woodson subcontracted the Salt Lake–to–Fort Laramie section with mails scheduled to be exchanged at Laramie on the 15th of each month. That year contracts were also let for a similar system between Salt Lake City and Sacramento, with George Chorpenning and Absolom Woodward receiving $14,000 per year for a monthly mail. Chorpenning inaugurated the service with his May 1, 1851, departure from the California city. . . .

Indian troubles were not uncommon (Absolom Woodward and two of his men were killed in 1851), and mail contractors regularly appealed for and received compensation for their losses. Troop detachments periodically escorted the mail stages or were dispatched to chastise Indians accused of molesting the mailmen. Annual payments to contractors had to be occasionally revised upward. Meanwhile overland emigrants continued to deposit letters at the several locations designated as mail stations, complaining on occasion that they were being charged an illegal fee. And from the mail carriers they encountered on the trails overlanders received the latest trail information, recent newspapers with local and national news, and quick letter service. For their part emigrants occasionally provided the mail carriers with something to eat.

With the awarding of a $190,000 contract for weekly mail service between Independence and Salt Lake to John M. Hockaday in April, 1858, federal mail service on the South Pass route entered an accelerated phase. New post office–stage stations now began to appear. At the other end of the route George Chorpenning received an 1858 contract for $130,000. It likewise specified weekly service between Placerville and Salt Lake. Hockaday's contract committed him to twenty-two-day service, Chorpenning's to sixteen—a mail service from Independence to Placerville of thirty-eight days. Since a semi-weekly overland mail had already been contracted for a southern route, this 1858 upgrading of service on the central route was prompted largely by the War Department's need for swift communication with its large army base near Salt Lake City. The southern-sympathizing postmaster general had awarded a 600,000-dollar yearly contract to John Butterfield in 1857 and essentially forced him to operate on a St. Louis, Memphis, Little Rock, El Paso, Tucson, and Fort Yuma route. Although Butterfield's Overland Mail rendered acceptable service, it did not quell demands for a mail line on the central route.

In 1859 a new postmaster general deemed economy measures to be in order. Cuts were made on the various overland mail operations, Hockaday and Chorpenning being reduced to semi-monthly service. These reductions were a severe financial blow, for by now it was obvious that massive governmental financing was crucial to any enterprise of this scope. Hockaday's and Chorpenning's financially troubled concerns were quickly subsumed by Russell, Majors, and Waddell's Central Overland California and Pike's Peak Express Company, which itself was soon in precarious financial straits. Then the ever-optimistic Russell conceived the Pony Express venture of 1860: a desperate attempt to convince the Congress of the year-round superiority of the central route and thereby secure the large federal stipend for overland mail service which was the last hope for Russell, Majors, and Waddell's financially troubled enterprise.

Russell's Pony Express relay stations strung along the overland trail in a bold attempt to win federal financing graphically demonstrated that within little more than a decade the U.S. government had been responsible for sweeping innovations in the trans-Mississippi West, innovations which much affected the nature and style of overland travel. By 1860 overlanders did not even need to travel in the traditional manner: they could bounce from Missouri to California as passengers in the stagecoaches specified in the government mail contracts. If, as almost all continued to do, they chose to travel in the customary covered wagon or by pack train, they did so on trails which had been surveyed, shortened, graded, and improved by government employees. Overlanders even enjoyed the luxury of crossing bridged streams and watering their stock at large reservoirs. For the injured or ill there were army hospitals along the route, and sutlers, blacksmiths, and generous commanding officers standing ready to distribute provisions to destitute travelers. There were even post offices where letters were mailed *and* received. More important, there were troops to escort overlanders along dangerous portions of the trail, and Indian agents to negotiate with chiefs and buy or bribe native acquiescence to overland travel. The government had transformed the trail into a road.

It is, of course, a moot point whether all these federal services were undivided benefits. The federal presence in the form of permanent forts, patrolling soldiers, and, occasionally, blundering and incompetent officers irritated Indians and sometimes provoked hostilities. It is at least possible that had there been no permanent federal presence along the trails there would have been less need for any. But that was more a question for future historians than for an emigrant of the 1850s. What mattered most to him was that Uncle Sam, that good fellow, had done and was doing much to expedite his overland journey.

Y *F U R T H E R   R E A D I N G*

Stephen E. Ambrose, *Undaunted Courage: Meriwether Lewis, Thomas Jefferson, and the Opening of the American West* (1996)
John Logan Allen, *Passage Through the Garden: Lewis and Clark and the Image of the American Northwest* (1975)
William A. Bowen, *The Willamette Valley: Migration and Settlement on the Oregon Frontier* (1978)
Vernon Cartensen, ed., *The Public Lands: Studies in the History of the Public Domain* (1962)
Richard M. Clokey, *William H. Ashley: Enterprise and Politics in the Trans-Mississippi West* (1980)
John Mack Faragher, *Women and Men on the Overland Trail* (1979)
Robert W. Frazer, *Forts and Supplies: The Role of the Army in the Economy of the Southwest* (1983)
Paul W. Gates, *History of Public Land Law Development* (1968)
William H. Goetzmann, *Army Exploration in the American West, 1803–1863* (1959)
——, *Exploration and Empire: The Explorer and the Scientist in the Winning of the American West* (1966)
Leroy R. Hafen and Ann W. Hafen, *Handcarts to Zion* (1960)
Harlan Hague, *The Road to California: The Search for a Southern Overland Route, 1540–1848* (1978)
David F. Hawke, *Those Tremendous Mountains: The Story of the Lewis and Clark Expedition* (1980)
Donald Jackson, *Thomas Jefferson and the Stony Mountains: Exploring the West from Monticello* (1981)
Turrentine W. Jackson, *Wagon Roads West: A Study of Federal Roads and Surveys and Construction in the Trans-Mississippi West* (1980)

Hildegard Birder Johnson, *Order on the Land: The U.S. Rectangular Land Survey and the Upper Mississippi Country* (1976)

David Lavender, *The Way to the Western Sea: Lewis and Clark across the Continent* (1988)

Merrill J. Mattes, *The Great Platte River Road: The Covered Wagon Mainline via Fort Kearney to Fort Laramie* (1969)

Gerland McFarland, *A Scattered People: An American Family Moves West* (1985)

Gary E. Moulton, ed., *The Journals of Lewis and Clark,* vols. 2–7 (1986–1991)

Roger L. Nichols and Patrick L. Halley, *Stephen Long and American Frontier Exploration* (1980)

John Philip Reid, *Law for the Elephant: Property and Social Behavior on the Overland Trail* (1980)

Roy M. Robbins, *Our Landed Heritage: The Public Domain, 1776–1970* (2nd ed., 1970)

Malcolm J. Rohrbough, *The Land Office Business: The Settlement and Administration of American Public Lands, 1789–1837* (1968)

James P. Ronda, *Lewis and Clark Among the Indians* (1984)

——, *Astoria & Empire* (1990)

Lillian Schlissel, *Women's Diaries of the Westward Journey* (1982)

Jerome O. Steffen, *William Clark: Jeffersonian Man on the Frontier* (1977)

Wallace Stegner, *Beyond the Hundredth Meridian: John Wesley Powell and the Second Opening of the West* (1954)

——, *The Gathering of Zion: The Story of the Mormon Trail* (1964)

The Legacy of Acquisition

Y

How did the United States acquire the lands that became the American West? For nationalists of the mid-nineteenth century, the answer seemed obvious. It was the "manifest destiny" of the United States to stretch from ocean to ocean and possibly beyond. Can this dramatic expansion be explained by a series of peaceful agreements? Certainly not. The Louisiana Purchase seemed like an amiable international arrangement, but only if one ignores the larger context of Europe's Napoleonic wars and the successful slave rebellion against the French in what became Haiti. Then, Louisiana appears to be a wartime fire sale by the French. No claims of peaceful acquisition can be made for the land added to the United States after war with Mexico in the mid-1840s. And, Native Americans in the nineteenth century lost much of their lands through a series of wars, forced removals, broken treaties, and inept government policies. The Gadsden Purchase of 1853 increased the southwestern territory of the United States for $10 million, whereas the even larger expanse of Alaska cost only $7 million in 1867. These additions came peacefully, but the farthest western land, the islands of Hawai`i, did not. As with Texas in the mid-1830s, a rebellion by pro-American residents in the 1890s led eventually to annexation. All these acquisitions added a grand diversity of landscapes and peoples to the enlarged United States. How ready were the proponents of Manifest Destiny in the nineteenth century to accept this legacy of diversity? Did their supreme confidence about westward expansion ignore the realities of cultures in collision?

Y *D O C U M E N T S*

The first three documents reveal attitudes about war between the United States and Mexico. Two Mexican military leaders, Mariano Arista and Anastasio Par-rode, address different audiences. To the American troops across the Rio Bravo—named the Rio Grande by the Americans—General Arista emphasized the unjust reasons for war between neighbors. He also wanted the soldiers to abandon their duties and join his ranks. How sincere was his offer? In the second document, Mexican commander Anastasio Parrode, addressed his own troops and vigorously urged them on to battle despite their recent defeat. The third document is a Texan's enthusiastic approval of the war. Charles DeMorse reminded his readers of those who had died during the Texas Revolution, especially at the "massacre of the Alamo." With Arista's and Parrode's fervent nationalism and DeMorse's demand for vengeance, could Mexicans accept the war's results and expect fair treatment from the Americans?

Documents four and five present the debate in the U.S. Congress in January of 1848 after the conclusion of the war. Senator John C. Calhoun of South Carolina, the great advocate of black slavery, argued that the conquered nation of Mexico should not be incorporated into the United States. He based his view on a system of racial hierarchy that placed some Indian tribes above the Mexicans. Senator John A. Dix of New York believed differently. He spoke of the inevitable expansion of the United States that, to his thinking, dictated the annexation of some of Mexico and its peoples. Both Calhoun and Dix expressed their opinions about the undesirable results of mixing races. Can it be assumed that many American leaders wished to acquire Mexican lands but did not wish to include Mexicans?

The final two documents consider another story of acquisition—Hawai`i. The last monarch of the kingdom of Hawai`i, Queen Lilioukalani had been forced to abdicate her throne on January 19, 1895. The descendants of Anglo-American missionaries working with pro-American business interests established the Republic of Hawai`i in 1894. On February 5, 1895, a military tribunal charged Lilioukalani with treason against the republic. On the day of her trial, she pleaded not guilty and spoke directly in Hawaiian. Document five is a transcription of her speech, which indicates the role played by the United States in the overthrow of her kingdom. Lilioukalani remained under arrest for twenty-one months. The United States formally annexed Hawai`i in 1898, but to many Native Hawaiians a bitter legacy remains. Document six is a statement by Haunani-Kay Trask published in 1993. A member of Ka Lāhui Hawai`i, an initiative by Native Hawaiians for self-government, Trask is also director of the Center for Hawaiian Studies at the University of Hawai`i. Her impassioned anger demonstrates that native peoples have a distinctly different view of the history of America's westward expansion.

Mexican General Mariano Arista's Advice to the Soldiers of the U.S. Army, 1846

Head-Quarters at Matamoros, April 20, 1846

Soldiers!—You have enlisted in time of peace to serve in that army for a specific term; but your obligation never implied that you were bound to violate the laws of God, and the most sacred rights of friends! The United States government, contrary to the wishes of a majority of all honest and honourable Americans, has ordered you to take *forcible* possession of the territory of a *friendly* neighbour, who has never given her consent to such

---

J'Nell L. Pate, *Document Sets for Texas and the Southwest in U.S. History* (Lexington, Mass.: D. C. Heath and Co., 1991), 62–63.

occupation. In other words, while the treaty of peace and commerce between Mexico and the United States is in full force, the United States, presuming on her strength and prosperity, and on our supposed imbecility and cowardice, attempts to make you the blind instruments of her unholy and mad ambition, and *force* you to appear as the hateful robbers of our dear homes, and the unprovoked violators of our dearest feelings as men and patriots. Such villany and outrage, I know, is perfectly repugnant to the noble sentiments of any gentleman, and it is base and foul to rush you on to certain death, in order to aggrandize a few lawless individuals, in defiance of the laws of God and man!

It is to no purpose if they tell you, that the law for the annexation of Texas justifies your occupation of the Rio Bravo del Norte; for by this act they rob us of a great part of *Tamaulipas, Coahuila, Chichuahua, and New Mexico;* and it is barbarous to send a handful of men on such an errand against a powerful and warlike nation. Besides, the most of you are Europeans, and we are the *declared friends* of a majority of the nations of *Europe.* The North Americans are ambitious, overbearing, and insolent as a nation, and they will only make use of you as vile tools to carry out their abominable plans of pillage and rapine.

I warn you in the name of justice, honour, and your own interests and self-respect, to abandon their desperate and unholy cause, and become *peaceful Mexican citizens.* I guarantee you, in such case, a half section of land, or three hundred and twenty acres, to settle upon, gratis. Be wise, then, and just, and honourable, and take no part in murdering us who have no unkind feelings for you. Lands shall be given to officers, sergeants, and corporals, according to rank, privates receiving three hundred and twenty acres, as stated.

If, in time of action, you wish to espouse our cause, throw away your arms and run to us, and we will embrace you as true friends and Christians. It is not decent nor prudent to say more. But should any of you render important service to Mexico, you shall be accordingly considered and preferred.

M. Arista,
Commander-in-Chief of the Mexican Army

Anastasio Parrode, Commander-in-Chief of the Department of Tamaulipas, to His Troops, 1846

Fellow-Citizens: The afternoon of the 8th of this month our brothers of Matamoros have fought with intrepidity and enthusiasm in the Fanques del Raminero. On the 9th they charged with the same ardour. But fate has not crowned our efforts. The enemy passed from the fort, favoured by the dense smoke of a wood on fire, which protected them from our shot. Thus have our enemies escaped!

J'Nell L. Pate, *Document Sets for Texas and the Southwest in U.S. History* (Lexington, Mass.: D. C. Heath and Co., 1991), 63–64.

Soldiers! another time we shall conquer. Such is the fate of war, a defeat to-day and glory tomorrow; that glory which shall be ours at the end of this holy struggle. The God of battles is trying our valour, but he had not abandoned us. We know how to conquer, and we know how to suffer.

Soldiers! the lamentation of the soldier for the companion who dies on the field of battle ought to be shot well-aimed at the enemy. Those are the tears which our brothers require of our love. Their tomb must be raised in the American camp. The corpses of the Yankees ought to form their mausoleums.

Soldiers! if we have lost some of our brothers, the glory will be greater, there will be fewer conquerors; it is not the number which gives victory. There were but three hundred Spartans, and the powerful Xerxes did not cross the Thermopylæ. The celebrated army of the great Napoleon perished in Spain at the hands of a defenceless people, but they were free and intrepid, and were fighting for their liberty.

Fellow-soldiers! shall we do less than they did? We are fighting for our liberty, our religion, our country, our cradles, our graves. Let him who does not wish to die a traitor, him who wishes to deserve the tears of his children, let him take breath and sustain his courage. He must not faint, he must not fear, but what have we to fear? The heart tells us that in it we shall find all that is requisite; and our hearts we will oppose to the enemy.

Soldiers! vengeance for our brothers! glory for our children! honour for our country!

We defend those cherished feelings. Do not fear. I swear to you that if the day be a laborious one, our glory will be sweeter; but glory we will have, and your general and companion will attain it with your loyalty and valour.

Anastasio Parrode
Tampico, May 13th, 1846

Charles DeMorse Gives a Texan's View of the War with Mexico, 1846

From the *Northern Standard* (Clarksville, Texas), May 13, 1846.

At last we have a real "sure enough" war on hand; something to warm the blood, and draw out the national enthusiasm. It seems that the "Magnanimous Mexican Nation" has at last come out of its chapparal of wordy diplomacy, treachery, meanness and bombast, and concluded for a little while, only a little while, to act like white people. There is at last—our pulses beat quickly with the thought—an opportunity to pay off a little of the debt of vengeance which has been accumulating since the massacre of the Alamo.

We trust that every man of our army, as he points his rifle and thrusts his bayonet, will think of his countrymen martyred at the Alamo, at Goliad,

Ernest Wallace, David M. Vigness, George B. Ward, eds., *Documents of Texas History* (Austin, Texas: State House Press, 1994), 163.

and at Mier, whose blood yet cries aloud from the ground for remembrance and vengeance, and taking a little closer aim or giving a little stronger thrust, will give his blow in his country's cause and an additional "God speed."

John C. Calhoun Opposes Incorporating Mexico, 1848

Sir, we have heard how much glory our country has acquired in this war. I acknowledge it to the full amount, Mr. President, so far as military glory is concerned. The army has done nobly, chivalrously; they have conferred honor on the country, for which I sincerely thank them.

. . . Now, sir, much as I regard military glory; much as I rejoice to behold our people in possession of the indomitable energy and courage which surmount all difficulties, and which class them amongst the first military people of the age, I would be very sorry indeed that our Government should lose any reputation for wisdom, moderation, discretion, justice, and those other high qualities which have distinguished us in the early stages of our history.

. . . It is without example or precedent, either to hold Mexico as a province, or to incorporate her into our Union. No example of such a line of policy can be found. We have conquered many of the neighboring tribes of Indians, but we never thought of holding them in subjection—never of incorporating them into our Union. They have either been left as an independent people amongst us, or been driven into the forests.

I know further, sir, that we have never dreamt of incorporating into our Union any but the Caucasian race—the free white race. To incorporate Mexico, would be the very first instance of the kind of incorporating an Indian race; for more than half of the Mexicans are Indians, and the other is composed chiefly of mixed tribes. I protest against such a union as that! Ours, sir, is the Government of a white race. The greatest misfortunes of Spanish America are to be traced to the fatal error of placing these colored races on an equality with the white race. That error destroyed the social arrangement which formed the basis of society. The Portuguese and ourselves have escaped—the Portuguese at least to some extent—and we are the only people on this continent which have made revolutions without being followed by anarchy. And yet it is professed and talked about to erect these Mexicans into a Territorial Government, and place them on an equality with the people of the United States. I protest utterly against such a project.

Sir, it is a remarkable fact, that in the whole history of man, as far as my knowledge extends, there is no instance whatever of any civilized colored races being found equal to the establishment of free popular government, although by far the largest portion of the human family is composed of these races. And even in the savage state we scarcely find them anywhere with such government, except it be our noble savages—for noble I will call

From *The Congressional Globe*, 30th Cong., 1st sess., 1848, January 4, 1848, 98–99, 136–137.

them. They, for the most part, had free institutions, but they are easily sustained amongst a savage people. Are we to overlook this fact? Are we to associate with ourselves as equals, companions, and fellow-citizens, the Indians and mixed race of Mexico? Sir, I should consider such a thing as fatal to our institutions. . . .

I come now to the proposition of incorporating her into our Union. Well, as far as law is concerned, that is easy. You can establish a Territorial Government for every State in Mexico, and there are some twenty of them. You can appoint governors, judges, and magistrates. You can give the people a subordinate government, allowing them to legislate for themselves, whilst you defray the cost. So far as law goes, the thing is done. There is no analogy between this and our Territorial Governments. Our Territories are only an offset of our own people, or foreigners from the same regions from which we came. They are small in number. They are incapable of forming a government. It would be inconvenient for them to sustain a government, if it were formed; and they are very much obliged to the United States for undertaking the trouble, knowing that, on the attainment of their majority—when they come to manhood—at twenty-one—they will be introduced to an equality with all the other members of the Union. It is entirely different with Mexico. You have no need of armies to keep your Territories in subjection. But when you incorporate Mexico, you must have powerful armies to keep them in subjection. You may call it annexation, but it is a forced annexation, which is a contradiction in terms, according to my conception. You will be involved, in one word, in all the evils which I attribute to holding Mexico as a province. In fact, it will be but a Provincial Government, under the name of a Territorial Government. How long will that last? How long will it be before Mexico will be capable of incorporation into our Union? Why, if we judge from the examples before us, it will be a very long time. Ireland has been held in subjection by England for seven or eight hundred years, and yet still remains hostile, although her people are of kindred race with the conquerors. A few French Canadians on this continent yet maintain the attitude of hostile people; and never will the time come, in my opinion, Mr. President, that these Mexicans will be heartily reconciled to your authority. They have Castilian blood in their veins—the old Gothic, quite equal to the Anglo-Saxon in many respects—in some respects superior. Of all nations of the earth they are the most pertinacious—have the highest sense of nationality—hold out longest, and often even with the least prospect of effecting their object. On this subject also I have conversed with officers of the army, and they all entertain the same opinion, that these people are now hostile, and will continue so.

But, Mr. President, suppose all these difficulties removed; suppose these people attached to our Union, and desirous of incorporating with us, ought we to bring them in? Are they fit to be connected with us? Are they fit for self-government and for governing you? Are you, any of you, willing that your States should be governed by these twenty-odd Mexican States, with a population of about only one million of your blood, and two or three millions of mixed blood, better informed, all the rest pure Indians, a mixed blood equally ignorant and unfit for liberty, impure races, not as good as the Cherokees or Choctaws?

We make a great mistake, sir, when we suppose that all people are capable of self-government. We are anxious to force free government on all; and I see that it has been urged in a very respectable quarter, that it is the mission of this country to spread civil and religious liberty over all the world, and especially over this continent. It is a great mistake. None but people advanced to a very high state of moral and intellectual improvement are capable, in a civilized state, of maintaining free government; and amongst those who are so purified, very few, indeed, have had the good fortune of forming a constitution capable of endurance.

John A. Dix Advocates Expansion onto Mexican Lands, 1848

Sir, no one who has paid a moderate degree of attention to the laws and elements of our increase, can doubt that our population is destined to spread itself across the American continent, filling up, with more or less completeness, according to attractions of soil and climate, the space that intervenes between the Atlantic and Pacific oceans. This eventual, and, perhaps, in the order of time, this not very distant extension of our settlements over a tract of country, with a diameter, as we go westward, greatly disproportioned to its length, becomes a subject of the highest interest to us. On the whole extent of our northern flank, from New Brunswick to the point where the northern boundary of Oregon touches the Pacific, we are in contact with British colonists, having, for the most part, the same common origin with ourselves, but controlled and moulded by political influences from the Eastern hemisphere, if not adverse, certainly not decidedly friendly to us. The strongest tie which can be relied on to bind us to mutual offices of friendship and good neighborhood, is that of commerce; and this, as we know, is apt to run into rivalry, and sometimes becomes a fruitful source of alienation.

From our northern boundary, we turn to our southern. What races are to border on us here, what is to be their social and political character, and what their means of annoyance? Are our two frontiers, only seven parallels of latitude apart when we pass Texas, to be flanked by settlements having no common bond of union with ours? Our whole southern line is conterminous, throughout its whole extent, with the territories of Mexico, a large portion of which is nearly unpopulated. The geographical area of Mexico is about 1,500,000 square miles, and her population about 7,000,000 souls. The whole northern and central portion, taking the twenty-sixth parallel of latitude as the dividing line, containing more than 1,000,000 square miles, has about 650,000 inhabitants—about two inhabitants to three square miles. The southern portion, with less than 500,000 square miles, has a population of nearly six and a half millions of souls, or thirteen inhabitants

From *The Congressional Globe*, January 26, 1848, pp. 181–182.

to one square mile. The aboriginal races, which occupy and overrun a portion of California and New Mexico, must there, as everywhere else, give way before the advancing wave of civilization, either to be overwhelmed by it, or to be driven upon perpetually contracting areas, where, from a diminution of their accustomed sources of subsistence, they must ultimately become extinct by force of an invincible law. We see the operation of this law in every portion of this continent. We have no power to control it, if we would. It is the behest of Providence that idleness, and ignorance, and barbarism, shall give place to industry, and knowledge, and civilization. The European and mixed races, which possess Mexico, are not likely, either from moral or physical energy, to become formidable rivals or enemies. The bold and courageous enterprise which overran and conquered Mexico, appears not to have descended to the present possessors of the soil. Either from the influence of climate or the admixture of races—the fusion of castes, to use the technical phrase—the conquerors have, in turn, become the conquered. The ancient Castilian energy is, in a great degree, subdued; and it has given place, with many other noble traits of the Spanish character, to a peculiarity which seems to have marked the race in that country, under whatever combinations it is found—a proneness to civil discord, and a suicidal waste of its own strength.

With such a territory and such a people on our southern border, what is to be the inevitable course of empire? It needs no powers of prophecy to foretell. Sir, I desire to speak plainly: why should we not, when we are discussing the operation of moral and physical laws, which are beyond our control? As our population moves westward on our own territory, portions will cross our southern boundary. Settlements will be formed within the unoccupied and sparsely-peopled territory of Mexico. Uncongenial habits and tastes, differences of political opinion and principle, and numberless other elements of diversity will lead to a separation of these newly-formed societies from the inefficient government of Mexico. They will not endure to be held in subjection to a system, which neither yields them protection nor offers any incentive to their proper development and growth. They will form independent States on the basis of constitutions identical in all their leading features with our own; and they will naturally seek to unite their fortunes to ours. The fate of California is already sealed: it can never be reunited to Mexico. The operation of the great causes, to which I have alluded, must, at no distant day, detach the whole of northern Mexico from the southern portion of that republic. It is for the very reason that she is incapable of defending her possessions against the elements of disorder within and the progress of better influences from without, that I desire to see the inevitable political change which is to be wrought in the condition of her northern departments, brought about without any improper interference on our part.

Queen Liliuokalani's Statement at Her Trial
for Treason, 1895

The only charge against me really was that of being a queen; and my case was judged by these, my adversaries, before I came into court. I remember with clearness, however, the attack upon me by the Judge Advocate, the words that issued from his mouth about "the prisoner," "that woman," etc., uttered with such affectation of contempt and disgust. The object of it was evidently to humiliate me, to make me break down in the presence of the staring crowd. But in this they were disappointed. My equanimity was never disturbed; and their own report relates that I throughout preserved "that haughty carriage" which marked me as an "unusual woman."

I said nothing to their taunts and innuendoes, and showed no emotion; but when the proper time came, I denied that I had been guilty of any treasonable action, and asked my counsel to submit the following statement:—

"In the year 1893, on the fifteenth day of January, at the request of a large majority of the Hawaiian people, and by and with the consent of my cabinet, I proposed to make certain changes in the constitution of the Hawaiian kingdom, which were suggested to me as being for the advantage and benefit of the kingdom, and subjects and residents thereof. These proposed changes did not deprive foreigners of any rights or privileges enjoyed by them under the constitution of 1887, promulgated by King Kalakaua and his cabinet, without the consent of the people or ratified by their votes.

"My ministers at the last moment changed their views, and requested me to defer all action in connection with the constitution; and I yeilded to their advice as bound to do by the existing constitution and laws.

"A minority of the foreign population made my action the pretext for overthrowing the monarchy, and, aided by the United States naval forces and representative, established a new government.

"I owed no allegiance to the Provisional Government so established, nor to any power or to any one save the will of my people and the welfare of my country.

"The wishes of my people were not consulted as to this change of government, and only those who were in practical rebellion against the constitutional government were allowed to vote upon the question whether the monarchy should exist or not.

"To prevent the shedding of the blood of my people, natives and foreigners alike, I opposed armed interference, and quietly yielded to the armed forces brought against my throne, and submitted to the arbitrament of the government of the United States the decision of my rights and those of the Hawaiian people. Since then, as is well known to all, I have pursued the path of peace and diplomatic discussion, and not that of internal strife.

"The United States having first interfered in the interest of those founding the government of 1893 upon the basis of revolution, concluded to leave to the Hawaiian people the selection of their own form of government.

"This selection was anticipated and prevented by the Provisional Government, who, being possessed of the military and police power of the kingdom, so cramped the electoral privileges that no free expression of their will was permitted to the people who were opposed to them.

"By my command and advice the native people and those in sympathy with them were restrained from rising against the government in power.

"The movement undertaken by the Hawaiians last month was absolutely commenced without my knowledge, sanction, consent, or assistance, directly or indirectly; and this fact is in truth well known to those who took part in it.

"I received no information from any one in regard to arms which were, or which were to be, procured, nor of any men who were induced, or to be induced, to join in any such uprising.

"I do not know why this information should have been withheld from me, unless it was with a view to my personal safety, or as a precautionary measure. It would not have received my sanction; and I can assure the gentlemen of this commission that, had I known of any such intention, I would have dissuaded the promoters from such a venture. But I will add that, had I known, their secrets would have been mine, and inviolately preserved.

"That I intended to change my cabinet, and to appoint certain officers of the kingdom, in the event of my restoration, I will admit; but that I, or any one known to me, had, in part or in whole, established a new government, is not true. Before the 24th of January, 1895, the day upon which I formally abdicated, and called upon my people to recognize the Republic of Hawaii as the only lawful government of these Islands, and to support that government, I claim that I had the right to select a cabinet in anticipation of a possibility; and history of other governments supports this right. I was not intimidated into abdicating, but followed the counsel of able and generous friends and well-wishers, who advised me that such an act would restore peace and good-will among my people, vitalize the progress and prosperity of the Islands, and induce the actual government to deal leniently, mercifully, charitably, and impassionately with those who resorted to arms for the purpose of displacing a government in the formation of which they had no voice or control, and which they themselves had seen established by force of arms.

"I acted of my own free will, and wish the world to know that I have asked no immunity or favor myself, nor plead my abdication as a petition for mercy. My actions were dictated by the sole aim of doing good to my beloved country, and of alleviating the positions and pains of those who unhappily and unwisely resorted to arms to regain an independence which they thought had been unjustly wrested from them.

"As you deal with them, so I pray that the Almighty God may deal with you in your hours of trial.

"To my regret much has been said about the danger which threatened foreign women and children, and about the bloodthirstiness of the

Hawaiians, and the outrages which would have been perpetrated by them if they had succeeded in their attempt to overthrow the Republic government.

"They who know the Hawaiian temper and disposition understand that there was no foundation for any such fears. The behavior of the rebels to those foreigners whom they captured and held shows that there was no malignancy in the hearts of the Hawaiians at all. It would have been sad indeed if the doctrine of the Christian missionary fathers, taught to my people by them and those who succeeded them, should have fallen like the seed in the parable, upon barren ground.

"I must deny your right to try me in the manner and by the court which you have called together for this purpose. In your actions you violate your own constitution and laws, which are now the constitution and laws of the land.

"There may be in your consciences a warrant for your action, in what you may deem a necessity of the times; but you cannot find any such warrant for any such action in any settled, civilized, or Christian land. All who uphold you in this unlawful proceeding may scorn and despise my word; but the offence of breaking and setting aside for a specific purpose the laws of your own nation, and disregarding all justice and fairness, may be to them and to you the source of an unhappy and much to be regretted legacy.

"I would ask you to consider that your government is on trial before the whole civilized world, and that in accordance with your actions and decisions will you yourselves be judged. The happiness and prosperity of Hawaii are henceforth in your hands as its rulers. You are commencing a new era in its history. May the divine Providence grant you the wisdom to lead the nation into the paths of forbearance, forgiveness, and peace, and to create and consolidate a united people ever anxious to advance in the way of civilization outlined by the American fathers of liberty and religion.

"In concluding my statement I thank you for the courtesy you have shown to me, not as your former queen, but as an humble citizen of this land and as a woman. I assure you, who believe you are faithfully fulfilling a public duty, that I shall never harbor any resentment or cherish any ill feeling towards you, whatever may be your decision."

From Haunani-Kay Trask, a Native Daughter in Colony Hawai`i, 1993

On the ancient burial grounds of our ancestors, glass and steel shopping malls with layered parking lots stretch over what were once the most ingeniously irrigated taro lands, lands that fed millions of our people over thousands of years. Large bays, delicately ringed long ago with well-stocked fishponds, are now heavily silted and cluttered with jet skis, windsurfers, and sailboats. Multistory hotels disgorge over six million tourists a year onto stunningly beautiful (and easily polluted) beaches, closing off access to locals. On the major islands of Hawai`i, Maui, O`ahu, and Kaua`i, meanwhile, military airfields, training camps, weapons storage facilities, and exclusive housing and beach areas remind the Native Hawaiian who owns Hawai`i: the foreign, colonizing country called the United States of America.

Because of the overthrow and annexation, Hawaiian control and Hawaiian citizenship were replaced with American control and American citizenship. We suffered a unilateral redefinition of our homeland and our people, a displacement and a dispossession in our own country. In familial terms, our mother (and thus our heritage and our inheritance) was taken from us. We were orphaned in our own land. Such brutal changes in a people's identity—their legal status, their government, their sense of belonging to a nation—are considered among the most serious human rights violations by the international community today.

As a result of these actions, Hawaiians became a conquered people, our lands and culture subordinated to another nation. Made to feel and survive as inferiors when our sovereignty as a nation was forcibly ended, we were rendered politically and economically powerless by the turn of the century. Cultural imperialism had taken hold with conversion to Christianity in the middle of the 19th century, but it continued with the closing of all Hawaiian language schools and the elevation of English as the only official language in 1896. Once the Republic of Hawai`i declared itself on July 4, 1894, the "Americanization" of Hawai`i was sealed like a coffin.

Today, Hawaiians continue to suffer the effects of *haole* colonization. Under foreign control, we have been overrun by settlers: missionaries and capitalists (often the same people), adventurers and, of course, hordes of tourists, nearly 7 million by 1993. Preyed upon by corporate tourism, caught in a political system where we have no separate legal status—unlike other Native peoples in the U.S.—to control our land base (over a million acres of so-called "trust" lands set aside by Congress for Native beneficiaries but leased by their alleged "trustee," the State of Hawai`i, to non-Natives), we are by every measure the most oppressed of all groups living in Hawai`i, our ancestral land.

Despite the presence of a small middle class, Hawaiians as a people register the same profile as other indigenous groups controlled by the United States: high unemployment, catastrophic health problems, low educational attainment, large numbers institutionalized in the military and prisons, occupational ghettoization in poorly paid jobs, and increasing outmigration that amounts to diaspora. Indeed, so great is the oppression-caused outmigration of Hawaiians from their island homes that, despite the highest birthrate in Hawai`i, we remain only 20 percent of the resident population. Some estimates report that more Hawaiians now live on the continent of the United States than in their Native land.

The latest affliction of corporate tourism has meant a particularly insidious form of cultural prostitution. The *hula,* for example—an ancient form of artistic expression with deep and complex religious meaning—has been made ornamental, a form of exotica for the gaping tourist. Far from encouraging a cultural revival, as tourist industry apologists contend, tourism has appropriated and prostituted the accomplishments of a resurgent interest in things Hawaiian (e.g., the use of replicas of Hawaiian artifacts such as fishing and food implements, capes, helmets and other symbols of ancient power to decorate hotels). Hawaiian women, meanwhile, are marketed on posters from Paris to Tokyo promising an unfettered "primitive" sexuality. Burdened with commodification of our culture and exploitation of our people, Hawaiians exist in an occupied country whose hostage people are forced to witness (and, for many, to participate in) our collective humiliation as tourist artifacts for the First World. . . .

Even for many residents of Hawai`i, the conditions and status of Native Hawaiians are little known and intentionally obscured by missionary-descended landowners, the State and Federal governments, local politicians and the media, as well as a complicitous university system economically dependent on the governor and the legislature. Like many a colony, Hawai`i has a very centralized political system, with the most powerful chief executive of all fifty American states. Of course, this sharp pyramidal structure is itself a product of our territorial period (1900–1959), when the all-white oligarchy feared (and therefore constrained) an organized majority "colored" population of Asian immigrants and Hawaiians.

Finally, there is always that particular variant of racism which fashions America's moral stupidity: vociferous denial of the presence, unique histories, and self-determination of America's conquered Natives. To Hawaiians, *haole* Americans seem to cherish their ignorance of other nations (especially conquered peoples who live wretched lives all around them) as a sign of American individualism. Americans have no cultural beliefs that connect them, as a people or nation, to other human beings or to the natural world as brothers and sisters in a familial cosmos. Therefore, peoples who suffer and die in the Third World, for example, or on Indian reservations, either deserve their fate or are unfortunate outcasts in an ordered world which finds white people at the top. From a Hawaiian perspective, this is not only incorrect, it is unbelievably cruel to family members.

In colony Hawai`i, not only the cruelty but the stench of colonialism is everywhere: at Pearl Harbor, so thoroughly polluted by the American military that it now ranks among the top priorities on the Environmental Protection Agency's Super Fund list; at Waikīkī, one of the most famous beaches in the world, where human excrement from the over-loaded Honolulu sewer system floats just offshore; at Honolulu International Airport, where jet fuel from commercial, military and private planes creates an eternal pall in the still, hot air; in the magnificent valleys and plains of all major islands, where heavy pesticide/herbicide use on sugar plantations and mammoth golf courses results in contaminated wetlands, rivers, estuaries, bays and, of course, ground water sources; on the gridlocked freeways which swallow up more and more land as the American way of life carves its path toward destruction; in the schools and businesses and hotels and shops and government buildings and on the radio and television, where white Christian American values of capitalism, racism and violent conflict are upheld, supported, and deployed against the Native people.

This is Hawai`i, once the most fragile and precious of sacred places, now transformed by the American behemoth into a dying land. Only a whispering spirit remains.

Y *E S S A Y S*

Thomas R. Hietala teaches history at Grinnell College in Iowa. His 1985 book, *Manifest Design: Anxious Aggrandizement in Late Jacksonian America,* took a fresh look at an old topic and made scholars reconsider the story of American expansion before the Civil War. The first essay is the concluding chapter of his book. It examines misconceptions about the era of "manifest destiny." In the second essay, John Whitehead, a historian at the University of Alaska Fairbanks, considers the historical connections of Hawai`i to the American West. He shows why United States nationalism could reach so far into the Pacific Ocean. For nineteenth-century proponents of American expansion, the westward surge of acquisition seemed an inevitable "destiny." Could these stories of acquisition have turned out differently? Are all the lands acquired by the United States up to 1898, clearly and comfortably part of the American nation?

The Myths of Manifest Destiny

THOMAS R. HIETALA

When John O'Sullivan coined the felicitous phrase "manifest destiny" in mid-1845, he provided Americans then and since with an invaluable legitimizing myth of empire. During the final phase of the Texas annexation crisis, he accused the European nations of "hostile interference" in American affairs, "for the avowed object of thwarting our policy and hampering our power, limiting our greatness and checking the fulfillment of our manifest destiny to overspread the continent allotted by Providence for the free development of our yearly multiplying millions." In his justification for American expansion, O'Sullivan reconciled democracy with empire while he implicitly sanctioned the dispossession of all non-Anglo peoples on the continent. During the mid-1840s, he repeatedly stressed that the United States must acquire abundant land for "the free development" of its "yearly multiplying millions"; without territorial expansion the novel experiment in free government and free enterprise might collapse.

The recurring emphasis on material factors in the Democrats' speculations about the need for expansion raises some important questions about the purported idealism of both "Jacksonian Democracy" and manifest destiny. To O'Sullivan and other Democrats, previous territorial acquisitions had been indispensable to the success of the American political and economic system. And though the Jacksonians were convinced of the superiority of popular government, they were much less certain about its viability. Their ambitions for a continental empire represented much more than simple romantic nationalism: they demanded land because they regarded it as the primary prerequisite for republican government and for an economy and society based upon individual acquisitiveness, geographical and social mobility, and a fluid class structure. These beliefs—best expressed by O'Sullivan but articulated by other Democrats as well—were crucial to most Jacksonian policies, especially those promoting territorial and commercial expansion. To consider manifest destiny in the context of such principles of political economy is a way of making more comprehensible the sustained drive for empire in the 1840s.

Misconceptions about manifest destiny still influence Americans' impressions about their nation's history. Although the civil rights struggle and the Vietnam War have led many Americans to question several of the prevailing orthodoxies of United States history, popular attitudes about the country's past—the self-concept of Americans and their definition of their nation's role in world affairs—have shown a remarkable resiliency, despite the challenges of revisionist scholars. Prevailing ideas about westward expansion are inextricably linked to the values associated with American exceptionalism and mission, fundamental components of the Jacksonian creed. The persistence of manifest destiny ideology under radically different political, economic, and military realities since the 1840s attests to the significant impact these legitimizing myths of empire have had on popular beliefs about United States history. Since continental expansion gave birth to and nurtured so many nationalistic myths, a reevaluation of the historical circumstances that spawned them is an essential exercise in the reassessment of the American past.

Complicating any separation of historical myth from historical actuality is the confusion surrounding the concept of territorial expansion as a policy implemented by national leaders and the concept of the frontier experience as a spontaneous process initiated by pioneers. Long before Frederick Jackson Turner began studying the evolution of a frontier area from "savagery" to "civilization," Americans speculated about the significance of westward expansion upon their institutions and character as well as about its effects upon the world at large. In their own minds, Americans believed that their progress provided a beacon light to a world in darkness. Moreover, though the ever-expanding frontier represented a process quintessentially American, it was also a process with ramifications for people across the Atlantic. From the very beginning of British settlement in North America, the expanding frontier and its pioneer inhabitants were as influential in historical development as were the seat of empire and its imperial officials. This preoccupation with the frontier and its impact on American character and destiny became even more pronounced after the Revolution, then reached new heights during the Jacksonian era. Images of mountain men, freedom fighters at the Alamo, wagon caravans, and prospectors rushing to California appeal more to romantic sensibilities than Calhoun's dispatches, [Robert J.] Walker's propaganda, or Polk's devious manipulations to gain title to the Spanish borderlands. The frontiersmen deserve the pages of print that have been devoted to them, though theirs is but half the story. The epic quality of the pioneers' adventures lends sanctity to American expansion and obscures the actual dynamics of empire building. Pioneers alone did not take possession of the continent, nor did policy makers alone acquire it. Two complementary assaults by national leaders and individual pioneers achieved a continental empire during the mid-1840s.

Jacksonians exalted the pioneer as the epitome of the common man, and they celebrated American expansion as an integral part of their mission to obtain a better nation and a better world based on individual freedom, liberalized international trade, and peaceful coexistence. The Democrats equated American progress with global progress and repeatedly argued that European oligarchs were actually opposing the interests of their own people by trying to discourage the expansion of the United States. Geographically and ideologically separated from Europe, the United States, under Jacksonian direction, tried to improve its democratic institutions, utilize the land's rich resources, and demonstrate to the world the superiority of a system allowing free men to compete in a dynamic society. Consequently, the impact of the pioneering process transcended the concerns of the frontiersmen. In forming "a more perfect union" on a continually expanding frontier, Americans thought that they were actually serving the cause of all mankind.

Such a melding of exceptionalism and empire permitted the Jacksonians the luxury of righteous denunciation of their critics at home and abroad. Their domestic foes could be paired with European monarchs as spokesmen for an old order of aristocracy, privilege, and proscription; American expansionism and the Jacksonian domestic program, on the other hand, represented the antithesis of traditional systems. Since territorial acquisitions and Democratic policies fostered opportunity and democracy, they liberated men from oppressive social and economic relationships. The Jacksonians' program promised so much for so little; no wonder messianic imagery appeared so frequently in their rhetoric.

Skeptical Whigs often challenged the Democrats' sincerity, however, sensing that the Jacksonians' motives for aggrandizement were more selfish than they usually admitted. The Democrats' rhetoric proved more resilient than the Whigs' trenchant criticisms of "manifest destiny," however, and so subsequent generations of Americans have underestimated the extent and the intensity of opposition to the policies behind expansionism in the 1840s, especially the Mexican War. Enduring misconceptions about the period have not only obscured the complexities of territorial and commercial expansion during the late Jacksonian era; they have also contributed to an erroneous impression of American history during the entire century from the close of the War of 1812 to the entry of the United States into World War I. A reassessment of these misconceptions shows a greater continuity between nineteenth- and twentieth-century foreign policy than is customarily supposed. The myths of manifest destiny perpetuate an unwarranted nostalgia for times past and conceal some of the striking similarities between the past and the present. The splendid half-century of American isolation and expansion had a darker side, too.

Since the advent of the atomic age, many historians have looked wistfully back to the nineteenth century as a simpler, more secure, and more innocent era in American history. During the national debate on the purported missile gap in 1960, for example, C. Vann Woodward observed that "throughout most of its history the United States has enjoyed a remarkable degree of military security, physical security from hostile attack and invasion. This security was not only remarkably effective, but it was relatively free." Woodward and many of his contemporaries stressed discontinuity in the relative security of the United States before and after its rise to world power. Before the twentieth century, the Atlantic and Pacific Oceans, a weak Mexico and Canada, and European distractions that diverted attention from American affairs gave the United States peace without onerous military expenditures, complicated diplomacy, or devastating wars. But free security disappeared with the quantum leaps in weapons technology in the twentieth century. No longer could the United States repose in the comforting knowledge that its sphere was insulated from the vicissitudes of the shrinking globe.

For most historians who wrote during the two decades following the Second World War, American security in the nineteenth century had not only been free; it had been innocent as well. Samuel Flagg Bemis observed in 1965 that "American expansion across a practically empty continent despoiled no nation unjustly." Whereas European empires had exploited and oppressed their colonial subjects, the United States had adhered to nonintervention, free trade, amicable diplomacy, and self-determination for all peoples. American leaders between the War of 1812 and the Spanish-American War based their foreign policy on what Bemis labeled the "two polestars" of United States foreign relations, "anti-imperialism and isolation." Noted diplomat and scholar George F. Kennan likewise viewed the nineteenth century as an era of detachment and naive innocence in American affairs. Kennan believed that American leaders during this period failed to recognize "the global framework" that buttressed the security of the United States. According to Kennan and others troubled by the exigencies of global conflict in their time, the United States during most of the nineteenth century had experienced the rare blessings of isolation and effortless security, an insularity and immunity from international strife that enabled Americans to devote virtually all their attention to domestic development. Spared from the wiles of European statecraft and war during much of its history, the United States seemed to Kennan ill prepared to deal with the ~~~ age of superpowers and superweapons after 1945.

American history books, including diplomatic history texts, reinforce dea that the United States became concerned with considerations of nal security only in the twentieth century. Historians of foreign relations usually cover the century from the winning of independence to the outward thrust of the 1890s only cursorily. After the American Revolution little of major importance is said to have occurred in American diplomacy except the proclamation of the Monroe Doctrine: the United States had seemed to lack anything resembling a foreign policy during that century of dramatic internal growth. Because 1898 represents for many scholars a sharp transition in the national experience, earlier continental expansion appears irrelevant to the global power politics of the twentieth century. The acquisition of Hawaii and the Philippines in 1898, for example, has received far more careful study than the annexation of Texas in 1845. Such neglect of the first century of American diplomacy and such inordinate emphasis on the period since the Spanish-American War conveys the impression that continental expansion was a foregone conclusion, a long but somewhat uneventful rehearsal for the emergence of the United States as a world power in the twentieth century.

Scholarly journals and monographs in American foreign relations repeat this pattern. An overwhelming proportion of recent articles and books on American diplomacy cover the period since World War I. By its virtual absence in both scholarly and popular publications, the pre-1898 era is rendered irrelevant by default, a mere antecedent to the more exciting and more perilous twentieth century. Scholars of American foreign relations have not carefully reexamined the territorial expansion of the United States in the late Jacksonian era and its relative importance in American history, though the fact that the United States doubled its domain in only three short years and fought its first sustained foreign war during the same period suggests that the period deserves some reconsideration.

The expansionism of the 1840s acquires a new significance, however, when it is considered within the context of the cultural, social, and political factors that motivated the Jacksonians to pursue a continental empire. In promoting the acquisition of new lands and new markets, the Democrats greatly exaggerated the extent of European hostility to the United States and refused to admit the duplicity and brutality behind their own efforts to expand their nation's territory and trade. By joining their concepts of exceptionalism and empire, the expansionists found a rationale for denying to all other nations and peoples, whether strong or weak, any right to any portion of the entire North American continent. If a rival was strong, it posed a threat to American security and had to be removed; if a rival was weak, it proved its inferiority and lent sanction to whatever actions were taken by pioneers or policy makers to make the territory a part of the United States.

The confusion surrounding expansion results in part from the ambivalence of the Jacksonians themselves, who demonstrated both compassion and contempt in their policies, depending on the racial and ethnic identities of the peoples to be affected by Democratic measures. Generous and humane toward impoverished Americans and poor immigrants from Europe, the Democrats showed far less concern for nonwhites whom they dispossessed or exploited in the process of westward expansion and

national development. Removal, eclipse, or extermination—not acculturation and assimilation—awaited the Indians, blacks, and mixed-blood Mexicans on the continent. Despite occasional statements to the contrary, the
expansionists regarded the incorporation of nonwhite peoples into the
country as both unlikely and undesirable. Without hint of hypocrisy the
Jacksonians sought lenient naturalization laws and opportunities for newcomers while strenuously defending policies to separate Indians and Mexicans from their lands and programs to relocate blacks to Africa and Central
America.

When expansionists did express concern for nonwhites, they did not
question the basic assumptions behind racial proscription and dispossession. They trusted masters to treat their slaves humanely; they urged that
the federal government compensate Indians adequately for their territorial
cessions. Few expansionists, however, could see any alternative to the
removal or extermination of Indians or the enslavement or proscription of
blacks. Indians had no legitimate claim to land; blacks had no legitimate
claim to freedom. Even Free-Soilers who opposed the extension of slavery
had little sympathy for the slave, arguing, in essence, that black freedom
was detrimental to white status. The racism in Washington was matched by
racism on the frontier: pioneers in both Oregon and California adopted
restrictive measures in the late 1840s to discourage or prohibit the migration of free blacks to the far West.

The expansion to the Pacific was not primarily an expression of American confidence. Anxiety, not optimism, generally lay behind the quest for
land, ports, and markets. A powerful combination of fears led the neo-
Jeffersonians of the 1840s to embrace territorial and commercial expansionism as the best means of warding off both domestic and foreign threats
to the United States. The Jacksonians were proponents of laissez-faire only
in a limited sense, and their sustained efforts to acquire land and markets
were their equivalents for what they saw as the Whigs' dangerous propen-
sity to meddle in the domestic economy. Rather than give an "artificial"
stimulus to the economy through protective duties or privileged charters,
the Democrats preferred to assist American producers by means of territorial acquisitions, reciprocity treaties, improvements in the navy, and a liberal land policy. Frightened by rapid modernization in the United States,
Democrats warned that both European monarchs and the Whig opposition
were threatening the Republic—the Europeans by their attempts to contain
American expansion, the Whigs by their resistance to Jacksonian foreign
policy and their support of legislation that would hasten industrialization,
urbanization, and class polarization in the United States.

Jeffersonian ideology, especially its romantic agrarianism, its fear of
industrialization, and its conviction that the United States had a natural
right to free trade, contributed significantly to the ideology of manifest destiny. To the Jeffersonians and Jacksonians, American farms raised good
republican citizens as well as corn, cotton, and wheat: cultivated fields produced virtuous, cultivated people. Whatever the realities of the late Jacksonian period, the expansionists insisted that agricultural societies fostered

opportunity and political equality, the essential features of American uniqueness. Moreover, the neo-Jeffersonians contended that only industrial nations became international predators; agricultural countries were self-contained and did not need colonies or privileged markets. These misconceptions cloak some of the more unflattering aspects of antebellum economy and society: slavemasters, not sturdy yeomen, dominated the social and political life of the South; the country's most important export crops, cotton and tobacco, were produced by forced labor; Indians were cruelly dispossessed of their lands and often their culture to make room for American producers; "go-ahead" Americans frequently seemed more interested in land speculation than in patient tilling of the soil; and the United States, like other empires, did prey upon other peoples and nations to augment its wealth, power, and security.

The fact that the United States acquired contiguous rather that noncontiguous territory makes American aggrandizement no less imperial than that of other empires of the mid-nineteenth century. The United States enjoyed several advantages that facilitated its enlargement and made it more antiseptic. Mexico's weakness, the inability of Indian tribes to unite and resist dispossession, the decline of France and Spain as colonizing powers in the New World, and geographical isolation from Europe all served the interests of the United States as it spread across the continent. In addition, the preference for an anticolonial empire embodied in the concept of a confederated Union also contributed to American success. But many Democrats wanted to venture beyond the continent, and had the party not become so divided during and after the Mexican War, the Polk administration probably would have taken steps to add Yucatán and Cuba to the United States, thereby extending the empire into the Caribbean.

The urge to expand beyond the continent was diminished by the fact that the continent itself was incredibly rich in resources. Those abundant resources provided the basis for unparalleled economic growth at home and power in relations with countries abroad. The expansionists regarded the nation's productivity as an irresistible weapon that could counterbalance the military strength of Europe. Here, again, an old Jeffersonian perception dating back to the 1790s came into play: the world desperately needed American commerce and would sacrifice a great deal to obtain it. Although the expansionists never had cause to drive the masses of Europe to starvation and revolution through an embargo on grain and cotton, their speculations on the subject showed them to be far more imperial than philanthropic in their attitudes toward their nation's wealth.

Distressed by many trends in American life, the Democrats formulated their domestic and foreign policies to safeguard themselves and their progeny from a potentially dismal future. They hoped to prevent domestic disturbances by acquiring additional territory and markets. Other measures were also devised to protect the country from various perils: the Democrats discouraged the growth of manufacturing and monopolistic banking, attempted to minimize the conflict over slavery, encouraged the sale and settlement of the national domain, and tried to discredit the efforts of dissidents to form third parties that might jeopardize the two-party system.

During the 1840s, then, national security was not "free," nor was it attained without constant effort. The expansionists utilized propaganda, personal vendetta, legislative legerdemain, confidential agents, covert military pressure, and offensive war to achieve their goals. The Jacksonians, in fact, felt as insecure in their world as their heirs felt in the 1940s, when the Soviet threat called forth a policy of ambitious containment. The insecurity of the 1840s prompted attempts to enlarge the United States; the insecurity of the Cold War prompted policies to hem in the Soviet Union. In both cases, anxiety was a major factor behind American actions.

Another myth of manifest destiny concerns the role of military power in American expansion. On May 11, 1846, President Polk informed Congress that "after reiterated menaces, Mexico has passed the boundary of the United States, has invaded our territory and shed American blood upon the American soil." War had begun, Polk observed, in spite of "all our efforts to avoid it." Much evidence, however, raises doubts about just how hard Polk tried to prevent war. Six weeks before Polk's war message, for example, Captain William S. Henry, a subordinate commander in Taylor's army en route to the city of Matamoras, noted in his journal, "Our situation is truly extraordinary: right in the enemy's country (to all appearance), actually occupying their corn and cotton fields, the people of the soil leaving their homes, and we, with a small handful of men, marching with colors flying and drums beating, right under the very guns of one of their principal cities, displaying the star-spangled banner, as if in defiance, under their very nose." This army's purpose was not limited to the defense of Texas. It is true that the United States claimed the Rio Grande as the border; it is also true that the United States, in the person of James K. Polk, claimed that the nation had a "clear and unquestionable" title to Oregon up to 54° 40′. But the issue for the Polk administration was not the validity of various boundary claims, but rather the issue of whether military pressure could force Mexico to relinquish the disputed territory between the Nueces and Rio Grande, and the undisputed territories of New Mexico and California besides. The Democrats chose war to defend an unclear and unquestionable title in the Southwest but retreated from a supposedly clear and unquestionable title in the Northwest. The hypocrisy did not escape the Whigs.

The war promised other benefits as well. Slidell encouraged the Polk administration to prosecute the war with vigor. "The navy should have an opportunity to distinguish itself," Slidell counseled after Taylor's army had already won its laurels. "The people *must* have something to huzza about." Americans rushed by the thousands to fight in Mexico, and several congressmen begged Polk for commissions to command them. The bloodshed elevated to prominence the next two elected presidents, Taylor and Pierce, as well as the future president of the Confederacy, Jefferson Davis. In Senator Benton's words, "gunpowder popularity" often served as "the passport to the presidency" at this time. Benton himself urged Polk to name him supreme commander in Mexico: the precedent of Jackson's meteoric rise to eminence through the killing of redcoats and redskins was not lost on ambitious Democrats. Benton did not become supreme commander and he never attained the presidency. To Polk's chagrin, the war's two most celebrated generals, Taylor and Winfield Scott, turned out to be Whigs. Contrary to the Democrats' expectations, the war did not help their party at the polls.

In contrast to the turmoil of the 1850s and the ordeal of the Civil War and Reconstruction, the 1840s appear in history books as years of stunning success. Within a thousand days the United States acquired its continental empire, adding vast territories at an unprecedented rate. After World War II, several historians who studied westward expansion depicted the 1840s as a golden age in American diplomacy, a time when enlightened self-interest and adequate power and resolve to attain it guided the United States foreign policy. Norman Graebner so assessed the decade, contending in 1955 that expansion to the Pacific "was a unified, purposeful, precise movement that was ever limited to specific maritime objectives. . . . It was . . . through clearly conceived policies relentlessly pursued that the United States achieved its empire on the Pacific," he concluded. Another prominent postwar scholar, Arthur M. Schlesinger, described Polk as "undeservedly one of the forgotten men of American history." Polk declared "certain definite objectives" for his term and achieved them all: a reduced tariff, an Independent Treasury, and the acquisition of Oregon and California. "By carrying the flag to the Pacific he gave America her continental breadth and ensured her future significance in the world," Schlesinger noted. Many postwar scholars who had witnessed the rise and fall of fascism only to face another menace in Cold War communism understandably assessed manifest destiny chiefly in terms of how the acquisitions had increased the wealth and power of the United States, equipping it to counter totalitarian regimes a century later. This perspective enhanced the reputations of the expansionists.

The Cold War view of manifest destiny is instructive not only for what it asserts but also for what it neglects or ignores. American policy makers in the 1840s did define the national interest in terms of acquiring land and markets, and they did find various ways to attain their ambitions. In fact, rarely have two presidents acted as audaciously as Tyler and Polk to overcome foreign and domestic opposition to their policies. The cavalier methods of the expansionists during the mid-1840s often appalled contemporaries such as the poet Emerson. "The name of Washington City in the newspapers is every day a blacker shade," he lamented in 1847, "all the news from that quarter being of a sadder type, more malignant. It seems to be settled that no act of honour or benevolence or justice is to be expected from the American government, but only this, that they will be as wicked as they dare." Cold War scholars, however, were often no more squeamish about the methods of aggrandizement than the expansionists themselves had been. Unlike Emerson and the anti-war Whigs, they seemed to accept the idea that the end justified the means.

A more detached analysis of the history of the 1840s—one less influenced by Cold War assumptions about the positive effects of nineteenth-

century expansion—demonstrates how high a price was paid for the acquisitions. The expansionists' shortcomings and mistakes were as historically
significant as their much touted strengths and accomplishments, for even
when they attained their immediate goal, it seldom lived up to their long-
term expectations. They acquired a continental empire but could not govern
it. Too certain that their political institutions could resolve fundamental
internal divisions and too complacent about the mounting sectional rancor
over the expansion of slavery, the Democrats failed to integrate the new
acquisitions into the Union and failed to keep the Union itself intact. No tri-
umphs of technology—no quantity of railroads, steamships, telegraphs, and
rotary presses—could sustain the expansive confederation. Limitations on
expansion did exist, though the Democrats seemed incapable of discerning
them during the 1840s. Their perceptions of the past and their fears for the
future blinded them to perils in the realignment of sections and politics.

The expansionists' far-fetched notions about nonwhites precluded their
thinking constructively about racial questions. By denying the likelihood of
a permanent black and Indian population on the continent, antebellum
Americans had difficulty preparing themselves and their descendants for
racial heterogeneity in the United States. The acceptance of racial diversity
as a reality of national life came largely through necessity, not choice. As
most European visitors realized, racial prejudice permeated the country and
transcended the sectional dispute over slavery. Americans, however, hardly
seemed to question the intense racial animus across the nation; it was such
a commonplace of life that it drew only isolated comment or criticism.
There were many gradations of racial feeling among Americans, of course,
and a small corps of radical abolitionists indicted the North for its failure
to practice racial egalitarianism in the free states. But there is no denying
that racial prejudice was a basic detriment of American domestic and foreign policy during the Jacksonian period.

The expansionists' ethnocentrism also sowed the seeds of future discord between the United States and the peoples of Latin America. The
annexation of Texas and the Mexican War created a legacy of suspicion and
anger toward the United States among peoples south of the Rio Grande.
However much the United States professed to be a "good neighbor" to other
countries in the hemisphere, those countries often held more ambivalent
views. This tension has complicated United States relations with Latin
America for well over a century and persists to the present. During much of
its history the United States has reserved its diplomacy for European countries. Usually a distinct lack of diplomacy has characterized relations with
Indians, Asians, and Latin Americans.

American arrogance was not confined to the Western Hemisphere. The
swashbuckling demeanor with which Caleb Cushing and his crew confronted the Chinese in 1844 demonstrated that Americans were, much like
the British, self-interested, presumptuous, and bound to create problems for
the unreceptive and understandably frightened Chinese. Americans stressed
their uniqueness and benevolence, but the Chinese tended to see greater
similarities than differences between the various Western intruders. The

persistent pattern of American condescension toward nonwhite peoples has made it difficult for twentieth-century leaders to adapt to the challenges of a shrinking globe and the recent dispersion of wealth and power away from Europe and America toward East Asia, the Middle East, and Africa. In their zeal to bring "the American way of life" to other peoples, several generations of United States policy makers have overlooked the fact that racism, aggressiveness, and self-righteousness have often been part of that way of life. The paradox of American benevolence coupled with awesome military power found expression more than a century before the United States intervened in Vietnam. During the Mexican War, for example, James Russell Lowell lampooned American pretensions in his "Pious Editor's Creed":

> I du believe wutever trash
>   'll keep the people in blindness,
> Thet we the Mexicuns can thrash
>   Right inter brotherly kindness,
> Thet bombshells, grape, an' powder 'n' ball
>   Air good-will's strongest magnets,
> Thet peace, to make it stick at all,
>   Must be druv in with bagnets.

Bayonet diplomacy (or "big stick" diplomacy) did not originate with Theodore Roosevelt and his interventionism in Latin America. Though not usually so described, the war against Mexico was the first instance of gunboat diplomacy. When a writer for the *Democratic Review* justified the invasion and occupation of Mexico in 1847, for example, he anticipated Roosevelt's 1904 corollary to the Monroe Doctrine. "It is an acknowledged law of nations," the *Review* writer maintained, "that when a country sinks into a state of anarchy, unable to govern itself, and dangerous to its neighbors, it becomes the *duty* of the most powerful of those neighbors to interfere and settle its affairs." Acting upon such assumptions, the United States has been doing its "duty" in Latin America for almost 140 years.

In many respects the expansionists' outlook turned out to be strikingly unrealistic. The United States was hardly overcrowded in the early 1840s: millions of acres within the existing national domain remained to be occupied and cultivated. Racial fears were also exaggerated. When southern slaves attained their freedom in 1865, no war between blacks and whites ensued. After the Civil War, scores of large cities and hundreds of factories and corporations spread across the country, yet democratic institutions and capitalism survived the transformation. Despite the undeniable hardships and radical adjustments precipitated by rapid industrialization, few Americans would argue that manufacturing weakened rather than strengthened the United States. The Democrats also overestimated the hostility of Britain. The British ministry acquiesced in the annexation of Texas; it did not incite Mexico to make war upon the United States; and it did not try to acquire California before the United States seized it in 1846. Several major premises behind the expansion of the late Jacksonian period proved erroneous.

The decade of the 1840s should be placed in a different historical context: United States policy in this crucial decade prepared the way for both late-nineteenth-century and twentieth-century imperialism. The expansion of the Tyler-Polk years, like that of the 1890s, grew largely out of a recurring domestic malaise that found expression in American aggrandizement. During both decades, ambitious and anxious policy makers welcomed war and expansion as alternatives to basic structural changes in American economics and politics. The methods of American foreign policy also suggest continuities over time. The tactics employed by Tyler and Polk to expand the empire suggest that the label "imperial presidency" should not be confined to presidents of the Cold War era: Polk, especially, acted as imperially as any of his twentieth-century successors. Democratic process and an aggressive foreign policy were as incompatible in the mid-nineteenth century as in the twentieth, as congressional critics frequently noted. In late 1846, for example, Whig Garrett Davis pointed out that the founding fathers had "entrusted to the president the national shield," but they had intentionally given the national sword and "the entire war power" to Congress. "To make war is the most fearful power exerted by human government," Davis warned, a power too momentous to be placed in any one man's hands. That admonition was out of fashion for two decades after World War II, but Vietnam gave it new meaning. In the 1840s and in the 1960s, Congress was remiss in its responsibility to scrutinize how American military power was used, for what purposes, and under what pretenses. In both cases a scheming president misled Congress into sanctioning a wider war than anticipated. Though Congress does delay while it deliberates, there are also drawbacks in granting the president the nation's sword as well as its shield: the skirmish on the Rio Grande, the attack in the Gulf of Tonkin, and, more recently, the meddling in Nicaragua, El Salvador, and Lebanon attest to that.

Orthodox historical "truths" possess considerable resiliency. By extolling the virtues and achievements of a self-conscious people, they appeal to nationalistic feeling, and through constant repetition they acquire an aura of unquestioned certainty over time. The idealism of westward expansion embodied in the concept of manifest destiny persists because it helps to reconcile American imperialism with an extremely favorable national image. The assumed benevolence and the supposedly accidental nature of American expansion are convenient evasions of the complexities of the past. In accepting the rhetoric of American mission and destiny, apologists for the expansionists of the 1840s have had to minimize or ignore much historical evidence. Perhaps more to the point, defenders of American exceptionalism and innocence have actually had to slight other crucial motives for expansion that the Democrats themselves often candidly admitted.

Though the phrase *manifest destiny* appears repeatedly in the literature of American foreign relations, it does not accurately describe the expansionism of the 1840s. It is one of many euphemisms that have allowed several generations of Americans to maintain an unwarranted complacency in regard to their nation's past, a complacency that has contributed in a fundamental way to the persistent quandary the United States has faced in trying to define a realistic role for itself in a world that seldom acts according to American precepts. Geographical isolation and a powerful exceptionalist ideology have insulated the United States from the complexities of culture and historical experience affecting other peoples, leaving Americans susceptible to myths and misconceptions at home and abroad. Often unaware of their own history, Americans frequently misunderstand foreign cultures and experiences as well. Myths and misconceptions often fill the void created by ignorance of history.

The expansionists of the 1840s should not be permitted to expropriate many of the best American ideals for their own purposes. Just as they manipulated the Census of 1840, the Democratic convention of 1844, and the Mexican-Texas border dispute for their own ends, so too did they exploit American exceptionalist ideology to ennoble their ambitions for riches and dominion. But rhetoric could not hide the chauvinism, aggressiveness, and design that were essential components of continental expansion. The United States used many tactics to expand its domain, and like other empires it created legitimizing myths to sanction that expansion. Some Americans, however, challenged the validity of those myths and condemned the conduct they excused. But critics of national policy seldom reach generations other than their own, for history—especially American history—often records only the dominant voices of the past. That the United States has changed dramatically since attaining its continental empire is obvious. That the American people have reassessed their basic assumptions about themselves, their national experience, and their approach to other nations is not so obvious.

Since impressions about the past affect consciousness in the present and help define possibilities for the future, the way in which historical events are interpreted significantly influences the ongoing process of defining national identity, national character, and national purpose. Because history involves both continuity and change over time, a historical work serves two crucial purposes: it provides a window to the past, and it furnishes a mirror to the present. However striking the changes in American life since the Jacksonian era, the persistence of certain principles and biases—the consistency of much of American political and diplomatic "culture" over several generations—ties the present to the past, and links both to the future. For that reason the legacy of the 1840s should be of concern to all Americans—not just historians.

Hawai`i: The First and Last Far West?

JOHN WHITEHEAD

What are the boundaries of the American West? The eastern limit causes some, though not great, consternation among western historians. While one camp claims the Mississippi River and another the 98–100th meridian, the argument here is a friendly one. To my knowledge no one has demanded that St. Louis's Gateway Arch be dismantled and moved to Abilene. The western limit provokes a heartier discussion. Robert Athearn excludes the Pacific Coast states from his "West," but most historians simply cannot dismiss California, Oregon, and Washington. Beyond the Pacific Coast and north of the 49th parallel, however, real problems develop. Western historians, with rare exception, resist including the nation's two westernmost states, Alaska and Hawai`i, in their region. . . .

Forging a link between Hawai`i and the West does not require new archival discoveries. A basic secondary literature on Hawai`i has been available for 25–50 years. For the most part, this has been compiled by historians of Hawai`i who do not omit Hawai`i's links to the West, but who often prefer to picture the islands as a world of their own or as part of a greater Pacific or Polynesia. They see Hawai`i as part of the general phenomenon of American and European colonialism in the Pacific, rather than as a part of American national expansion. Of course, historians can well debate whether national expansion and colonialism were not one in the same! The bulk of this secondary literature has been written by Caucasian historians. In the last decade, however, a renewed interest in Hawaiian studies has led to new historical studies by native Hawaiians. In general, the theme of this new work is dispossession of the islands' natives by foreigners.

In addition to the local chroniclers, American diplomatic and maritime historians have written extensively about the islands. Westerners rarely incorporate these findings in their regional histories. To my knowledge neither the traditional frontier or the "new" western historians claim Samuel Flagg Bemis or Samuel Eliot Morison as godfathers. While westerners have kept the door shut to Hawai`i, American historians in other fields have expanded their studies to the islands. Women's historians have written on missionary wives in Hawai`i and historical demographers have extended techniques estimating pre-Columbian native populations in the Americas to the islands. By painting an overview of the common themes of history between Hawai`i and the West based on this existing literature I hope to pry open that closed door. If a convincing case can be made for Hawai`i, Alaska should follow with relative ease!

The Hawaiian islands were discovered and settled by ocean going Polynesians sometime between 100 and 600 A.D. In the millennium and a half that passed between this original settlement and the arrival of the first Europeans, the islands' population grew substantially to a number ranging from a low estimate of 200,000–300,000 to a high estimate of 800,000–1 million. European contact with the Hawaiian islands and people commenced in January 1778 with the arrival of Captain James Cook at Waimea (Kaua`i) on the third of his famous Pacific voyages. Cook named these lands the Sandwich Islands after the Earl of Sandwich, First Lord of the Admiralty. After this initial encounter, Cook and his men ventured north from Hawai`i to Russian America, where they obtained an abundance of sea otter pelts. Upon returning to the islands from the North, Cook was killed in an altercation with the Hawaiians over stolen goods at Kealakekua Bay in February 1779. The surviving members of his crew, including an American, John Ledyard, finally left Hawai`i and eventually arrived in Macao. There they made one of the trip's most important discoveries: the sea otter furs obtained in the North fetched a handsome price in China. Within a decade, the Northwest-China fur trade was born, stimulated to a great extent by the publication of Ledyard's journal in 1783. Both American and English ships soon gathered furs on the Northwest Coast and then stopped in Hawai`i enroute to China. In 1790, the first American ship docked in Honolulu. America's westward expansion to Hawai`i, in a real sense the first Far West, had begun.

By 1800, Americans dominated the trans-Pacific fur trade, and Honolulu became the principal way station for the approximately twenty Boston-registered ships that plied this route annually. A decade later, American merchants received a monopoly on the islands' sandalwood trade from King Kamehameha I, thus adding an important product to their China-bound cargoes. From 1818–1821, Hawaiian sandalwood sold in Canton at an average of $100,000 annually. During the first two decades of the nineteenth century the total annual worth of the furs and sandalwood routed through Hawai`i to China was estimated from $300,000 to $1,000,000 annually. This constituted a substantial American commercial interest in Hawai`i and the Pacific. We might compare these figures to the $20,000–200,000 annual value of the more publicized Santa Fe trade in the 1820s.

The key to this early American commercial presence in the Pacific was Hawai`i's openness to foreigners and its readiness to provide and allow services such as ship repair, food acquisition, and trade. Hawaiian men and boys signed on for work aboard the Yankee ships, and American men and Hawaiian women formed relationships. Even in the first decade of American presence, sailors deserted their ships in Honolulu and remained in the islands, in some cases marrying native women and settling permanently. Though foreigners were forbidden to own land or construct permanent dwellings before 1820, a total foreign population of approximately 200 Americans and Europeans, *haoles* as the Hawaiians called them, resided in the islands by 1819.

American commercial involvement in Hawai`i surged in the quarter century between 1820 and 1845, as the American Pacific whaling fleet established its headquarters in Honolulu. The first whaling ships arrived in

1819; by 1829 over 100 ships a year called at the ports of Honolulu and Lahaina. In the 1830s and 1840s, 400–500 ships made semi-annual visits to the islands for reprovisioning, recreation, and trans-shipment of whale oil back to New England ports. The value of the Pacific whaling industry dwarfed that of the trans-Pacific fur trade and yielded products worth $6–10 million annually between 1830 and 1850. Hawai`i's role as the center for the Pacific whaling industry stimulated both the growth of mercantile houses and commercial agriculture ventures that supplied the ships. The reprovisioning function alone in Hawai`i produced an annual trade of $500,000 to $1 million in the late 1840s and early 1850s. Hawaiian agricultural products also supplied the Hudson's Bay Company in Oregon and the Russian-American Company in Alaska.

While agriculture grew to supply the whaling ships, the Hawaiian cattle industry developed. Cattle from California were first introduced to the islands in the 1790s by the English explorer George Vancouver as a gift to King Kamehameha I. Within a few decades these wild, roaming cattle were a nuisance to local farmers. By 1830, King Kamehameha III, son of Kamehameha I, imported Spanish and Mexican vaqueros from California, called *paniolos* in the islands (a shortened form of *Espanols*), to herd the cattle and train Hawaiians in ranching. By the late 1830s and 1840s, the Hawaiian cattle industry supplied beef to the whaling ships and hides for the emerging California hide and tallow trade. American inroads into the islands by this time were no better illustrated than in the life of John Palmer Parker, a Massachusetts sailor who jumped ship in Hawai`i in 1809. Parker won the favor of Kamehameha I and married his granddaughter Kipikane in 1816. In the 1830s, Parker herded and slaughtered cattle for Kamehameha III in the Waimea region on the island of Hawai`i. In 1847, Parker received two acres of land from Kamehameha III. This became the basis for the enormous Parker Ranch of Hawai`i, which has been in continuous operation by the same family to the present day. At over 200,000 acres, it is the largest cattle ranch under single ownership in the United States. Even before Moses and Stephen Austin contemplated their settlements in Texas, John Palmer Parker was in Hawai`i preparing for his cattle empire. So much for Senator Monroney's concern with the transportation of cows and horses to the islands!

The mercantile and agricultural enterprises that developed to serve the whaling industry were dominated by Americans. By 1843, Hawai`i's American-European or *haole* population numbered about 600, of whom 400 were American. This figure is remarkably similar to the 700 English and Americans present in California by 1845. Hawai`i's foreign population centered in Honolulu, the major commercial outpost for American trade west of the Rockies. According to Harold Bradley, one of the principal chroniclers of the early American presence in Hawai` i, "As the center of the sandalwood trade and later as the rendezvous for the whaling fleets, Honolulu had become the metropolis of the eastern Pacific. This position it proudly maintained until after the American occupation of California."

Hawai`i's position in the westward advance of the American commercial frontier was matched in the 1820–1845 period by its role in the west-ward expansion of American missionaries. In a pattern not dissimilar to that of the Nez Perce Indians,who ventured to St. Louis in 1831 and lured mis-sionaries to Oregon, the presence of native Hawaiians in Connecticut, usu-ally young boys brought home by sea captains for schooling or for work as personal servants, lured missionaries to Hawai`i a decade earlier. The most famous of these eastward moving islanders was a young sixteen-year old lad named Opukahaia, or Henry Obookiah as he was known in New England.

Shortly after his arrival in 1809, a group of Yale students found Obookiah weeping on the steps of the college. The Americans immediately began to instruct the young Hawaiian about Christianity and other aspects of New England life. The islander later lived with Yale's president Timothy Dwight for a time, and in 1816 went to the Foreign Mission School in Corn-wall, Connecticut, established to educate young men of the Polynesian and Indian races. While attending the school, Obookiah resolved to return to the islands and spread Christianity among his people.

Obookiah died in 1818, before he could return to Hawai`i. His example soon inspired the American Board of Commissioners for Foreign Missions to send a group of Yale men and their wives as missionaries to Hawai`i in 1819. Led by Reverend Hiram Bingham and Reverend Asa Thurston, the Puritan band arrived in Hawai`i in March 1820. The new king, Kame-hameha II or Liholiho, allowed the missionaries to come ashore. Unbe-knownst to the Americans, the traditional Hawaiian religious system had collapsed only months before their arrival. Though Liholiho had some mis-givings about the missionaries, he thought they might bring stability to the islands in light of the recent collapse of the old order.

Over the next quarter century the effect of the missionaries on the Hawaiian community was dramatic—infinitely more so than that of their later, more celebrated, counterparts in Oregon. In terms of saving souls the missionaries made rapid gains. In the mid-1820s, several influential mem-bers of the royal family were baptized and converted to Christianity. By 1840, some 20,000 Hawaiians had officially converted, though there would always be discussion as to how sincere many of the converts were.

The New Englanders also turned their attention to education. They devised an alphabet for the Hawaiian language and established schools that enrolled 52,000 native students, two-fifths of Hawai`i's population, by 1831. They constructed the first printing press west of the Rocky Moun-tains and soon produced a speller and other texts to be used in their schools. The missionaries and other foreigners also founded several schools specif-ically for their own children in the 1830s and 1840s. The O`ahu Charity School and Punahou School, or O`ahu College, as it was also called, so enhanced Honolulu's role as the Pacific metropolis that American mer-chants in Mexican California such as Thomas O. Larkin sent their children to school in the islands.

At times, there appeared to be no bounds to the role played by the American missionaries in Hawai`i. They soon moved from education and salvation to the shaping of public policy, largely in response to what they saw as the need to save the islands from the rowdiness, drunkenness, and prostitution brought on by the arrival of substantial numbers of American whalers. Their influence resulted in a set of blue laws regulating trade and outlawing prostitution.

In the 1830s and 1840s, missionary influence reached its ultimate impact in the organization of a constitutional monarchy for the islands. King Kamehameha III decided that the islands needed a stronger form of government to deal with the increasing presence of foreigners in the islands and called on the missionaries for help in 1838. William Richards resigned his holy calling and, by 1840, devised a constitutional monarchy with a representative assembly for the kingdom. Two years later, he became Hawaiian ambassador to the United States and secured diplomatic recognition for the islands.

While American missionaries, merchants, and whalers penetrated the Far West of Hawai`i between 1800 and 1845, Hawaiians themselves were active on the Pacific Coast of North America and its interior hinterlands. New England was not the only destination of eastward moving Hawaiians. In the 1810s and 1820s, some Hawaiians who had signed on to Yankee vessels left those ships and formed a substantial work force for the Canadian Northwest Fur Company. The death of three Hawaiian fur trappers in what is today southwestern Idaho has been remembered in the names of Owyhee County and the Owyhee River. When Marcus and Narcissa Whitman arrived in Oregon in the 1830s, Hawaiians were already there and formed part of the labor force to build the Whitman's mission. Hawaiians maintained a prominent place in the labor force of Oregon until the Donation Land Claim Act of 1850 specifically excluded them from obtaining free homesteads.

The presence of Hawaiians in the Northwest fur trade was matched by their participation in the California hide and tallow trade. Any reader of Richard Henry Dana's *Two Years Before the Mast* will recall the Bostoner's fond regard for the Kanakas or Sandwich Islanders he met on the beach in San Diego. When Dana returned to California in 1859, it was quite natural for him to extend his trip to Hawai`i. For Dana and others who went to early California, Hawai`i and Hawaiians were an integral part of the American experience in the Pacific. If California was a part of the West, then so was Hawai`i. The oceanic separation of the islands from the American mainland in no way hampered the interaction of the two. No one saw this connection more clearly than John Augustus Sutter. In 1838–1839, he first went to Hawai`i to make contact with Honolulu merchants before establishing his fort in California. A decade later, the strength and importance of the California-Hawai`i link was further reinforced in that seminal event of western expansion occasioned by Sutter—the California Gold Rush.

Reports of the gold discovery at Sutter's mill reached Honolulu in June 1848, the first place outside of California to get the news. By the fall of that year a score of ships from Hawai`i had reached the diggings, making the islanders, both natives and *haoles,* among the first argonauts. For the next two years, Hawai`i was the principal agricultural and mercantile supplier to the California mines with shipments of coffee, sugar, and potatoes—both Irish and sweet. Not only did Hawaiians go to California, but many miners chose to spend their winters in Hawai`i. Neither land nor horse trails were necessary to spur this multi-directional migration.

The spirit of Manifest Destiny that many gold seeking Americans brought to California quickly spread to Hawai`i, leading to the first overtures for American annexation in 1849. The move toward annexation was bolstered not only by Manifest Destiny, but also by fears in both Hawai`i and the United States that France might attempt to annex the islands. In 1851, King Kamehameha III first considered offering the islands to the United States should France make hostile overtures. Californians pushed for annexation because of Hawai`i's advantages in trade and for the protection it offered against other powers in the Pacific. Another spur to annexation sentiment in California was the dramatic decrease in Hawai`i's native population, which had fallen dramatically due to disease and low birth rate in the seventy-five years since Captain Cook's arrival. By 1832, the year of the first official census, the Hawaiian population had dropped to approximately 130,000; it continued to decline to slightly more than 70,000 by 1853. Many Californians saw Hawai`i as potentially virgin, or more accurately widowed, territory for westward migration. Some predicted the entire extinction of the Hawaiian people. As the *Alta California* (San Francisco) announced in 1851: "The native population are [sic] fast fading away, the foreign fast increasing. The inevitable destiny of the islands is to pass into the possession of another power. That power is just as inevitably our own."

With the election of the expansionist Democrat Franklin Pierce to the presidency in 1852, Americans looked ever more favorably on Hawai`i. Supporters for annexation in the Congress included delegates from California and from Maine where the ship building interest pushed Hawai`i. In Hawai`i, local annexation sentiment grew in 1853 because of fears of an internal revolution from foreign commercial interests even after the overt French threat subsided. There were also rumors that bands of filibustering Californians were ready to sail to the islands if an internal revolution broke out. King Kamehameha III entered into negotiations for a treaty with Secretary of State William L. Marcy in 1854, which would have provided for annexation as a state. Further negotiations came to an end with the death of Kamehameha III in December 1854. . . .

With the failure of the first annexation attempt, a pro-British monarchy assumed the throne in the Hawaiian kingdom. In less than a decade, American attentions were diverted to the great Civil War. Despite these changes in island and mainland perspectives, the commonly shared history of the ante-bellum era in no way ended. The Civil War, in fact, stengthened the bond. With Louisiana out of the union after 1861, Hawai`i began to export substantial quantities of sugar to the mainland via San Francisco refiners.

Sugar production, which had been stimulated by American merchants as early as 1835, boomed as a result of the war. Exports of 1.4 million pounds in 1860 soared to over 17 million pounds by 1866.

Sugar pushed the Hawai`i-California connection to heights unimagined before the war. Westerners were eager for news of island developments. In the pre-war tradition of Dana and Sutter, Mark Twain found it logical to travel to Hawai`i as part of a western sojourn. Wearied from his rambles in the mines of Nevada and California, Twain boarded a ship for Honolulu in 1866 with the intent of reporting the commercial opportunities of the islands to California businessmen. His letters for the *Union* (Sacramento) extolled the richness of Hawai`i's land, which yielded many more pounds of sugar per acre than did land in Louisiana. Though native Hawaiians were still the principal agricultural laborers in 1866, Twain pointed to the importation of Chinese coolies in the sugar fields as the wave of the future. Based on his observations in Hawai`i, he told California businessmen to increase their own use of Chinese labor.

A few years after his return to the mainland, Twain incorporated his letters from Hawai`i as the last chapters in his classic 1872 western adventure *Roughing It*. As late as the 1870s, Hawai`i was still a part of Mark Twain's West, but change was in the air. When Twain journeyed to Hawai`i, he was literally on the cusp of two eras. The islands he encountered in 1866 were still in the last phase of the whaling, missionary era. As Twain quipped of the average white man he met, "It is a safe bet that he is either a missionary or a captain of a whaler. I am now personally acquainted with seventy-two captains and ninety-six missionaries." The era in which a small group of whites mingled with a declining, but still numerically dominant, native population was in its final phase. The age of sugar and Asian labor that Twain glimpsed, and in fact proclaimed as the way of the future, was just beginning. Thirty years later the islands were a vastly different place. How fortunate it would have been if Twain had written about the islands again. But fate withheld him that opportunity. Though he returned to Hawai`i in 1895 on a world-wide lecture tour, he could not leave his ship because of a cholera epidemic in Honolulu. The peak of Diamond Head that he sighted from the harbor was much the same as in 1866, but what a different Hawai`i he would have found on shore. A few statistics will have to tell the story that Twain could not write.

Since Twain's departure in 1866, sugar production soared from 17 million pounds to 330 million pounds in 1893. The surge in sugar production resulted from a reciprocity treaty signed in 1875 between Hawai`i and the United States that allowed unrefined Hawaiian sugar to enter the U.S. duty free. The treaty quickly bound Hawai`i to the port of San Francisco, where locale refineries, predominantly those of sugar magnate Claus Spreckels, processed the crop. Though island merchants and planters controlled the majority of the harvest that moved eastward, Spreckels arrived in Hawai`i in 1876 and soon became the single largest planter in the islands. By 1891, the Californian and his Honolulu agent William G. Irwin controlled an estimated one-third of the islands' entire sugar production. Between 1875 and

1898, Hawai`i became more economically integrated into the American West than at any previous time.

The labor recruited to grow and harvest this augmented crop changed Hawai`i even more dramatically. The Chinese laborers Twain observed constituted a scant two percent of Hawai`i's 62,959 population in 1866 compared to 93.3 percent for native Hawaiians. By 1896, Asians—Chinese and Japanese—accounted for 42.1 percent of the islands' 109,020 population; Hawaiians had dropped to 36.2 percent of the total. The Caucasian population also grew in the same period as Portuguese laborers were recruited from Madeira. By 1896, Caucasians accounted for 20.6 percent of the population. However, the economically dominant American, English, and German *haoles* constituted only 6.7 percent of the total.

The Asian migration that transformed Hawai`i's population after 1875 clearly gave the islands a commonly shared social experience with many parts of the American West. But the mainland racism against the Chinese tended to exclude Hawai`i from the consciousness of the western region to which it was increasingly bound. Agitation against Chinese laborers in the West actually resulted in the migration of 8,000 Chinese from California to Hawai`i in the 1870s. . . . After the Chinese Exclusion Acts of the 1880s, white labor groups in California became increasingly hostile to any thought of Hawaiian annexation. Hawai`i would then be a source of the very laborers California was trying to exclude. Immigration could be halted from a foreign country but not from another part of the United States.

While the commonly shared experience of Asian immigration set up a barrier between Hawai`i and California in the western mind, the common economic tie of sugar wrought a similar aversion between the seemingly natural industrial partners in the islands and on the mainland. The post–Civil War sugar industry was characterized by constant economic warfare among eastern, midwestern, southern, and western refineries to gain dominance and control. The introduction of Hawaiian sugar, which would increase the power of California refiners, caused opposition from the other regions. When planters in Hawai`i and U.S. Secretary of State William Seward first championed a reciprocity treaty after the Civil War, easterners opposed it on the ground that it would aid only Pacific Coast refiners. The islands' planters thus had to search for other bonds of interest with the United States to secure the 1875 treaty.

Given its mid-Pacific location, Hawai`i had long been considered the key to Pacific security by American diplomats as early as the 1840s. By the mid-1870s American expansionists were well aware of the potential value of Hawai`i's Pearl Harbor as a coaling station for American ships. The Hawaiian monarchy was averse to ceding Pearl Harbor to the United States, but wondered if some appeal to American strategic interests could be used to gain reciprocity. American strategy did not necessarily require control of Hawai`i, but it did require that no other nation control the islands. Who could be persuaded to bind the economic interests of the islands to the strategic considerations of the mainland?

Though some westerners advocated the Pacific trade, congressional interest was more tied to eastern advocates of expansionism. In 1874, Hawai`i's new king David Kalakaua went to court them. He sailed from Honolulu to San Francisco and then journeyed by train to Washington and other eastern cities. Conjuring up memories of missionary and whaling days, Kalakaua generated goodwill and support for the reciprocity treaty his diplomats negotiated with President Grant. Though objections continued to be made by eastern and, by 1875, southern sugar growers and refiners, strategic considerations carried the day. The simple mention that Hawai`i would not "lease or otherwise dispose" of any "harbor, port or other territory" to another nation was enough to satisfy American imperial interests and gain Senate ratification.

A decade later the treaty was up for renewal. Again, the eastern and southern sugar interests, now alarmed at Spreckels's increasing power from his Hawaiian holdings, sought to thwart ratification. As in 1875, imperial, rather than western, considerations saved the treaty. In 1887, the insertion of a provision that the United States would have exclusive rights to develop a coaling station at Pearl Harbor, an advance over the simple 1875 provision that no other nation could do so, secured a continuation of the treaty. While Hawai`i's sugar exports bound the islands ever more tightly to the U.S. West Coast, it was East Coast expansionists who provided the rope to tie the knot. This pattern would continue over the next decade to the eventual annexation of the islands in 1898.

The impulse to annex Hawai`i originated in the islands. Like the Americans in Texas and California who decided to overthrow Mexican rule in the 1830s and 1840s, Americans in Hawai`i became dissatisfied with the indigenous rule of the Hawaiian monarchy, particularly of King David Kalakaua. Though Kalakaua secured the reciprocity treaty that so transformed the islands, he soon became distressed with the steady decline of the Hawaiian people within their own islands. The actual number of native Hawaiians continued to decline, as had been the case throughout the nineteenth century, as well as their proportion in the population. The ever growing economic power of the *haole* planters and merchants further eroded Hawaiian influence. To counteract this trend, Kalakaua decided to use the enormous tax revenues generated by sugar to expand and enhance the monarchy. He also decided to curtail the traditional *haole* influence in his government by placing more Hawaiians in appointed political positions. The older, more established portion of the *haole* community was particularly offended that Kalakaua was aided in his goals by Claus Spreckels and another American interloper Walter Murray Gibson, a political opportunist who first arrived during the Civil War as a representative of the Mormon church and became head of Kalakaua's cabinet in 1882.

By 1886, a portion of the *haole* community led by lawyer Lorrin Thurston decided that reforms must be made. Kalakaua's lavish expenditures and political maneuvers offended their sense of political stability and caused them to worry about the security of their economic assets. Thurston and his friends formed a group called the Hawaiian League in 1887. With the armed support of a voluntary militia group called the Honolulu Rifles, they forced Kalakaua to issue a new constitution in July 1887, known as the Bayonet Constitution, which increased the power of white property owners in the government.

The attempt of Thurston and the Hawaiian League to increase their political power encountered stiff opposition over the next few years. After Kalakaua's death in 1891, his sister and successor Queen Lili`uokalani pledged to restore Hawaiian power by issuing a new constitution. Concluding that they could no longer live under the monarchy, Thurston and his reformers formed the Annexation Club. Revolution and union with the United States was now the only answer.

Thurston journeyed to Washington in 1892, where the pro-expansionist administration of Benjamin Harrison indicated it would favor annexation if the monarchy were overthrown. When Lili`uokalani announced that she would issue a new constitution in January 1893, Thurston and his group, now called the Committee of Public Safety, acted. With the cooperation of American Minister John Stevens, who agreed to land a contingent of American troops from the U.S.S. *Boston* in Honolulu, the committee announced that the monarchy was abolished and that the provisional government was in power. Lili`uokalani surrendered to the American troops and appealed to Washington to restore her to the throne. Meanwhile, Thurston rushed to the American capital to secure annexation.

President Harrison submitted Thurston's treaty of annexation to the Senate. But as his administration ended only a few weeks after Thurston's arrival, no ratification vote was taken. His Democratic successor, Grover Cleveland, decided to investigate the revolution before proceeding with any new negotiations. He immediately dispatched a commissioner to Hawai`i, James H. Blount, who reported that both the revolution and the participation of American troops were unjustified. He also noted that annexation was not the desire of the native Hawaiian people. Based on these findings, Cleveland opposed annexation and proposed to restore the queen. However, when he found that the provisional government in Hawai`i would not agree to this, the president decided not to use American military force to restore the monarchy—even though it had been American military force that helped topple it. Secure in their power, the white revolutionaries formed the Republic of Hawai`i in 1894 and waited for the return of a Republican government in Washington more friendly to them. In the meantime, American imperial advocates such as Captain Alfred Thayer Mahan championed the cause of annexation by emphasizing the vital role of Hawai`i in Pacific expansion. The *haoles* in Hawai`i did not have to wait long. The election of 1896 brought them the American government they hoped for. By June 1897, President William McKinley sent a treaty of annexation to the Senate. The final congressional debate on Hawaiian annexation and of Hawai`i's "westernness" could now begin.

The principal opponents of annexation were, as usual, the sugar industry. In 1897, both the western and midwestern factions, including Claus Spreckels, opposed annexation because it threatened their control of refined sugar. Under the reciprocity treaties, only unrefined sugar could enter the United States. With annexation the planters in Hawai`i could build their own refineries and compete with Spreckels. The Californian and his western associates wanted to maintain a colonial hold on the source of so much of their wealth in the past decades. Midwestern beet sugar producers also saw Hawai`i as a competitor that could break the monopoly of the American sugar trust. They influenced the western state of Nebraska to join the opposition to the islands. In addition to the sugar trust, other western-ers opposed annexation. Anti-Oriental labor groups in California continued their opposition to Hawai`i and fueled fears in Congress that the islands might one day send a Chinese or Japanese representative to Washington, even though territorial status, rather than statehood, was being requested.

With such "western" opposition to Hawai`i, who supported the islands? Supporters of annexation were predominantly Republicans, particularly those in favor of imperial expansion. Despite this strong support, the treaty might well have failed without the fortuitous outbreak of the Spanish-American War in April 1898. The war's origins had little to do with Hawai`i or the West. But Hawai`i lay in the route of American ships headed for the Philippines. The Hawaiian Republic offered aid to the American fleet and garnered the benefits of the jingoistic enthusiasm generated by the war.

Before the war began, supporters of the treaty feared they could not get the necessary two-thirds vote in the Senate. Using the precedent of Texas annexation in 1845, they proposed annexation by a joint resolution in both houses. With war enthusiasm in the air, the Newlands Resolution passed both houses of Congress during June and July of 1898. Despite the decided opposition from certain western interests, the Pacific states supported Hawai`i in the final vote. Washington and Oregon voted unanimously for the islands in both houses. Calfiornia's Senate vote was split but the House delegation was 4-1 in favor. McKinley quickly signed the resolution on 7 July, and one month later the Republic of Hawai`i was formally transferred to the United States. Technically, the islands retained the government of the republic for another two years, until incorporated territorial status was finally conferred in 1900.

In 1898, Hawai`i, the last far western acquisition, became a part of the United States. A banner proclaiming "Westward The Course of Empire Takes . . ." adorned the balcony during a flag raising ceremony that Sanford B. Dole attended two days before he was inaugurated as Hawai`i's first ter-ritorial governor in 1900. Did these words not make it clear that Hawai`i was now a part of the American West? Over the ensuing century, historians have been willing to accept the "empire" but not the "westward" in the ban-ner. Despite the final support of the Pacific states for annexation and the enormous ties of the sugar trade between Hawai`i and California, the impe-rial overtones of Hawai`i's acquisition have continued to overshadow its westernness. Rather than being placed in western history texts in comple-mentary chapters to the acquisition of Texas and California, Hawai`i's rev-olution and annexation remain the province of diplomatic historians. . . .

Historically there have been a number of Wests. I have suggested that Hawai`i was a part of Richard Henry Dana's and Mark Twain's West. Hawai`i was an integral part of the pre–Civil War maritime West with its central role in the Pacific-Northwest fur trade, the whaling industry, the hide and tallow trade, and the California Gold Rush. Like California and Astoria, it was part of the West first reached by ships rather than by wagons and trains. After the Civil War, Hawai`i remained a part of that early western tradition with the sugar trade that still bound it in a mercantile and maritime fashion to California. But, in the years after 1865, other historic Wests emerged that left Hawai`i behind. The "classic" Old West that attracted so many frontier historians with its cowboys, miners, and Indian wars was, for the most part, a post–Civil War West heavily shaped and brought into being by the railroad. . . . It has been the advocates of these newer Wests who have protested most against Hawai`i.

Geographically, the inclusion of Hawai`i presents the American West with a true western frontier, with a border where one set of traditions and cultures meets others. As one moves toward Hawai`i, the American West meets Asia and Polynesia. The hula, the floral lei, and Japanese tourists compete as cultural symbols and designators with the whaling port of Lahaina [and] the mission houses. . . . There are people in Hawai`i who find the Asian and Polynesian ties stronger than the western ones. And some native Hawaiians might well feel that the inclusion of their islands in the American West is yet one more act of dispossession. But that is the nature of lands and peoples on the border. Westerners do not exclude San Diego and El Paso from the region because those cities border on Mexico. Westerners have come to grips with their southern frontier. Hawai`i provides the opportunity to come to grips with the region's western frontier, with its farthest West. . . .

Finally, Hawai`i places western historians on academic borders. I have suggested several times that diplomatic rather than western historians have embraced Hawai`i as their own. But diplomatic history is not antithetical to western history. From 1803 to 1898, the entire trans-Mississippi West was acquired by diplomatic negotiations between the United States and foreign nations with varying degrees of military force and mutual advantage. Possibly the most commonly shared history of the various regions of the American West has been the diplomacy of acquisition. In this diplomatic light, Hawai`i commands a prominent place in western history from the appointment of the first American consul in 1820 to the final annexation of the Republic of Hawai`i in 1898.

Diplomatically, geographically, and historically Hawai`i has long and deep connections to the American West. It was a part of the first maritime Far West, it was the nation's last far western acquisition, and it is truly a part of America's farthest western frontier. . . .

Y *FURTHER READING*

George M. Brack, "Mexican Opinion, American Racism, and the War of 1846," *Western Historical Quarterly* 1 (1978): 161–74
———, *Mexico Views Manifest Destiny, 1821–1846: An Essay on the Origins of the Mexican War* (1975)

Arnoldo De León, *They Called Them Greasers: Anglo Attitudes Toward Mexicans in Texas, 1821–1900* (1983)

Richard Drinnon, *Facing West: The Metaphysics of Indian-Hating and Empire-Building* (1980)

Michael Kioni Dudley and Keoni Kealoha Agard, *A Call for Hawaiian Sovereignty* (1990)

Jack Ericson Eblen, *The First and Second United States Empires: Governors and Territorial Government, 1784–1912* (1968)

John S. D. Eisenhower, *So Far from God: The U.S. War with Mexico, 1846–1848* (1989)

William H. Goetzmann, *When the Eagle Screamed: The Romantic Horizon in American Diplomacy, 1800–1860* (1966)

Norman Graebner, "The Mexican War: A Study in Causation," *Pacific Historical Review* 49 (1980): 405–26

Klaus J. Hansen, "The Millennium, the West, and Race in the Antebellum American Mind," *Western Historical Quarterly* 3 (1972): 373–90

Robert F. Heizer and Alan F. Almquist, *The Other Californians: Prejudice and Discrimination under Spain, Mexico, and the United States to 1920* (1971)

Ted Hinckley, *The Americanization of Alaska, 1867–1897* (1972)

Robert V. Hine, *Bartlett's West: Drawing the Mexican Boundary* (1968)

Reginald Horsman, *Race and Manifest Destiny* (1981)

——, *Expansion and American Indian Policy, 1783–1812* (1967)

Albert L. Hurtado, *Indian Survival on the California Frontier* (1988)

Robert W. Johannsen, *To the Halls of the Montezumas: The Mexican War in the American Imagination* (1985)

David Alan Johnson, *Founding the Far West: California, Oregon, and Nevada, 1840–1890* (1992)

Howard S. Lamar, *The Far Southwest, 1846–1912: A Territorial History* (1966)

Ernest M. Lander, Jr., *Reluctant Imperialists: Calhoun, the South Carolinians and the Mexican War* (1980)

Frederick Merk, *Manifest Destiny and Mission in American History: Reinterpretation* (1963)

——, *The Monroe Doctrine and American Expansionism* (1972)

David Montejano, *Anglos and Mexicans in the Making of Texas, 1836–1986* (1987)

Linda S. Parker, *Native American Estate: The Struggle over Indian and Hawaiian Lands* (1989)

David Pletcher, *The Diplomacy of Annexation: Texas, Oregon, and the Mexican War* (1973)

Earl S. Pomeroy, *The Territories and the United States, 1861–1890: Studies in Colonial Administration* (1947)

Philip Wayne Powell, *Tree of Hate: Propaganda and Prejudice Affecting United States Relations with the Hispanic World* (1971)

Francis Paul Prucha, *The Great Father: The United States Government and the American Indians*, 2 vols. (1984)

Morgan B. Sherwood, *Exploration of Alaska, 1865–1900* (1965)

Otis Singletary, *The Mexican War* (1960)

Joe A. Stout, Jr., *The Liberators: Filibustering Expeditions into Mexico and the Last Thrust of Manifest Destiny* (1973)

Robert M. Utley, *Frontier Regulars: The United States Army and the Indian, 1866–1891* (1973)

——, *The Indian Frontier of the American West, 1846–1890* (1984)

Charles Vevier, "American Continentalism: An Idea of Expansion," *American Historical Review* 65 (1960): 323–35

Walter L. Williams, "United States Indian Policy and the Debate over Philippine Annexation: Implications for the Origins of American Imperialism," *Journal of American History* 66 (1980): 810–31

CHAPTER
6

Cowboys, Outlaws,
and Violence

Y

Cowboys and outlaws are not just images created in Hollywood. Nonetheless, mass media in the form of dime novels, pulp magazines, radio programs, western films, and television series have presented many more shoot-outs and stampedes than can be found in the historical record. Did cowboys and outlaws lead exciting, adventuresome lives? How much violence did they encounter or create? Despite the tales of dramatic action set in the "Old West" of popular culture, what does the history of the "Real West" reveal? Especially troubling is the possibility that hard-working cowpunchers have become confused with gun-fighting desperados.

From the late 1860s to the late 1880s, in the era of the great trail drives and the open-range cattle bonanza, cowboys represented the racial diversity of the West, as did other wage laborers such as miners. Cow outfits could include Native Americans of mixed heritage, African Americans—often from Texas—Mexicans and Mexican Americans as well as Anglo Americans, Englishmen, and Scotsmen. Outlaw bands had some racial mixing, but several of the most famous relied on blood relations—exemplified by the sets of brothers who organized the James, Younger, and Dalton gangs. Ironically, violence for illegal gain did not preclude elevating outlaws to the status of folk heros. Individuals such as Billy the Kid and Jesse James acquired lasting fame through fierce action and dramatic death. Why have cowboys and outlaws acquired so much acclaim? To what extent do these popular heros reveal that in the West, or in the nation as a whole, many people approve of certain types of violence?

Y DOCUMENTS

The death of a famous outlaw sometimes produced dramatic accounts akin to pulp fiction. The first document is an excerpt from a book that appeared in 1882, the year of Jesse James's death. Its title page read, "Jesse James: The Life and Daring Adventures of this Bold Highwayman and Bank Robber and His No Less Celebrated Brother Frank James together with the Thrilling Exploits of the Younger Boys, written by *** (one who dare not NOW disclose his identity). The Only Book containing the Romantic Life of Jesse James and His Pretty Wife who clung to Him to the Last." The second document, another excerpt, appeared in 1925, in the posthumously published memoir of Granville Stuart, a well-known pioneer cattleman in central Montana. In 1884, Stuart led a band of vigilantes that executed, in less than one month, at least seventeen men suspected of rustling. "Stuart's Stranglers" may have hanged some honest individuals. His actions elicited criticism locally, but did not upset his fellow cattlemen. In 1885, they elected him president of the Montana Stock Growers Association.

As his memoirs revealed, Granville Stuart felt justified when he took the law into his own hands. Helen Wiser Stewart could not respond in a like manner when a hostile hired hand, Schyler Henry, who had quit working at the Stewart ranch in Nevada, killed her husband, Archie. Helen's letter of July 16, 1884, to a lawyer named Sawyer, reprinted here as the third document, gave details of the slaying and of her tragic predicament. She never explained the lies told by Schyler Henry that had so enraged Archie. No one stood trial for her husband's death. Helen, left with five children to raise, carried on with her husband's murderer possibly still nearby. Despite this frightening situation, she kept her ranch and over the next two decades expanded her holdings to more than two thousand acres, which made her the largest landowner in Lincoln County, Nevada. Helen Wiser Stewart did not allow one horrible act of violence to drive her off the land.

According to Granville Stuart, Theodore Roosevelt had advocated vigilante action against rustlers at a meeting of the Montana Stock Growers Association, which Roosevelt attended in Miles City on April 20, 1884. The fourth document is an article by the future president published in 1893 in *Century Magazine.* Roosevelt had not joined Stuart's Stranglers, nor had he experienced the murderous violence that transformed Helen Wiser Stewart's life. Instead, Roosevelt viewed both cowboys and outlaws as "wild rough-riders of the plains." He accepted much of the "lawlessness of life in the wilderness" as an admissible, almost heroic, aspect of men's lives on the frontier. The final document illustrates that lawless lives could end suddenly. The June 15, 1894 *Weekly Elevator* of Fort Smith, Arkansas, reported the death of Bill Dalton. Thousands of people came to view the corpse of the notorious outlaw in Ardmore, Indian Territory (later Oklahoma). What explains the popular fascination with the death of certain criminals, like Jesse James and Bill Dalton? Why are violent deaths approved by some, in the case of vigilante hangings, or ignored by others, as in the killing of Archie Stewart?

A Popular Account of the Death of Jesse James, 1882

The end of the play—The curtain falls—The lights turned down, and the King of American bandits makes a hasty exit!

On the morning of April 3d, 1882, Jesse James "died with his boots on." That it was a cowardly assassination I am forced to admit, but in writing of one that I knew well I have but this to say: he would have done the same to anyone whom he for one moment suspected! He would have killed the man and *inquired into the facts afterwards!* St. Joseph, Missouri, was the scene of his "taking off," and the Ford boys were "in at the death!"

He was shot down by two men who were in his confidence, and who had planned a raid for that very night. After the Blue Cut robbery in September, 1881, James was in hiding at his mother's house at Kearney, near Kansas City. He remained there for a few weeks and kept very quiet. Some time in November he went to St. Joseph and established himself in a little shanty in the southeastern part of the city. His wife, who was devotedly attached to him, and who is young and pretty, went with him. Although there had long been a price upon the heads of the James boys, Jesse paid no attention to it. His many hairbreadth escapades had made him oblivious to danger. Instead of going to Texas, as had been his custom when hunted down too closely, he remained in Missouri, only taking care to keep out of sight. He had been living very quietly in "Saint Jo," always kept himself well armed to guard against surprise, and his shanty was a regular arsenal.

After the shooting it was learned that Jesse had been planning another desperate raid, with the help of two brothers named Robert and Charles Ford. Just who these men were was not then known. It was believed they had been engaged in robberies with him before, but they claimed that they had been on his track for a long time, with the intention of capturing him and claiming the heavy rewards offered by the express companies, that have suffered from his depredations, and the State authorities. However that may be they were in his confidence. Charles had been at his house for several weeks, and Robert came a week or ten days before the assassination. These two men were the ones who shot down their chief without giving him a second's warning. James always wore a belt stuffed full of revolvers of the latest pattern. They were always loaded and he never took a step without them. If the Ford brothers had given him cause for the slightest suspicion he would have shot them down without hesitation. He had often treated detectives who had tried to gain his confidence in just that manner, and he would not have hesitated to do it again. It was thought for this reason that the Fords had been with him before and were well known to him, and it is not impossible that they became frightened at the general breaking up of the band and the many arrests, and sought to cover their own tracks and make themselves right at the same time with the authorities by taking the life of the great outlaw.

Jesse James: The Life and Daring Adventures of This Bold Highwayman and Bank Robber and His No Less Celebrated Brother, Frank James . . . (Philadelphia, PA: Barclay & Co., 1882).

At 9 o'clock on the morning of April 3d, 1882, the great outlaw and the two Fords were together in a front room in Jesse James' house. Unconscious of danger James unbuckled his belt and threw it on the bed preparatory to washing himself. He was unarmed. Jesse got upon a chair to arrange a picture. The brothers had determined to kill him and get the reward and this was their chance.

They exchanged glances and silently stepped between the pistols and their victim. Both drew their pistols. The click of the hammers fell on the ear of Jesse, and he was turning his head evidently to see what caused the warning sound when Robert, the youngest brother, sent a bullet crashing through his brain. The murdered bandit fell backward without a cry and rolled in his death agony on the floor.

Jesse's wife, who was in the next room, ran in and saw the two brothers scaling the fence and making off. Hardly had the shot been fired when there was a piercing scream. The dead man's wife flung herself upon the prostrate body and gave way to her grief in a flood of tears. The Fords gave themselves up and were hurried away to the court house and a guard immediately put on duty. The news spread like wildfire. The house was surrounded by excited people and hundreds of persons talked about the bloody deed on the streets. The body was taken in charge by the police and photographed. Persons who had known the outlaw were allowed to view the remains. They declared that there was no doubt this time and at last the great bandit had been killed. The face is fine-looking and intelligent and would not be taken for that of a cruel murderer. The house was searched and found to contain a quantity of firearms and ammunition. In the stable was several splendid horses.

Granville Stuart Recalls Cattle Rustlers and Vigilantes, 1883–1884

At the close of the fall roundup (1883) our tallies showed that we had suffered at least a three per cent loss from "rustling." These thieves were splendidly organized and had established headquarters and had enough friends among the ranchers to enable them to carry on their work with perfect safety.

Near our home ranch we discovered one rancher whose cows invariably had twin calves and frequently triplets, while the range cows in that vicinity were nearly all barren and would persist in hanging around this man's corral, envying his cows their numerous children and bawling and lamenting their own childless fate. This state of affairs continued until we were obliged to call around that way and threaten to hang the man if his cows had any more twins.

The "rustlers" were particularly active along the Missouri and Yellowstone rivers and our neighbors in the Dakota bad lands were great sufferers. . . .

Reprinted by permission of the Publishers, The Arthur H. Clark Company, from *Forty Years on the Frontier as seen in the Journals and Reminiscences of Granville Stuart,* Volume 2, Cleveland, 1925.

Billy Downs was located at one of the wood yards on the Missouri at the mouth of the Musselshell, ostensibly to trap wolves, but in reality to sell whiskey to the Indians. His place soon came to be headquarters for tough characters, and it was but a short time until Downs himself was stealing horses and killing cattle. Downs was a married man and his wife was at the wood yard with him. Because of sympathy for the woman, he was warned that he was being watched and that if he did not change his tactics he was sure to get into trouble. He paid not the least attention to the warning, but continued to surround himself with the worst characters on the river and kept on stealing horses and killing cattle.

On the night of July 4, [1884] a committee of vigilantes arrived at the Downs' place and called on him to come out. This at first he refused to do but after a short parley he did come out, accompanied by a notorious character known as California Ed. Both men plead guilty to stealing ponies from the Indians but denied that they had stolen from white men, but they failed to account for the twenty-six horses in the corral, all bearing well-known brands. They claimed that the quantity of dried meat found in the house was dried buffalo meat, notwithstanding the fact that there had not been a buffalo on the range for more than two years. In the stable was a stack of fresh hides folded and salted ready to be shipped down the river, all bearing the brand of the Fergus Stock Co. The two men were taken out to a little grove of trees and hanged.

At the time the vigilante committee started for the mouth of Musselshell, another party left for the vicinity of Rocky Point where two notorious horse thieves, known as Red Mike and Brocky Gallagher, were making their headquarters. They had stolen about thirty head of horses from Smith river, changed the brands and were holding them in the bad lands. They had also been operating over on the Moccasin range and stolen horses from J. H. Ming's ranch and from J. L. Stuart.

When the vigilantes arrived at Rocky Point the men were not there but had crossed over on the north side of the river. The party followed after, and captured them and recovered some of the horses. Both men plead guilty to horse stealing and told their captors that there were six head of the stolen horses at Dutch Louie's ranch on Crooked creek.

Fifteen miles below the mouth of the Musselshell, at an old abandoned wood yard, lived old man James, his two sons, and a nephew. Here also was the favorite haunt of Jack Stringer. There was a log cabin and a stable with a large corral built of logs, connecting the two buildings. One hundred yards from the cabin in a wooded bottom was a tent constructed of poles and covered with three wagon sheets. At the cabin were old man James, his two sons, Frank Hanson and Bill Williams. Occupying the tent were Jack Stringer, Paddy Rose, Swift Bill, Dixie Burr, Orvil Edwards, and Silas Nickerson.

On the morning of July 8, the vigilantes arrived at Bates Point. The men were divided into three parties. Three guarded the tent, five surrounded the cabin and one was left behind with the saddle horses. They then waited for daylight. Old man James was the first to appear. He was ordered to open the corral and drive out the horses. This he did but refused to surrender, backed into the cabin and fired a shot from his rifle through a small port hole at the side of the door. This was followed by a volley from port holes all around the cabin and in an instant the whole party was in action.

Two of the vigilantes crawled up and set fire to the hay stack and the cabin. The men inside stationed themselves at port holes and kept up the fight until they were all killed or burned up. The cabin burned to the ground. The tent was near the river bank and almost surrounded by thick brush and it was easier to escape from it than to get out of the cabin. Stringer Jack crawled under the tent and reached a dense clump of willows from which he made his last stand. Dixie Burr had his arm shattered with a rifle ball but jumped into an old dry well and remained until dark. Paddy Rose ran out of the tent, passed back of the men engaged at the cabin and concealed himself in a small washout and after dark made his escape. Nickerson, Edwards, and Swift Bill reached the river bank and crawling along through the brush and under the bank, succeeded in passing above the men at the cabin and hid in some brush and drift wood. Orvil Edwards and Silas Nickerson were the only ones that escaped without wounds. After the fight at the cabin the men went down the river and spent the day looking for the men who had escaped but failed to find them.

On the afternoon of the ninth, the fugitives rolled some dry logs into the river, constructed a raft and started down stream. At Popular creek agency they were discovered by some soldiers stationed there, ordered to come on shore and were arrested.

Notice of their arrest was sent to Fort Maginnis and Samuel Fischel, deputy U.S. marshall, started at once to get the prisoners and take them to White Sulphur Springs. At the mouth of the Musselshell a posse met Fischel and took the prisoners from him. Nearby stood two log cabins close together. A log was placed between the cabins, the ends resting on the roofs, and the four men were hanged from the log. The cabins caught fire and were burned down and the bodies were cremated.

Paddy Rose lay all day concealed in a little washout in the bad lands and at night struck for Fort Benton, where he had wealthy and influential relatives. With their influence and assistance he succeeded in reaching the Canadian border.

There were one hundred and sixty-five stolen horses recovered at Bates Point and one hundred and nineteen at other places. After the fight at Bates Point the vigilantes disbanded and returned to their respective homes. This clean-up of horse thieves put a stop to horse and cattle stealing in Montana for many years.

Several of the men that met their fate on the Missouri in July, 1884, belonged to wealthy and influential families and there arose a great hue and cry in certain localities over what was termed "the arrogance of the cattle kings." The cattlemen were accused of hiring "gunmen" to raid the country and drive the small ranchers and sheepmen off the range. There was not a grain of truth in this talk.

There were but fourteen members of the vigilance committee and they were all men who had stock on the range and who had suffered at the hands of the thieves. There was not one man taken on suspicion and not one was hanged for a first offense. The men that were taken were members of an organized band of thieves that for more than two years had evaded the law and robbed the range at will. The fact that the stock men loaned milch cows, horses, and farm machinery to settlers on small ranches, branded their calves for them at roundup prices, established schools for them, bought their butter and vegetables at high prices and in every way helped them to get a start is proof that any law-abiding person was welcome in this country.

Helen Wiser Stewart Writes of Her Husband's Murder, 1884

July 16, 1884
Las Vegas Rancho Nev.

Mr. Sawyer, Sir.

I write to you in great distress of mind hoping you as a husband and father will aid me to the best of your ability—I am left alone here and my little children fatherless by the hand of a murderer. My beloved husband and only friend was murdered Sunday the 13th at Mr. Kiels one mile and half from here while defending the honor of his family from a black-hearted Slanderers tounge. The evidence is all circumstantial. The man had been working here and while Mr. Stewart was in the El Dorodo Cañon left and went over to Kiels and was kept posted on every movement going on at the Vegas and was supplied with arms and a horse by men on the Ranch and vicinity. Archie came home Sunday about 10 o'clock after he had eaten dinner and rested a short time & told him of the Slander being talked about as it had been told to every one stopping on the place and passers by the day before. Mr. Stewart came home; they tried to frighten me into paying the man Schyler Henry off and letting him go. As he had got money and clothing of Mr. Stewart which I knew nothing of I could not settle as it was something I had never done before. About 2 O'Clock Willie the oldest boy saw his father saddle his horse and go down on the cattle range taking his Henry Rifle which is no unusual occurance, going in an opposite direction from Kiels. I supposed he was going down to see George Allen at his Coal camp on the road to the cañon 10 miles from here. Mr. Allen had been stopping here several days but left early Sunday morning for the cañon. The next I heard of my poor husband is this note which I copy as it was written by old man Kiel:

> Mrs. Stewart send a team and take Mr. Stewart away—he is dead—C Kiel

I left my little children with Mr. Frazier and went as fast as a Horse would carry me. The man that killed my husband ran as I approached as I got to

From *Women of the West* ed. by Cathy Luchetti (St. George, Utah: Antelope Island Press, 1982).

the corner of the house I said Oh where is he Oh where is he and the Old Man Kiel and Hank Parish said here he is and lifting a blanket showed me the lifeless form of my husband. I knelt beside him, took his hands, placed my hand upon his heart and looked upon his face and saw a bullet hole about two inches above the temple and about one inch into the hair and looking more closely I saw where the Rifle had been placed directly under the right ear and fired off that side of his face to a crisp. (He must have received that shot after he fell) and across the cheek bone & forehead on the right side he had been hit with some heavy instrument breaking the cheek bone and forehead starting in the opposite direction from the way the bullet went in; they told me he was shot in the shoulder. The hired men came with the Spring waggon and I took him home and on examination found he had been shot right above the left breast coming out under the right arm. The men said it was a pistol shot. It is evident that Mr. Stewart was finally Killed in the house with no one as witness except this Henry and old man Kiel. They are both Archie's enemies and would not tell the truth but swear against Archie. I am here with a lot of roughs and my life and Husbands property in danger. If I have friends in Pioche I think—pray they will come and help me. George Allen & James Wilson are here; also Mr. Frazier whose health is very poor he being hardly able to wait on himself but he has done all he can for me. Mr. Allen and Mr. Wilson both have business to attend to but say they will help me all they can in the time they can leave their business both inconvenienced themselves already.

PRIVATE

My friends here tell me I ought to be thinking of my children's interest. I do not know whether there is a will but think maybe there is but in case there is not I wish the guardianship of my children and to administer on the property. They tell me I will have to apply in 30 days from the 13th. They tell me I will have to go to Pioche right away. Write soon as possible and give me good legal instructions in regard to this matter. If there is a chance of anyone taking advantage of myself and childrens rights before I could get there I wish you to take measures to protect us. The man that murdered my husband is still at Kiels with a slight flesh wound in the hip. It is dangerous to say or do anything as we are overpowered by numbers and still threatened.

Yours in distress
Mrs. Archie Stewart
    you can give this to the public except what is marked private

Signed by,   These gentlemen sign their names here
Mr. Frazier   to corporate my statement—Mrs. Stewart
G. Allen
J. B. Wilson

Theodore Roosevelt Describes Cowboy–Land, 1893

Out on the frontier, and generally among those who spend their lives in, or on the borders of, the wilderness, life is reduced to its elemental conditions. The passions and emotions of these grim hunters of the mountains and these wild rough-riders of the plains are simpler and stronger than those of people dwelling in more complicated states of society. As soon as communities become settled and begin to grow with any rapidity, the American instinct for law asserts itself; but in the earlier stages each individual is obligated to be a law to himself, and to guard his rights with a strong hand. Of course the transition stages are full of incongruities. Men have not yet adjusted their relations to morality and law with any niceness. They hold strongly by certain rude virtues, and, on the other hand, they quite fail to recognize even as shortcomings not a few traits that obtain mercy in older communities.

Many of the desperados, the man-killers, and road-agents have good sides to their characters. Often they are people who in certain stages of civilization do, or have done, good work, but who, when these stages have passed, find themselves surrounded by conditions which accentuate their worst qualities, and make their best qualities useless. The average desperado, for instance, has, after all, much the same standard of morals that the Norman nobles had in the days of the battle of Hastings, and ethically and morally he is decidedly in advance of the vikings, who were the ancestors of these same nobles, and to whom, by the way, he himself could doubtless trace a portion of his blood. If the transition from the wild lawlessness of life in the wilderness or on the border to a higher civilization were stretched out over a term of centuries, he and his descendants would doubtless accommodate themselves by degrees to the changing circumstances. But, unfortunately, in the far West the transition takes place with marvelous abruptness, and at an altogether unheard-of speed, and many a man's nature is unable to change with sufficient rapidity to allow him to harmonize with his environment. In consequence, unless he leaves for still wilder lands, he ends by getting hung, instead of founding a family which would revere his name as that of a very capable, although not in all respects a conventionally moral, ancestor.

Most of the men with whom I was intimately thrown during my life on the frontier and in the wilderness were good fellows, hard-working, brave, resolute, and truthful. At times, of course, they were forced of necessity to do deeds which would seem startling to dwellers in cities and in old settled places; and though they waged a very stern and relentless warfare upon evil-doers whose misdeeds had immediate and tangible bad results, they showed a wide toleration of all save the most extreme classes of wrong, and were not given to inquiring too curiously into a strong man's past, or to criticizing him too harshly for a failure to discriminate in finer ethical questions. Moreover, not a few of the men with whom I came in contact—with

Theodore Roosevelt, *Ranch Life in the Far West* (Golden, CO: Outbooks, 1981), 88.

some of whom my relations were very close and friendly—had at different times led rather tough careers. This fact was accepted by them and by their companions as a fact, and nothing more. There were certain offenses, such as rape, the robbery of a friend, or murder under circumstances of cowardice and treachery, which were never forgiven; but the fact that when the country was wild a young fellow had gone on the road,—that is, become a highwayman,—or had been chief of a gang of desperados, horse-thieves, and cattle-killers, was scarcely held to weigh against him, it being treated as a regrettable, but certainly not shameful, trait of youth. He was regarded by his neighbors with the same kindly tolerance which respectable medieval Scotch borderers doubtless extended to their wilder young men, who would persist in raiding English cattle even in time of peace.

Of course, if these men were asked outright as to their stories, they would have refused to tell them, or else would have lied about them; but when they had grown to regard a man as a friend and companion, they would often recount various incidents of their past lives with perfect frankness; and as they combined in a very curious degree both a decided sense of humor, and a failure to appreciate that there was anything especially remarkable in what they related, their tales were always entertaining.

An Arkansas Newspaper on the Killing of Bill Dalton, 1894

BILL DALTON, THE BANDIT, KILLED

AT ELK, I.T., WHILE TRYING TO

ESCAPE FROM DEPUTY MARSHALS.

Bill Dalton, the notorious desperado and bandit, met his death on the 8th inst. at Elk, I.T. [Indian Territory]. C.L. Hart, a deputy marshal of the Paris district, fired the shot that sent the spirit of the outlaw to its home.

Last Friday afternoon a man named Wallace, accompanied by two women, rode into Ardmore and bought $200 worth of goods, for which they paid cash. Wallace, being a dissolute sort of a fellow, and known to be generally short of cash, his movements attracted attention. After purchasing the goods he went to the express office and called for a package which was given to him. This caused his arrest by the officers, who had been watching him, and the package upon being broken open was found to contain several gallons of whiskey. From the parties arrested and the incautious remarks the woman dropped the officials concluded the liquor was intended for the Longview bank robbers, who were thought to be camped near Elk, a small town 25 miles northwest of Ardmore. A posse of United States deputy marshals, consisting of D.E. Booker, S.F. Gladsay, S. Leatherman, E. Roberts, W.B. Freeman, M. Glover and Ross Hart, started for the freebooters' rendezvous. The Wallace place, where they had reason to believe their gang

Gaddy, Jerry J., ed., *Dust to Dust: Obituaries of the Gunfighters* (San Rafael, CA: Presidio Press/Old Army Press, 1977), pp. 60–61.

was in hiding, was surrounded by the posse about 8 a.m. that day, and while the men were taking their positions Dalton was seen to come out and look around and immediately return. The officers on the east side were discovered by him through a window or by some woman in the house, and, pistols in hand, he jumped through a window on the north and started to run east. Hart was less than thirty yards from the house and called on him to halt. Dalton half turned around, tried to take aim while running, and just then the officer shot. Two jumps in the air were the only motions made. His pistol fell from his hand, and with a groan he sank to the ground, and Hart ran up and asked him what he was doing there, but he was too near dead to reply.

The remains were taken to Ardmore, where they were viewed by thousands of people. Dalton's wife was one of the women who had been captured, and she identified the corpse as that of her husband. Cole Dalton and another brother of the outlaw called on the following day and made the identification more complete. The body will be sent to California for burial.

The house in which Dalton was staying was searched and a large lot of letters and notes found which had been addressed to the outlaw. Considerable evidences were found which prove that he was the leader of the bank robbery at Longview, Texas. Considerable money was found in the house, besides $275 on the body of Dalton. This was given to his wife.

The black hair of the corpse at first led to doubts as to whether Dalton had been killed. These doubts were removed during the process of embalming where it was discovered that the hair had been dyed.

Y *E S S A Y S*

Robert R. Dykstra is professor of history and public policy at the State University of New York, Albany. His essay in this collection combines two pieces that were published twenty-eight years apart. The first is from his prize-winning 1968 book, *The Cattle Towns,* which demonstrated that the historical record did not support the popular image of wide-open, lawless violence in famous end-of-the-trail communities such as Abilene, Ellsworth, Wichita, Dodge City, and Caldwell. Despite the great respect scholars gave to Dykstra's study, by the mid-1990s, he still found that the legend of cattle town killings and cowboy violence lived on in public expressions and popular fiction. Richard White of the University of Washington, and 1995–1996 president of the Western History Association, has won many prizes for his published work in western history, ethnohistory, and environmental studies. His essay considers whether western outlaws may be viewed as a social movement akin to the "social bandits" described by the European historian E. J. Hobsbawm. Did these outlaws fight for a better world even as they broke the law? White's careful analysis shows the limitations of such assumptions. His essay further explains how historical reality gave way to popular perceptions of the bandit and western hero. Dykstra and White trace different developments that emerged in the misrepresentation of violence in the West. Why do some murderous outlaws become popular heros and some lawful communities become synonymous with crime and killing?

The Cattle Towns Adjust to Violence (with a Postscript)

ROBERT R. DYKSTRA

As legend and literature have made all the world aware, the cattle town people confronted a peculiar social problem: personal violence. The traditional concept of the cattle trading center as an arena for almost unlimited homicide is not a twentieth-century product. Notoriety was a contemporary thing, born of the same vigorous sensationalism that underlies the present-day image. Three of the five major cattle towns, in fact, suffered from violent reputations even before their careers as cattle trading centers.

Ellsworth, which did not receive large numbers of longhorns until 1871, earned an unenviable community image immediately after its founding in 1867. Filled with a heterogeneous collection of teamsters, railroad workers, army scouts, soldiers, and the usual disreputable hangers-on—itinerant liquor dealers, gamblers, prostitutes—it was the scene of at least eight homicides during its first year of existence, all delightedly recorded by newspaper editors in better regulated towns up the line.

Dodge City experienced a similar early notoriety that it never outlived. Established four years before becoming an important reception point for Texas cattle, it entertained the same type of transients as had Ellsworth, plus a lethal increment of buffalo hunters. During its first year, 1872–73, news correspondents reported the violent deaths there of nine men, with another three as possibles. A quarter of a century later George M. Hoover, whose memory remained accurate about other matters, reported the true figure to have been fifteen. A year after its first settlement the commandant at nearby Fort Dodge finally had to intervene and rescue the town from a band of pseudo-vigilante terrorists.

Caldwell suffered much the same public relations fate. In the nine years between its founding in 1871 and its emergence as a cattle center in 1880, an assortment of vagrant whisky peddlers, livestock rustlers, and other frontier riffraff infested the tiny border community and its environs. Several murders and lynchings made its name a synonym for violence that, as in the cases of Ellsworth and Dodge, the passage of time never erased.

Primary responsibility for these initial homicides must be laid to the lack of any systematic efforts to suppress violence in these as yet municipally unorganized communities. Although the subsequent arrival of the Texas cattle trade hardly promised an end to the kind of transients who caused trouble, a new factor altered the situation considerably. The community economic base increasingly featured a variety of more or less orthodox businessmen interested in maximizing profits in a rational manner. By

Robert Dykstra, *The Cattle Towns* (New York: Alfred A. Knopf, 1968), pp. 112–148. Copyright © 1968 by Robert R. Dykstra. Reprinted by permission of Alfred A. Knopf, Inc. Available in paperback by the University of Nebraska Press.

and large the cattle town business firm represented a substantial investment over earlier enterprises both in stock and plant outlay, even the characteristic tent or shack saloon of earlier years giving way to a measure of bibulous elegance most attractive to drovers, buyers, and cowhands. Homicide, it seemed obvious enough, could easily lead to riot, and riot to property destruction—arson being particularly feared in those pre-brick days of almost prohibitive fire insurance rates.

In addition, as their profits mounted cattle town business and professional men increasingly invested surplus earnings in local opportunities, and such commitments caused an entrepreneur to identify the community's well-being with his own. Although the desire to suppress disorder could be, and was, rationalized in terms of making the town a good place to raise a family, townsfolk also feared that publicity about local violence inhibited the immigration of solid citizens, hard money, and permanent industry. "During the coming season," wrote a Wichita editor,

> Wichita desires law and order, with their consequent peace and security, and not bloodshed and a name that will cause a thrill of horror whenever mentioned and which will effectually deter the most desirable class of people from coming among us. Right speedily will the latter follow if the former are not maintained.

On the eve of his town's first cattle shipping season a Caldwell editor warned fellow citizens of the same danger. "We know," he reflected,

> that persons will frequent the city, at times, who, reckless in regard to law and order, having no interest in the good name and welfare of the place, acknowledge only their own inclinations and whims as their sole rule and guide for their conduct. Should this element . . . get the upper hand . . . then we may be certain that business men, men with capital and men having families, whom they love and respect, will steer clear of this place, and go to other localities, where law and order is the watchword of the day. Nothing would more surely kill the rapid growth, the substantial growth of our city.

Essentially entrepreneurial motives, in short, provided a powerful impetus for the systematic suppression of violence.

Legend implies that the cattle town people found themselves almost at the mercy of armed visitors, but such was not really the case. Responsible vigilante action always remained a decisive deterrent to any attempted terrorism by transients. The Kansas code empowered mayors to call upon all male inhabitants between the ages of eighteen and fifty to aid in enforcing the law. Yet local authorities held this alternative in reserve as an extraordinary measure to be used only when regular law enforcement had broken down—as at Ellsworth in 1873, at Wichita the following year, and at Dodge City and Caldwell in 1881. Whether justified by circumstances or not, collective citizen action invariably created ill feeling among the transients, most of whom, cowboys and drovers alike, were clannish Texans easily roused to a kind of ethnocentric defensiveness. The withdrawal of herds—

and consumers—from an "unfriendly" shipping center always remained a possibility. The problem for the cattle town people was not to rid themselves of visitors prone to violence, but to suppress the violence while retaining the visitors.

The community problem was unique in this respect, but the initial steps toward order were strictly conventional. Although many routine advantages accrued to communities that incorporated themselves as municipalities under Kansas law, at the cattle towns the immediate impetus to legal organization was fear of transient violence. Except in the case of Abilene, actual or anticipated acquisition of the cattle trade coincided roughly with municipal incorporation. The earliest city council proceedings at each town dealt with statutory limitations on disorder and violence, and the hiring of police officers was always among the first municipal business transacted.

The Abilene business community suffered through its first full cattle shipping season, 1868, without an attempt at control. In the summer of 1869 it became apparent that neither county nor township law enforcement officials felt responsible for coping with the special problems of the settlement. "While we were in Abilene," recorded one cowboy visitor of that summer, "we found the town was full of all sorts of desperate characters, and I remember one day one of these bad men rode his horse into a saloon, pulled his gun on the bartenders, and all quit business. When he came out several others began to shoot up the town." It was probably after such an incident as this that forty-four business and professional men petitioned their probate judge to grant the town corporate status. The judge favored the request in early September. But, recalled Theodore C. Henry, the land agent chosen as provisional mayor, "the [cattle shipping] season was so nearly closed by that time that active government was not attemp[t]ed." On May 2, 1870, a few weeks before the arrival of the new season's first herds, the governing council reconvened, drafting ordinances treating misdemeanors associated with transient disorder and creating a police force to enforce them. . . .

Statutes designed for the regulation of disorder in each of the Kansas cattle towns differed only in minor details from place to place and did not, of course, vary greatly from those of municipalities everywhere. State law already set penalties for many offenses, and municipal statutes routinely forbade vagrancy, disorderly conduct, intoxication, fighting, disturbing the peace, and resisting arrest. Discharging firearms within city limits was invariably proscribed, as was the carrying of dangerous weapons of any type, concealed or otherwise, by persons other than law enforcement officers. Local lawmakers also banned gambling, prostitution, and the frequenting of prostitutes. So much for statutory limits on disorder. Supplementary nuances, however, were sometimes unique, reflecting the heightened pertinence of these routine legal measures for the cattle town people.

The carrying of six-shooters by cattle trade transients proved of major concern. A long-standing state law prohibited any vagrant, intoxicated person, or former Confederate soldier from carrying "a pistol, bowie-knife, dirk or other deadly weapon" on pain of up to $100 fine and three months in jail. Cattle town authorities tended to ignore this severe injunction, preferring blanket ordinances against the carrying of arms by anyone and establishing a system for easy compliance. Wichita's evolving approach to the firearms problem provides an example. In 1871 the city marshal erected two signs warning against the carrying of firearms. In 1872 the toll-keepers at the privately operated Chisholm Trail bridge were sworn in as unpaid special policemen charged with exchanging metal tokens for weapons as riders entered town. This measure evidently proved unsuccessful, since in 1873 signboards ordered visitors to "LEAVE YOUR REVOLVERS AT POLICE HEADQUARTERS, AND GET A CHECK."

State law already forbade both prostitution and gambling if the latter involved special tables and devices—two kinds of professional amusement that, however socially obnoxious, cattle town businessmen considered absolutely indispensable to their hold on the Texas cattle trade. City fathers pragmatically softened the harsh punishments specified for those who would follow these illegal callings, their aim being local regulation rather than prohibition.

Of course these municipal statutes also ensured that all monetary penalties extracted from minor transgressors would accrue to the city's treasury rather than to that of the state. As misdemeanors, most routine misbehavior was handled in cattle town police courts. At Wichita in the twelve months following March 1, 1874, for instance, magistrates handed down a total of 439 convictions, all but 8 of them for misdemeanors. Only 12 of these cases were heard in district court, 53 by justices of the peace, and 374—or 85 per cent—in the Wichita police court. Police court fines thus constituted no small portion of the cattle town municipal income.

Of most importance was the establishment of the actual police machinery. Tradition relegates cattle town law enforcement to fast-drawing city marshals, each of whom operated virtually single-handedly in a sort of free-agent status, mainly motivated and guided by a personal commitment against lawlessness, divorced from prosaic police duties and the discipline or direction of a municipal employer. The image violates reality. In no case did any cattle town depend upon a lone marshal for its law enforcement. Police bodies of up to five men—carefully ranked as marshal, assistant marshal, and policemen—customarily supervised cattle trading seasons. Mayors appointed candidates to police posts at least annually, the chosen officers then being subjected to the often rigorous supervision of city councilmen who ratified appointments, determined pay and allowances, and removed officers at their discretion.

Local ordinances laid out the specific duties of the city marshal and his staff. The code drafted at Abilene in 1870 for the first cattle town police force remained fairly typical. The marshal, as "captain of police," was to supervise the city jail, maintain a "police record" of all persons arrested and confined, together with their offenses and ultimate dispositions, and "have charge of and control the entire police force of the town." The "several members of the town police" were to keep the peace, being specifically authorized to "enter any saloon, billiard hall or other place of public resort or amusement, and to arrest and confine in the jail of the town any person guilty of disorderly conduct or drunken[n]ess, who may refuse to be restored to order and quiet." An arresting officer was to report his action to some magistrate having jurisdiction within twenty-four hours of any arrest.

A few months after passage of this measure Abilene councilmen also invested their city marshal, Thomas J. Smith, with the duties of street commissioner at no increase in pay, a post bestowed on Marshal James B. ("Wild Bill") Hickok the following season. This less than glamorous office became a customary additional responsibility for cattle town lawmen. The job entailed investigating complaints about street obstructions, defects, and nuisances, both animate and inanimate, and seeing to their removal. Sometimes the police themselves hired others to perform this part of their task, such as the young Negro deputy employed by the Ellsworth force in 1873 "to arrest swine found at large," in the words of a waggish newspaperman. During winter months—periods of little law enforcement business—policemen might be made to earn their wages by direct attention to the streets. Thus at Wichita in early 1875 councilmen abolished the formal position of street commissioner and set the town's lawmen, including one Wyatt Earp, to repairing thoroughfares and sidewalks pending the advent of a new cattle season. Cattle town officers also acted as municipal sanitary inspectors each spring, and often made winter surveys of chimneys and flues. A man was sometimes added to the force specifically as a night watchman with the primary duty of keeping an eye out for fires. City fathers also occasionally employed "special" policemen to supervise particular trouble spots such as a theater or dance house, or allowed owners to do so.

Municipal contributions to support police officers constituted by far the largest cattle town expenditure for salaries. In the last three quarters of 1871, for example, the salaries of Abilene's police force amounted to 48 per cent of the town's total expenditure. For the same period at Caldwell in 1880 the proportion was 33 per cent. At Dodge City for the twelve months after April 9, 1884, police remuneration totaled 42 per cent of all expenditure.

In terms of specific salaries, Ellsworth's experience was probably typical. Through her first two years as a cattle center the scheduled allowances for her mayor, councilmen, treasurer, clerk, and city attorney, not counting special fees, totaled $1,410. During the same period police salaries were paid on a monthly basis, continually being adjusted to accord with the amount of police business. Except for one lapse from the pattern, the city marshal earned $150 per month during the cattle trading season (roughly June to November), and half that sum during the winter and spring—theoretically, therefore, $1,275 per year. In mid-1874, when other municipal salaries were drastically cut back to $725, the marshal's summer pay dropped to $100 per month. The salaries of his staff during the cattle trading years came to be fixed at $75 each per month. The city fathers manipulated this expense by simply adding policemen in the summer and removing them each autumn. Every member of the force in addition to his salary was normally allowed $2.50 for each arrest he made, a fee paid by the convicted lawbreaker as a part of court costs.

Experience soon indicated that whoring, gambling, and overindulgence in liquor were the three main causes of cattle town violence, and it seemed only fair that those enterprises that most stimulated this lethal circumstance should heavily subsidize its suppression. Saloon keepers already paid relatively high annual license fees into municipal coffers in accordance with state law. But prostitution and professional gambling, legally nonexistent, contributed nothing at all. It was soon decided that they too should join in supporting local police machinery, and consequently a system for covert regular assessment was devised.

The taxation of such underworld businesses clearly bears the stamp of the large urban center, from which it probably migrated to the western frontier. A New Englander who later sat on the United States Supreme Court, for example, introduced such taxation into a California mining camp in 1850. Although not publicized, the system was not unknown to Kansas. The law of 1871 establishing provisions for third-class cities, under which all the cattle towns functioned for periods, expressly forbade the practice.

Joseph G. McCoy, innovative father of the cattle trade at Abilene, deserves credit for instituting the system there after his election as mayor in 1871. Apparently acting on behalf of the saloon owners among his supporters, he forestalled an attempt to increase the liquor license fee and instead persuaded his councilmen to make up the difference by a covert assessment of gamblers and prostitutes. These fines remained in force throughout Abilene's last summer as a major cattle town. Always forward-looking, Wichita's authorities evidently introduced the system there in August of the town's first shipping season, 1872. The taxing of prostitutes commenced at Ellsworth in the autumn of the same year, the community's first important cattle season, with gamblers' fines added to regular civic revenues in the spring of 1873. Despite ample precedent from the older cattle centers, Dodge City—with its mayor probably on better personal terms than elsewhere with the disreputable elements—imposed illegal assessments only in 1878, when, in the midst of a desultory third cattle season and with the city deeply in debt, angry taxpayers convened and insisted on it. Caldwell's administrators, who invariably took their cue from Wichita, responded rapidly to precedent. In early 1880, six months after formally organizing itself and before the start of its first shipping season, the municipality began taxing gamblers regularly and in April extended the system to prostitutes.

The technical machinery involved did not vary substantially from place to place. If those on the books did not already provide them, new city ordinances introduced low minimum fines for prostitution and gambling convictions. These minimums then served as fees to be collected monthly. They usually amounted to from $5 to $10 for whores, the same for professional gamblers, and double these amounts or sometimes even higher for owners of brothels or places where professional gaming was sponsored.

The proceeds of these fines, together with tavern license fees and the income from routine misdemeanor convictions, evidently more than carried the weight of multiple peace officers. Wichita, in fact, by setting its illegal assessments rather higher than the norm and also altering its saloon license fees to monthly payments for easier collection, made the most of the system. Its spokesman boasted openly that the city thereby required no general business taxes such as were common elsewhere, a fact thought highly encouraging to prospective immigrants.

As elsewhere on the nineteenth-century frontier, the cattle town people, when it came to the matter of actual court action, tended to be lenient toward perpetrators of violence. This made penalties essentially discretionary and heightened the importance of selecting good law officers. Police judges customarily prosecuted participants in nonfatal encounters only for carrying weapons, being drunk and disorderly, or some other such light misdemeanor, although sending these cases to district court for comparatively severe assault and battery convictions always remained an alternative.

Generally speaking, the same leniency was granted to homicides. Only three persons ever earned the death sentence for cattle town killings, and none of these was ultimately executed by the state. Besides these three convictions, certain citizens of Abilene lynched one person as a penalty for murder. None of the three crimes for which these four men were punished was a gunfight or even a shooting homicide. In such cases townsfolk invariably were inclined to be forgiving, especially if the perpetrator could cite youth, intoxication, or some other extenuating circumstance. Of particular appeal was word that a youthful killer came from a good family, so that, with typical Victorian sentimentalism, it could be said of him that he fell temporarily upon evil ways. "We have no personal ill-will against the accused," mused Abilene's editor of a young Texan just acquitted of murder. "If he now reforms his life it will give us pleasure to note the fact, as it will certainly rejoice the hearts of his father and good mother, who are said to be highly respectable people." Another cowboy, a Georgian named Bob Shaw, wounded while trying to kill Dodge City's marshal, was exonerated by citizens as well as the authorities. "Shaw is not a desperado as would seem from this case," the local editor hastened to make clear. "Parties who have known him say he never was known to make a six-shooter play before this. . . . Shaw's family are highly respectable people, and he has concluded to quit the far west and go back to live under the parental roof."

A need to retain the good will—and the trade—of cattle town transients provided a more important motive for leniency. None of the four killers severely dealt with by cattle town justice was a cattleman or cowboy, and several specific incidents highlighted the fact that in the minds of a vocal citizen minority, at least, the law ought to rest lightly on Texans. At Wichita in 1874, for example, a group of cowboys calculatingly murdered a Negro laborer. When neither city nor county authorities moved to apprehend the killers, a local editor fumed. "If the law and its officers are powerless," he warned, "the sooner we know it the better. . . . A thousand men can be raised in Wichita and in this county, in three hours' notice, who will stand by their vindications." This stricture immediately provoked the wrath of many businessmen, who pounced on the surprised journalist for irresponsibly inflaming the public mind against those from whom they feared a retaliatory boycott.

Again, at Caldwell in 1882 two taut young fugitives from Texas justice who had come up the trail as cowboys gunned down the city marshal and fled into Indian Territory. The mayor hastily formed an impromptu posse, urging his volunteers to secure such horses as they needed from those hitched along the sidewalk. The Texans to whom the mounts belonged, however, refused to let them be requisitioned—and were supported by several businessmen. Nor could the intended pursuers learn the two killers' names or to which cattle outfit they belonged although, as an angry editor reported, "one or more persons knew all about them, but refused to give any information, fearing, perhaps, they might lose six bits of trade if they 'gave away' a cowboy, no matter what crime he might commit." During the following year at Dodge City, to cite a third instance, only the outspoken intervention of the influential Robert M. Wright kept boycott-obsessed businessmen from having the city marshal indicted for killing a cowboy who had been firing his pistol promiscuously.

The extent to which the choice of law enforcement personnel proved crucial in the cattle town adjustment to violence is evident in several unfortunate cases. Many different types of men served as cattle town law officers, from respected local citizens to virtually unknown transients. It is not true that lawmen all displayed a marked proficiency in that brand of personal combat known as gunfighting, but a military background or some other demonstration of familiarity with firearms, plus "nerve" and "pluck," were obvious requisites. Sometimes the desire for competency caused city fathers to hire men from those same disreputable elements they were supposed to govern. Lapsing into drunk and disorderly conduct became a routine occupational hazard with many such lawmen. Local authorities also risked the chance that such an individual would prove overly prone to the employment of violence as a deterrent, or that for the sort of discretionary firmness called for he might substitute mere bullying. This kind of "zealousness" often precipitated, rather than dispelled, trouble. At his worst, such an officer might display actual criminal propensities.

Caldwell's experience with city marshals proved especially distressing. By 1882 community opinion had split over whether a demonstrated gunfighter or a good local citizen would make the better law officer for the town. After various unsatisfactory experiments with both types, the advocates of the former triumphed. The city administration hired three polished gunfighters just up from Texas to administer justice. One of these, unknown to the community, was a graduate of the notorious Billy the Kid gang in New Mexico. Soon winning promotion to marshal, this young man, Henry N. Brown, though considered a bit quick on the trigger, gave Caldwell nearly two years of satisfactory service—until he was captured with his assistant marshal and two other comrades after trying to rob the bank at nearby Medicine Lodge and killing its president and cashier. All were killed in turn by angry citizens of that place. The damning notoriety brought upon Caldwell by the gunmen in whom it had placed its trust more than offset any previous benefits from Marshal Brown's efforts to contain violence.

Avoiding untrustworthy candidates was only one problem in officer procurement. Since the rationale behind cattle town law enforcement was the prevention of acts of violence rather than repression of those who were potential transgressors, both intelligence and a proper temperament were required. Treading the narrow margin between prevention and suppression, the ideal lawman promised no leniency for major infractions but at the same time avoided a hostile attitude that might simply provoke antagonism among these governed and serve as a standing challenge to physical encounter. Few officers existed with the natural qualifications of Abilene's popular Tom Smith, who kept his pistol concealed and often triumphed over violators of the peace merely with his fists. . . .

On the whole, law enforcement efforts proved generally effective, judging from the incidence of homicide. Many legendary desperadoes and gun-fighters sojourned in the cattle towns at one time or another, but few participated in slayings. Among those with clean records were such famed killers as Clay Allison, Doc Holliday, and Ben Thompson. The teen-aged gunman John Wesley Hardin was responsible for only one verifiable cattle town homicide, apparently having fired through the wall of his hotel room one drunken night to silence a man snoring too loudly in the adjoining cubicle. Nor did famous gunfighters serving as officers add much to the fatality statistics. As city marshal of Abilene in 1871, his only term as a cattle town lawman, the formidable Wild Bill Hickok killed just two men—one, a "special" policeman, by mistake. Wyatt Earp, who served as an officer (but never actually as marshal) at both Wichita and Dodge City, may have mortally wounded one law violator, though he shared credit with another policeman for this single cattle town homicide. The now equally renowned lawman William B. ("Bat") Masterson, at least according to contemporary sources, killed no one in or around Dodge, where he lived for several years.

With these celebrated personalities contributing far less than their supposed share, it is hardly surprising that the over-all homicide statistics are not particularly high. The table that follows is a compilation of all homicides—whether by police, resident citizens, or transients—for the periods in which each of the towns entertained the cattle trade. Only those killings that occurred in town have been counted, although fatalities in Abilene's and Ellsworth's suburban brothel districts are included because the communities attempted municipal control over these areas. On the other hand, homicides in West Wichita were excluded from Wichita's figures since city authorities took not the slightest responsibility for enforcement in that independent trans-river community. The statistics commence with the first

Cattle Town Homicides

TOWNS	YEARS																TOTAL
	1870	1871	1872	1873	1874	1875	1876	1877	1878	1879	1880	1881	1882	1883	1884	1885	
Abiline	2	3	2														7
Ellsworth			1	5	0	0											6
Wichita		1	1	1	1	0	0										4
Dodge City							0?	0	5	2	1	1	0	3	2	1	15
Caldwell										2	2	3	1	2	2	1	13
TOTAL																	45

full shipping season in which each town existed as a municipality, except in the case of Caldwell, which gained organized status only in mid-1879 but attempted some law enforcement pending approval of an incorporation petition.

The sources for the statistics are the cattle town newspapers, of which continuous runs survive for all pertinent years but one. For public relations purposes local editors sometimes chose to be circumspect about nonfatal affairs, making an adequate analysis of all lethal encounters impossible. But they inevitably succumbed to the newsworthiness of actual homicide, at which time public relations often went begging in the wake of hasty "extras" and reprinted regular editions, multiple copies of which citizens commonly bought to send to friends back East. Only when particularly useful or necessary have newspaper accounts been supplemented by other sources, secondary writings being in various degrees particularly unreliable.

As is evident, the number of homicides never topped five in any one cattle season year, and reached this figure only at Ellsworth in 1873 and at Dodge City five years later. In both instances, homicides may be said to have manifested "wave" dimensions, and were in fact thus considered by local residents. In at least six years no fatalities occurred at all. While not so significant in seasons of cattle trade decline as at Ellsworth in 1875 or at Wichita in 1875 and 1876, the zeroes recorded for two busy years at Dodge City seem particularly meaningful. The average number of homicides per cattle town trading season amounted to only 1.5 per year.

In the case of at least six of these killings—or well over 10 per cent—it is hard to identify any connection whatever with the existence of the cattle trade. Besides a Wichita insurance murder, and the murder of an Abilene tailor and the lynching of *his* murderer, . . . these included the shootings of a Wichita hotel keeper resisting arrest on a federal warrant, that of one Wichita Negro by another, and that of a Caldwell housewife by her drunken husband.

The majority of those involved in homicides, however, were indeed law officers, cowboys and drovers, or gamblers—the last a somewhat elastic category to accommodate four ex-lawmen without obvious means of support. Of homicide victims, nine were cowboys or drovers and nine were gamblers. Six were officers of the law. Aside from the non-cattle-trade killings mentioned above, victims included five townsmen with conventional occupations, three local rural settlers, two dance house proprietors, two miscellaneous visitors (one lawyer and a Pawnee Indian), and one female theatrical entertainer. The status of the remaining two victims is obscure. Analyzed in terms of perpetrators, sixteen cattle town homicides can be attributed to law officers, or citizens legitimately acting as such, twelve to cowboys or drovers, and eight to gamblers. The other nine homicides are distributed evenly among some of the categories already mentioned. These included two lynchings evidently carried out by cattle town residents rather than transients. Besides the episode at Abilene, a Caldwell gambler and bootlegger was hanged in somewhat mysterious circumstances. . . .

With the exception of killings by law officers and lynchings, the homicidal situations varied considerably. Seventeen apparently resulted from private quarrels, four were accidental or without discernible motive, two were committed by resisters of arrest, two avenged prior homicides, and two consisted of murders for profit. Homicidal disputes involving women, incidentally, exceeded by eight to one those mainly resulting from gambling disagreements. Of the six lawmen killed, interestingly enough, half met death in circumstances that must be termed accidental, although two of them—Ellsworth's Sheriff Whitney and the Abilene policeman killed by Marshal Hickok—were attempting to help quell trouble when shot. Only two officers died attempting to make arrests; the other fell in a private quarrel.

Lest tradition be completely overthrown, let it be noted that gunshots were far and away the principal medium of death. But tradition also would have it that the cattle town homicide typically involved an exchange of shots—the so-called gunfight. Actually, though thirty-nine of the forty-five victims suffered fatal bullet or buckshot wounds, less than a third of them returned the fire. A good share of them were apparently not even armed.

Despite all the shooting it seems fair to conclude that the cattle town people largely succeeded in containing the lethal tendencies of their situation, despite the odds involved in suppressing violence while remaining hospitable to the Texas cattle trade. The collective adjustment demanded wisdom and finesse at all administrative levels, and wisdom and finesse were often at hand. Legend does the cattle town people a double injustice—falsely magnifying the periodic failures of their effort while altogether refusing to take account of its internal complexities.

Postscript: Overdosing on Dodge City

ROBERT R. DYKSTRA

Louis stood in the path. . . . He pumped the stubby shotgun to put one in the chamber [and] held the sawed-off pointed down and against his leg. He said, "Man, . . . we like in the movies, huh? The two hombres facing each other out in the street."

"That's the only place it ever happened," Raylan said. "In the movies."

—Elmore Leonard, *Riding the Rap*

This passage from the latest offering by one of America's most respected crime novelists suggests that something I set out to do nearly thirty years ago may have had some good effect. *The Cattle Towns* was, and is, no polemic. But it did address two influential misconceptions about the Old West.

Copyright © by Western History Association. Reprinted by permission. The article first appeared as "Field Notes: Overdosing on Dodge City," by Robert R. Dykstra, *Western Historical Quarterly,* 27 (Winter 1996), 505–514.

The first is that the typical frontier community was sociologically cohesive—a kind of persistent Lockean husking-bee and barn-raising. The second misconception is that these particular frontier communities (forget Locke, think Hobbes) were relentlessly homicidal. The latter cliché—nurtured since the 1920s by "adult Westerns," in print and on screen, as well as by serious cultural historians—held that frontier communities such as cattle towns and mining camps routinely experienced virtually continuous handgun violence. . . .

As Elmore Leonard somehow discovered, nobody died in a Hollywood-style street duel; life may have imitated art *somewhere* on the frontier but not at the Kansas cattle towns. Within six years—the speed of light in scholarly circles—my demythologizing had taken hold among interested historians, as reflected in Eugene Hollon's survey of frontier violence, the fourth edition of Ray Billington's popular textbook, and Richard Bartlett's social history of the frontier, all published in 1974. Bartlett summarized everything especially well, I thought. "Such sobering analyses of these town," said he, "still do not make of them sleepy little religious communities. When the herds arrived, there was plenty of noise, fights, gambling, whoring, and general carousing—but it was under control."

Two years later I amiably offered my revelations at a glitzy big-budget Western film festival in Sun Valley, Idaho. My remarks for the most part prompted blank disbelief, although Henry King, prestigious director of the classic movie *The Gunfighter* (1950), rebutted me quite angrily. And a prominent folklorist who took a leading role in the conference dismissed me as a person who simply didn't like Westerns. The celebrity scholar of the moment was the author [Richard Slotkin] of *Regeneration through Violence* [1973], whose keynote speech offered us a foretaste of *The Fatal Environment* [1985] and who would ultimately—indeed, inevitably—give us *Gunfighter Nation* [1992]. I came away from Sun Valley with a renewed appreciation of America's weighty cultural investment in the received image.

Some years later, as if in response to this experience, Gary Wills employed my homicide data in his biography of ex-actor Ronald Reagan, thereby suggesting the foolishness of the movie industry's consumption of its own clichés. But my only other direct encounter with Hollywood came a few years ago when I was videotaped for an episode of a cable TV series, *The Real West.* The program was to be about the cattle towns, and during the lengthy taping I more than once reiterated the low body counts and the reasons for their being low. Two months later, however, as I glimpsed the very opening of the program, I knew that my best lines had ended up on the cutting-room floor. The name of the episode? "Bloody Dodge City."

Still, in the interim between major confrontations, my data continued to attract occasional lay interest. Most startling was my discovery of them summarized between the glossy covers of an upscale coffee-table magazine published in Paris. "De 1870 à 1885," read this abstract, ". . . dans les villes 'chaudes' d'Abilene, Dodge City, Ellsworth, Wichita et Caldwell, on n'enregistre que 55 morts par arme à feu."

Hmm, close but *pas de cigare*. Cattle town homicides totaled 45 not 55, and only 39 of the victims died from gunshot wounds. When in error, writers tend to err on the high side?

Certainly the most ambitious attempt to move the dialogue beyond the cattle towns has been Roger McGrath's study of two nineteenth-century California mining camps, Bodie and Aurora [published in 1984]. Strangely enough, however, McGrath's message cut both ways. The virtual absence of conventional crime in his towns led an important review of the book to appear under the headline "Not-So-Wild Frontier." Yet, McGrath had also found the local *homicide rate* so huge as to dwarf that of modern urban America. He managed this by devising rates according to the methodology of the FBI's Uniform Crime Reporting Program, which calculates a ratio for murders per every 100,000 of population.

McGrath was not the first historian to employ the FBI index. That honor accrues to two medievalists. James Given calculated a murder ratio for London in 1276 that almost matched the yearly average for Miami in the years 1948–1952. Barbara Hanawalt soon followed with a book arguing—even more elaborately—that medieval London's homicide ratio rose well *above* modern Miami's. But Hanawalt, an otherwise sophisticated historian, should have realized that it was the smallness of London's fourteenth-century population (35,000 to 50,000) rather than the average annual number of murders (18) that made its rate soar higher than that of the present era's most violent U.S. city.

Even more spectacularly does this fallacy of small numbers plague McGrath's mining camps, never larger than 5,000 souls each. For the more violent of his towns, McGrath calculated an enormous average annual homicide ratio of 116.0—as against Miami's 1980 ratio of only 32.7. The normally astute Richard White seemed quite impressed by this contrast [in his 1991 new history of the West]. But the fact is that while Bodie's body count was a mere 29 over several years, Miami's 1980 murders totaled 515. Which ought to remind one that there are lies, damned lies, and statistics.

Let Dodge City's example prove the point. Dodge was indeed the most violent of the cattle towns in terms of its total body count (N = 15), but its average was that of the five towns as a whole, 1.5 per cattle-trading year. It was thus no more homicidal than Abilene, Ellsworth, Wichita, or Caldwell; it simply had been a cattle town longer than any of the others.

And consider this. On 17 November 1880 a local layabout named John ("Concho") Gill shot and killed rancher Henry Heck in a quarrel over a woman. Bad business indeed—no man is an island and all that. Heck's demise, however, was Dodge City's *only* 1880 homicide. Since the village contained a resident population of merely 1,275 that year, this single killing yields a statistically huge homicide ratio of 78.4. Had Gill's bullet missed Heck, the town's 1880 ratio would have been zero. But because Gill's aim was true, Dodge City earned a rate twice that of violence-ridden Miami a century later.

Of course, there is nothing wrong with the FBI index. What's wrong is that comparing frontier Dodge City to modern Miami is comparing apples and oranges—or, more appropriately, an early pea and a prize-winning watermelon. The naiveté of such a venture, its frank display of statistical illiteracy, is inexcusable in this methodologically-advanced day and age, no? (Okay, make that *should be* inexcusable.)

Still, a simple comparison of the cattle towns' yearly average—1.5 victims—with that of McGrath's mining camps—4.75 victims, or four times higher—is not only plausible but surprisingly instructive. Even without doing the arithmetic, Richard White drew an especially intelligent conclusion from this difference. "Those towns such as the cattle towns that disarmed young men lowered the rates of personal violence considerably," he wrote. "Those towns such as Bodie and Aurora that did not disarm men tended to bury significantly more of them. Society as a whole was able to control personal violence when the community desired to do so."

The escalating 1990s debate over gun control has prompted some repetition of White's point. Thus *Newsweek* columnist Jonathan Alter asserted that "back in the 1870s, Wyatt Earp was called into Wichita because that rowdy cattle town was experiencing about one homicide a year, which the residents considered intolerable. Earp made sure that guns were checked at toll stations on the outskirts of town or confiscated." Gary Wills elaborated further in his syndicated column. The cattle town experience, he said, "showed that gun control, at many levels, was a fact of Western life. . . . We are often told that gun control laws will not work. But they seemed to have worked in the West. The cattle-drive towns had an average of $1\frac{1}{2}$ murders per year, and those usually had nothing [to do] with cowboys or 'shootouts.' They were the ordinary domestic stabbings and such."

Alter, of course, greatly exaggerated the leadership of Officer Earp in Wichita law enforcement. And Wills too sharply reduced both the proportion of cattle trade-related homicides and the incidence of fatal gunshot wounds. Yet the larger point seems well taken. . . .

When one looks closely at the Western experience beyond the cattle towns it *is* odd that actual body counts all over the place are not especially high. What, one might ask, is meant by "not high"? Certainly not as high as the body counts in metropolitan America today. But more pertinently, counts not as high as many historians have reported. For instance, the widely respected Daniel Boorstin described New Mexico's famous Lincoln County War, which featured Billy the Kid, as having claimed the lives of "more than sixty men." Yet the true total was a mere third of that—20 or 21 (depending on whether one Joe Bowers was or was not killed in the Five-Day Battle). Or body counts not as high as Hollywood mythologizing. For example, in Wyoming's famous but short-lived Johnson County War, on which the violent movie *Heaven's Gate* (1980) was based, actual homicides totaled two.

Other frontier body counts follow suit. During Deadwood's famous first year as a (literally) lawless mining camp homicides numbered four. And many legendary Western law officers and outlaws actually killed few men. Take the formidable Wild Bill Hickok. Over his lifetime, excluding his military service, Hickok accounted for either seven or eight kills (depending on whether he or Mrs. Horace Wellman should be credited with James Woods's demise at the Rock Creek fight). Call it seven plus an assist. Or consider another example: victims of the Jesse James gang during its lengthy career numbered 16—about one per year.

The local violence for which postbellum Texas is notorious offers other examples. The four *most* lethal of these outbreaks were the Sutton-Taylor feud, the Lee-Peacock feud, the McDade vigilante episode, and the San Saba County War. But the respective fatalities totaled 24, 20, 23, and 19. Judging from these cases and the similar total from nearby Lincoln County, about 20 to 25 victims was all a Western community would ultimately tolerate.

The Indian wars of the late nineteenth century are a special case. What gave them their unforgivably murderous quality were the massacre of noncombatants—women, children, the elderly—by testosterone-laden young males from both sides. In contrast, the number of *combat* deaths among soldiers and warriors was not particularly large. Between 1865 and 1898, regular troops killed while encountering Indians totaled 919. But well over a third of these—37 percent—died in two very exceptional engagements. One was the Fetterman ambush in 1866, which cost the lives of 79 officers and men. The other was the Little Bighorn Battle ten years later, in which 258 soldiers died. Absent those two bloodlettings, combat deaths averaged about 17 per year. As for Indian fatalities, they were probably even fewer over the long run. No more than 32 warriors, for instance, are known to have died at Little Bighorn.

The late nineteenth-century scholar looking for true mayhem and big body counts should forget Little Bighorn, forget Wild Bill and Wyatt Earp, forget Dodge City. Instead, consider the lethal character of simply working on the railroad. In the single year 1893 no fewer than 433 men died violently while attempting to couple railway cars. Now *that* would have made a blood-spattered epic worthy of Sam Peckinpah.

It seems to me that the cattle town experience points toward a remarkable truth: despite all the mythologizing, violent fatalities in the Old West tended to be rare rather than common. Does that mean it was a wholesome, tranquil place? Probably not. But it was clearly a safer—and one heck of a lot *saner*—West than ever dreamt of in our national imagination.

Regeneration through violence? The fatal environment? Gunfighter nation? Oh, please. Let's get a grip on ourselves.

Outlaw Gangs and Social Bandits

RICHARD WHITE

Americans have often regarded western outlaws as heroes. In popular culture—legend, folksongs, and movies—the American West might as well be Sherwood Forest; its plains and prairies teem with what E. J. Hobsbawm has called social bandits. Driven outside the law because of some act sanctioned by local conventions but regarded as criminal by the state or local authorities, the social bandit has been forced to become an outlaw. Members of his community, however, still consider him an honorable and admirable man. They protect him and are ready to reassimilate him if persecution by the state should stop. The social bandit is a man who violates the law but who still serves a higher justice. He robs from the rich and gives to the poor and only kills in self-defense or just revenge. As long as he observes this code, he is, in myth and legend, invulnerable to his enemies; he can die or be captured only when betrayed by friends.

In the American West, stories of this kind have gathered around many historical outlaws: Jesse James, Billy the Kid, Cole Younger, Sam Bass, John Wesley Hardin, Bob Dalton, Bill Dalton, Bill Doolin, and more. These men exert a surprising fascination on a nation that takes some pride in due process and the rule of law and where the standard version of western settlement is subordination of "savagery" to law and civilization. These bandits, however, exist in more than legend; as actual outlaws many enjoyed substantial amounts of local support. Such outlaws must be taken seriously as social bandits. Their appeal, while complex, is not mysterious, and it provides insights not only into certain kinds of western settlement and social conditions but also into basic paradoxes of American culture itself.

The tendency to justify certain outlaws as decent, honorable men despite their violation of the law is, in a sense, unique only because these men openly were bandits. In other ways social bandits fit into a continuum of extralegal organizations, such as claims clubs, vigilantes, and white-caps*—prevalent throughout the United States but most common in the West. In certain situations the differences between social bandits (criminals) and vigilantes (law enforcers) were not great, and although this may offend certain modern law and order sensibilities, it is a mistake to impose such contemporary distinctions on nineteenth-century conditions.

In the American West during this period, concepts of legality, extralegality, and illegality became quite confusing. Well into the late nineteenth century public law enforcement remained weak, particularly in rural areas where a variety of extralegal organizations supplemented or replaced the

*a type of vigilante group that sprang up in many different areas of the country toward the end of the nineteenth century and that was given to violence with racist overtones—e.g., flogging blacks in northern Texas and anti-Mexican actions in southern Texas.

constituted authorities. Members of claims clubs, vigilantes, and white-caps, of course, proclaimed their allegiance to community norms and saw themselves as establishing order, not contributing to disorder. On many occasions they were probably correct. Often, however, the line between extralegal organizations who claimed to preserve order and extralegal gangs accused of creating disorder was a fine one indeed. Claims clubs using threats of violence or actual violence to gain additional public land for their members, even when this involved driving off legitimate claimants, vigilante committees whose targets might only be economic or political rivals, or whitecaps who chose to upgrade the moral tone of the community through beatings and whippings may not be outlaws, but distinguishing them from criminals on moral or legal grounds is not very compelling. In the West, *criminal* could be an ambiguous term, and vigilantes often became the armed force of one racial, class, or cultural group moving against other groups with opposing interests. In such cases vigilantes often provoked retaliation, and local civil war resulted. American history is full of such encounters, ranging from the Regulator/Moderator conflicts of the colonial Carolina backcountry, through the anti-Mormon movements of the American frontier, to the Johnson County War of 1892.

Social bandits, however, did not represent this kind of organized opposition to vigilantes. They, too, arose where law enforcement was distrusted, where criminal was an ambiguous category, and where the legitimacy of vigilantism was questioned. Where social banditry occurred, however, the vigilantes and their opponents did not form two coherent groups, but instead consisted of numerous, mutually hostile factions. Regulator/Moderator struggles represented broad social divisions; social bandits thrived amidst personal feuds and vendettas.

Three gangs that seem most clearly part of a western social bandit tradition are the James-Younger gang of western Missouri and its lineal successors led by Jesse James (1866[?]–1882), the Dalton gang of Oklahoma Territory (1890–1892), and the Doolin-Dalton gang of Oklahoma Territory (1892–1896). Such a list is purposefully narrow and is not meant to be exclusive. These are only the most famous gangs, but an examination of them can establish both the reality of social banditry and the nature of its appeal.

Social bandits are almost by definition creations of their supporters, but this support must be carefully defined. Virtually all criminals have some people who aid them, since there will always be those who find profit and advantage in doing so. Social bandits, too, may have supporters who are essentially confederates. What separates social bandits from ordinary criminals, however, is the existence of large numbers of other people who aid them but who are only technically implicated in their crimes. Such people are not themselves criminals and are willing to justify their own actions in supporting outlaws on grounds other than fear, profit, or expediency. When such people exist in large enough numbers to make an area a haven for a particular group of outlaws, then social banditry exists. For the James-Younger, Dalton, and Doolin-Dalton gangs, this support had three major components: the kinship networks so important to western settlement in general, active supporters, and those people who can be termed passive sympathizers.

That two of these three gangs organized themselves around sets of brothers—the James brothers, the Younger brothers, and the Dalton brothers—is perhaps the most striking illustration of the importance of kinship in social banditry. Centered on blood relations, the James-Younger gang and, to a much lesser extent the Dalton gang depended on relatives to hide them, feed them, warn them of danger, and provide them with alibis. The James brothers recruited two of their cousins—Wood and Clarence Hite—into the gang, and even the Ford brothers, who eventually murdered Jesse, were recruited because they were related by marriage to Jim Cummins, another gang member. Only the Doolin-Dalton gang lacked widespread kin connections, and this forced them to rely more heavily on other forms of support, which were, however, common to all the gangs.

Besides kinspeople, the gangs drew on a larger group of active supporters who knew the outlaws personally and who duplicated many of the services provided by relatives of the bandits. The James-Younger gang recruited such supporters largely from among neighbors and the ex-Confederate guerrillas who had ridden with them in the Civil War. Such "friends of the outlaws" were, according to the man who broke the gang—William Wallace—"thick in the country portions of Jackson County," and many people in the region believed that no local jury would ever convict members of the James gang.

Similar support existed in Oklahoma. The Daltons—Bob, Emmett and Grat—had possessed "many friends in the territory" and had found aid not only among farmers but also on the ranches along the Cimarron River, in the Creek Nation, and in the Cheyenne-Arapaho country. The Doolin-Dalton gang apparently built on this earlier network of support. Frank Canton, who as undersheriff of Pawnee County pursued the Doolin-Dalton gang, distinguished their active sympathizers from the twenty-five to thirty confederates who fenced stolen goods for the outlaws.

> The Dalton gang and especially Bill Doolin had many friends among the settlers south of Pawnee along the Cimarron River, and along the line of Pawnee County. There is no doubt that Doolin furnished many of them money to buy groceries to live upon when they first settled in that country and had a hard struggle for existence. They appreciated his kindness even though he was an outlaw with a price upon his head, and there were plenty of people who would get up at the hour of midnight if necessary to ride to Bill Doolin to warn him of the approach of officers when they were seen in that vicinity.

U.S. Marshal Evett Nix, too, complained that "protectors and friends" of the Doolin-Dalton gang "were numerous." The small town of Ingalls in Payne County became a particularly notorious center of sympathy for the gang. Three deputy marshals died in the disastrous raid officers made on the town in 1893, and when a posse pursued the bandits into the surrounding countryside, local farmers misdirected the deputies. The frustrated offi-

cers retaliated by arresting a number of local citizens for aiding the outlaws. Probandit sentiment persisted in the region into 1894 when a local
newspaper reported that Bill Doolin was openly "circulating among his
many friends in the Sooner Valley" and pointedly remarked that deputy
marshals had been absent from the area as usual. Years later, when the state
erected a monument to the deputies who fell at Ingalls, at least one old local
resident complained that it had been erected to the "wrong bunch." In the
case of all three gangs, the network of primary supporters remained local-
ized. The James-Younger gang in its prime drew largely on Clay, Jackson,
and Ray counties in Missouri, while the Daltons and the Doolin-Dalton
gang relied heavily on people in Payne, Kingfisher, and Pawnee counties,
as well as ranchers in the neighboring sections of the Indian nations and the
Cherokee strip.

The final category of popular sympathy for outlaws was probably at
once the largest, the least important in terms of the bandits' day-to-day
activities, and yet the most critical in the transformation of the outlaws into
local heroes. This third group consisted of passive sympathizers—people
who probably had never seen an actual outlaw, let alone ever aided one.
Their sympathy, however, was quite real, and given a chance they publicly
demonstrated it. They mourned Jesse James, "lionized" Bill Doolin after
his capture, flocked to see Frank James after his surrender, packed his trial,
and applauded his acquittal. Such sympathizers appeared even in Coffeeville, Kansas, where the Dalton gang tried to outdo the James-Younger
gang by robbing two banks at once. The result was a bloody debacle—the
death of most of the gang and the killing of numerous citizens. Yet within
days of the fight, some people openly sympathized with the outlaws on the
streets of Coffeeville.

The mere existence of support, however, does not explain the reasons
for it. The simplest explanation, and one advanced by many anti-outlaw
writers, was that the bandits' supporters acted from fear. This is not very
persuasive. While arguing that fear brought support, many popular writers
have often simultaneously incorporated major elements of the bandits' legends into their own writings. They paradoxically argue against a sympathy
that they themselves reflect. Such sympathy seems an unlikely product of
fear, and there is little evidence for the reign of terror by these gangs
reported by outside newspapers for Missouri in the 1870s and Oklahoma in
the 1890s. Both Dalton and Doolin-Dalton gang members were welcomed
to the country dances and other community affairs in Oklahoma that they
attended. Certainly they had become locally notorious, but fear was not the
dominant note in their notoriety. In Payne County, for example, a Stillwater grocer fortuitously named Bill Dalton capitalized on outlaw Bill Dalton's fame in an advertisement with banner headlines proclaiming that:

> Bill Dalton's Gang Are After You And If You Can Give Them A Trial You
> Will Be Convinced That They Keep The Freshest & Best Goods In The
> City At The Lowest Prices.

Feared killers are not usually relied on to promote the sale of groceries.

Finally, if fear was the only cause of the bandits' support, it is hard to explain the continued expression of public sympathy after the outlaws were dead or imprisoned and no one had much to fear from them anymore.

A social bandit cannot survive through terror alone, and these bandits did not. They had ties to the local community predating their life of crime, and during their criminal careers social bandits reinforced those local ties. Gangs that did not have such connections or did not maintain them remained parasites whose lack of shelter and aid condemned them to destruction. The social bandits needed popular support; they could not undercut it by indiscriminately robbing the inhabitants of the regions in which they lived and operated. Those outlaws who simply preyed on local communities were hunted down like the stock thieves of Indian Territory. No one romanticized, and rarely even remembered, Dock Bishop and Frank Latham, or the more notorious Zip Wyatt-Ike Black gang, for example. The social bandits avoided such a fate by concentrating their robberies on railroads and banks. Thus, they not only avoided directly harming local people, but they also preyed upon institutions that many farmers believed were preying on them.

Beyond this, social bandits often did assist their supporters in at least small ways. There is no need to accept the numerous romantic stories of gallant outlaws paying the mortgages on the farms of poor widows to grant them an economic role in their local communities. Bill Doolin may very well have helped poor settlers through some hard times with groceries and small gifts; the Dalton and Doolin-Dalton gangs certainly did provide oysters and refreshments for local dances, and such small kindnesses were also probably practiced by the James-Younger gang. What was probably more significant to their supporters in chronically cash-short economies, however, was that all these gangs paid very well for the horses, feed, and supplies they needed. Their largess won them friends.

If fear fails as an explanation for what appears to be legitimate social banditry, then the next logical recourse is to the interpretation E. J. Hobsbawm offered to explain European bandits. According to Hobsbawm, social banditry is a premodern social revolt—a protest against either excessive exploitation from above or against the overturn of traditional norms by modernizing elements in a society. It is quintessentially a peasant protest. Hobsbawm mentioned Jesse James himself as following in this European tradition. The shortcomings of a literal reading of Hobsbawm are obvious. Jesse James could not be a peasant champion because there were no American peasants to champion. Yet Hobsbawm's analysis might be retrieved by reinterpreting the western outlaws more generally as champions of a "traditional" society against a "modern" society.

Such evidence as can be recovered, however, indicates that this interpretation, too, is badly flawed. Both the outlaws and their supporters came from modern, market-oriented groups and not from poor, traditional groups. The James-Younger gang had its origins in the Confederate guerrillas of the Civil War who were recruited from the economic and social elite of Jackson and neighboring counties. Usually guerrillas were the "elder offspring of well-to-do, slave holding farmers." The chief members of the James-Younger gang were ex-guerrillas with similar origins. Colonel Henry Younger, the father of the Younger brothers, owned 3,500 acres of land in Jackson and Cass counties before the Civil War. His wife was a daughter of a member of the Missouri legislature. The father of Jesse and Frank James was a Baptist minister who in 1850 owned a 275-acre farm. Their stepfather was a physician who resided with their mother on a Missouri farm worth $10,000 in 1870, and their uncle, George Hite, Sr., was said, probably with some exaggeration, to have been worth $100,000 before losing heavily in the tobacco speculation that forced him into bankruptcy in 1877.

Many of the gang's other supporters enjoyed similar social standing. Joseph Shelby, the Confederate cavalry leader, and members of the large Hudspeth family all aided the James-Younger gang, and all were prosperous farmers with sizable landholdings. The jury that acquitted Frank James of murder was composed of twelve "well-to-do thrifty farmers," and Clay County, in the heart of the bandit country, was "one of the richest counties in the state," inhabited by a people who were "well-dressed, well-to-do, and hospitable." These substantial farmers and speculators seem an unlikely source for premodern rebels or as leaders of a revolt of the rural poor.

Members and supporters of the Dalton and Doolin-Dalton gangs were not so prosperous, but then these gangs did not have such a firmly established rural region to draw upon. The Daltons were, by most accounts, an ordinary midwestern farm family. Three Dalton brothers became farmers; one was a deputy marshal killed in the line of duty; the other four eventually became outlaws. Bill Doolin was a ranch foreman and, according to local residents, a "respected citizen" before becoming a bandit. Bitter Creek Newcomb, Little Bill Raidler, and Dick Broadwell all had middle-class origins in families of merchants and farmers, and Raidler had supposedly attended college. The remainder of these two gangs included equal numbers of previously honest cowboys and small-time thugs and drifters without close family connections. Supporters of the Oklahoma gangs also apparently spanned class lines, ranging from small-scale farmers to large-scale ranchers like Jim Riley, who was locally considered well-to-do.

Neither class nor traditional values seem to be significant factors in the support of bandits, but the tendency of supporters to live in rural rather than urban regions suggest a third possible explanation of social banditry as an exotic appendage of the agrarian revolt of post–Civil War America. Some evidence, taken in isolation, seems to support such a connection with rural radicalism. Both local boosters and government officials interested in attracting capital attacked the gangs. They blamed them for discouraging investment and immigration. Governor Crittenden and Senator Carl Schurz of Missouri, for example, defended the assassination of Jesse James in ridding the state of "a great hindrance to its prosperity and as likely to give an important stimulus to real estate speculation, railroad enterprise, and foreign immigration."

On the other side, positions taken by some of the bandits after their careers were over make them appear to be radicals. Frank James credited his robberies with maintaining local prosperity because they had frightened eastern capital out of Jackson County and thus kept it free of mortgages. And in 1897 he declared: "If there is ever another war in this country, which may happen, it will be between capital and labor, I mean between greed and manhood, and I'm as ready to march now in defense of American manhood as I was when a boy in the defense of the South. Unless we can stop this government by injunction that's what we are coming to." Frank James was not alone in his swing to the left. James Younger became a socialist while in prison.

Put in context, however, all of this is considerably less compelling. While active criminals, none of the bandits took radical political positions. Nor did agrarian groups show much sympathy for the bandits. Contemporary writers pointed out that politicians and capitalists stole far more than bandits, and individual farmers aided the gangs, but organized agrarians did not confuse banditry with political action. The leading agrarian party in Missouri in the 1870s—the People's party—although it attacked banks and monopolies, also denounced lawlessness, particularly that of the James-Younger gang. It is also instructive to remember that the Farmers Alliance, which eventually spawned the Populist party, started out as a group to combat horse theft. The Populists themselves showed no more interest in banditry as a variant of political action than had the People's party of Missouri. In any case, if banditry were political in nature and inspired by agrarian resentment against banks and railroads, it is hard to explain why support for bandits was largely confined to Oklahoma in the 1890s while Populism spread all over the South and West.

A better explanation of social banditry is possible. It begins with the peculiar social conditions of western Missouri in the 1860s and 1870s and Oklahoma in the 1890s that allowed social bandits to emerge as variants of the widespread extralegal organizations already common in the West. The exceptional situations prevailing in both Missouri and Oklahoma encouraged popular identification with the outlaws whom local people supported not because of their crimes but rather because of certain culturally defined masculine virtues the outlaws embodied. In each locale there were good reasons to value such virtues. This emphasis on the bandits as symbols of masculinity, in turn, made them accessible to the larger culture at a time when masculinity itself was being widely worried over and glorified. The bandit's virtues made him a cultural hero and embarked him on a posthumous career (of a very conservative sort) which is far from over yet. All of this requires considerable explanation.

Public support of bandits can obviously exist only in areas where belief in the honesty and competency of public law enforcement has been seriously eroded. This was the case in both postwar Missouri and Oklahoma in the 1890s. In the Missouri countryside, ex-Confederates hated and feared Union sheriffs, who they believed used their offices to settle old scores from the war, and they regarded the state militia, called up to maintain order, as plunderers and freebooters. Wartime antagonisms and turmoil faded in time, but when the Pinkertons attacked the home of Zerelda Samuel, mother of the James boys, blowing off her arm and killing her young son—the halfbrother of Jesse and Frank—they rekindled hatred of the authorities. Governor Crittenden's subsequent solicitation of assassins to kill Jesse only deepened the prevailing distrust of the equity and honesty of law enforcement.

In Oklahoma settlers similarly distrusted U.S. deputy marshals, whom they often regarded as little better than criminals themselves. During the land rush, deputies used their office unfairly to secure the best lands and later spent much of their time arresting farmers who cut timber on the public domain or on Indian lands and prosecuting settlers who happened to be found with small amounts of whiskey in the Indian nations. Farmers believed that deputies sought only the fees they collected by persecuting "poor defenseless claim holders." On at least two occasions in the late winter and spring of 1893, resentment ran high enough for armed groups to attempt to attack deputy marshals and free their prisoners.

Although newspapers praised their bravery when they died in the line of duty, living marshals merited much less sympathy. Local newspapers rarely praised crimes social bandits committed, but they commonly ridiculed and denounced the lawmen who pursued them. In April of 1894, for example, the *Pond Creek Voice* reported that deputy marshals riding past the garden of an old woman who lived near the Cimarron River had mistaken her scarecrow for an outlaw and had riddled it with bullets before riding off in panic to report their ambush by the Doolin-Dalton gang. When Bill Dalton was actually killed, the *Stillwater Gazette* reported that it would come as a great relief to the deputy marshals "who have made it a practice to ride in the opposite direction from where he was every time they got him located." In the eyes of many people, the deputy marshals were simply another group of armed men, distinguished mainly by their cowardice, who rode around the territory posing a threat to life and property. The transition of the Dalton brothers from deputy marshals and possemen to open criminals was no fall from grace. Indeed, it may have gained the brothers support in some areas.

This distrust of law enforcement is particularly significant in the light of the widespread disorder existing in both areas. Following the Civil War, robbery and murder continued to occur in northwestern Missouri with appalling frequency. Gangs of ex-guerrillas from both sides pillaged and sought revenge for wartime acts; committees of public safety organized, and vigilantes remained active until the mid-1870s. Numerous armed bands, each protecting its own interests, clashed in the countryside. Legal protection was often unavailable. All this was not merely the last gasp of the Lost Cause; it was not a simple reflection of Union/Confederate divisions. Many local ex-Confederates, for example, opposed the James-Younger gang. The Confederate background of the outlaws certainly won them some sympathy, but only within the local context of chaotic, factional disorder.

The situation in Oklahoma in the 1890s was a remarkably similar mixture of predation, personal vengeance, and vigilantism. With the demand for Oklahoma land exceeding its availability, the government resorted to one of the most astonishing systems of distributing resources ever attempted by a modern state. Settlers in Oklahoma raced for their land. The races were spectacular, colorful, and virtually impossible to police. Numerous people—the "sooners"—stole over the line ahead of the starting time to stake claims. Sooners only increased the inevitable conflicts among people who claimed to have arrived first at a desirable plot of land. In the end the land rushes sowed a crop of litigation and violence. Even if nothing else divided a community, bitter factional struggles for land were sure to persist for years. In Payne County, the center of support for the Doolin-Dalton gang, the county attorney claimed, perhaps with some exaggeration, that there were fifty murders as the direct result of land claim cases in the early years. Such murders involved the leading citizens of Payne County. The first representative of Payne County to the Oklahoma legislature and speaker of the assembly, I. N. Terrill, terminated his political career in 1891 by murdering a man in a land dispute.

Given the distrust of local law enforcement, protection in such disputes often demanded organization and violence. In 1893, for example, the *Oklahoma State Capital* reported the presumed lynching of three sooners by a local vigilante committee. Apparently both sides—the alleged sooners and the vigilante committee—were armed and resorting to violence. Such actions, the reporter contended, were common: "Reports are coming in every day of white cap whippings and terrorizing and it is nothing to see the sooner pulling out every day, claiming that they have been threatened with hanging by vigilant committees if they did not go." The large numbers of horse and cattle thieves who had long existed in a sort of parasitic relationship with the large cattle operations and who now turned to stealing from settlers only increased the level of private violence.

The situation in Oklahoma was, however, more complicated than extralegal groups enforcing the laws against thieves and sooners. There was some ambiguity about what constituted theft. For example, Evan Barnard, an ex-cowboy and settler in Oklahoma who wrote one of the best of western memoirs, defended stock theft by his friend, Ranicky Bill: "He was generous and big-hearted . . . if he knew any settler who was hungry, he did not hesitate to rustle beef, and give it to the starving people. In the early days of Oklahoma, a man who did that was not such a bad person after all." According to Barnard, such attitudes were shared by many settlers. When it became clear that the large ranchers would lose their leases on Indian lands, the homesteaders moved in to steal wood, fencing, and stock. All the old-time cattlemen, Barnard contended, would admit that the "settlers were good rustlers." In practice *sooner, rustler, vigilante,* and *outlaw* were ambiguous terms; very often they were only pejorative names for those whose interests were not the same as other citizens.

In both Missouri and Oklahoma, pervasive lawlessness and widespread distrust of public law enforcement divided the countryside not into two clearly opposing groups, but rather into innumerable local factions. Conditions were ripe for factional violence and social banditry. A rather detailed example from Oklahoma is perhaps the best way to illustrate how tangled the relationship of gangs, vigilantes, and other armed groups could become; how supposed, and even demonstrated, criminal behavior might not cost people public sympathy; how private violence could be deemed not only necessary but admirable; and how social bandits garnered support in such situations.

In 1889, Evan Barnard, his friend Ranicky Bill, and other ex-cowboys banded together before the run for Oklahoma Territory to secure and protect land claims. It was a necessary precaution because "just staking a claim did not hold it." Barnard drove one man from his claim by flourishing a winchester and a six-shooter and telling him it was "a hundred and sixty acres or six feet, and I did not give a damn which it was." Bravado was not sufficient to drive off two other challengers, however; for them, Barnard had to demonstrate "the backing I had among the cowboys." This backing was available regardless of the merits of any specific case. One of Barnard's friends failed to secure a claim, but visits from Barnard's associates persuaded the legitimate claimant to sell out to him for $75. The claimant left but declared: "'If I had half the backing that you have, I would stay with you until hell froze over'. . . . He left the claim and Ranicky Bill remarked, 'hits sure hell to get things regulated in a new country.'" Ranicky Bill himself had to stop a contest on his claim by shooting up his opponent's camp. Private force clearly was both a necessary supplement to, and a substitute for, legal right.

Such bullying understandably stirred up resentment against Barnard and his friends, and some regarded them as sooners, which they were not. When these accusations were compounded by charges that Ranicky Bill was a horse thief, the vigilantes struck. They attacked Ranicky Bill's cabin, and although he escaped, the vigilantes threatened to hang Barnard and another neighbor. Ranicky Bill surrendered to authorities to clear himself, but his real protection came from thirty cowboys who gathered a day after the incident and offered to help him. Later, vigilantes seized another neighbor and twice hoisted him off the ground with a rope that cut into his neck. He refused to confess and was released, but now the entire neighborhood armed against the vigilantes, who ceased their operations.

According to Barnard, none of those accused by the vigilantes were thieves, but other incidents narrated in his book indicate how thoroughly such accusations were tied up in land disputes and factional quarrels. Friends and neighbors of Barnard apparently did steal a team of horses and other property from a claim jumper named Sniderwine during a land dispute. They considered this a legitimate means of driving him from his claim and probably perjured themselves to protect each other.

In such an atmosphere, the organization of settlers into armed groups or gangs for protection seems to have been common. The argument made by an actual stock thief to a new settler that in Oklahoma a man's legal rights and property were worthless without friends sometimes led to the corollary that if you were going to be denounced and attacked for supposed crimes, then you might as well have the "game as the name." And in practice, personal quarrels with each side denouncing the other as sooners and thieves sometimes left local newspapers totally unable to sort out the merits of the case. Personal loyalties and personal qualities in these situations took on larger than normal significance. Law, theft, and even murder became ambiguous categories; strong men who protected themselves and aided their friends could gain local respect transcending their separate criminal activities.

This respect for strong men who could protect and revenge themselves is the real heart of the social bandits' appeal. It is precisely this personal element that gang members and their supporters chose to emphasize. What distinguished social bandits and their supporters (as it distinguished peasant social bandits and theirs) from radicals and revolutionaries was their stubborn refusal to envision the social problems enmeshing them in anything but personal terms. The James and Younger brothers claimed they were hounded into banditry by vindictive Union men who would not leave them alone after the war. They fought only for self-preservation and revenge, not for a social cause. Supporters of Jesse James justified each of his murders as an act of vengeance against men who had attacked his comrades or family. Indeed, the chief propagandist for the James brothers, Missouri newspaper editor John Edwards, made personal vengeance the underlying theme of all their actions from the Civil War onward. Edwards distinguished the guerrillas from regular soldiers by saying these men fought not for a cause but to avenge assaults against themselves and their families. Personal defense and revenge, he claimed, dominated the entire career of the James and Younger brothers. Whether such a claim is accurate or not matters less than that it was credible. When John Edwards claimed these brothers were merely strong men seeking to defend their rights, the appeal could be felt deeply by those who knew that neither they nor the authorities could protect their own rights and property.

The Daltons' grievances, like those of the James and Younger brothers, were personal. They said they became outlaws because the federal government would not pay them for their services as deputy marshals and the express companies had falsely accused them of robbery. They were not radicals who fought against the system itself; they fought against what they regarded as its corruption by their enemies. Emmett Dalton declared that "our fights were not so much against the law, but rather against the law as it was then enforced." At least two members of the Dalton gang asserted that their criminal careers began with land problems, and Bill Doolin, like Cole Younger before him, claimed it was only the personal vindictiveness of his enemies and the corruption of the authorities that stopped him from surrendering. Many of the supporters of the outlaws agreed with these assertions of persecution, and movements for full or partial amnesty for the gangs were common.

Given social conditions in Oklahoma and Missouri, there was a decisive allure in strong men who defended themselves, righted their own wrongs, and took vengeance on their enemies despite the corruption of the existing order. Such virtues were of more than nostalgic interest. In praising bandits, supporters admired them more for their attributes than their acts. Bandits were brave, daring, free, shrewd, and tough, yet also loyal, gentle, generous, and polite. They were not common criminals. Lon Stansbery, who knew Bill Doolin from the 3-D ranch, was, for instance, forthright about the bandits' heroic stature and masculine virtue:

> The outlaws of that day were not hijackers or petty thieves, and some of them had hearts, even though they were outlaws. They always treated women with respect and no rancher was ever afraid to leave his family on the ranch on account of outlaws. While they would stand up and shoot it out with men, when women were around, they were the first to take off their Stetsons and act like real men.

And Red Orrington, a deputy marshal, called the Daltons "four of as fine fellows as I ever knew," brave men who went on the scout (the local term for banditry) for "love of adventure."

From the initial exploits of the James-Younger gang until the death of Bill Doolin, appraisals of the outlaws' character by their supporters, while sometimes allowing for an understandable laxity in regard to the sixth and eighth commandments, remained strong and consistent in their praise. The James and Younger brothers were "brilliant, bold, indefatigable roughriders," and in the words of an amnesty resolution introduced in the Missouri legislature, "brave . . . generous . . . gallant . . . honorable" men. The Daltons were "big hearted and generous" in every way, "like the average western man," while Bill Doolin was a "naturally . . . kind-hearted, sympathetic man." A contemporary diary from Ingalls comments that the Doolin-Dalton gang was "as a rule quite (*sic*) and peaceable," even though they moved about heavily armed, and residents later remembered them as "well behaved . . . quiet and friendly," a description close to an Oklahoma schoolteacher's memory of the Daltons as "nice and polite." Some supporters proclaimed them innocent of their crimes, others merely excused them, but all demanded sympathy not so much for the crime as for the criminal. Again it must be emphasized that what is being praised here is not lawlessness per se. Outlaw stories go out of their way to detach the social bandit from the ordinary criminal. Thus, in one story Bill Doolin turns a common thief who tried to join his gang over to a deputy marshal, since "they would have no men in their outfit who would rob a poor man or any individual." John Edwards also took pains to distinguish the James-Younger gang from common criminals.

> There are men in Jackson, Cass, and Clay—a few there are left—who learned to dare when there was no such word as quarter in the dictionary of the Border. Men who have carried their lives in their hands so long that they do not know how to commit them over into the keeping of the laws and regulations that exist now, and those men sometimes rob. But it is always in the glare of day and in the teeth of multitude. With them booty is but the second thought; the wild drama of the adventure first. These men

never go upon the highway in lonesome places to plunder the pilgrim. That they leave to the ignobler pack of jackals. But they ride at midday into the county seat, while court is sitting, take the cash out of the vault and put the cashier in and ride out of town to the music of cracking pistols.

And the *Ardmore* [*Oklahoma*] *State Herald* made the connections between the Doolin-Dalton gang and Robin Hood explicit:

Their life is made up of daring. Their courage is always with them and their rifles as well. They are kind to the benighted traveler, and it is not a fiction that when robbing a train they refuse to take from a woman.

It is said that Bill Doolin, at present the reigning highwayman, is friendly to the people in one neighborhood, bestowing all sorts of presents upon the children. It is his boast that he never killed a man.

This is as fully a romantic figure as Robin Hood ever cut.

Such Robin Hood descriptions only echoed those of the James-Younger gang twenty years before.

By the 1890s, in Oklahoma at least, the standards of how proper social bandits should behave seemed clear enough for the *Oklahoma State Capital,* a paper with little sympathy for outlaws, to lecture Bill Dalton on his duties as the heir of a great tradition. Bill Dalton, in an interview with a local reporter only the week before, had claimed he was considering teaming up with Frank James to open a saloon in Chicago to take advantage of their fame and the World's Fair. The saloon never materialized, and Bill Dalton had left Guthrie without paying his board bill. The *State Capital* had complained:

There is supposed to be honor among thieves. Men who presume to be great in any calling avoid the common faults of men. There is a heroism even in desperadoes, and the people admire an ideal type of that class. The James and Younger brothers are remembered as never having robbed a poor family or assaulted an unarmed man. Even the "Dalton boys"—they who really stood up to their "knitten" and looked down the muzzles of Winchesters—did brave and not ignoble deeds. But Bill Dalton—"Board Bill" Dalton—has besmirched the family escutcheon. The brothers, dead, when they hear what he has done, will turn over in their graves and groan—"Oh, Bill."

Bill Dalton's future specialization in bank and train robbery and his violent death presumably redeemed the family honor.

Social bandits thus did exist in a meaningful sense in the American West, yet their actual social impact, confined as it was to small areas with extreme conditions, was minor. They never sought social change, and the actual social evolution of Missouri and Oklahoma owes little to them. Nevertheless, their impact on American culture has been immense. The social bandits who metaphorically rode out of Missouri and Oklahoma into America at large quickly transcended the specific economic and political conditions of the areas that produced them and became national cultural

symbols. The outlaws were ready-made cultural heroes—their local supporters had already presented them in terms accessible to the nation as a
whole. The portrait of the outlaw as a strong man righting his own wrongs
and taking his own revenge had a deep appeal to a society concerned with
the place of masculinity and masculine virtues in a newly industrialized and
seemingly effete order.

Practically, of course, the outlaw as a model of male conduct was hopeless, and early popularizers of the outlaws stressed that although their
virtues and qualities were admirable, their actions were inappropriate.
Edwards portrayed the James and Younger brothers as men born out of their
time, and Zoe Tilghman (whose book ostensibly denied the outlaws were
heroic) claimed the Oklahoma bandits were cowboys "who could not bring
their natures to the subjection of such a change from the wild free life to
that kind that came to surround them. They were the venturesome spirits of
the old Southwest and could not be tamed."

Those who seriously worried about masculine virtue in the late nineteenth and early twentieth centuries romanticized toughness, loyalty, bravery, generosity, honor, and daring, but sought to channel it into muscular
Christianity or college football, not into robbing banks and trains. The outlaws' virtues were cherished, but their actions were archaic and antisocial.
In this paradox of accepted virtue without an appropriate arena in which to
exist lay the real power of the outlaws' appeal. The outlaw legend, rather
than the childish solutions of reformers who sought to provide for the
development of "masculine" virtues through organized sports or the dangerous solutions of chauvinists who praised war, retained the complexity,
ambivalence, and paradoxes of a personal experience in which accepted
male virtue had little relevance to an industrialized, bureaucratized world.

Ambivalence saved Jesse James and the mythical western hero that
sprang from his legends from becoming Frank Merriwell on a horse. The
position of the western hero reflects the paradoxical position most Americans occupy in an industrialized capitalist society. The traits and acts of the
outlaw become symbols of the larger, structural oppositions—oppositions
of law and justice, individualism and community, nature and civilization—
never adequately reconciled in American life. Assimilated into the classic
western, the social bandit becomes the western hero—a figure of great
appeal. The western is not the simple-minded celebration of the triumph of
American virtue over evil that it is so often ignorantly and unjustly presumed to be; instead it is the opposite. It plays on the unresolved contradictions and oppositions of America itself.

The entire structure of the classic western film poses the hero between
contrasting values both of which are very attractive: private justice and the
order provided by law, individualism and community, nature and civilization. The hero, posed between the oppositions, remains ambivalent. Like
the actual social bandit, the western hero never attempts to change the
structure itself, but rather tries to achieve a reconciliation through his own
courage and virtue. Western heroes personify culturally defined masculine
virtues of strength, self-reliance, and honor in a world where they have

ceased to be effective. More often than not the hero fails or only partially succeeds in his task and like the epitome of the classic western hero, Shane, is left wounded and out of place in a world he has himself helped to create. In the hero's dilemma, viewers recognize their own struggle to reconcile the cultural irreconcilables that society demands of them—individualism and community responsibility, personal dominance and cooperation, maximum productivity and respect for nature. The bandit and the western hero are social failures, and this paradoxically guarantees them their cultural success. It is as a cultural symbol that Jesse James would survive and thrive even though "that dirty little coward, that shot Mr. Howard [had] laid poor Jesse in his grave."

Y *FURTHER   READING*

Lewis Atherton, *The Cattle Kings* (1961)

Larry D. Ball, *Desert Lawmen: The High Sheriffs of New Mexico and Arizona, 1846–1912* (1992)

Richard Maxwell Brown, *No Duty to Retreat: Violence and Values in American History and Society* (1991)

——, *Strain of Violence: Historical Studies of Violence and Vigilantism* (1975)

——, "Violence" in *The Oxford History of the American West,* ed. Clyde A. Milner II, Carol A. O'Connor, and Martha A. Sandweiss (1994)

Lew L. Callaway, *Montana's Righteous Hangmen: The Vigilantes in Action* (1982)

John G. Cawelti, *The Six-Gun Mystique* (1984)

David Dary, *Cowboy Culture: A Saga of Five Centuries* (reprint, 1981)

Philip Durham and Everett L. Jones, *The Negro Cowboys* (1965)

Lawrence M. Friedman and Robert V. Percival, *The Roots of Justice: Crime and Punishment in Alameda County, California, 1870–1910* (1981)

C. Robert Haywood, *Cowtown Lawyers: Dodge City and Its Attorneys, 1876–1886* (1988)

W. Eugene Hollon, *Frontier Violence: Another Look* (1974)

Teresa Jordan, *Cowgirls: Women of the American West* (1982)

Terry G. Jordan, *North American Cattle-Ranching Frontiers: Origins, Diffusion, and Differentiation* (1993)

Robert Larson, "The White Caps of New Mexico: A Study in Ethnic Militancy in the Southwest," *Pacific Historical Quarterly,* 44 (1975): 171–86

David E. Lopez, "Cowboys Strikes and Unions," *Labor History,* 18 (1977): 325–40

Roger D. McGrath, *Gunfighters, Highwaymen, and Vigilantes: Violence on the Frontier* (1984)

Nyle H. Miller and Joseph W. Snell, *Great Gunfighters of the Kansas Cowtown, 1867–1886* (1967)

Frederick W. Nolan, *The Lincoln County War: A Documentary History* (1992)

Bill O'Neil, *Encyclopedia of Western Gunfighters* (1979)

Robert J. Rosenbaum, *Mexicano Resistance in the Southwest:"The Sacred Right of Self Preservation"* (1981)

Joseph G. Rosa, *Wild Bill Hickok: The Man and His Myth* (1996)

Julian Samora et al., *Gunpowder Justice: A Reassessment of the Texas Rangers* (1979)

William W. Savage, Jr., *The Cowboy Hero: His Image in American History and Culture* (1979)

William A. Settle, Jr., *Jesse James Was His Name . . .* (1966)

Glenn H. Shirley, *West of Hell's Fringe: Crime, Criminals, and the Federal Peace Officers in Oklahoma Territory* (1977)

Peter K. Simpson, *The Community of Cattlemen: A Social History of the Cattle Industry in Southeastern Oregon, 1869–1912* (1987)

Richard Slatta, *Cowboys of the Americas* (1990)

Richard Slotkin, *Regeneration through Violence: The Mythology of the American Frontier, 1600–1860* (1973)

——, *The Fatal Environment: The Myth of the Frontier in the Age of Industrialization* (1985)

——, *Gunfighter Nation: The Myth of the Frontier in Twentieth-Century America* (1992)

Kent Ladd Steckmesser, *The Western Hero in History and Legend* (1965)

Stephen Tatum, *Inventing Billy the Kid: Visions of the Outlaw in America, 1881–1981* (1982)

Robert M. Utley, *Billy the Kid: A Short and Violent Life* (1989)

——, *High Noon in Lincoln: Violence on the Western Frontier* (1987)

Don D. Walker, *Clio's Cowboys: Studies in the Historiography of the Cattle Trade* (1981)

John P. Wilson, *Merchants, Guns, and Money: The Story of Lincoln County and Its Wars* (1987)

Donald Worster, "Cowboy Ecology," in *Under Western Skies: Nature and History in the American West* (1992)

James A. Young and B. Abbott Sparks, *Cattle in the Cold Desert* (1985)

CHAPTER
7

Children, Marriage, and
Families

Y

Despite its celebrated adventurers and outlaws, the American West princi-
pally embraced families of many cultures. From indigenous people to immi-
grant newcomers, family provided the structure around which western
society thrived. Yet all families were not the same. Cultural values, lan-
guage, clan size, religious commitment, economic expectations, and social
opportunity covered a wide spectrum in the West. The Navajos of Arizona
differed from the Swedes of Minnesota, the Japanese of Oregon from the
German Jews of Kansas, the African Americans of Montana from the Mor-
mons of Utah. Even within cultures, dialects, spiritual disputes, and famil-
ial rivalries led to further breakdowns. Nonetheless, the West remained a
family region and its change, settlement, and expansion played out against
decisions made by families.

In part the changing face of the West accelerated these decisions. A fam-
ily opted for making the westward trek with a wagon train; another decided
to abandon mining and open a mercantile business. One Native American
family moved deeper into the New Mexico mountains, while a German cou-
ple agreed to try the perils of homesteading in the Dakotas. Families of all
cultures made decisions that moved them across and through the West.

Their movements brought them into direct and indirect contact with
each other. Families witnessed each others' lives. California-bound wives
looked with caution at Utah's polygamous women. Anglo children, moving
deep into Texas, watched Hispanic youngsters at play. African American set-
tlers crossed paths with Chinese laborers. Anglo women found in the West a
place to explore their capabilities. Native American women witnessed their
homeland taken up by others and developed strategies for preserving the
culture of their kin. In all cultures, the many challenges to domestic tradi-
tions affected families. What happened to the bonds between husbands and
wives? Did children's emotional and social development change? What
events brought disorder and violence to families? Ultimately, cultural ten-
sions, both positive and negative, surfaced for everyone and altered relation-
ships within many families.

PHOTO DOCUMENTS

The search for women's history leads the researcher to non-traditional sources. Women's lives are documented in the places where they lived and worked, especially the home. For this reason, family photographs often prove a rich trove of information about women's experiences in the American West. They cast light on the values women cherished and the commitments they made to themselves and their families.

David Hilton Homestead, Custer County, Nebraska, 1887   The disruption to family routines that accompanied a move to the West caused many women to seek ways to reestablish domestic order in new western homes. Often they used their most cherished possessions as symbols of family continuity, blending beloved eastern styles with unfamiliar western environments. Although the mother of this family, in Custer County, Nebraska, in the 1880s, wanted a photograph for her eastern friends, she could not bear to have it show the western sodhouse, now called "home." What does it say about perceptions of home and family that her husband and the photographer moved the pump organ into the animal-filled yard to accommodate the wife's wishes? This photograph, probably taken from the roof of the sodhouse, captures a family in transition. In what differing ways would such a transition affect the individual members of this family? (Solomon D. Butcher Collection, Nebraska State Historical Society)

Ira Watson House, Custer County, Nebraska, 1886   Migrating families often included several generations, as with the Ira Watson family of Nebraska shown here in 1886. In the endeavor to make a success of the demanding farm life, each family member, even young children, had to assume work responsibilities. Women often reached across the boundaries of their gender-specific duties and learned masculine skills. The youngest toddler gathered sticks for the fire or apples for the pie. Work filled each day and invaded family living space, so that leisure hours were also task-oriented. Even with all this communal effort, not every family succeeded well as agrarians. Homesteading could produce a spirit of great unity for western newcomers, but it could also result in financial ruin and family collapse. Because sodhouses enjoyed a reputation for solid construction, what could account for the unstable appearance of this one? How much comfort and privacy could the interior of this simple home be expected to provide this couple, a child, and a grandmother? What possible alternatives awaited a family that did not survive as homesteaders? (Solomon D. Butcher Collection, Nebraska State Historical Society)

Stewart Family in Spokane, Washington, 1889 Mrs. Stewart, who appears to be only in her early thirties, was already mother to eight children when this picture was taken in 1889. Note the distinct difference between the expressions of the children and that of the mother in this photograph. Women often had a new baby each year and had only their older daughters to rely on for household assistance. Despite these domestic hardships, parents and children looked on the western experience with different perceptions. Both boys and girls anticipated an adulthood that differed from their pioneering parents. These middle-class children, raised in the area of Spokane, Washington, may well have had the chance to pursue higher education. The introduction of coeducation in western universities expanded the career possibilities for many young girls, such as those pictured here. (Washington State Historical Society)

Alice Jasperson, Goshen, Utah, Sewing a Flag, c. 1917   Sewing and cooking skills of farm women meant more than a convenient talent for isolated families. For a successful farm, husbands and wives worked as coordinated teams. Women sold the butter, bread, and jellies from their kitchens and traded the eggs they gathered; at harvest time they fed the migrant crews, not as a courtesy but as part of the threshers' contract. They earned cash from handmade quilts and lace. They kept the family account books and they decided on the purchase of a new wagon or parcel of land. The unpaid labor of a wife and mother translated into essential dollars in the family budget. In their few spare moments women often turned their energies to religious or civic causes. Here, Utah's Alice Jasperson, complete with her apron, the badge of the farm wife, lends her patriotic support to World War I. Surrounded by photographs that explain her interest, Jasperson uses a foot-powered sewing machine to turn out an American flag. What might Alice Jasperson and Mrs. Stewart (see previous photograph) tell each other about their lives, if they could have a conversation? (Special Collections & Archives, Merrill Library, Utah State University)

Lincoln J. Smith and Margaret E. Breeden Smith with Their Children, in California, date unknown   African American families responded to the promise of the West, just as did white Americans. The expressions of the Smith family capture the aspirations and middle-class values that brought many African Americans to seek their family fortune in the West. Many headed for the farming regions of the Great Plains, and more than five thousand black men worked as cowboys on the open range. Some African Americans looked for economic advancement for themselves and their children in the western cities, where they opened small businesses or worked at trades. Margaret E. Breeden Smith's brothers, Charles and Richard Breeden, were businessmen in Marysville, California.

The equality that blacks sought in the West proved elusive. In several states, including California, Oregon, and Wyoming, antiblack laws restricted voting privileges, marriage regulations, and economic opportunity. It fell to the emerging black middle class to fight against these constraints and to become advocates of full equality in the West. Black women especially devoted themselves to church and club work with the specific goal of enlarging educational opportunities for all African Americans. (From the collection of the Community Memorial Museum of Sutter County)

A Chinese Family in California, date unknown   Asian immigrants were among the most marginalized of all western groups. Closed out from Caucasian society by their own cultural traditions, language barriers, and the hostility of the dominant society, Asian families developed a strong internal network and relied on each other. The women, however, became almost lost in the historical discourse for they worked and lived so completely inside the parameters of the Asian community. A Chinese woman faced many expectations within her own culture: assisting her husband in the family business, working in Chinese industries, and raising a large family of children. Despite the barriers of race and language that segregated Chinese and Caucasian women, they shared many similar values about families, children, and work. California missionaries tried to convert these women and their families to traditional Caucasian dress and manner, but as this photograph shows, the Chinese chose to retain their own sense of cultural identity. (California State Library, Charles Johnson Photography)

Joseph F. Smith and His Polygamous Family in Utah, c. 1900   It remained a mystery to non-Mormons why and how Mormon women entered into polygamous marriages. For those outside of Mormondom, the practice, which challenged long-held concepts of matrimony, appeared repressive and coercive. Nonetheless, within the Mormon culture, the taking of multiple wives, introduced by the religion's founder Joseph Smith and endorsed by his successor Brigham Young, had considerable support among many of its female practitioners. Although attention has centered on the husbands, such as Joseph F. Smith shown here with his wives and children, the motivation of the women is of greater interest. They counted among their numbers some of the nation's most thoughtful, literary women, who were forceful advocates for women's rights. At the same time, they expressed an unwavering loyalty to their spiritual commitment to "live life in the principle." Polygamous women gained support and comfort from each other during times of crisis and joy. The non-traditional family arrangements allowed rural women the company and the assistance of other females during work, leisure, and childbearing. Non-Mormons could not explain the refusal of Mormon women to come forward to "rescue homes" established to "save" them from their oppressive marriages; but to polygamous wives, the notion was ridiculous. (Courtesy of Church of Jesus Christ of Latter-day Saints Historical Department)

Chipeta and Her Family in Dragon, Utah, 1907   Native American women remain at the periphery of many discussions about the American West. Yet within their own tribes, women like Chipeta (Uncompahgre band of the Northern Utes), standing right of center with her hands on the shoulders of a young girl, exercised considerable power. Gender responsibilities were clearly drawn within Native American families, who steadily tried to avoid the encroachment of white culture. The futility of their efforts is typified by this picture, taken on the Ouray reservation in Utah after a mining town and railway station were established there. In these mixed cultural environments, Native American families had to make difficult decisions about adherence to traditional rituals or acceptance of white customs. This photograph places Native Americans within the visual context of the transitions their families faced. All the families shown in these last four photographs confronted challenges to their cultural and personal identities. What changes might each family have chosen to make and what alterations may have been beyond their control? (Courtesy of Vintah County Public Library)

Υ *E S S A Y S*

Elliott West, a professor of history at the University of Arkansas, has written extensively on social issues that shaped the American West. In this essay, he directs attention to the widely neglected subject of children in the pioneering experience. He reminds the reader that people of all ages contributed to the western epic and their perceptions and experiences varied from generation to generation. Paula Petrik, a member of the history department at the University of Maine, Orono, turns her historical lens to the subject of women and divorce. In this insightful essay, Petrik points out that within the legal system, standards for women differed from those for men; impressions about a woman's moral conduct could carry more weight than legal evidence that refuted any wrongdoing. In addition, Petrik demonstrates that not all domestic relations were marked by harmony and happy endings. For children, marriages, and families, does the history of life in the West allow us to determine what produced happy, successful lives?

Children and the Frontier

ELLIOTT WEST

Until its children are heard, the frontier's history cannot be truly written. The story of westward expansion has been a national inspiration and a global entertainment. It is a key to understanding America's precocious rise to power; from it, our people have taken their most enduring myths. But since its first telling, the story has been incomplete, and thus distorted. In all the human striving, failure, and accomplishment, a large portion of the actors have been left out. . . .

. . . We must take the children into account when describing the settlement of America's final frontier, and only through the frontier's evolution can we hope to understand those last generations born of three centuries of pioneering.

Western history looks very different when the children are included in it. Their story demands a drastic rewriting of the most familiar episodes of frontier history—those of conquest and economic development. In a typical textbook the traditional drama unfolds in an orderly march, chapter by chapter. . . .

This story has been written far too narrowly. For one thing, the leading actors have been almost all men. The reader assumes women and children were there, yet their roles are described so vaguely that, as one critic has suggested, the West might as well be labeled "Hisland" on the traditional historical map. Men did, of course, direct many of these great changes and did some of the most visible work—that of military conquest, diplomacy, and town building, for instance. To tell this story as primarily an enterprise of adult males, however, is absurd.

Elliott West, *Growing Up with the Country* (Albuquerque: University of New Mexico Press, 1989), 245–262. Copyright © 1989 by the University of New Mexico Press. Excerpted by permission of the University of New Mexico Press.

Children and women played an important part in much that is credited to their fathers and husbands. A new agricultural technology allowed boys, girls, and women to help with the arduous jobs of plowing, planting, and harvesting. Children handled much of the tedious but essential work of caring for growing crops; child herders were a common sight. On the thousands of smaller ranches and stock farms they were often the only ones in the field.

. . . Children who hunted, gathered wild plants, and tended gardens in many cases fed the men who farmed, ranched, and mined. When parents bought some item they could not make for themselves, they used cash earned by sons and daughters who helped make butter and gather eggs for sale and who herded neighbors' cattle, clerked in stores, hawked newspapers, and delivered laundry. Weary fathers ate and rested in homes where women and children did the cooking, canning, and washing.

. . . Children, in fact, were the frontier's most versatile workers. They gave their families what was needed most—an impressive adaptability. . . .

Most of all, the children remind us that the West was transformed through a complex economy of mutual dependence. . . . Yet pioneers did more than transform the country, and certainly they worried about more than making profits. . . .

Many parents chose their destinations according to opportunities—educational and social as well as economic—for their sons and daughters, and among the most common reasons for moving around the new country was the desire to be near schools or to escape society's corruptions. . . .

The powerful educational impulse, centering on children and the family, by its nature involved the westward transfer of information, values, and culture. Hard-worked mothers made time for teaching the basics of reading and mathematics. Fathers and mothers established common schools remarkably early, considering the trying circumstances, and educational officials argued for standardized curricula and instruction in good manners and patriotism as well as the "three R's." On many parts of the frontier, children could attend sabbath schools within the first years of settlement. Lyceums, literaries, and spelling matches stressed moral homilies almost as much as knowledge and fundamental skills. . . . A commitment to schooling became a useful tool in the pioneers' search for community, present and future.

Children . . . brought westward the rich lore of childhood—rhymes, word puzzles, songs, jokes, and games, some from a couple of centuries in the past. These spoke to the special concerns of the young; in laughing and playing, boys and girls used time-tested devices to amuse and soothe themselves in ways they knew best. Games, like some of what their parents did, created instant communities. With the rules and choreography of age-old contests, youngsters recognized a common heritage, and through the scrap and scramble, they introduced themselves. They used the traditions of their own complex culture to knit together this younger level of society. . . . Where adults greatly outnumbered children, the social and emotional value of youngsters increased, and lonesome, nostalgic men doted on the frontier's children, giving them gifts and special favors, reading to them, offering them advice and instruction. Most parents—not only those of the elite but also poorer farmers, ranchers, sheepherders, and saloonkeepers—showed their children affection and loving concern. Western children grew up with the message that their time of life was precious and to be prolonged as much as possible. . . .

In the darkest times, when death took their children, parents found comfort in another modern ideal. They faced the loss of sons and daughters with the new styles of mourning increasingly common in the East. These rituals proclaimed a sentimentalized vision of innocent youth. They spoke with assurance of children's heavenly ascent and of a family's rendezvous in paradise. These consolations soothed the special guilt of mothers and fathers who learned pioneering's blackest joke—that most children died, not at the hands and claws of savages and beasts, but through their parents' confident fantasies of controlling the land. . . .

Sooner or later, anyone interested in western children comes around to certain questions. How did the frontier's peculiar conditions shape its children? Did this heritage alone make western childhood distinctive? How did their early years prepare children for facing the challenges of adulthood? And how, finally, have frontier children left their mark on the modern West?

Children inevitably were influenced by conditions beyond their parents' control. The children's reality—their ideas of what the future held, their beliefs and attitudes, the ways they saw themselves—were formed partly through contact with surroundings that were different from those their elders had known. Work took them out into that environment—encouraging exchanges with it, helping them master their fears, and posing a variety of challenges and responsibilities. Play became another means of exploring the world around them, and through it they also learned to cope with anxieties and problems of frontier life. Around the children was a diverse, mobile society strikingly different from that to the east. Youngsters took on its aggressive, optimistic ways, even as they learned other lessons from its wide range of human types.

. . . Growing up in the West, girls and boys naturally acquired independent, self-motivated, confident, even brash personalities. Hard work was a given, for . . . "there was no life without it." As children matured, they were often eager to move on in search of better things. Many squinted hard at parents, teachers, and anyone else who tried to direct their lives too closely. Children likely acquired other, far less admirable traits linked to frontier life. Among these were an all-too-easy acceptance of violence, an exploitive frame of mind, a compulsive restlessness, and an unappeasable inner drive toward accomplishment and control of physical surroundings.

But when these traits are added up, they still fall short of describing the children's characters. Responding to the peculiar nature of the frontier, boys and girls were also absorbing what has already been noted—surviving traditions, the teaching of parents, the persistence of ideals from other places. Every generation has its mix of messages; because the world changes, parents' points of view always differ from their children's. But on the frontier, these normal differences were vastly exaggerated. . . .

Out of this . . . came what was, in the end, the most distinguishing characteristic of western childhood—its ambiguity. Children were told, through words and actions, that childhood was precious and should be prolonged as long as possible, then they were expected to play adult roles and to take on the tasks of men and women. They were admonished to tend to their studies and their moral betterment and then pushed into a society renowned for its open corruptions and its lusting for the almighty dollar. Look to your parents and obey them, they were urged, even as they were forced into situations bound to make them independent and emotionally self-reliant. Powerful bonds of love, affection, and respect drew families close together, while the generations' different perspectives and experiences, as well as the children's bonds among themselves, eroded family unity. . . . More than anything else, this—a garbling of messages, the push and shove of conflicting influences—set frontier childhood apart. . . .

Parents found their economic needs were great and their days crowded. Young children were pushed into heavy responsibilities and left to play and explore mostly on their own. To say the least, social controls were imperfectly enforced, and girls and boys grew up close to the West's famous vices and its sizable population of rakehells and shady characters. Theirs was no protected, choreographed upbringing. . . . No wonder so many adults worried about frontier children. . . . How could the future hold anything but trouble? . . .

Specifically, critics warned that children were bound to be corrupted. They need not have been concerned. The frontier did not produce a generation of moral anarchists. Mose Drachman roamed Tucson's streets and passed time with monte dealers. Later, as mayor, he fought to close saloons and gambling halls. Caesar Brock's daughter, Helen, grew from her wide-roaming, bronc-busting childhood to be a highly regarded rancher. Most children would mature not into outlaws and reprobates but responsible citizens respectful of institutions and prevailing values.

Another threat at first seems more serious. At an early age, far earlier than most youngsters today, frontier children were expected to deal with the demands and pressures of adulthood. They were given heavy responsibilities and exhausting work in some of the most difficult environments the country could offer. Many were expected to make important, even vital decisions. Frequently they saw the fruits of their efforts destroyed by natural disasters and human error, often their own. Then came hard times: short meals or outright hunger, scrambling to survive, or moving to another chance. This might seem to threaten a child's sense of himself and his ability to face the future. Frances Moore watching the hoppers eat the corn from her mother's arms, Owen McWhorter trying to coax freezing cattle from the snow, John Norton praying for rain that came too late—the stories make depressing reading. The lessons seemed to be of children's inadequacies, life's insurmountable difficulties, the likelihood of losing.

Yet these lessons were balanced by others. Under the right circum-

stances, hardships could have other, much more positive effects. . . . Many
. . . emerged with faith in themselves and their ability to form stable families of their own. . . .

These conditions describe well . . . most pioneer children. The companionate family was alive and healthy on the frontier, and most parents
treated their young with concern and an awareness of their emotional
needs. Mothers especially gave them affection and close attention during
infancy and early childhood, those first two years of life most crucial to
their emotional security. Children also made lives for themselves away
from their families, cultivating close friendships with others their ages and
making their surroundings into playgrounds. They enjoyed the affection,
advice, and encouragement of adults outside the home, surrogate parents
like Anne Ellis's Uncle Pomp and Marquis James's Mr. Howell. Certainly
youngsters grew up with a sense of their "required helpfulness." When a
child had such sources of emotional support, formidible challenges, even
when followed by failure, became sources of strength.

So what worried many critics most—the confused and unpredictable
nature of growing up, its harsh demands and grave responsibilities—could
be frontier childhood's finest virtue, not its greatest threat. Most children
grew up reasonably acquainted with their parents' heritage and strengthened by their families' affection and care. However trying, their lives gave
them a secure sense of worth and capability. Boys and girls entered adoles-
cence aware of life's adversities and of how people usually survived them.
They learned to adjust and to overcome, or at least endure, unexpected difficulties. They gained a healthy appreciation for human personalities and
oddities. Even those who moved often among the West's many settings
earned an intimate understanding of the country around them. Children
may have known only imperfectly from where they had come, but by any
measure they knew just where they were.

Unfortunately, the question of how the frontier prepared its children for
the future cannot be tied up so neatly. As the young matured, their ambiguous beginnings sometimes turned back upon them. The results could be
troubling. The most obvious examples had to do with gender and sexuality,
in particular how girls and boys identified with their elders and perceived
their futures as women and men. Though frontier daughters worked and
passed leisure time among women, much of their labor was alongside boys
and men in the fields, countryside, and boomtown streets. Their feelings of
accomplishment came largely from helping with men's work—those transforming tasks and celebrated changes linked to a grand national purpose.
Their play, too, was mostly out-of-doors, away from the houses that were
their mothers' domain. In short, they often identified less with women than
with fathers, brothers, and uncles. That left them freer to question the attitudes and roles that defined—and in many ways limited—their mothers'
lives, and it may have contributed to a strong sense of independence and
self-confidence among girls who grew up western. . . .

As these daughters approached womanhood, however, they were
expected to retreat from much of the life they had known and to perform

instead the traditional roles of wives and mothers. The result was an emotional confusion suggested in some of the most famous literary works by women influenced by the frontier as children. Mari Sandoz's *Old Jules,* Jean Stafford's *The Mountain Lion,* and Willa Cather's *My Ántonia*—a biography and memoir, a novella, and a novel—all celebrate accomplishments of the man's world. In all of them, young heroines find their greatest pleasure and sense of value while at work and at play with men and male friends. In contrast to the extraordinary contributions most mothers actually made, the ones in these books are either vague, insignificant characters or repressive figures resentfully portrayed. Even Cather's Ántonia Shimerda, ostensibly a fictional tribute to pioneer womanhood, grows up with an unappealing, almost shrewish mother. Ántonia "loved her father more than anyone else" when she was a girl and "stood in awe" of her older brother. She is most at home plowing and wandering through the meadows and along the creeks. "I like to be like a man," she tells the novel's narrator. Less famous reminiscences often suggest the same ambivalence of allegiance, even of sexual identity. Sometimes the titles alone make the point. Agnes Cleaveland called her memoir *No Life for a Lady.* Oello Martin chose "Father Came West," though it is obvious from the story that her mother was at least as responsible for their family's survival and achievements.

Boys also identified with the work and amusements of men. Yet they knew they would continue in these roles as adults, and this, ironically, allowed them to appreciate and sympathize more openly with their mothers. Frequently, in fact, they overstated the bleakness of pioneer women's lives. Hamlin Garland's angry memory of his mother's sacrifices is well known: "All her toilsome, monotonous days rushed through my mind with a roar like a file of gray birds in the night—how little—how tragically small her joys, and how black her sorrows, her toil, her tedium."

Frontier boys grew up to face their own contradictions, however. They naturally pictured a future of westering, developing new country, continuing a process through which their characters had been shaped. Their experiences prepared them for that life; public tributes to pioneering affirmed their inclinations. . . .

Yet many boys would live through the country's frontier stage to find themselves in a different West, a region of narrowing limits, where dwindling resources were pulled beyond their reach or kept firmly in the grasp of others. They saw a natural landscape that had seemed uniquely their own changed irrevocably into something else, transformed through a process in which they themselves had played a prominent part.

In a larger sense, all children faced this dilemma. Girls and boys grew up with the same presumptions—that their surroundings were full of grand potential, that there would always be more awaiting, and that they would be free to make of it what they could. Then, in the post-frontier West, they would confront the limits of the pioneer dream. Abuse of an abundant land led to ecological catastrophes; apparently boundless riches could be exhausted; government stewardship followed in the wake of a virtually unregulated pursuit of wealth. "The West was like a harlot who bore children," wrote a mother who reared two daughters on a Montana homestead, only to see them driven away by the dust bowl and the government's closing of land to new settlement: "We had brought them to the hard country. . . . They had grown up in the Badlands, knew what they could do there, but they were not allowed to."

The frustration of those daughters suggests the children's final lesson. Students today study the West both as frontier and as region. The first, at heart, is the story of a process, the interaction between invaders and the land invaded. The second is the story of a place—a part of the continent that, despite its diversity, has a few unifying elements, including natives who think of the West and westerners as a unique land and society. Historians are particularly curious about how the one experience became the other, how from conquest and settlement a distinctive part of the nation emerged with its own identity.

. . . The children's story, however, also has obvious implications for the study of the West as a region. As we try to understand how one era became the next, we should look to the lives of those who were shaped from their own beginnings by both the pioneering experience and the country's enduring nature.

The frontier is gone. It would be misleading, however, to suggest, as Avery Craven did nearly half a century ago, that the modern West shows the traces of the pioneer era only "as a landscape reveals the action of glaciers in ages long passed." No neat, precise line can ever be drawn between frontier and region, for the two eras have slid over one another, like sleeves of a spyglass, as pioneer youngsters have matured. Precisely because they were young, children were the persons most influenced by the frontier; as children, they had the most years ahead of them to live out the implications of that influence.

The contours of the recent West have been shaped by many forces. Among the most obvious have been a massive wave of new immigrants, especially since 1945, the reach of outside capital and technology, the continuing interaction among the region's various ethnic communities, and the weight of myth, the world's expectations of what the West ought to be. At least as important, however, have been those persons who matured as the new country was being settled. As adults, during the transitional decades of the early twentieth century, tens of thousands of these men and women helped determine the outlines of the modern West. As a new region emerged, they were most of its political and business leaders, educators and ministers, skilled workers and day laborers, housewives and merchants, criminals and drifters. They helped build new western institutions; more than any others, perhaps, they were responsible for regional attitudes and limitations.

Certainly the children can help us understand the most intriguing trait of the modern West—its deeply conflicted personality. Children grew up pulled between two sets of influences, their identification with the land about them and their parents' dogged efforts to instill values and traditions from another world. "I am a product of the American earth," Wallace Stegner would write of his boyhood on the plains just north of the Montana border, "and in nothing quite so much as in the contrast between what I knew through the pores and what I was officially taught." So westerners are fiercely loyal to their region and condescending toward outsiders who cannot understand and cope with the country; they are also excessively defensive about their lack of "culture"—defined, of course, in eastern terms. They are inordinately fond of art and fiction that romanticize frontier experiences unique to the West, yet they obsessively imitate alien architectural forms, building Cape Cod cottages and plantation-style banks against backdrops of buttes and craggy mountains. Growing up steeped in the virtues of free-wheeling enterprise and intimate with the natural setting, children matured into a region where individual opportunity was diminishing and the wilderness was under siege. Out of this dilemma has come the familiar harangue of modern westerners, who chafe at restraints and demand a free hand in development even as they wax nostalgic about the vanished beauty of an increasingly crowded land.

The frontier experience, we are told, gave Americans their greatest strengths and noblest virtues. Surely, however, this heritage has its troubled side. Westward expansion, Jackson Putnam has observed, "generated its own internal dynamic of ungratified aspiration." Driven by contradictory values, the character forged in the process was necessarily frustrated. Putnam's melancholy thought seems truer than ever when we consider the history of pioneer children and their passage to adulthood.

Just as surely, the frontier left a happier heritage. A child's life in the developing West encouraged traits especially useful in the contemporary world. Among these were a resilient strength, a self-reliance and sense of worth, and a tested understanding that hard times can be endured. Most children must have taken into their adult lives a faith in the family and its ability to adjust to trying circumstances. In the particulars of pioneer childhood were grounded qualities commonly associated with the modern West, among them an openness toward strangers, a confidence in dealing with fresh challenges, a kinship with what remains of the natural setting, and a pride—albeit an often grudging pride—in its contrariness.

Whatever the frontier's mark upon the children, their story, both the good and bad of it, is essential to understanding the region today. Only when we consider their history can we reconstruct what what one writer recently called "the unbroken past of the American West."

"How could any writer . . . know the details of our daily life?" asked Lee Whipple-Haslam seventy years after she began her time on the frontier. There is much to learn by trying to answer her question. Children were not passive observers of the making of western history. Just as the young always were far more in control of their own lives than their elders realized, so they shaped the course of western settlement in ways historians have ignored almost entirely. Their influence—and that of the pioneer experience—have not wholly disappeared. Long after the close of the frontier, its shaping force has survived, carried into our own day by those who grew up with the country.

Bordeaux v. Bordeaux: A Story of Divorce

PAULA PETRIK

One way American society confirmed definitions of womanhood has been to encode them in the legal canon. . . . Although most states adopted laws to safeguard women's rights in particular situations, women's prospects in divorce courts were problematic. Divorce generally was for women of means far into the nineteenth century.

The exception to these generalizations centered in the Rocky Mountain West. From 1850 to 1900, western states had the highest *per capita* divorce rate according to the Bureau of Labor Statistics. *Bordeaux v. Bordeaux,* a protracted turn-of-the-century Butte divorce case, illustrates how gender, class, and legal context influenced divorce cases involving middle-class women in Silver Bow County and, by extension, suggests how these variables operated in similar litigation in other jurisdictions.

John Bordeaux and Ella Bordeaux née Driggs were married in Butte, Montana, on June 2, 1886. . . . The deal struck, the couple jogged along until November 1889 when Ella returned to her parents' home because of her husband's harsh treatment. A few days later, John Bordeaux went down on bended knee to ask forgiveness, and the couple reconciled. This time all went well for a decade until John filed for divorce in Silver Bow County on January 26, 1899, claiming that his wife had deserted him on January 23, 1898. . . .

Unlike most defendants who did not bother to contest a divorce suit predicated on desertion, Ella responded on February 11, 1899, denying her husband's charges and filing a cross-complaint. Ella asserted that on January 23, 1898, John Bordeaux had ceased to live with her. Ella, moreover, reproached John with extreme cruelty, accusing him of "threatening conduct and language" and "abusive and intimidating behavior." The result of his behavior had caused Ella "great mental pain and anguish" and "disturbed her peace of mind." John Bordeaux had literally driven her from her home by his continual threats against her life with "loaded firearms."

Fearing for her life, Ella contended that she had been compelled against her will to leave her home for the safety of her parents' house in Salt Lake City. Immediately after her leave-taking, accordingly to Ella, her husband had dismantled the family dwelling and, since that time, had failed to provide a suitable residence for them. Because Ella had enjoyed a wide circle of friends and acquaintances among the "best people of Butte," her humiliation had been all the more acute, causing "lasting injury and destruction of her peace of mind and enjoyment of life." Ella's complaint detailed John

Paula Petrik, "Not a Love Story: Bordeaux v. Bordeaux," *Montana: The Magazine of Western History,* 41 (Spring 1991), 32–46. Excerpted by permission of the Montana Historical Society.

Bordeaux's property holdings: interests in the Mountain View, Prairie Flower, and St. Lawrence mines; ownership of several town lots; and proprietorship in additional but unknown mining camps. Valued at $100,000, these properties, Ella and her attorneys believed, provided a monthly income of $1,500, far in excess of the $90 to $120 monthly earnings of an average craftsman or miner. Ella claimed all the property was acquired jointly during their marriage. She petitioned the court for a restraining order to prevent her spouse from disposing of any property, for support of $500 each month while the suit was pending, and $5,000 in counsel fees. . . .

Ella's claim rested on . . . mental cruelty. Mental cruelty had been a feature of Montana law since *Albert v. Albert* (1885), in which the state supreme court had outlawed physical cruelty of any kind. Lower courts had elaborated on the court's ruling by extending the definition of cruelty to encompass mental cruelty—at least for divorcing middle-class couples. . . .

John Bordeaux denied all of his wife's charges. . . . While Bordeaux admitted that he owned the city property mentioned in Ella's cross action, he denied owning the more valuable mining property. His holdings he estimated at $33,000 and his monthly income at $517. He admitted that the property had been acquired since the couple's marriage but declared that Ella had never contributed "one cent."

On February 25, 1899, John Bordeaux upped the ante by filing an amended complaint, reiterating his earlier charge of desertion and adding adultery. Specifically, he alleged that his wife had committed adultery with an unknown man at a host of specified and unknown locations and times between August and November 1897. . . . Ella's attorneys promptly filed a demurrer, arguing that the amended complaint was vague, insufficient in its statements of facts, and ambiguous in that times and places for a majority of the charges were not specified. The judge agreed.

Bordeaux and his lawyers returned to court on March 3, 1899, to detail the times and places of Ella's alleged adulteries. These occasions included, among others, adultery with Lyman Sisley on September 21, 1897, in an unfinished house at 825 West Broadway, another liaison with Sisley at 825 or 827 West Park Street, another assignation on November 30, 1897, with Sisley at the Weyerhorst Block, and numerous illicit liaisons at the Bordeaux house. Again, Ella's attorneys demurred on the same grounds as before, but this time the court disagreed and overruled the defense demurrer.

Two months later Ella answered the amended complaint by denying *in toto* her husband's charges of adultery. She augmented her earlier complaint of mental cruelty with additional charges of physical cruelty, citing an incident in November 1889, others during the summer of 1894, and numerous other unspecified occasions. Finally, she added false accusations against her chastity. All of these things had contributed to her general humiliation and to the breakdown of her physical and mental health.

John Bordeaux challenged all of her statements and amplified his earlier claims, insisting he had not made false charges against his wife's chastity because she had been unchaste. Her health had in no way been injured. He claimed that Ella "was an extraordinary good sleeper," often keeping to her room and sleeping until 11 A.M. or very often until noon or 1 P.M. She was healthy enough "at any time to walk for hours with Lyman Sisley around the town of Butte." Not only had Ella not contributed toward the accumulation of the couple's estate, she had "never sought to save or economize or assist [Bordeaux] in any way whatever, but on the other hand [had] always been worthless and idle, and [had] spent thousands of dollars uselessly and unnecessarily."

When the flurry of legal maneuvering ended, John and Ella Bordeaux had accused one another of the worst that a husband and wife could do. From Ella's perspective her husband violated his marriage vows by forcing her from her home, accusing her of infidelity, and beating her. From John's viewpoint, Ella had violated her marital contract by her lewd and lascivious unfaithfulness and her failure to fulfill her wifely role because of laziness and profligacy. Both financially and socially much was at stake. The goal for John Bordeaux was to extricate himself from his marriage with the least possible economic liability; Ella's goal was the restoration of her good name and a goodly share of the couple's estate.

On August 15, 1901, roughly three years after filing of the initial complaint, court proceedings began in *Bordeaux v. Bordeaux* before Judge William Clancy. . . .

Because nineteenth-century divorce law involved assigning blame or fault, contested divorces were tried before a jury. . . . The first order of court business was the selection of a jury, and opposing counsels agreed upon twelve predominantly Catholic, working-class men. Next day, before a courtroom audience including many women, *Bordeaux v. Bordeaux* began. . . . John Bordeaux's lawyer called his first witness.

Robert Campbell summarized what he had seen at 825 West Broadway. He had watched the couple from the back door of the unfinished building.

> They were enjoying each other's company; he laid her down on the bench there, and pulled up her clothing; she had on a dark suit of underwear; it looked to me like a dark suit of combination underclothing; from where I was I could see that they were in the act of sexual intercourse.

He had seen Tom Bordeaux, John's brother jump from under the carpenter's bench and exclaim, "I have got you dead to rights," and immediately had seen Sisley run from the building heading across Broadway and then southwest. Ella Bordeaux got up, put on her hat, and set off east on Broadway toward home.

Under cross-examination, Campbell admitted that he had both a social and business relationship with John Bordeaux. He explained that he had been in the neighborhood of the Broadway house looking after business and had run into Tom Bordeaux, who asked him to go to the 825 address. He had known what the purpose was because Tom had intimated in a conversation the month before that Ella Bordeaux "was doing what was not right." . . . Under continued questioning, Campbell insisted the evening was balmy, very pleasant. He testified that he had waited a moment or two before following Tom and Ella Bordeaux east on Broadway. Mrs. Bordeaux had stepped along briskly. McHatton* asked Campbell, "did she [Ella] have her hat in her hand?" Campbell responded that Ella put a small-brimmed straw sailor hat on her head as she walked away.

Next McHatton asked about Ella Bordeaux's underwear, and Campbell acknowledged that it was a dark union suit. . . . Responding to McHatton's questions about the date, Campbell replied that he was sure of the date because he had made a note of the incident in his memorandum book. McHatton was incredulous that Campbell had noted an adultery with other entries pertaining to business. . . .

As credible as Campbell was, when he left the stand, McHatton had accomplished a good deal. He had established that Campbell's relationship with the Bordeaux brothers was more than casual, and he had elicited from Campbell numerous details that would set the standard for succeeding corroborating testimony. Finally, however slightly, McHatton had suggested the possibility of a conspiracy.

The second witness to take the stand was Charles L. Barnaman who testified that he had seen Ella Bordeaux and Lyman Sisley walking west on Granite Street sometime between 8:00 and 8:00 P.M. on September 21, 1897. . . . Barnaman lingered on the south side of Broadway and, a short time later, saw Lyman Sisley hurriedly leave an unfinished house and take off toward Alabama Street. Shortly afterward, Ella Bordeaux left the house and turned east on Broadway, fixing her hat as she went. Tom Bordeaux followed closely on her heels. Then Robert Campbell came around the side of the house and trailed after the Bordeauxs.

In cross-examination Barnaman admitted he had been to John Bordeaux's house and had been friends with Tom Bordeaux for some time. . . . Barnaman, too, admitted to writing about the evening's events in his memorandum book, which, unfortunately, had been misplaced. McHatton quizzed Barnaman about the book. Did he usually note occurrences of that kind? Sometimes, Barnaman admitted, he did.

The plaintiff's legal team was pleased with Barnaman's testimony, which corroborated Robert Campbell's version of the events. But McHatton was also gratified. He had enticed Barnaman into making some altogether outlandish admissions. Barnaman revealed himself to be a shady character, just the right sort to take part in a conspiracy.

On Friday afternoon, August 16, 1901, Tom Bordeaux took the witness stand. John Cotter* directed the cross-examination. He inquired into Tom Bordeaux's employment record in an effort to connect him with Barnaman and Campbell. . . .

Tom Bordeaux's rendition of what had occurred coincided with that of other witnesses. . . . Cotter ended his cross-examination by going over the condition of the building, and Bordeaux affirmed the details of the construction outlined by previous witnesses. . . .

---

*[Ella Bordeaux's attorney]

When court recessed for the weekend on Friday afternoon, Ella Bordeaux's case appeared bleak. Yet, the defense had scored against her husband's legal team by assembling evidence for business and social relationships connecting the plaintiff's principle witnesses. Charles Barnaman was a distinctly suspicious character, and Tom Bordeaux, as a constable and collection agent, had plenty of opportunity to meet Butte's petty underworld citizens, and he seemed entirely too involved in his brother's personal life. . . .

On Monday morning John Cotter . . . asked when Tom Bordeaux had told his brother about the incident at 825 West Broadway. This led to a discussion of the date of the adultery and the amazing disclosure by Bordeaux that the event actually had occurred on December 23 and not some three months earlier.

Startled, Cotter asked if Tom Bordeaux had testified the previous Friday that the adultery had occurred on September 21, 1897? Tom Bordeaux replied, "I said it was cold weather." How, continued Cotter, could he have made such an error? Had he consulted with the plaintiff's attorneys? . . . When, Cotter inquired, had Bordeaux discovered his error? Tom Bordeaux explained that he had examined his memorandum book the previous evening and realized his mistake. . . . Cotter asked about the adultery entry and learned that the book was empty except for the notation about Ella.

Cotter queried Bordeaux: Did he now wish to change his entire testimony to reflect the change in dates? Bordeaux answered affirmatively. McHatton then asked to know more about the notebook, its timely appearance, and its revelatory information. Why, McHatton wondered aloud, had Tom Bordeaux chosen that evening to refresh his memory? Had someone told him something very important about 825 West Broadway? Tom Bordeaux responded, "They might have suggested something to me as to the condition of that building over there at that date—September 21." Under further questioning, Bordeaux admitted that his brother had suggested he look into the house business. Cotter asked if Tom Bordeaux had tailored his evidence to the complaint or if he had testified to what he had actually seen. . . .

Tom Bordeaux's testimony revealed several important points. First, although Cotter intended to show that Bordeaux could have seen only two pairs of feet from under the bench or, later, a man and a woman in a room, the jurymen likely agreed with Bordeaux that what he had or had not seen in the way of criminal activity was immaterial; Ella Bordeaux had been in the wrong place at the wrong time.

Second, McHatton's cross-examination allowed the jurymen to hear *ad infinitum* the damaging details of the event at 825 West Broadway and permitted them ample time to reflect on them. McHatton's cross-examination technique was purposeful, however. The witnesses had thoroughly elaborated, detailed, and corroborated each other on all points. Much of their credibility rested on their agreement over the state of the house. But what if the house did not exist? Undoubtedly, McHatton planned to produce the building permit, like a rabbit out of a hat, to demonstrate that no such house, finished or unfinished, existed at the Broadway location in September 1897. Without the house, there could be no crime of adultery, and, in turn, without the adultery, John Bordeaux's case would collapse. The taint of conspiracy would have affected the other allegations of adultery, too, rendering them suspect. Between the adjournment of court on Friday, however, and its opening on Monday, someone—a courtroom spectator, one of the band of Barnaman-like Butte ferrets, an observant builder or contractor, a county official involved with the building trades—had indicated to John Bordeaux that the building dates were awry.

Third, Judge Clancy's rulings on the defense's various legal maneuvers tended to favor the plaintiff. His willingness to accept Tom Bordeaux's change in testimony was most obvious. Finally, the Monday testimony represented a setback for McHatton and Cotter. . . .

Following Tom Bordeaux, W. A. Ellsworth took the stand and testified that sometime around December 20, 1897, he too, had seen Ella Bordeaux and Lyman Sisley in the act of sexual intercourse. Upon completing his explicit description, Ellsworth added: "From where I was, I think I could have reached them with my hands."

McHatton and Cotter returned to their original plan of delineating the relationship between the witness and the plaintiff. Ellsworth admitted that he had been a constable in Meaderville in 1897 and had seen Tom Bordeaux frequently. He also had sold script to John Bordeaux. . . . On several points Ellsworth contradicted his own testimony and that of previous witnesses. . . .

Of all the plaintiff's witnesses, Ellsworth proved the least credible. His testimony supported Tom Bordeaux's revised date, however, and added a particularly graphic description of the couple's illicit liaison. . . . At this point in the trial the defendant's lawyers suspected that the conspiracy against Ella Bordeaux, no matter how jerrybuilt, would succeed. Accordingly, McHatton and Cotter began laying the foundation for an appeal to the state supreme court, and their exceptions increased apace. . . .

Finally, John Bordeaux took the stand and testified that he had heard about the West Broadway incident during the latter part of December. . . . Had he heard anything about his wife's conduct before December 1897? John Bordeaux replied:

> I just don't say when because I can't say. At first when I was informed of these various acts, I didn't believe; along towards the last they came so often until I had to; that was somewheres about the first of the year 1898. Since that time I have not lived or cohabited with her as my wife or otherwise.

McHatton opened his cross-examination asking if John Bordeaux had read, verified, and filed the complaint, attesting that his wife had committed adultery in September 1897? John Bordeaux excused his ignorance, "Oh, once in a while . . . say persons will bring in a paper and say it is so and so, and say you are to sign it, and you will not be particular in reading over everything, do you?" Was he willing to say he did not know what was in the complaint when he signed it, asked McHatton. Bordeaux said he knew the complaint's contents. Was not the information, McHatton continued, that John Bordeaux had given his attorneys stated in the complaint? Could he explain to the jury how he had sworn to certain dates in August and September of 1897 as part of the initial complaint? Could John Bordeaux account for this discrepancy? John Bordeaux supposed it was an error. McHatton proved relentless. How could this be when Bordeaux had his books for reference? "A man often has books and still makes an error, too," responded Bordeaux.

McHatton switched to the notebooks and reminded Bordeaux that he had examined his memoranda in preparation for conferences with his attorneys. Did he provide them with any dates other than those appearing in the complaint? McHatton then redirected his questions to discover if John Bordeaux had visited the owner of the house at 825 West Broadway over the weekend to determine the construction date and had changed the date accordingly. . . . At this juncture, Judge Clancy invited the plaintiff's lawyers to change the complaint to conform to the new date. The complaint was altered, and McHatton objected. . . .

Although defense lawyers introduced a cavalcade of witnesses to refute evidence for the adulteries and substantiate the conspiracy theory, the three most important witnesses were Ella Bordeaux; her uncle, William Farlin; and her father, A. E. Driggs. . . .

Unfortunately, both Farlin and Driggs were relatives; no independent witnesses were on hand to substantiate Driggs's or Farlin's version of the events.

Despite Farlin's relationship with the defendant, his testimony was significant for another reason. He furnished evidence that John Bordeaux had spent the nights immediately before his wife's departure in her company in a room with one bed. At issue here was the legal concept of condonation, defined by Montana civil law as the "conditional forgiveness of matrimonial offense constituting a cause of divorce." In essence once a husband or wife knowingly occupied the same bed with an unfaithful partner, the courts inferred sexual relationship and, by extension, condoning and forgiveness as well as restoration to marital rights. Surprisingly, plaintiff's counsel did little to contradict the evidence of condonation. Perhaps overly confident, they disregarded the small detail of a room with a single bed.

On Friday, August 23, 1901, Ella Bordeaux took the stand. . . . According to Ella, in the first three years of their marriage, John had beaten her with a stick kept in the bathroom for that purpose, choked her, and abused her verbally. At the end of November 1889, she had sent for her father to bring her home. John Bordeaux had come to her parents' home to plead on his knees for her return. The couple lived peaceably for several years after their reconciliation, but in 1894, John Bordeaux had beaten her so severely that she had been lame for three days. She recalled: "I didn't leave him at that time . . . because I didn't like it to be known to the public, and . . . I was afraid of him because he had threatened me so many times that he would kill me if I left him." . . .

Ella denied categorically any improper liaisons with Sisley, characterizing their relationship as simply social, having occurred in public in the presence of other ladies and gentlemen. Ella added that she had slept in the same room as her husband until the time she left.

B. S. Thresher* began Ella's cross-examination by returning to the disposition of the couple's furniture and worked his way toward questioning Ella about her lifestyle as John Bordeaux's wife. Ella acknowledged that the Bordeaux home was furnished nicely and that she received a generous allowance. When Thresher moved on to quizzing Ella about her housework, McHatton objected. . . . Thresher rejoined that Ella's cross-complaint raised the issue of cruelty, and the character of her husband's treatment of her was clearly important. McHatton was dumbfounded by Thresher's logic.

> Why may it please the court, many people have been cruelly murdered in the most elegantly furnished houses in the world. Does that in any wise extenuate or excuse or mollify or is it any defense to the act of murder committed? . . . No man with a retinue of servants is entitled or will be permitted to commit acts of cruelty against his wife.

Ella's testimony revealed steady employment of a servant and described the couple's domestic routine. The servant prepared breakfast and, when the couple ate together on those few occasions Ella joined her husband, they ate between 9:00 and 11:00 A.M. Ella said her husband gave her jewelry at Christmas and on her birthday. As to its value she was unsure; her only knowledge came from Bordeaux, who estimated the price of the jewelry at about $1,350. When Thresher asked Ella whether she needed such things, she responded, *"As to whether these were things that I needed, I will say that I think I did."* She testified further that she arose frequently after 9:00 A.M., rarely joined her husband for lunch, regularly went out in the afternoon, sometimes ate dinner with Bordeaux, and routinely visited with her mother in the evening.

From McHatton's perspective Ella Bordeaux's testimony was a disaster. Her task was to portray herself as a true woman replete with all the qualities associated with woman's role in the nineteenth century—selflessness, submissiveness, self-sacrifice, and domestic dedication. She had to convince the jury, first, that she was not the kind of woman who would enter into an illicit sexual relationship and, second, that her husband had treated her with such cruelty that she had to leave her home. During McHatton's questioning, Ella did very well. Her testimony reflected her efforts to keep her marriage together and to maintain the privacy of the family. Her descriptions of the confrontations between John and herself were dramatic and detailed.

Thresher's cross-examination undermined Ella's earlier self-portrait, and played on class differences between Ella and the jury. She was portrayed as spoiled, lazy, treacherous, indifferent, and a poor domestic man-

---

*[John Bordeaux's attorney]

ager. The jurymen could easily compare Ella's domestic efforts and her rewards with those of their own wives. To the working-class jurymen, Ella was a "bad wife."

In rebuttal John Bordeaux emphasized Ella's domestic failures, her indifference to him, her leisurely lifestyle, and her generally willful, peevish disposition. In addition, his attorneys carefully recorded that the Bordeauxs had no children—yet another indication of Ella's marital shortcomings. In his cross-examination, McHatton adroitly suggested to the jury that Bordeaux had accepted his wife's domestic failures without argument, but Bordeaux was equally successful in countering McHatton by saying that he was willing to indulge Ella up to a point. When it came to "running around with other men, he drew the line."

On August 26, 1901, nine of the twelve jurymen decided against Ella Bordeaux, finding her guilty of adultery with Lyman Sisley on several occasions. John Bordeaux had his divorce.

McHatton and Cotter petitioned for a new trial immediately on the basis of affidavits of several people involved in the case. The affidavits provided convincing evidence of a conspiracy among John Bordeaux's people and suggested jury tampering, but Judge Clancy denied the motion for a new trial. McHatton and Cotter appealed to the state supreme court on this and other issues.

The Montana Supreme Court first heard appeals involving Ella Bordeaux's petition for temporary alimony, suit money, and attorney's fees during the March 1902 term and decided the legal issues on June 2 and 5, 1902. The court dismissed Ella Bordeaux's appeal on the grounds that state law did not grant the supreme court the power to award monies prayed for; such power resided in the original Silver Bow County jurisdiction.

In February 1904, the high court heard arguments regarding the legal fees and substance of the case. Commissioner John Clayberg prepared an opinion for the court that addressed the three principal errors McHatton and Cotter urged on the court, the most important of which was condonation. Clayberg rightly pointed out that John Bordeaux had known about his wife's infidelity almost immediately after December 23, 1897, yet, he continued to live with her until January 1898. Under the circumstances and the weight of judicial precedent, John Bordeaux was not entitled to a divorce. Clayberg continued:

> We cannot refrain from saying that the record discloses in many instances a most reckless disregard for the truth on the part of some of plaintiff's witnesses, and also the character to some of plaintiff's witnesses which is not enviable to say the least.

The supreme court granted rehearing and remanded the case for a new trial in Silver Bow County.

In 1905 the supreme court entertained arguments—yet again—involving the Bordeaux divorce to contemplate the same three questions Commissioner Clayber had addressed earlier. It was on the third question—condonation—that the court's finding was most critical. It found that Judge

Clancy's court had erred in its failure to deny John Bordeaux a divorce because Bordeaux had condoned his wife's infidelity by sleeping with her in the same bed.

The high court recognized condonation as a delicate issue. State supreme courts were normally not in the business of reevaluating evidence. Their role was to safeguard procedure. Condonation was a special defense, and the defendant had to plead condonation initially, which Ella Bordeaux had not done. The justices conceded this but said the evidence in the testimony compelled them to consider condonation anyway. They based their rationale on a consideration of public interest, precedent, and statute.

Of the three, the justices' recourse to statute proved the most decisive and difficult. Although John Bordeaux's lawyers had argued that the evidence for condonation was conflicting and that the court had no business arriving at its own conclusions regarding the evidence, the justices looked to statute to support their right to do precisely that. In 1903 the Montana legislature had vested in the supreme court the power to examine questions of law *and fact* in equity cases. Such power gave the court the right to review the evidence and derive its own conclusions in light of a preponderance of evidence. With due warning to those who might construe the justices' pronouncement as a thoroughgoing precedent, the court recapitulated the evidence and found overwhelming evidence of condonation—that is, that John Bordeaux had condoned his wife's behavior.

In an interesting aside, the court added:

> . . . The evidence in the case is not of a satisfactory character, and . . . there are many features of the evidence introduced by the plaintiff which justify a very strong suspicion, to say the least, that the charges of adultery are the result of a conspiracy on the part of the plaintiff and some of his witnesses to establish a false charge against the defendant.

Justice Theodore Brantly reversed the judgment of the lower court and remanded the case to Silver Bow County, directing the court to dismiss the action.

Despite the supreme court's ruling and the strong language accompanying its opinion, John Bordeaux reinstituted his divorce suit in March 1907, claiming he had sought a reconciliation with Ella on March 15, 1906, and had been (perhaps understandably) spurned. Bordeaux sued on grounds of desertion, but the petition languished. The Bordeauxs remained married, and Ella kept alive her financial claims on her husband. In 1909, John Bordeaux revived his suit; Ella responded with the usual denials and complement of demands for legal fees. In May 1910 another jury heard the Bordeaux case but was discharged when it failed to agree on a verdict; the court then ruled that neither party was entitled to a divorce and dismissed the case. As a result, the Bordeauxs returned to the supreme court. *Bordeaux v. Bordeaux* finally ended in 1911 when the high court rejected Ella's financial claims one last time and directed the Silver Bow County Court to find in John Bordeaux's favor on the basis of his wife's desertion.

For the Bordeauxs, final disposition meant a mix of success and failure.

John Bordeaux escaped his marriage without having to pay alimony, but in the process had paid large sums to his successive groups of lawyers. Ella Bordeaux was vindicated, but she had not punished her husband as she had envisioned. They had spent the best years of their lives fighting with one another.

Any reasonable jury member would be hard put to find in favor of John Bordeaux on the basis of evidence presented in the case. As the supreme court underscored in two opinions, the plaintiff's case smacked of conspiracy. The alteration of the date of the Bordeaux/Sisley liaison alone suggested that the plaintiff and his cronies had concocted the incident on West Broadway. Other salient details such as Ella's straw hat and her dark underwear indicated that Bordeaux's confederates had made foolish errors in fabricating their story. No nineteenth-century, middle-class woman would have worn a straw boater in September, much less December, nor would she have sported dark underclothes. To understand why the case ended as it did is to conclude that Ella was innocent of adultery but guilty of being a bad wife.

John Bordeaux's attorneys introduced damaging evidence of Ella's total dereliction as a wife. Such a perception made it easier for the jury to believe in the possibility of Ella's moral failure. While the jury might perceive that the adultery incident at 825 West Broadway was phony, they could easily discount particular inconsistencies and contradictions on the supposition that, given Ella's general wifely conduct, she could be capable of adultery. . . . In combination with reports of Ella's domestic failure, tales of her adulteries tended to cast Ella as a wife capable of the worst marital errors. It was immaterial that the adultery at 825 West Broadway had not happened exactly as witnesses testified or even that it occurred at all, because Ella had certainly trespassed in thought, if not fact.

Social class further complicated Ella's position and helped the jury rationalize its findings. Clearly, two views of womanhood—one explicit, the other tacit—influenced courtroom proceedings. Both groups ostensibly espoused companionate marriage, a relationship characterized by mutual affection, respect, consideration, and responsibilities. They differed, however, on the definition of mutual responsibilities and appropriate response to default on these responsibilities.

For both the upper and working classes, men were the breadwinners and women were the household captains. But the role of the upper-class wife was less household labor and more household management; she was less a partner in a joint enterprise and more an affectionate companion. With a servant carrying out much of the domestic routine, Ella, and women like her, functioned in part as symbols of their husbands' status and success. When Ella responded to Stapleton's question regarding her entitlement to her husband's largesse by avowing her worthiness, she merely affirmed a class expectation. From her perspective, her rank in Butte society demanded that she maintain her status among her peers, and the requisite jewelry was only what a woman in her position deserved. To members of a working-class jury, however, Ella's response to this and questions dealing with the time she spent with her husband indicated her gross indifference to even a minimal role as a marital companion to her husband. Indeed, Ella's estimate of her "just deserts" painted her as an insolent, ungrateful wife.

Class considerations also tended to undermine Ella's claim that John Bordeaux had treated her with extreme cruelty. On the other hand, upper- and middle-class expectations decreed that men did not strike or otherwise abuse their wives. No provocation or reason could justify such behavior and, as McHatton said, no material circumstances, no matter how opulent, rationalized abuse. . . . John Bordeaux's attorneys, on the other hand, developed an idea they believed, rightly or wrongly, would appeal to the working-class jurymen. Largely by implication, Bordeaux's attorneys promoted a view that a husband need only provide material comforts. Comforts, however, demanded reciprocal wifely behavior. A wife's failure to comply with the "contract" could provoke her "correction."

John Bordeaux had upheld his part of the marital bargain by providing a substantial house, elegant household furnishings, clothes, generous amounts of pin money, a servant, and presents for his wife. From the perspective of the working-class jury, Ella had defaulted entirely on her part of the marital deal, and her conduct compared unfavorably with the jurymen's personal experience. Their wives labored long and hard in their homes, carrying out domestic tasks and raising children. Acknowledging their wives' contributions to familial well-being with presents of expensive jewelry was beyond the financial ability of most of them. Yet Ella Bordeaux, who did nothing, reaped rewards far beyond her merit and, apparently, did not appreciate them. Any man in John Bordeaux's situation, his attorneys hinted, would be frustrated—perhaps to the point of physical violence. . . .

Despite the mixed quality of Ella Bordeaux's *legal* victory, the supreme court's decision represented a *personal* triumph for her. By fighting John Bordeaux to a standstill she had, in a sense, won. *Bordeaux v. Bordeaux* represented a gloss on women's role in the operation of divorce law. Many women took the initiative and successfully obtained divorces from their husbands; many women, albeit fewer, found themselves in precisely Ella's position. Like other women who fought back, Ella adamantly refused to let her husband define their marriage even in its dissolution. She challenged directly her husband's estimate of her womanhood and sought to make him pay for his error. Ella was, in short, an "uppity" woman. While Montana women fared well generally when they approached the court for a divorce, an "uppity" woman who wanted more than a simple divorce could plan on obstacles, setbacks, and a long campaign. Yet women like Ella Bordeaux were responsible for pushing the Montana Supreme Court to interpret divorce law in ways ultimately beneficial to all women.

Y *FURTHER READING*

Patricia Albers and Beatrice Medicine, *The Hidden Half: Studies of Plains Indian Women* (1983)

Susan Armitage and Elizabeth Jameson, eds., *The Women's West* (1987)

John E. Baur, *Growing Up with California: A History of California's Children* (1978)

Rachel Calof, *Rachel Calof's Story: Jewish Homesteader on the Northern Plains* (1995)

Kathleen Neils Conzen, "A Saga of Families," in *The Oxford History of the American West,* eds. Clyde A. Milner II, Carol A. O'Connor, and Martha A. Sandweiss (1994)

Sarah Deutsch, *No Separate Refuge: Culture, Class, and Gender on an Anglo-Hispanic Frontier in the American Southwest, 1880–1940* (1987)

Jessie L. Embry, *Mormon Polygamous Families* (1987)

Carol Fairbanks, "Lives of Girls and Women on the Canadian and American Prairies," *International Journal of Women's Studies* (Sept./Oct. 1979): 452–72

John Mack Faragher, *Sugar Creek: Life on the Illinois Prairie* (1986)

James N. Gregory, *American Exodus: The Dust Bowl Migration and Okie Culture in California* (1989)

Robert L. Griswold, *Family and Divorce in California, 1850–1890* (1983)

Robert V. Hine, *Community on the American Frontier: Separate but Not Alone* (1980)

Larry M. Logue, *A Sermon in the Desert: Belief and Behavior in Early St. George, Utah* (1988)

Cathy Luchetti and Carol Olwell, *Women of the West* (1982)

Valarie J. Matsumoto, *Farming the Home Place: A Japanese American Community in California, 1919–1982* (1993)

Robert B. Moynihan, "Children and Young People on the Overland Trail," *Western Historical Quarterly,* 6 (1975), 279–92

Sandra L. Myres, *Westering Women and the Frontier Experience* (1982)

Nell Irvin Painter, *Exodusters: Black Migration to Kansas After Reconstruction* (1986)

Linda Peavy and Ursula Smith, *Women in Waiting in the Westward Movement: Life on the Home Frontier* (1994)

Paula Petrik, *No Step Backward: Women and Family on the Rocky Mountain Mining Frontier, Helena, Montana, 1865–1900* (1987)

Glenda Riley, *Building and Breaking Families in the American West* (1996)

——, *Women and Indians on the Frontier* (1984)

Lillian Schlissel, Bryd Gibbens, and Elizabeth Hampsten, *Far from Here: Families of the Westward Journey* (1989)

Lillian Schlissel, Vicki L. Ruiz, and Janice Monk, eds., *Western Women: Their Land, Their Lives* (1988)

Nancy Shoemaker, "Native American Families," in Joseph M. Hawes and Elizabeth I. Nybakken, eds., *American Families: A Research Guide and Historical Handbook* (1991)

Kathleen Underwood, *Town Building on the Colorado Frontier* (1987)

CHAPTER
8

Contested Reforms

Y

The nineteenth-century West served as a laboratory for political and social reform. Within its vastness, the appeal to new beginnings made the West an attractive place to adjust and improve on long-standing institutions. Certainly the Mormons, who arrived in the Great Basin in the 1840s, led the way with their experiment in polygamous marriage. They had no sooner made their changes to traditional wedlock and family arrangements, than others sought to outlaw the Mormon endeavor, calling for reformation of the polygamists. The clash between the two lifestyles resulted in years of acrimony on both sides. This episode showed that what is reform and progress for one constituency may be oppression and inequity for another.

In the West, other reforms produced similar contradictions. For example, the advancement of women's rights and the extension of suffrage to females predated these developments in eastern states. But to gain the necessary legislative support from male office holders, Anglo women in the West sometimes made choices based on racism and nativism.

In its more positive aspects, the West encouraged women's education and activism. From the United Negro Women's Club of Montana to the Kansas Equal Suffrage Association, social and political participation in the West took a decidedly female turn. Church groups and clubs formed the nucleus around which women planned their campaigns for urban improvements, charity fund raisers, and cultural activities.

Women of many interests joined western men in the expanding call for widespread reforms, especially to relieve the struggling farmers of the Great Plains. The great agrarian reformers, who called for the establishment of an income tax among their appeals, hailed from the Kansas and Nebraska plains. Less well-known were the men and women who labored for penitentiary reform in the West. By 1900, civic leaders in Colorado, Kansas, and Oklahoma lobbied for a reorganization of male prison life and the creation of separate reformatories for women prisoners. In these various reform endeavors, women steadily moved from the private to the public sphere, where they assumed a professional status among the male educators and public servants of the West.

Americans often point with pride to these reform impulses and their western successes. Certainly, the West stands as a national symbol for a fair chance and judgment by accomplishment rather than by social or political status. Reform designed to enhance the quality of life remains one of the hallmarks of the western epic. Yet the realities of racial and cultural bias present several questions. What did opportunity mean in the West? To whom was it accessible? And how did the mechanics of reform influence diverse groups?

Y *D O C U M E N T S*

The first three documents consider the question of polygamy, or more correctly polygyny—the taking by men of multiple wives. Sir Richard Burton, an international explorer who visited Salt Lake City, offers this 1860 assessment of polygamy. Burton writes almost in the tone of an observing anthropologist, which given his era produces a somewhat patronizing air. His comments are countered about twenty-five years later by Helen Mar Whitney, a member of the Church of Jesus Christ of Latter-day Saints. Her spirited defense of plural wives in no way sounds like the compliant mutterings of an oppressed woman. Further, her views on womanhood do not seem any different from those held by many non-Mormon females, raising the question of the real meaning of religious divisions among groups of women. The third Mormon document is a version of a folk song, collected in 1932. It points to the way that people use humor to criticize the cultural practices of others.

The next document includes excerpts from three witnesses testifying in California in 1876 on the matter of the desirability of Chinese immigration. Those testifying, Rev. Otis Gibson, Rev. A. W. Loomis, and Officer Alfred Clark, claim to have expert knowledge about the treatment of women inside the Chinese community. Highly sensationalized reports of Chinese prostitution and bondage prompted the movement to legislate against Asian immigration. Describing abuses toward women gave emotional ballast to the arguments of American labor leaders who opposed Chinese immigration on the grounds of job competition. Some voices were raised against this overwhelming portrayal of the Chinese as a criminal population bent on undercutting the American labor market by working for cheap wages. Professor Augustus Layres countered the general theme of the testimony, commenting on the importance of language and school segregation as divisive elements for Chinese immigrants. The painful impact of America's immigrant policy is explored in the poetry of Huang Zunxian, a Chinese consul-general stationed at San Francisco from 1882 to 1885. Huang Zunxian gives voice to the human aspects of the Chinese exclusion movement.

The last two documents consider the women's suffrage movement in Idaho. In the first, a letter from Carrie Chapman Catt to Emma Smith DeVoe, the national leader uses all the skills she learned as a classroom teacher—encouragement, humor, sympathy, inspiration, admiration—to infuse the Idaho workers with the spirit to continue their struggle for suffrage. The second document, a newspaper account of the victory of the Idaho campaign, shows the sophisticated and complex strategies western women used to advance the cause of women's rights.

Sir Richard Burton Examines Mormon Polygamy, 1860

The literalism with which the Mormons have interpreted Scripture has led them directly to polygamy. The texts promising to Abraham a progeny numerous as the stars above or the sands below, and that "in his seed (a polygamist) all the families of the earth shall be blessed," induce them, his descendants, to seek a similar blessing. The theory announcing that "the man is not without the woman, nor the woman without the man," is by them interpreted into an absolute command that both sexes should marry, and that a woman cannot enter the heavenly kingdom without a husband to introduce her. A virgin's end is annihilation or absorption, *nox est perpetua una dormienda;* and as baptism for the dead—an old rite, revived and founded upon the writings of St. Paul quoted in the last chapter,—has been made a part of practice, vicarious marriage for the departed also enters into the Mormon scheme. . . . The Mormons . . . see in the New Testament no order against plurality; and in the Old dispensation they find the practice sanctioned in a family, ever the friends of God, and out of which the Redeemer sprang. Finally, they find throughout the nations of the earth, three polygamists in theory to one monogame.

The "chaste and plural marriage" being once legalised, finds a multitude of supporters. The anti-Mormons declare that it is at once fornication and adultery—a sin which absorbs all others. The Mormons point triumphantly to the austere morals of their community, their superior freedom from maladive influences, and the absence of that uncleanness and licentiousness which distinguish the cities of the civilised world. They boast that if it be an evil they have at least chosen the lesser evil, that they practise openly as a virtue what others do secretly as a sin. . . . Like its sister institution Slavery, the birth and growth of a similar age, Polygamy acquires *vim* by abuse and detraction; the more turpitude is heaped upon it, the brighter and more glorious it appears to its votaries.

There are rules and regulations of Mormonism—I cannot say whether they date before or after the heavenly command to pluralise—which disprove the popular statement that such marriages are made to gratify licentiousness, and which render polygamy a positive necessity. All sensuality in the married state is strictly forbidden beyond the requisite for ensuring progeny,—the practice, in fact, of Adam and Abraham. During the gestation and nursing of children, the strictest continence on the part of the mother is required—rather for a hygienic than for a religious reason. The same custom is practised in part by the Jews, and in whole by some of the noblest tribes of savages; the splendid physical development of the Kaffir race in South Africa is attributed by some authors to a rule of continence like that of the Mormons, and to a lactation prolonged for two years. . . .

Besides religious and physiological, there are social motives for the plurality. As in the days of Abraham, the lands about New Jordan are broad

Richard F. Burton, *The City of the Saints and Across the Rocky Mountains to California* (London: Longman, Green, Longman, and Roberts, 1862), 519–520, 522–523, 523–524, 525.

and the people few. . . . To the unprejudiced traveller it appears that polygamy is the rule where population is required . . .

Helen Mar Whitney Defends Plural Marriage, 1884

Women, I willingly admit, are the weaker sex, and that men should lead, but how many of them are really capable of leading or governing? How many of them have caused the wife of his bosom to hide her face in very shame—the woman whom he had promised to love and to cherish till death did them part, but was too utterly selfish to make any sacrifice to insure her comfort or happiness, or that of his offspring. Such will indulge their appetites, and every pernicious and unhallowed lust must be gratified at the risk of her poor heart's breaking. Though this may be a slow process, it is murder nevertheless, and their offspring are receiving the legacy—handed down by a profligate father with the certainty of transmitting the same to the coming generations, who have been sinned against in having to take up with feeble and diseased frames, and no constitutions to begin life with. Thus human life is being shortened. Various and complicated diseases are continually multiplying, which baffle the understanding and skill of the most learned physicians. These diseases and defects are too often laid at the mother's door. There are laws laid down which should not be violated, and the greatest crimes have become so common that the world thinks little or nothing of them. Thousands of delicate women are united to men who show them not the least consideration—she being his "property" he can take license and she thereby becomes the most wretched of slaves. But through this patriarchal order (deride it as they may) is to come the emancipation of womankind, which has been decreed, as well as the restoration of all the human family who have not sinned against all hope of their redemption. That it is a trial, no sensitive woman nor sensible man will deny, but what is the whole of life if not a trial, and what righteous movement or reform was ever yet inaugurated, without human suffering to some degree?

But those who think that men have no trials in the plural order of marriage, are greatly deceived. The wives have far greater liberty than the husband, and they have the power to make him happy or very unhappy. For this cause, among others, there are not many men who are willing to take upon themselves these extra burdens and responsibilities, even for the sake of a higher glory hereafter. It certainly takes considerable religion and faith to stimulate a man who loves a quiet, easy-going life, to take up this cross, even with the hope of a future crown. . . .

There are few to be found in the world whose piety, purity of life and unselfish acts can be compared with the greater portion of these men and women of the covenant, who through faith and righteousness have gained power with God to go forth conquering and to conquer. They have more joy and pride in being descendants of the royal family of Abraham, who with

Helen Mar Whitney, *Why We Practice Plural Marriage* (Salt Lake City: *Juvenile Instructor* Office, 1884), 54–55, 62–63, 65–66.

his wives and children were so highly honored of God, than in all that earth and mortals could bestow. Could more of the eventful histories of our women be published they would furnish volumes of interesting reading—equal, I think, to any novels, with just this difference, they would be truths instead of fiction. They would show what women are capable of doing and that we have some leading spirits who have few, if any, equals. At all events they are bound to make a mark in the world, many thanks to their traducers for helping to bring them into notice. . . .

I have traveled considerably in Utah during the past two years and have had many opportunities of learning the minds of "Mormon" women upon the plural wife system. I know that there are scores who will endorse what I have expressed. I also testify that the ones who live up to the golden rule in this principle find blessings in it, even in this life. Instead of being man-worshipers, remaining in the same old grooves in which the human family have been at a stand still, or tending downward through many generations, we are rising above our earthly idols, and find that we have easier access to the throne of grace. Our Father says He will not accept of a divided heart. There can be no evil in a thing that inspires prayer, drives selfishness from the heart and lengthens the cords of human feelings, leading one to do greater deeds of kindness outside of his or her own little circle. Those who are so narrow minded as to think of no one's comfort and pleasure but their own, are not capable of enjoying any great amount of eternal glory. We can never enjoy anything to its fullest extent until we have first tasted of its opposite. But if a wife and mother does her part, is true to her husband and teaches her children to walk in the true path, holding out faithful to the end, all she suffers will but add greater laurels to her crown in the world to come. And the future happiness of such, could they obtain even the slightest glimpse of it, would repay them, and they would be willing, even anxious to endure all that was possible to make them deserving of that pure and unalloyed bliss of which I solemnly testify that I have had a foretaste.

I have not written with "the pen of the fanatic," but with the heart "of a woman," who is in earnest, and does not "prefer the glory of man above the glory of God."

"Brigham, Brigham Young," An Anti-Mormon Folk Song, Collected in 1932

Old Brigham Young was a Mormon bold,
    And a leader of the roaring rams,
And a shepherd of a heap of pretty little sheep,
    And a nice fold of pretty little lambs.
And he lived with five and forty wives
    In the city of Great Salt Lake

Mormon Songs: From the Rocky Mountains. A Compilation of Mormon Folksong (Austin: University of Texas Press, 1968), 176–178. Also to be found in Fife Folklore Archives, Utah State University.

Where they woo and coo as pretty doves do
  And cackle like ducks to a drake.

Chorus:
Brigham, Brigham Young;
  'Tis a miracle he survives,
With his roaring rams, his pretty little lambs,
  And five and forty wives.

Number forty-five was about sixteen,
  Number one was sixty-three,
And among such a riot how he ever keeps them quiet
  Is a right-down mystery to me.
For they clatter and they claw, and they jaw, jaw, jaw,
  Each one has a different desire;
It would aid the renown of the best shop in town
  To supply them with half what they require.

Old Brigham Young was a stout man once
  But now he is thin and old,
And I love to state, there's no hair on his pate
  Which once wore a covering of gold.
For his youngest wives won't have white wool
  And his old ones won't take red,
So in tearing it out they have taken turn about
  Till they've pulled all the wool from his head.

Now his boys sing songs all day,
  And his girls they all sing psalms;
And among such a crowd he has it pretty loud
  For they're as musical as Chinese Gongs.
And when they advance for a Mormon dance,
  He is filled with a greatest surprise,
For they're sure to end the night with a tabernacle fight
  And scratch out one another's eyes.

There never was a home like Brigham Young's,
  So curious and so queer,
For if his joys are double he has a terrible lot of trouble,
  For it gains on him year by year.
He sets in his state and bears his fate
  In a satisfied sort of way;
He has one wife to bury and one wife to marry
  And a new kid born every day.

Now if anybody envies Brigham Young,
  Let them go to Great Salt Lake,
And if they have leisure to examine at their pleasure
  They'll find it's a great mistake.
One wife at a time, so says my rhyme,
  Is enough for the proudest don,
So e'er you strive to live lord of forty-five
  Live happy if you can with one.

Testimonies Designed to Limit Chinese Immigration, 1876

San Francisco, April 12, 1876. Rev. Otis Gibson sworn.

Q. What is your profession?

A. A clergyman. . . . I was a missionary to the Chinese of the Methodist Episcopal Church. . . .

Q. Do you know upon what terms the Chinese are imported into this country?

A. They come free. I think all Chinamen come free, except the women. . . .

Q. Is it not a well-settled matter that a great many people are held in slavery here—bought and sold?

A. Only the women. I don't think there is a man so held. The women as a general thing are held as slaves. They are bought or stolen in China and brought here. They have a sort of agreement, to cover up the slavery business, but it is all a sham. That paper makes the girl say that she owes you four hundred dollars or so, passage money and outfit from China, and has nothing to pay. I being the girl, this man comes up and offers to lend me the money to pay you if I will agree to serve him, to prostitute my body at his pleasure, wherever he shall put me, for four, five, or six years. For that promise of mine, made on the paper, he hands him the four hundred dollars, and I pay the debt I owe you according to contract. It is also put in the contract that if I am sick fifteen days no account shall be taken of that, but if I am sick more than that I shall make up double. If I am found to be pregnant within a month, you shall return the money and take me again. If I prove to have epilepsy, leprosy, or am a stone woman, the same thing is done. . . .

Q. Then, so far as the women are concerned, they are in slavery? . . .

A. Yes, sir. And even after the term of prostitution service is up, the owners so manage as to have the women in debt more than ever, so that their slavery becomes life-long. There is no release from it.

Q. When these people become sick and helpless, what becomes of them?

A. They are left to die.

Q. No care taken of them?

A. Sometimes, where the women have friends.

Q. Don't the companies take care of them?

A. Not frequently.

Q. Is it not a frequent thing that they are put out on the sidewalk to die, or in some room without water or food?

A. I have heard of such things; I don't know. . . . Sometimes the women take opium to kill themselves. They do not know they have any rights, but think they must keep their contracts, and believe themselves under obligations to serve in prostitution.

"White Slavery," in *America's Working Women: A Documentary History—1600 to the Present,* Ed. Rosalyn Baxandall, Linda Gordon, Susan Reverby (NY: Vintage Books, 1976), 97–100.

Q. What is their treatment? Is it harsh?

A. They have come to the asylum all bruises. They are beaten and punished cruelly if they fail to make money. When they become worn out and unable to make any more money, they are turned out to die.

The Rev. A. W. Loomis, a Presbyterian clergyman, at the head of the Chinese Mission established by his church in San Francisco, says:

These Chinawomen that you see on the streets here were brought for the accommodation of white people, not for the accommodation of Chinese; and if you pass along the streets where they are to be found, you will see that they are visited not so much by Chinese as by others—sailors and low people. The women are in a condition of servitude. Some of them are inveigled away from home under promise of marriage to men here, and some to be secondary wives, while some are stolen. They are sold here. Many women are taken from the Chinese owners, and are living as wives and as secondary wives. Some have children, and these children are legitimate.

Q. These women engaged in prostitution are nothing more than slaves to them?

A. Yes, sir; and every one would go home to-day if she were free and had her passage paid.

Q. They are not allowed to release themselves from that situation, are they?

A. I think they are under the surveillance of men and women, so that they cannot get away. They would fear being caught and sold again, and carried off to a condition even worse than now.

Q. Are not the laws here used to restrain them from getting away—are they not arrested for crime?

A. Oh, yes. They will trump up a case, have the woman arrested ant bring people to swear what they want. In this way they manage to get possession of her again. . . .

Mr. Alfred Clark, for nineteen years past connected with the police force of San Francisco, and for the last eight years Clerk of the Chief of Police, testifies as follows: "In regard to the vice of prostitution, I have here a bill of sale of a Chinawoman, and a translation of the same." Witness submits a paper written in Chinese characters, and reads the translation, as follows:

An agreement to assist the woman Ah Ho, because coming from China to San Francisco she became indebted to her mistress for passage. Ah Ho herself asks Mr. Yee Kwan to advance her six hundred and thirty dollars, for which Ah Ho distinctly agrees to give her body to Mr. Yee for service of prostitution for a term of four years. There shall be no interest on the money. Ah Ho shall receive no wages. At the expiration of four years Ah Ho shall be her own master. Mr. Yee Kwan shall not hinder or trouble her. If Ah Ho runs away before her time is out, her mistress shall find her and return her, and whatever expense is incurred in finding and returning her Ah Ho shall pay. On this day of agreement Ah Ho, with her own hands, has received from Mr. Yee Kwan six hundred and thirty dollars. If Ah Ho shall be sick at any time for more than ten days, she shall make up by an extra month of service for every ten days sickness. Now, this agreement has proof—this paper received by Ah Ho is witness.

TUNG CHEE.

Twelfth year, ninth month, and fourteenth day (about middle
of October, eighteen hundred and seventy-three).

An Agreement to Assist a Young Girl Named Loi Yau

Because she became indebted to her mistress for passage, food, etc., and has nothing to pay, she makes her body over to the woman, Sep Sam, to serve as a prostitute to make out the sum of five hundred and three dollars. The money shall draw no interest, and Loi Yau shall serve four and one-half years. On this day of agreement, Loi Yau receives the sum of five hundred and three dollars in her own hands. When the time is out, Loi Yau may be her own master, and no man shall trouble her. If she runs away before the time is out, and any expense is incurred in catching her, then Loi Yau must pay the expense. If she is sick fifteen days or more, she shall make up one month for every fifteen days. If Sep Sam shall go back to China, then Loi Yau shall serve another party till her time is out; if, in such service, she should be sick one hundred days or more, and cannot be cured, she may return to Sep Sam's place. For a proof of this agreement, this paper.

Dated second, sixth month of the present year.

LOI YAU.

Augustus Layres Endorses Chinese Immigration, 1876

The Chinese are not, as it has been charged, a band of criminals and vicious, but on the contrary, a very laborious, frugal, quiet, and law-abiding people. There are no bummers among them, nor drunkards, nor bull-dosers, but with rare exceptions. The testimony of Alfred Clarke, Clerk of the Chief of Police, (an anti-Chinese witness) is very conclusive in this respect. "Prostitution, violation of the cubic air ordinance and gambling are the principal offenses for which arrests are made among the Chinese." But prostitution among the Chinese is no more common than among the other nationalities, as any person who takes a stroll through Dupont, Sacramento, and other streets of San Francisco, either by day or night, can soon discover. The municipal authorities, however, have deemed best to punish the Chinese alone for the infraction of the law.

The Chinese are fast learning both our language and customs, notwithstanding they are slow in adopting them. But why should they adopt them when they see so much bad example of dishonesty, drunkenness, and inhuman persecution against them, for no other reason except because they earn a morsel of bread by prolonged toil, day and night, which those who boast

Philip S. Foner and Daniel Rosenberg, eds., *Racism, Dissent, and Asian Americans from 1850 to the Present* (Westport, CT: Greenwood Press, 1993), 91–94.

of belonging to the superior race would fain take from their mouths and give to their white families? What right have they who set such barbarous and unchristian examples in this age of freedom and equal rights, to demand social assimilation from the Chinese? Do we, ourselves, wish to assimilate with any people whose practices and doctrines we condemn? If the Chinese are slow in adopting our civilization and Christian religion, not they, but the anti-Chinese crusaders themselves should bear the blame. And for them to appeal to Congress and the American people, and ask the restriction of Chinese immigration, on the ground that they do not assimilate with us, is the climax of impudence!

These men are constantly clamoring against the Chinese immigrants, yet complain because they do not as other immigrants come here to stay and do not conform with our habits and manners. What charming consistency!

However, as this allegation is likely to constitute the main ground for urging a restriction of Chinese immigration, before yielding to its weight, may we be permitted to inquire into the main and perhaps the only real cause of this want of social homogeneity on the part of the Chinese as well as of other foreigners, in order to see whether the blame attaches to them or to our civil government.

A tour of observation through the different colonies settled in our large cities, will disclose the fact that where a considerable people of foreign nationality form as it were a separate community, it is because they have not a sufficient knowledge of the English language. The necessity of a common medium of social intercourse which is afforded by their native tongue draws them together, and by their numbers they find ample supply among themselves for all their wants. . . .

The remedy universally adopted for conquering this aversion of certain foreigners to amalgamation and obtaining a homogeneous nationality is to *impart a free, and if necessary, obligatory education, particularly in the English language, to all the children of the people.*

The same theory applies to the case of the Chinese now under discussion, but with greater force. They too are compelled to live together as a separate people, chiefly because the great majority of them ignore the English language. But are they to blame for this lack of knowledge and want of assimilation? "They evince an eagerness for learning," says Dr. Loomis in his school report, "which is especially commented upon by strangers." They pay their pro-rata of the taxes for the support of public schools; but our benevolent, equitable and just civil government persistently refuses to grant admission to Chinese children into the public schools through prejudice and antipathy of race. And after suffering so great a wrong from the State and the Municipal Government, in violation of our treaty stipulations, shall the Chinese be subjected to a still greater wrong by way of punishment from the Federal Government, restricting their immigration on account of the lack of assimilation of which they are not the cause? Aye, the sense of right and justice is not yet dead in the American people and Congress!

These and other charges being disproved by fact and reason, why should Congress restrict Chinese immigration any more than that of any other nationality? Would not such a discrimination be a gross insult to the Chinese people and Government? Would it not be an act of flagrant injustice which would challenge the condemnation of the whole civilized world? What a sport would monarchical countries make of our boasted freedom, human equality, and independence! How would the enemies of popular government in our midst, who are constantly plotting its destruction, rejoice secretly in their hearts over this first departure from our national policy, successfully followed by us for one hundred years—"to make no discrimination between nations"—they would regard it as the first retrograde step in our career of liberty and civilization, as a tacit denial of one of the cardinal principles of the immortal Declaration of Independence, as the turning point of this great revolution of ideas wrought in this century by the United States of America. Let us fondly hope and pray that Congress will never consent to thus fatally stab our nation!

Huang Zunxian Expresses the Chinese Perspective in Poetry, c. 1884

EXPULSION OF THE IMMIGRANTS

Alas! What crime have our people committed,
That they suffer this calamity in our nation's fortunes?
Five thousand years since the Yellow Emperor,
Our country today is exceedingly weak.
Demons and ghouls are hard to fathom;
Even worse than the woodland and monsters.
Who can say our fellow men have not met an inhuman fate,
In the end oppressed by another race?
Within the vastness of the six directions,
Where can our people find asylum?

When the Chinese first crossed the ocean,
They were the same as pioneers.
They lived in straw hovels, cramped as snail shells;
For protection gradually built bamboo fences.
Dressed in tatters, they cleared mountain forests;
Wilderness and waste turned into towns and villages.
Mountains of gold towered on high,
Which men could grab with their hands left and right.
Eureka! They return with a load full of gold,
All bragging this land is paradise.
They beckon and beg their families to come;
Legs in the rear file behind legs in the front.
Wearing short coats, they braid their queues;

R. David Arkush and Leo O. Lee, trans. and eds., *Land Without Ghosts: Chinese Impressions of America from the Mid-Nineteenth Century to the Present* (Berkeley: University of California Press, 1989), 61–65. Copyright © 1989 The Regents of the University of California. Reprinted by permission.

Men carry bamboo rainhats, wear straw sandals.
Bartenders lead along cooks;
Some hold tailors' needles, others workmen's axes.
They clap with excitement, traveling overseas;
Everyone surnamed Wong creates confusion. . . .

Gradually the natives turned jealous.
Time to time spreading false rumors,
They say these Chinese paupers
Only wish to fill their money bags.
Soon as their feet touch the ground,
All the gold leaps out of the earth.
They hang ten thousand cash on their waists,
And catch the next boat back to China.
Which of them is willing to loosen his queue,
And do some hard labor for us?
Some say the Chinese are shiftless; . . .
Others say the Chinese are a bunch of hoodlums,
By nature all filthy and unclean.
Their houses are as dirty as dogs';
Their food even worse than pigs'.
All they need is a dollar a day;
Who is as scrawny as they are?
If we allow this cheap labor of theirs,
Then all of us are finished.
We see our own brothers being injured;
Who can stand these venomous vermin? . . .

From now on they set up a strict ban,
Establishing customs posts everywhere.
They have sealed all the gates tightly,
Door after door with guards beating alarms.
Chinese who leave are like magpies circling a tree,
Those staying like swallows nesting on curtains. . . .

Those who do not carry passports
Are arrested as soon as they arrive.
Anyone with a yellow-colored face
Is beaten even if guiltless.
I sadly recollect George Washington,
Who had the makings of a great ruler.
He proclaimed that in America,
There is a broad land to the west of the desert.
All kinds of foreigners and immigrants,
Are allowed to settle in these new lands.
The yellow, white, red, and black races
Are all equal with our native people.
Not even a hundred years till today,
But they are not ashamed to eat his words. . . .
The land of the red man is vast and remote;
I know you are eager to settle and open it.
The American eagle strides the heavens soaring,
With half of the globe clutched in his claw.

Although the Chinese arrived later,
Couldn't you leave them a little space? . . .

Grave, dignified, I arrive with my dragon banners,
Knock on the custom's gate, hesitant, doubtful.
Even if we emptied the water of four oceans,
it would be hard to wash this shame clean. . . .

(translation by J. D. Schmidt)

Carrie Chapman Catt Encourages
Idaho Suffragists, 1896

New York, June 25, 1896

Dear Mrs. [Emma Smith] DeVoe:—

Miss Serepta Sanders had written to me that she would be in St. Louis at the Republican Convention, but if she was there I failed to find her. . . . Of course, I did not get your report nor that of Dr. Atwater's about the Marysville Convention until after my return, but I probably would have gleaned from her that the county was not organized, and I should at least remind her that the State Constitution says, that "where there are two clubs there *must* be a County Association." I am surprised at her position, and, yet, there have come complaints from the Helena clubs all winter long. They have declared that she was standing in the way of the progress of the club and acted as an obstructionist. They had hinted about splitting or withdrawing, but I had begged of them to stock together until your visit, hoping that you may see a way out of the dark. It seems very strange that a woman like her who appears so much interested in suffrage, would stand in her own light to such a degree. . . .

It seems very ludicrous to me the way these western people in the small cities assume airs of society. I used to think there was one place where cast was unknown and where society was bound together only by congeniality. But it appears that wealth and show are gaining ground and trying to compel adoration. We have tried in vain to win society people to become workers in our cause. While there are many individuals who announce themselves as suffragists, I think we will all have to admit that we have not yet found a real society woman who has amounted to very much as a working force. I think we will have to organize them into societies by themselves where they will not be expected to do anything but to have their names referred to when they can do any good. Mrs. Johns has just got through with Boise. The club with "society" officers went to pieces and not one was organized by her. This time it was among the commonality and Mr. Balderston now regrets that the "society" people are left out. I have written him to say, that as the society people will not work somebody must, and we must take those who will toil. I will write to the "society" ladies and try to urge them

---

Emma Smith DeVoe Papers, Folder 15, Box 1, Idaho Historical Society.

to stand in line and show by their names that they are on our side. It is very amusing in that little town of only 2500 people, to find this condition of things. . . .

It is not yet settled as to my going to Idaho. I wrote to the Executive Committee and suggested speakers for the campaign. . . . I would like to have Mrs. Bradford of Colorado, go there for September and October, because her testimony of the good results in Colorado is most valuable, and I suggested her. I also told them, if they wanted to keep Mrs. Johns, who is now in the State, through the end of the campaign, they would have to do so at their own expense as our engagement would soon end. In this connection I offered my own services free to them for the month of August. In reply, they vote against every one of the speakers except me, and, of course, they are only willing to take me because I will cost them nothing. I now feel that it is hardly right for me to go for nothing if by so doing I am keeping others who would be paid from the work in the State. . . .

So far as the dissatisfaction of some towns in Montana with your work of last year, let me say that it should not give you a single heartache. . . . When we hear these things about ourselves it always hurts, and yet it is very foolish to think of them. There never was a speaker yet who did not sometimes hurt peoples' feelings and set them against it. . . . [If] there was a speaker who could always make speeches and never hurt anybody that she better be retired from the field at once as of too useless a character for us. However, I am sorry that these reports reached you for I did not intend that they should. . . .

Mrs. Nelson will have to close her work in Oklahoma before it is quite done owing to the intense heat. She writes day after day that the thermometer stands 102 in the shade. . . . It seems that September is a very hot month down in Oklahoma, and Miss Rees, the President, is inclined to think it is too early for work. But the work is very important in that Territory and we feel sure we shall get suffrage in the next Legislature. . . . Most of the places are now in fair condition and I do not think there would be any trouble about meetings where meetings have been held. . . . The work is very important. . . . We shall do nothing but be financially responsible. We would not expect you in this Territory to make a good record financially for the reason that there is little money to be had in Oklahoma, and, yet, you would do better than Mrs. Nelson as it has been very poor, because in the fall people have more money than at this time of year. However, it is not a prosperous place to go at best. What you fail to get in money you would win in final victory I feel sure. . . . If California and Idaho carry (and I must say I am not oversanguine about either), no power on earth could keep us from getting Oklahoma save the lack of work. . . . I hope things are better now and that the rest of the work will be more advantageously done.

With love, I am,

Yours truly,

Carrie C. Catt

Newspaper Account of Idaho Suffrage Vote, 1896

Idaho is the third state that has granted the full ballot to women within three years. So true is it that when the time is ripe for a movement it seems to sweep on of its own volition. For more than thirty years women, in less or greater numbers, had been knocking at the doors of legislative halls, asking for the right to vote. During all that time the matter was regarded with varying degrees of scorn, contempt and horror, while Wyoming, on the frontier, was looked upon as a practical joke. Then, like a thunder clap in a clear sky, Colorado quietly made her women voters one day. Two years later Utah did the same thing, resuming the form of government which she had held in former years. This fall Idaho followed suit and played trumps. . . .

The Idaho women who took an active part in this campaign can best tell the story themselves.

The state president, Mrs. Marcus Whitman of Montpelier, writes the News as follows:

> A most wonderful campaign has just ended in Idaho in behalf of equal suffrage. We say wonderful, because of the difficulties under which it was carried on. In the first place Idaho is a state of magnificent distances and inaccessible places. Only two lines of railroad traverse the state and as there are no connecting lines, it is necessary to travel through Oregon and Washington or Montana to go from one part of the state to the other. This of necessity makes it very expensive and almost impossible to properly work the state.
>
> Another great difficulty was the short time the association had for organization. . . .
>
> Preparations were immediately begun for the state political conventions. Headquarters were opened in Boise. Work was begun in the county conventions. Bear Lake county, the home of the president of the association, was the first to indorse the amendment and every delegate from that county went to the state convention instructed to stand firm for equal suffrage. The services of Mrs. Carrie Chapman Catt, and of Laura Johns of Kansas, who were then in the state, were secured, and in company with the officers of the association, they attended all the state conventions and secured a favorable plank in the platform of each party. Immediately after the conventions Mrs. Johns left for home and Mrs. Catt, after speaking at Mountain Home, Pocatello, Blackfoot and Idaho Falls, proceeded to California, their place being taken by Mary C. C. Bradford of Denver, who spent five weeks in the state and did excellent work for the cause. . . .

The people of Idaho have signified their desire for equal suffrage in no uncertain way. Ada County gave one of the largest majorities in favor. Only one county in the state gave a majority against it. This was Custer, an inaccessible county, where no work was done because of the difficulty of reaching the section. Custer cast the smallest vote on the amendment of any county in the state, and gave a majority of twenty-five against it. . . .

Three counties could not be reached at all by our workers on account of the long and difficult stage rides. Yet so thoroughly was the state organized

Rocky Mt. News, Denver, CO, Dec. 13, 1896.

by the day of election that not over a dozen precincts in the entire state but had parties pledged to work for us at the polls.

Another difficulty that had to be confronted by those managing the campaign was the lack of funds. The entire fund raised and disbursed by the association was $466. With this sum they sustained their headquarters, paid their secretary, carried on the work of the state, paid all their debts and had a balance remaining of about $16. . . .

Sixty-two per cent of all the electors voted on the amendment. The women who have been working for the amendment in Idaho are not in the least cast down. The present result was effected almost without organization, and with funds and resources which were pitifully small. . . .

One great source of opposition that the association had to meet was the old prejudice against the Mormons. The six southeastern counties are very largely Mormon in population. They are agricultural people, most of them having homes and families. While in the northern and western parts of the state the people are mostly miners and men without families. A fear became prevalent that placing the ballot in the hands of women would be giving the balance of power to the Mormons. Many refused to vote for the amendment on this account who were otherwise favorable.

As is always the case the liquor element of the state was against the cause and did all in its power to defeat it. The populists of the state were largely against the measure, citing for the reason that the women of Colorado had used the ballot to redeem the state from the populist rule and had voted against Governor Waite.

Mrs. Helen Young of Osborne enjoys the distinction of being the first woman admitted to the bar in Idaho. . . . Concerning the campaign in the northern counties and the legal status of the vote, she says:

> Though the Couer d'Alene district gave us 40 majority, I had hoped that it would be more. There are many miners' unions and Knights of Labor lodges here and their constitutions all favor the equality of the sexes. We presented our cause before each union, and were so cordially received that the vote was disappointing. . . .

Mrs. Athey, secretary of the state association, is a beautiful woman, very popular in Boise and proved exceptionally competent to fill her office. Concerning her work she writes:

> We opened headquarters August 1 and from that time campaign work was vigorously pushed. The secretary sent out to the clubs 7,000 copies of the resolutions passed at the convention July 1, and also wrote and mailed 2,000 letters, and to each club in the state sent a copy of an address presented to the cause by Mrs. Margaret Cain of Utah. Also 100 copies of the Woman's Tribune, 3,000 leaflets sent by Mrs. Clara Colby, and 9,966 leaflets purchased of the national association. From September 1 the secretary had charge of the press work and kept the papers of the state supplied with suffrage matter. Out of sixty-five papers, only three were opposed to the amendment. As many amendments fail of adoption because of the forgetfulness of the voters, the association caused to be printed and sent to every voting precinct small dodgers reminding voters of the amendment. Fifty thousand were sent out, and one was placed in the hands

of every elector when he went into the polls to get his ticket. The local club in Boise had 3,000 facsimiles of the amendment printed, and one was placed in the hands of each voter just before he received his ballot. This did us more harm than good since some of the voters marked the dodger instead of his ballot and folded it inside of the ballot. . . .

In the summer of 1895 Emma Smith de Voe, under the auspices of the committee on organization of the National American Woman Suffrage association, made a tour of the state, speaking in many of the principal towns along the railroads, and organizing eighteen clubs. The next November a state convention of a very quiet kind was called to meet in Boise, one delegate being invited from each county. . . . The active efforts of the Daily Statesman, a Republican paper, and the fact that many of the Boise ladies who were interested in calling this first meeting, were wives of prominent Republicans, caused political leaders of other parties to look upon the movement as a Republican scheme, and while these men seldom opposed the measure, only a few were ever active in its support. . . .

A convention of delegate members from all the clubs in the state was called to meet in Boise July 1. Special efforts were made to have this a representative convention and friends of all shades of political faith were placed on the programme. Mrs. M. J. Whitman was a popular candidate for president. Her portion of the state was considered strongly Republican and for this reason some of the delegates questioned the wisdom of electing her to that office, believing it impossible for anything to defeat the Democratic-Populist combination which was known to have been made in regard to state offices, and thinking that if the executive officer of the Equal Suffrage association was in harmoney with the leaders of that combination it might be beneficial to the cause. This view was not held by a majority of the convention, however, and Mrs. Whitman was elected.

During the month of August the different political parties held their conventions in Boise, and in each of the platforms was a resolution indorsing woman suffrage. Mrs. Catt was present and addressed all of these conventions, arousing Boise to an enthusiasm which seemed almost phenomenal. It is but just, however, to say that Mrs. Johns and the July convention had in a measure paved the way for Mrs. Catt's success.

Y *E S S A Y S*

In a prize-winning essay, Carol Cornwall Madsen, a member of the history faculty and a senior research historian in the Joseph Fielding Smith Institute for Church History at Brigham Young University, considers how Utah lawmakers shaped divorce law to accommodate the unique demands of polygamy. She shows how the law, crafted by Mormon and non-Mormon agencies, gave plural wives legal protection, but only temporarily. Margaret K. Holden, an assistant professor of history at the University of Nevada, Las Vegas, further develops the notion of women and legal status. She examines the ways in which white women endorsed the denial of rights to the Chinese as a way to advance support for female suffrage. These essays expose the roots of discrimination and raise a troubling question—Is negative bias an appropriate tool for supposedly positive reform?

Utah Law and the Plural Wives, 1850–1900

CAROL CORNWALL MADSEN

Various studies have examined the politics, the sociology, the economics, and the evolution of the relationship between the Mormon church and the federal government attendant to the Mormon practice of polygamy during Utah's territorial history. A relevant but lesser known aspect of the subject is the impact of Utah's domestic relations laws on plural wives, as these laws were shaped by polygamy and the federal efforts to abolish it. While all polygamists were at legal risk, plural wives were vulnerable not only to criminal prosecution but also to permanent legal discrimination, because of their unorthodox marital choice.

Joseph Smith, Mormon church founder, introduced the practice of plural marriage in 1843 as a restored biblical principle in Mormon theology. It was practiced privately until 1852, three years after the church settled in isolated Utah. Then it was publicly announced as a tenet of Mormon doctrine. While personal disputes arising from and within the practice were theoretically governed exclusively by ecclesiastical authority, the Mormon-dominated legislature sought to bring those issues under legal protection as well. Though never inserting the word "polygamy" into any statute, the Utah legislature framed laws that favored the practice without seeming unduly incongruent with the law in other states and territories, thus avoiding special scrutiny by the U.S. Congress.

Initial efforts to legally safeguard the practice were generally successful for several reasons. When Utah obtained territorial status in the Compromise of 1850, it became subject to the control of a federally appointed governor and judiciary. With the appointment of church president Brigham Young as first governor and the election of an all-Mormon legislature, however, Mormon legislative initiative was insured. Secondly, an unusual, though not unique, legislative move attempted to place judicial control in Mormon hands as well. One of the first acts of the legislature in 1851 was to extend the prerogatives of the probate courts, which normally heard only civil cases. Broadly construing the meaning of the territorial Organic Act, which stipulated that the authority of the probate courts "shall be limited by law," the legislature granted original jurisdiction in both civil and criminal cases to the probate courts, whose officers the legislature was also empowered to appoint. Thus, probate courts possessed concurrent jurisdiction with the district courts and offered an alternative to the federally appointed, non-Mormon officers of the district courts.

Another effort by the territorial legislature to enact protective legislation was rejection of the common law in 1854. Since bigamy was prohibited at common law, this legislative act could be construed as permitting legal recognition of plural marriage.

Thus, until Congress passed the Morrill Act in 1862, the first federal law specifically prohibiting bigamy, and the 1874 Poland Act restricting the jurisdiction of the Utah probate courts, the legal protection of Mormon institutions was relatively free of federal interventions.

Most Mormons simply avoided the courts, as far as possible, by settling their disputes within an ecclesiastical court system established early in the history of the church. Presided over by bishops of each ward (ecclesiastical unit) at the first level, it provided an appellate system rising from the bishop's court to the high council court (comprising representatives from several wards), and ultimately reaching to the first presidency of the church (the president and two counselors). . . .

Church courts were especially useful in settling domestic conflicts involving polygamy because of the practice's extralegal character. Nevertheless, Mormon legislatures also attempted to protect the women and children involved in plural marriage by enacting laws based on principles governing church court decisions. Most of these protective laws fell into the category of domestic relations, including marriage, divorce, and succession or inheritance. Their checkered history illustrates the escalating tension between local attempts to preserve a religious practice and federal efforts to destroy it and the legal consequences for plural wives.

For its first four decades, Utah law had no provisions for the civil licensing and registration of marriage. The only marriage law of the period was included in an ordinance incorporating the church, which authorized it to "solemnize marriages compatible with the revelations of Jesus Christ." This ordinance provided for "a registry of marriages," but it was to be kept only in the branches or stakes of the church. No civil record was required until the Edmunds-Tucker Act established regulatory measures in 1887. Thus, polygamous alliances did not need to become a matter of public record. In 1862, the Morrill Act specifically declared bigamous marriages illegal, but not until 1876 did the church-owned *Deseret Evening News* concede that the practice was "not recognized by the law of the land." Polygamy continued to be practiced by church members, however, for another fourteen years, until 1890, when church president Wilford Woodruff suspended the performance of any further plural marriages.

Though polygamy was denounced as a system of female bondage by non-Mormons, the liberality of Utah's divorce laws and the ease with which church divorces were granted belied this perception. As historian Lawrence Foster has noted, in polygamous Utah, contrary to prevailing opinion, women enjoyed more freedom in terms of marriage and divorce than women in other polygamous cultures. Though easy divorce seems incongruous with the Mormon theological focus on the eternity of marriage and propriety of plural marriage, the religious faithfulness and mutual affection of the participants were the primary determinants of a successful union. As early as 1842, according to one account, Joseph Smith taught that marriage was a covenant between two people and if it had not been conducive of blessings and peace, they were free to separate since "it was a sin for people to live together and raise or beget children, in alienation from each other." The sin, according to Mormon thought, was not in divorce but in perpetuating the form of marriage and the begetting of children without the cementing bond of affection. The decision in an 1847 divorce case brought before the high council in Winter Quarters, Nebraska, invoked this tenet: "No man or woman should ever be compelled to live together who cannot live in union. You two now are to separate and not come together again."

In 1861, Brigham Young, successor to Joseph Smith, reiterated this principle. "When a woman becomes alienated in her feelings and affections from her husband, it is then his duty to give her a bill and set her free," he said in a church conference. To continue to live together when a wife had become alienated from her husband was to violate the marriage covenant. Moreover, if a man proved to be an "unworthy" husband and father, he automatically forfeited his marriage covenants, and his wife or wives were "free from him without a bill of divorcement." The sanctity and perpetuation of a marriage, as a holy sacrament, were contingent on the righteousness of the couple and the retention of affection between them. Two cases brought before a Fillmore, Utah, bishop in 1883 illustrate the value placed on affection in marriage. "Although her [the applicant's] grounds are not just," the bishop reported to church president John Taylor (successor to Brigham Young), "in our opinion it would not be wise to compel her to continue to be the wife of her husband inasmuch as she claims that she does not now nor never did have any affection for him." In another instance, though the bishop again felt the complaining wife did not have sufficient grounds for divorce, she had expressed such hostility to her husband that he was willing to recommend a divorce and "leave the matter to the judgment of President [John] Taylor."

Church leaders continually preached against divorce and urged the reconciliation of estranged couples, but when conciliatory efforts failed, then they advised an expeditious separation and settlement. "Parties should be advised to learn how to live together in peace," Brigham Young counseled in 1851, "but if it is best for them to separate," the husband should give the wife and children "a large proportion of the property." Plural wives were particularly admonished to bear their burdens uncomplainingly and "not to expect heaven on earth but to prepare for it in due time." Nevertheless, they were speedily granted divorces when desired. Extant records show that more than 1,600 applicants, most of them women, received ecclesiastical divorces before polygamy was suspended in 1890.

While both men and women appealed to church courts for divorce, men were almost routinely refused, except in compelling circumstances, while women were seldom denied their requests. In typical earthy imagery, Brigham Young told one male petitioner, "If you have drawn a red hot iron between your legs and scorched yourself, bear it without grunting, and if it smarts, grease it. . . . I want the brethren to stop divorcing their wives, for it is not right. I do not want to grant divorces." The preferential treatment given women is consistent with Young's explanation of the sin of begetting children in alienation of affections and reflects the relative ease with which women could remarry in polygamous Utah, as well as the voluntary nature of the practice of polygamy. A church divorce confidentially and expeditiously released women unable to bear the emotional or physical burdens of plural marriage.

The governing policies for church divorces transferred into civil law in 1852, when the territorial legislature attached an incompatibility clause to the traditional grounds for divorce (impotency, adultery, desertion, habitual drunkenness, felony conviction, and abusive treatment). In words similar to those used in church divorce actions, the statute provided that divorce could be granted "when it shall be made to appear to the satisfaction and conviction of the court, that the parties cannot live in peace and union together, and that their welfare requires a separation." The law also provided a minimal residency requirement. Anyone who was or "wished to become" a resident of Utah could invoke the jurisdiction of the court. While various explanations have been tendered for Utah's adoption of such a liberal statute, it is consistent with Mormon legislative efforts to facilitate and protect the practice of polygamy with laws that reflected church court policies and practices.

Although Utah was among the 20 percent of states and territories with the highest divorce rate, it was lower than nearly all of its western neighbors during the first twenty-year period for which national divorce statistics were compiled (1867–1887). More than a third of Utah civil divorces during this time utilized the incompatibility clause, 71 percent of them granted during a single three-year period, 1875 to 1877. In fact, the total number of civil divorces granted in Utah more than tripled between 1875 and 1877, dropping back to its 1874 level in 1878. Four Utah counties registered precipitous increases, but the most dramatic occurred in the small southern Utah county of Beaver, where divorces jumped from two in 1874 to 108 in 1875 and 358 the next year. Of a total of 691 divorces in Beaver County during this twenty-year period, 91 percent were granted between 1875 and 1877. This aberration did not reflect an unusual season of marital discontent, but an exploitation of Utah's divorce law by non-Utah divorce lawyers, who found its open residency requirement and completion of the transcontinental railroad (in 1869) an irresistible combination. For example, of the 691 Beaver divorces, only seventy-five involved bonafide Utah residents. All the others were migratory divorces brought by residents of eastern states "wishing," for a day, to become residents of Utah. The probate judges in these counties facilitated the use of their courts by eastern divorce lawyers, creating a short-lived, but active, divorce mill in Utah.

Alarmed at the flagrant abuse of Utah's divorce law, Governor George W. Emery strongly urged the legislature to amend the law in 1876, but not until a grand jury investigation the following year and another urgent appeal by Governor Emery, in 1878, did the Mormon legislature reluctantly eliminate the offending provisions. A *Deseret News* article explained the reluctance: "Polygamy would be considered a system of bondage, if women desiring to sever their relations with a husband having other wives, were refused the liberty they might demand." Though plural wives could not utilize civil courts for divorce, first wives could. Moreover, the liberal divorce law contradicted the popular image of the enslaved wife in Utah. Thus, Mormon legislators agreed to reformulate the law only when convinced its abuse by non-Mormons had overshadowed its value to Mormons. . . .

While appeals for church divorces generally originated in bishops' courts, from which recommendations were sent to the first presidency for decisions, some applicants skirted this procedure and appealed directly to the church president. Moreover, Brigham Young sometimes suggested a choice of venue. In 1870, he advised Maria Jarman to apply "either to Bro. Elias Smith, Probate Judge of Salt Lake County, or to this office, and procure a bill at any time." It is not clear whether Maria Jarman was a first or plural wife, but it is clear that Young and Smith did not have comparable jurisdiction. Young also occasionally instructed probate judges on the disposition of cases, as he did in the divorce suit of Sarah Hutchenson, advising Judge Elias Smith "that it would be proper" to grant Sarah a divorce from her long-absent husband.

Numerous legal entanglements resulted from this blurring of jurisdictional boundaries. For example, in 1870 Eleanor and Elbridge Tufts decided to terminate their marriage of one year and were granted a church divorce. Both remarried. Upon learning twenty years later that the church divorce was not valid, Eleanor ceased living with John Wickel, her second husband, and sued Tufts for divorce. The divorce was still pending in 1895 when Tufts died. Eleanor then filed claim for a dower interest in his property as his only legal wife. The claim was granted by the trial court and affirmed by the Utah Supreme Court. In a similar case decided three years later, John R. Park, an early Utah educator, married Annie Armitage, a young convert, in 1872 at her bedside, believing her to be on her deathbed but wishing to secure an eternal marriage for them both. When Annie unexpectedly recovered, the two agreed to separate and obtained a church divorce the following year. Park never remarried, but Annie married and bore ten children. At Park's demise in 1902, Annie sued to recover a dower interest in property conveyed by Park before his death, claiming her right as his widow, since her church divorce from him was not valid. Though she lost her case in trial court, the Utah Supreme Court reversed the decision and she recovered her widow's share.

Divorce became less relevant following the 1890 suspension of church-sanctioned plural marriage, and a clear distinction between ecclesiastical and civil marriages and divorces took effect in Utah. The next several decades represented a period of legal adjustment for plural wives and children, many of whom found themselves in a state of legal limbo regarding their inheritance rights.

Like Utah's early marriage and divorce laws, laws of succession also attempted to accommodate the needs of plural wives and children. An 1852 statute rather ambiguously provided that in the absence of a will, and after payment of the liabilities of a man's estate, whatever property remained would "descend in equal shares to his children or their heirs; one share . . .

through the mother of such children . . . or if he has had more than one wife, who either died or survived in lawful wedlock, it shall be equally divided between the living and the heirs of those who are dead. . . ."

Written ten years before passage of the Morrill Act outlawing bigamy, the phrase "lawful wedlock" as it referred to additional wives was not necessarily contradictory. The following section, however, went beyond the implied rights of plural wives in the first section to provide that "illegitimate children and their mothers" shall inherit "in like manner."

Mary Ann Maughan, widow of Peter Maughan of northern Utah's Cache Valley, noted the inherent inequity in the "equal distribution to all heirs" of the property in a polygamous marriage. Though she was married thirty years and raised ten children, she was irked to learn that since it was ruled "best for all to share alike," the two-year-old son of her sister wife, Lissy, "was awarded just as much as I was."

A further provision of the 1852 law allowed illegitimate children and their mothers to inherit from the father, whether acknowledged by him or not, if it could be demonstrated that he was the father. Succession cases indicate this was the statute that granted plural wives inheritance rights.

In 1876, at the urging of Governor George W. Emery, the legislature amended the statute to require that the father acknowledge the illegitimate heirs before they inherit to avoid the possibility of fraudulent claims and to prevent injustice to legitimate heirs. It also reluctantly removed the heritable rights of mothers of illegitimate children to conform to the requirements of the Morrill Act, which not only made bigamy a crime, but also nullified all territorial laws that appeared to "establish, support, maintain, shield or countenance polygamy." Since the Mormon-controlled probate courts were allowed to retain jurisdiction in the settlement of estates after the federal Poland Bill of 1874 transferred all other civil and criminal jurisdiction to the district courts, succession claims could continue to be settled before sympathetic judges. Where succession or inheritance claims were heard, however, depended on the disposition of the first wife, who could press her legal claims in a territorial court or defer to an ecclesiastical court to decide the distribution of the estate. The Gunnell wives of Cache Valley, unlike Mary Ann Maughan, were subject to the later laws providing only for illegitimate children. When Francis Gunnell died in 1889, his second wife Emma "was left nothing, not being recognized by law as a wife. Everything was left to the first living wife, Aunt Esther, and some property divided among the children." The children combined their small inheritance and built a home for their mother. The silence of the law on plural wives' inheritance from their intestate husbands required them to find relief primarily through church courts or through the generosity of their children. Even plural wives who were beneficiaries of a will found themselves in a state of dependency. Emily Dow Partridge Young, widow of Brigham Young, shared in his estate, but found the limitations of her widowhood demeaning. A widow "is left to the mercy of his [sic] children," she complained. "They are given preeminence, while the wife and mother is ignored. Even my home, that I hold the deed of," she angrily noted, "is given to my children and I am not allowed the right to own anything but am fed with a spoon like a baby."

When prosecution of polygamists under the Morrill Act failed, Congress passed more stringent anti-polygamy legislation in 1882 (Edmunds Act) and 1887 (Edmunds-Tucker Act). The Edmunds Act affirmed the legality of the inheritance rights of illegitimate children born prior to January 1883, but did not acknowledge any rights of plural wives. In debate on the bill, Senator George F. Edmunds (R-VT) declared that "this bill does not leave any polygamous woman in any worse condition in point of law than she is at the moment, but it leaves her children in an infinitely better condition, because it makes them legitimate." The Edmunds-Tucker Act, while annulling all laws providing for the capacity of illegitimate children to inherit, also included a "saving clause" as to those children legitimated by the Edmunds Act and all others born within twelve months after its own passage in 1887.

In *Chapman* v. *Handley,* a suit brought in 1890 by the "illegitimate" offspring of George Handley, who died in 1874, and his plural wife Mary, the Utah Supreme Court held that the 1852 territorial law that gave illegitimate children the right to inherit from their fathers had been superseded by the 1862 Morrill Act, which disallowed any laws that supported polygamy. The Court thus denied the petitioners their claim of inheritance. The United States Supreme Court, however, ruling on a similar case, *Cope* v. *Cope,* reversed the judgment of the Utah court and found that the legislature was free to provide for illegitimate children to inherit from their mother, father, or both, declaring that it was "unjust to visit the sins of the parents on the heads of the children." The United States Supreme Court seemed more willing than Utah's judiciary to interpret the Morrill Act broadly, distinguishing between the rights of illegitimate children to legal protection and the illegal actions of their parents. The irony and ultimate tragedy, however, derive from the obvious disparity between the intent of Congress to protect the moral and social interests of Mormon women by freeing them from polygamy and its subsequent failure to protect their economic or legal status.

Nor were plural wives given legal status by the first legislature of the State of Utah that, in 1896, passed a law legitimating *all* issue of bigamous and polygamous marriages contracted prior to that year and providing that such children could inherit from both parents, but making no provisions for plural wives. The importance of writing wills was never so apparent. One astute daughter, Anne Leishman of Cache Valley, Utah, urged her father to make a will. "My mother would come in all right if he dies for a home and things," she explained, "but Aunt Betsy [his plural wife] would only be treated as a child. . . . She can't write a check, she can't sign a deed, she can't do anything." More than her husband or children, the plural wife experienced the penalties of living beyond the boundaries of the law.

The common law right of dower, granting a widow a one-third interest in her husband's real property, if he died intestate, and a one-third inchoate interest during his life-time, was obviously inoperative in polygamy, and the Utah legislature formally abolished dower in 1872. Since dower had been abolished, never enacted, or modified in other areas in the United States, Utah's legislation could not be construed as a wholly unique accommodation to the imperatives of plural marriage, but was clearly enacted to equalize the claims of plural wives on their husbands' estates. It also left polygamous husbands free to distribute their estates equitably by will. Mormon critics viewed the law as one more legal support of polygamy by breaking down the distinction between lawful and plural wives. One 1882 critic observed that abolition of dower rendered "a polygamous wife slavishly dependent on the husband's favor for any share of his property after his death" and urged repeal of the measure to protect the interests of the legal wife who, in polygamy, he said "is not the favorite as a general rule." Absence of dower effectively diminished a legal wife's claim, by withdrawing her inchoate interest in her husband's property during his lifetime and granting her only an equal share with all of her husband's direct heirs at his death.

In 1887, dower was reinstated by the Edmunds-Tucker Act. Its reinstitution continued to work against the legal interests of plural wives, even as sole surviving wives of their husbands. . . . Emily P. Raleigh sued for her dower right, as a sole surviving wife, in a piece of property willed by her husband to a mutual investment company. Though she had occupied the property for forty-six years and claimed it as a gift from her husband, the court ruled against her claim declaring that whatever misfortune she felt had befallen her was a result of her own volition. She made the choice to become a plural wife, the court asserted, "at her peril," failing thereby "to acquire the status of a lawful wife." She was, therefore, "without the pale of the law, of inheritance as to any property which her husband had acquired or might thereafter acquire."

Polygamy impinged less directly upon the development of Utah's property law. While dower clearly mitigated the property claims of a plural wife, passage of a Married Person's Property Act at the same time dower was abolished in 1872 protected the property owned by all women at marriage. The act allowed each spouse to retain and control the property each brought to the marriage, as well as that acquired afterwards. While the repeal of dower was opposed by non-Mormons, the Property Act was hailed by Mormon women as progressive and far more in keeping with the times respecting the advancing legal rights of married women.

Utah law was amended by federal statute or judicial decree in two nondomestic areas that also affected the status of plural wives. In 1870, the territorial legislature enfranchised women, only the second legislature in the country to do so. Originally proposed by several members of U.S. Congress as a means of empowering plural wives to throw off the yoke of polygamy, woman suffrage was seized on by Mormon lawmakers to counteract the perception of the subjugated plural wife. From 1870 until 1887, woman suffrage was inextricably linked to polygamy by non-Mormons, who feared it would strengthen Mormon political hegemony. Every congressional measure proposed to curtail the practice included repeal of woman suffrage in

Utah. Though eastern suffragists forcefully lobbied against repeal, the Edmunds Act finally denied polygamists the vote in 1882, and the Edmunds-Tucker Act disenfranchised all Utah women in 1887. While a presidential amnesty in 1893 restored the vote to men who gave up polygamy, women were not reenfranchised until statehood in 1896.

A major tool in the prosecution of polygamists was the testimony of plural wives. But Utah's civil code, adopted in 1870, exempted husbands and wives from testifying against each other, unless the action involved one against the other. It was later amended to allow testimony against one by the other in cases of crimes committed by one on the other. Federal prosecutors sought ways to circumvent this husband/wife privilege. While testimony from wives other than the first was admissible, since they were not legal wives, various approaches were applied to obtain testimony from first wives. In *United States* v. *Bassett,* in which the defendant's first wife agreed to testify, her testimony was ruled admissible by the Territorial Supreme Court, on the basis that polygamy was a crime against *her,* and, thus, under the civil code, she could testify. Moreover, it ruled that polygamy was also a crime of violence to her feelings, personal security, and her liberty, and she was, thus, allowed to testify under the criminal code as well. Since an exception to the husband/wife communication privilege was permitted under the criminal code when a "violent" crime was committed by one against the other, the prosecutors hoped to utilize that exception by declaring polygamy a crime of violence. When the case was appealed to the United States Supreme Court, however, it reversed the lower court's decision. It defined polygamy as a crime against the marital relation, rather than against the lawful wife and refused to acknowledge it as a crime of violence. Thus, the right of immunity excused first wives from testifying, but not being subject to this law, plural wives were required to testify against their husbands. Those who refused were cited for contempt, and several women were imprisoned. In one more instance, plural wives stood outside the boundaries of the law.

While in most respects the development of law in territorial Utah followed principles of the common law, despite legislative efforts to disclaim it, Mormon lawmakers attempted to shape the law, as far as possible, to fit the necessities of a unique family structure. Throughout Utah's territorial period, the law underwent repeated modification, as federal law and judicial decree reshaped it to match the legal contours of the larger society. The Mormon-federal conflict, among other things, demonstrated the fluidity of law in its response to the social factors influencing it. On the local level, Utah laws protecting Mormon interests continually met defeat by the federally appointed judiciary. Yet, on the national level, while congressional lawmakers carved away those protective statutes, the U.S. Supreme Court often exerted a meliorating influence. The weight of congressional legislation, however, ultimately prevailed. Though their children, as innocent victims, were granted legal protection, polygamous husbands faced criminal prosecution and their plural wives, legal discrimination. While many polygamists escaped federal prosecution altogether and others paid the requisite penalties of a fine and a relatively brief imprisonment, all plural wives experienced the legal consequences of living outside the protective limits of the law. Moreover, while polygamous husbands ultimately regained their legal and political rights through a presidential amnesty, plural wives did not. Because far more women than men practiced polygamy, the legal ramifications for women were not only more permanent, they were more pervasive.

While polygamy contributed to the shaping of Utah's territorial law, it is instructive to recognize that the law was so formulated as to accommodate a marital style involving only about 25 or 30 percent of Utah's residents. Rather than reflecting or regulating the practices of the larger population of the territory, the law, in this case, attempted to protect the rights of the minority, sometimes at the expense of the majority. Only when met by coercive measures did Utah/Mormon lawmakers finally "render unto Caesar" the legal prerogatives they had claimed for themselves in pursuit of the establishment of their religious commonwealth, yielding to federal measures to bring the territory into legal harmony with the rest of the nation.

Gender, Protest, and the Anti-Chinese Movement

MARGARET K. HOLDEN

Wars are often necessary—but evils, at the best.
They find our loyal citizens and their manly courage
test.
But our soldiers' widows are the sufferers, and often
cry in woe.
Our Children had no bread to eat; The Chinaman
must go.
Yes in their heathen land, across the raging main;
For coolie labor in their fair land we will ne'er
entertain.
They have robbed us our birthright, as every woman
knows.
In the cooking of your food, and the laundering of
your clothes.
They perform other domestic duties here, in prudence
I can't name.
And there is nothing left for us to do but lead a life of
shame.
We feel our position keenly, whilst tears down our
cheeks do flow.
Give us our Christian sympathy, say the Chinaman
must go.

Margaret K. Holden, "Gender and Protest Ideology: Sue Ross Keenan and the Oregon Anti-Chinese Movement," *Western Legal History,* 7 (Summer/Fall, 1994), 223–43. Used with permission of the Ninth Judicial Circuit Historical Society.

William Cole, an anti-Chinese sympathizer and Knights of Labor organizer, wrote these verses at the height of the anti-Chinese agitation in Oregon in the winter of 1886. Its language suggests a heretofore unexplored dimension of the anti-Chinese movement in the Pacific Northwest—the role that women and domestic ideology played in shaping the protest. As its imagery makes clear, anti-Chinese agitators believed that Chinese workers undercut women's domestic role and threatened the job opportunities for working women.

Among Cole's supporters were Euro-American women, one of whom was Sue Ross Keenan, an East Portland boardinghouse keeper and a member of the Knights of Labor. She became a highly regarded leader of the 1885–86 protests, and her anti-Chinese stance provides an example of female working-class political activism, pursued outside the more conventional middle-class moral-reform and suffrage organizations. In short, the anti-Chinese movement not only represented Euro-American workingmen's prejudices, interests, and demands, but also reflected the economic and domestic concerns, as well as the leadership, of working women.

Historians have long acknowledged that nineteenth-century Americans divided the world into separate spheres for men and women, the men traditionally being active in politics and the women in the private world of the home, where they cared for their families' moral and physical needs. Middle-class women pushed for reform from within the proscriptions of this domestic world, typically in organizations limited to women.

However, rural women joined the Grange, the Farmers' Alliance, and the Populist party in order to reform economic and social relations. Urban working women joined labor organizations such as the Knights of Labor to advance wide-ranging reforms. Although their activities seldom occurred in legislative chambers, governors' offices, or courtrooms, their efforts were political in the broad sense of the word. They acted formally and informally to change government and community behaviors and to forge an ideology of equal rights in their organizations.

Many of Portland's working women were among those breaking into public life, participating in anti-Chinese demonstrations at the city's largest public meeting grounds, and even attending bonfire-lit, open-air rallies. Perceiving Chinese labor as an economic threat, they joined anti-Chinese leagues and even the Knights of Labor, calling for equal rights for white men and women at the expense of the Chinese. Among the protesters, both men and women stressed domestic themes and emphasized traditional gender roles and domestic values to strengthen their free-labor ideology. This made for further opportunities within the movement for women.

Before Sue Ross Keenan joined the anti-Chinese movement, she played a vital role in Oregon's suffrage campaign. In the early 1880s, she worked for a suffrage amendment to the state constitution. . . . When the amendment failed, she lobbied the state legislature to pass a bill to extend the vote to women, to which end she testified before the Oregon Senate Judiciary Committee in February 1885.

Her testimony reveals her partisan nature and her attitudes about race and gender. She reminded the Judiciary Committee that Abraham Lincoln, a Republican president, had enfranchised the Negro. "We have waited long and anxiously for his Republican followers to enfranchise the women [*sic*]," she pointed out. "They have turned a deaf ear to our entreaties, and now our only hope lies with the Democratic party." . . .

Keenan also presented two nonpartisan arguments in favor of woman suffrage. Her testimony foreshadows her later stand on Chinese labor. First, she argued that women should have the vote because of their domestic role and moral superiority. "I come to you as a wife and mother, the mother of men, of voters," she told the committee. "I am proud of the name mother, and I ask a voice in making the laws that govern my children. I ask that a mother's voice be heard in your legislative hall." She molded her appeal carefully to fit the bounds of Victorian motherhood and domesticity, and demanded political equality on the basis of her special female qualities.

Her second contention drew on the conservative, anti-immigrant—and even racist—argument used by some suffragists after the Civil War. She told the committee that she did not belong to the inferior classes specifically forbidden from voting under the Oregon Constitution: "I am neither a Chinaman, Indian, idiot, lunatic nor criminal, and I stoutly and strongly protest against being classed with them any longer." For her, the state could legally classify Indians and Chinese on the basis of racial inferiority, but gender was not a legitimate category. In other words, she claimed the right to vote on the grounds that all people were not equal. White women and men—especially the civilized and the educated—shared an equality that excluded those she viewed as the inferior races and society's misfits. . . .

As the Oregon suffrage campaign dwindled after the 1885 legislature had voted against the suffrage bill, she turned her energies to a new cause—expelling the Chinese. Once again, to fight this battle, she marshalled her domestic ideology and her racist assumptions.

The anti-Chinese movement of 1885–86 had its immediate origins in the depression of 1884, which weakened the Pacific Northwest's economy. With the completion of the Northern Pacific Railroad in 1883 and the collapse of its stock the following year, the company let thousands of Chinese and Euro-American workers go. The unemployed floated to Portland in search of work and soup kitchens, but instead found fierce competition for jobs. In the autumn of 1885, Euro-American laborers formed anti-Chinese leagues to protest what they perceived as unfair Chinese competition. In less than a month, eight weekly anti-Chinese encampments organized in the Portland environs, springing up in the working-class neighborhoods of Albina, East Portland, Beaver Creek, and Oregon City. . . . Protesters called for the strict enforcement of the Chinese Exclusion Act of 1882, the legal removal of Chinese workers, and the boycott of all Chinese businesses, Chinese-manufactured goods, and employers of Chinese workers.

Simultaneously, the Knights of Labor began to form assemblies along the West Coast, recruiting heavily from the fledgling Oregon leagues. . . . A national labor organization headed by Terence V. Powderly, the Knights sought to create a producers' community based on mutual interdependence and citizen participation. Working men and women joined the movement, calling for an end to wage slavery and the factory system, which they believed crushed the economic independence of laborers. The Knights inherited an eighteenth-century republican tradition based on beliefs in the dignity of work, a republican form of government, and equal rights for men and women. Through organization, cooperation, and education, they hoped to restructure the economy into an interdependent society of producer-citizens.

West Coast Knights embraced this national agenda and equal-rights ideology, but also advocated the exclusion of Chinese laborers, at the expense of what one eastern visitor called the "humanitarian" nature of the national organization. In California, Washington, and Oregon, Knights assemblies demanded the exclusion of the Chinese on the grounds that the race was antithetical to the social, cultural, and economic values of Americans. A Knights newspaper in Pendleton complained that hardworking men and women refused to support Chinese rights because their "wages now are reduced almost below living rates on account of the inevitable influction of cooley l[a]bor." A sympathetic Portland editor predicted that the Knights would be effective in "defeating" corporations and capitalists that imported and employed coolie labor, and stated that only the Knights foresaw the "magnitude of the crisis" resulting from the degradation of white labor by the Chinese. . . .

Anti-Chinese protesters and Knights members encouraged women to join the leagues. Women frequently attended the anti-coolie meetings, and often numbered about "one-third" of the audience. At least two reasons explain why many of them became members. The precarious status of Euro-American working women meant that they often competed with Chinese men, and undoubtedly shared the racist attitudes that pervaded the movement.

Wage work was a fact of life for a growing number of women in the late nineteenth century. In Portland the percentage who worked outside the home—as boardinghouse keepers, seamstresses, mill operatives, and domestic servants—increased from about one-tenth in 1860 to almost one-quarter in 1880. More importantly, urban working women often competed directly with Chinese for jobs in domestic service, tailoring, and the mills. Between 1870 and 1890, Chinese workers in Oregon moved away from mining (which supported over three-quarters of the state's Chinese population in 1870 and less than one-tenth in 1890). By 1890 Chinese men were usually employed in domestic service, laundry washing, and common labor. Census takers in 1880 found nonfarming Euro-American working women predominantly in teaching, domestic service, dressmaking, tailoring, and millinery. Women in all these occupations except teaching competed with Chinese laborers for their jobs.

More telling, however, is a comparison of Chinese men and Euro-American women in specific industries in 1880. Over half the domestic servants were Euro-American women, while 40 percent were Chinese men. In laundry, Chinese men made up more than two-thirds of the workers, and Euro-American women less than 20 percent, while in the cotton and woolen mills employers hired about 9 percent Chinese men and one-third Euro-American women. In millinery and tailoring, 80 percent of the workers were Euro-American women, compared with 10 percent Chinese men.

Although the absolute number of Chinese men in these occupations was relatively small, their presence led to the perception that they were stealing
jobs from white women.

According to community leaders and anti-Chinese activists, women
attended protest meetings because they felt this economic threat. One newspaper editor, for instance, praised the "proper" open policy of the labor
movement because women suffered "from coolie competition as much as
men." A Knights of Labor leader called on women to join because so many
Chinese domestics competed for their jobs. A Democratic politician
observed that for "mothers and fathers" honest toil was now "disreputable"
because Chinese stole jobs for lower wages. One newspaper even blamed
Chinese competition for increasing the number of female prostitutes.
Protesters claimed that cheap Chinese labor forced Anglo women out of
work and into careers of "depravity." The *Daily News* reported a 33 percent
increase in "depraved" women in 1885, because of economic competition.
While this charge was most likely fabricated by a prejudiced editor, it
nonetheless illustrates the degree to which anti-Chinese agitators considered Chinese labor as "women's work" that threatened women's livelihoods.

When it came to the Chinese, Euro-American women could be as racist
as their male counterparts. Sue Ross Keenan revealed her own racial prejudices regarding suffrage, insisting that white women should gain the vote
before the "inferior" races did so. A similar prejudice appeared to be at
work during the winter of 1885–86. . . .

Portland's anti-Chinese agitators cited economic competition as the primary reason for Chinese expulsion, and contended that Chinese workers
competed unfairly with white laborers by working for lower wages and living in substandard conditions. At early meetings, Euro-American workers
complained that Chinese laborers in laundry, cigar manufacturing, tailoring,
and boot-and-shoe manufacturing took jobs from Portland's white men,
women, and children because they willingly worked for low wages.
Protesters charged that most Chinese worked in a "coolie" contract system,
selling their labor under contract at wages that, by local standards, were
"slave wages." . . . The *News* editor complained that "the whole contract
system is but one remove from slavery itself." He continued:

> The coolies are imported under contract and after their arrival in this country
> they are as much subject to the wills and orders of the contracted as were the
> negroes of the South under the old slave system. Chinese contractors operate
> like slave owners—their serfs are compelled to report their earnings promptly
> and contractors get a share.

In fact, few Chinese entered the country under contract and few were
employed in competitive industries. Still, agitators argued that this "coolie"
system created an immoral, flawed economy.

Workers in Portland believed that the future of their society and economy was in danger. . . . By focusing on the stark dichotomy between
Chinese slave labor versus free white labor, protesters veiled their attack on
industrial capitalism. They challenged capitalists for denigrating white

labor and encouraging "coolie" employment. Euro-American workers argued that West Coast capitalists created a labor system that artificially reduced wages by hiring cheap Chinese labor, which, in turn, undermined whites' economic independence. Their solution was to oust the Chinese from the state and restore their own wages.

The free labor rhetoric of Portland's anti-Chinese leagues sprang from antebellum American cultural and political values. The cult of the self-made man, the promise of equal opportunity, and the hope for social mobility were all linchpins of nineteenth-century political culture. . . .

Anti-Chinese advocates resurrected this free-labor ideology to remind capitalists of the ideals of social mobility and equal opportunity for whites. They believed that Chinese labor threatened economic prosperity and degraded white workers to the level of a "serf system" not unlike slavery. Racism led these workers to conclude that the ideal of free labor could not extend to Chinese workers, whom they believed to be incapable of assimilation and, thus, incapable of participating in a republic.

What appeared to be a straightforward ideology that drew a line between free Euro-American workers and unfree Chinese laborers was complicated by the interests of women. Anti-Chinese activists used gender to strengthen their cause by drawing on domestic values and women's traditional role in Victorian America. For instance, agitators stressed that white workingmen were family men with starving wives and children, unlike Chinese bachelors who sent money home to China. The *Oregonian*'s editor noted that the Chinese were a "menace to free institutions, to home, and family." League activists used gender to underscore their fight between "liberty and slavery." On one side were symbols of Victorian domesticity, including "elevation, morality, social purity," and "benevolence," as well as a few American political principles thrown in for good measure: "freedom, progress, and law." On the other side, the Chinese wallowed in "serfdom, foulness, filth, roguery, vice, theft, murder, [and] remorseless cruelty."

These domestic values also influenced the protesters' vision of the future. Agitators envisaged a classless society in which laborers and employers worked together to ensure a living wage and dignified labor for all citizens. One rank-and-file member imagined a future in which "every hard working and honest working man has his own home, his little vegetable and flower garden, his little library of useful books, his healthy, well-clad, and well-fed wife and children, a home where there dwells sunshine and happiness upon every face. No patricians, no plebeians, but a well-to-do community of happy and contented citizens." Once wages were restored, Euro-American workers planned to mimic middle-class gender roles, preferring women to be wives and not workers.

Women used similar language and symbols to attack Chinese labor. Keenan, the "chosen angel of the working class," frequently spoke at encampment meetings on women's duty to assist in the Chinese question, stressing the dignity of work and the family. She told one audience that as a mother she had worked hard to raise her family and wanted her children to have a chance to make an honest living "by the sweat of their brow." Without jobs, she lamented, her children would have no future. She appealed to mothers to join the Knights of Labor, which would rescue all families and reform society. She also echoed her male counterparts in insisting on the law-abiding nature of the group, and declared before a large rally that they were not "mobs, mudsills, [or] cranks," but "hungry" lawful citizens. A few nights later, she implored her audience to remove the Chinese without bloodshed "in the interests of our children."

Her leadership in the anti-Chinese movement challenged the notion of separate spheres, or, at the least, represented a woman's active extension of the domestic into the public realm. In the spring of 1886 Keenan spoke at Portland's anti-Chinese rallies and also toured eastern Oregon, lecturing for the Knights of Labor. In addition, her anti-Chinese cohorts nominated her to sit on the permanent committee for boycotting businesses that violated the leagues' principles.

Despite the leagues' claims of lawfulness, Portland erupted in violence in mid-February 1886, when Euro-American men embarked on a campaign of terror. The trouble started when the Anti-Chinese Congress met at Portland's Turn Hall on George Washington's birthday, and called for the Chinese to leave Oregon. The congress instructed all delegates to return to their homes and to "peaceably assemble and politely request the said Mongolian race to remove from the state . . . within thirty days."

A week after the congress adjourned, rioters forced thirty-nine Chinese loom operators at the Oregon City Woolen Mill to leave town on a steamer. A few days later, thirty Euro-American men armed with revolvers charged 180 Chinese woodchoppers and grubbers who were camped below the Albina flour mill. The mob ordered them to leave and paid their ferry fares. The Albina ferry made three crossings to Portland that night, carrying the men with their belongings on their backs. The exiled Chinese sought lodging and safety in the city. The following Friday, at 3 o'clock in the morning, exclusionists drove some one hundred to two hundred Chinese out of Albina and East Portland. Once again, the expelled took shelter in Portland's Chinatown. Later that morning, fifty masked men forced "coolie" woodchoppers in Mt. Tabor to the Albina ferry. The following week the *Oregonian* reported "another Ku klux raid" on fifty Chinese ranchers and gardeners north of Guild's Lake. Thirty men with blackened faces committed robbery and arson, destroying the vegetable gardens and hog ranches of the Chinese, attacking them and ordering them to walk to town.

Abandoning their goal of class cooperation and boycott, the anti-coolie leagues continued to brutalize and threaten many Chinese laborers. Sporadic violence against the Chinese continued into the summer as the protests waned. This dwindling enthusiasm coincided with the successful election of a labor-endorsed gubernatorial candidate and the revival of trade unions in Portland. Significantly, women could neither vote nor join the unions. In only a few years, they had moved from active protest to an auxiliary role.

This rapid transition did not stop Keenan. By the end of the decade, she was again pursuing political reforms. In 1892 she served as a delegate to a convention of the newly organized farmer-labor third party, the Populist party. However, without the right to vote, there was little room for female participation, and her name fades from the newspapers after the party's ini-tial organization. What ties all of her reform interests together was a deep faith in women's rights. The Oregon State Women's Suffrage Association, the Knights of Labor, and the Populist party each affirmed the right of women to participate in the public realm, as well as a rough equality between the sexes.

Sue Ross Keenan and other anti-Chinese leaders created a protest ide-ology that included notions about free labor and gender. Implicit within their speeches was the idea of equal rights for both sexes: white men and women deserved a decent wage and the opportunity to become republican citizens. The free labor ideology of the agitators distinguished race before that of gender. The notion of "free labor" was not a static, universal ideology, but one that could be shaped to fit local circumstances and spe-cific social conflicts. On the West Coast, Euro-American workers perceived Chinese laborers as economic competitors, which led them to call for Chinese exclusion. The Chinese, they reasoned, lacked the qualities essen-tial for social advancement. "Coolie" workers were unfit for American citi-zenship—the very foundation of the free labor ideology—whereas white citizens could, with self-improvement and economic independence, become part of the producers' republic. This notion of equality was not based on egalitarianism and natural rights. Race significantly narrowed the move-ment's equal-rights philosophy.

More important than the free labor ideal, however, was the ambiguous legacy of separate spheres. The Oregon anti-Chinese movement brought working women and men together to organize, deliberate, protest, and boy-cott. Their goal was to force government action, to compel capitalists' sup-port, and to pressure the Chinese to leave (in some cases using terror and vigilantism). Men, the principal actors in the movement, used gender refer-ences and domestic ideals to support their class and racial interests. On the surface, their rhetoric and social vision idealized home and hearth: women would tend to the home and family, while men would work in the public realm. By contrast, working-class women like Keenan used these same ideals—family domesticity and womanhood—to step out of the private sphere and organize with men. If the ideal of separate spheres had ever held any salience for working women, by the late nineteenth century it had finally begun to disintegrate. In the process, Keenan and other women in the labor and farmer protest movements of the Gilded Age carved out public roles for themselves. The precarious equality of men and women in Oregon's anti-Chinese movement was enhanced by the apparent erosion of their separate spheres.

Y *FURTHER READING*

Leonard J. Arrington and Davis Bitton, *The Mormon Experience: A History of the Latter-Day Saints* (1979)
Robert Smith Bader, *Prohibition in Kansas: A History* (1986)

Gunther Barth, *Bitter Strength: A History of the Chinese in the United States, 1850–1870* (1964)

Anne M. Butler, *Daughters of Joy, Sisters of Misery: Prostitutes in the American West, 1865–90* (1985)

Sucheng Chan, et al., eds. *Peoples of Color in the American West* (1993)

Sucheng Chan, *This Bitter-Sweet Soil: The Chinese in California Agriculture, 1860–1910* (1986)

O. Gene Clanton, *Populism: The Humane Preference in America, 1890–1900* (1991)

Norman H. Clark, *The Dry Years: Prohibition and Social Change in Washington* (1965)

William Deverell and Tom Sitton, eds., *California Progressivism Revisited* (1994)

Michael L. Goldberg, "Non-Partisan and All-Partisan: Rethinking Woman Suffrage and Party Politics in Gilded Age Kansas," *Western Historical Quarterly* 25 (Spring 1994): 21–44

Lawrence Goodwyn, *Democratic Promise: The Populist Movement in America* (1976)

Lewis L. Gould, *Progressives and Prohibitionists: Texas Democrats in the Wilson Era* (1973)

James R. Green, *Grass Roots Socialism: Radical Movements in the Southwest, 1895–1943* (1978)

Carl Guarneri and David Alvarez, eds., *Religion and Society in the American West* (1987)

Lee Clark Mitchell, *Witness to a Vanishing America: The Nineteenth Century Response* (1981)

Ruth Barnes Moynihan, *Rebel for Rights: Abigail Scott Duniway* (1983)

Walter K. Nugent, *The Tolerant Populists: Kansas Populism and Nativism* (1963)

Gary Okihiro, *Cane Fires: The Anti-Japanese Movement in Hawaii, 1865–1945* (1992)

Peggy Pascoe, *Relations of Rescue: The Search for Female Moral Authority in the American West* (1990)

Ferenc Morton Szasz, *The Protestant Clergy in the Great Plains and Mountain West, 1865–1915* (1988)

James Whiteside, *Regulating Danger: The Struggle for Mine Safety in the Rocky Mountain Coal Industry* (1990)

Railroad and Mining Labor

Y

*How much opportunity and wealth did the West offer to newcomers, espe-
cially hard-working newcomers? Bonanzas in mining, cattle, timber, and
railroads provided some glamorous tales, but stories of a few wildly successful entrepreneurs did not account for the West's economic transformation.
Ordinary men and women who eked out a daily existence as workers—both
as paid and unpaid laborers—built the economy of the West, a key ingredient in the nation's industrial structure. For this reason, western labor history, even as it merged with the national development of capitalism, opened
a window onto the lives of common folk, revealing both the accomplishments
and the struggles in day-to-day western work.*

*Of greatest importance is the illumination of race, class, and gender as ele-
ments in our western labor heritage. In the western work place, men and
women of differing cultural backgrounds came together, both as colleagues and
as competitors. There they participated in some of the most volatile labor history in this country, as allies or opponents, they traversed the rocky path of
western labor organization. Their experiences show how various groups—
Chinese, Irish, German, Japanese, Italian, African American, Greek, Hispanic,
Turkish, Jewish, Bulgarian—cooperated or opposed each other. The values of
each culture sustained the workers and explain many of the choices they made.*

*An examination of ethnic western groups clarifies the gender and class
patterns of the larger society. The cultural dynamics of labor communities
help us to develop a sophisticated appreciation for many subtle aspects
within race, class, and gender. Which racial and cultural groups stood
together and why? Who rose to power from within an immigrant community? What part did women workers play in the bitter struggle between the
companies and the unions in the West? How did the unpaid domestic work
of women enhance the efforts of western wageworkers? Why were labor disagreements so violent in the West? A consideration of these questions can
lead to a richer understanding of how the industrial development of the West
took shape and what it meant in the lives of individuals.*

Y *D O C U M E N T S*

The six documents in this section consider both the engineering and human
aspects of western industrial growth. In the first two documents, Albert D.

Richardson, a western traveler, and William A. Bell, a railroad surveyor, capture the sights and sounds of building the transcontinental railroad in 1865 and 1866. Their accounts describe the tremendous physical accomplishments of the workers, but also vibrate with the excitement and anticipation the nation felt as the eastern and western branches of the line moved together. The completion of the transcontinental railroad unleashed a great flush of national pride and an industrial giant that shaped western labor history for the next several decades. Although Richardson and Bell gave a precise account of the physical feats involved, they also casually recorded the seething cultural biases that marked western labor sites. In the third document, "Excerpts from the Annals of the Daughters of Charity at Virginia City," anonymous Catholic sisters show themselves to be keen observers of the social and economic deprivations in a bonanza mining town. Such insights might not be expected from a group of religious women retiring to the seclusion of a small convent, but they too joined the western working class. They earned a living in the bonanza mining community by providing, across religious boundaries, the educational and social services not yet institutionalized through public agencies. In the next document, Frank A. Crampton, a hard-rock miner, expands on the sisters' comments, describing the brutal reality of labor confrontation at Ludlow, Colorado, in 1915. He leaves no doubt about the bitter division between the workers and the managers at the mines. Each of these documents is further enhanced by the passionate message of Elizabeth Gurley Flynn in her appeal to women, an outgrowth of the class division she saw in the Ludlow episode. Her editorial, which appeared in the Socialist newspaper *Solidarity,* demonstrates the importance of women, as employees and as non-workers, in the events surrounding the formation of a western labor force.

These writings reveal the strong sentiment among western laborers, both women and men, who worked under extreme conditions. Clearly, these workers perceived of themselves as part of a great economic adventure, one that had regional and national significance. What do these readings reveal about workers' personal hopes? How does each document represent the story of economic, especially industrial, growth? Is it a tale of glory or of pain? Does rhetoric aimed at a particular audience limit the historical value of individual documents?

Albert D. Richardson Writes on Building
the Great Railroad, 1865

Ex-governor Leland Stanford, president of the Central Pacific Railroad, and the other gentlemen engaged in building it, were kind enough to organize a pleasant excursion that I might see the progress of their great work. By the Congressional charters, this company constructing the line from Sacramento California eastward, and the Union Pacific working from Omaha Nebraska westward, will each own and run as much road as it can build; so both are engaged in a hard race for Salt Lake.

Each corporation receives in Government bonds sixteen thousand dollars, thirty-two thousand dollars, or forty-eight thousand dollars for every mile of road finished—sixteen thousand where the route is level and grad-

Albert D. Richardson, *Beyond the Mississippi: From the Great River to the Great Ocean* (Hartford, CT: American Publishing, 1867), 401, 462, 566–69.

ing light; thirty-two thousand among the foot-hills, and forty-eight thousand in the Rocky Mountains and the Sierra Nevadas.

Each company also acquires absolutely thirteen thousand acres of land per mile along its line; and is allowed to issue first mortgage bonds in equal amount to the Government subsidy—the mortgage upon which these company-bonds are based having priority as a lien upon the property of the road over the mortgage given to the Government itself. In addition, the California corporation has a donation of nearly half a million dollars in bonds from San Francisco, and thirty acres of valuable land, in the city limits, from Sacramento. No other enterprise in our country was ever so magnificently endowed. . . .

Ten miles east of Sacramento the track is only one hundred and ninety feet above sea-level; at the crossing of the summit it is seven thousand feet. A peculiarly favorable route, where no elevation is lost after the climbing begins, alone enables it to rise nearly seven thousand feet in ninety-five miles. . . .

At the time of my visit the terminus was Colfax, fifty-five miles east of Sacramento. Thence, we took horses for twelve miles. Upon this little section of road four thousand laborers were at work—one-tenth Irish, the rest Chinese. They were a great army laying siege to Nature in her strongest citadel. The rugged mountains looked like stupendous ant-hills. They swarmed with Celestials, shoveling, wheeling, carting, drilling and blasting rocks and earth, while their dull, moony eyes stared out from under immense basket-hats, like umbrellas. At several dining-camps we saw hundreds sitting on the ground, eating soft boiled rice with chop-sticks as fast as terrestrials could with soup-ladles. Irish laborers received thirty dollars per month (gold) and board; Chinese, thirty-one dollars, boarding themselves. After a little experience the latter were quite as efficient and far less troublesome.

. . . Without the Chinese the California end of the great national thoroughfare must have been delayed for many years. Twelve thousand are now employed upon it. . . .

A hundred miles out, we passed Columbus, on the prairies. It promises to be a future railway focus. Mr. Train and his associates believe that it will be a great city, capital of Nebraska, and perhaps of the United States. Stranger things *have* happened. . . .

A few buffaloes had been killed here lately; and now we saw hundreds of antelopes from our train. . . . While in motion we aimed hundreds of rifle-shots at them from the car windows. A single one, from General Merrill, took effect, and sent its beautiful victim limping into the sand-hills.

At the end of the track, on the smooth, well-built road, we found long sleeping and eating-cars for the workmen, who press forward so fast that only portable dwellings will serve them. All supplies come from the east. The sleepers are brought down the Missouri, from Iowa forests. About half are soft cottonwood; but Burnetizing (infusing the zinc) is said to render them as durable as oak. Many of the timbers for bridges are of black walnut, often sixteen inches square. There are but two long bridges east of the Rocky Mountains—one of fifteen hundred feet across Loupe Fork; another of half-a-mile over the North Platte.

The charter permits only American iron. The rails are from Pennsylvania and New York. We found the workmen, with the regularity of machinery, dropping each rail in its place, spiking it down, and then seizing another. Behind them, the locomotive; before, the tie-layers; beyond these the graders; and still further, in mountain recesses, the engineers. It was Civilization pressing westward—the Conquest of Nature moving toward the Pacific. . . .

When the range is reached, rolling mills will be erected for making rails, iron dug from the hills, and ties cut from the forests. Though the highest summit-crossing contemplated is more than eight thousand feet above sea-level, it is believed that no heavier grade than eighty feet to the mile will be required.

The company design building a branch to Denver. . . . The chief Kansas fork, from Wyandotte up the Kaw and Smoky Hill, will join the main stem near Denver. It will probably make that connection about as soon as the California and Nebraska companies unite at Salt Lake. Of the two smaller Kansas forks the northern, from St. Joseph westward, will unite with the Platte valley line; and the southern, from Atchison, with the Smoky Hill. The Wyandotte and Atchison forks receive the same Congressional endowment as the Nebraska Union Pacific and the California Central Pacific— twelve hundred and eighty acres of land and sixteen thousand dollars in Government bonds for each mile completed. Passing no hilly regions, they do not obtain the higher subsidies.

The uniform width established upon the trunk line and all its branches is four feet eight and-a-half inches. That corresponds with most eastern roads, and will give an unbroken gauge from San Francisco to New York, via Omaha and Chicago.

. . . The summer of 1867 opens with twenty-five thousand men employed on the main stem of the Pacific Railway; *and the California and Nebraska companies expect their locomotives to meet in the vicinity of Salt Lake early in* 1870. Speed the day!

William A. Bell Describes the Engineering of the Railroad, 1867

The inland or Great Basin region of North America extends from the dividing ridge of the Wahsatch Mountains to the summit of the Sierra Nevada, 721 miles by the railroad. . . .

The road has been built, not by a staff formed of scientific engineers— they might have shrunk from so reckless a venture—but by a few go-ahead merchants of San Francisco, who left their counting-houses to become railway contractors. All last summer ten thousand Chinamen and about three thousand teams, were employed to grade and lay the track across the basin region. During the previous winter I saw them transporting long lines of

William A. Bell, *New Tracks in North America* (Albuquerque, NM: Horn and Wallace, Publishers, 1965), 487–91.

sledges, laden with iron rails and ties, across the summit to the valley of the Truckee and the Humboldt. When the snow had sufficiently thawed to enable them to complete the tunnels, an average of 500 tons of ties, rails, spikes, bolts, and chairs were carried over the Sierra, in fifty cars drawn by ten locomotives every day, and were sent from 300 to 400 miles to the scene of operations. Here two miles, and sometimes more, were laid per day, and each two miles required 500 tons of material for its construction. The rails usually weigh from 56 lbs. to 64 lbs. per yard. . . .

It is hard, after so much has been done, to be obliged to pronounce this summit railway a mistake. Yet there is no question about it. Had the Sierra Nevada been more thoroughly examined before this gigantic enterprise was undertaken, Beckworth's Pass—thirty miles to the north, and only 4,500 feet in height—would most certainly have been adopted. . . .

During 1868, 866 miles were added to the railway by the united companies; being an average of two miles and two-thirds a day, Sundays excluded, and the remaining 346 miles were completed in 107 days more. In the history of railway construction this rapidity has no precedent; and when it is remembered that for 1,600 miles wood for ties could only be obtained at three points accessible to the road, and also that the country is mostly an uninhabited desert, the result appears even yet more marvellous. The following quotation explains, in true American style, how the track is laid:—

"One can see all along the line of the now completed road the evidences of ingenious self-protection and defence which our men learned during the war. . . . The whole organisation of the force engaged in the construction of the road is, in fact, semi-military. The men who go ahead, locating the road, are the advance guard. Following these is the second line, cutting through the gorges, grading the road, and building bridges. Then comes the main line of the army, placing the sleepers, laying the track, spiking down the rails, perfecting the alignment, ballasting the rail, and dressing up and completing the road for immediate use. . . . Along the line of the completed road are construction trains constantly 'pushing forward to the front' with supplies. . . . The advanced limit of the rail is occupied by a train of long box cars, with hammocks swung under them, beds spread on top of them, bunks built within them, in which the sturdy, broad-shouldered pioneers of the great iron highway sleep at night and take their meals. Close behind this train come loads of ties and rails and spikes, &c., which are being thundered off upon the roadside, to be ready for the track-layers. The road is graded a hundred miles in advance. The ties are laid roughly in place, then adjusted, gauged, and levelled. Then the track is laid. . . .

"A light car, drawn by a single horse, gallops up to the front with its load of rails. Two men seize the end of a rail and start forward, the rest of the gang taking hold by twos until it is clear of the car. They come forward at a run. At the word of command the rail is dropped in its place, right side up, with care, while the same process goes on at the other side of the car. Less than thirty seconds to a rail for each gang, and so four rails go down to the minute! . . . The moment the car is empty it is tipped over on the side of the track to let the next loaded car pass it, and then it is tipped back again; and it is a sight to see it go flying back for another load, propelled by a horse at full gallop at the end of 60 or 80 feet of rope, ridden by a young Jehu, who drives furiously. Close behind the first gang come the gaugers, spikers, and bolters, and a lively time they make of it. It is a grand Anvil Chorus that those sturdy sledges are playing across the plains. It is in triple time, three strokes to a spike. There are ten spikes to a rail, four hundred rails to a mile, eighteen hundred miles to San Francisco. . . . Twenty-one million times are those sledges to be swung—twenty-one million times are they to come down with their sharp punctuation, before the great work of modern America is complete!"

Daughters of Charity Comment on Life in Virginia City, Nevada, c. 1875

Virginia City is built on the side of Mt. Davidson and in the Valley. The Gold Mines run under it. You will find shafts sunk in all parts of it—as they excavate the mountains, they arch it with plank, in order to prevent the houses from falling in, as they sometimes unfortunately do. We know of one instance, a grocery store supposed to be on a good foundation, the earth gave way and . . . swallowed the house. Fires also occur in those shafts or vacuums from powder they use for blasting rock, and lamps they are obliged to use, coming in contact. In some cases these unfortunate men cannot escape from this gulf of fire, and before water is made to reach them, they are consumed. Sometimes embankments fall in upon them: their lamentable cries are heartrending—no one can reach them. . . . Being a mining district, it is composed of all classes of people. The poor miners, who live in the bowels of the earth frequently suffer from ill health, and sometimes encounter serious accidents . . . never fail to be consoled by the care and sympathy of the Daughters of Charity, who carry to their poor "Shanties," little delicacies, and words of consolation, which are so valued by these Men of Faith. . . . At the time of our arrival it claimed a population of some fifteen thousand, and all day long, half or nearly half swarmed the streets, whilst the remainder was down among the drifts and tunnels of the "Comstock," hundreds of feet down, and often have we heard the faint boom of a blast down in the bowels of the earth. The mountain side is so steep that the entire City has a slant to it like a roof. Each street is a terrace, and from each to the next street below the descent is twenty or thirty feet. The fronts of the houses are level with the street they face, but their rear first floors are mainly propped up on lofty stilts. It was a laborious climb . . . one was panting and out of breath when they reached there—however, we generally got down a *little faster,* particularly if there happened to be what *we call* a "Washoe Zephyr" on the rampart (this is not *slang* for the Virginians—Eastern folks had better not attempt it!). . . . During the Christmas holydays . . . we had another Fair. . . . The result was most gratifying. But the time that saw such success, also

Excerpts from *Annals of Daughters of Charity*. From the Community Archives of the Daughters of Charity, Province of the West, Seton Provincialate, Los Altas Hills, CA. Reprinted by permission.

witnessed death in some . . . unfortunate household, and appeals were constant at our doors, some asking the kindness lost when a parent dies, others to receive care they never knew before, because of their poverty and distress. Limiting all to absolute necessities, we made place for them, but more room and more money than we had was needed. . . . A breakfast would cost three dollars, and if the traveller required more than was served at the table, he would pay one dollar each for every egg he got, and other things in proportion. . . . In May of 1870, Virginia City was visited by a disastrous conflagration at eleven o'clock a Planing Mill took fire and as the wind was very high; the flames devoured vast buildings. Despite the efforts of the fire companies which were finely organized, the fire could not be brought under control. For the space of an hour many imagined from the sound of the explosions that the entire City would be destroyed. . . .

Chinese Accounts of the Killings at Rock Springs, 1885

CHINESE CONSULATE-GENERAL,
San Francisco, Cal., October 5, 1885.

Sir: I have the honor to state that in compliance with your excellency's instructions, I proceeded with Col. F. A. Bee, Chinese counsul at San Francisco, and Mr. Tseng Hoy, interpreter, to Rock Springs, where we arrived on the 18th September, 1885, for the purpose of investigating the present condition of our countrymen in the latter place, and of ascertaining the facts connected with the recent riot that took place there against them.

As soon as we reached Rock Springs we ordered the remains of those Chinese killed in the riot to be disinterred and examined. We had fourteen coffins dug up, on opening which we found some bodies entire, some parts of bodies, the bones of separate bodies, and promiscuous heaps of bones; and we also dug up the remains of one without a coffin. Inquiring of the coroner at Rock Springs, he stated that since the 3d of September he had examined and interred nineteen persons, and I found that the Union Pacific Railroad Company had interred the remains of two. Besides five entire bodies, the remains of eight others were recognizable, while the bones of eight others were found wrapped up in separate bundles. We had, therefore, exhumed in all the remains of twenty one persons. . . .

Omitting those whose wounds have healed since the riot, I find that there are fifteen Chinese more or less severely wounded, several of whom, it is feared, will die, and several be disabled for life. . . .

With reference to the property destroyed by the mob, I find that every one of the surviving Chinese has been rendered penniless by the cruel attack. There are three reasons why the Chinese so completely lost their property: 1st, most of them when fleeing had no time to gather up their money, and those that did carry money with them were forcibly deprived of it by the

Providing Indemnity to Certain Chinese Subjects, 49th Congress, 1st Session, House of Representatives, 1886, pp. 26, 28–29.

mob; 2d, what they left in their houses was either plundered or burnt; 3d, the huts which they built for themselves were completely destroyed.

Since the riot took place it has been impossible for them to secure even a torn sheet or any article of clothing to protect them from the cold, or even the crumbs from the table to satisfy their hunger, or even a plank or mat to rest their bodies on. These poor creatures, numbering hundreds, are all hungry and clothed in rags. They look worn out and frightened, and most of them forlorn and absent-minded. Words fail to give an idea of their sufferings, and their appearance is a sad one to human eyes to witness.

Upon making inquiries as to the past, I found that the Chinese so savagely and unmercifully deprived of their property had been in Rock Springs, some for over ten years, others for a shorter time, for the purpose of working in mines or on railroads. Some of the Chinese locating at Rock Springs were afterwards joined by their fathers, brothers, or other relations, all settling themselves there as colonists, while others came with their goods for the purpose of peddling or trading. In the course of time they had built for themselves more than seventy huts, and the Union Pacific Railroad Company had also built more than thirty camp houses for its employés, thus forming quite a town. This town is now nothing but a mass of ruins.

The total value of the property lost belonging to over seven hundred persons is only about $147,000, this being an average of only a little more than $200 for each. I have concluded that no one has made any fraudulent claim.

. . . I beg to inclose for your consideration . . . a copy of the memorial addressed to me while at Rock Springs by five hundred and fifty-nine Chinese.

I am, your obedient servant,

HUANG SIH CHUEN,
Chinese Consul at New York.

ROCK SPRINGS, WYO., *September 18, 1885.*

HON. HUANG SIH CHUEN,
Chinese Consul:

YOUR HONOR: We, the undersigned, have been in Rock Springs, Wyoming Territory, for periods ranging from one to fifteen years, for the purpose of working on the railroads and in the coal mines.

Up to the time of the recent troubles we had worked along with the white men, and had not had the least ill-feeling against them. The officers of the companies employing us treated us and the white men kindly, placing both races on the same footing and paying the same wages.

Several times we had been approached by the white men and requested to join them in asking the companies for an increase in the wages of all, both Chinese and white men. We inquired of them what we should do if the companies refused to grant an increase. They answered that if the companies would not increase our wages we should all strike, then the companies would be obliged to increase our wages. To this we dissented, wherefore we excited their animosity against us.

During the past two years there has been in existence in "Whitemen's Town," Rock Springs, an organization composed of white miners, whose object was to bring about the expulsion of all Chinese from the Territory. To them or to their object we have paid no attention. About the month of August of this year notices were posted up, all the way from Evanston to Rock Springs, demanding the expulsion of the Chinese, &c. On the evening of September 1, 1885, the bell of the building in which said organization meets rang for a meeting. It was rumored on that night that threats had been made against the Chinese.

On the morning of September 2, a little past 7 o'clock, more than ten white men, some in ordinary dress and others in mining suits, ran into Coal-pit No. 6, loudly declaring that the Chinese should not be permitted to work there. The Chinese present reasoned with them in a few words, but were attacked with murderous weapons, and three of their number wounded. The white foreman of the coal-pit, hearing of the disturbance, ordered all to stop work for the time being.

After the work had stopped, all the white men in and near Coal-pit No. 6 began to assemble by the dozen. They carried fire-arms, and marched to Rock Springs by way of the railroad from Coal-pit No. 6, and crossing the railroad bridge, went directly to "Whitemen's Town." All this took place before 10 o'clock a. m. We now heard the bell ringing for a meeting at the white men's organization building. Not long after all the white men came out of that building, most of them assembling in the bar-rooms, the crowds meanwhile growing larger and larger.

About 2 o'clock in the afternoon a mob, divided into two gangs, came toward "Chinatown," one gang coming by way of the plank bridge, and the other by way of the railroad bridge. The gang coming by way of the railroad bridge was the larger, and was subdivided into many squads, some of which did not cross the bridge, but remained standing on the side opposite to "Chinatown;" others that had already crossed the bridge stood on the right and left at the end of it. Several squads marched up the hill behind Coal-pit No. 3. One squad remained at Coal-shed No. 3, and another at the pump-house. The squad that remained at the pump-house fired the first shot, and the squad that stood at Coal-shed No. 3 immediately followed their example and fired. The Chinese by name of Lor Sun Kit was the first person shot, and fell to the ground. At that time the Chinese began to realize that the mob were bent on killing. The Chinese, though greatly alarmed, did not yet begin to flee.

Soon after, the mob on the hill behind Coal-pit No. 3 came down from the hill, and joining the different squads of the mob, fired their weapons and pressed on to Chinatown.

The gang that were at the plank bridge also divided into several squads, pressing near and surrounding "Chinatown." One squad of them guarded the plank bridge in order to cut off the retreat of the Chinese.

Not long after it was everywhere reported that a Chinese named Leo Dye Bah, who lived in the western part of "Chinatown," was killed by a bullet, and that another named Yip Ah Marn, resident in the eastern end of the town, was likewise killed. The Chinese now, to save their lives, fled in confusion in every direction, some going up the hill behind Coal-pit No. 3, others along the foot of the hill where Coal-pit No. 4 is; some from the eastern end of the town fled across Bitter Creek to the opposite hill, and others from the western end by the foot of the hill on the right of Coal-pit No. 5. The mob were now coming in the three directions, namely, the east and west sides of the town and from the wagon road.

Whenever the mob met a Chinese they stopped him, and pointing a weapon at him, asked him if he had any revolver, and then approaching him they searched his person, robbing him of his watch or any gold or silver that he might have about him, before letting him go. Some of the rioters would let a Chinese go after depriving him of all his gold and silver, while another Chinese would be beaten with the butt ends of the weapons before being let go. Some of the rioters, when they could not stop a Chinese, would shoot him dead on the spot, and then search and rob him. Some would overtake a Chinese, throw him down and search and rob him before they would let him go. Some of the rioters would not fire their weapons, but would only use the butt ends to beat the Chinese with. Some would not beat a Chinese, but rob him of whatever he had and let him go, yelling to him to go quickly. Some, who took no part either in beating or robbing the Chinese, stood by, shouting loudly and laughing and clapping their hands.

There was a gang of women that stood at the "Chinatown" end of the plank bridge and cheered; among the women, two of them each fired successive shots at the Chinese. This was done about a little past 3 o'clock p. m. . . .

Some of the rioters went off toward the railroad of Coal-pit No. 6, others set fire to the Chinese houses. Between 4 o'clock and a little past 9 o'clock p. m. all the camp houses belonging to the coal company and the Chinese huts had been burned down completely, only one of the company's camp houses remaining. Several of the camp houses near Coal-pit No. 6 were also burned, and the three Chinese huts there were also burned. All the Chinese houses burned numbered seventy-nine.

Some of the Chinese were killed at the bank of Bitter Creek, some near the railroad bridge, and some in "Chinatown." After having been killed, the dead bodies of some were carried to the burning buildings and thrown into the flames. Some of the Chinese who had hid themselves in the houses were killed and their bodies burned; some, who on account of sickness could not run, were burned alive in the houses. One Chinese was killed in "Whitemen's Town" in a laundry house, and his house demolished. The whole number of Chinese killed was twenty-eight and those wounded fifteen.

Frank A. Crampton on the Ludlow Massacre, 1914

The coal mining industry of Colorado was dominated by the Colorado Fuel and Iron Company, the C. F. and I., a Rockefeller controlled outfit, whose officials from pit bosses to the top had little or no sympathy and little con-

Frank A. Crampton, *Deep Enough: A Working Stiff in the Western Mine Camps* (University of Oklahoma Press, 1982), 204–208. Copyright © 1982 by Frank A. Crampton. Excerpted by permission of the University of Oklahoma Press.

sideration for working stiffs. What the stiffs were paid didn't give them a chance; living and working conditions were a disgrace to the operating companies, which worked the mines on the theory that "men are cheaper than timber."

Many of the stiffs on strike were bohunks, imported by the companies employing them or furnished, at a fee, by professional importers of cheap labor. Once on a job, the bohunks had little choice other than to remain and accept whatever wage was offered, and to work under mining conditions that were a threat to their life every time they went underground.

The companies not only paid whatever they pleased, but also rented shacks to the stiffs, or put them in bunkhouses unfit for human habitation. The stiffs were obliged to trade at company stores where they were charged unreasonably high prices because there were no other stores in competition with the company-owned outfits where credit was freely given and the bill deducted from the stiff's time. Whenever a stiff complained, he was more often than not given his time, removed from his quarters, and denied the "privilege" of making purchases at the company store. The threat of deportation was ever present.

Not a few times conditions became so intolerable that a strike was called, with little or no success. The stiffs, who had no money when they went out, could not last very long and usually capitulated with gains that meant nothing. The strikes in the Walsenburg to Trinidad coal camps were a result of grievances against conditions that could no longer be tolerated. Feeling ran so high against the companies that Shattucky and I knew that the job we had come to do was an almost impossible one.

Not only were the working stiffs fighting against the coal companies, but also against officials of Colorado, who from the lowest constable on up to the governor's office, were, almost to a man, against the strikers and on the side of the coal mining companies. Particularly were they partial to the C. F. and I.

Shattucky and I found the Colorado National Guard keeping "order," not impartial order, but the kind of order the mine operators and the C. F. and I. demanded, at every mine or town we visited from Walsenburg to Trinidad. Unrest was at its worst around Ludlow, where the strikers had established a tent colony for themselves and their families.

At Ludlow, where Shattucky and I spent most of our time, Captain Carson commanded Cavalry Troop A, and Lieutenant Linderfelt Infantry Company B, although Major Hamrock should have been in command of B Company. Food among the strikers was scarce, and when shipments sent in by the miners' unions arrived by rail, Troop A and Company B, which were camped near the depot, would confiscate them on the pretext that arms and ammunition were concealed in the food cases.

During January, February and March, Horace Hawkins, attorney for the United Mine Workers, E. L. Doyle, a district secretary, Louis Tikis, and a score of others did a real job in smoothing things out. It appeared that, if the National Guard were withdrawn, a peaceful settlement might be made. A short-lived peace came when Governor Ammons recalled the National Guard and left the mine operators and the C. F. and I. to do as they pleased.

Company B under Lieutenant Linderfelt was left in Ludlow with thirty to forty "guardsmen," mostly mine guards, strikebreakers, and lesser company officials. After the National Guard pulled out, the operators of almost every coal mining town recruited companies of "militia," which were designated as "National Guard." The musters of the militia companies read as if they were payrolls of the mine operators. To the disgrace of the State of Colorado the militia companies were armed and equipped by the State, but paid by the operators, and the C. F. I., as later investigation proved.

Conditions became intolerable, and when rumors spread that the Ludlow tent colony was to be wiped out, resentment reached fever pitch. How true the rumors were was not known, but there was a precedent that the strikers had to guide them—that of the Forbes tent colony. On Sunday, April 19th, Shattucky, Louis Tikis, and others of the more level-headed, and I did all we could to ease the tension and to convince the strikers that the rumors were false. Quiet had been restored and everything was under control by late Sunday evening.

Tikis, Shattucky, and I went to see Linderfelt. We told him that if the C. F. and I. militia would cease their activities, we could guarantee that the strikers would cause no trouble. Linderfelt told us to go to hell, that he was in command and would be a judge of how to handle the strikers. Tikis, a cool-headed, intelligent man pleaded with Linderfelt to no avail. When we returned to our quarters, we were convinced that Linderfelt would do nothing to prevent serious trouble.

We were not mistaken. Early in the morning of the 20th, Company B, under command of Linderfelt, occupied the hill overlooking the tent colony. The hill gave the militia command not only of the colony but also of the surrounding hills and roads that led to it. A machine gun was in view on a rise on the hill, and the C. F. and I. militia stood with rifles ready and appeared to be awaiting orders to attack. The strikers hastily armed themselves as best they could with the few defensive weapons at their disposal and waited.

Shattucky, Tikis, and I, with a score of others did our best to control the strikers. The strikers did not want trouble, but were preparing to meet it. There might have been none had not Linderfelt's men let go with a couple of bombs, followed immediately by machine-gun and rifle fire.

Company B did not concentrate its fire on the strikers, most of whom had left the tents and had taken positions in the creek beds and on nearby hills, but poured rifle and machine gun fire into the strikers' tent colony where there were defenseless women and children.

The fighting lasted from morning until after dark, and during that time the militia swarmed into the colony, looted it of everything the men could lay their hands on, and attacked the women and children. The reign of terror finally ended when the militiamen poured coal oil on the tents and burned the strikers' shelters to the ground.

Shattucky and I got away, but Tikis and two others were captured, disarmed, and stripped of everything but outer garments and taken to Lieutenant Linderfelt's headquarters. We did not know it at the time, but it was disclosed in investigations that were made later, that Linderfelt, in a rage, brought a rifle butt down on Tikis' head, breaking the rifle stock and killing Tikis. Not to be denied their fun, his aids completed the job by killing the two other captives and putting bullets into the already dead Tikis.

Shattucky and I helped the strikers dig seven children and three women from the wreckage of their burned tent house homes. There were in all twenty-one killed in the massacre, and before order was restored thirty strikers were known to have died by militia gunfire. One militiaman was killed. While we were occupied in recovering the bodies, Lieutenant Linderfelt and some of his militiamen came to where we were working and took us prisoners. With others who had been with us, we were searched and everything on us taken away; money and personal effects were confiscated with whatever else was found. After the search and seizure, we were escorted out of town and told that if we returned we would be dealt with.

Every miner, coal and hard-rock, in Colorado was in arms and a statewide uprising was threatened with thousands volunteering to go to the aid of the strikers and their families. It was a situation that the C. F. and I. and the State of Colorado had not anticipated and could not control. Governor Ammons panicked and called on President Wilson for federal troops to put down the "insurrection" against the State of Colorado.

Before the federal troops arrived, the strikers took control of every coal mine between Ludlow and Trinidad and burned the buildings around them. Meanwhile, Governor Ammons called out the legitimate National Guard on April 23rd, and General Chase, who commanded it, occupied the mining areas between Walsenburg and Ludlow. The strikers were in such force south of Ludlow that the National Guard did not go farther than there; to have done so might have precipitated trouble more serious than that which had already occurred.

To make the situation more difficult, many guardsmen were hard-rock miners, and not a few were from the northern coal mines. They knew what the strike was about and what had happened when illegitimate militia were organized by the mine operators, supported by the State of Colorado, and erroneously called "National Guard." To complicate the difficulties, General Chase had made agreements with the strikers through Hawkins and Doyle, and then had violated them. The strikers no longer had confidence in the officials of Colorado, nor in the officers of the National Guard. Had the Federal troops not arrived when they did, more serious trouble would have developed.

Shattucky and I were in Trinidad when the Federal troops took over the whole area. Since there was nothing more that we could do to help improve the situation, we returned to Denver. I left Shattucky in Hawkins' office with Doyle and other labor leaders. I never saw him again. I went to Golden to get the stink of things I had seen out of my system and to forget: the stink departed, but the memory has not.

Elizabeth Gurley Flynn Calls
Women to Labor Action, 1915

In the tremendous process of merging all groups of labor into a unified whole; of infusing their humblest daily struggle with the urge of a great ideal—industrial freedom—women are as vitally concerned as men. But the I. W. W., the instrument through which "the world for the workers" is taking concrete form, makes no special appeal to women as such. To us society moves in grooves of class, not sex. Sex distinctions affect us insignificantly and would less, but for economic differences. It is to those women who are wage earners, or wives of workers, that the I. W. W. appeals. We see no basis in fact for feminist mutual interest, no evidence of natural "sex conflict," nor any possibility—nor present desirability—of solidarity among women alone. The success of our program will benefit workers, regardless of sex, and injure all who, without effort, draw profits for a livelihood.

I have seen prosperous, polite, daintily-gowned ladies become indignant over police brutality in the Spokane free speech fight of 1909, and lose all interest—even refuse to put up bail for pregnant women—when they realized that the I. W. W. intended to organize the lumber, mining and farming industries, whence the golden stream flowed to pay for their comfort and leisure.

Yet more horrible a glimpse into the chasm that divides woman and woman is afforded by the blood-thirsty approval of the Ludlow massacre by the "good women" of Trinidad, Colo. Mrs. Northcutt, wife of the lawyer said: "There has been a lot of maudlin sentiment about those women and children. There were only two women and they make such a fuss!" Mrs. Rose, wife of the superintendent of the coal railroad, said: "They're nothing but cattle! They ought to be shot!" Mrs. Chandler, wife of the Presbyterian minister, said: "The miners probably killed the women and children themselves, because they were a drain on the union!" and, "They ought to have shot Tikas to start with!" This of the Greek leader who had over thirty bullets in his body and his head laid open with the butt of a gun. The solution of labor troubles agreed upon by a dozen representative women was, "Shoot them down."

The "queen in the parlor" has no interest in common with "the maid in the kitchen"; the wife of the department store owner shows no sisterly concern for the seventeen-year-old girl who finds prostitution the only door to a $5 a week clerk. The sisterhood of women, like the brotherhood of man, is a hollow sham to labor. Behind all its smug hypocrisy and sickly sentimentality loom the sinister outlines of the class war.

. . . Women have been engaged in useful human toil since the dawn of time. True enough, much that once was "woman's work"—spinning, weaving, churning, etc.—has been absorbed by the factory system. The old divi-

Solidarity, July 31, 1915.

sion—men doing the outdoor and women the indoor tasks—ended with the advent of the power-operated machinery. But woman was not left idle-handed. Rather it was now possible and inevitable that she should follow her work and take her place with man, at the factory gate; 21 per cent of the total employes in the U.S. are women. . . . In Lawrence, Mass., mothers are toiling for $3 a week; department stores in New York city pay from $2.50 to $7; box, paper, handkerchief, garment factories pay as low as $8. Whatever superficial semblance of sex hatred appears, is due, like "race hatred," to the struggle for the pay envelope. The woman worker is no freer from "masculine domination," even though self-supporting, while mercilessly exploited by an employer; and the fundamental unity of interest between her and her brother is to organize as a class. . . .

The I. W. W. appeal to woman to organize side by side with their men folks, in the union that shall increasingly determine its own rules of work and wages—until its solidarity and power shall the world command. . . .

Where a secluded home environment has produced a psychological attitude of "me and mine"—how is the I. W. W. to overcome conservatism and selfishness? By driving women into an active participation in union affairs, especially strikes, where the mass meetings, mass picketing, women's meetings and children's gatherings are a tremendous emotional stimulant. The old unions never have considered the women as a part of the strike. . . .

Women can be the most militant or most conservative element in a strike, in proportion to their comprehension of its purpose. The I. W. W. has been accused of putting the women in the front. The truth is, the I. W. W. does not keep them in the back, and they go to the front. . . . The miners' union have followed the example of the I. W. W. and in Calumet and Colorado, women played as gallant a part as men. The spirit becomes infection when solidarity is a reality, and sex vies with sex, nationality with nationality—in courage and devotion.

A familiar query is, "What effect would the democratization of industry have on the family?" The I. W. W. is at war with the ruthless invasion of family life by capitalism, with the unnatural and shameful condition of a half million able-bodied unemployed men in New York City alone, last winter, yet there are 27,000 children under 16 years of age in cotton mills in the South. We are determined that industry shall be so organized that all adults, men and women, may work and receive in return a sufficiency to make child labor a relic of barbarism. This does not imply that mothers must work, or that women must stay at home, if they prefer otherwise. Either extreme is equally absurd. House work will probably be reduced to a minimum through the application of machinery, now more costly than the labor of women—but the care of children will remain an absorbing interest with the vast majority of women. The free choice of work is the I. W. W. ideal—which does not mean to put women forcibly back into the home, but certainly does mean to end capitalism's forcibly taking her out of the home. . . .

To the cynic the I. W. W. are "dreamers of idle dreams," to the beneficiaries of plunder, "a menace to society"—to those who cannot see beyond the barbarities of the past "chaos and disorder"—but to the women, who

have lived, struggled, suffered, triumphed with the I. W. W. for ten years—
it is the mighty arm of labor, cleaving a path to peace and freedom.

Y *E S S A Y S*

In the first essay, W. Thomas White, curator of the James Jerome Hill
Reference Library, an important center for railroad history, writes about the
complex patterns of labor relations in the Great Northwest. He not only chroni-
cles the competition between and among ethnic groups, female workers, and
native-born white laborers, but documents the role of railroad management in
promoting labor conflicts as a method for defeating union organization.
Gunther Peck, a member of the history department at the University of Texas,
Austin, in a prize-winning essay, further develops issues of cooperation and
hostility between diverse mine workers in Utah. His analysis demonstrates the
importance of understanding the inner workings of an immigrant community, if
we are to grasp the larger picture of western labor relations. Together the two
essays speak to whether regions within the West, although hosting different
industries, paralleled each other in the conduct of labor relations.

Race, Ethnicity, and Gender in the Northwest Railroad Work Force, 1893–1912

W. THOMAS WHITE

"A new destiny is upon us," the *Portland Oregonian* pronounced on
September 9, 1883, celebrating the completion of the Northern Pacific's
line to the Northwest Coast. . . . In the Far Northwest (Washington, Oregon,
Idaho, and Montana), as elsewhere, the railroads' arrival heralded a new era
of settlement and communication, at the same time profoundly influencing
the economic and cultural development that derived from the fast-growing
American-built environment in the region. With the burgeoning mines, the
railroads were the harbingers of large-scale corporate enterprise and all that
that implied in the Far Northwest.

Less appreciated is the significance of the roads' impact on labor relations in the Far West. With the railroads came a new, industrial work force,
possessed of a heritage of earlier conflicts with managers in the East. Their
experience, too, served as a model for other industries on the wageworkers'
frontiers. This case study will focus upon one segment of the new work
force—the unskilled laborers who performed the roads' maintenance-of-
way and construction work. Their experience contrasted sharply with that of

W. Thomas White, "Race, Ethnicity, and Gender in the Railroad Work Force: The Case of the Far
Northwest, 1883–1918," *Western Historical Quarterly*, 16 (July 1985), 265–83. Copyright by Western
History Association. Reprinted by permission.

skilled workers in the industry but was typical of that of many in the vast trans-Mississippi migrant labor pool that formed an indispensable part of the West's developing economy before the First World War.

The thousands of migrant laborers who built and maintained the roads received the least pay and endured the worst conditions in the industry. . . . Usually recruited by large labor contractors, workers often had to travel long distances to receive an average $1.75–$2.25 per day (Japanese and southern and eastern Europeans received less), out of which they paid $5.50–$7.00 per week for board, hospital fees, transportation, and a miscellany of other charges. Sanitary and housing conditions were "detestable" and the general treatment of workers "reprehensible." . . . For the laborers confronted by the grim realities of low pay, isolation, poor housing, and the other unfortunate aspects of unskilled, casual railroad work, those conditions formed an unhappy milieu that alternately spawned militant protests and later demoralized workers and hindered their success in those protest movements.

Like unskilled laborers everywhere, railway workers were divided sharply by race, ethnicity, and gender. Consequently, they were nearly powerless to overcome the many obstacles confronting them and realize any form of meaningful redress for their substantial problems. Only in the anti-Chinese campaigns of the mid-1880s and in the turbulence of 1894, when most employed on the roads were native white or north European men, did rank and file, skilled and unskilled workers alike, join together to launch serious, industry-wide challenges to management prerogatives. More typically, the Chinese, Japanese, Greeks, Bulgarians, blacks, women in a singular way, and others, many of whom also served as scapegoats for the accumulated grievances of others, proved unable to forge their own form of effective protest. For them the reality of the region's "new destiny" occasioned little cause for celebration.

The origins of the railroad labor movement can be traced to the completion of the Northern Pacific in 1883 and the Oregon Short Line the following year. The skilled operating brotherhoods earlier had established locals at Portland and other points, but they represented only a small minority of railway employees. It was the industrially organized Knights of Labor, which probably included many operating and shopcraft workers, that quickly became the most important force in the railway labor relations of the 1880s. . . . Despite its national jurisdiction, the Order's leadership was preoccupied with organizational problems and paid little attention to the activities of Knights in the Far Northwest. Consequently, the Order there was almost an indigenous labor organization. As such, it became an important vehicle for the expression of regional attitudes on race and labor organization. . . .

The sudden rise of the Knights of Labor in the Far Northwest cannot be attributed solely to the hard times occasioned by economic depression or the Order's early success in other areas. Much more important was the heavy reliance organizers placed on the widespread anti-Chinese prejudice in the region. Racial tensions had existed for some time as Chinese workers migrated to the region to labor in the mines and other developing industries. In their final construction phase, however, the railroads became their principal employers. As the Northern Pacific completed its line through the Pacific Northwest, it employed fifteen thousand Chinese construction workers in Washington Territory alone, and an estimated six thousand were at work in Montana and Idaho territories in 1882. With the completion of that line, thousands of Chinese workers reentered the Northwest's already overburdened labor market. White laborers' job fears then combined with smoldering racial and cultural resentments to lay the groundwork for a racial confrontation.

The Knights immediately capitalized on popular fears of being deluged with Chinese immigrants. They and, to a lesser extent, the International Workingmen's Association, a radical organization founded at San Francisco in 1881, led the movement to purge the Chinese from the region's burgeoning frontier communities. Their adopted mission was to establish a high degree of cultural and racial homogeneity within the Northwest and, by doing so, to preserve jobs for the large number of unemployed whites. Railway workers participated in the general exclusionist campaign and in the racial incidents that became commonplace throughout the region, finding their most spectacular expression in the Seattle and Tacoma confrontations of 1885–1886.

For all that, the Knights' strength was short-lived, and with the exception of the Spokane area, they had declined precipitously by the early 1890s. . . .

Nonetheless, the Knights left a fundamentally important legacy. Long after the Order's decline, exclusionist sentiment and the drive for industrial unionism remained constant themes in the experience of white railway workers. The potential danger to employers of an aroused, ethnically homogeneous, and united work force first became manifest in 1894 when the Panic reached its nadir. Coxeyism, the Great Northern Strike, and the Pullman Boycott demonstrated the Gilded Age pattern of labor militance at high tide in the Far Northwest. Freed from the internal divisiveness of great racial and ethnic diversity, native-born whites joined northern and western Europeans in industry-wide protests against the Grover Cleveland administration and the railroads. In the case of the Great Northern and Pullman strikes, that protest took the form of a resounding endorsement of Eugene V. Debs's infant American Railway Union, heir to the Knights' legacy of industrial unionism.

The emergence of Coxey's armies in the spring of 1894, the worst year of the 1893–1897 depression, dramatized the plight of the nation's unemployed. Several thousand men and women, including many recently laid off by the railroads, quickly imitated Jacob Coxey's Ohio example and formed their own "armies" in Butte, Spokane, Seattle, Tacoma, Portland, and smaller locales. Determined to carry their protest to the nation's capital and willing to hijack trains when all else failed, they were among the most militant of the country's "commonwealers." As such, they thoroughly alarmed local authorities as well as the Cleveland administration, which employed federal marshals and regular troops to check their progress in what became a dress rehearsal for intervention in the Pullman Strike. . . .

. . . Coxeyites in all the major (and many of the smaller) population centers worked hard to enlist community support by holding parades and benefits. In the case of the Seattle group, they established a women's auxiliary "to assist all poor working girls and unemployed women to earn an honest livelihood for themselves and aid those in distressed circumstances."

Further, they constructed an inclusive, Populist platform designed to appeal to a wide variety of potential supporters. Calls for the free coinage of silver and general currency reform held an obvious appeal for the region's mining communities as well as for those interested in currency inflation. Calls for immigration restriction and for restrictions on alien land ownership easily appealed to wage earners and farmers, whereas demands for government ownership of the railroads and telegraphs, public works, direct election of senators, and the initiative and referendum appealed to insurgent white communities throughout the region. Reflecting the views of their railroad members, as well as their support for strikers on the Great Northern, the Coxeyites reiterated their enthusiasm for the American Railway Union and urged "organized and unorganized labor to pull together for the good of all."

Called to protest repeated wage cuts and layoffs, the Great Northern Strike of April 1894 occurred simultaneously with the Coxeyite turbulence. Together they illustrated the unrest among unemployed and working railway men. In the GN Strike, unorganized white workers and members of the established brotherhoods alike flocked to the new American Railway Union, hopeful that at last they would have an effective organization. Later the myth that a great victory had been won further swelled the ARU's membership rolls.

The insurgent workers of the Far Northwest played a central role in that strike that so benefited the young industrial union. Ignoring President Eugene V. Debs's instructions, militants led by the youthful James Hogan (one of the ARU's national organizers) called the strike in western Montana when one of their number intercepted a coded message from the road calling for the dismissal of all ARU members in the Butte, Helena, and Great Falls yards. . . . Meanwhile, GN employees in the Cascade and coastal areas also ignored the initial calls for caution by Debs. In the case of the engineers, firemen, trainmen, and conductors, many defied their national leaders' explicit orders and joined the strikers.

After an arbitration board chaired by Charles Pillsbury awarded the ARU what essentially was wage parity with workers on the Northern Pacific, the new union claimed a great victory. The claim had little substance, but the widespread belief that a smashing victory had been won led directly to the ARU's tragic involvement in the Pullman Strike two months later.

At their first convention, held in June at Chicago, the ARU delegates ignored Debs's pleas for restraint and declared a sympathy boycott against the Pullman Palace Car Company. As the dispute escalated, it paralyzed all roads west of Chicago, with the exception of the Great Northern. Throughout the region, but again most strikingly in the northern Rockies, various elements of society threw their support to the ARU strikers. Farmers donated their crops. A host of elected officials, merchants, clergymen, professionals, labor organizers, and others vigorously protested the road's labor policies. . . . In Washington state, the Spokane and Sprague contingents of the National Guard refused to move against the strikers. Similarly, members of the railroad brotherhoods ignored direct orders from their national leaders to honor the boycott.

The fact that the ARU represented white, largely native-born, and northern and western European workers, many of whom were solid members of their respective communities, was an important element in the high degree of support accorded strikers in much of the region. Indeed, cultural affinity, combined with shared economic hardships occasioned by the Panic and with the rising Populist tide, worked to form a crucible of discontent in the Far Northwest. . . .

The turbulence of the 1890s, which the Pullman Strike demonstrated so spectacularly, triggered an abrupt change in the road's hiring policies. By the end of 1894, employers saw clearly that the racial and cultural homogeneity of the work force was a fundamental factor in the comparative unity exhibited by railway workers in all sectors of the industry and in the widespread community support they enjoyed. Since the anti-Chinese agitation of the 1880s, the roads had employed, for the most part, native whites and immigrants drawn from northern and western Europe. After 1894 the roads radically altered their employment practices, recruiting Japanese and southern and eastern European workers to fulfill the tasks in their unskilled sectors. Following the Pullman Strike, labor organizers in the industry were forced to deal, again, with the inescapable problem of ethnic and racial diversity.

The experience of Japanese workers, recruited largely into the unskilled maintenance-of-way and construction trades paralleled that of Mexican laborers in the Southwest and was decidedly different from that of the "labor aristocracy" of the operating brotherhoods. At the very bottom of the railroad labor hierarchy, they received less pay than "foreigners" (European immigrants) and "white men." They also bore the burden of anti-Asian prejudice, while they shared the harsh working conditions, routine exploitation by labor contractors, and general uncertainty connected with migrant work that beset all employed in that sector of the railroads' work force.

Japanese began arriving in the Far Northwest in significant numbers in the 1890s. By 1906 their number had risen to thirteen thousand, mostly construction and section hands employed on western railroads. Of those, the Northern Pacific, Great Northern, Southern Pacific, Union Pacific, and Milwaukee lines were the principal employers. Indeed, at its peak, the Great Northern alone employed five thousand of the newcomers, although their number declined rapidly in the wake of the Gentlemen's Agreement of 1907–1908.

To anxious managers desperate for large numbers of cheap tractable workers, Japanese immigrants, by the racial stereotypes of the day, seemed all ideal solution. "Jap section laborers . . . are certainly more reliable than either Greeks, Italians or white labor generally," GN Assistant Superintendent H. A. Kennedy wired from Spokane, adding that they "seem to be peculiarly adapted to section work." Kennedy's superior, F. E. Ward, seemed overjoyed that "the Japs are turning out so well" in Montana, and he entertained the notion of placing "our main reliance on them and having nothing to do with Italians or other outside labor."

The growing Japanese presence on the railroads and in other industries quickly ignited an intense opposition, spearheaded by organized labor. As the new century began, *Seattle Union Record* editor Gordon A. Rice commenced a long-term anti-Japanese campaign, warning: "The Northwest is on the verge of a gigantic struggle with Oriental labor" similar to that waged against Chinese workers in the 1880s. "Jim Hill [president of the Great Northern] will have Japs as yardmen, engineers and conductors if a check is not put upon his career of greed," Rice fumed, and the *Spokane Freemen's Journal* and other prolabor publications broadcast a similar message throughout the region. . . . To the east the *Butte Reveille* charged: "J. J. Hill is very fond of the Japs; they work cheaper than the Irishman, or Englishman, or Dutchman, and then besides they will stand all kinds of abuse from their employers."

Many factors played into the anti-Japanese stance adopted by labor in the Progressive Era. Fears of job displacement meshed with general apprehensions felt in the white community over the introduction of alien races and cultures. Anti-Japanese sentiment also held obvious institutional advantages for organized labor, as instanced in the fall of 1900 when the Great Northern replaced a number of white workers with Japanese immigrants at Everett, Washington. Local merchants joined with their white customers in the labor force to protest the road's decision, a development suggestive of the continuing force of community loyalties that had supported much of the nineteenth-century industrial protest. Spying the main chance for AFL organizers, the *Union Record* rejoiced: "Everett is fast coming to the front as a union town. . . . [T]he anti-Jap agitation is the chief incentive and it is a powerful one." Other labor papers immediately carried the story and its moral to the interior, and discussions of the "Asiatic labor question" became an important rationale for the formation of the Washington state federation.

Alienated from the labor movement and from the region's communities, Japanese workers had scant opportunity to remedy the conditions under which they toiled. In at least one instance, however, they did try to organize, forming their own union at Seattle in 1906. Angered by the exploitive practices of the Oriental Trading Company—the largest Japanese labor contractor in the region—the new union, led by K. Saskai and Jikei Hashiguchi, editor of *The Japan Current,* tried to strike up an alliance with the AFL organizations of western Washington. Predictably, their efforts proved unavailing, and no other effective agency emerged to challenge the roads' contractors.

In this hostile atmosphere, Japanese workers tended to signal their disaffection by voting with their feet. Some found work on other roads, such as the Milwaukee, which completed its line to the coast during those years.

Ultimately, however, most left railway work to find other jobs on farms, in the coastal cities, or, particularly after the outbreak of the Russo-Japanese War, they returned to Japan. When the Gentlemen's Agreement curtailed further Japanese immigration to the United States, the roads were compelled, once more, to discover new sources of unskilled laborers.

Suddenly, the new immigrants from eastern and southern Europe assumed a vastly greater importance. Although they had been arriving since the mid-1890s, the new Europeans now became the principal means of meeting the unskilled labor shortfall left by the 1907–1908 understanding. Generally, they were paid somewhat better than Asian workers—roughly twenty-five cents more per day—although they received less than native white workers until after 1911. Of course, all shared the same poor working conditions.

Like Japanese workers, most of the new Europeans were recruited by labor contractors. In its 1911 investigation, the Immigrant Labor Commission observed that each road employed one such agent to handle all non-English-speaking, European immigrant laborers. Like the Oriental Trading Company, the European contractors routinely exploited their charges through commissions, overpriced supplies, and a variety of other devices.

H. W. Osborn's Western Employment Company supplied immigrant laborers to the Great Northern in a fashion typical of other agencies throughout the country. With offices in Saint Paul, Duluth, Bemidji, Sioux City, Grand Forks, Fargo, Memphis, and in the northwestern cities of Seattle, Portland, and Spokane, Osborn's company possessed an extensive network for the recruitment and distribution of workers. Until the road dispensed with his services in 1910 because of overcharges against the company and exploitation of workers that resulted in slowdowns, Osborn was the principal supplier of Greek, Bulgarian, Austrian, and other European laborers. Clearly operating on a grand scale, in 1908 the Western Employment Company supplied over four thousand such workers (and 5,745 "white men") at Spokane alone.

Like Japanese workers, southern and eastern European railway laborers bore the additional burden of hostility and nativism levied by labor and the local populace. Though such sentiments were not as intense as those expressed toward Asians, nativist pronouncements by organized labor still served as a strong bar to any substantive improvement in the new immigrants' condition. Outside the region's communities, the new Europeans could not rely on the same social structure that had cut across class lines and supported earlier efforts at organization and militant action. . . .

At the 1913 Immigration Conference in Portland, in newspapers, and in other forums throughout Washington, Oregon, Idaho, and Montana, AFL spokesmen pounded home the constant refrain that the region was a "white man's country" and that the new European immigration benefited only "the great combinations of Capital that sponsored it." Equally significant, the weak Brotherhood of Maintenance of Way Workers, which had jurisdiction over that sector of the industry, seemed almost determined to obstruct its own growth by retaining its color bar and by reiterating its implacable opposition to "Italian and Greek labor that takes from honest American laborers the money and work that are rightfully theirs."

As in the case of Japanese workers, some of the new Europeans did attempt to organize and better their lot, principally through the United Brotherhood of Railway Employees and the Industrial Workers of the World. Although both groups were largely indigenous to the region, neither had any lasting impact in the railroad industry. They lacked both the popular, community base that the Knights of Labor and the American Railway Union had enjoyed and the strategic job skills and effective, nationally centralized organization and leadership that the operating brotherhoods were learning to use with such telling effect in the Progressive Era. . . .

Spurned by organized labor and excluded from even the marginal relief benefits conferred by agencies such as the Itinerant Workers Union (Hoboes Union), the new Europeans reacted much like their Asian counterparts, thereby aggravating the roads' chronic labor shortage. They sought other jobs or, particularly after the outbreak of World War I, returned to their home countries. To meet the new shortage, the railroads called for a reintroduction of Japanese workers. When that effort failed, they again were compelled to seek out new sources.

To meet the wartime challenge, the northwestern roads turned their recruitment efforts to enlist petty criminals, blacks, and women. Expressed resentments toward the newcomers, however, were more muted and decidedly different than those levied against their predecessors. In large measure, this comparative quiescence was due to the intervention of the federal government in the railroad industry. Anxious to prevent strikes or any further slowdowns on the roads, Woodrow Wilson created the Railroad Administration, which improved wages and working conditions throughout the nation. The RA also encouraged organization among the AFL unions, including the Maintenance of Way Brotherhood, which grew from only thirty thousand in 1917 to over three hundred thousand members by the end of 1920. While such policies defused worker unrest on the roads, they also deflected potential attacks on the new workers.

Desperate to employ more unskilled laborers, the carriers first attempted to obtain the services of men convicted of misdemeanors. Great Northern President Ralph Budd instructed his subordinates to utilize "laborers who have been jailed for petty offences at such points as Havre, Great Falls, etc., where help is hard to get." Refusing to be caught up in the anti-German hysteria, Budd also directed that no German-born applicant would be barred from the road unless there was firm evidence to "suspect him of being an enemy of the Government."

The roads also expanded their campaign to recruit black workers. Typical of that effort, the Great Northern obtained black workers through labor agencies such as the Minneapolis-based Fogg Brothers, which had connections to the Pinkerton's National Detective Agency and the Koenig Labor Agencies of Saint Louis and Kansas City, Missouri. In May 1917 the Fogg Brothers instructed their Missouri contacts "to get every possible negro you can get into Great Falls . . . the next bunch of nigers [sic] to Glasgow . . . and the next bunch . . . to Havre for pipe culvert work, [at] 20 cents per hour."

Black workers proved no more satisfied with low pay, poor conditions, and long hours than whites or Asians. "Negroes don't seem [to] be [a] paying investment," C. O. Jenks wired from Sand Point, Idaho, since "they don't stay long enough." As the surging wartime economy provided more and better paying jobs, there seemed little reason to settle for low wages and harsh working conditions in remote areas. With the possible exception of Pullman porters, blacks never became a numerically significant part of the Northwest's railway work force.

At the same time, the roads considered recruiting Puerto Rican and, like their counterparts in the Southwest, Mexican laborers. They quickly discarded such notions, however, largely because of the high cost necessary to transport such workers in large numbers over great distances. Further, Mexican railway workers could remain legally in the United States only for the duration of the war. Although the Southern Pacific employed some Mexican workers in Oregon, their large-scale importation into the Northwest made little economic sense to the officials of other roads in the region.

Women, however, did provide an important new source of labor for the roads. By the end of 1918, they numbered 2,384 on the Northern Pacific alone, including over 900 in Washington, Idaho, and Montana. Most held clerical jobs, but many women also worked in machine shops, on the tracks, and in roundhouses. They constituted only a fraction of the work force, but women employees attracted considerable attention from federal and state officials concerned with the type and conditions of their work.

RA Director William Gibbs McAdoo worried particularly about the employment of women in freight houses and on section gangs. Most "expressed themselves as thoroughly satisfied with the conditions of work," NP General Manager J. M. Rapelje reassured him, adding that "they are not asked to exert themselves beyond their strength." While he also tried to deflect McAdoo's anxieties, federal manager Jule M. Hannaford (formerly of the Northern Pacific) instructed his subordinates that although "the labor situation is [not] yet in such shape, especially on the West End, that we can dispose entirely with female labor in these classes . . . as rapidly as consistent, our officers will see that his [McAdoo's] wishes are complied with."

At the state level, Washington Commissioner of Labor C. W. Younger also worried about women's welfare on the roads, as well as their impact on society. While he seemed generally satisfied with women's working conditions in Washington and he applauded McAdoo's policy of nondiscrimination in wages, Younger cautioned: "Only under the sternest necessity should [women] be taken out from under the ancient shelter of the home." His bureau's investigation of the Tacoma, Parkwater, and Spokane railway shops revealed a generally beneficent new "shelter," but he could not "forbear . . . a few words of warning." "Woman is not always a good judge of her own strength," the labor commissioner fretted, while he worried over the "real danger that she will in an excess of zeal undertake tasks too heavy for her."

Younger failed to specify his principal concern about women in the industrial workplace. Certainly, the perceived dangers of women working outside the home included a potential threat to the traditional family structure, as Younger and others viewed it. Also, there were "moral risks" attendent upon "night work," which he felt "should be discouraged." Not least among Younger's and other progressives' apprehensions was the fear that if women worked night shifts they would "not get the requisite amount of rest, going home in the morning, preparing breakfast and then tackling the house work." Such pronouncements were hardly exceptional, and consequently, they illustrated the additional burdens women confronted in the industrial workplace, including those in comparatively well-regulated industries.

The wartime workers were last in the succession of varied groups that had entered the railroads' unskilled labor pool since the arrival of the first transcontinental in the Far Northwest. After the Great War, the roads' demand for such workers declined, while postwar legislation restricted immigration. In the lean years of the 1920s, the remaining unskilled wage earners fought hard, though unsuccessfully, to retain the benefits conferred upon them by the Railroad Administration. Not until the early days of the New Deal, however, did they obtain the legal tools to organize and bargain collectively to better their condition.

Between the years 1883 and 1917, unskilled workers in the Far Northwest, as elsewhere, proved unable to better their situation. Many factors militated against their success. The very nature of the railroad industry, which dictated that many workers be widely dispersed to maintain the road, was a constant underlying obstacle, one that proved particularly troublesome in the sparsely populated West. The intransigence of the region's railroad managers to wide-scale collective bargaining and union recognition, like that of their counterparts in other industries, remained an important hurdle for those interested in organization of the entire industry. Yet the same managers could and did make exceptions for smaller organizations representing skilled workers. On occasion, they utilized those relationships to their advantage by alliances with the national leaders of the Big Four— Brotherhood of Locomotive Engineers, Brotherhood of Locomotive Firemen and Enginemen, Brotherhood of Railroad Trainmen, and Order of Railway Conductors—and of the AFL to oppose industrial unionism, which threatened the established unions' jurisdictions and prerogatives no less than those of management.

The presence of such powerful forces did not automatically preclude effective attempts at mass organization. Both the Knights of Labor and the American Railway Union did present comparatively united, industry-wide challenges to management. In both cases, they were able to rely upon insurgent community support peculiar to the developing region, which, like much of the Far West, was almost entirely dependent on the railroads, subject to the vagaries of a largely extractive economy, remote from much of the national marketplace, and imbued with the fires of frustrated expectations. Yet their protests were, in one sense, an aberration, since they were launched when there was comparative ethnic and racial homogeneity in the railway work force.

After the great turbulence of the 1890s, the roads changed all that. In their perennial quest for cheap labor, the railroads, frightened by the Coxeyites and the ARU strikes of 1894, were no less aware than their counterparts in other industries and in other regions of the benefits to be gained by employing workers of diverse origins to do their unskilled, often seasonal, work. As the roads sought out new sources of labor, the resulting demographic challenge emerged as a decisive factor militating against unification of the work force, which was divided increasingly along the lines decreed by race, ethnicity, and gender. Subsequent attempts at mass organization, including the Japanese workers' organization in Seattle, the UBRE, and the IWW, proved to be short-lived, and finally only futile, experiments.

Consequently, nearly all involved in unskilled railroad work remained divided, unorganized, poorly paid, subject to the vicissitudes of casual labor, and victims of the generally harsh conditions imposed by employers and labor contractors. Not until the federal government intervened to resolve the transportation crisis of the First World War on a national level did the unskilled sector realize significant, albeit temporary, gains in pay, working conditions, and union organization. Aside from that brief moment, most workers in the industry experienced only lean years between the settlement of the far northwestern frontier and the onset of the New Deal.

"Old" Radicals and "New" Immigrants in Bingham, Utah, 1905–1912

GUNTHER PECK

In the fall of 1912, over one thousand employees of the Utah Copper Company in Bingham, Utah, walked off their jobs and armed themselves with rifles and dynamite in one of the most dramatic strikes in the Western Federation of Miners' (WFM) violent history. Twenty-four national groups cooperated in the walkout, digging trenches, breastworks, foxholes, even constructing a makeshift cannon. . . .

. . . In one of the most remarkable features of the Bingham strike, the American born leadership of the WFM, headed by union president Charles Moyer, maintained only marginal control of the strike movement. Immigrant strikers possessed their own agenda for striking. They advocated abolishing the padrone hiring system that had brought so many unskilled immigrants to Bingham in the first place. Although the Utah Copper Company never recognized their union, immigrant strikers succeeded in

Gunther Peck, "Padrones and Protest: 'Old' Radicals and 'New' Immigrants in Bingham, Utah, 1905–1912," *Western Historical Quarterly,* 24 (May, 1993), 157–78. Copyright by Western History Association. Reprinted by permission.

forcing the company to fire its most powerful and notorious labor agent, Greek entrepreneur Leonidas Skliris. . . .

This article explores the complex relationships between Bingham's "new" immigrants—principally Japanese, Italian, Slavic, and Greek—and the American-dominated union local before, during, and after the 1912 strike. How does an understanding of the ethnic and racial tensions between "new" immigrants and "old" American-born radicals change our story of western radicalism—its origins, its growth, and its decline? . . .

It is important to establish what I mean by "radical" and to assess briefly the content and context of the Western Federation of Miners's radicalism in 1912. For the purposes of this essay, I use "radical" in the literal sense to refer to any individual or group ideologically committed to changing society at its roots. Although the WFM had recently affiliated with the allegedly conservative and craft-oriented American Federation of Labor in 1911, the WFM's constitution of 1912 still proclaimed that "a class struggle in society" would continue "until the producer is recognized as the sole master of its product." In Bingham, the WFM local remained strongly committed to organizing a working class of skilled and unskilled male workers and supporting the Socialist party, which represented a powerful minority party throughout the first decade of the twentieth century. The Socialists attained a powerful position in Bingham's City Council, electing members every two years between 1905 and 1911. . . .

In spite of the WFM local's commitment to the Socialist party, very few of Bingham's new immigrants were enlisted into the local class struggle. . . . Although the union accepted Greek, Italian, and South Slavic workers into its membership and promoted Slavic immigrant Yanco Terzich to its executive board, its relationship to these new immigrants remained ambivalent. In Bingham, only a handful of Italians and Greeks joined the union before the 1912 strike, even though they attained numerical prominence in the work force by 1907. Local union leaders E. G. Locke and Thomas Burlison discussed "the Greek problem," including their grievances against the padrone hiring system, as early as 1908 when they proposed using the union library to teach Greek workers the English language. But little appeals to have come from their inclusionist proposal; the number of Greeks joining the local remained very low—one or two a month—before and after the union's discussion about whether to encourage Greeks to join. Efforts to publish local union news and announcements in foreign languages were sporadic at best, despite a smattering of Greek and Italian members and a more sizeable number of Slavic and Finnish members. In 1905, the only occasion for translation came when union officials posted signs in three languages demanding the immediate payment of back dues. Declarations of class solidarity, by contrast, such as the local's support for the Industrial Workers of the World, were read, delivered, and published only in English.

The strength of nativism in Bingham reflected the intensity of economic and social change that the community had experienced between 1900 and 1910. In 1900, the population of Bingham, already something of an anomaly in the state of Utah, consisted mostly of non-Mormon men, nearly half of them foreign born. Most of Bingham's labor force worked underground in silver mines and had emigrated to the United States from Sweden, Ireland, England, and more recently, Finland. By 1910, however, not a single silver mine remained in Bingham and newly arrived Greek, Italian, and Japanese immigrants comprised nearly half the local work force. The overall skill level of the work force dropped significantly as the number of unskilled laborers in Bingham increased elevenfold.

The spectacular growth of the Utah Copper Company, which pioneered the largest and most successful open-pit copper mine in the world, fueled a dramatic demographic and social transformation. Incorporated in 1903 and backed by Guggenheim family capital, the company, by 1907, had begun mining and smelting an entire mountain of low-grade copper ore above Bingham Canyon, using steam shovels that operated on train tracks to dig and load the ore directly onto boxcars for smelting. A booming market for copper ensured the company's rapid growth and hastened the displacement and deskilling of Bingham's underground silver miners. Deskilling proved a complex and uneven process in Bingham. Certain immigrant groups such as the Swedes seemed to have benefited from the reorganization of work by becoming skilled machine tenders. Former skilled miners did not usually fill most of the new unskilled positions at the Utah Copper Company. Instead Greek, Italian, and Japanese immigrants, who performed the arduous tasks of laying and relaying railroad track for the cumbersome steam shovels, moved into those positions. Though deskilling affected different national groups in strikingly different ways, citizens of Bingham across the occupational and political spectrums blamed the community's wrenching dislocations on these new unskilled workers, a pattern evidenced in the rapid growth of the anti-immigrant and anti-Mormon American party.

. . . In 1911, the Utah Copper Company's modern expansion produced two paradoxical developments. Not only did mechanization with steam shovels greatly increase the amount of pick and shovel work performed in Bingham, it also necessitated the expansion of a seemingly archaic method of obtaining these strong arms and backs—the ethnic padrone system. A labor contractor who imported his countrymen and provided them with jobs in America, the padrone also exploited his intermediary position by charging fees to all immigrant workers for getting and keeping their industrial livelihoods. In Bingham, three men imported unskilled immigrants for the burgeoning number of railroad and mining jobs: Leonidas Skliris, also known as the "Czar of the Greeks," imported all Greek and Slavic workers; Edward Daigoro Hashimoto, importer of Japanese laborers into Utah; and Moses Paggi, labor agent for Bingham's Italians.

While nativism and cultural differences kept many new immigrants from joining the WFM local, class solidarities nonetheless quickly developed within Bingham's immigrant communities. Paid the least, Greek, Italian, Slavic, and Japanese workers formed the bottom tier of the Utah Copper Company's ethnic and skill hierarchy and assumed some of the greatest occupational risks in the open pit. Most Greek and all Japanese workers earned $1.75 a day as muckers, laying track for the steam shovels in the open pit, or unloading ore with pick and shovel at the smelter. Most muckers, in work gangs of five or six people, labored next to and were supervised by one of their own countrymen. Although the localistic organization of mucking prevented much interaction between different ethnic groups of workers, job-related disputes and dangers could provoke moments of intense class feeling among muckers. In 1908, when an American foreman attempted to fire a Greek worker without notifying his fellow workers, six Greek workers "beat their American supervisor with sticks, fists, and stones." . . .

If class solidarities among immigrant workers developed within ethnic boundaries at the smelter and open pit, Bingham's many saloons encouraged bonds both within and between groups of immigrant workers. By 1911, nearly every major ethnic group in Bingham possessed its own drinking establishment. But such facilities did not serve merely as safe havens where immigrants spoke their own languages. One of the most popular sporting events in Upper Bingham's Greek coffee houses, the weekly wrestling contests between Japanese and Greek workers encouraged immigrants of many nationalities to bet on the likely winner. . . .

Though few Greek immigrants had much contact with the union prior to the 1912 strike, they nonetheless demonstrated a remarkable capacity for collective action. In August 1908, over three hundred Greek laborers walked off their jobs at the Utah Copper Company's smelter and demanded a restoration of a pay cut made during the recent recession. . . . Just one week later, the Utah Copper Company granted Greek workers their demand and restored the former wage rate of $1.75 a day. Although Greek workers struck without any union affiliation or cooperation from other immigrants, their success derived from the existence of the WFM local in Bingham, which company officials loathed; better, after all, to grant the demands of Greek workers without union recognition than to drive them into the arms of the Western Federation. The walkout did not produce a single comment in the local union's minutes, however, suggesting just how much cultural and political distance continued to exist between Greek and American workers.

Class loyalties in Bingham did not emerge only in union hall meetings, nor did they develop roots purely within the work place or Bingham's many ethnic saloons. Perhaps the most crucial factor in Greek workers' growing awareness of their exploited condition was their volatile relationship with the padrone, Leonidas Skliris. Born in the village of Vresthena, high in the mountains above Sparta, Skliris's career in the United States began in 1898 when he arrived in New York and began selling flowers to businessmen on Wall Street. Skliris quickly mastered English and, by 1901, moved to railroad work as a section foreman on the Baltimore & Ohio Railroad. A year later, Skliris had moved to Utah, at the exhortation of childhood friend and labor agent, William Caravelis of Pocatello, Idaho. . . .

By 1911, Skliris had greatly expanded his operations as a labor contractor. Unlike the Greeks who immigrated to Bingham in 1908, most of those arriving in 1911 came from the island of Crete rather than from villages near Skliris's own hometown in the southern Pelopponese. Skliris had also expanded his power in America by purchasing the Panhellenic Grocery store in Bingham from a Cretan businessman. Like many company town

superintendents, Skliris required that Greek workers shop there or risk losing their jobs. Such extensions of the tribute system galvanized the militancy of Greek workers, few of whom would have proclaimed Skliris a
defender of the laborer.

To the contrary, Greek immigrants, led by the Cretans, began organizing themselves to remove Skliris as the Utah Copper Company's labor agent
and to abolish the padrone system altogether. In the spring of 1911, fifty
Greek laborers sent a letter to the governor of Utah, William Spry, demanding the abolition of Skliris's tribute system:

> Do you think this is right for Skliris to sell livelihoods to the poor workman . . .
> and to thus suck the blood of the poor laborer? Where are we? In the free
> Amerika [*sic*] or in a country dominated by a despotic form of government?
> Hoping you liberate us from this padrone, who is ravaging the blood of the poor
> laborer, and that too, of his fellow countrymen.

These Greek workers did not describe Skliris as a bad protector, or a Turk,
but in stark class terms, as an oppressor of the "poor laborer," a man whose
authority violated their rights as workers in America. When Governor Spry
failed to reply, over five hundred Greek immigrants, all of them employees
of Utah Copper, wrote him another letter. The workers typed this one,
refined the English usage, and demanded that "Skliris and his agents be
restrained," that all immigrants be hired directly by the company, and that
all Greek employees be "at liberty to do their purchasing wherever they
wish." Spry replied this time, but suggested they take their complaint
directly to the Utah Copper Company management for "an impartial hearing." Most Greeks recognized that the company had facilitated Skliris's
rise to power and began searching for more direct means of abolishing
padronism.

Although Greek workers were increasingly well organized during the
summer of 1911, tensions continued to divide American and immigrant
workers. The appeal to a more powerful and supposedly neutral authority in
Governor Spry was itself a revealing commentary on Greek workers' distrust of the American-led union local. By 1912, however, local union leaders, such as E. G. Locke, recognized the organizing potential of the padrone
system and wrote a letter to the ambassador of Turkey, with copies to
Governor Spry, demanding that he investigate the existence of peonage
among "his subjects from Crete." By publicizing Skliris's villainy, Locke
hoped to win allies among Bingham's militant Cretan miners. Locke, however, overlooked the fact that these same miners loathed their official
Turkish protectors as much as their new-world protector Skliris. Not surprisingly, Locke's letter earned the union little support from Bingham's
patriotic Cretans. . . .

Until the summer of 1912, working-class Greeks in Bingham remained
unclear about what kind of Americans they planned to become. As Greek
workers' anger against Skliris and the padrone system mounted, their sense
of cultural distance from the Bingham local narrowed. Having witnessed
the indifference and complicity of one group of Americans, they soon
turned to the only group of Americans willing to listen to their complaints,
E. G. Locke and the Bingham local. The union's membership grew spectac-

ularly that summer, from 250 members in June, to 700 in July, to nearly 1200 by September. Precisely who encouraged the Greeks' participation remains unclear. Certainly the handful of Greeks in the Bingham local had some influence in recruiting their countrymen as did John Leventis, a Cretan immigrant who owned Bingham's most popular coffee house and who proved an outspoken champion of labor during the strike. Although the union hired no official Greek organizer, it did translate its entire constitution and organizing literature into Greek that spring and probably relied on E. G. Locke and Greek union members to disseminate the WFM literature. The federation also hired an Italian organizer, Steve Oberto, who worked in Bingham throughout the summer of 1912.

The Greek immigrants demonstrated their already established internal mobilization in the way they took over the union's business. In early September, recently initiated Greek immigrants decided to exercise their new found rights by pressing American union leaders for a strike vote. When Charles Moyer, president of the WFM, heard of their plans, he rushed to Bingham by train to dissuade the strike-hungry immigrants. Moyer's reluctance to strike highlighted some of the growing tensions in the WFM between its radical constitution and its organizing strategy. With a strike fund nearly bankrupt and the union's legal resources stretched thin, Moyer hoped to avoid a protracted and expensive strike, as had recently occurred at the Homestake Mining Company in Lead, South Dakota. Perhaps more important, Moyer remained reluctant to relinquish control over the expanding Bingham local to recently initiated Greek and Italian immigrants, whose militancy and solidarity with Japanese workers challenged the authority of American-born radicals such as himself and the organization they had built.

After an impassioned speech by Moyer against striking, the membership, led by Greek miner John Stanopolis, voted to walk and began celebrating with gunshots and victory toasts. The next morning, over one thousand immigrants laid down their tools and set up pickets around the Utah Copper mine and smelter works. Hundreds of non-union immigrants soon followed them, including all two hundred Japanese laborers in Bingham, many of whom joined the picketing effort. By contrast, a number of skilled American workers, many of them union members, refused to join the strikers and attempted to go to work. When American steam shovel operators began revving up their engines, "a number of strikers, principally Greeks, appeared on the mountainside above the workman [*sic*] and pelted them with stones and rolled boulders down the mountainside, driving the workers from their places." By noon of the first day, over five thousand workers were idle and "the greatest industrial sight on earth" had been completely shut down.

The drama of the Bingham strike inspired reporters of all political stripes to discern and define the event's meaning and significance. . . . The Salt Lake City *Deseret Evening News* reported that:

> The "white" element has been forced against its will [to strike]. . . . The Bingham camp is today a divided camp. . . . On one side is a mob of . . . 3500 aliens. . . . On the other . . . are perhaps 1500 men who refused to strike . . . and in addition to these the merchants and citizens of Bingham itself.

By defining Greeks, Italians, and South Slavs as nonwhite, this reporter reduced to race what [others] had reduced to class.

Given the popularity of these competing reportorial narratives—the emergence of race war or a raceless working class—how did union leaders in Bingham negotiate such reductive alternatives? Moyer's strategy, consistent throughout the strike, focused on winning public support for the union's cause by attempting to "Americanize" the efforts of its militant immigrant membership. For Moyer, this meant not only obeying American laws regarding firearms, but respecting the authority of the union's American leadership. Initially, this seemed an impossible task because immigrant strikers controlled the mine with guns and dynamite and fired at all who came near, including Moyer himself. Subsequently, Moyer distanced himself publicly from Greek laborers. To the *Deseret Evening News,* Moyer disavowed violence and stated that he could not be held "responsible for the individual conduct of 4000 members." Moyer feared that a nativist backlash would ruin his chance to win political support for an arbitrated settlement of the strike. Moyer's concession to Utah's nativist political climate seemed double-edged, however, for by distancing himself from Greek strikers, he also undercut his authority and reputation as a union leader to an American public. . . .

Moyer sought to regain control over the rebellious membership by orchestrating an open-air meeting between strikers, himself, the governor of Utah, and middle-class immigrant leaders. Nicholas Stathakos spoke first to the crowd of angry strikers: "For the glory of our nation, you should be law-abiding here." Not surprisingly, Stathakos's appeal to Greek patriotism "deeply agitated" a great number of Greek strikers. Greek Orthodox priest Vasilios Lambrides followed Stathakos, but the priest's appeal to patriotism likewise failed to calm the angry strikers. Greek workers' angry reaction to Stathakos and Lambrides underscored the sharply different meanings that honor and patriotism possessed for working-class and middle-class Greeks. After Lambrides left the podium, a number of Greek strikers denounced Skliris as a capitalistic traitor and demanded that company officials abolish the padrone system. One laborer from Crete emphasized the importance of this demand by asserting that Greek strikers would return to work if Skliris were fired. The meeting ended with a stern speech by Governor Spry, who warned immigrants not to take the law into their own hands; afterwards Spry took a walking tour of the strikers' fortifications with Moyer as his guide.

Moyer's effort to regain control of the Bingham strike by attempting to Americanize the immigrant workers' struggle had produced quite a different result. If Moyer regained a measure of control over the strikers, immigrants succeeded in redefining the strike's agenda and purpose. This mutual accommodation marked the beginning of a more cooperative and coordinated relationship between immigrant strikers and the WFM. Greeks became the core of a disciplined but now unarmed strike force that patrolled company grounds, inspected all incoming trains for strikebreakers, and manned the picket lines. The fusion of immigrant and union demands was dramatically evident just one week after the open-air meeting when

Leonidas Skliris announced his resignation from the Utah Copper Company. Greek workers promptly held a meeting to consider the possibility of returning to work, and although they engaged in an animated discussion, they voted unanimously to continue striking for both union recognition and the abolition of padronism.

Skliris responded to the worst crisis of his career by wrapping himself in the paternalistic ideology that had once undergirded his power as a padrone. In a two-page letter printed in the *Deseret Evening News* on the day of his resignation, Skliris asserted that his Greek countrymen loved him because he alone served as their true defender. His letter conveyed a clear sense of betrayal and exemplified the ties of reciprocity that had once existed between himself and his compatriots in Bingham. Yet it likewise illustrated the profound ideological distance that had developed between Skliris and Greek workers. Skliris refused to believe that Greek strikers remained committed to unionism and the abolition of the padrone system. In his own mind, he had always been a good padrone, providing his countrymen with jobs and job security at a fair and reasonable price. Rather than criticize his countrymen for being radical, and therefore both un-Greek and un-American, Skliris embraced the notion that a Greek rival had conspired to take his rightful place as the protector of Greek workers. . . .

Skliris's resignation produced a crisis within Utah's small middle-class Greek community, which tried to distance itself from Skliris while simultaneously defusing the public perception that Greek strikers were in fact committed to industrial unionism. On the day after Greek workers voted to continue striking, George Photopoulos, editor of the Greek newspaper *To Fos* (The Light), stated in the *Salt Lake Evening Telegram* that "the Greeks in Bingham do not understand the significance of a union" and "are ignorant of such American customs." On the same day, Stathakos announced the formation of a local chapter of the Panhellenic Union, whose purpose in Utah was to "establish schools where Greeks can become familiar with the American language and customs . . . and learn to respect the laws of America and in that way become more desirable citizens." Clearly, industrial unionism was not one of the "American customs" the Panhellenic Union would teach. Founders of the union in Utah committed themselves to an upwardly mobile, middle-class type of Americanization, one that stood in direct opposition to the working-class form of Americanization that Greek workers had embraced in the WFM. . . .

If the accommodation of working-class Greeks into the WFM left Skliris and Stathakos bewildered, its implications for other members of Bingham's working class were all too obvious. The Japanese workers who had walked out with other immigrants remained excluded from the union. The boundaries of working-class organization continued to be racialized in Bingham, boundaries that in fact eased the Americanization of working-class Greeks and Italians. Although the boundaries of race appeared highly mutable in Bingham, the term "Americanization" connoted whiteness for all classes during the conflict. Joining the WFM thus culminated a process of both working-class acculturation and racial assimilation for Greek and Italian immigrants. Mexican sugar beet workers in Oxnard, California, who refused to join the AFL in 1903 unless the offer included their Japanese cohorts, Bingham's formerly nonwhite Greeks sundered ties with their Japanese co-workers as WFM leadership brought the strike under more direct control. The Utah Copper Company attempted to take advantage of these enduring racial divisions by offering special wages to the Japanese during the strike. Most Japanese laborers responded to this tragic dilemma with their feet, however, and left Bingham altogether.

The continued exclusion of the Japanese from the union weakened the WFM's ability to maintain pressure on the Utah Copper Company. Nevertheless, Moyer succeeded in building a tension-fraught alliance between unskilled immigrants and skilled American workers in Bingham during the strike. By the second week, even skilled craft unions such as the American Brotherhood of Railway Workers had joined the shutdown. The union was also successful in increasing the economic pressure upon the Guggenheim copper interests by pulling out an additional four thousand copper workers from Ely and McGill, Nevada. But such collective economic leverage proved too little to gain a union contract. . . .

The Utah Copper Company broke the strike not merely with superior financial resources, but by dividing working-class ethnicity from within each immigrant group, thus pitting Italian worker against Italian worker and Greek laborer against Greek laborer. In this endeavor, the company benefited from events far from Bingham. On 1 October 1912, the Greek government issued an executive draft order recalling to active duty all male subjects between the ages of eighteen and thirty. For Bingham's Greek strikers, the outbreak of the Balkan Wars posed a profound dilemma: Should they return to Greece to vanquish their traditional enemy or finish the fight against labor padronism and the Utah Copper Company? Initially, most Greeks stayed in Bingham in solidarity with other strikers; they also stayed because Skliris assumed control of Utah's repatriation effort to the Balkan War.

With the help of Stathakos and former business partner Will Caravelis, Skliris transformed the newly created Panhellenic Union from an organ of middle-class Americanization to one of Greek nationalism, and took on the task in Utah of exporting "patriotic" Greeks back to their homeland. Skliris made the most of his self-appointed role as the nationalistic spokesman of Utah's Greek community in the *Salt Lake Tribune:*

> To be sure, the empire of the Ottoman is great and its soldiers are fierce and fanatic fighters, but history has yet to show where the Caucasian Race . . . ever went down to defeat in a war so important as this will be. The Turk is doomed.

More than a touch of irony shadowed Skliris's bravado, given his own recent experience with "fierce and fanatic fighters." Perhaps more remarkable, however, was Skliris's identification of Greeks as "Caucasian." Like Moyer, Skliris also sought to redeem Greek workers to a nativist public by emphasizing their Americanness and whiteness. Skliris thus used the Balkan War not only to rehabilitate the padrone system, but to whiten himself and his rebellious constituency in the eyes of Utah's middle class.

The Utah Copper Company capitalized on these events by acquiring much-needed strikebreakers. Although Leonidas Skliris had resigned as the company's labor agent, his subordinate, Gus Paulos, sent one hundred Greek strikebreakers to Bingham on 10 October. Hundreds of angry Greek strikers confronted their countrymen at the mine gates, but enough of these newly imported workers remained on the job to start up three steam shovels that day. . . . During the ensuing weeks, hundreds more Italian, Greek, and Mexican workers poured into Bingham, enabling the Utah Copper Company to resume full production by 15 November. . . .

For the Greek strikers and strikebreakers who remained in Bingham, the 1912 episode left enduring ideological divisions that would take more than a generation to heal. Not coincidentally, copper miners in Bingham remained without a union until 1946, when the International Union of Mine, Mill, and Smelter Workers, an offspring of the WFM, finally won a union contract. Many of the 1912 strike's most militant Greek participants scattered throughout the West; some, such as Louis Theos, became organizers for the IWW, while others joined fellow union members in the coal fields of Ludlow, Colorado, the site of the infamous Ludlow Massacre of 1914.

If immigrant workers emerged from 1912 a class divided, padrones emerged more unified than ever before. The reorganization of padronism that occurred during the strike became dramatically evident in the cross-ethnic alliances that resulted. In December 1912, as the strike wound down, Skliris formed a seven-year business partnership with Italian padrone Moses Paggi to provide immigrant laborers to the Utah Power & Light Company. Skliris and Paggi charged immigrant workers five cents a day rather than a dollar a month, and deducted the tribute directly from workers' wages, bypassing any troublesome problems of collection or enforcement. Equally if not more significant, padrones also imported men from beyond their home country's borders. The Mexican strikebreakers who arrived in Bingham in 1912 were not brought there by a Mexican padrone, but by Japanese contractor E. D. Hashimoto, whose connections among nonwhite workers in Mexico served him well after 1912. In the process, Mexicans became the newest of Bingham's many new immigrants—like the Japanese, a nonwhite group whose admission into American labor unions would be vigorously resisted for years to come.

For Bingham's American-born residents, the strike thoroughly discredited any formal working-class organizations. The Bingham local survived for a few years, but only as a shell of its former self. Although the Socialists still commanded 20 percent of Bingham's electorate during the strike, they polled barely 3 percent in congressional elections two years later. At the city council level, the Republicans acquired a virtual monopoly on power, polling 74 percent of the vote and winning all five seats in the fall of 1913. Formerly one of Utah's most politically radical communities, the town of Bingham Canyon had quickly become one of its most conservative. For the American-born radicals who stayed in Bingham such as E. G. Locke, the Bingham defeat meant not only the loss of his job as the union's financial secretary, but a subsequent lifetime of blacklists and temporary work.

For western social historians, the significance of the impressive, but short-lived militancy of Greek, Italian, and Japanese workers does not lie in the event's typicality or its far-reaching impact on the western labor movement. The WFM's loss of the Bingham local did not cripple the union, nor did other groups of unskilled immigrants subsequently begin "taking over" WFM locals. Rather, it is precisely the atypical features of the Bingham strike—the unusual prominence of rank and file immigrants and their demands against both immigrant elites and would-be union leaders—that suggest its importance to western social historians. The tensions and loyalties within and between immigrant groups underscores just how intertwined and mutable racial, ethnic, and class formations could be in the West. Organizers mobilized Greek strikers as both workers and immigrants, and, at different moments of the strike, as both white and non-white workers. The relationships between race, ethnicity, and class could cut in different and sometimes unpredictable directions, inducing the same Greek workers to fight both Leonidas Skliris and Charles Moyer at distinct moments. The choices Greek workers and Skliris made about their ethnicity occurred within an intensely nativist and polarized political context, one that at least partially defined the very meaning of being Greek in racial and political terms. Ethnicity for these immigrants existed as an invention of American society, as suggested by Werner Sollors, but it emerged as an identity whose meaning was forged out of conflicts between different classes and different races of immigrants. The struggle to construct ethnicity in Bingham also demonstrated the conflict over the elastic but always racialized definitions of both Americanization and radicalism, a struggle in which an immigrant working class, an immigrant middle class, and American radicals all participated.

The Bingham strike also suggests ways of rethinking some of the conceptual challenges—both new and traditional—confronting western labor history. It is only by examining the intersections between race, ethnicity, and class, so richly intertwined during the Bingham strike, that their historical meaning and significance begins to emerge. Recognizing how the category of Caucasian worker changed and expanded during the Bingham strike, for example, helps us make distinctions between different ethnicities and different forms of racism; and it encourages us to avoid flattening the meaning of race and ethnicity across the nineteenth and twentieth centuries. To conclude that the WFM declined in Bingham merely because it accepted racist practices and therefore could no longer be considered truly radical, would obscure the complexity of the union's social history by failing to historicize the meaning of *either* racism or radicalism. From its inception, the WFM's socialist politics coexisted with a commitment to excluding non-white workers, a connection that problematizes idealized definitions of western labor radicalism and narratives of its growth and decline. If race and ethnicity constituted highly mutable social constructs in Bingham, so too did radicalism and Americanization remain contested concepts whose meanings developed out of the conflicts between working-class and middle-class immigrants, "old" radicals and "new" immigrants. Recognizing the tensions between Charles Moyer and Greek strikers does not mean the WFM was conservative, but suggests that more and more diverse kinds of radicals worked and organized in Bingham than previously thought. It was the militancy and, by 1912 standards, the radical cross-ethnic and cross-racial solidarity of Greek, Italian, and Japanese immigrants that redefined the union's strike agenda and challenged, at least temporarily, the WFM's increasingly nativist politics. The challenge to western labor historians should not be to examine how ethnicity and race necessarily weakened the growth of an indigenous and ideologically pure western radicalism, but how the ethnicity and race of western radicals—"old" native-born and "new" immigrant alike—shaped *both* the growth and decline of western labor radicalism.

Y *FURTHER READING*

James B. Allen, *The Company Town in the American West* (1966)

Ronald C. Brown, *Hard-Rock Miners: The Intermountain West, 1860–1920* (1979)

James W. Byrkit, *Forging the Copper Collar: Arizona's Labor-Management War of 1901–1921* (1982)

Cletus E. Daniel, *Bitter Harvest: A History of California Farmworkers, 1870–1941* (1981)

Melvyn Dubofsky, *We Shall Be All: A History of the Industrial Workers of the World* (1969)

James H. Ducker, *Men of the Steel Rails: Workers on the Atchison, Topeka and Santa Fe Railroad, 1869–1900* (1983)

James C. Foster, ed., *American Labor in the Southwest: The First One Hundred Years* (1982)

Howard M. Gitelman, *Legacy of the Ludlow Massacre: A Chapter in American Industrial Relations* (1988)

Rudolph Lapp, *Blacks in Gold Rush California* (1977)

Janet LeCompte, ed., *Emily: Diary of a Hard-Worked Woman* (1987)

Irene Ledesma, "Texas Newspapers and Chicana Workers' Activism, 1919–1974," *Western Historical Quarterly,* 26 (Autumn 1995): 301–31

Richard E. Lingenfelter, *Hardrock Miners: A History of the Mining Labor Movement in the American West, 1863–1893* (1974)

Hugh T. Lovin, ed., *Labor in the West* (1986)

Philip J. Mellinger, *Race and Labor in Western Copper: The Fight for Equality, 1896–1918* (1995)

Stuart Creighton Miller, *The Unwelcome Immigrant: The American Image of the Chinese, 1785–1882* (1969)

Carey McWilliams, *Factories in the Field: The Story of Migratory Farm Labor in California* (1939)

Bruce Nelson, *Workers on the Waterfront: Seamen, Longshoremen, and Unionism in the 1930s* (1988)

Rodman Wilson Paul, *Mining Frontiers of the Far West, 1848–1880* (1963)

William G. Robbins, *Hard Times in Paradise: Coos Bay, Oregon, 1850–1986* (1988)

Vicki L. Ruiz, *Cannery Women, Cannery Lives: Mexican Women, Unionization, and the California Processing Industry 1930–1950* (1987)

Alexander Saxton, *The Indispensable Enemy: Labor and the Anti-Chinese Movement in California* (1971)

Carlos A. Schwantes, *Hard Traveling: A Portrait of Work Life in the New Northeast* (1994)

————, *Radical Heritage: Labor, Socialism, and Reform in Washington and British Columbia, 1885–1917* (1979)

————, "Wage Earners and Wealth Makers," in *The Oxford History of The American West,* ed. Clyde A. Milner II, Carol A. O'Connor, and Martha A. Sandweiss (1994)

David F. Selvin, *A Place in the Sun: A History of California Labor* (1981)

Duane A. Smith, *Rocky Mountain Mining Camps: The Urban Frontier* (1967)

Clark C. Spence, *Mining Engineers and the American West: The Lace Boot Brigade, 1849–1933* (1970)

Mark Wyman, *Hard Rock Epic: Western Miners and the Industrial Revolution, 1860–1910* (1979)

Otis E. Young, Jr., *Black Powder and Hand Steel: Miners and Machines on the Old Western Frontier* (1976)

Liping Zhu, "'A Chinaman's Chance' on the Rocky Mountain Frontier," *Montana, The Magazine of Western History,* 45 (Autumn/Winter 1995): 36–51

CHAPTER
10

Living on the Land,

Leaving the Land

Y

The story of the agricultural settlement of the West is one of high hopes and shattered dreams, of living on the land and leaving the land. In the 1870s, farmers moved out into the central plains of Kansas, Nebraska, and Colorado drawn by cheap land and the promise that rain follows the plow. The realities of aridity forced most to beat a belated retreat until new ways of dealing with the environment emerged. Only a few years later, new settlers followed—immigrants enticed by railroad promotions and "free" government lands. Agricultural science inflated farmer hopes. Irrigation and dry farming techniques developed by land-grant universities in the West persuaded many individuals that the high-plains areas would support family farms. The first two decades of the twentieth century saw a rush of homesteaders to the northern tier of western states. There they faced the harsh winters, thin soils, and insect infestations. The rains never seemed to come when needed, and their bleak isolation made some doubt the usefulness of both science and human effort. Many either failed before 1920 or were dragged under by the agricultural depression following World War I.

At the same time farmers were failing in the West, the federal government committed itself to turning western Indians into small independent farmers as a means of civilizing and saving them from extinction. Few Indian groups readily cooperated with this planned transformation. After passage of the 1887 Dawes General Allotment Act, the government set about breaking up reservations into small 80 to 160 acre individual allotments, opening "surplus" lands to non-Indian farmers. Between 1887 and 1934, American Indians lost 83 percent of their 156 million acres of reservation land, ushering in a period of increased dependency, but not of cultural extinction.

Making a living from the arid lands of the interior West has always been difficult. Why, then, did so many men and women try to make a life as farmers in this region? Even as they were struggling and failing, why did the government persist in its belief that Indians should become farmers too?

Does "leaving the land" carry the same meaning for Indians as it did for non-Indian homesteaders?

Υ D O C U M E N T S

The first three documents survey the experience of Indians with settled reservation and allotted agriculture. The first is an excerpt from an extended council meeting on the Uintah-Ouray Reservation in eastern Utah in 1903, a document full of Indian voices. Special Agent James McLaughlin, the Indian Bureau's point-man for difficult negotiations, explains the government's reasons for breaking the reservation into individual allotments. In turn, Ute speakers try to explain why—legally, culturally, and economically—they oppose such actions. Pay attention to the metaphors these Ute speakers use to express their arguments. This is a frustrating document, a classic example of the cultural and conceptual gulf separating Indians and whites. The next two documents are reminiscences of reservation farming in Montana. John Stands-in-Timber, a Northern Cheyenne leader, recounts the problems of learning how to farm. In the same selection, Ella C. Deloria, a Yankton Sioux scholar and educator, recalls how farming disrupted traditional patterns of native life. The third document is Martin Charlot's account of the futility of Flathead-Salish farming.

The final three documents describe the decision to move out on the land. The fourth document narrates the reminiscences of a Danish father and son. The Jorgensens moved from Waupaca, Wisconsin, to Dagmar, Montana, in 1906. The father, Jorgen, is motivated to move in order to live with fellow Danes, whereas the son, Otto, sees the move west as a great American adventure. The fifth document is Elinore Pruitt Stewart's 1913 letter to a friend expressing her enthusiasm for women taking up homesteading. Her words convey the seemingly realistic dreams that lured so many onto the land. The final document is Montana farmer Edward J. Bell's account of his family's efforts at dry farming between 1911 and 1923. He provides a more realistic assessment of the successes and failures, the aspirations and broken hopes of farming in a marginal environment, that led many to leave the land.

Northern Utes Respond to the Break-up of Their Reservation, 1903

Minutes of Council held at Uinta Agency, Whiterocks, Utah, by James McLaughlin, United States Indian Inspector, with the Uinta and White River Ute Indians belonging on the Uinta Reservation, Utah, for discussion and consideration of the provisions of the Act of May 27, 1902, affecting said Indians, and as amended by the Indian Appropriation Act approved March 3, 1903.

Uintah Reservation Allotment Council Proceedings, 1903. National Archives, Record Group 75, Bureau of Indian Affairs, Uintah Reservation, Special Case 147.

Monday, May 18, 127 Indians in attendance

Inspector [James] McLaughlin: My Friends, I am pleased to see such a large representative gathering, and I shake hands with each and every one of you here assembled. . . .

Until quite recently, the policy of our Government has been that Indians had unquestioned right to all lands of their respective reservations, but a recent decision of the Supreme Court of the United States is that Indians have no right to any part of their reservations except what they may require for allotments in severalty or can make proper use of.

This was the decision of the Supreme Court on January 5th last in the case of a Kiowa Indian of Oklahoma named Lone Wolf, which involved the question of the Indian's title to lands. The court decided that the Government had the right to legislate in regard to the surplus lands of Indians without consulting the Indians concerned. But if they take allotments, they cannot be disturbed,—their title to the lands allotted to them being secured to them by law. . . . The Secretary of the Interior and the Commissioner of Indian Affairs are very anxious that you consent to the provisions of the Act so that you may get the best of your reservation lands for yourselves. . . .

After you have taken your allotments the remaining land is to be opened for settlement, and every person who takes any of this remaining land must file upon it under the homestead law and pay $1.25 per acre for it, and the proceeds will be for your benefit. The expenses of alloting your lands will be charged to that fund, and the remainder will be expended for the benefit of the Uinta and White River Utes in the discretion of the Secretary.

I do not know, my friends, that I can make this any plainer. . . . I am here to obtain the consent of you people to accept allotments as specified by the law, 80 acres to every head of a family and 40 to each other member, and 250,000 acres pasture land south of Strawberry River for use of your cattle and horses, and the remaining land, after the 1st of October 1904, to be opened for settlement to homesteaders who must pay $1.25 per acre.

My friends, if I had my choice in this matter I would be glad to see you occupy all of this country but this is impossible. The White people are coming into that country and no power can keep them out. The only land the Indian is sure of is that which he takes as his allotment. . . .

I do not want to say too much to day so that you might forget or get mixed, so I think we had better adjourn till tomorrow at ten o'clock, and I hope you will be able to tell me what you think of the proposition. . . .

Tuesday, May 19, 120 Indians in attendance

Inspector McLaughlin: My friends, we have met again and I am very glad to see so many of you assembled here to day. I explained the object of my visit here very carefully yesterday, and I hope that you all understand it fully. If there is anything that you do not understand clearly, I wish you to ask questions so that I can explain it to you. . . .

Tim Johnson: You are here now to ask these Indians a question. What do you want to ask about? We hav'nt got a whole lot of things to talk about with you. This land is ours and we hav'nt got it for sale. The Indians say that they want to keep it and hold it if they can. When they put us on this reservation, it means the President told us to hold this reservation and they were not to open it. He said "I put you on that land, and I want you to stay on it." This whole land used to belong to the Indians at one time.

That is the reason I talk so. He is not going to break this reservation and settle anyone upon it. I was born here on this land and we do not want to give it up. . . .

Inspector McLaughlin: . . . Now my friends, Tim Johnson has raised a question that I am very glad to have brought up. He says there was a large tract of country set apart for your people, that you were to have for your-selves for all time. . . . The reservations were made large in days gone by when you could make a living by hunting and large reservations were then necessary and possible, but with the tide of immigration coming into the country, game has become scarce and you can no longer live by hunting: and therefore you must take to agriculture to make a living for yourselves and families. . . . Now, Congress has enacted a law affecting you people. It says you are to have lands allotted to you and I have been sent out here to explain the Act and obtain your consent to accept your allotments. . . . If the consent of you people cannot be obtained by June 1st, that is in eleven days from now, the Secretary must proceed to allot the lands to you under the Act. . . . The policy of the Government in regard to Indian reservations has changed during the past year. There will be no more treaties made with Indians. The surplus lands will be opened to settlement but the Indians will be protected in their homes. . . .

Appah: You are my friend. What have you been telling these Indians? I do not like that. When the Indians were given this land and when they pulled the chain over and surveyed it, they told us that this land would be ours always and that it would never be opened. That is the reason we do not know anything about opening our reservation. The Indians have lots of horses, and when you tell us that we must take farms, we do not like that on account of our horses. I have a father in Washington. It is on account of this reservation that I have that father. That is the reason the Indians think of their father in Washington upon whom they depend for these things. We do not listen to any White Man out here. We do not listen to the Mormons here. That is the reason I do not like what you tell us.

Sowsonocutt: They did not put us here on this reservation for nothing. They put us here a long time ago. That is how we came on this reservation. That's the reason we like this land here and we are holding it tight. All this land belongs to us and this reservation here belongs to the little children growing up. We do not like what you tell us when you talk about giving us little pieces of land. It is not good. The Indians have lots of cattle and horses. When we take the Government's little pieces of land, how are we to run our horses inside on little pieces of land? . . .

Capt. Parank: I do not want you to steal my money. I heard all you had to say. I heard you, and I think I understand you all right, but I do not believe what you tell me. . . .

Capt. Woods: I like this reservation, this land. I hold on to it tight. I do not want to let it go. This land here don't belong to the people back there who make the law: it belongs to these people who have black hands. They do not want to see this reservation opened. We like this reservation here, and we want to keep it. We do not Want to give any of the water away or let any of it go.

Wapsock: We do not want this reservation line changed in any way. We want to keep it now just as it is; that's the way the other reservations are. . . . We have an Agent here to watch it. The Indians do not understand anything about being put on a little farm. Even if they talk about that in Washington, we do not like it. . . .

Shatkwitch: . . . Here is our own reservation line over here. Here is water running from both ranges of mountains here. That belongs to the Indians. The Indians here are holding it back because they like it. I do not like this making ditches over the reservation. . . . How are our horses going to range? We do not know anything about selling this land. . . . I do not want any of it cut off. . . . We need all that country down there for our horses to graze it, and the horses come to the streams for water. That is the reason I like this land. I do not want to sell it. . . .

Black Hawk: I have listened to what you have said to these people. I can understand some of what you say myself. I do not like it. After you allot the land and sell it, I do not like that. I have no sense, and I know it, I just play with this land, but when I had money, I threw it away. I am here on this land. That is what holds me up. I do not want you to steal it from me. . . .

Ebenezer: That is all right. These fellows here are holding their reservation. It is the truth. I have been put on this reservation here. They tell me, "You raise what you want to eat." and I do that. Washington says that, and I do what Washington tells me to do. . . . This is my land. I am holding this wood back to burn. These streams of water here, I am holding them. We want them all. . . . I am on this reservation, and I do not want this land thrown open.

Inspector McLaughlin: Now my friends, I have listened to you and every word has passed into my ears. . . .

Now my friends, the statements of your speakers have convinced me that you do not understand what I have said. From your speeches you are evidently laboring under a mistake by thinking that I am here to negotiate an agreement with you people. You seem to be impressed with the belief that I am sent here to make a treaty with you for the opening of your reservation. You lose sight of the fact, or do not understand, that this which I present to you is already a law of Congress. I am here to submit this law to you and explain every feature of it that you may understand, so that you may consent to take your allotments. . . .

My friends, your holding the reservation as in the past is out of the question. As certainly as the sun rises to-morrow it is to be opened. . . .

Now, it is your duty to listen to reason and to the arguments which I have presented. Remember that our talk must be with no hard feelings. We must have our discussion in a friendly manner. I make this explanation to you because I see your talk has been all along one line. . . .

Thursday, May 21, 112 Indians in attendance

Appah: I do not understand what that new law is. I do not understand about our reservation line made by that old treaty, how this new law can thrown that off. . . . You are pulling me round from this line here. I do not feel very happy when you do that. . . . When you cut our land up and put me on a piece of land I don't understand it. . . . I can't understand why you are pulling me round over the country, but you are pulling me round like a horse. You are pulling down the Agency and you are pulling the school down too. . . . I am not going to think the way of this new law. Why don't you throw that law away? You are just like a storm coming down from the mountains when the flood is coming down the stream and we can't stop it. I have this reservation line fixed and you can't throw it aside.

Friday, May 22, 120 Indians in attendance

Little Jim: I am going to talk to you anyhow, even if you have no ears. This reservation has not been put here for the fun of it. Washington put this reservation here and all other reservations all over this land. This Agency is Washington's thoughts, and it is good. That's the reason you cannot open this reservation. . . . Washington said,—"No one can take any part of this land I will not allow it." Now you did not know about this treaty so I am telling you that now. I know this because I heard Washington tell it. Now this land was put here for the Indians, not for everyone; it was put here for us. That's the reason we want to keep it. We keep it for these young people growing up. . . .

Grant: I want to talk and will talk now. I have a mind of my own. I think that Congress should have sent a man out here before this law was passed, to talk with the Indians and have an understanding with them. Then we would have got along easier. I do not know anything about this allotment business and I sit back here and listen to the two sides. I do not know which way to go. It hurts me a whole lot. They pull me one way and the other, and I don't know which way to stay. I work on my farm and raise crops. Now, when they come here cutting the land into little pieces it looks as though they would do me up. That's the reason I do not like it. What are my horses going to do when I have only a little piece of land? Must I tie my horses in that little field? That's the reason I do not like it . . . .

John Star: I have just come down from the saw mill where I have been working. I just got here now. You see me and I see you. My flesh is black: you have good flesh, you are white like this paper here. My flesh looks like the ground. That's the reason I am going to keep it. Why should I give it away? I like it: I was raised here. That's the reason I have got it right in my heart. I am pretty well acquainted with the White Man. I know him. The White Men want something all the time. They want everything. They are after this land and are troubling me all the time. If I have cattle the White men will come in and drive them off. Then there will be trouble. That's the reason I will not give it away. . . .

Sockive: Can you hear what I say? We will not give this land up.

Inspector McLaughlin: I have heard all your speakers have said, but do not think it is the real sentiment of a majority of the people of this reservation.

Sockive: You keep saying the same thing. That's the reason I keep saying the same thing to you. I talk to you the same as you have talked to me.

Inspector McLaughlin: . . . There is a great difference between the talk I am giving you and what you are giving me. I am here to represent the great Government of the United States in this matter. I explained to you the law which has been enacted by the Great Council, the law that has been approved by the President of the United States, whom you call Washington. I have explained to you that it will make no difference what you say as to whether the law will be carried out or not. . . . Your talk has been simply along one line, and that is protesting against the opening of your reservation. My friends, you seem not to have grasped the thought that what you have been discussing is already past, and all your talk on that line amounts to nothing. You are on record as being opposed to it. The reservation, my friends will be opened up notwithstanding your protests. . . .

Wanrodes: My friend, I like these mountains and I like this water; I like the timber; I like the coal in the coal mine. The mountains have range for my horses. I do not think Washington will take away what he told me I had got. . . . We want a place for our horses to graze. . . . We have farms down here on the Bench where there is no timber: we want to hold those farms, and we want to hold some of this timber up here in the mountains too. . . .

I do not like this 250,000 acres of pasture land. I have a cattle range at Rock Creek west of here and north of Strawberry River. What will they do with my cattle range? I want you to fix it so I can hold that piece of land. . . . I would feel more satisfied if you could say it was more than 40 acres for one person. I have lots of cattle. I hear that if we do not come to you and say that we agree, you will go back and say: "These Indians would not agree to this." Then they will come back and give me land. I do not like that. I want to pick my own land.

. . . I have my farm that Colonel [Agent James E.] Randlett made for me and I want to hold it. I have a good farm from which I sell hay and get $8.00 a ton. Some times I get 400 dollars from it and I put it in my pocket, and I like that. I like what you say. I like it that I can go where I wish without a pass. I can go and see my friends the Bannocks or anyone else.

Now I want you to give me my piece of land on Rock Creek where my cattle are. . . .

Charley Mack: . . . Before they passed such a law, someone ought to have come here and spoken to the Indians first. That is the reason the

Indians are so scared,—it has come so sudden. They were not expecting anything like this. That is the reason they are so scared.

What are the Indians going to do? It is like sand. You throw water upon sand and it will cave in and wash off: so with Indians, after a while there will be none left. The reason the Indians are so scared is there is no more land. If they take this land away from us we can find no more land to go to. We are done for. We are afraid of the Mormon people. They do not like the Indians. If an Indian goes into a Mormon's pasture for his horses, the Mormon would kill him. That's the reason they are afraid. This opening business is the same way. The Indians will have a farm near a White Man's. If the Indian tries to get water for his farm, some White Man will stop this, and maybe take a shovel and strike him on the head. There will be a lot of drawbacks. Many of these young men here, cannot talk English. There will be disagreements and quarrels all the time. . . .

Tim Johnson: These White Men who have farms on the bench take too much water for their grass. If many White men come in here they will hold all the water and make the Indians pay for what they want. These Indians will gain nothing by letting their land go. You will not listen to the Indians. You are getting a lot of money, you are getting paid for this. . . .

Saturday, May 23, 134 Indians in attendance

Inspector McLaughlin: . . . My friends, we have held six councils and have been discussing this matter for the past six days. This is the last public council that I intend holding with you for this purpose. When we adjourn to day it will be the final adjournment. I feel that I have done my full duty in placing this matter before you people that you might understand every clause and phase of it. And I am confident that each and every one of you understands the full meaning of this new law, and it is now for you to determine whether you consent or not to the acceptance of your allotments under the provisions of the Act. . . .

. . . My friends, I repeat again, that I am very much pleased with your courteous treatment of me since I have been here with you, but before closing our council I am going to give you another piece of advice. This paper which I have read to you will be at the Agency Office while I remain here, and I would like to see all of you come in and sign it, at least a sufficient number to make it acceptable to the Department, so that I can have the required number of names attached to the paper that will go forward to Washington. The Government at Washington is your best friend and does not wish to impose any hardship upon you people, and does that which is for your best interests. . . .

I shake hands with each and every one of you with a good heart. I leave with no enmity against any of you people and I hope you feel the same towards me. . . .

[Editor's Note: Of 280 adult Uintah and White River Ute males, only 82 signed the Allotment Agreement.]

John Stands-in-Timber and Ella C. Deloria Recall the Early Days of Reservation Farming, 1877–1900

[John Stands-in-Timber:] The government started the Indians raising gardens as soon as they surrendered. Some had gardens of corn and other crops. . . . They had forgotten how, though they all used to garden in the old days before they hunted buffalo. Now they were learning about new crops as well, things they had never seen before. The Dull Knife people got to Oklahoma in 1877 about the time the watermelons ripened, and when the Southern Cheyennes gave them some they cut them up and boiled them like squash. They did not know you could eat them raw. But later when they planted their own they put sugar with the seeds. They said it would make them sweeter when they grew.

When they reached Tongue River every man was supposed to have a garden of his own. A government farmer went around to teach them. And many of them worked hard, even carrying buckets of water from the river by hand. One man, Black White Man, wanted to raise cotton. He had seen it in Oklahoma. He plowed a piece of ground and smoothed it up, and when it was ready he took his wife's quilt and made little pieces from the inside and planted them with a garden hoe. When his wife missed the quilt, she got after him. He was afraid to tell her, but finally he said, "I got it and took out the cotton and planted it. We will have more quilts than we need, as soon as it grows."

When they first learned to plow in Oklahoma the farmer told them to get ready and come to a certain place and he would show them. They did not understand. They thought "Get ready" meant fancy costumes and not their new pants and shirts. So everybody had feathers on their heads and necklaces and leggings and fancy moccasins. It looked like a dance, not a farming lesson. And all the women and children went along to see them.

The farmer told one man to grab the handles while he started ahead with the team. But the plow jumped out of the ground and turned over, and the Indian fell down. But he tried again, and by the time they got back around he was doing pretty well. Then they all tried. At last they came to one man who had been watching closely. When he started off the dirt rolled right over and he went clear around that way, and the criers started announcing, "Ha-aah! See that man!" The women made war cries and everybody hollered just as if he had counted coup.

Another time when they practiced plowing down there, one man plowed up a bull snake and the next man plowed up a rattlesnake, and after that they were all afraid to go.

In Montana they began to help each other. The government issued plows to quite a few men, and in Birney the Fox Military Society used to

Reprinted from John Stands-in-Timber and Margot Liberty, *Cheyenne Memories*, 276–78, by permission of Yale University Press. Copyright © 1967 by Yale University Press. Excerpted by permission of Yale University Press.

Reprinted from *Speaking of Indians*, 60–63, by Ella C. Deloria. Copyright 1979, University of South Dakota Press.

plow together as soon as the frost was out. They would all gather at the farthest place up the river and work together until that was done, and then move to the next. They had seven or eight plows and it went faster that way. Besides, it was more fun.

[Ella C. Deloria:] At length there came the time when individual allotments of land were made. Families were encouraged to live out on them and start to be farmers forthwith. Equipment for this, as well as some essential furniture, was given the most docile ones by way of inducement. But again, it wasn't easy to make the spiritual and social adjustment. The people were too used to living in large family groups, cooperatively and happily. Now here they were in little father-mother-child units (with an occasional grandparent, to be sure), often miles from their other relatives, trying to farm an arid land—the very same land from which, later on, white farmers of Old World tradition and training could not exact even a subsistence living. Enduring frightful loneliness and working at unfamiliar tasks just to put himself ahead financially were outside the average Dakota's ken. For him there were other values. The people naturally loved to foregather; and now the merest excuse for doing so became doubly precious. For any sort of gathering it was the easiest thing to abandon the small garden, leave the stock to fend for themselves, and go away for one to four weeks. On returning, they might find the place a wreck. That was too bad; but to miss getting together with other Dakotas was far worse.

After a time, however, they were making better, larger houses—neater, too, with the logs planed so as to fit closer and requiring less of the mud chinking that was always coming loose in the first cabins. The doors and windows fitted better, there were floors, and the roofs were of boards. The people began to make ingenious adaptations of some elements in their old life to the new. For instance, at one period they transferred the art decorations of the tipi to the loghouse. Out of G.I. muslin they made very large wall coverings, a carry over from the dew curtain of a tipi and called by the same term, *ozan*. On these they painted beautiful designs and made lively black and white drawings of historical scenes of hunting or battles or peacemaking between tribes, and courtship scenes, games, and such like activities of the past. People went visiting just to see one another's pictographs and to hear the stories they preserved. . . .

My impression is that the women took special pride in caring for their new homes and new furniture. Once my mother took me along to call on Nancy Gall, daughter of the famous chief, and we found her vigorously scrubbing her pine floor to a brilliant yellow and cleaning house generally. "I promised the *tiwaheawanyaka* [guardian-of-the-family] to do this every Floorwashing Day [Saturday], and I have never missed yet!" she explained, rising from her knees to greet my mother.

A salute right here to the government field matrons, those guardians-of-the-family! Attached to the agency staffs, they did a great deal of good in helping the women to a fine start and inspiring them to learn. It was a pity they were withdrawn, for, in a way, they were the most constructive influence exerted by government at that period. They were no Home Ec. Ph.D's, that's true. They were only sensible, motherly women, usually elderly with *hearts that were right*. And that, I think, is nearly enough in practical work with so called backward peoples. Feeling their warmth and sympathy, the people responded well in numerous cases and spoke of them later on with respectful gratitude. Among other things, those women taught the Dakota housewives to make "lung bread," as yeast raised bread was named because of the air holes. Formerly only baking-powder dough was known, but now there was a definite preference for the new kind. The field matrons taught many. Others made long journeys to our mission to be taught there.

I can imagine the delight of the husbands when their wives wished to make the trip. With what sudden alacrity they must have stepped around, getting the team hitched to the wagon! To their monotonous new life, it was a welcome break to get together with other men also camping around the mission for one reason or another. "We are here while *winunhca* learns how to make lung bread." So they would account for themselves, temporarily happy again, as they sat in circles upon the ground to smoke the endless pipe and talk about past glories.

They needed those breaks, poor things! It was they who suffered the most from the enforced change, whether they realized it or not. It was their life primarily that was wrecked; it was their exclusive occupation that was abruptly ended. The women could go right on bearing children and rearing them. They could cook, feed their families, set up and strike camp unaided, pack and unpack when on a trip. Even embroidery, exclusively a woman's art, was not cut off suddenly. It tapered away as the buffalo and deer skins on which the work was done became more and more scarce. By slow degrees, meanwhile, they could learn other work and were able to make the shift more easily.

The man was the tragic figure. Frustrated, with his age old occupation suddenly gone, he was left in a daze, unable to overcome the strange and passively powerful inertia that stayed him from doing anything else. And so he sat by the hour, indifferent and inactive, watching—perhaps envying— his wife, as she went right on working at the same essential role of woman that had been hers since time immemorial. In such a mental state, what did he care that unsympathetic onlookers called him "lazy Indian" and accused him of driving his wife, like a slave, while "he took his ease"! As though he enjoyed it! If, as he sat there, someone had called, "Hey! There's a herd of buffalo beyond that hill! Come quick!" he would have sprung into life instantly again. But, alas, no such thing would ever happen now. All he could do, or thought he could do, on his "farm" was to water the horses mechanically, bring in fuel and water, cut a little hay, tend a little garden. He did it listlessly, almost glad when the garden died on his hands for lack of rain. His heart was not in what he was doing anyway—until something human came up: a gathering of the people, where he could be with many relatives again; or a death, when he must go to help with the mourning; or a cow to be butchered, reminiscent of the hunt; or time to go to the agency for the biweekly issue of rations. That he must not miss. For him and his family, that was what still gave meaning to life.

Martin Charlot Speaks to the Futility of
Flathead-Salish Farming, 1890–1910

In the Bitterroot when my grandfather, Victor, was chief, we Salish started farming. The government told us to do it and we did. We had no equipment except the few things the agent gave us, such as harness and plows. We made fenceposts in the mountains and hauled them home by packing them on our horses. Each of the Indian families fenced small acreages and protected their grain. Then time went on and my grandfather died. My father, Charlot, became chief.

We continued farming. The agent told my father to tell the people they would receive wheat and oat seed. My father told the tribesmen to do more farming and get the seed. They did. We got more plows and harness. We helped each other with the farm work. One Indian farmer had two or three plows going at the same time. Everyone helped everyone else in the harvest. We didn't have any threshing machines. We put the grain on buffalo hides that the women had sewed together. Then we led horses over the grain to separate it. Several of the men would lift the robes and shake them to let the wind blow the chaff out. We also had two mills going and we used to fetch the grain to the mill on pack horses. The mill was about 12 miles from where we lived.

Everything was going along fine. We were making a good living and learning the White man's way. Then Garfield came to see us. He came to visit my father, for Charlot was the head man among the Salish. Garfield told my father that we would have to move out of the Bitterroot and go to the Jocko.

"I am doing some farming," my father said. "I am getting good crops and my people and I are living here as the agents and priests have taught us to do. I am not going to move."

"If you don't move you will be treated like a fish in dirty water," Garfield said.

"This is my home," my father answered. "By the 1855 treaty, we don't have to move. We will stay in the Bitterroot."

A general who was with Garfield spoke up and told my father that he would send an army in there and kill us if we didn't move. Still my father would not agree to go. Some of the other tribesmen pulled out and went to the Jocko. Arlee led them.

About a year later, the general came back and told my father that we had to move. He said that my father was no longer the head man of the tribe now that Washington considered Arlee the head man. That made my father mad because Arlee was not a full-blooded Salish. He was mostly Nez Percé. So every year for about three years this same general came back and asked us to go, and every time my father said he wouldn't do it. Finally, my father said that he would move to the Bannock tribe or the Shoshoni tribe and live

From "Samples of Pend d'Oreille Oral Literatures and Salish Narratives," by J. Verne Dusenberry, in *Lifeways of the Intermontane and Plains Montana Indians,* ed. by Leslie B. Davis. (Occasional Papers, No. 1, Bozeman: Museum of the Rockies, 1979). Reprinted courtesy of Montana State University, Bozeman.

with them on their reservation, but that he would not go to the Jocko to live. The government men would not agree to that so we stayed in the Bitterroot.

We tried to keep on farming, but Whites came in and homesteaded our land. We could not keep the little patches where we had fenced and had raised our crops. The wild game kept getting scarcer and scarcer. Nearly 20 years went by. We had no money or supplies from the government. Our young men were getting lazy, my father said. Also, many of them wanted to move to the Jocko. One of the leaders of the Salish, Vanderberg, asked my father to take us over. He said that the time had come for us to go. My father sent word that we would move.

A man from the government came to see us. He promised that we could have some livestock. Every family would get one cow and one calf of their own. Besides that, the government would have a herd of steers for us so that every Saturday seven head of steers would be butchered and distributed to us. My father knew some White men in the Bitterroot who had good cows, so he asked if the government would buy the cows and calves from him. The agent said "no," because the cattle would drift away and we would lose them coming over.

We were told also that we should leave behind our belongings such as furniture and equipment, for we would get new things once we got to the Jocko. Some of the people really owned some good machinery and some pretty good household equipment, and they hated to leave it but thought they would get new things, so they just left it. The government man also told my father that the government would buy him a new team and buggy to make the trip over in.

"When you go through Missoula," the government man said, "you look at the residences and see the best-made house that you like. Our carpenters will make one for you just like it."

But when we got to the Jocko, things were not the way they were promised. Whatever we got, we had to work for. There was no new machinery nor household stuff for those people who had left theirs behind. We never saw or heard of the seven head of steers that were to be butchered every Saturday. We never got the cow and the calf apiece like we were promised. My father did not get his new house. Instead, we cut logs and had to haul them to the mill to make lumber for our houses. Then we built our cabins, some near the Agency and more of them along Jocko Creek in the timber. Then, we were told to fence off the land we wanted. Only a few people did that. The next instruction we got was to start farming. Again, only a few people did that. My father refused to do it, although he had put in an irrigation system.

The men in the tribe did all that work digging ditches without getting much pay for it. After the irrigation system was in, many more people started farming. They were successful in farming on both sides of the Jocko River. In time, we even had a threshing machine. Just as we had done in the Bitterroot before the trouble began, we started helping each other out and got quite a bit of farming done. After the harvest, we took the grain to the flour mill and had it made up into flour for our winter provisions. The surplus grain we sold. All in all, we made a good living.

But those days didn't last either. Pretty soon, maybe in 15 years, engineers surveyed the reservation. When my father asked why they were doing it, they told him that the government was just making a survey to determine the acreage. But it wasn't long before we were allotted and the Whites moved in. Then, the government took hold of the irrigation system. They made it bigger, all right, but the Indians didn't get the water when they wanted it and needed it. Their crops burned up. Some of them went in debt. Pretty soon, most of them quit farming. The White man took over everything.

Jorgen and Otto Jorgensen Remember the Decision to Homestead in Montana, 1906

[Jorgen:] One would think that we would have been satisfied to settle down where we were but such was not the case. We had constantly longed for fellowship with other Danes in a Danish congregation in a Danish settlement with a Danish school. There was a Danish Church in Waupaca [Wisconsin] but that was a distance of seven miles away. Our neighbors were all native Americans. Most of them were uneducated and not too intellectual. They were congenial and friendly enough but we got little satisfaction or enjoyment from fellowship with them. The language was a handicap too because Kristiane [his wife] had not had as good an opportunity to learn it as I who had mixed with other people more. She could make herself understood alright but has since improved a great deal. She reads English books quite well but when it comes to writing I have to do it.

In the meantime we had managed to get all the land under cultivation that I was able to handle without hired help. All we had to do was to plant potatoes in the spring, dig them up in the fall, and haul them to town during the winter which was a little too tame an existence. I have mentioned two reasons why we wanted to move but there was a third. The older girls were growing up, and what if one of them should come home some day with one of these individuals with a foreign background and present him as her sweetheart. This was unthinkable. (Strangely enough after we came to Montana one of the girls actually did come and present an American as her sweetheart but he was a high class individual. He was a lawyer who later became district judge for Sheridan and other counties.)

When E. F. Madsen's call came in "Dannevirke" in 1906 to establish a Danish colony in eastern Montana, I immediately said, "That's where we are going," and Kristiane immediately agreed. I think people thought we were crazy to abandon what was, as far as people could tell, the comfort and security we had for insecurity and a cold, harsh climate. "You'll freeze to death out there," they said and related terrifying experiences of people who had succumbed in snowstorms. But it didn't seem to make much of an impression on us. I was past 50 years of age and if we were to build up another farm it was time to get started.

Small Collections 178. Typescripts at Montana Historical Society Archives, 225 N. Roberts Street, Helena, MT 59620.

E. F. Madsen from Clinton, Iowa had been out in Montana on October 6, 1906 to find a place for a new Danish colony and had selected the place where it now is located in the northeast corner of Montana about 25 miles from the Canadian line and close to the Dakota boundary. Madsen named it "Dagmar." Its full name is "Dronning Dagmar's Minde" (Queen Dagmar's Memorial), and is the first such colony in the United States. The land is fertile with smooth rolling prairies. The land was not surveyed but could be claimed by anyone over 21 years of age under Squatter's right. The 160 acres allowed was later increased to 320 acres. . . .

[Otto:] My first recollection of any talk of moving or living anywhere else but where we were, was the folks, setting at the kitchen table one night—it must have been in 1906. Mother was fidgeting with something or other on the table, listening to Pa read aloud from the weekly Danish publication, *Dannevirke,* with a bright, faraway look in her eyes; and when he had finished, she said: "Skul' vi?" (should we?) We kids sat around, I for one, with open mouth, sensing something special was in the wind, and when the word Montana was mentioned,—MONTANA!! Montana to me was a magic word! That's where Falsbuts' were going to go! And Falsbuts' boys had thoroughly briefed me on what could be expected there: buffalo, cowboys, and wild horses—Oh boy! Free land, homesteads, Montana and the West! No one has any idea of what those magic words could conjure up in a 10-year-old boy's mind!

As I have grown older, I have often wondered what prompts the pioneering spirit in some people and leaves others completely devoid of it.

As the folks became serious about the matter, the idea crystallized, as was evidenced by the preparations such as a new cookstove, a swell big kitchen range, new harnesses, etc. It was now "for sure" that the big adventure was about to become a reality. But it was not until the spring of 1908 that all the difficulties of such an undertaking were overcome. Selling the farm, auction sale, getting the cash, etc. We didn't sell much—everything was stuffed into the immigrant-car, (special homeseekers rates) and when I say "stuffed" I mean just that! Cows and calves, chickens, pigs, horses, dogs, (no cats). All household goods, all the farming implements, wagons, mower, hayrake, and hayrack. The hayrack was used to double-deck the chickens above the cows.

I have often wondered what Pa's reactions were to all this. He never showed anything, outwardly. I remember when we left the farm for the last time, and we were about to get into the wagon. He was buttoning his coat with one hand and with the other, reached down to stroke the big old gray tom-cat, which was to be left behind; and he said, "Kitty, Kitty!" I was dumbfounded, for I had never seen him do a thing like that before. He straightened up and looked around at the good new house and big new red barn; and in his slow, easy-going and deliberate way, climbed into the wagon. I have often wondered what his innermost thoughts were at that moment. But like so many thousands before him who have pulled up stakes for the unknown future in the West, he left little room for sentiment. In tribute to my father, I think this was his staunchest moment. Of course, the die was cast; the decision had been made some time before, which also took courage—but the final last look at the fruits of 12 to 14 of his best years, brought from him no outward sign of regret. Nor did he, I'm glad to say, ever live to regret it. To turn his back on all this, against the advice of well-meaning neighbors and friends; and at the age of 51 years, take a family of eight children out into the un-tracked prairies fifty miles from the railroad and "nowhere" with measly small capital, took courage and fortitude, to say the least. That kind of spirit and courage, I'm afraid, is fast becoming a thing of the past in these United States.

Elinore Stewart Advocates Homesteading for Women, 1913

January 23, 1913.

Dear Mrs. Coney,—

When I read of the hard times among the Denver poor, I feel like urging them every one to get out and file on land. I am very enthusiastic about women homesteading. It really requires less strength and labor to raise plenty to satisfy a large family than it does to go out to wash, with the added satisfaction of knowing that their job will not be lost to them if they care to keep it. Even if improving the place does go slowly, it is that much done to stay done. Whatever is raised is the homesteader's own, and there is no house-rent to pay. This year Jerrine [her daughter] cut and dropped enough potatoes to raise a ton of fine potatoes. She wanted to try, so we let her, and you will remember that she is but six years old. We had a man to break the ground and cover the potatoes for her and the man irrigated them once. That was all that was done until digging time, when they were ploughed out and Jerrine picked them up. Any woman strong enough to go out by the day could have done every bit of the work and put in two or three times that much, and it would have been so much more pleasant than to work so hard in the city and then be on starvation rations in the winter.

To me, homesteading is the solution of all poverty's problems, but I realize that temperament has much to do with success in any undertaking, and persons afraid of coyotes and work and loneliness had better let ranching alone. At the same time, any woman who can stand her own company, can see the beauty of the sunset, loves growing things, and is willing to put in as much time at careful labor as she does over the washtub, will certainly succeed; will have independence, plenty to eat all the time, and a home of her own in the end.

Experimenting need cost the homesteader no more than the work, because by applying to the Department of Agriculture at Washington he can get enough of any seed and as many kinds as he wants to make a thorough trial, and it does n't even cost postage. Also one can always get bulletins from there and from the Experiment Station of one's own State concerning

---

Elinore Pruitt Stewart, *Letters of a Woman Homesteader* (Boston: Houghton Mifflin Company, 1914), pp. 213–217.

any problem or as many problems as may come up. I would not, for anything, allow Mr. Stewart [her husband] to do anything toward improving my place, for I want the fun and the experience myself. And I want to be able to speak from experience when I tell others what they can do. Theories are very beautiful, but facts are what must be had, and what I intend to give some time.

Here I am boring you to death with things that cannot interest you! You'd think I wanted you to homestead, would n't you? But I am only thinking of the troops of tired, worried women, sometimes even cold and hungry, scared to death of losing their places to work, who could have plenty to eat, who could have good fires by gathering the wood, and comfortable homes of their own, if they but had the courage and determination to get them.

I must stop right now before you get so tired you will not answer. With much love to you from Jerrine and myself, I am

Yours affectionately,

ELINORE RUPERT STEWART.

The Bell Family Tries Dry Farming, 1911–1923

During the first five years on the farm [in Wibaux County, Montana] our wheat averaged about 15 bushels an acre. That was considerably less than the 23 bushel average for Montana for the same period. All our wheat was on spring or fall plowing as we had not yet learned about summer fallowing. Prices for wheat at Wibaux ranged from about 65 cents to one dollar a bushel. These yields and prices now seem extremely low but we thought our income for those years was fairly satisfactory.

In 1916, when the state had an average yield of 19 bushels an acre of wheat, we got only six or seven because of the rust in our area. The price that year was around $1.50 a bushel and we would have made a killing had it not been for the rust.

In 1917, we harvested 1,021 bushels of wheat from 158 acres and 132 bushels of flaxseed from 19 acres. At wartime prices of $2.05 a bushel for wheat and $3.02 for flaxseed, our returns from these crops were about $2,500. We also sold a few steers. My mother got $5.00 a week from eggs and butter but that was for only part of the year. The weather in 1917 was not as good as we had hoped. Summer showers passed us by and we had some hail damage on our southwest corner.

In 1918 we again complained that rains were not coming our way. Wheat yielded about six bushels an acre compared with six and a half the year before. We had about 200 bushels of flaxseed which sold for $3.30 a bushel and about 800 bushels of wheat at $2.00 a bushel giving us $2,260 from the sale of grain. All our spring wheat that year was Marquis, a new variety that had replaced the old Haynes Bluestem after the rust epidemic of 1916.

Reprinted from *Homesteading in Montana: 1911–1923. Life in the Blue Mountain Country,* 57–60, by Edward J. Bell, Jr. 1975. Courtesy of Montana State University, Bozeman, MT.

In 1919 my father and I decided to go all out for production. Returns from the previous two years of high prices had been very disappointing but dryland farmers always think next year will be better. We planted over 300 acres of wheat and rye and about 50 acres of feed grains.

We had an open winter and got an early start in the spring, but were delayed by snow in late March and early April. The fall and winter had been dry. A little precipitation in May raised our hopes temporarily, but no rain fell after that. The oats failed to germinate; we had little or no garden and wheat prospects dwindled.

Then came the grasshoppers. We got a circular from the Agricultural Experiment Station at Bozeman and used their formula in mixing poisoned bran. After spreading the bran over our fields we saw hordes of insects coming from the draws and rangeland over too wide an area for us and our neighbors to cover. In the circular from Bozeman we also found a diagram for a catching machine. Papa made one and I caught 100 bushels of grasshoppers. At the end of each round the box was full of hoppers. For a scoop I used a square five-gallon oil can with the top cut out. Dry grasshoppers were hard to get from the catcher box into a sack. I finally hauled a tub of water to the field and used a hand sprayer to wet the insects, after which they were easier to manage.

We put the hoppers in the 100-bushel grain tank, resting on posts behind the granary. It was clear that we would have no other use for the grain wagons that year. When the tank was full I quit catching. This operation didn't really benefit the wheat as the damage had already been done, but it was better than to sit around and worry when there wasn't anything else to do. The folks used the hoppers for chicken feed that winter. By the middle of July the grasshoppers had disappeared. We thought this was partly due to parasites and partly because there wasn't anything left for the grasshoppers to eat.

In spite of all this, we had a little wheat at harvest time. The 20 acres of summer fallow was full of Russian thistles but tall enough to use the binder. Other wheat was too short for the binder but Papa made a header by extending the elevator canvas on our eight-foot binder. We made header boxes from a couple of bundle racks and got two neighbor boys to drive the teams. By harvesting around the edges of the draws and other places where any wheat had survived, we were able to cut 200 acres.

The feed grains were complete failures and we got only six loads of rye hay from the 25 acres planted the fall before. I mowed the grass on the hill tops and in the draws. These were places where we had not cut hay in former years when other native grasses were available. We also put up two stacks of Russian thistle hay.

Our 200 acres of wheat yielded 425 bushels of which 99 bushels came from 20 acres of spring wheat on land that had been summer fallowed the year before. This was our first experience with summer fallow.

There wasn't any income that year from the sale of grain because we needed to save the wheat for seed. My father sold a few steers and for a while Mother had a little money from eggs and butter. They also ground some wheat in the feed mill and used it for breakfast food. The bank continued to make loans for current expenses. Averill and Papa spent a rather frustrating winter bringing the cattle through on Russian thistles and the meager amount of other hay and straw. I was a senior in high school then.

In the period 1920–1923, yields were better but prices broke sharply in the fall of 1920 and continued to decline. In view of the depressed situation it was decided that Averill and I should get our college education as soon as possible. During his freshman year, 1920–1921, he found that we could support ourselves while going to college. The folks stuck it out until the 1923 failure of the Wibaux County Bank. This took all their property, because my father was a director with double liability on his stock. Then they also moved to Bozeman where they spent the rest of their lives.

Y *E S S A Y S*

In the first essay, David Rich Lewis, associate professor of history at Utah State University, presents a case study of Indian farming in the arid West. Focusing on the experiences of the Northern Utes of eastern Utah, Lewis describes how federal Indian policies, Ute cultural responses, environmental realities, and the market economy precipitated agricultural failure and ultimately a state of dependency. The story is a common one of Indians living on the land and ultimately losing the land while retaining their sense of identity, place, and cultural value. In the second essay, Gilbert Fite, professor emeritus of history at the University of Georgia and a past president of the Agricultural History Society and both the Western and Southern History associations, considers the lives of his own grandparents and parents in South Dakota. He describes the difficult situation facing Dakota farmers and the poverty and prosperity that kept them going. Although his own grandparents lost their land, Fite maintains that they did enjoy a reasonable standard of living and found joy in their activities. He concludes that farming in the late nineteenth and early twentieth centuries helped raise a new generation of Americans who lived on and ultimately left the land.

Farming and the Northern Ute Experience

DAVID RICH LEWIS

Nineteenth-century American Indian policy rested on the belief that Indians were deficient, and that if they were to survive they must be raised through the social evolutionary stages from savagery to civilization. The idea was to transform Indians into yeomen farmers and farm families, settled and self-sufficient market agriculturalists, the backbone of an idealized Jeffersonian democracy. Applied broadly, agrarian-based policies like allotment had disastrous effects on native environments and subsistence systems, in many cases inducing the very dependency that officials hoped to end. What follows is one case study of this agrarian policy applied to the Northern Utes

David Rich Lewis, "Environment, Subsistence, and Dependency: Farming and the Northern Ute Experience, 1850–1940," from *Overcoming Economic Dependency,* C. Matthew Snipp, ed. Copyright © 1997 by C. Matthew Snipp. Reprinted by permission of the University of Oklahoma Press.

on the Uintah-Ouray Reservation, and their responses to the fundamental cultural changes entailed by a settled agrarian lifestyle.

The Ute (*Núciu*) peoples were a culturally self-identifying group of affiliated Numic-speaking bands inhabiting the intermountain region of modern Utah and Colorado at contact. Utah Ute bands included the Cumumba, Tumpanuwac, Uinta-at, San Pitch, Pahvant, and Sheberetch (later called collectively the Uintah Utes). The Yamparka and Parianuc (White River Utes), the Taviwac (Uncompahgre Utes), and the Wiminuc, Kapota, and Muwac, (Southern and Ute Mountain Utes) comprised the Colorado Ute bands. For most of the year, Utes moved in extended family hunting groups ranging from 20 to 100 people. Band or inter-band congregations for any extended period of time were rare. Notably individualistic, Utes maintained no central councils. Leadership remained local and consensual, based on the proven ability of individuals to perform specific tasks.

Ute subsistence strategies were elegantly adapted to the relative scarcity and local resource concentrations in their environments. The cyclical movements of family groups through familiar, non-exclusive hunting and gathering territories allowed them to exploit the periodic abundance of a wide variety of resources during the season of their precipitous maturation. . . .

Spanish colonial intrusions into the southern reaches of Ute territory were limited, and only a handful of missionary explorers ventured through the heart of the region. Utes readily adopted horses and Spanish trade goods, raided their pueblos and supply lines, aided them against the Comanches, and contracted their diseases, but never submitted to colonial administration. In 1800, at least 8,000 Utes from twelve major bands inhabited the region. Contacts between Utes and Euro-Americans increased after 1810 as fur trappers appeared bringing trade goods and guns in exchange for Ute furs, hides, and horses. Northern Ute bands remained aloof and independent during this "middle ground" period. Only after the appearance of Mormon settlers in 1847 and the Colorado gold rush of 1859 did Northern Utes experience the full impact of intercultural contact and directed change.

The original Mormon settlement site in the Salt Lake Valley occurred in a buffer occupancy zone between Ute and Shoshone peoples and generated little immediate conflict. But when Mormon settlers moved south into Utah Valley in 1849 they began a cycle of competition with Utes for the relatively scarce subsistence lands and resources of the region. Utah Valley was a prime subsistence area and fishery, as well as a crossroads for interband trade. As the settlers appropriated the grass and fish, plowed up the land and killed off the game, Tumpanuwac Utes turned to an alternate food source— Mormon livestock. Mormon militiamen retaliated in 1850, driving the Utes from the valley.

An uneasy peace reigned for the next few years, but Mormon settlers continued to move southward along the Wasatch Front, disrupting the finely balanced Tumpanuwac, San Pitch, and Pahvant subsistence strategies, precipitating the recurring patterns of Ute starvation, begging, and depredation on Mormon crops and property. In 1851 Superintendent J.H. Holeman warned that Utes increasingly distrusted Mormons who appropriated "all the most valuable lands." "The Indians have been driven from their lands," he continued, "and their hunting grounds destroyed without compensation wherefore they are in many instances reduced to a state of suffering, bordering on starvation. In this situation some of the most daring and desperate approach the settlements and demand compensation for their lands, where upon the slightest pretexts, they are shot down or driven to the mountains." What followed was a series of uncoordinated raids known as the Walker War (1853–54), a conflict symptomatic of gradual Ute subsistence displacement.

Mormons were the first to offer Utes an agricultural alternative. In 1855, Agent Garland Hurt announced the creation of three "Indian farms," staffed by white farmers. Ute leaders expressed their interest in the projects and desired the promised crops, but resisted the idea of settling down, doing the work themselves, and surrendering their diversified subsistence strategy. They told Hurt that, "they were very poor, and had to hunt most all the time to keep from starving, and if they laid down their bows to work in the fields they would soon be obliged to pick them up again." A few Utes settled near the farms each summer to watch white farmers work for them, but drought and grasshoppers limited the harvest each year, forcing Hurt to encourage the people to go hunting or face starvation.

After closing the farms in 1860, Bureau officials decided to remove Utah Utes to the Uintah Valley of eastern Utah. . . . Since the Mormons did not want it and Utes showed no inclination to farm anyway, officials deemed the valley suited to their "savage" condition and set aside over two million acres as the Uintah Valley Reservation. The Uintah Basin was not exactly a wasteland, but neither was it an ideal year-round environment. Utes led by *Auten-quer* resisted removal and continued a series of subsistence raids against Mormon settlements known as the Black Hawk War (1863–68). Those who did move to the reservation found little waiting for them and refused to settle near the agency as long as they could hunt and gather in the surrounding mountains.

During the 1860s, agents moved the Uintah Agency several times in search of adequate agricultural lands, but the 70 or 80 acres they managed to cultivate suffered from periodic droughts and grasshopper plagues. Most of the agency's annual budget went to feed and clothe the people when they came into the agency each winter. . . . Ute agents managed to attract a few families to settle and work on the scattered "garden-patch" agency fields, but admitted that there existed a "great antipathy to work on the part of the men, the greater part of what [farming] was done being by the squaws and children." Ute men continued to hunt while agency farmers attempted to illustrate "the dignity of labor." The reproduction of Ute social norms in this reservation setting precluded male agricultural labor—digging in the earth for plant foods, after all, was the subsistence province of women.

Ute agents worried about this attitude and the growing dependence on rations. Upon his arrival in 1871, Agent J.J. Critchlow complained that, "There seems never to have been anything more done for them than to keep them quiet and peaceable by partially feeding and clothing them and amusing them with trinkets." He started a campaign to transform the increasingly dependent Uintah Utes into self-sufficient farmers, but he and his staff ran into the same cultural and environmental problems. Utes continued to reproduce their subsistence round in the reduced environment of the Uintah Basin. In 1875, Critchlow reported 80 families with garden patches totaling 200 acres, but that his staff did the plowing and planting. Families would return from their summer travels to harvest what wheat and vegetables managed to grow during their absence. Nor could Critchlow interest them in cooperative farming, for their individualistic traditions precluded extended communalism. Ute men refused to farm calling it "squaw's work," assuring each other and their agent that "Washington did not intend that they should work," and that the "Great Spirit" created whites to "work and plant for the Indian."

The environmental limitations of the Uintah Basin made it difficult for agents to demonstrate even the potential benefits of farming. . . . Critchlow reported that, "The broken character of the land, by streams, slough, rocky and alkaline patches, makes it discouraging, even to skilled laborers; much more is it so to those [Utes] unaccustomed to habits of industry." At roughly 5,000 feet, growing seasons were short and the Basin remained isolated from Utah markets by rugged mountains and poor roads.

By 1880, most of the Utah Ute bands resided within the boundaries of the reservation and were well on the way to a dependent economy. Traditional foods supplemented by agency rations formed their basic diet, and the handful of Uintah families who did any farming became increasingly dependent on agency resources and rations. Ute leaders blamed whites and evil shamans for the disappearance of game animals and for the diseases which plagued them. Hopes for a self-sufficient reservation economy diminished even further after the forceable removal of the Yamparka, Parianuc, and Taviwac Ute bands from their mountain strongholds in Colorado to the Uintah Basin.

Beginning in 1849, Colorado Ute bands entered into treaties with the federal government designed to get them to settle down. Over the next 30 years, Anglo and Hispanic miners and ranchers flooded into Colorado, forcing Utes to sign new treaties ceding the eastern two-thirds of the state. In return the Indian Bureau created agencies staffed with blacksmiths and farmers to teach Utes the "civilized arts." Most Taviwac (Uncompahgre) Utes moved toward their reserved area and a few settled near the Los Pinos Agency in the Uncompahgre Valley. Some tried their hand at farming small garden plots, but Ute women did most of the actual work after agency employees plowed and planted their fields. The majority of Yamparka and Parianuc (White River) Utes refused to recognize the treaties and only visited their agency along the White River periodically to collect rations and annuity gifts. In both cases their agencies were in agriculturally inhospitable environments, high and dry and lacking irrigation. . . .

In 1878, Nathan C. Meeker, an idealistic agrarian socialist, became the White River agent. Meeker tried to force agriculture on the already restive Utes and failed. One faction led by Douglas began working the agency fields for pay, but Meeker discovered that the men worked irregularly and would quit when they accumulated enough to buy ammunition in order to hunt, leaving women to tend the gardens—reproducing cultural patterns via a different short-term economic endeavor. Another faction opposed all Meeker's efforts and grew angry when he moved the agency to Powell's Valley in 1879 and started plowing up a valuable horse pasture and race-track. Meeker tried withholding rations, but peer ridicule was enough to keep Ute males from farming. Meeker failed to realize that Ute horses represented status and wealth and were valued more than cattle. When he told some Utes to shoot their horses to make room for fields and cattle the situation turned violent. After years of passive resistance to farming, years of broken promises and increasing subsistence deprivation, White River warriors attacked and destroyed the agency, killing Meeker and his staff. The warriors managed to hold off regular army troops for nearly a week, but negotiated a peaceful settlement when they found that Uncompahgre Utes would not join them in the uprising.

Predictably the incident increased agitation for the complete removal of Utes from Colorado. In an effort to avoid removal, Ute leaders—particularly Ouray of the Uncompahgre Utes who mediated the final peace—stressed that they did not object to the idea of plowing the land for farms, but that, in this case, the White Rivers objected to the *location* of the plowing. Ouray used this subtle, politically sophisticated distinction to reassure the investigating commission that peaceful agricultural settlement *on their own lands* was still possible. Investigators agreed, placed the blame on Meeker's aggressive agrarianism, but were powerless to halt the removal of the peaceful Uncompahgre. Between 1881 and 1882 the army forcibly removed White Rivers to the Uintah Reservation, and the Uncompahgres to their own executive order reservation adjoining Uintah—the two million acre Ouray Reservation. . . .

Whatever improvement Agent J.J. Critchlow saw in the Uintahs' participation in agriculture before 1881 slowed to a crawl when the White Rivers arrived. Never truly defeated they were, "indolent and know nothing of farming or caring for themselves by civilized pursuits, and what is worse many of them have no desire to learn. . . . They laugh at the Uintahs for farming, and say they ought to fight and then Washington would furnish them plenty to eat." The Uncompahgres were unhappy on their reservation, feared further relocation, and resisted opening farms on land which their agent deemed agriculturally worthless without an expensive irrigation system. In 1882, Uintah and Ouray agents reported 280 cultivated acres for the 2,825 Northern Utes, most worked by Uintahs and agency staff. Critchlow encouraged Uintahs to expand production and trade their surplus to the other bands in exchange for agricultural labor and firewood, but the local market economy he envisioned never materialized. Instead, all three became increasingly dependent on government rations as a subsistence alternative to both farming and hunting. . . .

Through the rest of the nineteenth century Utes passively resisted a settled agrarian lifestyle and continued to reproduce typically Ute patterns of behavior. Officials described Ute farms as small subsistence gardens of from one to four acres, scattered along the reservation watercourses. They noted that Uintahs appeared to be more "progressive" in their farming

efforts than White River or Uncompahgre Utes, but that Ute women continued to perform the bulk of the agricultural labor after agency employees
prepared their fields. Agent Robert Waugh candidly admitted that Ute men
were, "the most practical & least theoretical of any beings I ever came
across. He wants the least & enjoys the most with the least care or effort.
He views with a jealous eye any & all efforts to intrude the White Mans
ways & wants upon him, & would resist them by force only that he thinks
that would be harder. . . ."

Agents also complained that Utes maintained horse herds well beyond
practical agricultural needs, reproducing their own value system within a
changing reservation economy. Agent E.W. Davis reported that, "In the matter of stock raising the Indians have a decided preference to ponies over cattle. Four or five Indians of the Uintah tribe own nearly all the Indian cattle
on this reserve. Their influence among the tribe is measured by the number
of ponies they possess, and as long as this custom obtains among them they
will raise horses in preference to cattle." What was worse, he thought, was
that they trained the best horses for racing, not plowing, and that their
horses allowed them to continue seasonal hunting and visiting patterns
instead of staying home to farm.

In the mid-1890s as Bureau officials and state game wardens curtailed
treaty hunting rights, more Ute families attempted to farm or raise livestock. Agents reported that with the aid of agency employees some 260
families from a population of 1,800 Utes had farms totaling nearly 2,500
acres (not all planted) on the combined four million acre Uintah-Ouray
Reservation. Due to limited irrigation and the physical isolation of the
reservation, Utes produced little salable surplus and had virtually no market
outside the agency and Fort Duchesne military post. By 1900, alfalfa and
hay replaced wheat and oats, reflecting the increase in Ute livestock holdings. . . . Agents estimated that 20 to 30 percent of Ute subsistence came
from their own labor in "civilized pursuits" (farming and wage labor), 10
percent from hunting and gathering, and 60 to 70 percent from government
rations. Utes also leased their extensive grazing lands in the western
Strawberry Valley, earning a small per-capita income which became, in
some minds, a viable economic alternative to agricultural labor.

Between 1894 and 1905 federal officials moved to allot Northern Ute
lands in severalty—the ultimate realization of their agrarian ideal for
American Indians. At Uintah-Ouray, allotting commissioners surveyed the
land and found that aside from river bottoms and adjacent benches, little of
it was fit for agriculture. Rocky and alkaline soils, climate, and the broken
nature of the country would make even the best lands difficult and expensive to clear and irrigate, but they went ahead with their orders to allot each
family head 80 acres and each family member 40 acres of arable land.

In councils with Bureau officials, Ute leaders found common voice in
opposing allotment. They understood the connection between severalty and
farming and in their speeches rejected allotment through metaphorical
attacks on things that would separate the people and break up their lands
(fences), that would tie them to a specific plot (log houses), that would
make their land agriculturally viable (irrigation), and undercut their land

use patterns and resistance to farming. "The Indians have lots of horses," Appah, a White River, told his listeners, "and when you tell us that we must take farms, we do not like that on account of our horses." "What are my horses going to do when I have only a little piece of land," asked Grant, a Uintah. "Must I tie my horses in that little field?" John Starr, a White River, told the allotting agent, "You see me and I see you. My flesh is black: you have good flesh, you are white like this paper here. My flesh looks like the ground. That's the reason I like this land: my flesh is like the ground. That's the reason I am going to keep it."

Above all, Utes worried about neighboring Mormons who were already encroaching on their land and water, and the flood of new settlers who would destroy their communality. Captain Joe insisted that "The Indian reservation was not put down for nothing. It is held down by something heavy," by the treaties he witnessed as a young man. "This is the Indian's land. . . . We don't want this reservation opened, and we do not want White people coming in among us." Warren, a Uintah, told his listeners that the land "is not buckskin or deer's hide, and I do not want to sell it." Charley Mack concluded, "What are the Indians going to do? It is like sand. You throw water upon sand and it will cave in and wash off: so with Indians, after a while there will be none left." Allotment threatened a more collective Ute identity and lifestyle that had arisen over time as their elders died, as paths to leadership changed, and as individual families found fewer opportunities to live without help from the larger group. Allotment represented an effort to re-individualize Utes economically after years of collectivist policy and of informal cooperation necessitated by a dependent reservation economy.

Utes responded to the allotment threat in several ways. Most continued their passive resistance by refusing to choose or even visit their surveyed allotments. Others, particularly the Uncompahgres, subverted the agricultural intent of allotment by specifically choosing land remote from the agency, fit only for carrying on an independent hunting and herding lifestyle. In other cases, White Rivers threatened band members who accepted allotments, destroyed allotment survey markers, and made life difficult for the survey crews. In 1906 nearly 400 White River and Uintah Utes fled the allotted reservation in protest and remained around Pine Ridge, South Dakota for two years before returning to the Uintah Basin.

Perhaps the most dramatic response to counter the individualistic thrust of allotment was the adoption of the Sun Dance religion—a collective group ceremony in which individuals danced for "Power" (*Puwa*), not for themselves, but for the welfare of the group. Utes embraced the dance at a point in their history when the real and perceived deprivations of reservation life and allotment threatened to overwhelm them. They danced to counter their economic and political dependency through group unity. In later years Utes even cloaked the Sun Dance in agricultural imagery, calling it a "harvest festival," in order to protect it from official suppression.

Allotment fulfilled Utes' worst fears by immediately reducing their four million acres to only 353,265 acres, including a 250,000-acre tribal grazing reserve. As whites purchased and moved onto opened lands surrounding the checkerboard Ute allotments, disputes arose over boundaries, trespass, and the right to use and divert stream water. In 1906 the government moved to protect Ute water rights and make agriculture more viable by appropriating $600,000 for the Uintah Irrigation Project. Indian Irrigation Service planners expected to bring water to 80,000 allotted acres and reimburse the government for construction through the sale of unallotted reservation lands.

Irrigation officials soon ran into unanticipated problems. Utes roundly rejected both the construction and costs of the irrigation project. Many refused to work on the ditches or to prepare their allotments for water. Others who took canal construction jobs had little time to farm. Perhaps more troubling was an unforeseen deadline. Project officials found that the reservation was opened and water rights established under state law, thus forfeiting federal protection guaranteed by *Winters v. U.S.* (1908). Utah law required "beneficial use" of the water within fourteen years (by 1919) to maintain primary rights over settlers with secondary or tertiary water claims.

While work on the ditches went forward as quickly as possible, agency officials realized that Utes would hardly be able to prove beneficial use in time to save primary rights on even 10 percent of their lands. Without water they would lose the productive capability and resale value of their allotments and any hope of a self-sufficient agricultural economy. Bureau officials decided to act. With or without the consent of allottees, officials leased Ute lands to white homesteaders on condition that they prepare the land for irrigation. Agents suggested that Ute lessors could live on a corner of their allotment and perform wage labor for the white lessee, that they could sell part of their land to raise money for capital improvements, or that elders and those with inherited allotments could sell their land with the primary water right intact in order to gain some immediate benefit. In 1911 alone, agents arranged the sale of 67 (5%) of 1,365 Ute allotments. Many Utes, particularly White Rivers, tried to prevent band members from signing away heirship properties, but the sales and leasing continued. Between 1915 and 1917, Superintendent Albert H. Kneale arranged 1,764 leases totaling 54,000 (52%) allotted acres. In 1916, Kneale reported that they had 85,150 allotted acres under 22 irrigation canals, with 39,760 acres leased (46%), and 17,354 acres sold or pending sale.

Statistically, agricultural activity at Uintah-Ouray increased dramatically. From 131 Ute farms totaling 4,572 acres (most unplanted) in 1905, agents reported 13,260 cultivated acres in 1914. However, Utes [controlled] only 6,147 acres on 222 allotments (again, most unplanted). White lessees worked the [rest] while 68,869 allotted acres (84%) remained idle. Leasing became a common and, in some cases, preferred method of land use for Ute allottees. One extension agent noted that, "The present prevailing custom is for the Indian owner to employ a white man to run the farm, paying him a definite share of the products." Some Ute leaders opposed leasing, arguing that it brought more whites onto Indian land, or, like William Wash, that, "This leasing of land to the whites is a swindle. . . . The Indians do not know how to make money off their land. They don't know w[h]ether the white man is handling it right or not." Despite frequent disagreements between Indian landlords and white tenants, many Utes found leasing a comfortable way to earn a living, please agents concerned with statistics, and avoid the routine of agricultural labor.

This attitude frustrated bureau officials who expected Utes to embrace allotment, the Protestant work-ethic, and become self-sufficient farmers overnight. Superintendent Kneale lamented Ute reliance on rations and their "unearned" income from leases and a small land claims settlement, observing that they were "wholly content to make their living expenses conform to this income, so there is little occasion to perform manual labor." Those who farmed did so intermittently, leaving their fields unattended in mid-season to grow as they would. Few actually lived on their own allotments, preferring instead extended family groupings on a single plot. Officials struggled to get even a slight majority to live in frame houses and not use them as horse stables or destroy them in accordance with mortuary practices. In these ways, Utes continued to reproduce cultural elements in the transformed reservation environment.

Aside from the cultural resistance, there were more practical obstacles to successful agriculture—obstacles which contributed to continued Ute economic dependency. Ute farmers lacked the capital or credit necessary to purchase modern farm equipment and relied on older horse-drawn implements loaned or purchased through the agency. Utes received meager instruction in irrigation and dry farming crops and techniques from the handful of agency farmers hired to supervise scattered operations across the region. Even with an irrigation system the Uintah Basin remained a difficult environment for successful, small-scale subsistence farming. Finally, like other reservations, Uintah-Ouray remained physically and economically isolated from the American marketplace. Until the 1910s, the lack of markets was not a problem since Utes traded what little surplus they produced—mainly hay, oats, and wheat—at the agency or Fort Duchesne. But the fort closed in 1912 just as production from irrigated Ute farms and white homesteads increased, flooding local markets. High freight rates kept their forage and grain crops uncompetitive even in a vigorous regional economy.

By 1920, the Uintah Irrigation Project covered 80,306 arable acres at double the original reimbursable cost, but the costs to the Ute people went well beyond that. Agency officials arranged the sale of over 25,000 acres of the best land to non-Utes. Faulty surveys and canal construction left some allotments without adequate water, and improper irrigation techniques increased erosion and brought up alkali rendering other lands worthless. Some white lessees failed to make adequate improvements or abused the land, leaving it barren and alkaline, while others who purchased Indian lands defaulted on their payments. The irrigation project proved to be an expensive benefit to those Utes who actually used the water and a federal gift to those whites who bought Ute allotments or ultimately used their canals. Its legacy was one of tribal and individual indebtedness and further land sales far outweighing, in Ute terms, the economic or cultural worth of the project.

Despite all these problems, the period between 1920 and 1928 was a high point for Northern Ute agricultural activity, a rather discouraging high as far as Bureau officials were concerned. The completed irrigation system and Bureau-sponsored agricultural fairs and clubs stimulated some competition among mixed-blood and Uintah band families who were more often active farmers than Uncompahgres or White Rivers. However, the emergence of a marketable product advanced farming more than anything else. In the late 1910s, plant scientists found the isolated Uintah Basin an ideal location for producing new genetic strains of alfalfa seed for national markets. Ute and white farmers took advantage of this economic boom. The number of adult male Utes with farms rose from 176 (66%) in 1912 to 218 (79%) in 1920, and average farm size jumped from 32 to 41 acres, about half of it leased to whites. By 1928, Utes irrigated 15,243 acres and did "more farming . . . than the Indians of any other reservation," but that assessment by irrigation specialists belied the fact that half that acreage remained unplanted or leased to whites.

Throughout this boom period, farming at Uintah-Ouray remained largely a subsistence enterprise for most Ute families. Alfalfa and hardy grains comprised 95 percent of Ute crops, most of which was consumed locally by Ute livestock. Gardens, ration issues, and game animals supplied families with food, while Utes generated cash through livestock and alfalfa seed sales and land leases. Annual Ute farm income ranged from only $200 to $300 per family. After the alfalfa seed boom peaked in 1925, declining prices, insect infestations, bad weather years, and the costs of water assessments cut into Ute production, profits, and ultimately Ute farming itself.

The national economic depression and environmental degradation of the early 1930s nearly finished Ute farming. The alfalfa seed market collapsed leaving Basin farmers overextended without a viable cash crop. The land itself was exhausted from overcropping and improper irrigation practices. Overgrazing and widespread drought exacerbated these problems, deepening the depression in the Uintah Basin. One agency farmer noted in 1932 that most of the remaining 169 Ute farmers were "making a living" by simply "existing" on their farms. By the mid-1930s, cultivation on Ute allotments dropped 42 percent and yields on those acres declined by 50 percent. With white farmers in the same boat, leasing became nearly impossible, yet the bills for water assessments and reimbursable loan payments continued, forcing many Utes to turn their land over to the new Northern Ute Tribal Council organized under the Indian Reorganization Act of 1934. Unemployment and relief reached 75 to 90 percent in Uintah and Duchesne counties generally, and nearly every Ute family depended on agency rations.

A few Ute farmers continued to cultivate their land in the 1930s and 1940s, concentrating on forage and grain crops for livestock, but by the 1950s most Utes forsook their fields to live on income from oil and gas royalties, agricultural leases, and federal claims case payments. Unable to compete with white ranchers who out-produced them on the same land, Utes resumed leasing a majority of their irrigable lands—as much as 78 percent in 1950. By 1956 there were only 37 Ute farmers, and between 1958 and 1964 observers noted only 11 individuals doing any farming. Aside from several family operations and the maintenance of some alfalfa fields associated with a tribal cattle industry, Northern Utes do virtually no farming today.

Ranching had the potential of becoming a more successful agricultural enterprise among the Northern Utes in the twentieth century, but the division of the reservation into small allotments and the loss of the best grazing lands in the Strawberry Valley limited its potential success. Agents had little luck encouraging Utes to reduce their horse herds and replace them with cattle and sheep until the 1920s when changing economic values, increased alfalfa production, and per-capita payments from a claims case made livestock purchases more practical. In 1923, a core group of Ute stockmen owned about 4,000 cattle, 6,500 sheep, and over 5,000 horses. By the late 1920s, Ute livestock ownership broadened as sheep replaced cattle—a cheaper, more productive animal in terms of wool, meat, and offspring, especially on an increasingly overgrazed range. Ute livestock production peaked in 1932 with 3,546 cattle and 14,850 sheep, followed by deep herd reductions as overgrazing, drought, and depressed markets caught up with Basin ranchers. Ute participation in ranching faltered after World War II for many of the same reasons farming did. In the 1960s Utes organized a tribal cattle enterprise which continues to date, but it has never proven very profitable nor has it provided a significant number of jobs.

The history of farming on the Uintah-Ouray Reservation is one example of how federal policies, economic and environmental realities, and Northern Ute cultural responses to those changes contributed to a state of dependency. While case specific, this history mirrors the agricultural experiences of many other western native groups and their progression from cultural self-sufficiency to dependency and enforced marginality. . . .

In hindsight it is easy to see why agriculture alone offered Indian peoples in the western United States little more than short-term subsistence and long-term economic dependence. Most refused to simply abandon their diversified subsistence strategy and conform to American agrarian ideals or farming techniques. They saw the failure of early farm efforts and the cultural costs of conforming to that way of life. Their reservations were mere remnants of once vast estates, unable to support the people, so they turned to rations and periodic wage labor. Reservations were generally unwanted, marginal agricultural lands to begin with, often arid and better suited to ranching or some other activity. Most were isolated from transportation facilities and regional or national markets, making it difficult for Indians to become successful market agriculturalists.

Native peoples generally received inadequate agricultural instruction and equipment to work the land. With little access to capital for improvements, they fell further behind and became dependent on the government for reimbursable loans. Resistance, both passive and active, and the reproduction of cultural norms within the altered reservation environment contributed to farming's limited success. Finally, the agrarian nature of federal

Indian policy launched Indians into farming small allotments at the very time white farmers were expanding their farms, increasing the intensity of cultivation with power equipment, and cooperatively marketing their produce in order to survive in an increasingly corporate, increasingly urban and industrial world. While the Indian Bureau abandoned allotment in the 1930s and encouraged cooperative tribal enterprises in the 1950s, they did little to restore alienated native lands or Indian confidence in future agricultural development. . . .

A Family Farm Chronicle

GILBERT C. FITE

During the last quarter century, historians have talked and written a good deal about doing history from the bottom up. Historians, it was said, had been too much enamored with society's elites. To better understand our history, these critics insisted that we needed to look at the lives and activities of common men and women. Furthermore, scholars argued, local records which more fully revealed the life of the common people should be explored in depth. Dusty county court house basements with their land, tax, assessment, mortgage, and other records became a favorite place to dig into the lives of ordinary individuals.

Not having any great theory of history to propound and wanting to be in one of the main streams of current American historiography, I decided to talk about one of those common men who settled on the Dakota frontier. Moreover, the information on this pioneer farmer has come almost exclusively from those county records which dirty your hands and ruin your eyes. The fact that the individual whose farming career I intend to discuss happens to be my maternal grandfather, makes this exercise no less legitimate as a study of common, ordinary citizens.

The free and cheap land of the American West drew people like a powerful magnet. Unlike a magnet that draws and holds metals to it in a fan and lasting grasp, many Americans were held by the land only temporarily. Rather than realizing their Jeffersonian dreams of establishing a successful farm and living a happy, contented life under their own vine and fig tree, they were battered and defeated by nature and ruined by economic conditions over which they had no control. Many western pioneers on the last frontier filed on government land in a spirit of hope and optimism only to find that natural and man-made barriers defeated their hopes and aspirations.

One such man was Benjamin Franklin McCardle. Born in Virginia in 1862, he was the son of Samuel McCardle, who moved to Mason County, West Virginia where the family lived in 1880. After holding jobs in different parts of the state, in the spring of 1888, Frank, as he was generally known, struck out for the West. After a journey of some twelve hundred miles, he arrived at Wessington Springs in Jerauld County, Dakota Territory. He must have made the last part of the journey on foot or by stage because the railroad did not reach this village of about three hundred people in east-central Dakota until 1903.

By the time McCardle, now twenty-six years old, arrived on that prairie-plains frontier, the Great Dakota boom had burst. During 1883 and the spring of 1884, thousands of settlers had flocked to the region between the James and Missouri Rivers in search of free land. But by 1886 drouth, poor farm prices, and marketing problems had brought shock and discouragement to many of those optimistic pioneers. Territorial Governor Gilbert A. Pierce reported in 1886 that the year had been less than prosperous for many settlers. In translation the Governor's political rhetoric really meant that times were very hard. Conditions got worse in 1887 and 1888, the year McCardle arrived. The drouth was so bad in 1889 in parts of Dakota Territory that thousands of farmers were overwhelmed by want and destitution. Many accepted public charity, while others left Dakota to escape starvation and complete ruin.

McCardle, then, reached the Dakota frontier at a most unfavorable time. But he was determined to establish himself in the community. There was still some government land that could be filed on, and relinquishments could be purchased cheap from settlers who were discouraged and ready to leave. McCardle, however, made no immediate effort to obtain land. He had no capital to begin farming, even on free land. Thus, he obtained a job on the farm of H. G. Gilbert, who lived in Harmony township a few miles northwest of Wessington Springs.

That same year Mary E. Alguire, a young woman who had been born in New York state in 1862, settled with her foster family in Jerauld County. After being orphaned she was raised by the A. S. Fordham family, with whom she traveled to Dakota. Mary Alguire got a job as a housekeeper with the J. R. Eddy family, who lived not far from the Gilberts where Frank worked. Frank and Mary, the hired girl and hired man of neighboring farmers, soon became acquainted and were married in the fall of 1890. In December 1889, just a few months before her marriage, Mary had homesteaded on a quarter section of land five miles west and four north of Wessington Springs. Like many other homesteaders, she managed to fulfill the legal residence requirement, although she did not live on the homestead for any substantial period of time.

In 1891, a few months after their marriage, the young couple moved to Dale township in the east-central part of the county. They rented a farm located on the southwest quarter of section twenty-six. Their first daughter, Mary Jane, was born there on 5 September 1891. The McCardles lived on this rented farm for two years.

Meanwhile, Frank filed a timber culture claim on a quarter section two miles north of where he was living. Most of the 160 acres lay just above the Firesteel Creek flat, an area extending back from the mostly dry creek bed some three-fourths of a mile and which grew abundant salt grass. The soil on the flat was a dark gumbo which, when wet, stuck to a person's feet and to buggy and wagon wheels. The upland part of the McCardle land had a sandy base in which crops usually failed when moisture was short. The average rainfall in Jerauld County, which was situated on the ninety-ninth meridian, was eighteen to twenty inches a year, which meant that crop production was marginal. The one good thing about the McCardle land was that it had an abundant supply of underground water only fifteen to twenty feet below the surface. A windmill standing over a shallow well could supply unlimited amounts of water for household and livestock needs.

Frank and Mary moved to their tree claim late in 1892 or early in 1893. In November 1892 another daughter, Frances Hazel, arrived. Frank got to his own farm in time to meet the assessor, whose report—in the middle of 1893—showed how this young farmer, his wife, and growing family were faring on government land. The McCardles had 2 cows and 2 calves, and 2 other cattle, but no additional livestock. These 2 "other cattle" were probably a team of oxen. A year earlier, when he was still on his rented farm, he had reported 4 working oxen to the assessor. The McCardles had no hogs or chickens. At least they reported none to the assessor. The assessed value of their personal property was only $15.

The same year that McCardle moved to his tree claim, the Panic of 1893 set off a long and severe depression. Farm prices dropped drastically, and, to make matters worse, in 1894 much of the Great Plains fell victim to extreme drouth and heat. Many farm families had a difficult time eking out a living of any kind. There are no diaries, letters, or account books which reveal how the McCardles weathered the hard times of the 1890s, but, like many unnamed pioneers, they somehow managed to survive. They even added slightly to their personal property, as well as to their family. In March 1895 a son, Lincoln Elwood, was born. A few months later when the assessor called, he could record that the McCardles owned 4 horses, 4 cows, 2 calves, and 2 hogs. Their taxes on personal property, however, went unpaid even though they amounted to only $4.87.

Times continued to be hard, and the McCardles made little economic progress. It was not until 1899 that Frank and Mary McCardle began to increase their personal property substantially, especially in the form of livestock. By that time they owned 8 horses, 1 stallion, 3 cows, 50 sheep, and 7 hogs. While the value of their agricultural machinery was assessed at only $15, this was three times what it had been listed at two or three years earlier. By 1900 McCardle's sheep herd reached a little over 400 head. Considering the time, the McCardles were doing rather well compared to many of their neighbors. Between 1890 and 1900 several hundred farmers in Jerauld County had given up and called it quits. The number of farms in the county dropped from 790 to 487, or by about 300 in that depression-filled decade.

After farming for ten years, McCardle actually appeared to be on the road to becoming a successful family farmer and livestock man. Moreover, the family finances received a boost in February 1901 when his wife sold her homestead for $500. In September 1902 Frank received the patent for his farm from the United States Land Office.

It was not long, however, before the McCardles were wrestling with a common problem that plagued most frontier farmers—lack of capital. On 23 November 1904, just a few days after McCardle's land had been registered in the Land Patent Record, he borrowed $900 at six percent interest secured by a mortgage on his land. The loan was to run for five years. He also borrowed another $54 which was to be repaid in a similar period. In his case the lender took out the interest in advance so McCardle received $45 which was to be repaid at $9 a year. He paid off the small loan within a few months, but when the $900 mortgage was due in 1909 he was unable to meet his obligation. Consequently, on 1 December 1909 he borrowed $1,000 from the South Dakota School Fund at five percent interest and paid off his old note. The new loan was due in 1913. It is not clear whether McCardle did not have the money to pay off his mortgage, or whether he preferred refinancing, but he renewed his loan from the School Fund in 1913 and again in 1916. In other words, McCardle managed to extend his borrowing until June 1921 when payment would be due. From 1909 to 1921 he borrowed money to pay off previous loans.

Although McCardle continued in debt, he greatly improved his economic condition in the first two decades of the twentieth century. He benefited from that more prosperous period to which farmers sometimes referred as the Golden Era of American Agriculture. Farm commodity and land prices both rose sharply during those years. By 1910 McCardle had 11 head of horses and mules, 65 head of cattle and calves, 6 hogs and a fair supply of agricultural implements. He had been able to build a comfortable five-room house and a large stock barn. He sent his two daughters to Wessington Springs Seminary, a secondary and junior college institution which had been established by the Free Methodist Church in the 1880s. The furnishings in the McCardle home were adequate. He even bought a piano for his daughter, Mary. The assessed valuation of his personal property was nearly $1,000, and his quarter section of land was on the tax rolls at $1,333, up from $475 in 1902.

Things got even better for the McCardle family during the next decade. Although there were occasional drouths in the area, McCardle raised enough feed for his livestock and built up his assets. He also improved his standard of living. McCardle was one of the few farmers in the area who had an automobile as early as 1914. By 1915 he was one of the leading livestock raisers in Dale township. He owned 156 cattle and had become a well-known horse and mule trader. His personal property was assessed at $6,776. Higher prices generated by the outbreak of war in Europe were bringing a taste of genuine prosperity to this established farmer, who was now far removed from his hard-scrabble pioneer days. By 1917 his personal property was valued at $8,861, which included nearly 200 head of cattle, a large number for any farmer in that community.

A quarter century after they began farming on a rented quarter section of land, Frank and Mary McCardle seemed to have achieved the dream of many Americans, that of owning their own farm and enjoying a decent, middle-class standard of living. With hard work, fair management, and some luck, they had moved from bare subsistence with scarcely any property, to a comfortable living, and land and personal property worth between $30,000 and $40,000. Surely he was better off than if he had stayed in West Virginia and found work in the coal mines or steel mills.

Like most farmers Frank McCardle wanted more land. He needed additional acreage for his growing livestock herds, and he hoped to leave a farm to each of his three children. What could be more a part of the American dream than to leave a good inheritance to his son and daughters? So, in 1911, he began to buy land. In that year he purchased 160 acres in an adjoining section. Four years later he bought 320 acres next to his home place. He also acquired what was known as a short quarter of 128 acres some three miles from the home farm. By 1917 he owned 768 acres, including the 160 acres he had acquired under the Timber Culture Act. The average size farm in Jerauld county in 1920 was 404 acres, making McCardle's holdings nearly double the county average.

Meanwhile, his daughters did not wait around for their prospective inheritances. In the summer of 1916, Hazel and her husband Arthur Shoff, and McCardle's oldest daughter, Mary, headed for northwest South Dakota to find land of their own. Their search took them to Perkins County, about seventy-five miles from the Montana border. The Shoffs and Mary McCardle first bought a quarter section from James B. Carter of Baker, Montana. The land was located about twenty miles south of Bison, the county seat, and near the Moreau River. Then Mary, an independent spirit who believed that women should do their own thing a generation before the emergence of the women's liberation movement, filed on 277 acres close to the land she and the Shoffs had purchased together. She filed under the Enlarged Homestead Act of 1909, which was extended to South Dakota in 1915. Her land was along Rabbit Creek, a small stream that flowed into the Moreau River. She was among the thousands of pioneers who moved into the Western Dakotas and Eastern Montana between 1900 and 1920. This was chancy country, where rainfall usually ranged from twelve to sixteen inches a year, but it did not intimidate the McCardle girls. Perhaps it should have!

In July 1917 Mary McCardle married Clyde Fite who had migrated to South Dakota from Ohio in 1914 as a magazine salesman. They settled down on Mary's homestead until Clyde was called for military service in January 1918. After he returned from France a year later, they resumed a small farming and livestock operation on Rabbit Creek. Mary received title to her land on 27 January 1922.

Meanwhile, things were turning sour for Frank McCardle on his Jerauld County farm. The prosperous times of World War I suddenly ended, and by 1921 farmers were suffering from a severe economic slump. Commodity and land prices fell with a sickening thud, placing farmers who were in debt in a particularly unfortunate position. In the previous decade McCardle had gone heavily into debt purchasing, mainly on credit, some 600 acres of land.

As prices fell in late 1920 and 1921, his debts became a crushing burden. In South Dakota, however, hard-up farmers had a possible way out. In 1917, under the governorship of Peter Norbeck, the South Dakota legislature had passed a rural credit law which permitted the state to make thirty-year real estate loans to farmers at relatively low interest rates. With his back against a wall of debt, McCardle applied for and received a loan of $5,000 in March 1921. He applied this amount against his other indebtedness.

Paying off some old loans with new borrowings did nothing to relieve the economic pressure on McCardle. As commodity prices continued to fall, his expenses remained high. Like hundreds of thousands of farmers all over the United States, he found himself in a severe cost-price squeeze. For example, as cattle prices dropped from $14.95 to $7.31 a hundred pounds between 1919 and 1921, McCardle's taxes on land and personal property remained at wartime highs. In some cases tax rates in the early 1920s were actually higher than in 1918 or 1919. In 1921 McCardle had 11 horses and mules, over 100 head of cattle, 69 sheep, and other personal property that was assessed at nearly $4,000, the fourth highest in the township. By community standards McCardle did not appear to be bad off. But he was. During the early 1920s he continued a general family farm operation, but he simply could not produce enough income to service his debts, pay taxes, meet operating costs, and make a living. What he made he spent for operational costs and living expenses, leaving debts to multiply and his interest obligations unpaid.

Financially pressed from every side, McCardle decided to convey his children's land inheritance to them at once. They would get deeds to their land, and he would be rid of his debts. The fact was, McCardle was land poor in those hard times after World War I. On 6 October 1923 he legally transferred a half section of grass land to his daughter and son-in-law, Mary and Clyde Fite. He deeded his home quarter to his daughter, Hazel, and 128 acres to his son, Mike. Then he deeded his last 160 acres to his wife. When the papers were all signed, McCardle did not have an acre in his own name. Incidentally, he had not done his children any favors. All of the land was transferred "subject to encumbrances," the legal jargon for assuming mortgage debt and unpaid interest. Unless conditions got better, the land would not produce enough to service the debt in the depressed 1920s.

Nevertheless, the Fites decided to make a determined effort to save the land McCardle had given them. In 1924 they left their homestead west of the Missouri River in Perkins County and returned east to live with the McCardles on the old home place. By this time Frank and Mary McCardle were sixty-two years old and needed help with farm and household work. This joint farm family made enough for a modest living, but debts continued to accumulate. Both Mary and Clyde Fite took off-farm jobs teaching nearby in rural schools in hopes of earning enough cash to make principal and interest payments on their land. Their efforts, however, proved futile.

The financial roof began falling in on the McCardle family in 1927. After giving notice of foreclosure on August 10, McCardle's home place, where he and the Fites lived, was sold at public auction on the court house steps in Wessington Springs. The only bidder was the State of South Dakota which held a mortgage on the land. McCardle had not made a single principal or interest payment on his $5,000 loan, negotiated in 1921 with the Rural Credit Department. By then the principal, interest, delinquent taxes, and miscellaneous expenses amounted to $7,994.14. In effect, McCardle had sold his land to the state in 1921 and lived on it for six years without making payments of any kind. Thousands of South Dakota farmers did the same thing in the 1920s. The same day the sheriff sold the land owned by McCardle's son. Again, the state was the only bidder. The Fites managed to hold onto their land in Jerauld County until April 1929 when it, too, went under the auctioneer's hammer. By 1929 all of the 768 acres of McCardle family land had been foreclosed on except one quarter. Somehow, the family held that last 160 acres until 1936. Meanwhile, beginning in 1927, unpaid taxes were building up on Mary McCardle Fite's 277-acre homestead. In 1934 the Perkins County Treasurer billed her for $533.77 in delinquent taxes. In the depth of the Great Depression, the figure might just as well have been $5,000 or $5 million as far as her ability to pay was concerned. After years of trying to collect taxes, Perkins County officials finally resorted to legal action and gained title to the land in 1942.

By any economic criteria, Frank McCardle was an economic failure. A pioneer settler on the last frontier, he won some initial successes, but after farming for more than forty years he died a virtual pauper in 1948, twelve years after his wife's sudden death in 1936. He experienced only one fairly prosperous period, the era of World War I. Otherwise, it was a constant struggle with debt, and he experienced that final humiliation feared by every farmer—loss of his land.

How should historians assess the thousands of Frank McCardles who occupied the western frontier in the late nineteenth and early twentieth centuries? I submit that it is inaccurate and unfair to judge them and their contributions only by their land holdings or bank accounts—or, in other words, by their economic progress. Adverse economic and climatic conditions combined to ruin the dreams of tens of thousands of these hardy pioneers as they came to the end of their working lives in the 1920s and 1930s. The Rural Credit Department foreclosed on nearly 7,000 farms in South Dakota alone during those years, to say nothing of the banks, insurance companies and other lenders who foreclosed on thousands of additional farmers in that vast prairie-plains region from Canada to Texas.

Yet until he gave up farming in 1934 at age seventy-two, Frank McCardle and many other pioneer farmers on that last frontier had enjoyed a fairly decent standard of living for the times. He and his wife raised three children, all of whom eventually left the farm for better things. The McCardles paid taxes to support schools, roads, and other needed facilities, and they helped organize the political and social institutions of their community. They contributed to nation-building by helping to open up the vast cattle and wheat lands valuable to the country's welfare.

While the land occupied by these last American pioneers provided only a modest living for most settlers, it did support a transitional generation.

That is, the children and grandchildren of those farmers represented by Frank McCardle gained sustenance from the farm long enough and in sufficient amounts so that the next generations could enter into the expanding manufacturing, commercial, and service economy of the nation. Farms, of course, had been fulfilling that function in American society for generations. But the McCardle generation was the last in which the farm supported a large number of people and then launched them into society with their rural values and outlooks intact. Jefferson may have exaggerated the values people supposedly derived from a close association with the land and farming, but agricultural fundamentalism was one of the dominant strains in American thought up through the early twentieth century.

. . . I would illustrate my point by mentioning two individuals well known to [historians of the American West]. The late Robert G. Athearn, a former president of the Western History Association, forsook land that had been homesteaded to pursue a brilliant career in teaching and writing about the region he knew so well. Wayne D. Rasmussen, too, left the homestead of his parents in Montana in the 1930s and trekked to the East Coast, where he worked for the United States Department of Agriculture for some fifty years, becoming the outstanding authority in the field of agricultural history. Not all of those who were temporarily supported by homesteads on the last frontier gained such distinction as Athearn and Rasmussen, but the time and place produced its quota of outstanding Americans. This was made possible by the hard work and sacrifices of the tens of thousands of unknown and unheralded pioneers typified by Frank McCardle. Those who have been calling on historians to spend more time studying the lives of common people are on the right track. The unknown and unrecognized legions contributed to nation-building and deserve our best scholarly efforts. I say hail to the ordinary men and women on that frontier such as Frank and Mary McCardle.

Y *FURTHER READING*

Barbara Allen, *Homesteading the High Desert* (1987)
Robert R. Alvarez, Jr., *Familia: Migration and Adaptation in Baja and Alta California, 1800–1975* (1987)
Leonard Arrington, *Great Basin Kingdom: An Economic History of the Latter-day Saints, 1830–1900* (1958)
John W. Bennett and Seena B. Kohl, *Settling the Canadian-American West, 1890–1915: Pioneer Adaptation and Community Building* (1995)
Peter G. Boag, *Environment and Experience: Settlement Culture in Nineteenth-Century Oregon* (1992)
Allan G. Bogue, "An Agricultural Empire," in *The Oxford History of the American West*, ed. Clyde A. Milner II, Carol A. O'Connor, and Martha A. Sandweiss, 275–313 (1994)
———, *From Prairie to Cornbelt: Farming on the Illinois and Iowa Prairies in the Nineteenth Century* (1963)
Marshall E. Bowen, *Utah People in the Nevada Desert: Homestead and Community on a Twentieth-Century Farmers' Frontier* (1994)

Brian Cannon, "Struggle Against Great Odds: Challenges in Utah's Marginal Agricultural Areas, 1925–39," *Utah Historical Quarterly,* 54 (Fall 1986): 308–327

Leonard A. Carlson, *Bureaucrats and Land: The Dawes Act and the Decline of Indian Farming* (1981)

William E. DeBuys, *Enchantment and Exploration: The Life and Hard Times of a New Mexico Mountain Range* (1985)

Gilbert C. Fite, *American Farmers: The New Minority* (1981)

———, *The Farmer's Frontier, 1865–1900* (1966)

Robert A. Goldberg, *Back to the Soil: The Jewish Farmers of Clarion, Utah, and Their World* (1986)

Mary W.H. Hargreaves, *Dry Farming in the Northern Great Plains, 1900–1925* (1957)

———, *Dry Farming in the Northern Great Plains: Years of Readjustment, 1920–1990* (1992)

Katherine Harris, *Long Vistas: Women and Families on Colorado Homesteads* (1993)

Thomas D. Isern, *Bull Threshers and Bindlestiffs: Harvesting and Threshing on the North American Plains* (1990)

Peter Iverson, ed., *The Plains Indians of the Twentieth Century* (1985)

Alvin M. Josephy, Jr., *Now That the Buffalo's Gone* (1982)

David Rich Lewis, *Neither Wolf Nor Dog: American Indians, Environment, and Agrarian Change* (1994)

———, "Still Native: The Significance of Native Americans in the History of the Twentieth-Century American West," *Western Historical Quarterly,* 24 (May 1993): 203–228

Elaine H. Lindgren, *Land in Her Own Name: Women as Homesteaders in North Dakota* (1991)

Alice Littlefield and Martha C. Knack, eds., *Native Americans and Wage Labor: Ethnohistorical Perspectives* (1996)

Frederick C. Luebke, ed., *Ethnicity on the Great Plains* (1980)

Dean L. May, *Three Frontiers: Family, Land, and Society in the American West, 1850–1900* (1994)

Janet A. McDonnell, *The Dispossession of the American Indian, 1887–1934* (1991)

D. Aidan McQuillan, *Prevailing Over Time: Ethnic Adjustment on the Kansas Prairies, 1875–1925* (1990)

Melissa L. Meyer, *The White Earth Tragedy: Ethnicity and Dispossession at a Minnesota Anishinaabe Reservation, 1889–1920* (1994)

Paula M. Nelson, *After the West Was Won: Homesteaders and Town-Builders in Western South Dakota, 1900–1917* (1986)

Mary C. Neth, *Preserving the Family Farm: Women, Community, and the Foundation of Agribusiness in the Midwest, 1900–1940* (1994)

John Opie, *The Law of the Land: 200 Years of American Farmland Policy* (1987)

Donald L. Parman, *Indians and the American West in the Twentieth Century* (1994)

Donald J. Pisani, *From Family Farm to Agribusiness: The Irrigation Crusade in California and the West, 1850–1931* (1984)

Sherry L. Smith, "Single Women Homesteaders: The Perplexing Case of Elinore Pruitt Stewart," *Western Historical Quarterly,* 22 (May 1991): 163–83

Richard White, *Land Use, Environment, and Social Change: The Shaping of Island County, Washington* (1980)

C H A P T E R
11

Dam Water, Damn Dust

Y

By the late-nineteenth and early-twentieth centuries, a growing number of
Americans—this "people of plenty"—recognized the myth of the land's
inexhaustible abundance. Some embraced conservation as a response to
individual greed and corporate exploitation of resources, and supported
enlightened government regulation based on progressive principles of technological efficiency and scientific management. Others desired the preservation of resources based on their intrinsic natural values. The West became
the focus for this conservation-preservation debate, especially as it related to
water.

In 1878, John Wesley Powell pointed out that aridity unified the West,
but that irrigation could unlock its potential prosperity. Based on his observations of Utah Mormons ("the Lord's Beavers"), Powell envisioned a West
filled with a million forty-acre farms, with grazing and timber lands ratio-
nally distributed and wisely managed to promote the greatest good for the
greatest number of citizens. In later years as director of the U.S. Geological
Survey and National Irrigation Survey, Powell's democratic agrarian vision
faded as he realized there wasn't enough water to nourish even a fraction of
the arid lands. But irrigation boosters ignored Powell's warnings and
Congress implemented national reclamation programs on a scale Powell fundamentally distrusted. Bigger and bigger dams stored water, but alienated
local concerns. Dams came to serve other interests—power generation, urban
centers, distant agribusinesses. In the meantime, settlers overextended their
use of marginal range land and its water resources trying to take advantage
of the agricultural boom of the 1910s. By the time the boom went bust, reclamation projects proved no match for the natural processes of drought, wind,
and erosion. The land lay exposed by plow and grazing animals. When the
rains stopped, the dusty topsoil blew away.

This chapter examines some responses to the environmental realities of
aridity in the twentieth-century West by focusing on the related extremes of
water and dust. What do the following readings tell us about Americans'
perception of and relationship to the arid lands? What different roles are
assigned to or taken on by the federal government? What are the economic
and social costs of dam water and damn dust?

⋎ D O C U M E N T S

The first four documents consider dam water. The first is an extract from John Wesley Powell's 1878 *Report on the Lands of the Arid Region*. In it, Powell defines the arid West, lauds cooperative agrarian settlement and the power of irrigation, and proposes a radical new system for classifying and distributing the land, water, and resources of the public domain. The second document is by irrigation booster William E. Smythe who takes Powell's vision and spins it into the grand story of agrarian conquest and nationalism. Aridity and irrigation become virtues, the foundations for true democracy and social progress. The third document is an outgrowth of Powell's proposals and Smythe's boosterism. In 1902, Congress passed the National Reclamation or Newlands Act, establishing a reclamation fund for dam and irrigation works in the West and laying the basis for the Bureau of Reclamation. The fourth document excerpts oral histories about the construction of Hoover Dam between 1929 and 1935. In these histories, men and women describe the reasons for the dam, their personal experiences working on and living near the dam site, and assess the dangers involved. The document ends with excerpts from President Franklin D. Roosevelt's dedication of the dam, uniting the democratic agrarian vision of irrigation in the arid West with the positive role of government.

In the final three documents we turn to damn dust, the ecological nightmare of the "dirty thirties." The fifth document is a letter written in 1935 by Caroline A. Henderson of Eva, Oklahoma, to a friend living in Maryland. Having lived on the farm with her husband for five years, Henderson describes the drought, dust storms, and activities of the federal government in trying to combat the loss of topsoil. She also speaks about the spirit of the local people who faced overwhelming ecological and economic odds. The sixth document is the narrative script for Pare Lorentz's 1936 documentary, *The Plow That Broke the Plains*. This 21-minute New Deal propaganda film, funded by the Resettlement Administration, explained the reasons for the dust storms and reassured citizens that technology, harnessed by enlightened government planning and public conservation efforts, could save the day. The final document was written by the father of soil conservation, Hugh Hammond Bennett who headed the U.S. Soil Conservation Service at its inception in 1935. His is a more telling critique of the frontier and agrarian myths, of the lack of an American land ethic, and the need for government programs to protect our soil.

John Wesley Powell Demands
Reclamation of the Arid Lands, 1878

The eastern portion of the United States is supplied with abundant rainfall for agricultural purposes, receiving the necessary amount from the evaporation of the Atlantic Ocean and the Gulf of Mexico; but westward the amount of aqueous precipitation diminishes in a general way until at last a region is reached where the climate is so arid that agriculture is not successful without irrigation. This Arid Region begins about midway in the

---

J. W. Powell, *Report on the Lands of the Arid Region of the United States* (Washington, D.C.: Government Printing Office, 1878).

Great Plains and extends across the Rocky Mountains to the Pacific Ocean. . . . [I]t embraces something more than four-tenths of the whole country, excluding Alaska. In all this region the mean annual rainfall is insufficient for agriculture, but in certain seasons some localities, now here, now there, receive more than their average supply. . . .

Irrigable Lands

Within the Arid Region only a small portion of the country is irrigable. These irrigable tracts are lowlands lying along the streams. On the mountains and high plateaus forests are found at elevations so great that frequent summer frosts forbid the cultivation of the soil. Here are the natural timber lands of the Arid Region—an upper region set apart by nature for the growth of timber necessary to the mining, manufacturing, and agricultural industries of the country. Between the low irrigable lands and the elevated forest lands there are valleys, mesas, hills, and mountain slopes bearing grasses of greater or less value for pasturage purposes.

Then, in discussing the lands of the Arid Region, three great classes are recognized—the irrigable lands below, the forest lands above, and the pasturage lands between. . . .

Advantages of Irrigation.   There are two considerations that make irrigation attractive to the agriculturist. Crops thus cultivated are not subject to the vicissitudes of rainfall; the farmer fears no droughts; his labors are seldom interrupted and his crops rarely injured by storms. This immunity from drought and storm renders agricultural operations much more certain than in regions of greater humidity. Again, the water comes down from the mountains and plateaus freighted with fertilizing materials derived from the decaying vegetation and soils of the upper regions, which are spread by the flowing water over the cultivated lands. It is probable that the benefits derived from this source alone will be full compensation for the cost of the process. . . .

Coöperative Labor or Capital Necessary for the Development of Irrigation.   Small streams can be taken out and distributed by individual enterprise, but coöperative labor or aggregated capital must be employed in taking out the larger streams.

The diversion of a large stream from its channel into a system of canals demands a large outlay of labor and material. To repay this all the waters so taken out must be used, and large tracts of land thus become dependent upon a single canal. It is manifest that a farmer depending upon his own labor cannot undertake this task. To a great extent the small streams are already employed, and but a comparatively small portion of the irrigable lands can be thus redeemed; hence the chief future development of irrigation must come from the use of the larger streams. . . . [B]ut when farming is dependent upon larger streams such [poor] men are barred from these enterprises until coöperative labor can be organized or capital induced to assist. . . .

In Utah Territory coöperative labor, under ecclesiastical organization, has been very successful. Outside of Utah there are but few instances where it has been tried; but at Greeley, in the State of Colorado, this system has been eminently successful. . . .

Increase of Irrigable Area by the Storage of Water.   There are two methods of storing the waste waters. Reservoirs may be constructed near the sources of the streams and the waters held in the upper valleys, or the water may be run from the canals into ponds within or adjacent to the district where irrigation is practiced. This latter method will be employed first. . . .

The greater storage of water must come from the construction of great reservoirs in the highlands where lateral valleys may be dammed and the main streams conducted into them by canals. On most streams favorable sites for such water works can be found. . . .

The increase by storage will eventually be important, and it would be wise to anticipate the time when it will be needed by reserving sites for principal reservoirs and larger ponds.

Timber Lands

Throughout the Arid Region timber of value is found growing spontaneously on the higher plateaus and mountains. These timber regions are bounded above and below by lines which are very irregular, due to local conditions. Above the upper line no timber grows because of the rigor of the climate, and below no timber grows because of aridity. Both the upper and lower lines descend in passing from south to north; that is, the timber districts are found at a lower altitude in the northern portion of the Arid Region than in the southern. The forests are chiefly of pine, spruce, and fir, but the pines are of principal value. Below these timber regions, on the lower slopes of mountains, on the mesas and hills, low, scattered forests are often found, composed mainly of dwarfed piñon pines and cedars. . . .

. . . In general it may be stated that the timber regions are fully adequate to the growth of all the forests which the industrial interests of the country will require if they can be protected from desolation by fire. No limitation to the use of the forests need be made. The amount which the citizens of the country will require will bear but a small proportion to the amount which the fires will destroy; and if the fires are prevented, the renewal by annual growth will more than replace that taken by man. . . .

In the main these fires are set by Indians. . . . On their hunting excursions they systematically set fire to forests for the purpose of driving the game. This is a fact well known to all mountaineers. Only the white hunters of the region properly understand why these fires are set, it being usually attributed to a wanton desire on the part of the Indians to destroy that which is of value to the white man. The fires can, then, be very greatly curtailed by the removal of the Indians. . . .

[L]umbermen and woodmen will furnish to the people [in the land] below their supply of building and fencing material and fuel. In some cases it will be practicable for the farmers to own their timber lands, but in general the timber will be too remote, and from necessity such a division of labor will ensue. . . .

Pasturage Lands

The irrigable lands and timber lands constitute but a small fraction of the Arid Region. Between the lowlands on the one hand and the highlands on the other is found a great body of valley, mesa, hill, and low mountain lands. To what extent, and under what conditions can they be utilized? Usually they bear a scanty growth of grasses. These grasses are nutritious and valuable both for summer and winter pasturage. . . .

Though living water is not abundant, the country is partially supplied by scattered springs, that often feed little brooks whose waters never join the great rivers on their way to the sea, being able to run but a short distance from their fountains, when they spread among the sands to be reëvaporated. These isolated springs and brooks will in many cases furnish the water necessary for the herds that feed on the grasses. When springs are not found wells may be sometimes dug, and where both springs and wells fail reservoirs may be constructed. . . .

The Farm Unit for Pasturage Lands.   The grass is so scanty that the herdsman must have a large area for the support of his stock. In general a quarter section of land alone is of no value to him; the pasturage it affords is entirely inadequate to the wants of a herd that the poorest man needs for his support.

Four square miles may be considered as the minimum amount necessary for a pasturage farm, and a still greater amount is necessary for the larger part of the lands; that is, pasturage farms, to be of any practicable value, must be of at least 2,560 acres, and in many districts they must be much larger. . . .

Farm Residences Should Be Grouped.   These lands will maintain but a scanty population. The homes must necessarily be widely scattered from the fact that the farm unit must be large. That the inhabitants of these districts may have the benefits of the local social organizations of civilization—as schools, churches, etc., and the benefits of cooperation in the construction of roads, bridges, and other local improvements, it is essential that the residences should be grouped to the greatest possible extent. This may be practically accomplished by making the pasturage farms conform to topographic features in such manner as to give the greatest possible number of water fronts.

The great areas over which stock must roam to obtain subsistence usually prevents the practicability of fencing the lands. It will not pay to fence the pasturage fields, hence in many cases the lands must be occupied by herds roaming in common; for poor men cooperative pasturage is necessary, or communal regulations for the occupancy of the ground and for the division of the increase of the herds. Such communal regulations have already been devised in many parts of the country.

William E. Smythe Envisions Conquest of Arid America, 1900

The ninety-seventh meridian divides the United States almost exactly into halves. East of that line dwell sixty-four million people. Here are overgrown cities and over-crowded industries. Here is surplus capital, as idle and burdensome as the surplus population. West of that line dwell four or five millions—less than the population of Pennsylvania, and scarcely more than that of Greater New York. And yet the vast territory to the West—so little known, so lightly esteemed, so sparsely peopled—is distinctly the better half of the United States.

The West and East are different sections, not merely in name and geographical location, but in physical endowments and fundamental elements of economic life. . . . It was the destiny of the one to blossom and fruit in an epoch distinguished for the accumulation of wealth, with its vast possibilities of evil and of good. It was the destiny of the other to lie fallow until humanity should feel a nobler impulse; then to nurse, in the shadow of its everlasting mountains and the warmth of its unfailing sunshine, new dreams of liberty and equality for men. . . .

The distinguishing characteristic of the vast region west of the ninety-seventh meridian is, then, its aridity—the lack of rainfall sufficient to insure the success of agriculture. . . .

It was not, however, until a few pioneer settlements had demonstrated undreamed-of results, nor until Major John W. Powell, by utterances as daring as his explorations, had furnished a scientific basis for a brood of new hopes, that the real character of Arid America began to glow, like the belated sun through a morning fog, upon the popular imagination. . . .

The Blessing of Aridity.   The anomaly that its foremost blessing should consist in the fact which gave it a wide-spread reputation for worthlessness is interesting, but unimportant. Nature frequently conceals her raw materials of greatness, alike in men and in countries, until time and opportunity are ripe. In the aridity of the West we shall find the true key to its future institutions. Climate may produce a healthy race, and mineral resources may enrich it, but the natural conditions which determine the character of social and industrial organization, and mould the habits and customs of men, are the potent influences which shape civilization. . . .

William E. Smythe, *The Conquest of Arid America* (NY: Harper & Brothers, 1900), 19, 22, 24, 30, 43–48.

The Miracle of Irrigation. The essence of the industrial life which springs from irrigation is its democracy. The first great law which irrigation lays down is this: There shall be no monopoly of land. This edict it enforces by the remorseless operation of its own economy. Canals must be built before water can be conducted upon the land. This entails expense, either of money or of labor. . . . For these reasons men cannot acquire as much irrigated land, even from the public domain, as they could acquire where irrigation was unnecessary. . . . A large farm under irrigation is a misfortune; a great farm, a calamity. Only the small farm pays. But this small farm blesses its proprietor with industrial independence and crowns him with social equality. That is democracy. . . .

The canal is an insurance policy against loss of crops by drought, while aridity is a substantial guarantee against injury by flood. Of all the advantages of irrigation, this is the most obvious. Scarcely less so, however, is its compelling power in the matter of production. Probably there is no spot of land in the United States where the average crop raised by dependence upon rainfall might not be doubled by intelligent irrigation. The rich soils of the arid region produce from four to ten times as largely with irrigation as the soil of the humid region without it. As the measure of value is not area, but productive capacity, twenty acres in the Far West should equal one hundred acres elsewhere. . . .

This is the miracle of irrigation on its industrial side.

As a factor in the social life of the civilization it creates, irrigation is no less influential and beneficent. Compared with the familiar conditions of country life which we have known in the East and central West, the change which irrigation brings amounts to a revolution. The bane of rural life is its loneliness. . . . The starvation of the soul is almost as real as the starvation of the body.

Irrigation compels the adoption of the small-farm unit. This is the germ of new social possibilities. . . .

Where settlement has been carried out upon the most enlightened lines irrigated farms range from five to twenty acres upon the average, rarely exceeding forty acres at the maximum. It is perfectly obvious, of course, that a twenty-acre unit means that neighbors will be eight times as numerous as in a country settled up in quarter-sections—that where farms are ten acres in size neighbors will be multiplied by sixteen. . . .

A very-small-farm unit makes it possible for those who till the soil to live in the town. The farm village, or home centre, is a well-established feature of life in Arid America, and a feature which is destined to enjoy wide and rapid extension. Each four or five thousand acres of cultivated land will sustain a thrifty and beautiful hamlet, where all the people may live close together and enjoy most of the social and educational advantages within the reach of the best eastern town. . . . The great cities of the western valleys will not be cities in the old sense, but a long series of beautiful villages, connected by lines of electric motors, which will move their products and people from place to place. In this scene of intensely cultivated land, rich with its bloom and fruitage, with its spires and roofs, and with its carpets of green and gold stretching away to the mountains, it will be difficult for the beholder to say where the town ends and the country begins.

This is the miracle of irrigation upon its social side.

Irrigation is the foundation of truly scientific agriculture. Tilling the soil by dependence upon rainfall is, by comparison, like a stage-coach to the railroad, like the tallow dip to the electric light. The perfect conditions for scientific agriculture would be presented by a place where it never rained, but where a system of irrigation furnished a never-failing water supply which could be adjusted to the varying needs of different plants. It is difficult for those who have been in the habit of thinking of irrigation as merely a substitute for rain to grasp the truth that precisely the contrary is the case. Rain is the poor dependence of those who cannot obtain the advantages of irrigation. . . .

This is the miracle of irrigation upon its scientific side.

An Excerpt from the Reclamation Act, 1902

An Act Appropriating the receipts from the sale and disposal of public lands in certain States and Territories to the construction of irrigation works for the reclamation of arid lands.

Be it enacted by the Senate and House of Representatives of the United States of America in Congress assembled, That all moneys received from the sale and disposal of public lands in Arizona, California, Colorado, Idaho, Kansas, Montana, Nebraska, Nevada, New Mexico, North Dakota, Oklahoma, Oregon, South Dakota, Utah, Washington, and Wyoming . . . shall be, and the same are hereby, reserved, set aside, and appropriated as a special fund in the Treasury to be known as the "reclamation fund," to be used in the examination and survey for and the construction and maintenance of irrigation works for the storage, diversion, and development of waters for the reclamation of arid and semiarid lands in the said States and Territories, and for the payment of all other expenditures provided for in this Act: . . .

SEC. 3 . . . that public lands which it is proposed to irrigate by means of any contemplated works shall be subject to entry only under the provisions of the homestead laws in tracts of not less than forty nor more than one hundred and sixty acres, . . .

SEC. 5. That the entryman upon lands to be irrigated by such works shall, in addition to compliance with the homestead laws, reclaim at least one-half of the total irrigable area of his entry for agricultural purposes, and before receiving patent for the lands covered by his entry shall pay to the Government the charges apportioned against such tract, as provided in section four. No right to the use of water for land in private ownership shall be

Carolyn Merchant, ed., *Major Problems in American Environmental History* (Lexington, Mass.: D.C. Heath and Co., 1993), 347–348.

sold for a tract exceeding one hundred and sixty acres to any one landowner, and no such sale shall be made to any landowner unless he be an actual bona fide resident on such land, or occupant thereof residing in the neighborhood of said land, and no such right shall permanently attach until all payments therefor are made.

Voices of Those Who Built Hoover Dam, 1929–1935

Charles Squires: In the long fight for the passage of the Boulder Canyon Project Act, certain characters are worthy of special mention. For Nevada [Senators] Tasker L. Oddie, Key Pittman, and Congressman Sam Arentz were particularly active. In California the people of the Imperial Valley particularly were enlisted in the cause, as well as the Los Angeles Bureau of Water and Power. In this bureau there were several men without whose aid this work could not have been accomplished. Among those were W. B. Mathews, attorney for the Los Angeles Bureau of Water and Power, and William Mulholland, the distinguished engineer who built the great aqueduct from Owens Valley to Los Angeles. During all those years Senator Hiram Johnson, Senator Black, and Congressman Phil Swing were the Californians active in the fight for the Colorado Project. . . .

Erma Godbey: We had heard a lot about the Boulder Canyon Project while we still lived in Colorado and took the *Denver Post,* because the regional offices of the Bureau of Reclamation were in Colorado. . . . Also there were men who had helped do diamond drilling to find out where they could build a dam that had later come up to Silverton and worked in the mines, that we had talked to personally, so we thought what we'll do is come over here.

My mother and stepfather came down from Colorado to visit us. They were driving an old seven-passenger Dodge touring car. We had no car, so we had them drive us over here. We put a mattress and two baby cribs and two baby mattresses on the top of the car and tied them on. Then all of us got in the car. We brought a few cooking utensils and very few clothes and some bedding with us—and that's all. We had four children, and my baby was only five months old. We came from Oatman down to Needles and around by way of Searchlight.

It was terrifically hot. My God, it was terribly hot and dusty. None of the roads were paved in those days. It was just ungodly, it was so hot. . . . We went down to what is now the middle of [Lake Mead]. It was called Ragtown, but it was officially Williamsville, after Claude Williams, who

Andrew J. Dunar and Dennis McBride, *Building Hoover Dam: An Oral History of the Great Depression* (NY: Twayne Publishers, 1993), 14, 39–42, 90, 147, 150, 158, 163, 268, 311, 312. Copyright © 1993 by Twayne Publishers. Excerpted with permission of Twayne Publishers, an imprint of Simon & Schuster Macmillan.

was in charge of it. It looked like anyplace that is just built out of paste-board cartons or anything else. . . .

We got ahold of some clothesline, and we had some safety pins. We put some poles in the ground and pinned these beautiful wool blankets with safety pins to these poles to try to make a little bit of shade from the terrible heat. It would get to be 120 by nine in the morning, and it wouldn't get below 120 before nine at night. It just seemed like the river just drew the heat right down there. You could just see the heat dancing off of the mountains, the black cliffs down there. I would wrap my babies in wet sheets so they could sleep. But for my littlest baby, the one that was only five months old, Ila, I would put the wet sheet around her crib so the air would blow through it. But it wasn't enough. . . .

We had no furniture. Nobody had furniture. . . . Eventually we got two powder boxes. I set them up in the tent, and I put the ironing board across, so that way we had a bench.

We had to haul drinking water from the river. They had dug a couple of holes a little bit in from the river, and the river would seep through the sand and it would be pretty good. . . .

We had to go down to the river and bathe. I wore my dress but no petticoat and stuff, and we'd wash up underneath and do the best you could without becoming naked for other people to see us. One day I was holding the baby by one leg, and I darn near lost her in the river. My husband managed to rescue her before she floated on down the river. I couldn't swim.

People would dig a hole in their tent floor. They would put one of these powder boxes down in the hole, and they would try to keep things a little bit cool that way. We hauled water from the river and had to let it settle to wash clothes and things. And here I had a baby in diapers. We didn't have Clorox and stuff like that in those days, so I had to boil the diapers on the campfire. . . .

They would go to work at 7:00 in the morning. It was so terribly hot by noon that men were passing out with the heat. So they decided that they would go to work at 4:00 in the morning and work until noon. Another shift would come on at 4:00 in the afternoon and work until midnight. But nobody would work during the very heat of the day between noon and 4:00. So then my husband had to be at work at 4:00 in the morning. That meant I had to get up at about 2:30 in the morning and get some breakfast going for him and get his lunch packed. . . .

Harry Hall: I got a job working graveyard as what they called a pitman. They were scaling the diversion tunnels at that time on day shift. Graveyard shift would go down there with a 2,300-volt electric Marion shovel and muck out the material that they had shot during the day shift. My job was to back the trucks in so the operator on the shovel would not have to swing too much to load the trucks. . . .

Joe Kine: My first job high scaling was over the Nevada valve house, cutting down to put the valve house in. That was the steepest canyon wall of all. We had a crew of men, and they came and went together all the time. I'd have a buddy that worked with me, and we'd be together all the time unless he took a day off or something. We tied our rope to a steel in the ground at the top of the canyon wall. We tied our safety belts and our bos'n chair on that. We had inch ropes. We had good ropes. They didn't break. . . .

We dropped ourselves over. Then we slid down to where we wanted to work, whether it was close or way down. We could move back and forth pretty good with our ropes. . . .

We didn't have expert powdermen. We done the whole business ourselves: drilled, loaded the holes and shot, barred down. Whatever was loose, we'd stick a bar behind it and pry it off and let it drop down. The engineers would mark it how far back we wanted to go. They'd take their transits and shoot and check it and tell you whether you had enough off or didn't have enough off. They had that all figured out. They'd mark it. Then we'd drill some more and go ahead. . . .

But that was a good job. I got paid $5 a day to start with. Afterwards I got $5.60. I believe that was one of the safest jobs they had. I think there was less people that got hurt on high scaling than there was on lots of the other jobs. It wasn't any worse than anything else. One thing, you were sitting down all the time. It was a sitting-down job.

Tommy Nelson: Those trucks never turned their ignition off unless they were broke down. When they were hauling that debris out of the river bottom, a man coming down assigned to a certain truck might take any truck until he found his own. They would change shifts right on the run.

I recall one little incident, just to give you an idea how highball this job was. During the change of a shift—I was working a swing shift—I heard the swish of an air hose way up high there. I looked up there, and here comes a high scaler. He looks like a little ant. Apparently he got knocked off before he got tied on. He was coming all the way down. He lit very close to where I was flagging these trucks.

There was a shovel operator by the name of Red Wixson operating a shovel nearby where this fellow fell. I took a quick look to see if there were any trucks coming. I didn't think there was much I could do for this guy, but best I take a look. So I went over to him real fast. Red jumped out of his shovel. There wasn't nothing you could do for him. But there was trucks coming, and they were stacking up. Along came a hard-boiled superintendent. I won't use the language he used. But he said, "Get those blankety-blank trucks moving." I said, "Carl, there's a man killed over here." "Well, he won't hurt anybody; get 'em going."

Tex Nunley: You could say the first [concrete] was poured with a water bucket. It was on the lower portal railroad. They benched off on the cliff up there to put in the track. They had steel beams going up. They poured concrete with a water bucket around some of those beams. When they took the beams out, the concrete stayed. That was the first concrete that ever went into the mix. The dam was built on up to that, so that pour was taken in. Sounds funny, but that's the way it was. . . .

Bob Parker: A girl wrote a few months back that her grandparents had told her that her uncle was buried in Hoover Dam in the concrete. I did find out that he was in an accident down in the slot when one of the forms gave way and concrete poured down in there. He and another man were on this scaffold down in there carrying a big plank. The concrete tore down the scaffold that they were on and dumped him and the plank down in the bottom in the wet concrete. Somehow the man that was with him hung onto the scaffold and was saved. Her uncle wound up in the bottom, and it took them a few hours to dig him out, but they got him out of that concrete. Of course, he was dead. But they never left anybody buried in the dam.

Harry Hall: The filling of the lake and the tremendous amount of weight from the water caused the crust of the earth to change position. We had a tremendous number of earthquakes—not fatal ones, but you could see the dust fly, you could hear, you could feel some of them. . . . After the lake filled, the seismic activity ceased.

President Franklin D. Roosevelt's Address at the Dedication of Boulder Dam 30 September 1935

Senator Pittman, Secretary Ickes, Governors of the Colorado's States, and you especially who have built Boulder Dam, this morning I came, I saw and I was conquered, as everyone would be who sees for the first time this great feat of mankind. . . .

We are here to celebrate the completion of the greatest dam in the world, rising 726 feet above the bed-rock of the river and altering the geography of a whole region; we are here to see the creation of the largest artificial lake in the world—115 miles long, holding enough water, for example, to cover the State of Connecticut to a depth of ten feet; and we are here to see nearing completion a power house which will contain the largest generators and turbines yet installed in this country, machinery that can continuously supply nearly two million horsepower of electric energy. . . .

Beautiful and great as this structure is, it must also be considered in its relationship to the agricultural and industrial development and in its contribution to the health and comfort of the people of America who live in the Southwest.

To divert and distribute the waters of an arid region, so that there shall be security of rights and efficiency in service, is one of the greatest problems of law and of administration to be found in any Government. The farms, the cities, the people who live along the many thousands of miles of this river and its tributaries—all of them depend upon the conservation, the regulation, and the equitable division of its ever-changing water supply.

What has been accomplished on the Colorado in working out such a scheme of distribution is inspiring to the whole country. Through the cooperation of the States whose people depend upon this river, and of the Federal Government which is concerned in the general welfare, there is being constructed a system of distributive works and of laws and practices which will insure to the millions of people who now dwell in this basin, and the millions of others who will come to dwell here in future generations, a just, safe and permanent system of water rights. In devising these policies and the means for putting them into practice the Bureau of Reclamation of the Federal Government has taken, and is destined to take in the future, a leading and helpful part. . . .

Caroline A. Henderson Sends a Letter from the Dust Bowl of Oklahoma, 1935

EVA, OKLAHOMA
June 30, 1935

MY DEAR EVELYN:—

Your continued interest in our effort to 'tie a knot in the end of the rope and hang on' is most stimulating. Our recent transition from rain-soaked eastern Kansas with its green pastures, luxuriant foliage, abundance of flowers, and promise of a generous harvest, to the dust-covered desolation of No Man's Land was a difficult change to crowd into one short day's travel. Eleanor has laid aside the medical books for a time. Wearing our shade hats, with handkerchiefs tied over our faces and vaseline in our nostrils, we have been trying to rescue our home from the accumulations of wind-blown dust which penetrates wherever air can go. It is an almost hopeless task, for there is rarely a day when at some time the dust clouds do not roll over. 'Visibility' approaches zero and everything is covered again with a silt-like deposit which may vary in depth from a film to actual ripples on the kitchen floor. I keep oiled cloths on the window sills and between the upper and lower sashes. They help just a little to retard or collect the dust. Some seal the windows with the gummed-paper strips used in wrapping parcels, but no method is fully effective. We buy what appears to be red cedar sawdust with oil added to use in sweeping our floors, and do our best to avoid inhaling the irritating dust.

In telling you of these conditions I realize that I expose myself to charges of disloyalty to this western region. A good Kansas friend suggests that we should imitate the Californian attitude toward earthquakes and keep to ourselves what we know about dust storms. Since the very limited rains of May in this section gave some slight ground for renewed hope, optimism has been the approved policy. Printed articles or statements by journalists, railroad officials, and secretaries of small-town Chambers of Commerce have heralded too enthusiastically the return of prosperity to the drouth region. And in our part of the country that is the one durable basis for any prosperity whatever. There is nothing else to build upon. But you wished to know the truth, so I am telling you the actual situation, though I freely admit that the facts are themselves often contradictory and confusing.

Early in May, with no more grass or even weeds on our 640 acres than on your kitchen floor, and even the scanty remnants of dried grasses from last year cut off and blown away, we decided, like most of our neighbors, to

---

Caroline A. Henderson, "Letters from the Dust Bowl," *Atlantic Monthly,* 157 (May 1936), 540–51.

ship our cattle to grass in the central part of the state. We sent 27 head, retaining here the heifers coming fresh this spring. . . .

The day after we shipped the cattle, the long drouth was temporarily broken by the first effective moisture in many months—about one and one-quarter inches in two or three gentle rains. All hope of a wheat crop had been abandoned by March or April.

Contrary to many published reports, a good many people had left this country either temporarily or permanently before any rains came. And they were not merely 'drifters,' as is frequently alleged. In May a friend in the southwestern county of Kansas voluntarily sent me a list of the people who had already left their immediate neighborhood or were packed up and ready to go. The list included 109 persons in 26 families, substantial people, most of whom had been in that locality over ten years, and some as long as forty years. In these families there had been two deaths from dust pneumonia. Others in the neighborhood were ill at that time. Fewer actual residents have left our neighborhood, but on a sixty-mile trip yesterday to procure tractor repairs we saw many pitiful reminders of broken hopes and apparently wasted effort. Little abandoned homes where people had drilled deep wells for the precious water, had set trees and vines, built reservoirs, and fenced in gardens,—with everything now walled in or half buried by banks of drifted soil,—told a painful story of loss and disappointment. I grieved especially over one lonely plum thicket buried to the tips of the twigs, and a garden with a fence closely built of boards for wind protection, now enclosing only a hillock of dust covered with the blue-flowered bull nettles which no winds or sands discourage. . . .

The coming of the long-desired rain gave impetus to the Federal projects for erosion control. Plans were quickly made, submitted to groups of farmers in district gatherings, and put into operation without delay.

The proposition was that, in order to encourage the immediate listing of abandoned wheat ground and other acreage so as to cut down wind erosion, the Federal Government would contribute ten cents per acre toward the expense of fuel and oil for tractors or feed for horses, if the farmers would agree to list not less than one fourth of the acreage on contour lines. Surveys were made promptly for all farmers signing contracts for either contour listing or terracing. The latest report states that within the few weeks since the programme was begun in our county 299,986 acres have been ploughed or listed on these contour lines—that is, according to the lay of the land instead of on straight lines with right-angled turns as has been the usual custom.

The plan has been proposed and carried through here as a matter of public policy for the welfare of all without reproach or humiliation to anyone. It should be remembered that 1935 is the fourth successive year of drouth and crop failure through a great part of the high plains region, and the hopelessly low prices for the crop of 1931 gave no chance to build up reserves for future needs. If the severe critics of all who in any way join in government plans for the saving of homes and the restoration of farms to a productive basis could only understand how vital a human problem is here considered, possibly their censures might be less bitter and scornful.

At any rate the contour listing has been done over extensive areas. If rains come to carry forward the feed crops now just struggling up in the furrows, the value of the work can be appraised. The primary intention of the plan for contour listing is to distribute rainfall evenly over the fields and prevent its running off to one end of the field or down the road to some creek or drainage basin. It is hoped that the plan will indirectly tend to lessen wind erosion by promoting the growth of feed crops, restoration of humus to denuded surfaces, and some protection through standing stubbles and the natural coverage of weeds and unavoidable wastes. One great contributing cause of the terrible dust storms of the last two years has been the pitiful bareness of the fields resulting from the long drouth.

I am not wise enough to forecast the result. We have had two most welcome rains in June—three quarters of an inch and one-half inch. Normally these should have been of the utmost benefit, though they by no means guarantee an abundant feed crop from our now sprouting seeds as many editorial writers have decreed and they do nothing toward restoring subsoil moisture. Actually the helpful effects of the rains have been for us and for other people largely destroyed by the drifting soil from abandoned, unworked lands around us. It fills the air and our eyes and noses and throats, and, worst of all, our furrows, where tender shoots are coming to the surface only to be buried by the smothering silt from the fields of rugged individualists who persist in their right to do nothing.

A fairly promising piece of barley has been destroyed for us by the merciless drift from the same field whose sands have practically buried the little mulberry hedge which has long sheltered our buildings from the northwest winds. Large spaces in our pastures are entirely bare in spite of the rains. Most of the green color, where there is any grazing, is due to the pestilent Russian thistles rather than to grass. Our little locust grove which we cherished for so many years has become a small pile of fence posts. With trees and vines and flowers all around you, you can't imagine how I miss that little green shaded spot in the midst of the desert glare.

Naturally you will wonder why we stay where conditions are so extremely disheartening. Why not pick up and leave as so many others have done? It is a fair question, but a hard one to answer.

Recently I talked with a young university graduate of very superior attainments. He took the ground that in such a case sentiment could and should be disregarded. He may be right. Yet, I cannot act or feel or think as if the experiences of our twenty-seven years of life together had never been. And they are all bound up with the little corner to which we have given our continued and united efforts. To leave voluntarily—to break all these closely knit ties for the sake of a possibly greater comfort elsewhere— seems like defaulting on our task. We may *have* to leave. We can't hold out indefinitely without some return from the land, some source of income, however small. But I think I can never go willingly or without pain that as yet seems unendurable. . . .

We long for the garden and little chickens, the trees and birds and wild flowers of the years gone by. Perhaps if we do our part these good things may return some day, for others if not for ourselves. . . .

"The Plow That Broke the Plains":
The Film Narrative, 1936

General Summary

"The Plow That Broke the Plains," America's first documentary motion picture, is a saga of the land of the Great Plains area of the United States.

Reproduced in ten principal sequences, the film traces the story of the plains country from that period in American history when the territory was a great windswept continent of grass peopled only by the aborigines and native fauna to the present day. From the days when the buffalo roamed the Great Plains through the successive invasions of range cattle, the homesteader and the large scale wheat farmer to the present time when dust storms whip across once fertile acres carrying away the fertile topsoil and bringing tragedy and disaster to the Plains people in this saga of the soil.

As an addendum to the picture the producers have added sequences of narration and pictorial explanation of the work of the Resettlement Administration and other federal agencies in reconstruction of land and in the resettlement of impoverished farmers giving them new hope and a better chance to wrest a living from the good earth.

Synopsis by Sequences

Sequence 1: *Grass*

The Great Plains country was once an uncharted range, an unfenced and inexhaustible pasture a thousand miles long.

Sequence 2: *Cattle*

It was a cattlemen's paradise with southern plains for winter grazing and mountain sweeps for summer grazing. Fortunes were made in beef as the railroads brought the markets to the edge of the plains. Cattle syndicates and land speculators followed the steers to the grasslands and by 1866 hardly an acre was unclaimed. After the cattle came the sheepman and the dirt farmer.

Sequence 3: *The Homesteader*

The homesteader came to find a new land in the great fervor of national expansion. As the fence was strung and the first posts driven, America saw the last of the free range. The homesteader began to plow the range, ripping the grass cover that held the loose topsoil. With the homesteader came modern machinery and with it, increased culture of the soil bringing bounty in the good years there were rains. And still the homesteaders came impelled by land companies and offers of 320 acres of government land.

James J. Lorenre, ed., *Enduring Voices,* Vol. 2 (Lexington, MA: D.C. Heath and Co., 1993), 227–229. Synopsis attached to Rexford G. Tugwell to William L. Brown, April 2, 1936. Copyright Office, Dept. of Motion Pictures, Broadcasted and Recorded Sound, LOC.

Sequence 4: *Warning*

But when the rains failed, homesteaders failed. Nature brought forceful retribution for breaking the sod of the plains. The homesteaders moved onward—there was plenty of land.

Sequence 5: *War*

When the World War came, new life came to the plains. Highgeared machinery, combines, night harvesting, additional farmers—all hands turned to the plains to answer the appeal that "Wheat will win the war! Plant wheat!" With a martial background the Great Plains yielded broad acres of wheat for the Allied cause.

Sequence 6: *Speculation*

But speculation always comes and with it the highest order of power machinery is thrown immediately into use. The world was our market! We had the land, the manpower and modern machinery. We welcomed the golden harvest of wheat and money as the rains held forth. Speculation was rife. The days of bouncing prosperity and of jazz age pleasure were here. The ticker tape sent stocks to a new high until the market, topheavy with its own distortion, toppled as the crash of 1929, wreaking financial and economic havoc throughout the nation.

Sequence 7: *Drought*

But when the rains held off, acres of once fertile land were left baking under the hot plains sun. Machinery rusted and in 1930 came the worst drought in our history, 1931, 1932, 1933 more drought and winds swept across the once verdant grasslands.

Sequence 8: *Dust Storm*

Striking with a stirring fury, the winds came and swept away the good earth imperilling life, wrecking hopes, bringing chaos and disaster.

Sequence 9: *Devastation*

For six years the people of the plains fought drought and dust. Most of their livestock starved or were choked by sandstorms. Many people left, but many stayed when everything was gone—all but life itself. But the misery and devastation of drought and dust swept a tide of invasion westward once again—toward the West Coast. In 1935 more than 30,000 refugees hit the trail out of the drought country every month. Homeless, penniless, bewildered, they joined the luckless army of the highway. As the emigres swept into California, historians pondered the problem of the plains and saw that in 50 years America had turned the grasslands into a great dust bowl—almost into a veritable desert waste.

Sequence 10: *Conclusion*

But the Federal Government is attacking the plains problem on two broad fronts. Congress has appropriated millions for drought relief to save farmers from starvation and dire poverty. On the second front the Government is carrying forward a program of permanent reconstruction of the land. Sod, seeds, and trees are being put into the plains. The Forestry Service, Soil Conservation Service, cooperating with the Department of Agriculture are uniting efforts to restore damaged lands. Farmers are being taught best methods of farming to prevent erosion.

The Resettlement Administration is taking title to 5,000,000 acres of land in the Great Plains and turning it back to grass and its natural uses. The Resettlement Administration has moved three divisions into the field and has loaned money for seed, feed, equipment for those who can stay and is moving thousands of others out, giving them a new chance to make a living. It is establishing farmstead communities where they can have advantage of public services, technical advice and assistance and an opportunity to secure homes and farms on long term credit.

But the sun still bakes the land and the winds still sweep across broad acres. It is the job of all agencies, private, state and federal to cooperate in reconstruction to prevent the Great Plains from becoming a desert—we must all cooperate in a battle to save our greatest natural resource—the soil.

Hugh Hammond Bennett Insists on Soil Conservation, 1939

In fifteen decades, Americans have transformed a wilderness into a mighty nation. In all the history of the world, no people ever built so fast and yet so well. This will be a land of liberty, they said in the beginning, and as they hacked the forest, drove their ploughshares deep into the earth, and spread their herds across the ranges, they sang of the land of the free that they were making. All that they finally built upon this continent is founded in that faith—that here there would be opportunity and independence and security for any man.

Those things are the power and the hope of this democracy. And they have sprung, very largely, from the goodness of our land, its capacity to produce rewardingly. Yet with astonishing improvidence, Americans have plundered the resource that made it possible to realize their dream.

Moving across this country in the greatest march of occupation ever known, they have exploited and abused this soil. As a result, our vital land supply has been steadily sapped by the heavy drain of soil erosion. . . .

Millions of acres of our land are ruined, other millions of acres already have been harmed. And not mere soil is going down the slopes, down the rivers, down to the wastes of the oceans. Opportunity, security, the chance for a man to make a living from the land—these are going too. It is to preserve them—to sustain a rewarding rural life as a bulwark of this nation, that we must defend the soil. . . .

Today the nation has an abundance of land, but not enough *good* land. Probably, if there had not been so much good land in the beginning, there would not have developed the early idea that the productive soil of America was limitless and inexhaustible. . . .

From Hugh Hammond Bennett, *Soil Conservation* (New York: McGraw-Hill Book Company, 1939), v–vii, 1–3, 5–6, 8–9, 11–15.

All our experience has demonstrated that erosion can be controlled in a practical way. The need is for forthright, determined, nation-wide action. Today's necessity for public action is the outgrowth of yesterday's failure to look more carefully to our land. . . .

. . . Both the march of land occupation and the ensuing national development were accompanied . . . by a prodigious wastage of the resources with which nature originally stocked the land. The white inhabitants of this country, in their "conquest of the wilderness" and their "subjugation of the West," piled up a record of heedless destruction that nearly staggers the imagination. Slopes once clothed with mighty forests now lie bare and stark. Formerly rich lands are riddled with gullies. Level plains country that once supported lush stands of native "short" grasses is overgrown with weeds or covered with shifting sands left in the wake of dust storms.

What caused this tragic transformation? What happened to the bountiful land that inspired early explorers to enthusiastic comment and rhapsodic description? The answer lies largely in a false philosophy of plenty, a myth of inexhaustibility, which prevailed generally for many years and persists, in some quarters, even at the present time. . . .

. . . The plain truth is that Americans, as a people, have never learned to love the land and to regard it as an enduring resource. They have seen it only as a field for exploitation and a source of immediate financial return. In the days of expanding frontier it was customary, when land was washed, cropped, or grazed to a condition of impoverishment, to pull up stakes and move on to fresher fields and greener pastures. Today such easy migration is no longer possible. The country has expanded to the full limits of its boundaries, and erosion is causing a progressive shrinkage of the tillable area. The early frontier psychology of land treatment must be abandoned once and for all. In its place a new frontier has appeared. A restricted area of land—an indispensable area, subject to still further restriction by the inroads of uncontrolled erosion—has taken the place of a former abundance of land. Now, man must move rapidly over this diminishing area in order to clear away not trees or prairie grasses but old methods of wasteful land use and substitute therefore new methods of conversation that will provide security for the soil and for those living by the soil. . . .

. . . National action may be led and aided by government, but the soil must be conserved ultimately by those who till the land and live by its products. Without a widespread recognition of this latter responsibility, any governmental program of soil conservation must be doomed to eventual futility and failure.

Y *E S S A Y S*

Wallace Stegner (1909–1993), the Pulitzer Prize–winning novelist, historian, biographer, and short story writer, spent his life describing the western character and defending the western landscape. For many years he directed the creative writing program at Stanford University where he remained professor emeritus. He was also a key figure in the modern conservation movement. Stegner delivered this essay as one of the William W. Cook Lectures at the University of Michigan Law School in October 1986. Stegner provides a trenchant assessment of western water use and the Bureau of Reclamation, pointing out the perversion of John Wesley Powell's perhaps naive prescription for the arid West by the William Smythes of the world. The second essay by Donald Worster, Hall Distinguished Professor of American History at the University of Kansas and one of the leading environmental historians of our time, describes the dust storms of the 1930s in the southern plains. Worster maintains that the dust bowl was primarily the work of man, not nature, and that this ecological disaster in the long run far outweighed the economic disaster of the Great Depression. His evocative account captures the physical violence and the psychological impacts of drought, wind, and that damn dust.

Striking the Rock—Water and the Arid West

WALLACE STEGNER

The summer of 1948 my family and I spent on Struthers Burt's ranch in Jackson Hole. I was just beginning the biography of John Wesley Powell, and beginning to understand some things about the West that I had not understood before. But during that busy and instructive interval my wife and I were also acting as western editors and scouts for a publishing house, and now and then someone came by with a manuscript or the idea for a book. The most memorable of these was a famous architect contemplating his autobiography. One night he showed us slides of some of his houses, including a million-dollar palace in the California desert of which he was very proud. He said it demonstrated that with imagination, technical knowhow, modern materials, and enough money, an architect could build anywhere without constraints, imposing his designed vision on any site, in any climate. . . .

That desert house seemed to me, and still seems to me, a paradigm—hardly a paradigm, more a caricature—of what we have been doing to the West in my lifetime. Instead of adapting, as we began to do, we have tried to make country and climate over to fit our existing habits and desires. Instead of listening to the silence, we have shouted into the void. We have tried to make the arid West into what it was never meant to be and cannot remain, the Garden of the World and the home of multiple millions.

That does not mean either that the West should never have been settled or that water should never be managed. The West—the habitable parts of it—is a splendid habitat for a limited population living within the country's rules of sparseness and mobility. If the unrestrained engineering of western water was original sin, as I believe, it was essentially a sin of scale. Anyone who wants to live in the West has to manage water to some degree.

Ranchers learned early to turn creeks onto their hay land. Homesteaders not on a creek learned to dam a runoff coulee to create a "rezavoy" as we did

Wallace Stegner, *The American West as Living Space* (Ann Arbor, The University of Michigan Press, 1987), 31, 33, 36–38, 42, 44–60. Copyright © 1987 by the University of Michigan Press. Reprinted by permission of the University of Michigan Press.

in Saskatchewan in 1915. Kansas and Oklahoma farmers set windmills to pumping up the underground water. Towns brought their water, by ditch or siphon, from streams up on the watershed. Irrigation, developed first by the Southwestern Indians and the New Mexico Spanish, and reinvented by the Mormons—it was a necessity that came with the territory—was expanded in the 1870s and 1880s by such cooperative communities as Greeley, Colorado, and by small-to-medium corporate ventures such as the one I wrote about in *Angle of Repose*—the project on the Boise River that after its failure was taken over by the Bureau of Reclamation and called the Arrowrock Dam.

Early water engineers and irrigators bit off what they and the local community could chew. They harnessed the streams that they could manage. Some dreamers did take on larger rivers, as Arthur Foote took on the Boise, and went broke at it. By and large, by 1890, individual, corporate, and cooperative irrigators had gone about as far as they could go with water engineering; their modest works were for local use and under local control. It might have been better if the West had stopped there. Instead, all through the 1890s the unsatisfied boosters called for federal aid to let the West realize its destiny, and in 1902 they got the Newlands Act. This *permitted* the feds to undertake water projects—remember that water was state owned, or at least state regulated—and created the Bureau of Reclamation.

Reclamation projects were to be paid for by fees charged irrigation districts, the period for paying off the interest-free indebtedness being first set at ten years. Later that was upped to twenty, later still to forty. Eventually much of the burden of repayment was shifted from the sale of water to the sale of hydropower, and a lot of the burden eliminated entirely by the practice of river-basin accounting, with write-offs for flood control, job creation, and other public goods. Once it was lured in, the federal government—which meant taxpayers throughout the country, including taxpayers in states that resented western reclamation because they saw themselves asked to pay for something that would compete unfairly with their own farmers—absorbed or wrote off more and more of the costs, accepting the fact that reclamation was a continuing subsidy to western agriculture. Even today, when municipal and industrial demands for water have greatly increased, 80 to 90 percent of the water used in the West is used, often wastefully, on fields, to produce crops generally in surplus elsewhere. After all the billions spent by the Bureau of Reclamation, the total area irrigated by its projects is about the size of Ohio, and the water impounded and distributed by the bureau is about 15 percent of all the water utilized in the West. What has been won is only a beachhead, and a beachhead that is bound to shrink.

One of the things Westerners should ponder, but generally do not, is their relation to and attitude toward the federal presence. The bureaus administering all the empty space that gives Westerners much of their outdoor pleasure and many of their special privileges and a lot of their pride and self-image are frequently resented, resisted, or manipulated by those who benefit economically from them but would like to benefit more, and are generally taken for granted by the general public.

The federal presence should be recognized as what it is: a reaction against our former profligacy and wastefulness, an effort at adaptation and stewardship in the interest of the environment and the future. In contrast to the principal water agency, the Bureau of Reclamation, which was a creation of the boosters and remains their creature, and whose prime purpose is technological conversion of the arid lands, the land-managing bureaus all have as at least part of their purpose the preservation of the West in a relatively natural, healthy, and sustainable condition. . . .

The protection provided by these various agencies [the National Park Service, the Bureau of Land Management, and the National Forest Service] is of course imperfect. Every reserve is an island, and its boundaries are leaky. Nevertheless this is the best protection we have, and not to be disparaged. All Americans, but especially Westerners whose backyard is at stake, need to ask themselves whose bureaus these should be. Half of the West is in their hands. . . .

The bureaus need, and some would welcome, the kind of public attention that would force them to behave in the long-range public interest. Though I have been involved in controversies with some of them, the last thing I would want to see is their dissolution and a return to the policy of disposal, for that would be the end of the West as I have known and loved it. Neither state ownership nor private ownership—which state ownership would soon become—could offer anywhere near the disinterested stewardship that these imperfect and embattled federal bureaus do, while at the same time making western space available to millions. They have been the strongest impediment to the careless ruin of what remains of the Public Domain, and they will be necessary as far ahead as I, at least, can see.

The Bureau of Reclamation is something else. From the beginning, its aim has been not the preservation but the remaking—in effect the mining—of the West.

A principal justification for the Newlands Act was that fabled Jeffersonian yeoman, the small freehold farmer, who was supposed to benefit from the Homestead Act, the Desert Land Act, the Timber and Stone Act, and other land-disposal legislation, but rarely did so west of the 98th meridian. The publicized purpose of federal reclamation was the creation of family farms that would eventually feed the world and build prosperous rural commonwealths in deserts formerly fit for nothing but horned toads and rattlesnakes. To insure that these small farmers would not be done out of their rights by large landowners and water users, Congress wrote into the act a clause limiting the use of water under Reclamation Bureau dams to the amount that would serve a family farm of 160 acres.

Behind the pragmatic, manifest-destinarian purpose of pushing western settlement was another motive: the hard determination to dominate nature . . . as part of our Judeo-Christian heritage. Nobody implemented that impulse more uncomplicatedly than the Mormons, a chosen people who believed the Lord when He told them to make the desert blossom as the rose. Nobody expressed it more bluntly than a Mormon hierarch, John Widtsoe, in the middle of the irrigation campaigns: "The destiny of man is to possess the whole earth; the destiny of the earth is to be subject to man. There can be no full conquest of the earth, and no real satisfaction to humanity, if large portions of the earth remain beyond his highest control."

That doctrine offends me to the bottom of my not-very-Christian soul. It is related to the spirit that builds castles of incongruous luxury in the desert. It is the same spirit that between 1930 and the present has so dammed, diverted, used, and reused the Colorado River that its saline waters now never reach the Gulf of California, but die in the sand miles from the sea, that has set the Columbia, a far mightier river, to tamely turning turbines; that has reduced the Missouri, the greatest river on the continent, to a string of ponds; that has recklessly pumped down the water table of every western valley and threatens to dry up even so prolific a source as the Ogalalla Aquifer; that has made the Salt River Valley of Arizona, and the Imperial, Coachella, and great Central valleys of California into gardens of fabulous but deceptive richness; that has promoted a new rush to the West fated, like the beaver and grass and gold rushes, to recede after doing great environmental damage.

The Garden of the World has been a glittering dream, and many find its fulfillment exhilarating. I do not. I have already said that I think of the main-stem dams that made it possible as original sin, but there is neither a serpent nor a guilty first couple in the story. In Adam's fall we sinnéd all. Our very virtues as a pioneering people, the very genius of our industrial civilization, drove us to act as we did. God and Manifest Destiny spoke with one voice urging us to "conquer" or "win" the West; and there was no voice of comparable authority to remind us of Mary Austin's quiet but profound truth, that the manner of the country makes the usage of life there, and that the land will not be lived in except in its own fashion.

Obviously, reclamation is not the panacea it once seemed. Plenty of people in 1986 are opposed to more darns, and there is plenty of evidence against the long-range viability and the social and environmental desirability of large-scale irrigation agriculture. Nevertheless, millions of Americans continue to think of the water engineering in the West as one of our proudest achievements, a technology that we should export to backward Third World nations to help them become as we are. We go on praising apples as if eating them were an injunction of the Ten Commandments.

For its first thirty years, the Bureau of Reclamation struggled, plagued by money problems and unable to perform as its boosters had promised. It got a black eye for being involved, in shady ways, with William Mulholland's steal of the Owens Valley's water for the benefit of Los Angeles. The early dams it completed sometimes served not an acre of public land. It did increase homestead filings substantially, but not all those homesteads ended up in the hands of Jeffersonian yeomen: according to a 1922 survey, it had created few family farms; the 160-acre limitation was never enforced; three-quarters of the farmers in some reclamation districts were tenants.

Drought, the Great Depression, and the New Deal's effort to make public works jobs gave the bureau new life. It got quick appropriations for the building of the Boulder (Hoover) Dam, already authorized, and it took over from the state of California construction of the enormous complex of dams and ditches called the Central Valley Project, designed to harness all the rivers flowing westward out of the Sierra. It grew like a mushroom, like an exhalation. By the 1940s the bureau that only a few years before had been hanging on by a shoestring had built or was building the four greatest dams ever built on earth up to that time—Hoover, Shasta, Bonneville, and Grand Coulee—and was already the greatest force in the West. It had discovered where power was, and allied itself with it: with the growers and landowners, private and corporate, whose interests it served, and with the political delegations, often elected out of this same group, who carried the effort in Washington for more and more pork barrel projects. In matters of western water there are no political parties. You cannot tell Barry Goldwater from Moe Udall, or Orrin Hatch from Richard Lamm.

Nevertheless there was growing opposition to dams from nature lovers, from economists and cost counters, and from political representatives of areas that resented paying these costs in subsidy of their competition. Uniting behind the clause in the National Park Service Act that enjoined "use without impairment," environmental groups in 1955 blocked two dams in Dinosaur National Monument and stopped the whole Upper Colorado River Storage Project in its tracks. Later, in the 1960s, they also blocked a dam in Marble Canyon, on the Colorado, and another in Grand Canyon National Monument, at the foot of the Grand Canyon.

In the process they accumulated substantial evidence, economic, political, and environmental, against dams, the bureau that built them, and the principles that guided that bureau. President Jimmy Carter had a lot of public sympathy when he tried to stop nine water-project boondoggles, most of them in the West, in 1977. Though the hornet's nest he stirred up taught him something about western water politics, observers noted that no new water projects were authorized by Congress until the very last days of the 99th Congress, in October 1986.

The great days of dam building are clearly over, for the best dam sites are used up, most of the rivers are "tamed," costs have risen exponentially, and public support of reclamation has given way to widespread and searching criticism. It is not a bad time to assess what the big era of water engineering has done to the West. . . .

Begin with some environmental consequences of "taming" rivers, if only because the first substantial opposition to dams was environmental.

First, dams do literally kill rivers, which means they kill not only living water and natural scenery but a whole congeries of values associated with them. The scenery they kill is often of the grandest, for most main-stem dams are in splendid canyons, which they drown. San Francisco drowned the Hetch Hetchy Valley, which many thought as beautiful as Yosemite itself, to ensure its future water supply. Los Angeles turned the Owens Valley into a desert by draining off its natural water supplies. The Bureau of Reclamation drowned Glen Canyon, the most serene and lovely rock funhouse in the West, to provide peaking power for Los Angeles and the Las Vegas Strip.

The lakes formed behind dams are sometimes cited as great additions to public recreation, and Floyd Dominy even published a book to prove that the Glen Canyon Dam had beautified Glen Canyon by drowning it. But drawdown reservoirs rarely live up to their billing. Nothing grows in the zone between low-water mark and high-water mark, and except when brimming full, any drawdown reservoir, even Glen Canyon, which escapes the worst effects because its walls are vertical, is not unlike a dirty bathtub with a ring of mud and mineral stain around it.

A dammed river is not only stoppered like a bathtub, but it is turned on and off like a tap, creating a fluctuation of flow that destroys the riverine and riparian wildlife and creates problems for recreational boatmen who have to adjust to times when the river is mainly boulders and times when it rises thirty feet and washes their tied boats off the beaches. And since dams prohibit the really high flows of the spring runoff, boulders, gravel, and detritus pile up into the channel at the mouths of side gulches, and never get washed away.

Fishing too suffers, and not merely today's fishing but the future of fishing. Despite their fish ladders, the dams on the Columbia seriously reduced the spawning runs of salmon and steelhead, and they also trapped and killed so many smolts on their way downriver that eventually the federal government had to regulate the river's flow. The reduction of fishing is felt not only by the offshore fishing fleets and by Indian tribes with traditional or treaty fishing rights, but by sports fishermen all the way upstream to the Salmon River Mountains in Idaho.

If impaired rafting and fishing and sight-seeing seem a trivial price to pay for all the economic benefits supposedly brought by dams, reflect that rafting and fishing and sight-seeing are not trivial economic activities. Tourism is the biggest industry in every western state. The national parks, which are mainly in the public lands states, saw over three hundred million visitors in 1984. The national forests saw even more. A generation ago, only five thousand people in all the United States had ever rafted a river; by 1985, thirty-five million had. Every western river from the Rogue and the Owyhee to the Yampa, Green, San Juan, and Colorado is booked solid through the running season. As the rest of the country grows more stressful as a dwelling place, the quiet, remoteness, and solitude of a week on a wild river become more and more precious to more and more people. It is a good question whether we may not need that silence, space, and solitude for the healing of our raw spirits more than we need surplus cotton and alfalfa, produced for private profit at great public expense.

The objections to reclamation go beyond the obvious fact that reservoirs in desert country lose a substantial amount of their impounded water through surface evaporation; and the equally obvious fact that all such reservoirs eventually silt up and become mud flats ending in concrete waterfalls; and the further fact that an occasional dam, because of faulty siting or construction, will go out, as the Teton Dam went out in 1976, bringing disaster to people, towns, and fields below. They go beyond the fact that underground water, recklessly pumped, is quickly depleted, and that some of it will only be renewed in geological time, and that the management of underground water and that of surface water are necessarily linked. The ultimate objection is that irrigation agriculture itself, in deserts where surface evaporation is extreme, has a limited though unpredictable life. Marc Reisner predicts that in the next half century as much irrigated land will go out of production as the Bureau of Reclamation has "reclaimed" in its whole history.

Over time, salts brought to the surface by constant flooding and evaporation poison the soil: the ultimate, natural end of an irrigated field in arid country is an alkali flat. That was the end of fields in every historic irrigation civilization except Egypt, where, until the Aswan Dam, the annual Nile flood leached away salts and renewed the soil with fresh silt.

Leaching can sometimes be managed if you have enough sweet water and a place to put the runoff. But there is rarely water enough—the water is already 125 percent allocated and 100 percent used—and what water is available is often itself saline from having run through other fields upstream and having brought their salts back to the river. Colorado River water near the headwaters at Grand Lake is 200 parts per million (ppm) salt. Below the Wellton-Mohawk District on the Gila it is 6,300 ppm salt. The 1.5 million acre feet that we are pledged to deliver to Mexico is so saline that we are having to build a desalinization plant to sweeten it before we send it across the border.

Furthermore, even if you have enough water for occasional leaching, you have to have somewhere to drain off the waste water, which is likely not only to be saline, but to be contaminated with fertilizers, pesticides, and poisonous trace minerals such as selenium. Kesterson Reservoir, in the Central Valley near Los Banos, is a recent notorious instance, whose two-headed, three-legged, or merely dead waterfowl publicized the dangers of draining waste water off into a slough. If it is drained off into a river, or out to sea, the results are not usually so dramatic. But the inedible fish of the New River draining into the Salton Sea, and the periodically polluted beaches of Monterey Bay near the mouth of the Salinas River, demonstrate that agricultural runoff is poison anywhere.

The West's irrigated bounty is not forever, not on the scale or at the rate we have been gathering it in. The part of it that is dependent on wells is even more precarious than that dependent on dams. In California's San Joaquin Valley, streams and dams supply only 60 percent of the demand for water; the rest is pumped from wells—hundreds and thousands of wells. Pumping exceeds replenishment by a half-trillion gallons a year. In places the water table has been pumped down three hundred feet; in places the ground itself has sunk thirty feet or more. But with those facts known, and an end clearly in sight, nobody is willing to stop, and there is as yet no state regulation of groundwater pumping.

In Arizona the situation is if anything worse. 90 percent of Arizona's irrigation depends on pumping. And in Nebraska and Kansas and Oklahoma, old Dust Bowl country, they prepare for the next dust bowl, which is as inevitable as sunrise though a little harder to time, by pumping away the groundwater through center-pivot sprinklers.

Add to the facts about irrigation the fact of the oversubscribing of rivers. The optimists say that when more water is needed, the engineers will find a way—"augmentation" from the Columbia or elsewhere for the Colorado's overdrawn reservoirs, or the implementation of cosmic schemes such as NAWAPA (North American Water and Power Alliance), which would dam all the Canadian rivers up against the east face of the Rockies, and from that Mediterranean-sized reservoir supply water to every needy district from Minneapolis to Yuma. I think that there are geological as well as political difficulties in the way of water redistribution on that scale. The solution of western problems does not lie in more grandiose engineering.

Throw into the fact barrel, finally, a 1983 report from the Council on Environmental Quality concluding that desertification—the process of converting a viable arid-lands ecology into a lifeless waste—proceeds faster in the western United States than in Africa. Some of that desertification is the result of overgrazing, but the salinization of fields does its bit. When the hydraulic society falls back from its outermost frontiers, it will have done its part in the creation of new deserts.

The hydraulic society. I borrow the term from Donald Worster, who borrowed it from Karl Wittvogel. Wittvogel's studies convinced him that every hydraulic society is by necessity an autocracy. Power, he thought, inevitably comes to reside in the elite that understands and exercises control over water. . . .

The hydraulic society involves the maximum domination of nature. And the American West, Worster insists, is the greatest hydraulic society the world ever saw, far surpassing in its techniques of domination the societies on the Indus, the Tigris-Euphrates, or the Yellow River. The West, which Walter Webb and Bernard DeVoto both feared might remain a colonial dependency of the East, has instead become an empire and gotten the East to pay most of the bills.

The case as Worster puts it is probably overstated. There are, one hopes, more democratic islands than he allows for, more areas outside the domination of the water managers and users. Few parts of the West are totally controlled by what Worster sees as a hydraulic elite. Nevertheless, no one is likely to call the agribusiness West, with most of its power concentrated in the Iron Triangle of growers, politicians, and bureaucratic experts and its work done by a permanent underclass of dispossessed, mainly alien migrants, the agrarian democracy that the Newlands Act was supposed to create.

John Wesley Powell understood that a degree of land monopoly could easily come about in the West through control of water. A thorough Populist, he advocated cooperative rather than federal waterworks, and he probably never conceived of anything on the imperial scale later realized by the Bureau of Reclamation. But if he were alive today he would have to agree at least partway with Worster: water experts ambitious to build and expand their bureau and perhaps honestly convinced of the worth of what they are doing have allied themselves with landowners and politicians, and by making land monopoly through water control immensely profitable for their backers, they have made it inevitable.

How profitable? Worster cites figures from one of the most recent of the mammoth projects, the Westlands, that brought water to the western side of the San Joaquin Valley. Including interest over forty years, the cost to the taxpayers was $3 billion. Water is delivered to the beneficiaries, mostly large landholders, at $7.50 an acre foot—far below actual cost, barely enough to pay operation and maintenance costs. According to a study conducted by economists Philip LaVeen and George Goldman, the subsidy amounted to $2,200 an acre, $352,000 per quarter section—and very few quarter-section family farmers were among the beneficiaries. Large landholders obliged by the 160-acre limitation to dispose of their excess lands disposed of them to family members and cronies, paper farmers, according to a pattern by now well established among water users.

So much for the Jeffersonian yeoman and the agrarian democracy. As for another problem that Powell foresaw, the difficulty that a family would have in handling even 160 acres of intensively farmed irrigated land, both the corporate and the family farmers solve it the same way: with migrant labor, much of it illegally recruited below the Rio Grande. It is anybody's guess what will happen now that Congress has passed the Immigration Reform and Control Act, but up to now the border has been a sieve, carefully kept open from this side. . . .

What should one make of facts as depressing as these? What do such facts do to the self-gratifying image of the West as the home of freedom, independence, largeness, spaciousness, and of the Westerner as total self-reliance on a white stallion? I confess they make this Westerner yearn for the old days on the Milk and the Missouri when those rivers ran free, and we were trying to learn how to live with the country, and the country seemed both hard and simple, and the world and I were young, when irrigation had not yet grown beyond its legitimate bounds and the West provided for its thin population a hard living but a wonderful life.

Sad to say, they make me admit, when I face them, that the West is no more the Eden that I once thought it than the Garden of the World that the boosters and engineers tried to make it; and that neither nostalgia nor boosterism can any longer make a case for it as the geography of hope.

The Black Blizzards Roll In—The Dust Bowl Begins

DONALD WORSTER

The thirties began in economic depression and in drought. The first of those disasters usually gets all the attention, although for the many Americans living on farms drought was the more serious problem. In the spring of 1930 over 3 million men and women were out of work. They had lost their jobs or had been laid off without pay in the aftermath of the stock market crash of the preceding fall. Another 12 million would suffer the same fate in the following two years. Many of the unemployed had no place to live, nor even the means to buy food. They slept in public toilets, under bridges, in shantytowns along the railroad tracks, or on doorsteps, and in the most wretched cases they scavenged from garbage cans—a Calcutta existence in the richest nation ever. The farmer, in contrast, was slower to feel the impact of the crash. He usually had his own independent food supply and stood a bit aloof from the ups and downs of the urban-industrial system. In the twenties that aloofness had meant that most farm families had not fully shared in the giddy burst of affluence—in new washing machines, silk stockings, and shiny roadsters. They had, in fact, spent much of the decade in economic doldrums. Now, as banks began to fail and soup lines formed, rural Americans went on as before, glad to be spared the latest reversal and just a little pleased to see their proud city cousins humbled. Then the droughts began, and they brought the farmers to their knees, too. . . .

During the thirties serious drought threatened a great part of the nation. The persistent center, however, shifted from the East to the Great Plains, beginning in 1931, when much of Montana and the Dakotas became almost as arid as the Sonoran Desert. Farmers there and almost everywhere else watched the scorched earth crack open, heard the gray grass crunch underfoot, and worried about how long they would be able to pay their bills. Around their dried-up ponds the willows and wild cherries were nearly leafless, and even the poison ivy drooped. Drought, of course, is a relative term: it depends upon one's concept of "normal." But following the lead of the climatologists of the time, we can use a precipitation deficiency of at least 15 per cent of the historical mean to qualify as drought. By that standard, of all the American states only Maine and Vermont escaped a drought year from 1930 to 1936. Twenty states set or equaled record lows for their entire span of official weather data. Over the nation as a whole, the 1930s drought was, in the words of a Weather Bureau scientist, "the worst in the climatological history of the country."

Intense heat accompanied the drought, along with economic losses the nation could ill afford. In the summer of 1934, Nebraska reached 118 degrees, Iowa, 115. In Illinois thermometers stuck at over 100 degrees for so long that 370 people died—and one man, who had been living in a refrigerator to keep cool, was treated for frostbite. Two years later, when the country was described by *Newsweek* as "a vast simmering caldron," more than 4500 died from excessive heat, water was shipped into the West by diverted tank-cars and oil pipelines, and clouds of grasshoppers ate what little remained of many farmers' wheat and corn—along with their fenceposts and the washing on their clotheslines. The financial cost of the 1934 drought alone amounted to one-half the money the United States had put into World War I. By 1936, farm losses had reached $25 million a day, and more than 2 million farmers were drawing relief checks. Rexford Tugwell, head of the Resettlement Administration, who toured the burning plains that year, saw "a picture of complete destruction"—"one of the most serious peacetime problems in the nation's history."

As the decade reached its midpoint, it was the southern plains that experienced the most severe conditions. During some growing seasons there was no soil moisture down to three feet over large parts of the region. By 1939, near Hays, Kansas, the accumulated rainfall deficiency was more than 34 inches—almost a two-year supply in arrears. Continued long enough in such a marginal, semiarid land, a drought of that magnitude would produce a desert. Weathermen pointed out that there had been worse single years, as in 1910 and 1917, or back in the 1890s, and they repeatedly assured the people of the region that their records did not show any modern drought lasting more than five years, nor did they suggest any long-range adverse climatic shift. But farmers and ranchers did not find much comfort in statistical charts; their cattle were bawling for feed, and their bank credit was drying up along with the soil. Not until after 1941 did the rains return in abundance and the burden of anxiety lift.

Droughts are an inevitable fact of life on the plains, an extreme one occurring roughly every twenty years, and milder ones every three or four. They have always brought with them blowing dust where the ground was bare of crops or native grass. Dust was so familiar an event that no one was surprised to see it appear when the dry weather began in 1931. But no one was prepared for what came later: dust storms of such violence that they made the drought only a secondary problem—storms of such destructive force that they left the region reeling in confusion and fear.

"Earth" is the word we use when it is there in place, growing the food we eat, giving us a place to stand and build on. "Dust" is what we say when it is loose and blowing on the wind. Nature encompasses both—the good and the bad from our perspective, and from that of all living things. We need the earth to stay alive, but dust is a nuisance, or, worse, a killer. . . .

Dust in the air is one phenomenon. However, dust storms are quite another. The story of the southern plains in the 1930s is essentially about dust storms, when the earth ran amok. And not once or twice, but over and over for the better part of a decade: day after day, year after year, of sand rattling against the window, of fine powder caking one's lips, of springtime turned to despair, of poverty eating into self-confidence.

Explaining why those storms occurred requires an excursion into the history of the plains and an understanding of the agriculture that evolved there. For the "dirty thirties," as they were called, were primarily the work of man, not nature. Admittedly, nature had something to do with this disaster too. Without winds the soil would have stayed put, no matter how bare it was. Without drought, farmers would have had strong, healthy crops capable of checking the wind. But natural factors did not make the storms—they merely made them possible. The storms were mainly the result of stripping the landscape of its natural vegetation to such an extent that there was no defense against the dry winds, no sod to hold the sandy or powdery dirt. The sod had been destroyed to make farms to grow wheat to get cash. But more of that later on. It is the storms themselves we must first comprehend:

their magnitude, their effect, even their taste and smell. What was it like to be caught in one of them? How much did the people suffer, and how did they cope?

Weather bureau stations on the plains reported a few small dust storms throughout 1932, as many as 179 in April 1933, and in November of that year a large one that carried all the way to Georgia and New York. But it was the May 1934 blow that swept in a new dark age. On 9 May, brown earth from Montana and Wyoming swirled up from the ground, was captured by extremely high-level winds, and was blown eastward toward the Dakotas. More dirt was sucked into the airstream, until 350 million tons were riding toward urban America. By late afternoon the storm had reached Dubuque and Madison, and by evening 12 million tons of dust were falling like snow over Chicago—4 pounds for each person in the city. Midday at Buffalo on 10 May was darkened by dust, and the advancing gloom stretched south from there over several states, moving as fast as 100 miles an hour. The dawn of 11 May found the dust settling over Boston, New York, Washington, and Atlanta, and then the storm moved out to sea. Savannah's skies were hazy all day 12 May; it was the last city to report dust conditions. But there were still ships in the Atlantic, some of them 300 miles off the coast, that found dust on their decks during the next day or two.

"Kansas dirt," the New York press called it, though it actually came from farther north. More would come that year and after, and some of it was indeed from Kansas—or Nebraska or New Mexico. In a later spring, New Hampshire farmers, out to tap their maples, discovered a fresh brown snow on the ground, discoloration from transported Western soil. Along the Gulf Coast, at Houston and Corpus Christi, dirt from the Llano Estacado collected now and then on windowsills and sidewalks. But after May 1934 most of the worst dust storms were confined to the southern plains region; less frequently were they carried by those high-altitude currents moving east or southeast. Two types of dusters became common then: the dramatic "black blizzards" and the more frequent "sand blows." The first came with a rolling turbulence, rising like a long wall of muddy water as high as 7000 or 8000 feet. Like the winter blizzards to which they were compared, these dusters were caused by the arrival of a polar continental air mass, and the atmospheric electricity it generated helped lift the dirt higher and higher in a cold boil, sometimes accompanied by thunder and lightning, other times by an eerie silence. Such storms were not only terrifying to observers, but immensely destructive to the region's fine, dark soils, rich in nutrients. The second kind of duster was a more constant event, created by the low sirocco-like winds that blew out of the southwest and left the sandier soils drifted into dunes along fence rows and ditches. Long after New York and Philadelphia had forgotten their taste of the plains, the people out there ate their own dirt again and again. . . .

In the memory of older plains residents, the blackest year was 1935, particularly the early spring weeks from 1 March to mid-April, when the Dust Bowl made its full-blown debut. Springtime in western Kansas can be a Willa Cather world of meadowlarks on the wing, clean white curtains dancing in the breeze, anemones and wild verbena in bloom, lilacs by the porch, a windmill spinning briskly, and cold fresh water in the bucket—but not in 1935. After a February heat wave (it reached 75 degrees in Topeka that month), the dust began moving across Kansas, Oklahoma, and Texas, and for the next six weeks it was unusual to see a clear sky from dawn until sundown. On 15 March, Denver reported that a serious dust storm was speeding eastward. Kansans ignored the radio warnings, went about their business as usual, and later wondered what had hit them. Small-town printer Nate White was at the picture show when the dust reached Smith Center: as he walked out the exit, it was as if someone had put a blindfold over his eyes; he bumped into telephone poles, skinned his shins on boxes and cans in an alleyway, fell to his hands and knees, and crawled along the curbing to a dim houselight. A seven-year-old boy wandered away and was lost in the gloom; the search party found him later, suffocated in a drift. A more fortunate child was found alive, tangled in a barbed wire fence. Near Colby, a train was derailed by dirt on the tracks, and the passengers spent twelve dreary hours in the coaches. The Lora-Locke Hotel in Dodge City over-flowed with more than two hundred stranded travelers; many of them bed-ded down on cots in the lobby and ballroom. In the following days, as the dust kept falling, electric lights burned continuously, cars left tracks in the dirt-covered streets, and schools and offices stayed closed. A reporter at Great Bend remarked on the bizarre scene: "Uncorked jug placed on side-walk two hours, found to be half filled with dust. Picture wires giving way due to excessive weight of dust on frames. Irreparable loss in portraits anticipated. Lady Godiva could ride thru streets without even the horse see-ing her." . . .

By 24 March southeastern Colorado and western Kansas had seen twelve consecutive days of dust storms, but there was worse to come. Near the end of March a new duster swept across the southern plains, destroying one-half the wheat crop in Kansas, one-quarter of it in Oklahoma, and all of it in Nebraska—5 million acres blown out. The storm carried away from the plains twice as much earth as men and machines had scooped out to make the Panama Canal, depositing it once again over the East Coast states and the Atlantic Ocean. Then the wind slackened off a bit, gathering strength, as it were, for the spectacular finale of that unusual spring season—Black Sunday, 14 April.

Dawn came clear and rosy all across the plains that day. By noon the skies were so fresh and blue that people could not remain indoors; they remembered how many jobs they had been postponing, and with a revived spirit they rushed outside to get them done. They went on picnics, planted gardens, repaired henhouses, attended funerals, drove to the neighbors for a visit. In midafternoon the summery air rapidly turned colder, falling as many as 50 degrees in a few hours, and the people noticed then that the yards were full of birds nervously fluttering and chattering—and more were arriving every moment, as though fleeing from some unseen enemy. Suddenly there appeared on the northern horizon a black blizzard, moving toward them; there was no sound, no wind, nothing but an immense "boogery" cloud. The storm struck Dodge City at 2:40 p.m. Not far from there John Garretson, a farmer in Haskell County, Kansas, who was on the road with his wife, Louise, saw it coming, but he was sure that he could beat it home. They had almost made it when they were engulfed; abandoning the car, they groped for the fencewire and, hand over hand, followed it to their door. Down in the panhandle Ed and Ada Phillips of Boise City, with their six-year-old daughter, were on their way home too, after an outing to Texline in their Model A Ford. It was about five o'clock when the black wall appeared, and they still had fifteen miles to go. Seeing an old adobe house ahead, Ed realized that they had to take shelter, and quickly. By the time they were out of the car the dust was upon them, making it so dark that they nearly missed the door. Inside they found ten other people, stranded, like themselves, in a two-room hut, all fearing that they might be smothered, all unable to see their companions' faces. For four hours they sat there, until the storm let up enough for them to follow the roadside ditch back to town. By then the ugly pall was moving south across the high plains of Texas and New Mexico.

Older residents still remember Black Sunday in all its details—where they were when the storm hit, what they did then. Helen Wells was the wife of the Reverend Rolley Wells, the Methodist minister in Guymon. Early that morning she had helped clean the accumulated dust from the church pews, working until she was choking and exhausted. Back in the parsonage she switched on the radio for some inspiring music, and what she heard was the hymn "We'll Work Till Jesus Comes." "I just had to sit down and laugh," she recalls; she had worn out her sweeper but still had a broom if that was needed. Later that day her husband, partly to please two visiting *Saturday Evening Post* reporters, held a special "rain service," which concluded in time for the congregation to get home before the dust arrived. . . .

The last of the major dust storms that year was on 14 April, and it was months before the damages could be fully calculated. Those who had been caught outside in one of the spring dusters were, understandably, most worried about their lungs. An epidemic of respiratory infections and something called "dust pneumonia" broke out across the plains. The four small hospitals in Meade County, Kansas, found that 52 per cent of their April admissions were acute respiratory cases, thirty-three patients died. Many dust victims would arrive at a hospital almost dead, after driving long distances in a storm. They spat up clods of dirt, washed the mud out of their mouths, swabbed their nostrils with Vaseline, and rinsed their bloodshot eyes with boric acid water. Old people and babies were the most vulnerable to the dusters, as were those who had chronic asthma, bronchitis, or tuberculosis, some of whom had moved to the plains so they might breathe the high, dry air.

Doctors could not agree on whether the dust caused a new kind of pneumonia, and some even denied that there were any unusual health problems in their communities. But the Red Cross thought the situation was so serious that it set up six emergency hospitals in Kansas, Colorado, and Texas, and it staffed them with its own nurses. In Topeka and Wichita volunteers worked in high school sewing rooms to make dust masks of cheesecloth;

over 17,000 of those masks were sent to the plains, especially to towns where goggles had been sold out. Chewing tobacco was a better remedy, snorted some farmers, who thought it was too much of a bother to wear such gadgets when driving their tractors. But enough wore the Red Cross masks or some other protection to make the plains look like a World War I battle-field, with dust instead of mustard gas coming out of the trenches. . . .

The medical remedies for the dust were at best primitive and makeshift. In addition to wearing light gauze masks, health officials recommended attaching translucent glasscloth to the inside frames of windows, although people also used cardboard, canvas, or blankets. Hospitals covered some of their patients with wet sheets, and housewives flapped the air with wet dish towels to collect dust. One of the most common tactics was to stick mask-ing tape, felt strips, or paraffin-soaked rags around the windows and door cracks. The typical plains house was loosely constructed and without insu-lation, but sometimes those methods proved so effective that there was not enough air circulation inside to replenish the oxygen supply. Warren Moore of southwestern Kansas remembers watching, during a storm, the gas flame on the range steadily turn orange and the coal-oil lamp dim until the people simply had to open the window, dust or no dust. But most often there was no way to seal out the fine, blowing dirt: it blackened the pillow around one's head, the dinner plates on the table, the bread dough on the back of the stove. It became a steady part of one's diet and breathing. "We thrived on it," claim some residents today; it was their "vitamin K." But all the same they prayed that they would not ingest so much it would maim them for life, or finish them off, as it had a neighbor or two.

Livestock and wildlife did not have even those crude defenses. "In a ris-ing sand storm," wrote Margaret Bourke-White, "cattle quickly become blinded. They run around in circles until they fall and breathe so much dust that they die. Autopsies show their lungs caked with dust and mud." Newborn calves could suffocate in a matter of hours, and the older cattle ground their teeth down to the gums trying to eat the dirt-covered grass. As the dust buried the fences, horses and cattle climbed over and wandered away. Where there was still water in rivers, the dust coated the surface and the fish died too. The carcasses of jackrabbits, small birds, and field mice lay along roadsides by the hundreds after a severe duster; and those that sur-vived were in such shock that they could be picked up and their nostrils and eyes wiped clean. In a lighter vein, it was said that prairie dogs were now able to tunnel upward several feet from the ground.

Cleaning up houses, farm lots, and city stores after the 1935 blow sea-son was an expensive matter. People literally shoveled the dirt from their front yards and swept up bushel-basketfuls inside. One man's ceiling col-lapsed from the silt that had collected in the attic. Carpets, draperies, and tapestries were so dust-laden that their patterns were indiscernible. Painted surfaces had been sandblasted bare. Automobile and tractor engines oper-ated in dust storms without oil-bath air cleaners were ruined by grit, and the repair shops had plenty of business. During March alone, Tucumcari, New Mexico, reported over $288,000 in property damage, although most towns' estimates were more conservative than that: Liberal, Kansas, $150,000; Randall County, Texas, $10,000; Lamar, Colorado, $3800. The merchants of Amarillo calculated from 3 to 15 per cent damage to their merchandise, not to mention the loss of shoppers during the storms. In Dodge City a men's clothing store advertised a "dust sale," knocking shirts down to 75 cents. But the heaviest burdens lay on city work crews, who had to sweep dirt from the gutters and municipal swimming pools, and on housewives, who struggled after each blow to get their houses clean.

The emotional expense was the hardest to accept, however. All day you could sit with your hands folded on the oilcloth-covered table, the wind moaning around the eaves, the fine, soft, talc sifting in the keyholes, the sky a coppery gloom; and when you went to bed the acrid dust crept into your dreams. . . . After 1935 the storms lost much of their drama; for most people they were simply a burden to be endured, and sometimes that burden was too heavy. Druggists sold out their supplies of sedatives quickly. An Oklahoman took down his shotgun, ready to kill his entire family and himself—"we're all better off dead," he despaired. That, to be sure, was an extreme instance, but there were indeed men and women who turned distraught, wept, and then, listless, gave up caring.

The plains people, however, then as now, were a tough-minded, leather-skinned folk, not easily discouraged. Even in 1935 they managed to laugh a bit at their misfortunes. They told about the farmer who fainted when a drop of water struck him in the face and had to be revived by having three buckets of sand thrown over him. They also passed around the one about the motorist who came upon a ten-gallon hat resting on a dust drift. Under it he found a head looking at him. "Can I help you some way?" the motorist asked, "Give you a ride into town maybe?" "Thanks, but I'll make it on my own," was the reply, "I'm on a horse." They laughed with Will Rogers when he pointed out that only highly advanced civilizations—like ancient Mesopotamia—were ever covered over by dirt, and that California would never qualify. Newspaper editors could still find something to joke about, too: "When better dust storms are made," the *Dodge City Globe* boasted, "the Southwest will make them." Children were especially hard to keep down; for them the storms always meant adventure, happy chaos, a breakdown of their teachers' authority, and perhaps a holiday. When darkness descends, as it did that April, humor, bravado, or a childlike irresponsibility may have as much value as a storm cellar.

Whether they brought laughter or tears, the dust storms that swept across the southern plains in the 1930s created the most severe environmental catastrophe in the entire history of the white man on this continent. In no other instance was there greater or more sustained damage to the American land, and there have been few times when so much tragedy was visited on its inhabitants. Not even the Depression was more devastating, economically. And in ecological terms we have nothing in the nation's past, nothing even in the polluted present, that compares. Suffice it to conclude here that in the decade of the 1930s the dust storms of the plains were an unqualified disaster.

Y *FURTHER READING*

Thomas G. Alexander, "Stewardship and Enterprise: The LDS Church and the Wasatch Front Oasis Environment, 1847–1930," *Western Historical Quarterly,* 25 (Autumn 1994), 341–66

F. Lee Brown and Helen M. Ingram, *Water and Poverty in the Southwest* (1987)

Terrence M. Cole, "Wally Hickel's Big Garden Hose: The Alaska Water Pipeline to California," *Pacific Northwest Quarterly,* 86 (Spring 1995), 59–71

William Cronon, "Landscapes of Abundance and Scarcity," in *The Oxford History of the American West,* eds. Clyde A. Milner II, Carol A. O'Connor, and Martha A. Sandweiss (1994), 603–37

Robert G. Dunbar, *Forging New Rights in Western Waters* (1983)

Dan Flores, "The Rocky Mountain West: Fragile Space, Diverse Place," *Montana The Magazine of Western History,* 45 (Winter 1995), 46–56

Mark W.T. Harvey, A *Symbol of Wilderness: Echo Park and the American Conservation Movement* (1994)

Samuel P. Hays, *Beauty, Health, and Permanence: Environmental Politics in the United States, 1955–1985* (1987)

Norris Hundley, Jr., *The Great Thirst: Californians and Water, 1770s–1990s* (1992)
———, "Water and the West in Historical Imagination," *Western Historical Quarterly,* 27 (Spring 1996), 5–31
———, *Water and the West: The Colorado River Compact and the Politics of Water in the West* (1975)

R. Douglas Hurt, *The Dust Bowl: An Agricultural and Social History* (1981)

Helen Ingram, *Water Politics: Continuity and Change* (1990)

James R. Huger, *Turning on Water with a Shovel: The Career of Elwood Mead* (1992)

Michael Lawson, *Dammed Indians: The Pick-Sloan Plan and the Missouri River Sioux, 1944–1980* (1982)

David Rich Lewis, "Native Americans and the Environment: A Survey of Twentieth-Century Issues," *American Indian Quarterly,* 19 (Summer 1995), 423–50

James C. Malin, *History and Ecology: Studies of the Grassland,* ed. Robert P. Swierenga (1984)

Russell Martin, *A Story That Stands Like a Dam: Glen Canyon and the Struggle for the Soul of the West* (1990)

Daniel McCool, *Command of the Water: Iron Triangles, Federal Water Development, and Indian Water* (1987)

M. Catherine Miller, *Flooding the Courtrooms: Law and Water in the Far West* (1993)

Roderick Nash, *Wilderness and the American Mind,* 3d ed. (1982)

Susan Rhoades Neel, "A Place of Extremes: Nature, History, and the American West," *Western Historical Quarterly,* 25 (Winter 1994), 489–505

John Opie, *Ogallala: Water for a Dry Land* (1993)

Charles S. Peterson, "Headgates and Conquest: The Limits of Irrigation on the Navajo Reservation, 1880–1950," *New Mexico Historical Review,* 68 (July 1993)

Donald J. Pisani, *To Reclaim a Divided West: Water, Law, and Public Policy, 1848–1902* (1992)

Marc Reisner, *Cadillac Desert: The American West and Its Disappearing Water* (1986)

Pamela Riney-Kerberg, *Rooted in Dust: Surviving Drought and Depression in Southwestern Kansas* (1994)

A. E. Rogge, et al., *Raising Arizona's Dams* (1995)

William D. Rowley, *Reclaiming the Arid West: The Career of Francis G. Newlands* (1996)

Robert A. Rutland, *A Boyhood in the Dust Bowl* (1995)

James E. Sherow, *Watering the Valley: Development Along the High Plains Arkansas River, 1870–1950* (1990)

Joseph E. Stevens, *Hoover Dam: An American Adventure* (1988)

Lawrence Svobida, *Farming the Dust Bowl* (1986)

John Walton, *Western Times and Water Wars: State, Culture, and Rebellion in California* (1992)

Richard White, *The Organic Machine* (1995)

Donald Worster, *Rivers of Empire: Water, Aridity, and the Growth of the American West* (1986)

———, *An Unsettled Country: Changing Landscapes of the American West* (1994)

———, *Under Western Skies: Nature and History in the American West* (1992)

CHAPTER
12

The Other Western Homefront

Y

Most scholars agree that World War II contributed to the transformation of
the American West. Federal military installations popped up everywhere.
War mobilization launched hundreds of new defense-related industries and
stimulated tens of thousands of existing businesses and shops receiving government contracts. Coal, oil, gas, and mineral production and processing
expanded. New war plants and the influx of soldiers and civilian war workers generated a construction boom. Women and minority groups moved into
industrial production to replace men called away to military service. Rapid
urban population growth and a dramatic rise in personal income stimulated
service industries. Federal spending invigorated the region, but increased the
West's dependency on the government. However, this "transformation" was
not solely the result of the war, nor was it a uniquely western event. World
War II had the same impact on the social, political, and economic structures
of the nation as a whole.

This chapter shifts the focus to a less discussed aspect of the World War II
homefront—race relations in the West. In the early years of the war, the government organized the evacuation of targeted racial and ethnic groups from
the west coast of the United States. Japanese Americans faced internment in
hastily constructed camps in the interior West. The military relocated Aleuts
for their own protection and against their wishes. Those who escaped wholesale removal, like Italian Americans, were restricted in their movements and
activities along the coast. Their lives and loyalties became a matter of public
scrutiny. Racial tensions increased as Native American, African American,
Mexican American, and Mexican workers moved into the factories and fields
of the West. Segregation and discrimination, often considered Southern phe-
nomena, were equally evident throughout the West. Although transformed
by the war, the West remained discouragingly like the rest of the nation in
many respects.

Y DOCUMENTS

The first two documents deal with the relocation and internment of Japanese
Americans during World War II. Roger Daniels, professor of history at the

University of Cincinnati, traces in quantitative terms the impact of forced relocation. The second document converts Daniels' numbers into human beings. Yoshiko Uchida provides a personal reminiscence of what it was like to be interned at the Tanforan Assembly Center in San Bruno, California, and then transferred to Topaz, Utah, "jewel of the desert." The third document is a collection of oral histories describing the restrictions placed on Italian Americans living in coastal California, a little recognized set of circumstances dubbed "the unknown internment." The fourth document is a statement by Flore Lekanof, Sr., Tribal Operations Coordinator for the Aleutian/Pribilof Islands Association, representing twelve tribes in the Aleutian Islands. Lekanof describes the process and impact of Aleut removal as part of a plea for reparations and an apology from the U.S. government.

The final two documents focus on the importation and repatriation of Mexican and Mexican American laborers during and after the war. Writing in 1943, Charles M. Smith of the Farm Security Administration provides an operational outline and positive assessment of the Bracero Program, wherein American farmers could obtain needed seasonal laborers and Mexican laborers could find good paying jobs. The final document is a 1946 essay by journalist and political commentator Daniel L. Schorr. He describes the backlash against Mexican Americans in San Antonio, Texas as representative of racial attitudes and the problems of social and economic reconversion following World War II.

What were the social, economic, and psychological impacts of relocation, internment, or reconversion? Why was relocation deemed necessary? Does the experience of Mexican farm laborers differ from the ideal described by the Farm Security Administration? Were the situations and experiences of these ethnic and racial groups during the war a distinctly western variation on an American problem?

Roger Daniels Quantifies the Forced Migrations of Japanese Americans, 1942–1946

It is often assumed that all Japanese Americans suffered a common fate during World War II: imprisonment in a War Relocation Authority concentration camp. This was not the case; the purpose of this note is to indicate the variety of Japanese American experiences during the war and to establish a uniform terminology.

According to the Census of 1940, there were 126,947 persons of Japanese ancestry living in the United States, another 157,905 in the Territory of Hawaii, and 263 in the Territory of Alaska, for a total of 285,115 persons. More than two-thirds of these were native-born American citizens. Because, except for a few World War I veterans, no Japanese person could be naturalized, there were close to 100,000 aliens of Japanese birth who became, after Pearl Harbor, enemy aliens.

Some of these enemy aliens were the first forced migrants of the war. Starting on December 7, some 3,000 adult aliens, almost all of them male, were arrested by the FBI and interned in such places as Missoula, Montana,

"The Forced Migrations of West Coast Japanese Americans, 1942–1946," by Roger Daniels in *Japanese Americans: From Relocation to Redress,* 72–74, edited by Roger Daniels, Sandra C. Taylor and Harry H. L. Kitano, 1986. Permission granted by University of Utah Press.

or Lordsburg, New Mexico. This was a well-established governmental policy, recognized in international law, and represented no innovative action. The men were interned under military guard but were in the custody of the Immigration and Naturalization Service (INS), part of the Department of Justice. Eventually, each man interned received a hearing, and some were freed as a result of those hearings. The vast majority of adult male enemy aliens were not interned, nor were any women and children. Several hundred of the internees were repatriated during the war on the exchange ship *Gripsholm,* a Swedish passenger liner.

In December and January 1941–42, most, but not all, of the more than 3,000 Japanese American citizens who had been inducted into the armed forces since the institution of the draft in October 1940, were discharged because of their ancestry, and they, and all other Japanese Americans were placed in a special category, IV-C, normally reserved for enemy aliens, and making them ineligible for military service.

After the promulgation of Executive Order 9066 by President Franklin D. Roosevelt on February 19, 1942, the U.S. Army took control of all persons of Japanese ancestry—aliens and citizens, men, women, and children—who lived in California, in the western parts of Oregon and Washington, and in part of Arizona, and forced them to leave their homes for the duration of hostilities. According to the 1940 census, 111,938 persons lived in what became the forbidden zone. In the more than two years between the census and the forced removal, that population gained from natural increases and was also affected by voluntary migration. According to the army's statistics, 117,116 persons were "eligible" for *incarceration* between March and October 1942. But it took charge of only 110,723. They were *incarcerated,* first in assembly centers under the jurisdiction of the army, and then in relocation centers under the jurisdiction of the War Relocation Authority.

This process has been given many names. Franklin Roosevelt was willing to call the places of confinement *concentration camps.* The War Relocation Authority abhorred that term and preferred to talk about the process as "relocation," although it sometimes referred to its prisoners as "evacuated" or "impounded people." The problem with the word "relocation," apart from its euphemistic nature, is that it also has been used to describe the process by which some Japanese Americans "voluntarily" moved out of the forbidden zone, and to the process by which, during and just after the war, thousands of Japanese Americans moved out of the camps to new homes and businesses in the interior of the United States. To further the semantic confusion, it has become common in recent years to speak of the "internment" of Japanese Americans as describing all the procedures affecting aliens and citizens, a practice that has been given official sanction by Congress, which created the Commission on the Wartime Relocation and Internment of Civilians (CWRIC) in 1980.

Most of the few thousand Japanese Americans resident on the West Coast who were neither interned nor incarcerated were allowed to migrate voluntarily outside of the forbidden zone. Japanese Americans who already lived in such places as Salt Lake City, Chicago, or New York were, if they were not interned, left in nervous liberty. The army's data indicate that nearly 5,000 voluntarily migrated east between March and October 1942. Clearly, others had already done so between December 7 and the beginning of March, but there are no good data on the numbers involved.

To complicate matters further, some Japanese Americans not subject to incarceration because of their residence returned to the forbidden zone to join their families, as did some discharged servicemen. In addition, some 1,000 persons were in various institutions, medical and penal, and not otherwise incarcerated; however, some patients were concentrated into a few institutions, such as Hillcrest Sanitorium outside of Los Angeles.

According to the War Relocation Authority, it had, at one time or another, 120,313 individuals in custody. It received 111,236 from the army, 1,118 from Hawaii, 1,735 who were transferred from INS internment camps, 219 "voluntary residents" (mostly individuals who joined families already in camp), and 24 from various institutions. In addition, 5,981 U.S. citizens were born to incarcerated mothers.

The overwhelming majority of Hawaiian Japanese Americans were left at liberty; all but a few thousand of the mainland Japanese Americans were interned or incarcerated, as was every such person who had lived in Alaska. . . .

At the very outset, even before the relocation centers had been filled, several hundred persons received "work release furloughs" to assist in harvesting crops, such as sugar beets in the western states outside of the forbidden zone. Others were allowed to volunteer for service with military intelligence units of the U.S. Army. In the fall of 1942, hundreds of students were allowed to leave to attend colleges and universities outside of the forbidden zone. And, particularly after the beginning of 1943, a process of controlled resettlement in the interior states was encouraged.

Thousands were moved from camp to camp: while some transfers were to reunite families and others at the convenience of the government, the major reason for intercamp migration was caused by a desire to *segregate* those considered disloyal in one camp—Tule Lake, California. Loyalty was largely determined by inmate answers to a questionnaire administered to all adults in WRA custody early in 1943. The two crucial questions asked were:

27. Are you willing to serve in the armed forces of the United States on combat duty, wherever ordered?
28. Will you swear unqualified allegiance to the United States of America from any or all attack by foreign or domestic forces, and forswear any form of allegiance or obedience to the Japanese emperor, to any other foreign government, power or organization?

Those who answered "No" to one or both questions—some 6,700 of the 75,000 respondents—were considered disloyal and most of them were segregated in the camp at Tule Lake. This segregation involved moving some 13,000 inmates, for about 6,200 "loyal" persons were moved from Tule Lake to other camps and some 6,800 persons were moved to Tule Lake.

Input-Output Data for WRA Centers, 1942–1946

	FROM		TO
90,491	assembly centers	54,127	return to West Coast
17,491	direct evacuation	52,798	relocated to interior
5,918	born in camp	4,724	Japan
1,735	INS internment camps	3,121	INS internment camps
1,579	seasonal workers (furloughed from assembly centers to work crops, then to camp)	2,355	armed forces
1,275	penal and medical institutions	1,862	died
1,118	Hawaii	1,322	to institutions
219	voluntary residents (mostly non-Japanese spouses)	4	unauthorized departures
120,313	Total population ever under WRA control	120,313	

By the end of the war almost half of the incarcerated people were out of camp, having received what the WRA came to call "leave clearance" to work, to go to college, or to enter the armed forces. By March 20, 1946, the last camp was empty. The accompanying table shows the movement of people in and out of the camps.

Yoshiko Uchida Remembers a Desert Exile in Utah, 1942

The bus made a sharp turn and swung slowly into the racetrack grounds. As I looked out the window for a better view, I saw armed guards close and bar the barbed wire gates behind us. We were in the Tanforan Assembly Center [San Bruno, California] now and there was no turning back. . . .

As soon as we got off the bus, we were directed to an area beneath the grandstand where we registered and filled out a series of forms. Our baggage was inspected for contraband, a cursory medical check was made, and our living quarters assigned. We were to be housed in Barrack 16, Apartment 40. Fortunately, some friends who had arrived earlier found us and offered to help us locate our quarters. . . .

Everywhere there were black tar-papered barracks that had been hastily erected to house the 8,000 Japanese Americans of the area who had been

Yoshiko Uchida, *Desert Exile* (Seattle: University of Washington Press, 1982), 68–70, 75, 77, 102–103, 105–106, 109, 113–115. Copyright © 1982 by University of Washington Press. Used with permission of University of Washington Press.

uprooted from their homes. Barrack 16, however, was not among them, and we couldn't find it until we had traveled half the length of the track and gone beyond it to the northern rim of the racetrack compound.

Finally one of our friends called out, "There it is, beyond that row of eucalyptus trees." Barrack 16 was not a barrack at all, but a long stable raised a few feet off the ground with a broad ramp the horses had used to reach their stalls. Each stall was now numbered and ours was number 40. That the stalls should have been called "apartments" was a euphemism so ludicrous it was comical.

When we reached stall number 40, we pushed open the narrow door and looked uneasily into the vacant darkness. The stall was about ten by twenty feet and empty except for three folded Army cots lying on the floor. Dust, dirt, and wood shavings covered the linoleum that had been laid over manure-covered boards, the smell of horses hung in the air, and the whitened corpses of many insects still clung to the hastily white-washed walls. . . .

About one hundred feet from our stable were two latrines and two washrooms for our section of camp, one each for men and women. The latrines were crude wooden structures containing eight toilets, separated by partitions, but having no doors. The washrooms were divided into two sections. In the front section was a long tin trough spaced with spigots of hot and cold water where we washed our faces and brushed our teeth. To the rear were eight showers, also separated by partitions, but lacking doors or curtains. The showers were difficult to adjust and we either got scalded by torrents of hot water or shocked by an icy blast of cold. Most of the Issei were unaccustomed to showers, having known the luxury of soaking in deep pine-scented tubs during their years in Japan, and found the showers virtually impossible to use. . . .

For four days after our arrival we continued to go to the main mess hall for all our meals. . . . Meals were uniformly bad and skimpy, with an abundance of starches such as beans and bread. I wrote to my non-Japanese friends in Berkeley shamelessly asking them to send us food, and they obliged with large cartons of cookies, nuts, dried fruit, and jams. . . .

On the sixteenth of September [1942], our family was assigned to Group IV of the four groups departing that day for Delta, Utah. We were to have supper at 4:00 P.M. and be at the departure point by 5:00 P.M., but we had no appetite at such an early hour and were too nervous to eat. . . .

About 8:00 P.M. the train, loaded with five hundred internees, was ready at last to begin its journey to Utah. We all clustered at the windows for a final look at Tanforan, scanning the crowds for friends staying behind. There were people gathered along the fence, on rooftops, on barrack steps, any place where they could get a glimpse of the train. They shouted and waved as though they would not see us for a long time, although they knew they would be following us in just a few weeks. . . .

As the train approached our destination we watched the landscape closely, hoping it would give us some indication of what the Topaz "relocation center" would be like. I felt cautiously optimistic as we reached the town of Delta for the land didn't appear to be too unfriendly or barren. A cheerful man boarded the train and passed out copies of the first issue of *The Topaz Times,* which gave us instructions regarding procedures at the new camp. I could tell a public relations man was already at work for the masthead contained a picture of a faceted topaz gemstone and in large print the words, "Topaz—Jewel of the Desert."

Once more we were counted as we got off the train and then were transferred to buses for the final leg of our journey to Topaz. As we rode along, I continued to feel fairly hopeful, for we were passing small farms, cultivated fields, and clusters of trees. After a half hour, however, there was an abrupt change. All vegetation stopped. There were no trees or grass or growth of any kind, only clumps of dry skeletal greasewood.

We were entering the edge of the Sevier Desert some fifteen miles east of Delta and the surroundings were now as bleak as a bleached bone. In the distance there were mountains rising above the valley with some majesty, but they were many miles away. The bus made a turn into the heart of the sun-drenched desert and there in the midst of nowhere were rows and rows of squat, tar-papered barracks sitting sullenly in the white, chalky sand. This was Topaz, the Central Utah Relocation Center, one of ten such camps located throughout the United States in equally barren and inaccessible areas. . . .

As the bus drew up to one of the barracks, I was surprised to hear band music. Marching toward us down the dusty road was the drum and bugle corps of the young Boy Scouts who had come with the advance contingents carrying signs that read, "Welcome to Topaz—Your Camp." It was a touching sight to see them standing in the burning sun, covered with dust, as they tried to ease the shock of our arrival at this desolate desert camp.

A few of our friends who had arrived earlier were also there to greet us. They tried hard to look cheerful, but their pathetic dust-covered appearance told us a great deal more than their brave words. . . .

The entire camp was divided into forty-two blocks, each containing twelve barracks constructed around a mess hall, a latrine-washroom, and a laundry. The camp was one mile square and eventually housed 8,000 residents, making it the fifth largest city in the state of Utah. . . .

Each barrack was one hundred feet in length, and divided into six rooms for families of varying sizes. We were assigned to a room in the center, about twenty by eighteen feet, designed for occupancy by four people. When we stepped into our room it contained nothing but four army cots without mattresses. No inner sheetrock walls or ceilings had yet been installed, nor had the black pot-bellied stove that stood outside our door. Cracks were visible everywhere in the siding and around the windows, and although our friends had swept out our room before we arrived, the dust was already seeping into it again from all sides. . . .

Just as at Tanforan, we had to deal in our early days at Topaz with the matter of physical adjustment. Because of the daily extremes in temperature, the altitude (4,600 feet above sea level), and the ever pervasive dust, it took many weeks for us to become acclimated and to overcome the despondency caused by the inadequacy of everything from housing to food. . . .

None of us felt well during our incarceration in Topaz. We all caught frequent colds during the harsh winter months and had frequent stomach upsets. Illness was a nuisance, especially after we began to work, for memos from a doctor were required to obtain sick leave. Much of our energy simply went into keeping our room dusted, swept, and mopped to be rid of the constant accumulation of dust, and in trying to do a laundry when the water was running. . . .

The shortage of barracks caused unhappiness, not only among the new arrivals, but among the groups trying to organize the camp's activities. The Education Department, for instance, wanted barracks for schools, and the Recreation Department was equally anxious to secure barracks for its projects. The Placement Bureau also had its troubles. It had begun placing residents at various jobs throughout camp, but was accused by many of favoritism and patronage, and the administration, caught in the middle, quickly became the target of everyone's ire. A call for sugar beet workers on outside farms was immediately filled, because there were any number of men who wanted to escape the confusion and disarray of life inside the barbed wire.

Italian Voices from the Unknown Internment, 1942

Nida Vanni, Arcata, CA: The order to move came in the papers. General DeWitt ordered it. He did it for the Italians and Germans and—who else was it?—the Japanese. 'Course we didn't have any Japanese here. We had a certain date that we had to move. G Street [Highway 101 through downtown Arcata] was the street that was OK on the other side. It was crazy . . . crazy. Everybody that I knew in Arcata was just dumbfounded. The Italians were suddenly enemies because of the war. It was just the idea of this general. I don't know how he got it passed. That's what baffled everybody.

My mother, who lived here, too, was born in France, so she was able to stay in her house even though she was Italian. I was able to stay because I was born here. But my dad and husband had to go across the street. They both lost their jobs. That's why everybody became a citizen in 1942. They tried to take out their papers right after the law was passed. My dad had been here since 1902; nobody ever bothered you, so you didn't become a citizen. He was working night and day and he just didn't have time to study. It was a hard thing to do. You had to learn all that Constitution. Everybody was trying to learn, and they were teaching it to each other and going to school. They finally got their papers; my husband got his in 1942. . . .

My mother took the Italian paper that came from San Francisco, and she would read everything that was going on down there. It was really bad because in San Francisco they put thousands and thousands on trains and sent them back to concentration camps some place, just like they did with the Japanese. . . . Even us here, you know—the papers would say, "Well, they might send you up to Trinity County and make a concentration camp," all kinds of rumors. We didn't know what was going to happen. . . .

Alessandro Baccari, Jr., San Francisco, CA: As a little boy, I witnessed the trauma of those of Italian origin who were not American citizens during the outbreak of World War II. At the time, my father had a photographic studio. To the studio came nearly a thousand Italians to have their photographs taken for placement on their alien registration papers. I would witness my mother attempting to console them as they waited for my father to take their photographs. And, after their picture was taken, they would say in Italian, "But I'm not a criminal. What have I done?" "I've lived here forty years; I love America." "I'm not intelligent enough to pass the citizenship test." "Why do I have to be in at eight o'clock?" "Why can't I go to my boat? What kind of living will I have?" "They take my sons into the service, but I'm considered an enemy. What have I done, Signor Baccari?" It was very difficult for my father to answer these people.

I never forgot their sadness, their tears. It was a very emotional experience for me. And of course I got to see it daily because of my father's photography. My parents also wrote letters for them in English to explain their feelings. Many had no relatives here, just themselves. They couldn't turn to anybody. There was no social agency. There was no one to go to. It was a very trying time.

The only organization which helped was the Roman Catholic church. Saints Peter and Paul Church on Filbert Street became a sanctuary for these Italian aliens. At the church, mass was said daily in Italian so that the people would not feel that they were being forsaken.

I'll never forget Mr. Maniscalco. He was a fisherman, the most respected at the wharf. I went to grammar school with his son, John. One day, I was visiting their house and he greeted me by saying, "Alessandro, I can no longer go aboard my boat at the wharf." Italian aliens were compelled to remain fourteen blocks away from the waterfront. He couldn't comprehend. With tears in his eyes, he told me, "I'm gonna breaka the law. My boat is my life." He would sneak out to see his boat and the waterfront. . . .

Marino Sichi, San Francisco, CA: My dad came over in October of 1920, and my mother and I came in November 1922, when I was two. Right after Pearl Harbor, General DeWitt issued an order. That son-of-a-bitch, I hope he rots in his grave. Anybody of Japanese, German, or Italian descent could not live west of Highway 101. That was the demarcation line. We had applied for our citizenship papers and were in the process of getting them. My parents hadn't gotten theirs yet because they couldn't read or write English. If my father had gotten his, then I would have automatically been a citizen before I was eighteen. But he didn't get his in time, so we had to apply individually. Then, with the war on, they froze it [naturalization] and we had to move out. . . .

I was courting my wife at the time [spring 1942], and we weren't allowed out after eight o'clock at night. We had to be inside, but I figured,

"Oh, to hell with it." I'd go where I'd want. Went all my life, so why not now? I was twenty-one at the time. Well, somebody turned me in. Called the FBI. . . .

They confiscated all of our guns. I had a .22 and a .410, and my dad had a .22. That's about all the things that we had at the time. I had just bought my folks a brand new Zenith console radio, which I still have. We took it down to the shop and had the shortwave component disconnected. They were afraid I'd use it for receiving or transmitting some way. . . .

The guy who arrested me was nobody local. Even the police chief said afterwards, "Heck, I've known you all my life. I never knew you weren't born here."

"No, I've been living here since I was two years old." I didn't know any other country, really.

So they locked me up in the county jail for five days, waiting for transportation, I guess. . . . It turned out they took us to Sharp Park, near Pacifica. They had quite a concentration camp there, a holding camp I guess you'd call it.

I remember the camp was divided in half. The Japanese were on the left side as you went in, and we were on the right. I don't know, it seemed like there were thousands of people; it was quite a large gathering. There were Germans, English, French, Italians, every nationality you could think of.

We didn't get to talk to the Japanese. They had us separated by a big fence. It was a double fence, big enough to drive a truck between and they patrolled it steadily, on foot and by truck. And barbed wire. It must have been at least ten feet high with barbed wire coming up on the ends on both sides. Couldn't get in or out. . . .

Flore Lekanof, Sr., Lambasts the Government Evacuation of Alaska's Aleuts, 1942

Just six months after the bombing of Pearl Harbor on December 7, 1941, Unalaska and Dutch Harbor were bombed on June 3 and 4, 1942, by the Japanese.

I was drafted into the U.S. government work force in May 1942, after the elementary school was closed for the summer. As long as I lived on St. George Island, I would never return to the classroom for schooling. This was the normal practice of the U.S. federal government on the Pribilof Islands since the purchase of Alaska by the U.S. in 1867 from the Russian government.

It was while a handful of U.S. work force was repairing the landing dock that a messenger brought word of the Dutch Harbor bombing. It was

Fern Chandonnet, ed., *Alaska at War, 1941–1945: The Forgotten War Remembered* (Anchorage: Alaska at War Committee, 1995), 307–308. Copyright © 1993 by Alaska at War Committee. Reprinted with permission of the Alaska at War Committee and the Alaska Humanities Forum.

about lunch time. We were told to stop working and go to our homes. People all over the village were scared to death. On that foggy day, some of us heard airplanes flying over the island. The fog was so thick that we could not see whether they were American or Japanese planes. I heard my grandmother say it was time for the Creator (God) to come back.

A few days later, my family and others attended the local Russian Orthodox church, where my father was a reader. After church on that beautiful Sunday afternoon, we had our usual Sunday brunch of coffee and bread. While we were gathered around the kitchen table, shocking news was delivered to our home. At once we were to prepare to board a ship. The village was to be evacuated. Every person was to leave on the ship. Where we were to be taken, we did not know. We were instructed for each person to take the clothing they wore and a sack of personal clothing and effects to the ship. Domestic animals, such as cows and pigs, were disposed of by shooting. After much commotion, we were on the U.S. Army transport ship *Delarof.* The St. Paul people were already on that ship.

Although there were pleasantries exchanged by the St. Paul and St. George people as they met, one could see anxiety on their faces.

In later years, my Uncle Gabriel Stepetin told me that my maternal grandmother on St. Paul Island went into her bedroom to take her own life. She did not want to leave her home. My uncle was able to stop her, but she died in Funter Bay that winter.

Much illness, physical and mental, was experienced by the Aleut people at Funter Bay, where we were taken. St. Paul people were put on one side of the bay at an old dilapidated cannery site, while the St. George people were put two miles across the bay at an old gold mining camp. Ten percent of the Pribilof people died at the camp during the two years of encampment. Most of these were the elderly and the very young. Many of the deaths were caused by unhealthy living conditions and by pneumonia, tuberculosis, measles, and general mental depression. I lost both of my grandmothers and a sister at Funter Bay. My father suffered from pneumonia and I contracted tuberculosis of the lungs and spent three-and-a-half years in a sanitarium where I nearly died.

Because of the evacuation from their homelands, the Aleut people suffered not only the loss of their loved ones, but their ethnic culture was shaken by exposure to a strange environment. For three years, the elders were not able to guide their people in their customary manner. The government took charge for three years. The usual caring nature of the Aleut people for their own was halted. This was to take away the practice of my people always looking after the interest of everyone living in a village.

Today, one has to pay cash for services—such as fish and a ride to the local store for groceries. Young people are inducted into the American mainstream culture through media and schools to the point that the respect for elders, once held sacred, is almost nonexistent. People are indoctrinated into the concept of cash economy as opposed to subsistence economy. Rendition of some kind, usually cash, is expected and given for services rendered. . . .

Charles M. Smith Praises Farm Workers from Mexico, 1943

Eager to help the Allies defeat the Axis, thousands of Mexican nationals are pouring into the United States today to produce and harvest Food for Freedom. Often waving little United States and Mexican flags and shouting "Viva, Mexico" and "Viva, Los Estados Unidos," they are crossing the border by rail at the rate of about 2,000 every 8 days. As they arrive, they are speedily distributed to labor-short farms in a large number of vital growing areas west of the Mississippi.

Although Mexican farm laborers are no novelty in the United States, especially in California and the Southwest, the current movements are unique in the history of the two Nations. They are made in accordance with the provisions of an international agreement between the United States and Mexico. This agreement, the first of its kind ever entered into by the United States, was arranged last summer by the State Department, acting at the request and with the advice of the United States Department of Agriculture, when it became apparent that domestic sources of supply would be inadequate to meet the need for seasonal farm workers in all areas. It provides for the orderly emigration and use of Mexican nationals as agricultural laborers here and is designed to protect the interests of both the growers and the workers.

The Department called on the Farm Security Administration to work with the Mexican Government and other United States agencies in selecting Mexican workers, transporting them to the United States, and providing needed health and welfare services.

First Mexican workers transported under the agreement left Mexico City last September 25 to harvest California sugar beets. Through May 9 this year, a total of 17,308 Mexican workers had been recruited and transported, with California receiving the largest number—12,495—and the States of Arizona, Washington, and Idaho the remainder. In addition to sugar beets, the Mexicans have worked, or are working, in fruits, vegetables, and guayule in California, vegetables in Arizona, and sugar beets in Washington and Idaho, and are now being moved into sugar beet areas of Colorado, Montana, Wyoming, South Dakota, and Nebraska. The War Food Administration, which is now directing and supervising all farm labor activities of the Federal Government, plans to bring in up to about 50,000 Mexican nationals this year as part of the United States crop corps program.

Under the international agreement, the WFA pays for the transportation of the Mexicans to the work area in this country and for their return. The contracts which each worker signs with the WFA on the one hand, and which each employer, or organization of employers, signs with the WFA on the other, provide that the worker should be paid the prevailing wage for the agricultural work he does, with a minimum of 30 cents an hour, and employment for at least 75 percent of the contract period. Workers also are

Charles M. Smith, "Farm Workers from Mexico," *Agricultural Situation,* 27 (June 1943), 12–14.

guaranteed shelter, sanitary and medical facilities of a reasonable minimum standard. If FSA farm labor supply centers are not available, the Mexicans live in growers' housing approved by the WFA. Ten percent of their wages is deducted and sent back to Mexico for deposit to their credit and is handed over to them after their return to Mexico.

Selection machinery in Mexico City is geared to select only healthy, experienced farm workers for transportation to the United States. The workers arrive in groups of from 400 to 1,200 from farm communities in the states of Jalisco, Michoacan, Zacatecas, and Guanajuato at Mexico City. There, in the National Stadium, the men's agricultural experience and character are carefully reviewed and their health checked by representatives of the health, agricultural and immigration offices of both countries. The physical examination includes X-rays of lungs and digestive tract and also a blood test. No individuals are accepted for contract until they have passed the physical examinations. Applicants may be rejected for health reasons or other causes, including inexperience with farm work.

A transportation crew, representing the WFA, takes charge of the workers when they are put on the train for the United States. Members of this crew arrange for meals and necessary medical attention en route and divide the men into groups of 10, each of which selects its own leader. When the train reaches the border, the first WFA crew returns to Mexico City and takes over, accompanying the workers to their destination points in the United States. The new crew has a list of growers and the number of workers required at each destination, and groups the workers in accordance with this list.

Most growers thus far have expressed themselves as generally satisfied with the Mexican workers they have employed. Last fall, Earl Coke, general manager of California Field Crops, Inc., an organization of sugar beet operators formed to employ the first 3,000 Mexican nationals brought into California, said: "The workers imported from Mexico have saved the sugar-beet harvest in this State." Other employers have issued similar statements. However, as was to be expected, there have been a number of disputes between employers and workers involving such factors as wages, housing, living and working conditions. In most cases, these have been straightened out through on-the-farm mediation, but when this method fails the formal complaint proceeding is brought into use. If either an employer or worker files a complaint against the other, a hearing is held at which the worker and the employer can be represented, as well as the Mexican consul in the area, if he wishes. If the worker is found to be at fault, he is repatriated or transferred to another employer. If the employer is found at fault, he can be required to remove the cause of the complaint and keep the worker or, if he refuses to do so, suffer the loss of his workers.

Aside from the valuable work the Mexicans have been doing in helping to save war-essential crops, their presence in the United States has done much to solidify the "good neighbor" relationship between the United States and Mexico. This is due in part to the spirit of patriotism and good will of the workers. Before they leave Mexico, they are told that they are "soldiers of the soil" whose job it is to help produce the food needed to defeat the Axis, that idleness or bad behavior will not be condoned, and that they will receive no sympathy in Mexico if they are repatriated for misconduct. But it is also due to the friendly attitude demonstrated by the people of this country toward them. Celebrations and fetes are held in their honor and educational and recreational programs are arranged for their benefit. As long as this attitude continues, hemispheric solidarity can only be strengthened.

Daniel L. Schorr Decries the Exploitation of Mexican Americans, 1946

"If there's anything I hate worse than a Nigger, it's a damn Mexican," said the soldier from south Texas, speaking what he had been taught. This attitude is behind a postwar "reconversion" process in Texas, aimed at depriving Mexican Americans of the few economic and social gains they won during the war and restoring the segregated, underpaid, uneducated pool of cheap labor that south Texas has always sought to maintain. The campaign, in which the authorities, business and the newspapers all play their part, amounts to a conspiracy.

There are about one million Mexican Americans in Texas—out of a total of approximately three million, who form the third largest minority in the United States. They are most densely settled in south Texas and make up about one-third of San Antonio's 300,000 population. For years they have done the sweated work that has helped to make this district rich. During the war the manpower shortage opened a scattering of skilled, occasionally even supervisory, jobs for Mexican Americans. Children left school to go to work. Although there was never more than five percent of the group in wartime industry in Texas, the taste of better living standards brought yearnings for social equality. Now that "reconversion" has set in, these Mexican Americans may not want to return to their former status.

Therein lies a potentially explosive situation. Tension is rising and there has already been some reaction to the mounting repression. In San Antonio's slum-ridden West Side, it is possible to collect a gang of bellicose youngsters by simply promising a fight against Anglo-American kids. The process produces increased repression and threats from the authorities, further heightening the tension.

An incident that has aroused widespread indignation among Mexicans concerns a winner of the Congressional Medal of Honor, Staff Sergeant Macario Garcia. While home on furlough, Garcia stopped for a cup of coffee at the Oasis Café in Sugarland, Fort Bend County, near Houston. The proprietor, Mrs. Donna Andrews, told him no Mexicans were served there. When he insisted on being served, there was a fight between Garcia, aided by two sailors, and customers in the café. A deputy sheriff arrived, told all

Daniel L. Schorr " 'Reconverting' Mexican Americans," *The New Republic,* 115 (Sept. 30, 1946), 412–413.

concerned to forget the incident and sent Garcia home. Later the story was reported in Mexico City and then picked up by the Associated Press and by Walter Winchell. The publicity led the county authorities to seek vindication of their honor. Garcia was belatedly arrested on a charge of "aggravated assault" against Mrs. Andrews.

This was not the first case involving a Congressional Medal winner. Some time before, Sergeant Jose Mendoza Lopez, of Brownsville, after his return from a good-will tour of Mexico, arranged with the coöperation of the United States Army, was thrown out of a restaurant in a small town in the Rio Grande Valley. I have examined dozens of affidavits made by Mexican Americans, testifying to discrimination in south Texas towns.

Social discrimination is no new phenomenon in a state where the defense of the Alamo still gets top billing in school history books and children are taught from the cradle that Mexicans are "dirty," "lazy," "shiftless" and "dishonest." The intensification of pressure, accompanied in some cases by terrorism, makes the Mexican Americans unwilling to accept the situation. . . .

The Mexican American's economic frontiers, which were widened somewhat during the war, are beginning to close in on him. The regional office of the Fair Employment Practice Commission closed in December. When war industries began laying off men, Mexican Americans were among the first to go. Frequently this is justified on a basis of seniority, which is another way of saying that previous discrimination makes new discrimination unnecessary; Mexican Americans were usually the last to be hired. It is expected that Help Wanted advertisements for skilled or responsible jobs will soon be carrying the note, "No Mexicans Need Apply." An FEPC official who had dealt with anti-Mexican discrimination during the war told me: "I don't think the Latin Americans will accept this situation. They can be trodden on just so long." . . .

Every attempt to check anti-Mexican discrimination has been blocked. A bill to outlaw discrimination, introduced in the legislature by Senator J. Franklin Spears of San Antonio, has been defeated at three sessions. During the war Texan bigotry and economic discrimination fought a holding action. Now a counter-offensive is talking shape to wrest from the Mexican Americans their economic and social gains. But bitterness at this "reconversion" is growing and will not long be contained.

Y   E S S A Y S

Historically, African Americans and the South have been a convenient focal point for discussing racial segregation; however, the West offers cases as well. In the first essay Terrence M. Cole, associate professor and chair of the History Department at the University of Alaska, Fairbanks, explores the racial segregation and "Jim Crow" policies applied to Alaskan natives. His essay reveals that although Alaskan natives outnumbered the permanent white population of Alaska until the late 1930s, natives had few rights and little political voice.

Establishment of the Alaska Native Brotherhood, appointment of a progressive territorial governor, and incidents such as the removal of Alberta Schenck from a Nome movie theater precipitated changes in Alaskan civil rights that presage later national victories in race relations. In the second essay, Erasmo Gamboa, associate professor in the American Ethnic Studies Department at the University of Washington, traces the history of the Bracero program in the Pacific Northwest. His account balances program ideals against what happened to Mexican laborers. Although the program offered benefits for both American farmers and Mexican workers, the reality of racial discrimination and difficult working and living conditions demonstrates the gulf between paper contracts and worker experiences.

Jim Crow Segregation in Alaska

TERRENCE M. COLE

Americans have long believed that the western frontier offered more free-dom, justice, and equality than the overcrowded, class-conscious cities of the East. This familiar theme of an egalitarian western society expressed by Frederick Jackson Turner and his followers has been sounded repeatedly in American history and literature. Though the Turner Thesis may no longer be fashionable among professional historians who advocate the "new western history," the significance of the frontier in the modern popular culture and politics of Alaska has never dimmed. No matter what political philosophy they espouse, most residents of the "Last Frontier" share the conviction that Alaska's geographical isolation has made the northernmost state vastly dif-ferent from the other forty-nine in the Union. Modern Alaskans prefer to think that their state offers greater freedom and opportunity than the more densely settled "Lower 48," and that Alaska is relatively free from the worst ills of the outside world, including poverty, pollution, racism, and crime. A popular bumper sticker often seen in Alaska claims, "We don't give a damn how they do it Outside."

Modern Alaskans are therefore surprised and shocked to learn that before World War II racial segregation and Jim Crow policies towards Alaska natives were standard practice throughout much of Alaska. So few blacks lived in the territory, especially before World War II, there was little organized discrimination against them. Natives, however, actually outnum-bered the permanent white population of Alaska, and it was not until the late 1930s that whites became the permanent majority. In those prewar years, pioneer Alaskans often refused natives the right to vote, prayed every Sunday in segregated churches, and sent their children to segregated schools.

Some Alaskans may have been blind to the inequities of their own soci-ety, but the unfair treatment of natives was plainly evident to outsiders who

Terrence M. Cole, "Jim Crow in Alaska: The Passage of the Alaska Equal Rights Act of 1945," *Western Historical Quarterly,* 23 (November 1992), 429–449. Copyright by Western History Association. Reprinted by permission.

could afford to be more truthful. During World War II, a visiting war correspondent noted in 1943 that the social position of Indians and Eskimos in Alaska "is equivalent to that of a Negro in Georgia or Mississippi."

The Second World War laid the foundation for the great advances in racial equality that occurred in America during the 1950s and 1960s. As C. Vann Woodward once explained, U.S. pronouncements against the Nazis and Hitler's hated racist doctrines highlighted the "inconsistency" between American "practice at home and propaganda abroad." In Alaska, as elsewhere in the American West, World War II thoroughly transformed virtually every aspect of life in the territory. Among the sweeping social, economic, and political changes that the war brought to the North, none was perhaps more painful than the successful battle in the 1940s to outlaw racial segregation in Alaska.

Eleven years before Rosa Parks refused to give up her seat on a bus in Montgomery, Alabama, a similar scene took place in Nome, Alaska. Alberta Schenck, a young half-Eskimo woman, was arrested in Nome in 1944 for daring to sit in the "white only" section of the local theater. Schenck's one-woman protest in Nome, and the fight against segregation across Alaska in the 1940s by crusaders such as Governor Ernest Gruening, native rights advocates Roy and Elizabeth Peratrovich, and the other Tlingit leaders of the Alaska Native Brotherhood and Sisterhood, illustrate that Jim Crow was a scourge to Alaska, as well as to Alabama. The majority of white residents in prewar Alaska took public discrimination against natives for granted. Scars from such discrimination were largely invisible to those who did not have to suffer it. This hidden plague of prejudice was especially hard to cure in Alaska, because so many whites chose to believe it never existed.

The early years of American control of Alaska in the late nineteenth century coincided with the peak of the Indian wars in the western states, and the gradual legal entrenchment of segregation and white supremacy in the southern states. In 1896, the same year as the Klondike gold strike, the U.S. Supreme Court issued its landmark decision in *Plessy v. Ferguson,* which formally approved segregation as the law of the land with the "separate but equal" rule.

The general American attitude towards Native Alaskans, as with blacks in the South, was reflected in a persistent pattern of discrimination. Presbyterian missionary, trader, and territorial governor John G. Brady, according to his biographer Ted C. Hinckley, preferred to refer to Alaskan Indians as natives or "Alaskans," because "for too many whites *Indian* was synonymous with *nigger.*" Hinckley explains that Brady ran a general store in Sitka in the 1880s, but quit the business when his partner insisted on putting in two separate entrances with completely separate departments for natives and whites "so that tourists would no longer be obliged to rub elbows with smelly, lamp black-smeared Tlingits."

The situation at Brady's store in Sitka was not unique. Numerous bars, restaurants, and hotels in various Alaskan communities posted permanent signs stating "No Natives Allowed," while movie theaters habitually restricted natives to seats in the balcony with signs such as "For Natives

Only." Native residents who migrated to white mining and fishing communities invariably settled in Indian ghettos on the outskirts of town. There were no legal prohibitions against natives settling wherever they chose in Alaska, but economic, social, and cultural reality dictated that natives live apart from whites. By both law and custom, however, Alaskan children attended segregated schools. As elsewhere, the deep feelings of parents for their children made the schools in Alaska a flash point for racial strife. . . .

The quest for native citizenship and equality with whites inspired the establishment in 1912 of the Alaska Native Brotherhood (ANB), an association that evolved into the first significant native political organization in Alaska. The mission-trained native leaders of the ANB patterned their goals on the teachings of the missionary school teachers, from whom they had learned that Christianity and complete acculturation were the keys to both heaven and the American dream. Anything less would doom native people to certain extinction. The ANB, whose official song was "Onward, Christian Soldiers," and whose official lapel pin was a prospector's gold pan, supported three major initiatives: citizenship for natives, better education for native children, and abolition of "uncivilized" native customs.

In the 1920s, under the leadership of William and Louis Paul, the ANB became a highly effective political machine. William Paul, a skilled Tlingit attorney, successfully battled in the courts for the natives' right to vote, and created a native voting block that held the balance of power in southeastern Alaska. William Paul himself became the first native to run for and win a seat in the territorial legislature in 1924, the year that all Native Americans were granted U.S. citizenship. Fear of Paul's political machine and his alleged manipulation of the many natives who could not read (like a big city ward boss, he distributed cardboard cutouts to his followers to enable illiterate voters to make their Xs in the right places on the ballot) helped spur passage of the 1925 Alaskan literacy law designed to limit native voting.

Some white residents responded with anger to the increasing signs of native political power. A 1926 editorial in the *Fairbanks Daily News Miner* under the headline "Alaska—A White Man's country," expressed the fears of many when it charged that Indians were threatening to take control of Alaska. . . .

High on the ANB's list of political priorities was the reform of the native educational system. The ANB targeted the dual system of education as a cruel hoax on those who had abandoned their own traditions, only to be rejected by the white culture they had tried to embrace. The native schools stressed rudimentary education, primarily teaching English and vocational training, while the white schools, in contrast, generally had "a high percentage of high school graduates who continue education in institutions of higher learning." In the larger communities of southeastern Alaska, such as Wrangell, Ketchikan, Juneau, and Sitka, native children were generally barred from the local public schools and forced to attend the federal Indian schools. Paul nearly succeeded in 1921 in convincing the bureau of education to close the Indian school at Wrangell, in order to forcibly integrate education in the community. . . .

School segregation remained one of the core problems of Alaska's racial dilemma. But race discrimination in other public places, such as restaurants, theaters, playgrounds, and swimming pools also emerged as a battleground in the 1930s and 1940s. When a grand officer of the ANB was told to sit in the native-only section in a Juneau movie theater in 1929, he walked out and vowed never again to suffer such an insult. At a meeting of the executive council, the ANB agreed to stage a boycott of the offending theater, not because its policies were any worse than other theaters in town, but because it had a chain of theaters throughout southeastern Alaska and appeared to be more vulnerable to a boycott. In conjunction with the theater boycott, the ANB also recommended that its members refuse to patronize any establishment that discriminated against natives. The action proved effective throughout much of southeastern Alaska. Within a month the "No Natives" signs at the theater and other businesses began to come down. . . .

Though the ANB succeeded in forcing some white businessmen in southeastern Alaska to learn to value native patronage, there were still glaring examples of blatant discrimination against natives in the region and throughout Alaska in 1939, when Franklin D. Roosevelt appointed a crusading New Deal Democrat named Ernest Gruening as governor of the territory. Gruening was shocked by the signs he saw excluding natives from public facilities. The new governor met few white Alaskans who seemed to share his sense of outrage. "I found relatively little encouragement . . . from Alaskans with whom I discussed the matter," Gruening later wrote. "It was, they said, 'the custom of the country.' When I proposed to some that these discriminations be forbidden by legislation, I was told that it would stand little chance of enactment by the Territorial Legislature."

On his first visit to Alaska, Gruening said he had been haunted by a sign that hung in Anchorage's leading restaurant, the Anchorage Grill on Fourth Avenue, which said, "We Do Not Cater to Native and Filipino Trade." In 1940, he returned to have a chat with the owner, George Grames, a naturalized American from Greece. In his memoirs, *Many Battles,* Gruening described how he rebuked Grames for the sign and asked him how he would like to see a sign that read "We Do Not Cater to Greeks." Gruening wrote, "I then gave George a pep talk about the meaning of America. He went over and removed the sign. 'It will never be up again,' he said."

In Alaska, as in many other American communities, World War II demonstrated the contradictions between the nation's fight for freedom overseas and its denial of equal opportunity at home. On 30 December 1941, about three weeks after Pearl Harbor, Elizabeth Peratrovich, the grand vice president of the Alaska Native Sisterhood, and her husband Roy Peratrovich, the grand president of the Alaska Native Brotherhood, sent an angry letter to Governor Gruening complaining about the "No Natives Allowed" sign over the door of the Douglas Inn, across Gastineau Channel from Juneau. They complained that natives in Alaska were being treated like Jews in Germany, and challenged the hypocrisy of such prejudice. The Peratrovichs wrote that especially because of "the present emergency, when unity is being stressed," wasn't such a sign "very Un-American?" "In the present emergency," their angry letter continued, "our native boys are being called upon to defend our beloved country, just as the White boys. There is no distinction being made there but yet when we try to patronize some business establishments we are told in most cases that natives are not allowed." The Peratrovichs said they appealed to Gruening because, "We know you have the interest of the native people at heart and we are asking that you use your influence to eliminate this discrimination, not only in Juneau or Douglas, but in the whole Territory."

In fact, Gruening had already taken action. He had previously asked both the mayor of Anchorage and the mayor of Douglas to use their influence to have any signs in their communities "indicating discrimination between natives and whites removed." The governor had also personally asked the owner of the Douglas Inn, John Marin, an immigrant from Italy whose real name was Martini, to remove his offensive sign. Marin claimed he kept the sign up because, "I can't have a lot of dirty, drunken natives in my place." . . .

When Marin still refused to remove the sign from the Douglas Inn, Gruening determined that legislation specifically outlawing such practices was the only answer. In July 1942, the governor informed Guy J. Swope, director of the Division of Territories and Island Possessions, about the situation and asked for the opinion of the solicitor's office on preparing "a suitable bill for introduction into the next Territorial Legislature." The war provided a strong rationale for legislative action. Signs forbidding natives from entering a public establishment, the governor wrote, were not only offensive, but "are in my judgement distinctly destructive of morale and furnish . . . a psychological impediment to the war effort. They are in effect a replica of Hitlerist policies and cannot be justified." . . .

Unfortunately, the most powerful person in Alaska during World War II, General Simon Bolivar Buckner, Jr., the commanding officer of the Alaska Defense Command, demonstrated an intense prejudice against Alaska natives. Son of the famous Confederate general of the same name, who surrendered to U.S. Grant at Fort Donelson in 1862, General Buckner's racial views in the 1940s were little different from those of any rabid southerner during the Civil War. Apparently on Buckner's orders (though he denied it), Alaskan military posts issued regulations prohibiting soldiers from fraternizing with native women, ostensibly to protect native virtue and to stop the spread of venereal disease among the troops. To ensure the separation of whites from natives, the army encouraged soldiers to patronize restaurants, stores, and hotels that denied access to natives. Military officials actually placed some establishments that welcomed all races off limits to military personnel, simply because they did not discriminate against natives.

Roy Peratrovich of the ANB protested bitterly to congressional delegate Tony Dimond and Governor Gruening against the army's discriminatory policies. "The matter of race discrimination is rather getting out of hand in Alaska," Peratrovich wrote in the spring of 1943. "Before the present war, it was the civilians that discriminated against the Indians. Now it is the civilians and the soldiers." . . .

. . . Buckner justified the separation of the races on both moral and practical grounds. He explained that just as a white oak tree is different from a willow, "Similarly, the Lord in His infinite wisdom has, for reasons beyond our knowledge, created in the Indians a human being differing in many respects from a white man." According to Buckner, the only problem with race relations in Alaska was troublemakers who hoped to exploit the situation, as the general explained in a letter to the assistant secretary of war in July 1943. Buckner claimed that only "shyster lawyers," ambitious politicians, "fifth columnists," and misguided individuals "who see no appreciable differences between the Chinese, the Caucasians, the Japs, the Negroes, and Papuans, the Indians and the Australian Bushmen and who would be happy to intermarry with any of them," were inciting trouble among the Indians in Alaska. When Buckner stubbornly failed to revoke his discriminatory policies, Governor Gruening and Delegate Dimond went over his head, taking their complaints about race discrimination all the way to Secretary of War Henry L. Stimson and to President Roosevelt himself, who ordered a stop to the exclusion of Alaska natives from USOs.

One of the most notorious incidents of racial discrimination in Alaska during World War II was the U.S. government's botched handling of the 1942 forced evacuation of nearly nine hundred Aleuts from their homes in the Aleutian Islands. Unlike the internment at about the same time of 120,000 Japanese Americans in concentration camps, an overtly racist measure born of wartime hysteria, the removal of the Aleuts from a combat zone for their own protection was theoretically a sounder public policy. In fact, the Aleut evacuation was administered so poorly that it caused a horrendous amount of death and hardship among the native people. Many of the Aleuts died after their evacuation, while those who survived until the end of the war and returned to the Aleutians found entire villages burned to the ground and their personal belongings looted by American military personnel.

The decision to evacuate the Aleuts came after the Japanese bombing of Dutch Harbor on 3 June 1942 and their subsequent occupation of Attu and Kiska Islands; the Aleuts were given no notice before U.S. Navy ships arrived to take them away. Though virtually all natives were required to leave the Aleutian Chain, some whites were permitted to stay. For instance Charles Hope, a white man who lived at Unalaska, was allowed to remain in the village, while his native wife was forced to leave.

After the hasty government round up of the Aleuts, most of the natives were warehoused in abandoned canneries and camps in southeastern Alaska for the duration of the war. Sanitary conditions in the camps were deplorable. Small children and the elderly suffered most. About forty of three hundred people died at Funter Bay, where a physician who visited the camp in the fall of 1943 wrote, "As we entered the first bunkhouse the odor of human excreta and waste was so pungent that I could hardly make the grade." Residents of Ketchikan feared that the two hundred Aleuts housed in an old CCC camp at Ward Cove eight miles from town would spread an epidemic of venereal disease and tuberculosis among the white population. The city of Ketchikan quarantined the camp and businessmen urged the Aleuts be moved farther from the city. The proprietor of the Totem Inn said she wanted to keep Aleuts out of her establishment because "they were unsanitary and diseased and thus obnoxious to her regular customers besides requiring an unusual amount of trouble in sterilizing of their dishes."

The cavalier attitude of the U.S. government towards the welfare of the Aleut people was due in part to the exigencies of war. But it was also part of a deeper problem: Alaska natives were second-class citizens in their own land. In an effort to remedy that situation and to outlaw discrimination against natives, Governor Gruening submitted an anti-discrimination bill to the territorial legislature in early 1943. Passing the bill proved to be difficult, especially because of the complete lack of native representation among territorial lawmakers. At the time, there was not a single native member of the Alaska legislature. Though natives comprised about one-half the population of the territory, only one Alaska native had ever been elected to the territorial legislature in its history—William Paul, who had served in the mid-1920s.

The anti-discrimination bill failed to pass in the 1943 session by the narrowest margin possible, an 8–8 tie vote in the house. "While I am greatly disappointed in this result," Gruening wrote Secretary of Interior Harold Ickes in March 1943, "and consider it shocking that in this international crisis the Alaska Legislature should put itself on record before the whole world as in favor of discrimination—an incident which may well be utilized by enemy propagandists—the outcome was a good deal closer than I would have expected." . . .

In November 1943, Gruening sent a written message to the annual convention of the Alaska Native Brotherhood, urging the group to find native leaders willing to serve in the legislature. The proof that natives were needed in Juneau, he said, was the shameful rejection by the old guard of the anti-discrimination bill. The governor stated that "Native people have both a right and a duty to exert themselves, to assert themselves, and, by taking an active part in our political life, to see that such an unfortunate exhibition of prejudice and bigotry is not repeated." When the votes were counted in the 1944 fall elections, two Tlingit Indians had been swept into office with overwhelming support: Frank Peratrovich of Klawock, older brother of ANB Grand President Roy Peratrovich, and Andrew Hope of Sitka.

In the spring of 1944, during Gruening's campaign to win support for the anti-discrimination bill in the next legislature, he received an emergency telegram from a seventeen year old Nome girl named Alberta Schenck, who had spent the previous night in jail for violating the segregated seating arrangements in the local theater. Her arrest was destined to inspire much debate in the battle for the equal rights bill in the coming legislative session.

Nome, like most other Alaskan towns, had its share of Jim Crow practices. . . .

The threat of spreading tuberculosis was a common justification for keeping Eskimos separate from whites, as was the smell given off by native skin boots, which were usually tanned in urine. According to one war correspondent, Eskimos and whites had "complete equality" in Nome in the early 1940s, except at the hotel and the movie theater. "They can't live at the hotel," Howard Handleman wrote in 1943, "and they have to sit on their own side of the theater." The balcony, nicknamed "Nigger Heaven," was completely reserved for full-blooded Eskimos.

In the spring of 1944, the forced seating arrangements at the theater particularly bothered Alberta Schenck, a young school girl whose mother was an Eskimo and whose father was a white man. Two of her brothers were on duty with the U.S. Army, and her father was a veteran of World War I. Alberta worked as an usher at the Dream Theater after school and felt ashamed every time she had to tell Eskimos that if they found no seats on the right side of the theater or in the balcony they had to leave, even if there were empty seats on the left side.

She explained her frustrations to Major Marvin "Muktuk" Marston, the head of the Alaska Territorial Guard, and a staunch fighter for equal treatment of Alaska natives. . . .

Alberta told Marston that she had been fired from her job at the theater for complaining about the management's segregated seating policies. She could not understand why such unfair treatment of those with a different color skin could be allowed in a land that professed such love for freedom and justice. When the major read an essay Alberta had written at school describing her feelings, he was astounded at the pain and suffering that came through her simple language. "There was no use in evading the issue nor in pretending to this intelligent adolescent that all was well," Marston wrote. "She knew and I knew that here was a festering core of racial prejudice and social injustice wholly incompatible with our loudly proclaimed 'equality and justice for all.'"

Marston suggested that Alberta submit her essay to the editor of the *Nome Nugget* and ask him to publish it. When the next issue of the paper came out he was surprised to find her hard hitting letter to the editor on page three.

"I believe we Americans and also our Allies are fighting for the purpose of freedom," Alberta wrote. "I myself am part Eskimo and Irish and so are many others. I only truthfully know that I am one of God's children regardless of race, color or creed. You or I or anyone else is not to blame [for] what we are." She then addressed the situation at the Dream Theater. "What has hurt us constantly is that we are not able to go to a public theater and sit where we wish, but yet we pay the SAME price as anyone else and our money is GLADLY received." Such actions, she said, were not in the spirit of Thomas Jefferson's Declaration of Independence or the U.S. Constitution that she was studying in school, but were instead "following the steps of Hitlerism."

Alberta's letter caused a furor in Nome. The next issue of the paper carried an angry rebuttal from an anonymous reader. "The theater is a private institution, and has the right to make its own house rules and until the native people as a whole live up to public health standards, it would be hard for the management to change their present system even though some of the natives themselves do not like to sit next to 'odoriferous' persons. . . . I therefore, suggest that those of the native group who are intelligent enough to complain and criticize, start working from within the native population, raise their own standards and earn the right for which they are asking."

Marston said that Alberta wrote a second article in response, but the "newspaper was anxious to drop so hot an issue and the printed discussion came to a sudden close." A few nights after Alberta's letter was published, she went out on a date to see a movie with a white army sergeant stationed at the Nome base. The sergeant escorted her down the aisle and they sat together on the white side of the theater. Suddenly, the manager came down the aisle and ordered her to move to the native side of the auditorium with the other Eskimos and "half-breeds." When the sergeant told Alberta not to get up, the manager rushed out and returned with the Nome chief of police. When she still refused to get up, Marston said the chief "seized Alberta by the shoulders and literally pulled her into the aisle, pushed her down to the door, and out onto the street."

Alberta Schenck spent that night in the Nome city jail. She was released the next day. Her arrest infuriated the local native population, who threatened legal action, but felt helpless to fight the long established policies of discrimination. As "Muktuk" Marston later wrote, "when the white man called the law in the Arctic, the native was always in the wrong and the white man was always in the right." According to Marston, on the Sunday night following the incident with Alberta, a group of Eskimos purchased tickets and stormed into the theater, sitting wherever they chose. Alberta's father, Albert Schenck, reportedly hired O. D. Cochran, a prominent local attorney and territorial senator, to represent Alberta in a suit against the theater manager and the Nome chief of police.

Marston also helped Alberta compose a telegram to Governor Gruening describing what had happened. When the governor received the news, he immediately wired Nome Mayor Edward Anderson demanding an explanation. The mayor, ashamed of what the local police had done, wired back a brief response: "A mistake has been made. It won't happen again." In a personal letter to Alberta, Gruening praised her for refusing "very properly" to sit in the native section. "The discrimination which crops out here and there in Alaska against people of Native blood . . . is very objectionable to me," Gruening wrote. "I consider it un-American. I feel that it violates the principles upon which our nation was founded. I deem it contrary to the spirit of our country and directly in conflict with the issues on which this great war is being fought. In this war, American boys of all races and creeds are enlisted. There is no discrimination when they are called upon to lay down their lives for their country and for liberty." Gruening promised Alberta that he would again push for passage of an anti-discrimination bill in the next legislature, and "if it becomes law, you may be certain that the unpleasant experience which has been yours will not happen again to anyone in Alaska. It should never have happened—in America."

A sign of how deeply Alberta's arrest angered some members of the Nome community came only a few weeks later in the annual election of the Queen of Nome. The yearly spring carnival was the highlight of the Nome social scene. In April 1944, only about a month after her experience in the city jail, Alberta Schenck, with massive support from the soldiers of the Nome garrison, was elected the Queen of Nome for 1944. She won the popularity contest by an overwhelming margin, thanks to soldiers who had been angered by the way she had been treated. Individuals could vote as often as they liked at various businesses around the community, and Alberta tallied 63,850 votes, three times the total of her nearest competitor. "The so called 'Four Hundred' of Nome were dumbfounded," Major Marston wrote in his memoirs published twenty-five years later. "I suspect they have not yet fully recovered from the shock." . . .

[On 22 January 1945, the] Alaska legislature convened in Juneau. Near the top of its agenda was the equal rights bill that would abolish segregation as practiced at Nome's only theater. In his message to the legislature, Governor Gruening urged the lawmakers to meet the challenges of the postwar world. "First, let us live up, at home, to the principle for which American boys of every race, creed and color are giving all they have," Gruening said. "Let us get rid of the soul-searing race discrimination in our midst to the extent that we can do it by legislative action."

The bill to make segregation a crime was introduced in the house by Representative Edward Anderson of Nome, who as city mayor had apologized to Governor Gruening for Alberta Schenck's arrest. Alberta's lawyer, Senator O. D. Cochran, introduced a senate version. Crowded hearings were held in both bodies to debate the measure, which would guarantee "full and equal accommodations, facilities and privileges to all citizens" throughout Alaska. As one newspaper account of the house proceedings stated, "The ghost of Abraham Lincoln, the Great Emancipator, trod heavily through the halls of the House of Representatives yesterday as that body convened in a committee of the whole before a jammed gallery on the non-discrimination bill introduced by Anderson of Nome." Speaking forcefully from the gallery in favor of the Anderson bill was Roy Peratrovich, the president of the Alaska Native Brotherhood. The ANB president blasted the "unscrupulous white men in our midst" whose actions were "a disgrace to the Democratic form of Government." . . .

Opponents of the equal rights bill argued that it would not eliminate racial discrimination. An editorial in the conservative Juneau *Empire* admitted the next day that those who said there was no discrimination in Alaska were either "very much mistaken or else not very observant. Racial discrimination certainly does exist in Alaska as it exists not only in every State and Territory of the United States but throughout the world." According to the *Empire,* however, the bill would only make matters worse. "No law can force a business man, who is of one race, to deal pleasantly with a customer who happens to be of another race." The newspaper continued, "We honestly believe that a law which would attempt to force an elimination of racial discrimination, such as this measure now in question, would only serve to heighten racial discrimination." The *Empire* pointed with pride to the fact that it was no longer the custom in southeastern Alaska to have segregated seating in movie theaters. "Many more places of public accommodation are now opened to Indians than was the case 20 years ago. Not because laws were passed, but because this disease of the mind is being cured gradually."

In both the house and senate debates, Senator O. D. Cochran used the Dream Theater as a "prime example" of the injustice of racial discrimination. The notorious case of Alberta Schenck was a vivid reminder of how painful prejudice could be. Several of O. D. Cochran's Nome colleagues in the senate, including Tolbert Scott and Frank Whaley, bitterly opposed the equal rights measure. Scott claimed that "mixed breeds" who wished to associate with whites were causing all the problems, and that the issue had only been raised to "create political capital for some legislators." Senator Allen Shattuck of Juneau argued that rather than bring the races closer together, they should be kept farther apart for their own good. The natives needed time, he said, to adjust to one thousand years of white civilization. "Eskimos are not an inferior race," said Senator Grenold Collins of Anchorage, another opponent of the measure, "but they are an individual race."

After hearing all of the white senators expound on their racial views for nearly two hours, Elizabeth Peratrovich, wife of Roy Peratrovich, took the floor. In her moving testimony she told how it felt to be turned away from a place of business or denied the right to live in a certain neighborhood because of the color of one's skin. She said the opponents of the bill claimed the law would not stop racial discrimination, but that was hardly a reason to vote against it. "Do your laws against larceny and even murder prevent those crimes?" she asked the opponents of the bill. When Mrs. Peratrovich finished, one reporter wrote, the shrill opposition had been shamed into a "defensive whisper," and she drew "volleying applause from the galleries and Senate floor alike, with a biting condemnation of the 'super race' attitude."

Though the anti-discrimination bill provoked hours of bitter debate in the legislature, in the end it proved to be one of the most popular pieces of legislation during the 1945 session. The legislature passed the equal rights measure by an overwhelming margin: 19–5 in the house and 11–5 in the senate. Governor Gruening signed the equal rights bill into law on 16 February 1945, officially abolishing Jim Crow practices in the Territory of Alaska. Standing behind Ernest Gruening as he put his signature on the bill were the key figures in its passage: Roy and Elizabeth Peratrovich, Senator N. R. Walker of Ketchikan, and the two Nome politicians who had come to Alberta Schenck's defense, Senator O. D. Cochran and Representative Edward Anderson.

With the passage of the 1945 Alaska equal rights bill, the signs in Alaskan businesses prohibiting natives came down. Discrimination did not end in Alaska, but the 1945 law was nevertheless a significant step forward as it recognized that no one had the right to post their policies of race discrimination.

Even to this day, however, many Alaskans have blind spots when it comes to the subject of race discrimination towards Alaska natives. Racism is virtually an invisible topic in Alaska's historical literature, and some old timers would prefer it stay that way. As one former white resident of Nome wrote me in 1989, regarding the Alberta Schenck incident: "I am sorry that I have no additional knowledge of the occurrence you are writing about probably because to me there was nothing unusual happening. Whenever two or more groups intermingle, be they of different races or just groups of the same race, there will be friction that will gradually be eradicated if no one keeps poking the embers." With the massive social, political, and economic challenges that still face Alaska natives today as they struggle for equality and cultural survival, it seems wishful thinking to believe that the problems of the past should be so easily forgotten, or, worse yet, to pretend that they never happened at all.

Mexican Laborers in the Pacific Northwest

ERASMO GAMBOA

Between 1943 and 1947, the United States government contracted with approximately 47,000 bracero agricultural laborers in Mexico to work in the northwestern states of Idaho, Oregon, and Washington. Despite the large number, little is known about the experiences of these men. In contrast, the history and administrative details of the agricultural bracero program in California and other southwestern states have been well documented. This essay examines the social and work experiences of the braceros on farms in the Northwest and compares their record with those of braceros elsewhere in an attempt to provide a broader understanding of the national wartime labor program.

During the Second World War, the U.S. War Manpower Commission's call for record-shattering farm production exerted tremendous pressure on an already labor-starved western agricultural economy. One result was a demand for Mexican workers to which Congress responded in August 1942 with Public Law-45 (PL-45), a binational agreement authorizing the importation of agricultural workers from Mexico. Two months later, the Utah-Idaho Sugar Company at Toppenish, Washington, announced that 500 braceros would arrive for the October beet harvest. Within a year, Mexican nationals had become a vital mainstay in northwestern farm production; only California recruited more workers. Of the 220,640 laborers who entered the country under PL-45, approximately twenty-one percent were contracted by northwestern farmers.

The braceros' experiences in the Pacific Northwest were shaped by their background, the attitude of growers and northwestern communities, and the federal bureaucracy. Government officials expected the workers to live in tent camps under spartan conditions with few organized social activities. Overall, the men endured much racial discrimination from employers and local communities alike. On the job, they suffered many accidents not only

Erasmo Gamboa, "Braceros in the Pacific Northwest: Laborers on the Domestic Front, 1942–1947," *Pacific Historical Review,* 56 (August 1987), 378–398. Copyright © 1987 by Pacific Coast Branch, American Historical Association. Excerpted by permission.

because of their unfamiliarity with farm machinery, but also because farmers had little regard for their safety. As a rule, braceros received low wages, and when they organized strikes to win increases, they encountered quick and sometimes violent resistance from growers and local officials. Although these experiences differ little from those of braceros in the Southwest, the record of the workers in the two regions significantly diverged.

Life was difficult for the braceros because they were young and came from rural areas steeped in traditional Mexican culture. Typical were the eighty men housed at the camp at Lyndon, Washington, where the greater number were between twenty and thirty years of age with only two over forty. For most, their sojourn to the United States would be the first separation from their immediate and extended families which were (and are) so important in Mexican culture. Thus they arrived ill-prepared to cope with the strain of hostile and unfamiliar circumstances and the tensions and emotion surrounding the war effort. Not surprisingly, many men became distraught and feigned illness or wrote to their families asking to be recalled for reasons of supposed sickness or death before the end of their seasonal contracts. In one week alone at Preston, Idaho, twelve men returned home before their contracts had expired. Federal farm labor officials from Portland expressed concern that many braceros in the Northwest would use any means to return early. They "definitely want to be sent home now," observed one official in what became a common complaint. "If there is a way to hasten their departure, they will find it . . . either by refusing to work or violation of the [wage] ceiling." In 1945, the Chief of Operations at Portland reported that ten percent of all braceros contracted to the Pacific Northwest were either missing or had been granted an early repatriation.

Poor living conditions also heightened the desire of many workers to return to Mexico. In the Northwest, the braceros generally lived in mobile tent camps designed to go where needed among the widely dispersed agricultural areas. As a rule, six workers lived together in a 16' by 16' tent furnished with folding cots, one blanket per person, and stove heaters when available. Although each individual was entitled to bring seventy-seven pounds of personal effects from Mexico, in reality most arrived with little more than a change of clothes. Within time, the workers scavenged for discarded crates or boxes and placed them inside the tents for storage and seating. These makeshift creations, along with personal pictures of loved ones, tokens of remembrance, or knick-knacks purchased locally, completed the interior.

During the summer, the men were often driven from the tents by 100 degree temperatures, and in fall and winter, the fabric structures offered little protection from the inclement Northwest weather. Stoves, if provided, were virtually ineffective because the loose sides of the tent allowed heat to escape quite easily. Moreover, the frequent lack of adequate supplies of kerosene, coal, or dry wood meant that the stove heaters were often useless. As early as October, the camp manager at Hazelton, Idaho, found it nearly impossible to keep the braceros inside their assigned quarters because insufficient fuel and the lack of stoves in some tents resulted in "unusually cold" lodgings. Although the specter of hypothermia was present, the braceros faced a more serious threat from fires as they struggled to keep warm with the combination of kerosene, old stoves, and highly flammable tents. Besides frequent tent fires, there were also destructive explosions. In one instance in October 1944, some braceros at Marsing, Idaho, barely escaped injury when an oil-burning water heater exploded and destroyed everything around it.

When fires occurred, the design of the mobile camps' water systems added to the danger. Water tanks, pipes, and pumps were entirely above ground and readily froze increasing the peril of fire. Water barrels with handpumped fire extinguishers were also useless during freezing temperatures. "We have these 2 ½ gallon water extinguishers which are no good in cold weather and our fire hydrants freeze up at night," complained a worried camp manager. "We try to keep the water faucets dripping at night but the Mexicans are taught to conserve water in Mexico and turn them off at night."

Although the braceros complained strongly about their living accommodations, they grumbled most about the poor quality of food served in the camps. The meals lacked variety and appeal because the kitchen facilities in the tent camps were often makeshift and deficient by most standards. Moreover, northwestern federal officials, unlike those in the Southwest, gave local grower committees the responsibility for feeding the braceros in the labor centers. In 1944, federal officials ordered the camp manager at Wendell, Idaho, to suspend all food services because of the lack of refrigeration and a vehicle to bring fresh provisions from town. The kitchens themselves posed particular problems because they were usually housed in large tents. The mess tent at Wilder, Idaho, for example, was 150 feet long. Not only was such a tent unstable in strong winds, but dust entered easily and blanketed the food.

In the Northwest, as in California, meals were the source of more discontent and work stoppages than any other single aspect of camp life. In July 1943, Mexicans at the Skagit County camp north of Seattle went on strike in order to call attention to the terrible kitchen services. Workers there started their daily routine with breakfast at 4:30 a.m. Seven and a half hours later, they stopped work to eat a noon lunch consisting of three sandwiches: one contained meat, one egg spread, and another jelly. A sweet roll and half pint of milk were also provided. The camp, improvised at the county fairgrounds, had no refrigeration; therefore by lunch time, the sandwiches, prepared the day before, were unappetizing and the milk was "sour or blinky." The type of sack lunches served in the Northwest were found in most bracero camps throughout the country. Although the men had a strong dislike of white bread and lunch meats, cooks served such sandwiches because they were easy to prepare. In California, camp kitchens continued to serve sack lunches for many years after the war.

Contributing to discontent over meals was wartime rationing which meant that desirable quantities and varieties of food were not always available. The Agricultural Workers Health Association, a government sponsored cooperative which provided health care to farm workers in the Northwest, supported the complaints of the braceros. In 1945, it reported that the poor, iron deficient food was the main cause of nutritional anemia among the men. This disclosure prompted the Mexican embassy to take action that led to improvement in the quality of food served to the braceros.

The poor kitchen services were exacerbated by the camp managers who were often inept supervisors and inexperienced. At Weiser, Idaho, a hopeless but outspoken manager described the workers' food as a "lamentable situation," because "any jelly or jam has soaked through the bread; cheese had begun to harden, and prepared meats run the chance of becoming spoiled before the sandwich is eaten." On the other hand, a more resourceful manager at Milton-Freewater, Oregon, instructed the growers to return to the camp to pick up the sack lunches between 10 and 11 a.m. so that the meals would be fresher and more appetizing. The attitude of the camp official at Payette, Idaho, illustrates how managers could also worsen food-related problems. At the beginning of the work season, the camp kitchen had 300 spoons. By the middle of the year, there were seven spoons left and in November a single spoon remained for 110 men. Though more were available, the camp manager refused to request them because he believed the workers were stealing or losing the spoons. Other camp supervisors did everything possible to improve the food services, including simple but important considerations designed to prevent health risks. The camp manager at Stanwood, Washington, translated signs reading "Wash Your Hands" into Spanish and recommended to his supervisor that similar safety regulations in other camps be translated. Otherwise, he stated, the signs amounted to little more than "wasted effort."

Food services were inadequate in other ways. Workers were not provided containers to carry coffee or milk, so they used anything they could find without much thought to sanitation. This doubtlessly contributed to bracero camps in the Northwest having an unusually high incidence of food poisoning. In 1946 in a period of nine months, there were five outbreaks of food poisoning. The most serious outbreak had occurred three years earlier on a hop ranch near Grants Pass, Oregon, where 500 of 511 braceros fell sick and 300 required hospitalization. The Pacific Northwest was not unusual in this respect, for elsewhere gastrointestinal disorders also developed as the most common health problem among Mexican workers.

Leisure time activities, a key to the physical and social well being of most persons, were just as precious to the braceros—yet the men had little to do during their off hours. In most camps, Mexican movies projected outdoors on tent walls were a bright spot in an otherwise dull routine. Among the films making the rounds of the camps and enjoying great popularity were *Jalisco Nunca Pierde, Huapango, Dos Mujeres, Un Don Juan, Ojos Tapatios,* and *El Héroe de Nacozarí.* Among the reasons for their popularity were the themes emphasized by Mexican producers of the 1940s: an exaltation of rural life in prerevolutionary Mexico, veneration and respect for family and authority, resignation to poverty and personal hardship. Simply stated, the films not only aroused nostalgia for the homeland, but also appealed to the Mexicans with their conservative and nationalistic message. The braceros cheered the underdog and empathized with the romanticized life portrayed on the screen, thereby temporarily forgetting the harsh conditions that had compelled them to come to the United States. Still others seemed to equate their experiences as braceros with the scenes of hardship and heroic adventure brought to life on the canvas walls and resolved to persevere in spite of their adversities. The popularity of the films was so great that growers would occasionally transport several hundred men by truck to a camp where one of the movies was being shown.

When films were not available, the braceros found other ways to pass time during nonworking hours. On Sundays, they sometimes requested Catholic priests to offer mass in camp. They also frequently pooled their resources to purchase radios or jukeboxes, which they stocked with Spanish records. Others passed idle hours with handicraft work, such as fashioning rings out of scrap pipe or suitcases from discarded wood.

Beyond the limited leisure activities, the social highlight of the year at most camps was the celebration of Mexican Independence. The Office of Labor, in the War Food Administration, sanctioned the festival because officials recognized it as an excellent way to sustain morale and a dedication to task among the imported work force. State farm labor officials also encouraged local communities to cooperate with the celebrations at the labor camps. In California, where Mexico's national holidays were also observed, Mexican government officials frequently delivered patriotic speeches, a practice described by Ernesto Galarza as "worn thin" and ineffective by 1944. Independence day festivities in most northwestern camps were largely improvised but still provided a welcomed break from the daily routine. At Wilder, Idaho, for example, the workers organized an impromptu evening dance but because "Mexican senoritas" were not available, some of the men agreed to dress in women's clothes in order to provide partners for the camp population.

Another much-celebrated occasion in the camps was Cinco de Mayo, the anniversary of the defeat of the French in Mexico. At Medford, Oregon, in 1944, more than a thousand attended the celebration, including U.S. Senator Rufus Holman (a member of the Senate Appropriations Committee), the mayor of Medford, members of the chamber of commerce, students in local high school Spanish classes, many farmers with their wives and families, and "several of the local barmaids." The local radio stations broadcast the day's festivities, while Mexican music from the camp jukebox and musicians from the camp population gave the day some authenticity. Three pigs were butchered for the noon meal and visitors dined on two thousand tortillas, fifty gallons of ice cream, and a thousand soft drinks. As a symbol of friendship, the workers raised the flags of both countries in a special ceremony as bugles called the crowd to attention. In the evening, the camp hosted a dance, complete with orchestra, where women from the community and the growers' wives and daughters danced with the Mexican workers.

These two celebrations, which brought the braceros and public together, stood in stark contrast to widespread anti-Mexican sentiment usually faced by the workers. In the Northwest, Idaho developed the most notorious reputation for discrimination. Prejudice became so common and deep-seated that in 1946 the Mexican government threatened to forbid its workers to go into the state and two years later made good on its threat. Consequently, Idaho, like Texas, was blacklisted by the Mexican government for its mistreatment of braceros. This action resulted from the blatant racism of some Caldwell and Nampa merchants and businesses. A Mexican government official found that "signs in both Nampa and Caldwell business houses forbid the Mexicans to enter. Seven beer parlors in Caldwell and 11 in Nampa have such signs posted. . . ." The members of the Notus Farm Labor Committee, which had contracted the braceros, denounced the Caldwell Chamber of Commerce for violating the prohibitions against discrimination in PL-45 and cautioned that the practice jeopardized the growers' work force. The committee requested that certain stores remain open in the evening so that workers could make necessary purchases without harassment. "We have worked hard to get that labor in here," declared a committee spokesperson, "and it is doing us a service. If by our discriminating signs we are to lose the labor it will be a blow to the farmers in this area." Few heeded the warning and Mexico put Idaho off limits.

Antipathy against Mexicans developed outside of Idaho as well. In Seattle, the Reverend U. G. Murphey, chairman of the Evacuees Service Counsel which worked on behalf of Japanese Americans relocated in internment camps, was unsympathetic toward the Mexican men, and although PL-45 did not provide for permanent residency, he opposed any settlement of braceros. Meanwhile, the school superintendent at Boardman, Oregon, asked Senator Rufus C. Holman why the braceros in the state could not be conscripted into the military. At Stanwood, Washington, braceros had an altercation with some high school students and a local marshall outside a restaurant resulting in a near "race riot." Not long thereafter, the camp manager at Medford, Oregon, reported that a Mexican national was attacked in public "without provocation" and severely injured by five young men. After the assault, the battered man was arrested on a charge of being intoxicated. During his arraignment the judge acknowledged that "those who made the attack should have been arrested instead." As it turned out, the bracero had been staggering and presumed drunk "due to the beating received and not due to alcoholism as claimed." Such instances were not everyday occurrences, but they did reveal a pattern of racial animosity toward the Mexican workers.

In Idaho the braceros asked I. A. Pesqueira, the Mexican consul at Portland, to intercede on their behalf against the discriminatory practices. It was their protest, coming on the heels of the earlier complaints about conditions in Idaho, that finally resulted in the state being placed off-limits in October 1948 for Mexican laborers. "I have been directed by my government," wired Pesqueira to Idaho growers, ". . . that farmers in Idaho are hereby suspended from importation of nationals of my country for any purpose until further notice. This suspension is prompted by discrimination against our nationals on social and economic grounds and by violations of the international agreement and the individual workers' contracts."

Braceros faced another severe form of discrimination from health authorities. Some hospitals refused to treat them, and this prejudice prompted the chief of operations at the U.S. Office of Labor in Portland to suggest that the federal government establish infirmaries in areas where Mexicans could not obtain needed medical care. Sometimes, the workers were denied treatment on racial grounds, while on other occasions health practitioners doubted the men's ability to pay their medical expenses and feared they would be left with outstanding bills. . . .

When medical authorities and community hospitals treated the braceros, the workers usually received minimal attention. On one occasion in 1945, a Mexican worker received a gunshot wound in the abdomen (cause not stated), and died six weeks later. The Agricultural Workers Health Association, which worked with the braceros, strongly condemned the doctor who treated the victim. "Burial visually eliminated medical incompetence," stated a spokesperson for the association, and "it is indeed unfortunate in such cases that the physician cannot be given as the cause of death." The same year in Idaho, a group of braceros had been summoned to fight forest fires. On the third day a tree fell on one of them, Ramón Carrillo, and injured his leg. He was examined at the hospital in Grangeville, found fit, and returned to duty. Back fighting fires he continued to experience considerable pain in his leg. Six or seven days later, Ramón was examined once more but the doctor found no reason for the suffering. Finally, Ramón made his own way to a nearby War Food Administration office where he explained what had happened. Subsequent x-rays disclosed that Ramón's leg was fractured. Twice, he wrote to the Mexican consul at Salt Lake City to seek compensation for the time lost from work. Then in despair, he sent a letter in Spanish to President Franklin D. Roosevelt. "They do as they please," he complained to the President, "because I cannot speak English." Ramón was more fortunate than another injured worker who died after failing to recover from anesthesia administered to set a fractured arm.

In addition to poor living conditions, discrimination and minimal health care, braceros faced unpleasant and dangerous work conditions because some farmers had little concern for the welfare of the men. At times, growers required that the braceros work during extremely cold weather, although the men were not acclimatized and lacked proper clothing. For instance, in 1946, freezing temperatures and blizzard conditions hit southern Idaho causing braceros recently transferred from California to refuse to work. This prompted the sugar beet growers to threaten them with fines and intimidate them to return to work for as little as $2.50 for eight hours. In the judgment of the camp manager, it "was not right" to expect the braceros to work under such conditions. The growers were unfair, he stated, because "I noticed on some of these days the local help was not in the fields. In general, I believe that Nationals were not treated as they should have been."

The growers' lack of concern for the men's welfare was reflected in numerous work-related accidents which resulted from poor safety and the braceros' inexperience with the hazards of working near powerful farm machinery. At Weiser, Idaho, Apolinar Calderón accidentally severed a finger while working on a seed harvester. In Oregon, Primitivo Mosqueda suffered serious injuries to the temporal region, lacerations, and a fractured skull when his head was pinned between two pieces of farm equipment causing "a portion of an end of a bolt to pierce down in the skull to an unbelievable distance." In another instance, as workers were having lunch, a tractor ran over a milk bottle sending glass flying into the braceros' food. One worker accidently swallowed a fragment and spent three days in the hospital after doctors removed the glass from his throat. At Kennewick, Washington, Pedro Correa Armenta lost his sight in a work-related accident. Following an unsuccessful operation to restore his vision, he was repatriated to Mexico. Often the braceros were killed or critically injured in accidents while being transported to and from work in open flatbed trucks. The return trip was the most dangerous because the workers had to ride atop loose loads of potatoes, sugar beets, or lightly secured vegetable and fruit boxes. The men exacerbated this dangerous practice by dangling their legs over the sides of the vehicles or standing without the benefit of safety rails. "Another Mexican National lost his life yesterday while being transported by truck," reported the Oregon state supervisor for farm labor in 1943. At Hillsboro, Oregon, a man fell from a truck, striking his head and seriously injuring his spinal column. In Idaho, another worker received a compound fracture of the skull and a broken shoulder blade when he jumped off a moving vehicle.

The hazardous use of flatbed trucks to transport the braceros was a problem in the Southwest, but, according to medical officers in the Department of Labor, the number of accidents involving trucks was particularly grave in the Northwest. In 1946 federal farm-labor authorities initiated a safety campaign to end the practice, but most farmers refused to cooperate. "It can't be done" was the response. This attitude prompted the camp manager at Weiser, Idaho, to complain to his supervisor in Portland. "One committee member [grower]," he reported, "told me . . . to leave the farmers alone," because they had insurance to cover such accidents. Three months later, the camp supervisor wrote that growers continued to haul the workers on top of loosely loaded potato trucks with "no consideration as to the safety of the men." This time he requested assistance in getting the "practice stopped." Following the second letter, the Portland supervisor directed all northwestern camp managers to enforce a ban on "transporting workers on flat-bed trucks and on top of loads." Unfortunately, the directive was not issued in time for José Guerrero Rodríguez who was killed when a flatbed truck carrying twenty-two braceros to fight a forest fire overturned near Payette, Idaho. . . .

The braceros could legally do little more than complain to Mexican government officials to improve working conditions because their contracts prohibited work stoppages or strikes. In the Southwest these prohibitions kept labor disturbances to a minimum. As Ernesto Galarza noted, dissatisfied workers had but two alternatives: "either shut-up or go back." Doubtlessly, southwestern braceros staged labor protests—there was a serious disturbance near Fullerton, California, in 1943—but no general pattern of strikes emerged. In the Northwest, on the other hand, braceros were constantly on strike, and this made the region unique among other parts of the country.

Just months after the braceros arrived in the Northwest, they initiated the first strike and established a pattern that continued until PL-45 expired in 1947. At Burlington, Washington, a local Mexican American convinced the braceros to halt work because farmers were paying higher wages to Anglos doing similar work. The growers ended the work stoppage by reminding the Mexicans that strikes were prohibited under the terms of their contract and by giving the Mexican American a "friendly warning against inciting a riot in a government camp." The "instigator" at once left and the workers returned to their jobs.

Most bracero strikes were not so easy to put down. Idaho, which had the lowest wage scales and the most recalcitrant farmers, experienced many serious labor disturbances despite the state legislature's approval, in February 1943, of a strong measure to curb labor unrest. The law prohibited union organizers from entering, without the owner's consent, "any ranch, farm, feeding and shearing plant or other agricultural premise" to solicit members, collect dues, or promote a strike. Picket lines and consumer boycotts were also illegal.

The law notwithstanding, in June 1944 the braceros at Preston, Idaho, went on strike over wages. "Those breaking their contracts," warned the growers, "would be taken out to the road where they would be out on their own, the proper immigration authorities would be notified, they would be picked up by these authorities, placed in jail to await court action; in the meantime while awaiting for court they would have to work for 90 days without compensation, except board and room." Under this threat, the braceros resumed work. However, five months later, the same workers struck again over wages, and this time they sought the Mexican consul's assistance. The farmers responded with violence and ended the strike. "Last Friday," noted the camp manager, "one of the farmers in the area assaulted one of the Mexicans and gave him a right good mauling." In this and similar cases, investigations followed but no one was charged. The lack of repercussions made growers aware that they would not be held accountable by the federal government or local authorities. They also understood that once the braceros were in the United States, the workers and Mexican government officials had little to say in the conditions of employment or wages short of black-listing an entire state.

The threat of violence did not stop 170 Mexicans from striking for over a week at Idaho Falls in July 1945. The strike started when fifty braceros, who were new to the camp, refused to pick cherries at the prevailing rate. Farmers responded by ordering the camp kitchen closed in an effort to end the strike. Several times some of the men attempted to leave the camp, but they were turned back by the boos and harassment of the more militant braceros. This gave the Bonneville County Sheriff and the Idaho State Highway Patrol the pretext to enter the camp in order to prevent a "riot." They offered to escort any bracero willing to cross the picket line. Still, no one left the camp for nine days until the lack of food ended the strike.

The longest and best coordinated work stoppage involved more than 600 braceros from four camps near Nampa, Idaho, in June 1946. The timing of the walkout was critical to the growers primarily because their crops were ready for harvest and because prisoners of war, who had earlier been used as agricultural workers, were no longer available. The strike was in protest to a higher wage scale in the western part of Canyon County where growers had to compete with Oregon farmers. Government labor officials described the walkout as a "general strike," because it included the four camps and the men were demonstrating in the streets of Nampa in open defiance of the growers. In an attempt to control the strike, a Spanish-speaking farm labor supervisor negotiated with the braceros until they finally agreed to call off the strike on the promise that the Mexican consul would push for a hearing before the county wage stabilization board.

Twelve days later, the workers and growers got an opportunity to testify before the wage board. The braceros presented their case for a uniform wage of $.70 an hour. The growers responded that some workers were paid as much as $.75 because they were skilled "American laborers" employed year around, but as for the braceros, they were paid adequately at a $.60 rate. In the end, the growers convinced the hearing examiners to rule that "there was no evidence presented that warranted a change, either increase or decrease, in the existing scale."

The Mexican consul, in a move to force an increase in wages, threatened the growers: "Considering that ample opportunity has been given Farmers Associations [of the] Nampa District to revise discriminatory attitudes toward contracted Mexican Nationals, please proceed to remove workers at your earliest convenience unless seventy cents per hour prevailing wage in nearby areas is recognized before Monday, July 22nd." This threat was reinforced by Carl G. Izett of the Federal Production and Marketing Administration offices in Portland who argued that a solution to the workers' protest was "critical" to the continuation of the bracero program. The labor dispute ended, however, without either an increase in wages or repatriation. Although made uneasy by the consul's threat and the braceros' "extremely rebellious attitude," the growers persuaded local law enforcement officials to break the strike by arresting the strikers on spurious felony charges. . . .

The pattern of labor unrest among braceros in the Pacific Northwest must be seen in light of circumstances peculiar to the region and the men's motive for coming to the United States. They came to earn sufficient money to take back to Mexico but this was not always possible because of working conditions or low wages. Most braceros left terrible living conditions in Mexico, yet the tent camps left much to be desired and the food was deplorable. When the workers protested, northwestern farmers searched for another source of cheap labor.

The expiration of PL-45 in April 1947 gave growers added reason to stop bringing braceros in the Pacific Northwest. The new legislative authorization for the bracero program, PL-40, contained major administrative changes, including payment by employers of all transportation costs from Mexico. As a result, braceros were replaced by Mexican American workers on northwestern farms, although southwestern states continued to recruit Mexican nationals in record numbers until 1964.

As in the Southwest, the war caused the northwestern agricultural economy to boom. Growers faced critical labor shortages that could be met only through the use of cheap imported Mexican workers. These men came with their civil rights formally protected by contract, but no sooner were they on northwestern farms than employers set aside the agreement. The braceros sought to improve their wages and treatment on and off their jobs, but the federal government, which had authority over any violation of the workers' contracts, offered them little support.

Despite this record, the wish for a return to a national bracero or "guest worker" program has never completely gone away. The lessons of the last bracero program should serve as a forceful reminder of the gulf between paper agreements and the reality for the contracted workers themselves.

Y FURTHER READING

Carl Abbott, "The Federal Presence," in *The Oxford History of the American West,* ed. Clyde A. Milner II, Carol A. O'Connor, and Martha A. Sandweiss (1994), 469–99

Karen Anderson, *Wartime Women: Sex Roles, Family Relations, and the Status of Women During World War II* (1981)

Beth Bailey and David Farber, "The 'Double-V' Campaign in World War II Hawaii: African Americans, Racial Ideology, and Federal Power," *Journal of Social History,* 26 (Summer 1993)

Howard Ball, *Justice Downwind: America's Atomic Testing Program in the 1950s* (1986)

Alison R. Bernstein, *American Indians and World War II: Toward a New Era in Indian Affairs* (1991)

Albert S. Broussard, "Strange Territory, Familiar Leadership: The Impact of World War II on San Francisco's Black Community," *California History,* 65 (March 1986)

Kitty Calavita, *Inside the State: The Bracero Program, Immigration, and the I.N.S.* (1992)

John Christgau, *"Enemies": World War II Alien Internment* (1985)

Roger Daniels, *Prisoners Without Trial: Japanese Americans in World War II* (1993)

Peter H. Eichstaedt, *If You Poison Us: Uranium and the Native Americans* (1994)

Louis Fairchild, *They Called It the War Effort: Oral Histories from World War II, Orange, Texas* (1993)

Philip L. Fradkin, *Fallout: An American Nuclear Tragedy* (1989)

Erasmo Gamboa, *Mexican Labor and World War II: Braceros in the Pacific Northwest, 1942–47* (1990)

Michelle S. Gerber, *On the Homefront: The Cold War Legacy of the Hanford Nuclear Site* (1992)

Sherna B. Gluck, *Rosie the Riveter Revisited: Women, the War, and Social Change* (1987)

Camilie Guerin-Gonzales, *Mexican Workers and American Dreams: Immigration, Repatriation, and California Farm Labor, 1900–1939* (1994)

Peter Irons, ed., *Justice Delayed: The Record of the Japanese American Cases* (1989)

Kevin A. Leonard, " 'Is This What We Fought For?: Japanese Americans and Racism in California, the Impact of World War II," *Western Historical Quarterly,* 21 (November 1990), 463–82

Roger W. Lotchin, "The Historians' War or the Home Front's War?: Some Thought for Western Historians," *Western Historical Quarterly,* 26 (Summer 1995), 185–96

———, "WWII and Urban California: City Planning and the Transformation Hypothesis," *Pacific Historical Quarterly,* 62 (May 1993)

Ryan Madden, "The Forgotten People: The Relocation and Internment of Aleuts During World War II," *American Indian Culture and Research Journal,* 16, no. 4 (1992)

Gerald D. Nash, *The American West Transformed: The Impact of the Second World War* (1985)

———, "The West and the Military-Industrial Complex," *Montana, The Magazine of Western History,* 40 (Winter 1990), 72–75

———, *World War II and the West: Reshaping the Economy* (1990)

Richard S. Nishimoto, *Inside an American Concentration Camp: Japanese American Resistance at Poston, Arizona,* ed. Lane Ryo Hirabayashi (1995)

Richard Polenburg, *War and Society: The U.S., 1941–1945* (1972)

Allan Kent Powell, *Splinters of a Nation: German Prisoners of War in Utah* (1990)

Ray C. Ringholz, *Uranium Frenzy: Boom and Bust on the Colorado Plateau* (1989)

Ferenc M. Szasz, *The Day the Sun Rose Twice: The Story of the Trinity Site Nuclear Explosion, July 16, 1945* (1984)

John Tateishi, *And Justice for All: An Oral History of the Japanese American Detention Camps* (1984)

Sandra C. Taylor, *Jewel of the Desert: Japanese American Internment at Topaz* (1993)

———, "Leaving the Concentration Camps: Japanese Americans and Resettlement in the Intermountain West," *Pacific Historical Review,* 60 (May 1991), 169–94

Constandina Titus, *Bomb in the Backyard: Atomic Testing and American Politics* (1986)

Nobiya Tsuchida, *American Justice: Japanese American Evacuation and Redress* (1988)

Emilio Zamora, "The Failed Promise of Wartime Opportunity for Mexicans in the Texas Oil Industry," *Southwestern Historical Quarterly,* 45 (January 1992), 323–50

C H A P T E R
13

New Cities, New Lives

Y

The modern West presents a horizon that differs from the open range of the nineteenth century. Houston boasts of magnificent skyscraper architecture; Denver opens a colossal new airport; Seattle draws tourists to its futuristic Space Needle. In the 1990s Salt Lake City wins the Olympics; Los Angeles owns a powerful basketball team; Dallas repeatedly claims the professional football championship. The cities of the West are no longer remote towns. For the past one hundred years, these cities have grown into cultural, economic, and political centers, not just of the West, but of the country. Especially since 1900, western cities have beckoned to American families, immigrants, and corporations with the promise of the good life in the land of wide-open skies. By 1990 almost half of the nation's fifty largest cities lay in the West.

Urbanization transformed the entire region. Once Americans thought of the West as a vast rural environment, ideal for agricultural life. However, technology, politics, and modern demographics altered that western landscape and the economic expectations of its inhabitants. The twentieth century has seen western urban centers emerge as the locus of regional development. As this occurred, the fundamental relationship between the urban and rural communities shifted, helping to change the balance of power economically and politically.

At the same time, other issues surfaced which underscored the less desirable aspects of city life. Lack of sufficient housing, inadequate sanitation, waning job markets, rising crime, a weak tax base, overextended public agencies, racial and ethnic clashes—all these problems now plague western cities, even as they have eastern ones. Western cities face the dual task of managing their internal structures and balancing their ecological and economic relationship with the hinterland. Urban residents have had to consider whether their cities made efficient decisions in times of rapid growth.

How much and what kind of urban planning shaped western cities? How will cities handle the competition for water in a region that stretches across arid and semi-arid geography? Can Americans, especially the elderly, continue to move into western cities, pushing the suburban boundaries farther into the countryside? Will westerners recognize the benefits, as well as the stresses, that a culturally mixed, urban population produces?

⅄ *PHOTO DOCUMENTS*

A few photographs cannot illuminate the entire history of Los Angeles, but they can touch on overarching themes that have shaped the city. These images highlight developments in the means of transportation, consumption of resources, and diversity of population. The photographs suggest the nature of cooperation and competition within communities, and the allure of an urban area as it changed from a provincial town to a sophisticated metropolis. These themes are not restricted to Los Angeles for they highlight the urban transformation of the West. Often in the same picture, these photographs combine grand dreams of urban improvement with the gritty realities of urban life. Is the challenge for western cities to fulfill dreams or to replace them with reality?

Second Street Cable Railway, Looking West, 1888   As Los Angeles residents moved beyond the small central town core, private entrepreneurs responded to commuters' needs by building cable car and electric railways. Before the city established a public transportation system, these small rail companies enhanced the business opportunities of diverse organizations and made daily commuting more convenient for area residents. Previously undeveloped land escalated in value because it became accessible. A systematic alteration of the urban landscape was under way. How many beneficiaries of improved transportation can be identified in this late-nineteenth-century photograph? Department of Special Collections, University Research Library, UCLA.

Jawbone Siphon Construction Site, c. 1910   It can be argued that the
ultimate success or failure of western cities hinges on their ability to deliver
water for urban consumption, which shows no trend toward reduction.
Cities of the arid West transport water great distances, across difficult terrain. This reality was evident during the building of the Los Angeles aqueduct, 1908–1912. Since the completion of Jawbone Siphon, pictured here
during its construction north of Mojave, California, the needs for water in
Los Angeles have increased dramatically, but the western water supply has
not. Past strategies for finding new sources of water have included tapping
underground aquifers, diverting rivers, and building dams. Perhaps no other
issue pits western jurisdictions against each other more intensely than the
expensive competition for control of water, a matter that is highly politi-
cized at both the city and state levels. What changes will western cities need
to make if the supply of water declines? Courtesy of CALTRANS.

Construction of the Harbor Freeway, 1956   In advance of any other major U.S. city, the automobile dominated as the mode of transportation most chosen by Los Angeles residents. As a result, after World War II, a complex system of freeways and super highways took over the urban landscape through and around the city. The freeways served as facilitators to mobility and as barriers to communication, introducing both urban access and obstruction. The process by which the owners of private property yielded to government right-of-way clearances changed the visual boundaries of city neighborhoods, and the relationships within those communities. Not only were families cut off from each other, but resentments grew over how officials selected a community for dismemberment and how they assessed property compensation rates. These issues concerned the African American neighborhood depicted here in 1956. What adjustments did residents face after their middle-class community became a freeway boundary? Courtesy of L.A. Dept. of Water and Power.

Disneyland, 1955   Walt Disney carefully planned the environment that he wanted for his first theme park, Disneyland, shown here shortly after it opened in the 1950s. With this park, Disney introduced an entertainment product that depended on convincing families to enter a make-believe world with children's storybook characters brought to life by scriptwriters and costume designers. This aerial photograph taken during the experimental phase of that marketing scheme captures both the meticulous arrangement of the interior and the orderly exterior of the partially filled parking lot on the right. The two blend seamlessly to create an image of clean western spaciousness, far different from amusement parks of the East. Despite Disney's goal to construct an idyllic leisure enterprise, removed from environmental reality, he planted this space for organized relaxation in the midst of urban freeway construction, seen in the background. Courtesy of Anaheim History Room, Anaheim Public Library (Aerial #32).

Disneyland, 1967   Like the West itself, Disneyland underwent constant transformation. Shown here only twelve years after the preceding photograph, note the growth both inside and outside of Disneyland. As the acreage for expansion shrunk, park engineers made space for new exhibits by building up into the air and down under the ground. The original boundaries of the park area have been pushed back, and visitors have more attractions to keep them amused. The ongoing appeal of the Disneyland escape, which sold attitude as much as entertainment, is evident from the change in the parking lot, now considerably enlarged and filled with cars. However, the impression that Disneyland draws its visitors into a pleasant haven removed from urban disorders has diminished as the borders of the park butt up against the fiercely crowded Anaheim and Santa Ana freeways. Courtesy of Anaheim History Room, Anaheim Public Library (P13029).

Burning Building in Watts Uprising, 1965   The appealing fantasy of Walt Disney aside, in the real world of twentieth-century Los Angeles, the gulf between the rich and the poor, whites and people of color, widened. Those with the means fanned out from the urban core, using the freeway complex to escape to upper-middle-class communities, thus further decentralizing the city. The people who remained sorted themselves out along racial lines, but shared equally in the municipal economic segregation that kept most in poverty. Crowded into the ghettos and barrios of the city, African Americans and Hispanics lived in the poorest housing, attended the most impoverished schools, and labored in the most menial jobs. These problems were made worse for ethnic communities by occasions of violence that originated from the Los Angeles police department. The long-simmering inequities, given voice by those leading the struggle for civil rights, finally erupted in August of 1965 with a massive disturbance that swept through the Watts district of Los Angeles. Department of Special Collections, University Research Library, UCLA. Photo by George R. Fry, Jr.

A Korean American Stands Guard During the Los Angeles Riots, 1992
By the 1990s, racial tensions in Los Angeles had accelerated, as more ethnic groups poured into the overtaxed inner city. African Americans, Latinos,
Koreans, Chinese, and Japanese, all jockeyed for space and power within a
shrinking economic base. In 1992, the acquittal of four white police officers
videotaped viciously beating a black motorist triggered a new explosion of
racial animosity in Los Angeles. As the riot gained momentum, the complexity of race relations became clear when Latinos and African Americans
directed much of their violence at Korean-American merchants. Attacks on
people and places of business crossed and recrossed ethnic lines, making
this a complicated battle for community and identity. This young Korean
American, who sends conflicting messages between his peace symbol and
his T-shirt, stands guard over a family business. Photograph 1992 © Jean-
Marc Giboux, Gamma Liaison, New York.

Dodger Stadium, 1962   Out of the tangle of the freeway system rises the majestic Dodger Stadium—a symbol of Los Angeles as a big league city. Relocated from Brooklyn, New York in 1958, the Dodgers quickly became identified with their new western home. Photographed in 1962, the brand new stadium reflected the pace of the fast-moving community that swirled around it as thousands of citizens made their way toward its glowing lights. The stadium, part of the heart of Los Angeles, radiates with the glamour and vibrancy that mark the promise of western urban life. Despite significant problems, Los Angeles resonates with distinctive and interesting features that continue to attract the native born and the immigrant. It is a center of cultural and economic sophistication, with the potential to transcend its problems. The future course of Los Angeles may be determined by the recognition, across cultural groups, of that dazzling possibility for all its citizens. Unidentified photographer. Dodger Stadium. Gelatin Silver Print, 1962. Bruce Henstell Collection.

Y *E S S A Y S*

Quintard Taylor, who teaches history at the University of Oregon, has written several important studies of African Americans in the West. His essay considers the interaction between competing cultural groups. Rather than the usual Caucasian versus ethnic group construction, he focuses on two minority communities and compares their social and economic experiences. Taylor assesses how the impact of a dominant white society influenced work, education, and perspective for African-American and Japanese-American citizens. Carl Abbott, whose writings have won many awards, is professor of urban studies and planning at Portland State University. His essay looks to the future of the West and explains how the major challenge for westerners will be to "think urban." What ideas developed in Abbott's essay also might be applied to Taylor's study?

Blacks and Asians in a White City

QUINTARD TAYLOR

In 1909, against a backdrop of rising racial tension in Seattle, a Japanese restaurant that previously accepted black customers refused service to city residents Powell and Katherine Barnett. Powell Barnett described the incident in an interview thirty years later: "We went into this place and were told that management had changed their [sic] policy and we couldn't be served because we were colored. I never went back." Edward Pitter, however, recalled an episode at another downtown Japanese restaurant in 1930 when a white patron came in and demanded, "[G]et these negroes out." The owner promptly responded, "These my people, you get out." These two widely disparate accounts of Japanese-black interaction reflect the complexity of understanding race relations where multiple racial groups find themselves sharing urban neighborhoods. . . .

In Seattle, the Japanese constituted the city's largest racial minority until World War II and competed with African Americans for employment and housing. Moreover, the virulent racism usually directed against blacks in eastern urban communities was diffused in Seattle among the Japanese, Chinese, Filipinos, and African Americans.

White residents subjected Seattle's African Americans and Japanese to discrimination. Early twentieth-century Japanese were singled out because they allegedly acted as clannish foreigners who resisted assimilation while competing successfully with white produce merchants and farmers. Blacks, considered unmotivated, uneducated workers, given to sexual promiscuity and pretensions to social equality with whites, faced their own set of slurs.

Though other Americans had specific rationalizations for ostracizing each group, African Americans and Japanese Americans experienced strikingly similar treatment. Public accommodations in the city either excluded them or made the rare Japanese or black patron uncomfortable. Both groups were barred from union participation and, thus, in the first decades of the twentieth century, saw their opportunities in manufacturing decline concomitantly with the rising political power and economic influence of the city's white unions. And, as with blacks, Japanese college graduates were denied employment commensurate with their educations. . . .

If Seattle's Japanese Americans and African Americans recognized the similarity of discrimination against them, each group responded to its social status in ways reflective of its particular culture, history, and perception of

Quintard Taylor, "Blacks and Asians in a White City: Japanese Americans and African Americans in Seattle, 1890–1940," *Western Historical Quarterly,* 22 (November, 1991), 401–29. Copyright by Western History Association. Reprinted by permission.

destiny in America. . . . Each group arrived in the city with differing expectations and definitions of success and moved on trajectories that would end in distinct destinations. Moreover, each community held contrasting ideas of the appropriate responses to discrimination. African Americans voiced concern for economic opportunity and the end of formal discrimination—the "campaign for human dignity," to use the typical NAACP characterization during the interwar years. Japanese Americans, while aware of discrimination and its impact on their economic progress, chose to wage their campaign for human dignity with entrepreneurial success and stellar academic achievement, and repudiated the confrontational tactics associated with African American civil rights organizations. . . .

Prior to 1890, black Seattleites lived throughout the city. But the spectacular growth of the city between 1880 and 1900, when its population leaped from 3,533 to 80,671, fueled economic segregation. Before 1880, rich and poor shared the same neighborhoods. But, as city officials annexed surrounding suburbs as soon as city transportation became available, wealthy and middle-class residents relocated in the hills, while the poor of all races remained behind in the flatlands that hugged the harbor. This growing economic segregation fostered two black residential concentrations; the Yesler-Jackson, a working class, transient area just south of downtown, bordering the city's Chinatown; and the East Madison Street area, the hilly, heavily forested section on the northeastern edge of the city that soon was to be the home of Seattle's small, upwardly mobile African American population.

Yesler-Jackson, initially a residential area of Victorian homes, had become, by 1890, a neighborhood of "third class" hotels, lodging houses, saloons, and shops that catered to Seattle's sailors, loggers, and railroad workers. The low rents and proximity to the railroad station and downtown hotels attracted single black males—railroad porters, cooks, and waiters. . . .

Middle-class blacks found homes in East Madison, an area on the city's northeastern fringe similar to nearby white, street-car suburbs such as Rainier Heights or Madison Park. . . . East Madison remained an underdeveloped, heavily wooded area outside the city limits, until the Madison Street cable car line extended east to Lake Washington in 1889. With public transportation available, the area attracted black professionals, business-owners, and skilled artisans. . . .

Both Yesler-Jackson and East Madison generated distinct images that, regardless of their accuracy, most Seattle residents held until well into the twentieth century. Yesler-Jackson, the larger of the two, emerged as impoverished, squalid, yet risque, while East Madison quickly evolved into a bastion of middle-class conformity. Although few people discerned it at the time, these two different neighborhoods expanded toward each other and ultimately merged in the Central District, Seattle's twentieth-century African American community. . . .

The first Japanese immigrants, or Issei—as they called themselves, arrived as unskilled laborers in Seattle in 1883. They were, according to Japanese historian Yasuo Wakatsuki, "uncomplicated farm boys . . . younger

SALE
07-07-06 11:15
REG#12 TRAN#8554 CSHR#460

AMERICAN LEGAL HISTORY
978019516225   47.95
U MAJOR PROB IN THE HIST
978066941580+7   34.15

SUBTOTAL	$82.10
TAX 7.000%	5.75
TOTAL	87.85
Visa	87.85

ACCOUNT # XXXXXXXXXXXX2679
NAME : LAMBERT CHRISTOPHER
EXPIRATION DATE: 03/08
APPROVAL CODE: 01583
CHANGE DUE $0.00

sons with no prospect of inheriting land." Like the blacks who preceded them by two decades, the Issei were lured by high wages. Japanese railway workers in the Pacific Northwest could earn seven times their average salary in Japan, farmhands four times, and domestic servants, nearly twenty-three times their wages at home. . . .

The Japanese population grew slowly until the 1880s, when anti-Chinese agitation culminated in Seattle's only nineteenth-century race riot (1886) and the forcible removal of the Chinese population in the city. The following year, approximately two hundred Japanese men, viewed for the moment as an acceptable alternative to Chinese labor, arrived from San Francisco to work in the canneries and logging camps in western Washington Territory. . . .

The demand in Seattle for Japanese unskilled labor remained high most of the first decade of the twentieth century, and the city's Japanese population tripled. In 1910, the Japanese were the fifth largest (pop. 6,127) ethnic group in Seattle, following Canadians, Swedes, Norwegians, and Germans. This population, unlike the smaller black community, could support extensive community institutional development. By 1916, the community had five Japanese language newspapers, the largest, *Hokubei Jiji,* with a circulation of 7,000, was distributed throughout Washington. The community also sustained ten churches and a variety of social and civic clubs. . . .

The Nihonmachi and African American communities of Seattle entered their fourth decade in the early 1920s. Each community had developed an array of social, economic, and cultural organizations and institutions. newspapers, churches, clubs. Moreover, each community sought to advance its economic and political interests in manners consistent with its respective history and culture. If the communities were moving along different trajectories, a comparison of particular features of these two communities may account for the growing divergence between them. Three features—entrepreneurial activity, the campaign for civil rights, and community attitudes toward education should prove insightful for analysis of the then existing populations and as an indication of future trends.

Of the three features of community that account for divergent action, the most easily comparable is entrepreneurial activity. . . . A cursory examination of the statistics for business development in the two communities indicates a commanding advantage for the Japanese during the entire 1900 to 1940 period. In 1916, for example, the Nihonmachi had three banks, ninety-five hotels, eighty restaurants, eighty-one fruit and grocery stores, forty-seven clothing stores, three movie theaters, fifteen hospitals and clinics, and seven drugstores. The small, but growing, number of Japanese entrepreneurs served a predominantly white clientele. Nearly half of the restaurants were "western," meaning their patrons were largely non-Japanese. By 1935, despite the Great Depression, 183 hotels, 148 grocers, 39 "American" restaurants, and 24 Japanese restaurants operated in Seattle's Nihonmachi. According to the 1930 census, 898 Japanese businesses in Seattle averaged $26,600 in annual income and employed 2,304 people, eighty-four percent of whom were Japanese and thirty-eight percent of whom were members of the proprietors' families. . . . Seattle's Japanese immigrants were more entrepreneurially oriented than the Chinese, the blacks, or for that matter, other West Coast Japanese.

Japanese entrepreneurial success could be traced to two sources, the *tanomoshi,* a collective fund supported by individual merchants that provided venture capital for additional Japanese businesses, as well as a sizable regional population. Seattle's Japanese merchant associations, usually composed of immigrants from the same prefecture, established this collective fund, which served as a rotating credit system. Monies collected from regular assessments of the members provided venture capital for newer businesses, freeing Japanese businesses from relying on white banking institutions for their initial capital.

But the success of the sizable Japanese population in Seattle can also be attributed to economic links with the Japanese in the rural areas of western Washington. By 1920, Seattle's Nihonmachi, with 7,800 residents, was the second largest Japanese community in America. Augmented by another 2,700 in surrounding King County and 2,000 in neighboring Pierce County (Tacoma), that population numbered nearly 13,000. Moreover, Seattle, along with Los Angeles and San Francisco, was the site of American branches of Japanese banks and trading companies such as the Sumitomo Bank. By 1930, twelve such foreign-based firms employed 167 persons. The symbiotic relationship between the rural and urban populations is best seen in Seattle's Japanese green grocers' links with nearby Japanese truck farmers, who controlled 16,000 acres in western Washington, and in the hiring preferences of Japanese firms in the United States for Japanese immigrants. This rural-urban bond allowed the Japanese an economic independence and prosperity far greater than any found in Seattle's black community.

Historian Ronald Takaki . . . offers an additional reason—racial discrimination. Racist employers denied work to the Japanese in the manufacturing economy and in the emerging consumer-culture dominated by large department stores and neighborhood supermarkets. Consequently, the Issei were pushed into small-scale entrepreneurial activity and turned to self-employment and the employment of other Japanese to insure community survival.

The Immigration Act of 1924 ended Japanese emigration to the United States. With no new immigrant members, Seattle's Nihonmachi population stabilized by the end of the 1920s and began to decline in the 1930s. The earlier spectacular growth of the Japanese business community was curtailed by the drop in population coupled with the effects of the Great Depression. Nevertheless, despite state and federal laws that prevented the Issei from owning land or voting, and employers that excluded many skilled and unskilled Japanese laborers from the city's industrial occupations and Japanese college graduates from commercial enterprises outside the Nihonmachi, the community, during the interwar years, established an enviable record of economic success and helped to "reinvent" the image of the Japanese.

If Japanese workers increasingly became business owners and, in the process, began serving a growing number of non-Japanese, the city's African American business community appeared headed on the opposite course. Many nineteenth century Seattle blacks had been entrepreneurs— barbers, restauranteurs, boarding house owners and shopkeepers, serving a predominately white, male clientele. Establishing a barbering business or a restaurant in frontier Seattle required little capital and, occasionally, produced a handsome living for African Americans. . . .

But, as the frontier town gave way to a rising metropolis, both the clientele and the locations of black businesses evolved with the African American community, which operated on the periphery of the city's rapidly growing economy. Consequently, nineteenth-century notions of serving "all people," which typically meant an overwhelmingly white clientele, now capitulated to twentieth-century realities that directed black businesses to service, predominantly, black customers.

Though few in number in comparison to Japanese American enterprises, Seattle's early twentieth-century "race" businesses encompassed a diverse spectrum. Most of the businesses were, predictably, barber shops, beauty parlors, pool halls, and grocery stores. Occasionally, local entrepreneurs entered uncharted ground. Black Seattle counted among its enterprises the Anzier Movie Theater, the sixty-one room Golden West Hotel, which touted itself as the finest "colored" hostel west of Chicago, and the Lincoln Discount Corporation, a local finance company that, in 1931, was successful enough to absorb the Central Washington Finance Holding Corporation of Wenatchee, Washington. . . . Attucks Realty, owned by local dentist Dr. Felix B. Cooper, the North American Produce Company, and the most ambitious African American enterprise in the city, N. J. Graffell's Liberian-West African Transportation and Trading Corporation, founded in 1927, all suggested the range of black business possibilities.

The *Seattle Northwest Enterprise,* founded in 1920 by William H. Wilson, was the most widely known black business, and arguably, the most successful. Capitalizing on the isolation of small African American communities throughout the Pacific Northwest, Wilson targeted the *Enterprise* beyond black Seattle to the regional market. Shrewdly utilizing a network of correspondents, who reported social affairs in small black communities in such diverse cities as Billings, Montana; Pocatello, Idaho; and Eugene, Oregon; the *Enterprise* developed a regional circulation that, by March 1927, reached 25,000.

Despite these successes, local African American leaders recognized that black Seattle's economy was underdeveloped and urged blacks to become entrepreneurs. In November 1933, the *Northwest Enterprise* gave extensive coverage to a presentation by Urban League Executive Secretary Joseph S. Jackson titled "Black Money in a White City," in which he reported that local blacks spent $2,000,000 in Seattle annually. He went on to say that virtually all of this money was draining out of the black community because of the absence of black businesses. Rev. H. B. Ganntt, of the First AME Church, sounding a theme that would be increasingly supported, at least among middle-class blacks, for the remainder of the decade, declared, "Negroes should support and patronize their professionals and businessmen even at some sacrifice."

Nowhere was the contrast between black Seattle and Japanese Seattle more apparent than in their business communities. Although Japanese Seattle, in 1930, had a population of 8,448, opposed to 3,303 in black Seattle, the 1930 census listed 402 Asian male, (primarily Japanese) retail store owners in Seattle as opposed to fifteen black male store owners; 150 male Asian hotel owners and managers (thirty-six percent of the city-wide total), compared with one African American in that category; and seventy-three male Asian restaurant owners, and only six black male restaurant owners.

This palpable lack of success of African American businessmen and women, compared with their Japanese counterparts in Seattle, is often explained by describing the industry, honesty, and frugality of the Japanese. While such attributes are critical in entrepreneurial success, it may be profitable to recall the particular difficulty African Americans had in developing their business expertise. Black Seattle was not Chicago's South Side, New York's Harlem, or Seattle's Nihonmachi. Its firms did not develop a rotating credit system to provide venture capital for new enterprises as did the Japanese, nor could such businessmen and women rely on bank loans or a "captive market" generated by a large local residentially-segregated African American population. And, unlike the Japanese, blacks had long been immersed in American culture and, thus, had far fewer food or clothing requirements that necessitated specialized restaurants or stores. Moreover, if the owners of white restaurants, hotels, and movie theaters shunned black patronage, the Asian entrepreneurs welcomed it. Japanese grocers provided food, hotel owners offered rooms at affordable prices, southside Japanese restaurants welcomed working class black customers when other establishments turned them away, and one cafe near the railroad depot developed a menu of "soul food" to entice porters and ship stewards. Thus, despite often self-serving exhortations to "support the race," from groups such as the Seattle Negro Business League and the Seattle Association of Professional Men, black Seattle never developed a major commercial community. . . .

As other groups enhanced their range of opportunity, black occupational mobility continued to be restricted by educational limitations and ongoing employer discrimination. . . .

Black Seattle's employment dilemma and economic underdevelopment were prompted by a common source: the exclusion of African Americans from the vital center of the local economy. The words of the first Seattle Urban League Annual Report in 1930 were just as telling in 1920, or, for that matter, on the eve of World War II. After seven decades in Seattle, the African American was still prevented from going "forward in the industrial economy of [the] city." And "his home and family life . . . his health, and his education" were compromised accordingly.

If many Japanese chose self-employment over paid labor or, as Ronald Takaki has suggested, were forced into entrepreneurship, then Seattle blacks just as certainly chose militant protest and confrontational tactics over the ameliorative approach of the city's Japanese citizens. The objectives and tactics of the two leading civil rights organizations for the respective communities, the National Association for the Advancement of Colored People (NAACP) and the Japanese American Citizen's League (JACL) illustrate the contrasting political agendas of Seattle's largest non-white communities.

The Seattle branch of the NAACP, founded in 1913, reflected a legacy of protest that extended to the 1890s, when black Seattleites, numbering slightly more than 400, founded branches of two national civil rights organizations, the Afro-American League and the Afro-American Council, to challenge national and local discrimination. Following that tradition, the Seattle NAACP emerged from the efforts of Letitia A. Graves, a beautician, to protest President Woodrow Wilson's newly instituted policy of segregating black federal employees. Formed only three years after the national association was established in New York, the Seattle NAACP was one of the earliest branches west of the Mississippi River.

Once established, the Seattle NAACP embarked on a number of fronts. Between 1914 and 1919, it staged protest marches, filed lawsuits, and sponsored celebrations of Emancipation Day and Lincoln's birthday. In 1915, the NAACP confronted theater owners who planned to show the anti-black, *Birth of a Nation*. Although initially unsuccessful, the chapter persisted in its efforts and, finally, in 1921, persuaded the city council to order the chief of police to ban the film.

In the 1920s, the NAACP, plagued by a small membership and irregular participation, nevertheless protested selected instances of discrimination or offered aid and relief to other African Americans. In 1921, for example, the Seattle branch persuaded the state legislature to table an anti-intermarriage bill; in 1927, it organized relief for Mississippi River flood victims and two years later forced a public apology from the *Seattle Post-Intelligencer* for publishing a racially-offensive story on a community-sponsored health clinic.

During the 1930s, however, the NAACP, challenged by radical groups such as the Communist-backed League of Struggle for Negro Rights, and buoyed by a core of politically astute activist members led by Lodie M. Biggs, the city's only black bacteriologist; William H. Wilson, editor of the *Northwest Enterprise;* and Clarence Anderson, an attorney, emerged to play a crucial role in protecting community interests. The NAACP, again, blocked anti-intermarriage bills introduced in the state legislature in 1935 and 1937, and the following year it led a successful campaign to indict three white police officers in a police brutality case involving the death of black Seattle hotel waiter, Berry Lawson. Moreover, the Seattle NAACP protested dozens of individual cases of employment discrimination and racial harassment that, in earlier decades, would have gone unnoticed. . . .

Just as the NAACP was a largely middle-class organization in Seattle, the JACL evolved from the efforts of the city's increasingly well-educated and affluent second generation Japanese Americans. By 1930, the Nisei— as the second generation (those born in the United States) were called—had become a slight majority within Seattle's Nihonmachi and comprised forty-nine percent of Japanese America. Although respectful of the values and traditions of their parents, and of the Imperial Japan revered by their elders, the second generation felt an equally compelling loyalty to the land of their birth. Two prominent Seattle Nisei, newspaper editor James Sakamoto and attorney Clarence Arai, were founding members of the JACL. Sakamoto, who, in 1928, started the *Japanese American Courier,* the city's first English language Japanese weekly newspaper, recognized the dilemma of the Nisei. . . . Addressing those of his generation who remained culturally adrift between the land of their birth and the homeland of their parents, Sakamoto urged an unambiguous embracing of American culture and citizenship. "It is high time," he told them in unequivocal terms, "to lower the anchor." To that end, Sakamoto, Arai, and other West Coast Japanese community leaders founded the JACL to defend their rights as American citizens. Between 1930 and 1940, the JACL expanded from eight charter affiliates to fifty chapters, with nearly six thousand members. Composed primarily of Nisei professionals and businessmen, its self-defined role was to educate the larger society about Japanese Americans, while reminding the second generation of their commitment to America.

Sakamoto and other JACL leaders charted a course in contra-distinction to the militancy of the Seattle NAACP. "Agitation begets agitation," declared Sakamoto, "and this can never lead to the best results." While acknowledging the existence of discrimination in employment, Saburo Kido, another founder writing in the *Nikkei Shimin,* the newspaper of the JACL, urged the Nisei not to complain. "In technical or commercial vocations, we cannot afford to work with talents inferior to Americans. It is not enough even to be their equals; we must surpass them—by developing our powers to the point of genius if necessary. . . . Complaints against race prejudice . . . are not justified. They only show that something is lacking in the initiative or ability of the one who complains." . . .

The radically differing approaches to the question of civil rights in Seattle rested not, as is often suggested, on the distinctive "cultures" of African Americans and Japanese Americans, as much as on the approaches of specific community leaders. Indeed, Japanese community leaders in Hawaii, as Ronald Takaki reminds us, were heir to a long tradition of confrontational politics not unlike the approach of Seattle's African Americans. Seattle's black leadership—William H. Wilson, Lodie Biggs, and Clarence Anderson, among others—operated in a protest style common to middle-class blacks throughout the nation. Moreover, they were spurred by local African Americans associated with Marcus Garvey's Universal Negro Improvement Association in the 1920s and the Communist Party in the 1930s. Seattle's Japanese leadership did not have a comparable challenge. Indeed, James Sakamoto, the most prominent local Nisei leader, struck a pose similar to Booker T. Washington a generation earlier and reflected the thinking of a significant section of Nihonmachi community leadership when he stressed accommodation to the racial status quo, educational advancement, and economic self-sufficiency. Sakamoto, according to his biogra-

pher, Mayumi Tsutakawa, seldom defended Nisei or Issei rights or challenged Asiaphobes who called for Japanese exclusion. The Japanese, he
said, should "stay within their own community, support small businesses
within their area and emulate the patriotism of white America."

Moreover, the economic success of the Japanese seems to have precluded assertiveness in the face of discrimination. Japanese restaurants and
green grocers, dependent upon white patronage, were unwilling to be
involved in public challenges that might alienate their clientele. Black
workers, by necessity, sought such acts to expand their employment opportunities. Of course, direct black competition with white labor engendered
corresponding hostility.

. . . Not unexpectedly, education became a central issue for both groups,
in vastly differing ways. Remembering the inferior education that was the
lot of most southern blacks, and stressing education and family cohesion as
prerequisites for racial progress, black Seattleites gave the education of
their children top priority. . . .

Southern migrants to Seattle, like their counterparts throughout the
urban North, recognized the greater educational opportunity offered in the
city. Parents encouraged school attendance in the early grades and city
school officials made no effort to segregate or isolate black pupils. Still,
regular school attendance in the early years did not automatically translate
into high school or college graduation. In 1940, blacks completed 8.4 years
of school, slightly ahead of the immigrant rate, but well below the city average of 10.8 years. Only 2.7 percent of the blacks completed college while
the city average was 8.3 percent. Conversely, sixteen percent of the black
population completed less than five years of schooling, a percentage far
higher than the city-wide average of 4.8 percent.

The high percentage of African Americans completing fewer than five
years of schooling obviously reflects the deficient education of many southern migrants, but the high rate of school attendance in the early grades compared with the small number of high school and college graduates, is more
problematic. Why were so many black children, given their parents' regard
for formal training apt to leave school before graduation? Some apparently
dropped out to supplement parents' meager incomes, others to establish
independent households. The depression forced large numbers of African
Americans, and in fact all groups, into the work force at younger ages. But
perceived opportunity and pervasive discrimination also induced many
black teenagers into the labor pool earlier than other groups. . . . They realized that education alone would not guarantee access to professional careers
or more lucrative occupations; it would, in fact, interfere with wage earning
during their younger, more productive years. . . .

Even well-educated, solidly middle-class black parents were unable to
pass their educational advantages on to their children. Madge Cayton,
daughter of Seattle's most prominent black couple and granddaughter of a
former U.S. Senator, graduated from the University of Washington in 1925
with a baccalaureate degree in international business. Nevertheless, she
could not find a job outside the black community unless she chose to "pass"

(for white). Refusing that option, she became a waitress and cashier in small restaurants in the black community, before moving to Chicago in 1935 to become a social worker. Maxine Pollard, daughter of Dr. Charles Maxwell, black Seattle's most prominent physician in the 1930s, chose not to enter college because she feared she could not get a position on a par with her education. . . . Pollard remained in Seattle and worked as a maid and stock-clerk through World War II.

A comparison of the educational achievements of Seattle's blacks and that of its Japanese is revealing. Because they shared the Yesler-Jackson residential neighborhood, both groups attended the same schools. As physically distinct minority groups, both Japanese and black students often encountered social ostracism, particularly in junior high and high school. And like black students, Japanese college graduates faced pervasive discrimination that barred them from virtually all positions appropriate to their level of education. The first Japanese American graduate of the University of Oregon Law School, for example, could find employment only with a Japanese consulate. A Nisei essayist's lament in 1937 that while he "would much rather [be] a doctor or lawyer" but instead had been forced to be a "professional carrot-washer," expressed the profound sense of grievance of all non-whites hindered by restricted opportunities.

Nevertheless, the Japanese community, which was about twice the size of the African American community in the 1930s, generated during the decade ten times more University of Washington students than the black community. Even taking into consideration the black Seattle students who matriculated at southern black colleges, it was clear that the Japanese were far more likely to attend college.

The primary reason for the differing rates was the relative affluence of each community. Seattle's *Nihonmachi,* with its much larger middle class supported by ethnically oriented businesses, could absorb far more Japanese college graduates than black Seattle could, or, for that matter, than could the city's Chinese or Filipino communities. Nisei graduates bitterly complained of their constrained opportunities. Nonetheless, employment prospects in an increasingly middle-class, business-oriented Japanese community, with a growing demand for the services of doctors, lawyers, and accountants, provided Japanese graduates with a significant advantage over the impoverished black population of working-class people. A comparison of the level of financial support for education is indicative of the relative affluence of the two communities. While black Seattle was proud of its $100 scholarships given during the 1930s, Seattle's Nihonmachi, as early as 1920, offered to contribute $10,000 toward the construction of a public school in its neighborhood. . . .

The important differences in educational emphasis and attainment that surfaced in black and Japanese Seattle in the 1920s and 1930s stemmed not so much from the background of the parents, although the better schooled parents could provide arguments for education based on intrinsic and economic reasons, as from the divergent rewards of education in a city that widely and routinely practiced racial discrimination. This reality persuaded many black students not to stay in school. Such a choice, no matter how rational in the context of the era, however, did not augur well for the future of black Seattle. The larger number of Japanese college graduates, while not substantially altering white attitudes in the 1920s and 1930s, nevertheless positioned this Asian group to advance rapidly once barriers to employment were dismantled after World War II. Thus, choices made by Seattle African Americans in the 1930s, rational given the contemporary circumstances in the 1930s, insured that neither they nor their children would be similarly positioned in the 1960s to take advantage of falling barriers.

Early twentieth-century Japanese and African Americans forged tentative links across a broad cultural divide. Throughout the interwar years, black, Asian, and white groups invited their counterparts to share aspects of their culture or discuss common problems. Typical of such gatherings was the May 1932 meeting of the Aeolian Society, a Japanese American club created to stimulate interest in classical music. The group invited Idel Vertner, secretary of the Phyllis Wheatley YWCA, to lecture on Negro spirituals and to give renditions of "Deep River" and "Go Down Moses." William H. Wilson's 1932 presentation to the University of Washington Interracial Society, where he challenged his listeners to support intermarriage and full social equality for blacks, was another example of attempts at multi-racial understanding. In 1941, six months before the attack on Pearl Harbor, representatives of the Jewish, Japanese, and black communities spoke on the contributions of their groups to Seattle and to the United States at a symposium on interracial justice sponsored by a Catholic community center near Jackson Street. Additionally, inter-ethnic athletic contests, such as the highly publicized 1928 meeting of the Japanese Girls' Club all-star basketball team with a black all-star team, provided regular contact in an informal setting.

The Japanese evacuation from Seattle in 1942 tested the prejudices of all Seattleites, including African Americans. The *Northwest Enterprise,* in 1941, became one of the few Seattle newspapers to oppose the evacuation of the Japanese from the West Coast. "Don't lose your head and commit crimes in the name of patriotism," warned the paper in a front page editorial five days after the attack on Pearl Harbor. "As treacherous as was this unheralded attack on our country, it should bring no reprisals [on] innocent Japanese citizens on our shores. The same mob spirit which would single them out for slaughter, has trailed you through the forest to string you up at some crossroad. The Japanese are not responsible for this war. They certainly are good citizens. . . ."

The words of the *Northwest Enterprise* were echoed by the actions of some African Americans. Thomas Bodine, a Society of Friends interpreter who assisted the Japanese in their relocation, described an unnamed black man who drove a Japanese family to the train scheduled to take them to a relocation center. The man helped the family unload and then stood with them on the sidewalk, waiting for the boarding order for their designated car. He said to the Japanese woman, "You know that if there's ever anything I can do for you whether it be something big or something small, I'm here to do it." He then turned to the husband and said, "Goodbye now and good luck." Finally, he got on his knees and embraced the three children.

We know far less of what the Japanese thought of African Americans, but some information is suggestive. While intent on establishing their colonial empire in Asia, Japanese nationalists portrayed themselves as defenders of "colored" peoples. In that context, local Seattle Japanese expressed sympathy for the plight of Seattle's blacks. In a 1921 U.S. Naval Intelligence report of Japanese links with West Coast branches of the Universal Negro Improvement Association, the black nationalist organization founded by Marcus Garvey, one government informant described an unsuccessful attempt by Japanese nationalists and UNIA members in Seattle to create a "Colored Peoples' Union" inclusive of all "except the whites or Teutonic races."

There is little evidence, however, of any organizational links between African American and Asian American groups after the decline of Seattle's UNIA branches in the late 1920s. James Sakamoto's *Japanese American Courier* occasionally denounced attempts to restrict interracial marriage, and his paper refrained from the negative stereotyping and derogatory cartooning that often appeared on the pages of the major daily Seattle newspapers, but the *Courier* rarely commented on discrimination against blacks and other minorities. . . .

Did the Japanese discriminate against blacks? The evidence is mixed. Black Seattleites, Gertrude Simons and Muriel Pollard, remember the Japanese restaurants as less discriminatory than white establishments. Gertrude Simons specifically described the welcome extended to black porters and ship stewards by Asian restauranteurs and landlords. "The one thing I can say for them . . . the ones that had the hotels down around Jackson Street, you can always find a place to live." One restaurant near the railroad station that had an overwhelmingly black clientele of railroad workers, served, according to Muriel Pollard, "soul food." Yet, Edward Pitter, a ship's steward in the 1930s, remembers the disturbing paradox of entering restaurants during his visits to Japan, while being denied entry into Japanese American establishments in Seattle. No blacks would be served in Seattle, according to Pitter, if whites were eating there. Perhaps the Japanese, mindful of their dependence on white patronage, chose, like nineteenth century black Seattle barbers, to exclude African Americans, because they feared unsettling white sensibilities on race. Occasionally, however, as the Pitter account cited at the beginning of this article indicates, a rare restauranteur challenged that view.

Fragmentary evidence from varied sources indicates that Japanese Americans and their African American neighborhood were tolerant, if not understanding of each other. Irene Burns Miller and Juanita Proctor describe rare interracial marriages between black men and Japanese women, although Proctor's account indicates the Japanese community disowned the women involved. But the daughter of a reporter for the Japanese-language newspaper, recalling her racially and ethnically integrated neighborhood of "Negroes, Yugoslavians, and other Caucasians, as well as the Japanese," said, "we never did think about race. I guess Seattle was more or less a melting pot. We all got on well together."

Asian-black rivalry, however, was evident in Seattle, particularly in employment and housing. When Bernard E. Squires, the new executive director of the Seattle Urban League arrived in the city in 1939, he and his wife, Melvina, were surprised to find Japanese redcaps at the train station and Japanese bellboys in their hotel, two occupations traditionally identified with African Americans. Because Japanese Americans were excluded from industrial jobs, they competed with Seattle blacks for positions as hotel and railroad porters, janitors, houseboys, and maids. The Japanese, however, had advantages over black migrants in this employment competition; they arrived in Seattle in large numbers earlier, they could rely on kinship networks to obtain jobs, and Seattle's white residents were more familiar with the Japanese than with blacks as servants.

Those Japanese Americans and African Americans who attempted to bridge the wide cultural chasm between their respective groups often met with skepticism, indifference, or occasionally, open opposition from their ethnic and racial kinspeople. Yet, the difficulty of such attempts rested, not with internal opposition, language barriers, or a failure of cultural understanding—although all of these forces had some bearing on the continued divisions—but with the vastly differing aspirations that propelled these groups along separate routes.

By World War II, Seattle's Japanese American and African American communities had moved further apart physically and emotionally. Seattle's Nihonmachi disappeared from 1942 to 1945; its residents evacuated to internment camps in the interior West. The wartime disruption of the community, coupled—ironically—with a dramatic lowering of anti-Japanese enmity after World War II, prevented the reestablishment of the spatial community. Post-war Japanese Seattle, far more middle-class and well-educated than black Seattle, was, fortunately, poised to exploit the liberalizing attitudes.

Black Seattle also underwent profound change. The huge wartime migration to the city quadrupled the pre-war population and made African Americans indisputably the largest minority, a distinction they held until 1990, when Asians, augmented by continued Chinese immigration and rising numbers of Vietnamese refugees, again overtook blacks. But from 1945 to the 1970s, the African American migration to Seattle generated an extensive ghetto that shared many characteristics with the rest of urban black America and that intensified white opposition to African American aspirations, at least through the 1960s.

Thus, internal forces in the Japanese American community, such as the impetus toward private commercial activity and educational achievement, and external forces, including the striking decline in anti-Japanese prejudice after World War II, converged to promote upward mobility in the Nihonmachi—at least for the young and well-educated. Although the rapid success and relatively easy integration of Japanese Americans is celebrated and frequently advanced as a "model" for other racial minorities to emulate, we would do well to remember the historical circumstances that provided the backdrop for their achievements. "The Issei," Roger Daniels reminds us, "were a small, self-confident group entering a fertile region with a rapidly expanding population. They came with almost all the skills and technological know-how necessary to reach the bottom rungs of the ladder of success. They brought with them the ethnic pride of a successfully emerging nation about to assume the leadership of a continent. They came at a unique time in the history of their two countries: their experience [and the Japanese America they created] cannot be repeated."

African American Seattle was to have a different history. Seattle blacks found it exceedingly difficult to generate entrepreneurial opportunities comparable to that of the Japanese in the 1920s and 1930s. And, growing racial tensions, sparked by the influx of black southerners during and immediately after World War II, propelled the African American community in a separate direction. This population growth culminated in a protracted civil disobedience campaign in the early 1960s and bloody racial confrontations in the city, as elsewhere in urban America, by the end of the decade. Truly, the two paths were different.

The Urban West and the Twenty-First Century

CARL ABBOTT

In 1964 Oregon novelist Ken Kesey published *Sometimes a Great Notion,* the impassioned story of a fiercely . . . independent family of loggers on the southern Oregon coast. The novel is much admired by Oregonians, who read it as a tribute to the vanishing American pioneer. The urban West appears only by implication in the form of a fumbling labor organizer who longs to return to the civilized cities of California.

In 1990 Thomas Pynchon's frantic and fantastic *Vineland* fictionalized the same territory. The story starts and ends in the environs of Eureka, California, in a complex landscape inhabited by timber workers, aging hippies, and pot farmers. In between, it stretches easily and instantly to San Francisco, Los Angeles, Las Vegas, Tokyo, and Washington, D.C. Like it or not, Pynchon's Vinelanders are firmly connected to the rationalized, bureaucratic society that radiates from the office towers of the contemporary city. The redwood country may still bear some superficial resemblance to a nineteenth-century frontier, but Pynchon knows that the region is a full participant in the new worlds of the 1990s.

The difference between Kesey's West and Pynchon's rejects the impacts of the "third urban revolution."

To explain my terminology, the "first urban revolution" involved the independent creation of cities in the Middle East, India, China, and Middle America between 5,000 and 2,500 years ago. Preindustrial cities differed

Carl Abbott, "The Urban West and the Twenty-First Century," *Montana: The Magazine of Western History,* 43 (Spring 1993), 62–68. Excerpted by permission of the Montana Historical Socie from rural villages by their concentration of non-agricultural occupations and their roles in organizing large-scale social and political systems. A handful of such communities appeared in the future American West during the "long eighteenth century" that stretched from the Spanish reconquest of New Mexico in 1692 to the colonization of the Northwest Coast in the years around 1810. Colonial Santa Fe, San Antonio, St. Louis, and Sitka represented the efforts of European officials to incorporate western North America into a system of mercantile capitalism centered on the North Atlantic.

If the era of preindustrial cities is measured in millennia, the effects of the "second urban revolution" were concentrated in the nineteenth and early twentieth centuries. The industrial city was "invented" in Manchester and London, imitated in France and Germany, and exported to the United States. Industrializing nations shifted from largely rural to substantially urban societies in the course of two generations. The rate of change peaked in Britain between 1800 and 1850, in Germany and the United States between 1850 and 1890, and in Japan between 1870 and 1920. The climax products of this second urban revolution were the manufacturing and commercial cities that crowded northern Europe, Japan, and parts of eastern North America at the opening of the twentieth century—Glasgow, Essen, Osaka, and Pittsburgh as well as London, Berlin, Paris, and New York. Industrial cities enlisted new territories and populations as suppliers of resources and markets for manufactured goods. The result was a global geography that Immanuel Wallerstein has termed the second world-system. The Atlantic core nations controlled the periphery through a greatly expanded network of colonial cities in Africa and Asia and quasi-colonial cities in the Americas. Bombay, Melbourne, Denver, and San Francisco all facilitated the entrance of European capital, organized access to regional markets, and funneled regional products to factory cities on both sides of the North Atlantic.

. . . Western settlement and organization spread outward from the key cities of San Francisco and Denver and their ancillary centers of Portland, Los Angeles, Salt Lake City, and Santa Fe between the 1840s and 1870s. As railroad builders added more links to the western transportation system in the 1880s and 1890s, isolated metropolitan regions merged into the national hierarchy of cities focused on New York and Chicago. At the climax of the industrial era in the 1920s, economist N. S. B. Gras and sociologist Robert Park could both summarize the West as a collection of a dozen metropolitan regions that connected farming market centers and mining towns to the national capitals of commerce.

The last half century has brought a third global restructuring of urban form and functions, with Mexico City and Los Angeles replacing Manchester and Chicago as the symbols of the era. New technologies and institutions of communication have brought people into a single marketplace for ideas as well as goods, driving a further integration and elaboration of the global system of cities. One obvious consequence has been the explosive urbanization of the southern two-thirds of the globe, whose urban population will quadruple between 1960 and the end of the century.

In the developed world, the ongoing revolution in urban technology is bringing a new balance of centralization and decentralization. Commuting zones of individual cities may now reach more than a hundred miles from the city center. Changes in trade, financial systems, and travel have vastly extended multilateral ties within and across national systems of cities. Within the American West, urban-regional growth has responded to the reinternationalization of the American economy, the global shift toward services (especially those involved in the leisure economy of recreation and retirement), and the expansion of the science-based garrison state. In the world under creation by the third urban revolution, prosperous cities are increasingly specialized players in a global economy, whether they are Brussels or Barcelona, Honolulu or Houston, San Diego or Seattle.

With this context, I want to project the urban West of the later twentieth century into the twenty-first century. In a ten-second sound bite, my argument is that *what we see is what we're going to get.* That is, the coming decades are likely to see the American West continue to work through the impacts of the third urban revolution. It will be no more possible to re-create the world of Hank Stamper and the loggers of the Wakonda Auga watershed than the worlds of William Bent or Juan de Oñate. In particular, I want to touch on four points:

1. the end of "urbanization" in the American West;
2. the consolidation of control functions in a handful of supercities;
3. the continued "urbanizing" of what used to be the western backcountry;
4. the policy-making environment of western cities.

(1) In the technical definition used by demographers, "urbanization" has essentially reached its end. In this useage, urbanization refers to the shift of national or regional population from rural to urban residence. As a measurable social indicator, urbanization theoretically ranges between 0 and 100 percent. Over the last two centuries, urbanization in every industrial nation has traced a logistic curve or "S" curve. A rapid upturn—the first bend or up-curve of the S—reflects the impacts of the second urban revolution. A leveling off—the second bend or down-curve of the S—has led highly developed societies to a stable urbanization level of roughly 80 percent.

In the United States, demographers usually measure the level of urbanization by the proportion of population living within the boundaries of metropolitan areas. The West as a whole (nineteen states) has shifted from 43 percent metropolitan in 1940 to 64 percent in 1960, 78 percent in 1980, and 80 percent in 1990.

The case is even more extreme in the eight states of the Far West—California and its historic satellites of Alaska, Washington, Oregon, Idaho, Nevada, Arizona, and Hawaii. The overall proportion of metropolitan population in these states has increased from 64 percent metropolitan in 1940 to 76 percent in 1960 and then to a plateau of 88 percent since 1970. This level of saturation urbanization equals that in the most developed nations of western Europe—the United Kingdom at 87 percent, the Netherlands at 89 percent, and Germany at 90 percent.

Absolute numbers of city and suburban residents, of course, can and will continue to grow, but the balance is unlikely to change. For every new resident of nonmetropolitan areas, there will be seven or eight new city people. Since 1970, in fact, the metropolitan population of the eight far western states has increased by nearly 12 million, while the nonmetropolitan population has increased by about 1.4 million for a ratio of 8.5 to 1.

(2) Within this profoundly urbanized West, we have every reason to expect the continued concentration of advanced services and nonroutine information industries in the handful of biggest metropolitan centers. Virtually every observer thinks that the rich get richer when it comes to headquarters activities, nonroutine finance, consulting, research, advanced education, and similar economic sectors. The advantages of agglomeration and propinquity attract the activities that produce and process nonroutine information, making a few favored locations even more attractive for more such activities. At the top of the global hierarchy are a handful of "world cities," perhaps including Los Angeles. Following are international gateways like San Francisco, Seattle, and Vancouver and specialized international cities like Honolulu.

These advanced service cities will be increasingly detached from their region and tied into national and international networks. Examples of income sources that transcend or bypass the regional context are many—international tourism in Honolulu, overseas trade through Los Angeles and Long Beach, federal research grants to Seattle universities and think tanks, international contracts for Boise and Corvallis engineering firms, supervision of multinational corporate business from San Francisco office towers.

The unpredictable element in this scenario will be the character and location of the sunrise industries of the fifth long wave in the world capitalist economy. The fifth Kondratieff cycle should begin its takeoff sometime in the late 1990s, following the twenty-year slump that began in 1974. We cannot be certain, however, which industries will drive the new wave of economic expansion—bioengineering? communications industries? personal leisure and entertainment industries? Nor do we know whether the West will be the preferred location for the early twenty-first-century equivalent of the aerospace and electronics industries.

(3) The uncertainties of industrial change aside, the West will continue to see metropolitan influence filter down the urban hierarchy and incorporate the sparsely settled West into the use zones of metropolitan areas.

Cost equilibrium factors will favor smaller cities over larger cities as locations for manufacturing assembly, back office data manipulation, and similar routine production activities. Within the Northwest, for example, Portland and the Willamette valley have proved an attractive location for electronics production and assembly plants. Spokane has benefited economically from the transfer of credit card and data processing activities by Seattle banks.

Beyond Portland industrial parks and Spokane offices, the third urban revolution will continue to erode the isolation of the rural West. The western backcountry of the nineteenth century has been embraced within urban recreation, commuting, and amenity zones in the later twentieth century.

This extraordinary penetration of the "empty" West by the urban West involves the appropriation of natural resources for new purposes—grazing land for garbage disposal and nuclear waste, forests for scenic preservation, farming districts for sources of water.

This process has been accelerating since the 1950s. It is likely to continue for at least two more decades as members of the "double-boomer" generation born between 1940 and 1965 reach their fifties and sixties. A few of the nonmetropolitan remnant of westerners will operate the remaining farms and ranches. Many more will tidy up motel rooms, tend ski lifts, build retirement dream homes for their metropolitan neighbors, and develop fax-based businesses serving metropolitan customers. In a sense, what I am describing is a double "insult" to the traditional western backcountry. It will be monopolized and subordinated to city uses through metropolitan political and economic influence, but it will be far less important than the wider world to the key cities of the West. The question is less how to preserve the fragments of the rural West than how to ease the transition from a resource economy.

(4) The last question is the possibility of leadership in public policy. In comparison with the urban East or South, the cities of the West are marked by institutional openness. In important ways, they still reflect the positive effects of the "frontier" as a challenge that demanded wide participation, voluntary association, and support for public institutions and government.

At the end of the twentieth century, the most promising future for the United States as a civil community may well be found in the middle-sized cities of the West. A pessimistic critic might plausibly argue that America's small towns retain a Tocquevillian consensus but lack the resources to carry out civic agendas or the willingness to accommodate new ideas. Many of our largest cities are deeply riven by ethnic divisions and chasms between rich and poor that have destroyed their ability to unite around a conception of the common good.

Instructive contrasts to deeply divided Philadelphia or Chicago are Portland and Seattle. Portland, says *The Economist,* is the city "where it works." The latter has been described by one enthusiast as "a paragon and an inspiration, testimony to what urban living could be like if cities were, like Seattle, moderately populated, surrounded by water, hemmed in by mountains, favored by a mild climate and watched over by a citizenry that knows how lucky it is." Over the past generation that watchful citizenry has taxed itself to clean up Lake Washington, to create a regional park system, and to anticipate the impacts of rapid growth. Voters have responded passionately if not always effectively to preserve a human-scale downtown and to maintain affordable housing. In part because of such civic commitment, metropolitan Seattle earned first place in rankings of general quality of life among American cities by Arthur Louis in 1975 and *Places Rated Almanac* in 1989. In between it has placed first, fifth, twelfth, first, and second in various specialized and comprehensive ratings. An *international* comparison of one hundred large metropolitan areas showed Seattle-Tacoma in a tie with Melbourne and Montreal as the best cities for average residents.

Apart from obvious advantages of climate, setting, and prosperity, what underlies the high rankings for western cities is a shared commitment to the public interest. The health, education, and social components of Ben-Chieh Liu's most thorough quality-of-life study (1976) measured such items as per capita investment in education and medical facilities, school enrollment, newspaper circulation, and the ratio of public library books to population. Overall, twenty-four of twenty-six far western metropolitan areas rated good or better on the health, education, and social components.

The civic culture of the West has also been receptive to women in positions of leadership. An obvious indicator has been the long list of women elected as mayors of major western cities in the last twenty years, including the chief executives of Phoenix, Santa Barbara, San Jose, San Francisco, Stockton, Modesto, Portland, and Spokane. Since western states took the lead in granting voting rights to women before the Nineteenth Amendment, it is also not surprising that women constituted at least 15 percent of state legislators in all but one far western state (California) at the end of the 1980s, compared with only fourteen of thirty-one eastern states.

The recent experience of cities such as San Jose, Sacramento, and Portland tends to confirm several hypotheses about the political empowerment of women in western cities. First, the cities of the postwar West have been communities filled with newcomers who lack ties and obligations to extended families, churches, and other community institutions. Women who have satisfied their responsibilities to nuclear families have been relatively free to devote time and energy to political activity. Second, the spreading suburbs of western cities have been "frontiers" that require concerted action to solve immediate functional and service needs like adequate schools and decent parks. Since pursuit of the residential amenity package has often been viewed as "woman's work" (in contrast to the "man's work" of economic development), burgeoning suburbs have offered numerous opportunities for women to engage in volunteer civic work, to build capacity as political activists, and finally to run for local office. Third, western cities have had weak political machines and parties. The alternative of personalized, nonparty politics is far more open to the influence of energetic women.

Women's participation in local politics has also drawn on their success in filling executive, professional, and managerial jobs. The relative hospitality of western cities can be measured by the high proportion of such jobs held by women. Among large metropolitan areas nationwide in 1980, the proportion ranged from 23 percent in Scranton to 38 percent in Washington, D.C. The West had only one metropolitan area under 30 percent, with especially strong opportunities in San Diego, San Francisco, San Jose, Sacramento, and Honolulu. Statewide census data show that the West is also receptive to women entrepreneurs as measured by the ratio of women-owned businesses to population.

One consequence of this openness to the full range of talents and ideas is that western cities as a group have strong records on issues of physical livability. Many of them have reinvested in mass transit systems. They also

have begun to give serious if not always effective attention to land use planning. We can expect growth management and open space preservation to
continue to dominate local political agendas into the new century.

To balance an optimistic evaluation of western cities as centers of policy innovation, however, it is necessary to remember that many of these
well-governed cities have small minority populations. Large cities such as
Portland and Seattle and smaller cities such as Billings and Boise have been
at the far ends of northward migration tracks from the rural South, the
Caribbean, and Latin America. As is also true in Minneapolis-St. Paul, it is
relatively easy to generate civic consensus in homogeneous communities.
During the war migrations of the 1940s, these cities were no better than any
others at dealing fairly with African American newcomers or Japanese
American exiles. Since 1980 many have had to face another rapid expansion
of Hispanic, Asian, and black populations. It remains to be seen whether
official welcomes for increased diversity manage to fend off the social divisions that threaten to paralyze many cities in all parts of the nation.

We can gain a clear idea of the spatial and demographic character of the
metropolitan West in the early twenty-first century if we understand the
trends of the last two decades. As the third urban revolution continues to
work itself through in the Far West, perhaps the biggest challenge for westerners will be to "think urban."

Tensions between urban realities and rural imagery are reflected in
western literature. Regional novelists choose their contemporary protago-
nists from ranchers, farmers, loggers, rodeo riders, and river rafters. Their
topics are Native Americans, nature, and life in the land of wind and storm.
Indeed, the importance of cities as inspiration for western writers is
obscured by the tendency to recognize as "western" only those artists who
deal with small towns and open landscapes. Wallace Stegner and Ivan Doig
are "western" writers but Maxine Hong Kingston is an ethnic or feminist
writer. Robert Stone, Joan Didion, and Thomas Pynchon are "mainstream."
Literary histories remember Walter Van Tilburg Clark's stories about nineteenth-century westerners far more often than his novel about twentieth-
century Reno.

The same contrast is summarized by the public response to two painters
who came to the Southwest as outsiders and remained to be captivated by
the clarity of southwestern light. Englishman David Hockney's reaction to
Los Angeles in the 1960s was a series of stunning depictions of lawn sprinklers, high-rise buildings, and swimming pools. The surfaces glare and stare
back at the viewer in the "Technicolor daylight" of California. The clear
light of New Mexico similarly drew easterner Georgia O'Keeffe to paint
and repaint the sun-bleached relics of the desert. The international art world
has recognized and applauded Hockney's urban and suburban imagery. The
middlebrow public in the United States has adopted O'Keeffe's traditionally regional subject as a national icon. As with literature, Americans prefer
to neglect the urban West and to admire what they know to be comfortably
western.

As these examples suggest, the myth of open spaces has proved extraordinarily persistent. One of our jobs as historians will be to interpret not

only the facts but the feel of the West as an *urbanized* region that is about
to enter a new century.

Y *F U R T H E R   R E A D I N G*

Carl Abbott, *The Metropolitan Frontier: Cities in the Modern American West*
(1993)
———, *The New Urban America: Growth and Politics in Sunbelt Cities* (1981)
———, "Regional City and Network City: Portland and Seattle in the Twentieth
Century," *Western Historical Quarterly* 23 (August 1992), 293–319
Diana Meyers Bahr, *From Mission to Metropolis: Cupeño Indian Women in Los
Angeles* (1993)
Gunther Barth, *Instant Cities: Urbanization and the Rise of San Francisco and
Denver* (1975)
David Brodsly, *L.A. Freeway: An Appreciative Essay* (1981)
Albert Broussard, *Black San Francisco: The Struggle for Racial Equality in the
West, 1900–1954* (1993)
William Cronon, *Nature's Metropolis: Chicago and the Great West* (1991)
Mike Davis, *City of Quartz: Excavating the Future in Los Angeles* (1992)
Robert B. Fairbanks and Kathleen Underwood, *Essays on Sunbelt Cities and Recent
Urban America* (1990)
John M. Findlay, *Magic Lands: Western Cityscapes and American Culture After
1940* (1992)
Robert M. Fogelson, *The Fragmented Metropolis: Los Angeles, 1850–1930* (1967)
Lionel Frost, *The New Urban Frontier: Urbanization and City-building in
Australasia and the American West* (1991)
Richard Griswold del Castillo, *The Los Angeles Barrio, 1850–1890: A Social
History* (1979)
David Hamer, *New Towns in the New World: Images and Perceptions of the
Nineteenth-Century Urban Frontier* (1990)
William Issel and Robert W. Cherney, *San Francisco, 1865–1923: Politics, Power,
and Urban Development* (1923)
Kenneth T. Jackson, *Crabgrass Frontier: The Suburbanization of the United States*
(1985)
Marilyn S. Johnson, *The Second Gold Rush: Oakland and East Bay in World War II*
(1993)
Wesley G. Johnson, Jr., *Phoenix in the Twentieth Century: Essays on Community
History* (1993)
Lawrence H. Larsen, *The Urban West at the End of the Frontier* (1978)
Mary Lou Locke, "Out of the Shadows and into the Western Sun: Working Women
of the Late Nineteenth-Century Urban Far West," *Journal of Urban History,* 16
(February 1990), 175–204
Roger W. Lotchin, *Fortress California: From Warfare to Welfare* (1992)
———, *The Martial Metropolis: U.S. Cities in War and Peace* (1984)
Bradford Luckingham, *Phoenix: The History of a Southwestern Metropolis* (1989)
———, *Minorities in Phoenix: A Profile of Mexican American, Chinese American,
and African American Communities, 1860–1992* (1994)
Delores Nason McBroome, *Parallel Communities: African Americans in
California's East Bay, 1850–1963* (1993)
Gerald D. Nash, *The American West in the 20th Century: A Short History of an
Urban Oasis* (1973)
Carol A. O'Connor, "A Region of Cities," in *The Oxford History of the American
West,* eds. Clyde A. Milner II, Carol A. O'Connor, and Martha A. Sandweiss
(1994)

John W. Reps, *The Forgotten Frontier: Urban Planning in the American West before 1890* (1981)

Joseph A. Rodriguez, "Ethnicity and the Horizontal City: Mexican Americans and the Chicano Movement in San Jose, California," *Journal of Urban History* 21 (July 1995), 597–620

Raphael J. Sonenshein, *Politics in Black and White: Race and Power in Los Angeles* (1993)

Arthur C. Verge, *Paradise Transformed: Los Angeles During the Second World War* (1993)

Richard C. Wade, *The Urban Frontier: The Rise of Western Cities, 1790–1830* (1959)

CHAPTER
14

Owning the West

ϒ

The West has always belonged to the federal government, but it seems few people have ever been entirely happy with that arrangement. During the 1780s and 1790s, the original thirteen states ceded their claims to western lands, a compromise to ensure the creation of a functional national government. After securing land in the trans-Mississippi West through the Louisiana Purchase of 1803, the United States embarked on a century of territorial acquisition. The government in turn distributed the land—cheap land, not free land—to settlers, and established procedures for creating new territories and states out of the public domain.

A large percentage of the land did not come under state, local, or private control, and so remained "public"—that is, under federal administration. In the twentieth century, a host of federal agencies emerged to administer these public lands such as the bureaus of reclamation and land management, the forest and national park services, and fish and wildlife service. Because many Americans highly value individualism and private property, government ownership and regulation are not always happily accepted. In the West, the rhetoric of "states' rights" precipitated a series of campaigns against the "feds." By the late 1970s, the "Sagebrush Rebellion" became the general term applied to these anti-government protests. Essentially a debate over land use and ownership, the Sagebrush Rebellion is an expression of a deeper philosophical concern regarding the constitutional balance of power between individuals, states, and the federal government. This larger argument has given rise to extremes of rhetoric and action by self-proclaimed "patriots," "constitutionalists," and "militias."

But the issue of owning the West is not just a matter of "feds" versus citizens, or extremists versus the courts. It is also a debate between residents of western states over who is, and what it means to be, a "westerner." Which group of westerners should decide the fate of western lands? Caught up in the various assertions of western identity is the airing of resentment against "easterners" and other "newcomers," and a warning of the existing chasm between the rural and urban West. Ultimately the western landscape both joins and divides westerners in their heated debate over the future of the region.

In the following readings, note the rhetoric about public lands. What are the arguments of the Sagebrush Rebels and their opponents? Who benefits

*from the use of the public domain? In a multiple-use model, how do we
arrive at an equitable balance between competing interests, politically and
ideally? Is state ownership preferable to federal control? Why might western
states* not *want to be responsible for all of the land within their boundaries?
What is the future of the public domain?*

Y D O C U M E N T S

The first document is from the 1931 Committee on the Conservation and
Administration of the Public Domain, also known as the Hoover Committee. It
represents the first in a series of attempts to transfer federal lands to state control—attempts that come to be known as the Sagebrush Rebellion. The second
document illustrates the opposition that arose to this proposed transfer from
westerners themselves. Governor George H. Dern of Utah agreed that states
should control their own lands, but argued that the proposed transfer gave
western states only the most arid, overgrazed, and economically worthless
lands. He and other public land users viewed the costs of rehabilitating the
land (decimated by these very same users) as prohibitive compared to the minimal costs of continuing to lease it from federal land managers.

The next three documents trace the Sagebrush Rebellion viewpoint into the
1970s and 1990s. In the third document, a Nevada state senator explains the
reasons for the rebellion, and an official of the Council of State Governments
reports on the status of public land policy in the West. The fourth document, a
1986 newspaper account by James Coates of the *Chicago Tribune,* reports on
what happened to the Sagebrush Rebellion. He suggests that the show is over
because the highly urbanized West now has other concerns. The fifth document
indicates that Coates penned his epitaph prematurely. Journalists Tom Wharton
and Christopher Smith of the *Salt Lake Tribune* describe the latest, and most
personal, backlash against federal western land managers and policies.

The final document consists of four cartoons published between 1980 and
1995. They editorialize on the relationship of western public land users and the
federal government, divergent attitudes toward proper land use, and the last two
reincarnations of the Sagebrush Rebellion. In the fourth cartoon, Utah Governor
Michael Leavitt personifies the current western states' rights movement.

Report of the Committee on the Conservation and Administration of the Public Domain, 1931

To the President of the United States:

The committee appointed by you, in accordance with the act of
Congress approved April 10, 1930, to make a study of and report on the

Report of the Committee on the Conservation and Administration of the Public Domain, January, 1931
(Washington, D.C.: U.S. Government Printing Office, 1931).

conservation and administration of the public domain, respectfully submits the following report: . . .

General Policies

It is the conclusion of the committee:

1. That all portions of the unreserved and unappropriated public domain should be placed under responsible administration or regulation for the conservation and beneficial use of its resources.

2. That additional areas important for national defense, reclamation purposes, reservoir sites, national forests, national parks, national monuments, and migratory-bird refuges should be reserved by the Federal Government for these purposes.

3. That the remaining areas, which are valuable chiefly for the production of forage and can be effectively conserved and administered by the States containing them, should be granted to the States which will accept them.

4. That in States not accepting such a grant of the public domain responsible administration or regulation should be provided.

5. We recognize that the Nation is committed to a policy of conservation of certain mineral resources. We believe the States are conscious of the importance of such conservation, but that there is a diversity of opinion regarding any program which has for its purpose the wise use of those resources. Such a program must of necessity be based upon such uniformity of Federal and State legislation and administration as will safeguard the accepted principles of conservation and the reclamation fund. When such a program is developed and accepted by any State or States concerned, those resources should be transferred to the State. This is not intended to modify or be in conflict with the accepted policy of the Federal Government relating to the reservation stated in conclusion No. 2 above.

Special Recommendations

1. That Congress pass an act granting to the respective public-land States all the unreserved, unappropriated public domain within their respective boundaries, conditioned, however, that in order to make the grant effective, the States desirous of accepting it shall so signify by act of legislation. A copy of the accepting act signed by the governor and attested by the great seal of the accepting State, when transmitted to the President of the United States, shall operate as an application for the clear listing of the lands granted, and the proceedings thereon shall follow under the direction of the Secretary of the Interior, as in the case of selections heretofore made by public-land States under State land grants.

2. That for States not accepting the grant Congress shall include in the act a provision that upon the application of the State land commission, or State land commissioner, as the case may be, authorized thereto by the State

legislature, the President should by Executive order designate the unreserved, unappropriated public domain in such State as a national range. . . .

4. Areas of unreserved and unappropriated public domain granted to the States shall be clear listed by the Department of the Interior in accordance with established procedure as to mineral or nonmineral character. In the case of lands classified as nonmineral in character, those passed to the States should be in fee simple, and pending the transfer of lands to the States the Federal Government should recognize in so far as possible any method inaugurated by the States to regulate the movement of livestock on such lands to prevent overgrazing that is not discriminatory between the States. . . .

11. As to all grants provided for in the act, the land should pass to the States impressed with a trust for administration and rehabilitation of the public domain and for public institutions and with such restrictions as Congress might deem appropriate. . . .

15. In the administration of the public domain as a national range it is recommended that consideration be given to those methods which will perpetuate the best interests of the livestock industry, including long-time permits for grazing, and developing watering holes to permit the complete use of the range. The program should include consideration of a year-round permit system allocated so as to make the best use of the entire grazing areas of the State.

Careful consideration should be given to those areas vital for both grazing and watershed protection to the end that both interests receive constructive administration. . . .

19. It is the conclusion of the committee that as to agricultural and grazing lands, private ownership, except as to such areas as may be advisable or necessary for public use, should be the objective in the final use and disposition of the public domain. . . .

Utah Governor George H. Dern Responds to the Public Lands Debate, 1932

It is proverbially impolite to look a gift horse in the mouth, but if at first glance the horse looks as if he would eat more than he can produce the donee may be pardoned for examining his teeth.

Comes now the Government of the United States tentatively offering us what looks at a distance like a fine, large horse. As we get closer we have some difficulty in discerning whether it is actually a fine, large horse, or a fine, large white elephant.

I am referring, of course, to the proposition that the United States shall cede to the States the control of the surface rights of all public lands not included in reservations or withdrawals, in national parks or monuments, or in the national forests. . . .

Hearings Before the Committee on the Public Lands, House of Representatives (Washington, D.C., Government Printing Office, 1932), 13–20.

The Western States appreciate the compliment of being assured that they are now man grown and that they can be trusted to administer the proposed new heritage more wisely than it can be done from offices in the National Capital, but they can not help wondering why they should be deemed wise enough to administer the surface rights but not wise enough to administer the minerals contained in the public lands.

The remaining public lands of the United States are open for entry by any citizen, who may have them for a nominal sum if he is willing to live upon them for a while; but they remain vacant and spurned. If private citizens will not accept them as a gift from the National Government, by what process of reasoning are they worth anything to the States? If the National Government can not sell them, how can the States sell them? If the National Government can not lease them, how can the States squeeze any revenue out of them? . . .

I have no elaborate statistics to present, but, in my opinion, it must be obvious to everyone familiar with conditions in the more arid sections of the West, as typified by Utah, that in its present depleted state the surface of the remaining vacant and unappropriated public domain, excluding the national forests, can not be made to produce enough revenue to pay the cost of administration. The States already own, in their school-land grants, millions of acres of this same kind of land, which they can neither sell nor lease, and which is yielding no income. Why should they want more of this precious heritage of desert?

If this proposed gift included all the public lands except the national parks, and if it carried with it all the minerals therein contained, I am sure we should all rise up and rejoice over an act of justice long deferred. . . .

But we have here quite a different proposition. In the first place, it is not proposed to turn the national forests over to the States. Now, it happens that the national forests are about the only part of the remaining public domain that is worth having, so far as the surface rights are concerned. They are valuable either as grazing lands or as timber lands. . . .

We live in a semiarid country, where the precipitation varies from 5 inches to 31 inches per annum and where the altitude ranges from 2,000 to 14,000 feet above sea level. The lower areas, with scanty precipitation and no water for irrigation, predominate, and in these areas there is so little vegetation that the land has a very low value. Over a large area in southern Wyoming it requires 10 acres to graze one sheep three months. Such land is considered worth probably 40 cents an acre. We have some in Utah that is even worse. This is the land that the Government, in a sudden burst of generosity, now threatens to give us. . . .

The proposition before us for consideration therefore is that the Government shall keep the good land and give the States the poor land. . . .

But the facts that these lands do not promise to become sources of much-needed State revenue is not the only thing to be taken into consideration. If that were all, we might take them and say we are no worse off than we were without them. Actually, however, we might be paying a big price for them, and it is pertinent to inquire whether they are worth the price.

The first item in the price is the possible sacrifice of Federal reclamation. The extension of agricultural development in the Western States is dependent upon reclamation works built by the Federal Government. . . .

Shall the States assume the burden of reclaiming the public lands without at the same time having turned over to them the mineral royalties which the Government now devotes to that purpose? . . .

Hence I repeat that the reclamation act and the leasing act combined have constituted a fine, enlightened, constructive program of unselfish cooperation among all the public-land States. It is the kind of neighborly cooperation that is essential to the growth and development of the great West, which must move forward regardless of State lines. . . .

It is not necessary to own a piece of land in order to get the benefit of it. Notwithstanding the fact that the title to the public lands and minerals is in the United States, they have been administered largely for the benefit of the States in which they are situated. . . .

Since the States already get the benefits derived from the public lands, it is pertinent to inquire how much better off they will be if the title and the responsibility and the management are turned over to them. . . .

Two Statements from Nevada on the Sagebrush Rebellion, 1979

State Senator Richard E. Blakemore, Nevada:

The "sagebrush rebellion" is a catchy but somewhat misleading term used to describe the western states' demands for a greater role in determining the future of the west.

Unlike the dictionary definition, in this rebellion there is no armed or unlawful resistance to government. Neither is western land desolate or worthless as the term "sagebrush" connotes.

Moreover, if much of the land in the west ever was considered of little worth, the need for energy has changed that.

Statistics show that much of the west is controlled by the federal government. The federal government controls about one third of the 2.1 billion acres of land in this country or 700 million acres. Over 90 percent of all federal land is from the Rockies west. The federal government controls 96 percent of Alaska, 87 percent of Nevada, 66 percent of Utah, 64 percent of Idaho, and 45 percent of California. The lowest percentage of western federal lands is in Washington at 29 percent. On the average, the federal government controls 52.6 percent of the land in the 12 western states, excluding Hawaii.

By contrast, the federal government controls only 4.3 percent of the land in the other 38 states. Many counties in the west are 99 percent federal land.

Two Reports from Nevada on the Sagebrush Rebellion, 1979, in *State Government News,* 22, No. 10 (November 1979) 3–5. Reprinted by permission of The Council of State Governments, Publisher.

What does this large federal presence mean to westerners and why are westerners protesting?

For many years, the public domain was open to ranching, mining, and outdoor recreation. But a number of federal acts, passed to protect and conserve the environment, have closed great parts of the public domain to traditional uses. Westerners see these restrictions in the use of public lands as a portent of things to come—that eventually most of today's public lands will be locked up in wilderness or other restrictive uses. Matters are made worse for agricultural interests by urban growth, which gobbles up the little private land open to development.

Meanwhile, the west today is at the confluence of two major movements—that for protection of the environment and that for production of energy.

To a great extent, the success of the attempt for U.S. energy independence depends upon resources of the west. In addition, the west is looked to for increased agricultural production and for its reserves of minerals necessary to modern industry.

The environmental movement prompted the passage of federal legislation aimed at protecting the environment and maintaining great portions of the country in a natural state. Among the major environmental acts of the past 15 years are the Wilderness Act, the National Environmental Protection Act, the Federal Land Policy Management Act (BLM Organic Act), the Wild and Scenic Rivers Act, and the National Forest Management Act.

The genesis of the sagebrush rebellion can be found in the conflict between the desires to protect and preserve the environment and the demands for food, minerals, and energy from the west.

The rebellious spirit in the west today can be traced to several federal policies and actions in recent years.

Constraints on the uses of public lands and obstacles to disposal of public lands into nonfederal ownership have increased over the past 15 years.

Most federal land is managed by two agencies—the U.S. Forest Service and the Bureau of Land Management (BLM). The BLM never even processed most proposals for land exchanges to eliminate checkerboard patterns of private-public ownership. Privately owned land can be exchanged for public lands, but appraisals must be made so the values are equivalent. Exchanges make it possible to consolidate ownership of contiguous land tracts. However, the BLM has not given staff priority to exchanges.

Of the 275,000 acres of public land in Nevada for which exchanges have been proposed since 1968, only 3,000 acres have been exchanged. In those 10 years, there have been denials on less than 20,000 acres, meaning that the BLM has not rendered decisions on 92 percent of the land requested for exchange.

This illustrates the general opposition of land management agencies to land disposal or any changes in ownership patterns. These attitudes were sanctioned by Congress in 1976 with passage of the Federal Land Policy Management Act, commonly called the BLM Organic Act. (Until then it was U.S. policy to dispose of public lands, although there was very little disposition in the preceding 30 years. The Organic Act made retention of public lands the policy, unless land use planning under the act showed disposal was in the national interest.)

At the same time, the Forest Service was engaged in a wilderness review, known as RARE II. The Organic Act also required the BLM to begin wilderness review on the land it administers.

Another blow to the west was President Carter's hit list of western water projects, which was issued without consultation with governors of the affected states.

Also in the water area, a recent opinion by the U.S. Department of the Interior could open the way to federal intervention in state administration of water laws. The opinion, not yet tested in court, concludes that the Department of the Interior should comply with state water law, but that compliance would not prevent the federal government from taking whatever water rights it needs.

These federal policies and activities make the west apprehensive about what's next. Nonwesterners may appreciate this frustration with federal land policies more if they consider the growth in federal regulation throughout the country in the past 15 years.

Overregulation is bad anywhere. Imagine how much worse it is for states in which the federal government is also the landlord over most of the land in the state. Excessive regulation and heavy-handed bureaucracy are magnified where land is federally controlled.

While the particular issues on which the sagebrush rebellion are based are more common to the west, the principles behind the movement are national in scope. It is a question of the extent to which the destiny of the country is controlled by federal agencies and bureaucrats. States, local governments, and the people should make more of these determinations and the federal government less.

Because of the federal omnipresence in the west, westerners have reached the crisis first. But reversing the trend towards centralization that threatens the economy, our lands, and our freedoms is of concern to all Americans.

Westerners have started drawing lines and pushing back. We ask nonwesterners to join with us for the benefit of all.

Susan S. Munroe, Council of State Governments, Washington Office:

Approximately 300 state and county officials making up the Western Coalition on Public Lands met in Reno, Nevada, September 5–7, to hammer out policy proposals that would remedy what members believe to be growing federal encroachment into states' purview over land and water use.

The Nevada legislature's introduction of a measure to secure transfer to the state of a portion of federally owned lands has been dubbed a "sagebrush rebellion." The move, which could end up in the U.S. Supreme Court, appears only to be a first salvo.

The state and county officials proposed other possible remedies to federal intervention, including:

- Expeditious disposal of unmanageable and isolated tracts of federal lands;
- Full payments to counties under the payments in lieu of taxes program to compensate for the tax immunity of federal lands;
- Support for wilderness decisions based on the multiple-use concept of public lands;
- Support for Alaska lands legislation that would guarantee the conveyance of statehood entitlement lands to that state;
- Support for a comprehensive energy impact assistance program;
- Support for the goals of the National Forest and Rangeland Resources Planning Act; and
- Support for comprehensive state and local land use planning.

The recommendations were subsequently approved, with some modifications, by the Western Conference of the Council of State Governments and the Western Interstate Region of the National Association of Counties (NACo).

Soon after the Western Coalition meeting, the U.S. Senate passed a measure to speed energy development that will further diminish western states' land and water rights. By a vote of 68–25, the upper house moved to establish a powerful, four-member Energy Mobilization Board.

Opponents believe the legislation will mandate far-reaching energy efforts that will trample federalism and ignore environmental consequences.

If the bill passes undiluted by the U.S. House (where action is expected shortly) and is signed into law, once again western attempts to control land use will have been thwarted, this time in favor of federal governmental interest in expediting massive energy development.

Passage of the Energy Mobilization Board bill would add substantial fuel to the already flaming sagebrush rebellion. By giving the energy board such broad powers, particularly a grandfather clause that allows waiver of any laws enacted after beginning construction of a priority project and authority to make decisions for state, local, and federal agencies which miss deadlines, Congress and the president will almost assure a barrage of lawsuits that will result in a slowdown of project developments for perhaps years to come.

Lawsuits are but one weapon in the sagebrush rebellion's arsenal to protect and regain land from federal control.

For example, western interests are pushing S. 1680, introduced August 3 by U.S. Senator Orrin Hatch (R-Utah), and companion legislation in the U.S. House, H.R. 5426, introduced by U.S. Representative James Santini (D-Nevada), that will provide for conveyance of federally owned, unreserved lands to the states by Congress.

The measures provide for states to set up their own land commissions and protect existing leases and revenues prior to transfer by application to a federal land transfer board.

The Western Conference of the Council of State Governments and the National Association of Counties' Western Interstate Region support the bills, which are still in committee.

James Coates Asks,
Is the Sagebrush Rebellion Dead? 1986

Lean and lanky as the Marlboro man, David Flitner sat behind James Watt's old desk at the Mountain States Legal Foundation here and told how the "Sagebrush Rebellion" had been shackled by conservationists' victories and modern urban problems.

The Sagebrush Rebellion, which captured the spotlight during Ronald Reagan's 1980 presidential campaign, was a package of legislative proposals that would have allowed the federal government to sell large amounts of the land in the American West and speed up development of natural resources.

"I happen to be one who cheers and supports the Sagebrush Rebellion," Reagan said in a campaign speech in Salt Lake City. "Count me in as a rebel."

As interior secretary, the newly elected president chose Watt, the first director of the foundation, which had been set up in 1977 by conservative Colorado braumeister Joseph Coors and others as a mirror of such liberal groups as the Sierra Club.

With the help of the administration and a Republican-dominated Senate, pro-development forces won some big battles—increased offshore oil exploration, mining on national forest lands and a freeze on federal grazing fees.

But though the rebels continue to "fight the good fight" on many fronts, the rebellion has become a holding action, Flitner said.

"Things were going well at first but the bureaucracy is so entrenched. It's almost immaterial in the end which administration gets in. So, yes, things have slowed down for us," he said.

A coalition of ranchers, sheepherders, miners and other leaders of the wide open West had formed the Sagebrush Rebellion with the goal of taking control of about 500 million acres of mostly arid land west of Omaha that is owned by the federal Bureau of Land Management.

"We were getting our fannies kicked all over the place," recalled Flitner, a wealthy Wyoming rancher who succeeded Watt as director of the foundation in 1981.

"People were getting so frustrated that the most intimate policies about our lives—how our grazing was done, how our forests were managed, how our water was used—were being made by bureaucrats in far-away big cities."

The Reagan administration came riding to the rescue with proposed sales of massive Western coal tracts and of offshore oil and gas leases. Cuts were attempted in the creation of new wilderness areas and there even were plans to allow mining within the boundaries of the country's sacrosanct national parks.

The coal sales created a furor in Washington.

Meanwhile, plans to develop mineral rights in national parks were stalled by a raft of lawsuits filed by such groups as the Sierra Club, Wilderness Society and Friends of the Earth. The drive to halt wilderness areas also fizzled.

A major bid to expand timber cutting in the national forests was stymied when environmentalist lawsuits forced the U.S. Forest Service to cut back on plans to build access roads for the loggers. The Wilderness Society showed that the roads would cost more than the timber companies paid the government for taking its trees.

And the rebels' key proposal to sell off public land—the Western Lands Distribution and Regional Equalization Act—also ran into a mass of environmentalist lawsuits and finally was shelved by administration leaders beset by Gramm-Rudman deficit-cutting issues.

Today, as the sagebrush rebels look for support among their fellow Westerners, they find a highly urbanized society in which roughly 75 percent of the population live in towns and big cities; it is a society that has moved on to other concerns.

Return of the Sagebrush Rebels, 1995

Federal land managers are under new orders as they patrol an increasingly unfriendly American West: Back off it confronted by hostile locals.

In a region where much of the land belongs to the federal government, grazing reform, environmental regulations and even the reintroduction of wolves into Yellowstone National Park has started a minirevolution.

"Are we going to have the Confederate States of the West, or do we have a federation?" asks environmental writer Ted Williams. "These laws are enforced on the ground. If we do away with the enforcement of the Endangered Species Act because extracting industries like loggers, ranchers and miners don't really like it, then we really don't have a law."

Since March, rangers and wildlife officers have been directed to travel in pairs, stay in radio contact with district offices and approach people with caution. If detained by angry citizens, officers must cooperate, not resist.

And now that anti-fed zealots have been linked to the bombing in Oklahoma City, edgy agents face more uncertainty while patrolling wide-open public lands.

Tom Riley, senior special agent in charge of the U.S. Fish and Wildlife Service, was shocked Friday to hear a man on a Merdian, Idaho, radio station express pleasure with the bombing of the Oklahoma federal building, where hundreds are feared dead.

The caller said the federal government was at war with the white male population of United States, adding that civil war was the only way to resolve it.

He boasted that the Oklahoma City bombing was only the beginning.

Tom Wharton and Christopher Smith, "West's Rebels Take Fight to the Feds," *Salt Lake Tribune,* April 23, 1995, pp. A1, A6–A7. Reprinted by permission of the Salt Lake Tribune.

Throughout the West, evidence of violent militancy has been piling up:

- Three weeks ago, a bomb in the Forest Service's Carson Ranger District office in Carson City, Nev., shattered windows and reduced a computer on the district ranger's desk to microchip rubble. Hours later, three pipe bombs destroyed a Forest Service outhouse in Elko County. A bomb threat was phoned into the supervisor's office of the Toiyabe National Forest in Sparks, Nev.

- Last month, the sheriff of Lemhi County, Idaho, refused to allow three U.S. Fish and Wildlife Service officers to execute a federal search warrant as they investigated the killing of a recently reintroduced gray wolf. Instead, agents say, Sheriff Brent Barsalou helped lend his voice to the hail of threats thrown at officers. Barsalou counters that the agents were dumb to approach ranchers already angry about the Endangered Species Act.

- With an armed crowd looking on last July 4, Nye County, Nev., Commissioner Dick Carver climbed aboard a bulldozer and punched open a long-closed road on federal land. A Forest Service special agent dodged the advancing blade while attempting to warn angry citizens that their acts were illegal. The agent's remarks were drowned out by the straining diesel engine and the cheering crowd.

The movement is worrying law-enforcement branches of agencies like the Bureau of Land Management, National Park Service and U.S. Forest Service. Twice monthly, special agents hold a national conference call to discuss winds of war on the Western range.

Last month, wallet-sized "contact cards" bearing the phone numbers of the U.S. Attorney's office and the FBI were issued to field-going Forest Service employees in case they are detained by citizen militias or vigilante groups. The cards bear a statement by Forest Service Chief Jack Ward Thomas:

> Because you are a Forest Service employee, we will do everything necessary to ensure your safety and protect your rights. Everything will be done to have you released as quickly as possible.

But some "home rule" advocates say the feds are overreacting.

"This is an orchestrated effort to put fear in their own peoples' minds to make them believe they are under some sort of attack, when in actuality they are not," says Ruth Kaiser, executive director of the National Federal Lands Conference, a Bountiful, Utah-based group spearheading a "county rights" movement. "When we tell [federal agents] that we don't feel they have any authority, that's not a threat, it's a direct communication."

While many federal officials are loathe to publicize potential terrorism, they are taking the talk seriously.

"The threat is real and it's there," says Michelle Barrett of the BLM's Nevada State Office in Reno, where an unsolved bombing on Halloween night 1993 caused $100,000 in damage. "It seems all the rhetoric being raised sends a small fringe over the edge, inciting them to believe violence is the way to resolve a public policy debate. What's worse, the media tend to romanticize these people and paint our employees as the big, bad faceless bureaucrats."

With the bombings, vigilante posses and increasing refusal to obey federal land-use laws, an old outlaw mythos is resurfacing.

"What gives us a lot of concern is the groups that want to settle disputes at the cattle guard instead of in the courtroom," says Greg Stover, president of the Federal Wildlife Officers Association. "That attitude is going to get someone hurt."

Indeed, many Western rebels have made martyrs of separatists like Randy Weaver, whose wife and child along with a federal marshal were killed in an Idaho siege, and the Branch Davidians who met fiery deaths in Waco, Texas.

David Helvarg, author of *The War on the Greens,* believes there's a convergence of gun-rights advocates, local militia organizers, "Wise Use" advocates, anti-environmentalists and white supremacists into the sovereignty movement.

"You've got a revolution of rising expectations, with the feeling that now is the time to drive the feds off 'their' land," says Helvarg.

Meantime, the Western states' rights movement, once espoused by fringe presidential candidates like Col. James "Bo" Gritz, has become a populist cause embraced by mainstream political leaders like Republican Gov. Mike Leavitt of Utah.

Last spring at the Western States Summit in Phoenix, Leavitt unveiled his "Conference of the States" plan to end what he sees as the federal government usurping local authority. The cowboy governor's self-styled Magna Carta proclaims, "The message here is that the time of hoping, begging and waiting has ended. The time for action has come."

William Perry Pendley is president of the Mountain States Legal Foundation, which was established by former Interior secretary James Watt to help protect property owners from intrusive government regulation. He likens angry Westerners to the patriots of the American Revolution.

"In report after report, in decision after decision, in legal pleading after legal pleading, the federal government concludes that Westerners are irrelevant," Pendley says. "All that Nye County and others are doing is responding, with the only mechanism they believe to be available to them, to protect their citizens from an oppressive and unresponsive federal regime." . . .

Faced with a classic Western standoff, federal employees are unsure where they stand in trying to enforce the law. With a Republican-dominated Congress united under the banner of less government interference, "the Justice Department isn't sure whether to prosecute these violations," says one Forest Service official.

Riley says field agents have been advised to avoid any conflicts over the Endangered Species Act now that the landmark legislation is up for reauthorization in Congress. "That might cause Congress to not pass the law," he says. "That's the political reality and we understand that. But we don't want our agents and the public getting hurt."

National Park Service Director Roger Kennedy says his rangers are wary when they approach people in the field.

"You put on your [bulletproof] vest more often. You want a partner in the car with you. Spouses worry about you more," he says. "On the positive side, it means you have to be more polite with people."

If anything, Barsalou says, federal employees are learning they can't run roughshod over Westerners.

"The attitude I got from the federal officers is that they could come in and do what they wanted to do and that they were not answerable to anybody," he says. "Well, we proved them wrong. This went from Iron Creek, Idaho, to the halls of Congress in two weeks. Now they realize they're responsible to someone."

Four Editorial Cartoons Capture the Angry West

Source: *High Country News,* August 23, 1993, 15. Feature TOLES, copyright 1993 The Buffalo News. Reprinted with permission of Universal Press Syndicate. All rights reserved.

Camp Followers.

Source: Calvin Grondahl, *Deseret News,* September 8–9, 1980, A-5.

Source: Pat Bagley 1995, The Salt Lake Tribune. *High Country News,* March 20, 1995, 3.

Source: Pat Bagley, *The Salt Lake Tribune,* May 22, 1994, A20.

Y *E S S A Y S*

R. McGreggor Cawley, associate professor of political science at the University of Wyoming, has produced one of the most cogent pieces of analysis of twentieth-century western land politics. In an objective assessment of a highly emotional topic, Cawley traces the roots, issues, tactics, and politics surrounding the various incarnations of the Sagebrush Rebellion. He explores how interest group and party politics, public opinion, and administrative latitude in implementing programs have shaped land policy. The second essay is by Bruce Babbitt, former Arizona governor and Interior Secretary during the Clinton presidency. As both a westerner and the nation's leading land manager, Babbitt gives a personal assessment of interagency responsibilities and squabbles, the balance between preservation and multiple use, and the need to reform reclamation in the arid West. Both essays speak directly to the issue of who owns or controls the West, and what that ownership has meant and should mean in the future.

The Sagebrush Rebellion and Environmental Politics

R. McGreggor Cawley

As part of an annual public opinion survey, the Advisory Commission on Intergovernmental Relations (ACIR) asks a sample of national respondents:

R. McGreggor Cawley, *Federal Land, Western Anger: The Sagebrush Rebellion and Environmental Politics* (Lawrence: University of Kansas Press, 1993), 71–89, 92–119, 123–124, 141–142, 160–168. Copyright © 1993 by the University Press of Kansas. Reprinted by permission of the publisher.

"From which level of government do you feel you get the most for your money?" In 1978, 35 percent of the total sample and 32 percent of the western sample picked the federal government. A year later, however, only 29 percent of the total sample and 18 percent of the western sample picked the federal government. . . .

Indeed, the cover of the September 17, 1979, issue of *Newsweek* carried a photograph of a cowboy on horseback below the title: "The Angry West: 'Get Off Our Backs, Uncle Sam.'" The accompanying story noted:

> Suddenly the Old West has become the Angry West, a region racked by an increasingly bitter sense of isolation and political alienation. . . . One measure of the anger now firing up the West is the way it has united an otherwise maverick group of states and rugged individualists with a sense of common cause— and a conviction that the rest of the country doesn't share, understand or sympathize with the region's most vital concerns.

In short, public land users were not the only ones who expressed frustration with the federal government during the late 1970s.

It is not surprising then, that the Sagebrush Rebels believed their complaints might have currency with an audience larger than disgruntled public land users. As Nevada state Senator Richard Blakemore, one of the sponsors of the Nevada Sagebrush bill, explained: "While the particular issues on which the Sagebrush Rebellion is based are more common to the west, the principles behind the movement are national in scope. It is a question of the extent to which the destiny of the country is controlled by federal agencies and bureaucrats. States, local governments, and the people should make more of these determinations and the federal government less." . . .

Rebellions Past and Present

There have been at least two controversies similar to the Sagebrush Rebellion during this century. The first occurred in the 1920s after the U.S. Forest Service announced plans to increase grazing fees for the national forests. In response, Senator R. M. Stanfield (R-Ore.) held hearings throughout the West that, in the words of Samuel Dana, "not only permitted but encouraged the malcontents to air their grievances, real and imaginary, against the Forest Service."

Though unsuccessful in blocking the proposed increase, this controversy did force the Forest Service to replace its original plan with one designed in consultation with representatives of the national livestock associations. The hearings also focused national attention on the public lands, leading President Herbert Hoover to establish a Committee on the Conservation and Administration of the Public Domain in 1929. The primary recommendation offered by the Hoover committee was that states be given the remaining public domain on one condition: the federal government retained title to the mineral estate. The committee further proposed that any lands not accepted by the states be placed under active federal management.

The prevailing response in the West to this apparently generous offer was skepticism. Utah Governor George H. Dern explained:

> The Western States appreciate the compliment of being assured that they are now man grown and that they can be trusted to administer the proposed new heritage more wisely than it can be done from offices in the Nation's Capital, but they can not help wondering why they should be deemed wise enough to administer the surface rights but not wise enough to administer the minerals contained in the public lands.

Dern went on to ask if the national government had been unable to sell, lease, or even give the public lands away, "by what process of reasoning are they worth anything to the states?" Refusal by the states to pursue the title issue, in turn, set the stage for the next round of controversy.

Realizing that federal management of the public lands was inevitable, western stockgrowers redirected their energies to the task of designing a management scheme that simultaneously acquiesced to federal intrusion but retained as much of the status quo as possible. The result of this effort was the Taylor Grazing Act of 1934. The Taylor Act directed the secretary of Interior to create grazing districts and regulate their use through a permit/fee process, but it also required that "preference shall be given in the issuance of grazing permits to those within or near a district who are landowners engaged in the livestock business."

This conspicuous tilt in favor of western stockgrowers did not pacify all ranchers, however. In 1936 Nevada ranchers instigated a legal battle over the authority of the Grazing Service to assess a uniform grazing fee. After finding early success in the Nevada courts, the stockgrowers' cause was ultimately defeated by the U.S. Supreme Court. Undaunted by this setback, the stockgrowers mobilized a replay of the Stanfield gambit, directed this time by Senator Pat McCarran (D-Nev.).

From 1941 to 1946 McCarran conducted hearings throughout the West, assembling over six thousand pages of nearly uniform criticism directed at the Grazing Service. Out of this controversy emerged two legislative strategies. In 1946, Senator Edward V. Robertson (R-Wyo.) revived the disposal issue by introducing legislation calling for the conveyance to the states of virtually all federal lands. Although this proposal generated some interest, in the end a more complicated ploy by McCarran resolved the dispute.

Using . . . a "triple play between a Senate committee which refused to allow increased fees, a House committee which cut appropriations because fees were not raised, and a powerful interest group which supported both committees," McCarran succeeded in cutting the Grazing Service's 1946 budget almost in half, reducing it to little more than a "paper organization." The Grazing Service was then merged with the General Land Office to create the Bureau of Land Management. And to add insult to injury, for a brief period during this time the salaries of many BLM field personnel were actually paid by the stockgrowers from the portion of federal grazing fees returned to the states.

When viewed against this background, it is not surprising that many critics dismissed the Sagebrush Rebellion as merely the latest in a long series of attempts by exploiters to "rip off" public property. Indeed, the basic form of the Sagebrush Rebellion—a noisy protest against federal management policies—does fit the general pattern established by these earlier episodes. But this similarity in form masks important contextual differences. . . .

The Sagebrush Rebellion emerged in an arena reflecting at least three important structural changes brought about by the events of the 1960s and 1970s. First, the transformation of the BLM into a multiple use agency converted the earlier monopolitical culture into a more competitive marketplace. . . .

Second, legislative mandates and the redefinition of conservation served to provide land managers with real alternatives in making public land regulatory decisions. The train of events beginning with the Multiple Use Classification Act of 1964 and culminating in the Federal Land Policy and Management Act of 1976 offered conclusive evidence that grazing was no longer the dominant use of the public lands, even though the Taylor Grazing Act was never repealed. . . .

Third, the Sagebrush Rebels, unlike their predecessors, had to confront the opposition of a national environmental movement. Although certainly not a monolithic force, environmentalists did maintain a relatively unified front in federal land policy discussions. And perhaps more important, environmentalists could buttress their claims by pointing to an apparent groundswell of public support for environmental concerns.

Thus, the political milieu that had previously underpinned commodity users' dominance in public land policy no longer existed in the late 1970s. Moreover, the experiences of the 1970s suggested that little would be accomplished as long as the discussion was confined to the public land policy arena. Indeed, the kind of intervention contemplated by the Sagebrush Rebels required demonstrating that their frustration involved more fundamental issues than the relative balance between preservation and development in public land policy. . . .

"Second War between the States"

In his 1978 keynote address to the first annual meeting of the Western Governors' Policy Office (WESTPO), Colorado Governor Richard Lamm warned: "We meet at a time when feelings of sectionalism and regionalism are the most intense of any time since the Civil War. . . . Unlike the last war between the states—which pitted the North against the South and only tangentially involved the West—in the 'Second War between the states,' the West is very much involved. In fact, the West appears to be the chief area under attack." The primary situation prompting this caution was the pronounced population shift from the northeastern and northcentral (the frostbelt) regions of the country to the South and West (the sunbelt) that developed in the first half of the 1970s. But as might be suspected, more was at stake than the relocation of people. Like the Civil War, the frostbelt-sunbelt controversy emerged from growing regional economic disparities. . . .

The initial ammunition for this attack came from a 1976 *National Journal* article. Using per capita federal spending and per capita federal tax burden by state and region in the nation for 1975, the authors of this article created a ratio that measured the amount of money returned to the states and regions per tax dollar raised. Their results seemed to provide graphic evidence supporting the frostbelt's claims. For example, for every dollar they generated in federal tax revenue, the Northeast got 86 cents back in federal spending, while the Midwest got only 76 cents. In contrast, the West received $1.20 and the South $1.14. In aggregate terms, the Northeast and Midwest sent over $30 million more to the federal government than they received from it, while the South and West received over $22 million more from the federal government than they sent to it. . . .

As the battle over federal funding took shape, regional tensions emerged in the energy arena as well. In 1970 Congress adopted the Clean Air Act, which gave coal-burning facilities two options for reducing smokestack emissions: installation of scrubber technology, or increased use of low-sulfur (hence "compliance") coal. The cost of scrubber technology, as well as questions about its durability, made compliance coal the preferred option. Since about 85 percent of the nation's stripable, low-sulfur coal is located in the West, the Clean Air Act stimulated a flurry of western coal production. With the advent of the energy crisis, western coal production became a full-fledged boom. . . .

Although the boom in western coal production carried obvious economic benefits, it also carried costs. Surface mining may be a cost-effective production technique, but as the coal fields of Appalachia have demonstrated, it leaves serious, long-term environmental disruption in its wake. . . . The coal boom also created other costs for the human environment, most notably a surge in the population of small, rural towns located close to federal coal fields. The rapid influx of people disrupted lifestyles, and more important, overburdened the towns' infrastructures (schools, hospitals, police and fire protection, water and sewer systems). Westerners also understood that the energy boom was temporary. Eventually the energy resources would be depleted, leading to an economic bust of about the same magnitude as the boom.

It remained to be seen, then, whether the benefits from western energy development would outweigh the costs. However, it was clear that a passive stance would not bring attention to western concerns. In consequence, western states began to mobilize around a theme summarized by New Mexico Governor Jerry Apodaca: "Let there be no mistake—the West will not become an energy colony for the rest of the nation. We will not sacrifice our greatest assets—our blue skies and clear streams, our unblemished plains and mountains—to an endless national thirst for energy." The point for Apodaca and other western governors was not to stop energy development, but to insure that the development proceeded in an orderly, controlled manner. . . .

While never particularly cordial, the relationship between the West and the federal government became increasingly antagonistic during the 1970s, especially after Jimmy Carter moved to the White House. . . .

The West Against the Feds

Historically, confrontations between the federal government and western states over land use decisions have followed a fairly predictable script. They usually begin with an aggressive assertion of national prerogative by the federal government that precipitates an equally aggressive assertion of states' rights. The political climate in the 1970s, then, made confrontation virtually inevitable. The rise of the environmental movement, in combination with the energy crisis, led to an expression of national prerogative that rivaled the activism of the early conservationists. At the same time, pressures from growth and emerging regional tensions made western leaders especially defensive about decisions affecting their states. Thus, it was just a matter of time until these countervailing forces exploded in open conflict. . . .

On February 21, 1977, about one month after his inauguration, Carter announced: "I have identified 19 (water) projects which now appear insupportable on economic, environmental, and/or safety grounds. . . . I am recommending at this time that no funds be provided for these projects in FY78." Only eight of the projects on this so-called hit list were located in the West, but this fact did not seem to matter to westerners. Immediate reaction throughout the West portrayed Carter's move as a direct attack on the region. A political cartoon portrayed Carter showing two maps to the western congressional delegation: one depicting the location of the water projects on the hit list, and the other showing the states that did not vote for Carter in the 1976 election. The maps were identical: the western third of the nation. . . .

Had the announcement of the hit list been an isolated event, western animosity might have been dismissed as arising more from parochial self-interest than states' rights issues. As it turned out, however, the hit list was only a prelude to the more dramatic moves by the Carter administration in the battle over Alaskan lands. The Statehood Act of 1958 had granted Alaska the right to claim over 110 million acres from the unreserved federal estate within its boundaries. This grant, justified by the fact that roughly 99 percent of Alaska was federal property at the time it joined the Union, became mired in a complex set of controversies that lasted over twenty years. . . .

On December 1, 1978, Carter invoked the Antiquities Act of 1906 to set aside 56 million acres as seventeen new national monuments in Alaska. This classification barred all development activity on the land unless Congress subsequently removed it from national monument status. . . . In one set of proclamations, Carter doubled the area of the national park system by adding a land mass roughly the size of Minnesota.

Not surprisingly, Alaskans were less than receptive. As one disgruntled Alaskan exclaimed: "Environmentalists have infiltrated the government too far. And now those park planner parasites are locking up Alaska as wilderness and excluding mankind. They want food for the soul. *We* need food for the body. The federal government has always acted like a foreign power up here." . . . In contrast, the environmental community's reaction was perhaps best summarized by Edgar Wayburn's assertion: "The President's quick and decisive actions place him in history as the greatest conservation president of our time."

The environmental community's assessment of Carter soon changed, however. . . . The event that led to this reassessment was Carter's "crisis of confidence" speech.

The topic of the speech was the national energy crisis. . . . Escalating crude oil prices fueled rampant inflation and created a balance of payments problem that drove down the value of the dollar in international money markets. In many respects, these economic implications were more troublesome than the shortages themselves, because they lacked a focal point for mobilizing public attention. And though Carter's attempt to link the energy crisis with broader public alienation was an accurate reading of the times, his solutions were fraught with ambiguity.

On the one hand, Carter seemed to side with the environmental community in its ongoing insistence that reducing energy consumption (conservation) was the most appropriate response to the energy crisis. . . . But on the other hand, increased domestic production remained a major component of the overall national energy plan. Carter called for the creation of an "energy security corporation" to implement an $88 billion plan for converting coal, oil shale, and tar sands into synthetic fuel sources (synfuels), which could be substituted for oil and natural gas. Indeed, Carter argued that this proposal could "replace 2 ½ million barrels of imported oil per day by 1990." . . .

. . . Synfuel development presented potentially serious environmental consequences. Synfuel production creates a rather nasty mix of carcinogenic compounds, toxic substances, and trace metals, which means that both the production process and disposal of its by-products pose dangerous health threats. In addition, the Council on Environmental Quality (CEQ) estimated that synfuel production at levels proposed by Carter would require strip mining five hundred square miles of western lands for coal and mining another one hundred to two hundred square miles for oil shale. Water presented yet another problem. CEQ noted that mining, reclamation, and production of synfuels would consume enough water to "irrigate roughly 100,000 acres of agricultural land per year." To this list can be added a host of secondary impacts created by the population influx needed for expanded mining operations, as well as the construction and operation of the synfuel plants. . . .

If Carter had intended to rekindle confidence in the federal government, his speech produced exactly the opposite effect in the West. Portraying Carter's initiatives as tantamount to declaring large portions of the West "national sacrifice areas," a broad coalition of western political leaders, environmentalists and indigenous western commodity interests (primarily stockgrowers) quickly mobilized opposition. But even as battle lines were being drawn over the administration's energy proposals, Carter launched yet another salvo.

In September 1979 Carter formally approved an air force proposal to develop a multiple protective shelter (MPS) basing mode for MX missiles. . . . Although various basing modes had been considered by the air force, the preferred system at the time of Carter's approval seemed to be the "race track" MPS located in the Great Basin area of western Utah and eastern Nevada. The basic design of this system required the construction of two hundred tunnels (race tracks) connecting 4,600 shelters. Missiles would then circulate through the race tracks to the shelters on a secret schedule. . . .

Despite historically strong support for national defense in the West, the prospect of being made the potential target for 9,200 Soviet missiles was unsettling. As Senator Paul Laxalt (R-Nev.) asked rhetorically: "Wouldn't Nevada, as home of the nation's top defense apparatus, be subject to a mighty nuclear attack if war comes?" The possibility of nuclear holocaust was less troublesome, though, than the more immediate environmental and social impacts associated with the construction of the MX system. . . .

Stockgrowers and mining interests opposed the system because it would restrict access to large areas of the public lands far more effectively than wilderness designation. Environmentalists objected to the long-term, perhaps permanent, destruction of the desert's fragile ecosystems. State and local officials recited the familiar litany of socioeconomic impacts associated with the boom conditions the system would bring. And everyone wanted to know where the air force intended to get the water needed both for construction and operation of the system.

Though certainly not the only points of disagreement between the West and the federal government, these issues provide a clear picture of the frustrations that produced the Angry West. . . .

The Sagebrush Rebellion

In November 1980, over five hundred people gathered at the Little America convention center in Salt Lake City to attend a national conference on federal land policy sponsored by the League for the Advancement of States' Equal Rights (LASER). According to its promotional literature, LASER was a nonprofit foundation organized "to create a broad base of support in favor of divesting the federal government of the public domain." Calvin Black [a former Utah State legislator] who had consistently raised complaints about federal land policy since deliberations over the Federal Land Policy and Management Act (FLPMA) in the early 1970s, served as chairman of LASER's board of directors. Other members of the board included Senators Barry Goldwater (R-Ariz.), Orrin Hatch (R-Utah), and Ted Stevens (R-Alaska).

The conference program read like an inventory of the issues and interests that characterized the Sagebrush Rebellion. One set of panel discussions served as a forum for grazing, mineral, timber, recreation, and other public land user interests to voice complaints about federal management policies. Another set offered legal, political, and economic arguments in support of state ownership of the federal public lands. In his keynote address, Hatch told the participants that they were involved in an event of "great historical significance," an event, he argued, that "will constitute the major factor in the political and economic future of the West." But after the LASER conference, history seemed to be repeating itself. Reminiscent of the tactics used by both Stanfield and McCarran during earlier conflicts, hearings of the House Subcommittee on Mines and Mining were scheduled by James Santini to begin in Salt Lake City immediately following the close of the LASER conference.

A mood of excitement permeated these meetings, and for good cause. It had been a little over a year since Nevada launched the Sagebrush Rebellion, and much had happened in that time. As Dean Rhoads explained to the subcommittee: "Some months ago, in January 1979, I never realized that when I walked down the hall and put the first bill on the chief clerk's desk in the Nevada Legislature that it would ever grow into the movement that it is today. It has grown from a handful of legislators and supporters in Nevada to broad-based Western support that now has seven Western States that have passed some type of sagebrush rebellion legislation." The Sagebrush Rebellion, it seemed, had become more successful than anyone dared imagine a few months earlier.

Important as these efforts were, the outcome of the 1980 elections clearly overshadowed them. President-elect Ronald Reagan sent a telegram to the conference that read in part: "I renew my pledge to work toward a Sagebrush solution." Equally important, Republicans gained control of the U.S. Senate, which meant that western senators sympathetic to the Sagebrush Rebellion would move into key leadership positions. Combined, these events indicated that a major policy realignment loomed on the horizon. . . .

What the participants did not anticipate, however, was that some members of the new administration would use the Sagebrush Rebellion to advance their own political agenda. . . .

State Ownership

Whether or not the Sagebrush Rebels' view of events during the 1970s represented an accurate assessment, they believed it did. Summarizing that view, Nevada State Senator Richard Blakemore argued:

> For many years, the public domain was open to ranching, mining, and outdoor recreation. But a number of federal acts, passed to protect and conserve the environment, have closed great parts of the public domain to traditional uses. Westerners see these restrictions in the use of the public lands as a portent of things to come—that eventually most of today's public lands will be locked up in wilderness or other restrictive uses.

The question, then, was how to articulate these complaints within the political landscape of the late 1970s.

It seemed clear that the existing pluralist bargaining arena did not provide an acceptable avenue. Environmentalists had been largely successful in portraying environmentally disruptive activities as at best a necessary evil associated with the concept of multiple use, and at worst a violation of the national interest connected with the public lands. The Carter administration, in turn, had expressed little sympathy with either the Sagebrush Rebels' complaints or the broader concerns of the western governors. In consequence, there appeared to be little recourse for them but to provoke a showdown in the hope that such a disruption would create the possibility for restructuring the dialogue.

Invocation of the traditional call for state control of the public lands offered an appropriate text. On the one hand, it created a bridge between the Sagebrush Rebels' demands and the frustration expressed by western governors. On the other hand, if articulated correctly, it could also undermine environmentalists' influence without violating the basic principle of multiple use management. The initial strategic move entailed securing passage by the state legislature of AB 413, asserting Nevada's moral and legal claim to BLM lands. This maneuver accomplished several purposes. First, it guaranteed attention from the national news media and therefore a national platform from which the Sagebrush Rebels could voice their complaints. Second, it accentuated the intergovernmental character of the issue, thus subordinating the preservation/development debate. Indeed, AB 413 specifically excluded "congressionally authorized national parks, monuments, national forests, [and] wildlife refuges," as well as lands controlled by the Department of Defense, Department of Energy, Bureau of Reclamation, and Indian reservations. In addition, AB 413 required the conveyed federal lands to be managed "in such a manner as to conserve and preserve natural resources, wildlife habitat, wilderness areas, historical sites and artifacts, and to permit the development of compatible public uses for recreation, agriculture, ranching, mining and timber production . . . under principles of multiple use which provide the greatest benefit to the people of Nevada." Interestingly, this management mandate was virtually identical to that contained in FLPMA. Change in ownership of the public lands, therefore, did not imply a change in management philosophy.

But the most sophisticated aspect of the Nevada strategy was that it formulated a confrontational situation based on threat rather than action. Asserting a claim to the public lands, even through state law, represented nothing more than a statement of philosophy unless it was coupled to an attempt to actually take control of the public lands. Hence, the federal government and other opponents were more or less without options for action until Nevada officials decided to make good on their threat. But the Sagebrush Rebels were in no hurry to take the next step.

The Sagebrush Rebels intended to escalate the controversy by seeking passage of bills similar to AB 413 in other states as a prelude to initiating an original jurisdiction case in the U.S. Supreme Court. Recognizing that the legal precedents were not encouraging, the rebels hoped these legislative efforts, if successful, would strengthen their position by demonstrating broad-based support for their cause. Such support, in turn, might help sway the court.

Moreover, politicizing the issue also offered the possibility of engendering a conciliatory attitude among federal land managers, which had certainly been the case during earlier controversies. Equally important, the process of working bills through the state legislatures would delay the need to take further action until after the 1980 elections. And while it was too early to make predictions, a major controversy like the Sagebrush Rebellion might well catch the attention of campaigning politicians. In short, far from a spontaneous outburst of frustration, the Nevada strategy was a skillfully designed ploy that allowed the Sagebrush Rebels to mobilize public opinion before initiating legal action. . . .

There was another reason to postpone legal action: the Sagebrush Rebellion had begun attracting attention in Congress, and the Constitution vests Congress with the power to dispose of public lands. Thus, if Congress enacted legislation that authorized the transfer of federal lands to the states, then there would be no need to take the matter to the Supreme Court.

The Western Lands Act: Several bills addressing the transfer issue emerged during the ninety-sixth Congress. By the fall of 1979, they had been harmonized into the Western Lands Distribution and Regional Equalization Act (the Western Lands Act), introduced in the Senate as S. 1680 by Hatch (R-Utah), and in the House as H.R. 5436 by Santini (D-Nev.). The purpose of the Western Lands Act was to provide a mechanism for the conveyance of BLM and Forest Service lands, including mineral rights, to the states. However, it specifically excluded the transfer of national parks and monuments, military lands, Indian reservations, and national wildlife and bird sanctuaries created prior to January 1, 1979.

The governors were given five years from the enactment date to initiate the conveyance process by requesting that the president establish a Federal Land Transfer Board (FLTB) for their state. . . .

The actual conveyance process required the state to submit an application to the FLTB, but the amount of land claimed in the application was left a matter of state discretion. Thus adoption of the Western Lands Act did not necessarily imply a wholesale transfer of federal land to the states. . . .

On the face of it, then, the Western Lands Act seemed to define a carefully constructed process that allowed states to claim federal lands while preserving both the public character of those lands and the principles of multiple use management. What made this bill especially attractive to Sagebrush Rebels, and troublesome to their opponents, was that it avoided the awkward legal arguments for state ownership. Indeed, if the Western Lands Act was adopted, there would be little, if anything, opponents could do to block the transfer.

It remained to be seen whether or not the Western Lands Act could successfully traverse the legislative process. . . . However, the general elections were approaching, and even though divestiture of the federal estate was a radical idea, the Western Lands Act provided a convenient vehicle for mobilizing public complaints about the federal government. Equally important was the question of whether or not the western states were willing and/or able to carry out a multiple use management program. . . .

State Management: The Sagebrush Rebels' assurances that state ownership would not alter the fundamental character of public land management created something of a quandary for their opponents. If the states embarked on a full-fledged multiple use management program, then conveyance represented far less of a threat than critics charged. Indeed, guarantees of protection for wilderness and other environmental values contained in both the Western Lands Act and bills under consideration by the state legislatures seemed to affirm the Sagebrush Rebels' sincerity. The major change brought about by conveyance appeared to be simply the relocation of the conflict from the nation's capital to the various state capitals. But opponents realized this move carried other implications. . . .

[To them,] the Sagebrush Rebellion represented nothing more than the most recent chapter in the ongoing land heist saga initiated during the Stanfield era and continued in the McCarran era. In that case, the language of the Sagebrush legislation was less important than the intent behind it. The real strategy . . . involved transfer of federal lands to the state as a prelude to converting public lands into private property. . . .

In a *Wall Street Journal* editorial, Interior Secretary Andrus pointed out: "There are institutional barriers to balanced management of public lands by the states. In Idaho, for example, the state constitution says state lands must be managed for the highest return to school endowment fund. If they followed that to the letter, as the State Land Board must do, it would mean a lot of those lands would be sold, or leased for single-purpose harvest—either timber or mineral." . . . In short, it seemed that the existing legal mandates would leave the states little recourse but to manage conveyed federal lands for revenue maximization. Under such a mandate, moreover, uses that did not generate revenue (such as wilderness) would have to be ignored. . . .

Another objection raised by opponents proved more troublesome for the Sagebrush Rebels—the cost of managing public lands. Assuming the states were willing to mount a full-fledged multiple use program, critics asked, would they also be willing to appropriate the funds necessary for the program? This was an appropriate question to ask in light of the traditional fiscal conservatism of western legislatures and the developing national tax revolt, exemplified by California voters' approval of Proposition 13 in 1979. . . .

Despite questions and uncertainties surrounding both the legal and management issues, Sagebrush Rebels pursued the conveyance strategy throughout 1979 and 1980, chalking up an impressive track record along the way. Arizona, New Mexico, and Utah enacted bills similar to AB 413, with the Arizona legislature overriding Governor Bruce Babbit's veto. Wyoming also adopted a Sagebrush bill, which claimed both BLM and Forest Service lands. Colorado, Idaho, and Alaska passed legislation calling for feasibility studies of land transfers, and the Hawaii legislature adopted a resolution endorsing the Sagebrush Rebellion without actually joining the movement. . . .

Defusing the Rebellion

Testifying before an interim committee of the Colorado legislature in August 1980, Dean Rhoads explained that court action on the Sagebrush Rebellion would be initiated sometime after the general elections. During a subsequent telephone interview in October 1980, one of Rhoads's staff members indicated that court action was planned for April 1981. However, in an interview at the LASER Conference, Rhoads suggested that although the Supreme Court would eventually have to rule on the issue, litigation might not be instigated for "ten years." He went on to identify two factors accounting for this change in strategy: an assessment predicting that the Sagebrush Rebels would lose on a five to four decision if the existing Court heard the case; and the outcome of the 1980 elections, which opened new and unanticipated possibilities. The likely future of the Sagebrush Rebellion, Rhoads concluded, lay in the direction of "piece-meal legislation, administrative actions, executive orders, and revamping of regulations," all geared to addressing the grievances underlying the movement. Conveyance, either through court or congressional action, no longer seemed to be the dominant goal of the Sagebrush Rebellion.

Herein lies a definite parallel between the Sagebrush Rebellion and the controversy of the 1940s. As William Voigt observed, the resolution of the McCarran era carried disturbing consequences:

> It would be nice to say that the victory against the land grab had lasting values, but it would be untrue. That turned out to be little more than a holding action followed by a more subtle threat. Somewhere along the way the livestock leadership came to the conclusion that outright ownership was not necessary if other measures could assure the perpetuation of its privileged status on the public lands. Why own if you could have all or nearly all the prerogatives of ownership without the cost and bother?

Although Reagan's election did not suggest that Sagebrush Rebels would necessarily gain the "prerogatives of ownership," it did mean that the Sagebrush Rebellion was suddenly transformed into a profound threat.

Reagan's open support for the movement combined with his equally open criticism of environmental regulation in general created a potentially devastating blow to opponents of the Sagebrush Rebellion. If Reagan fulfilled his campaign promises, the argument that federal management would be more sympathetic to environmental concerns than state management no longer carried the certainty it had before the election. Moreover, Reagan's election in spite of his blunt attack on environmental regulations challenged the environmentalists' insistence that the public supported their cause. As one *Wall Street Journal* editorial suggested: "Environmentalism is a worthwhile cause, but the voters have grown tired of environmental excesses."

The situation was further aggravated by the Republican senatorial victory. . . . Among the more influential members of this coalition were Jake

Garn and Orrin Hatch of Utah, Paul Laxault of Nevada, Malcolm Wallop of Wyoming, Harrison Schmidt of New Mexico, James McClure of Idaho, and Jesse Helms of North Carolina. . . .

After the 1980 elections, this coalition not only remained intact, but moved into various leadership positions within a Republican-controlled Senate. For example, James McClure became chairman of the Energy and Natural Resources Committee, and Jesse Helms became chairman of the Agriculture, Nutrition, and Forestry Committee. Both of these committees had oversight power on federal land policy matters, and both new chairmen had publicly supported the Sagebrush Rebellion.

Thus it is clear why the Sagebrush Rebels were willing to set aside conveyance in favor of less dramatic policy adjustments. Indeed, the root complaint raised by public land users during the 1970s was that federal land managers consistently *interpreted* federal management policies as a call for environmental protection. Thus, a sympathetic secretary of Interior could accomplish a great deal by simply altering the interpretation of existing policies. And on December 22, 1980, this possibility became a reality when Reagan announced that James Watt was his choice for secretary of the Interior.

Environmentalists lost little time in mounting opposition to Watt's appointment. Concentrating on his involvement with Mountain States Legal Foundation and his support for the Sagebrush Rebellion, environmentalists portrayed Watt's nomination as a blatant conflict of interest. . . .

Affirming that he was "part of the Sagebrush Rebellion," Watt maintained that the conveyance effort was a "waste of money." The cause of the controversy, he argued, was a Department of Interior that had "become almost hostile to many interests of the West." Watt admitted, "BLM has a right to dictate how leased federal lands should be used, but BLM goes beyond that, dictating to the land user how he must use the state-leased lands, and private land he owns or leases." The goal of his administration, then, would be to "manage [the public] lands as a good neighbor . . . and let the sagebrush rebellion die because of friendly relations." . . .

Once confirmed, Watt approached his new task with the enthusiasm of a general leading an invasion. He initiated budget and personnel changes directed at increasing the department's development emphasis and decreasing its environmental planning efforts. He also proposed changes in policies and regulations for virtually every area under the department's administration. Among the more controversial of these changes were plans to begin processing mineral lease applications for areas within the wilderness system; accelerate leasing of OCS [Outer Continental Shelf] lands and federal coal reserves; reduce public participation in the BLM land planning process; reduce the likelihood of future grazing cuts; redirect Land and Water Conservation Fund revenues from land acquisition to park maintenance efforts; and dismantle both surface mining and ORV [off-road vehicle] regulations. Although the environmentalists stepped up their attacks, it seemed that Watt represented a more formidable adversary than they had anticipated. . . .

Thus the Sagebrush Rebels had cause for guarded optimism. As an appraisal in the January 1982 edition of *Coalition Comments* suggested, "many of the goals of the Sagebrush Rebellion have been accomplished since James Watt became Secretary of Interior. The main future thrust . . . must now be to institutionalize and make permanent the changes that have been made through administrative decisions and changed attitudes of the new administration." But once initiated, political controversies frequently develop in unexpected ways.

In June 1982 the Nevada Select Committee on Public Lands adopted a resolution that reaffirmed "its total dedication to the original 'Sagebrush Rebellion' concept." The event that triggered this change in attitude was a proposal in Reagan's budget message of February 8, 1982. Explaining that the federal government owned 775 million acres of land and 405,000 buildings, he went on to suggest: "Some of this real property is not in use and would be of greater value to society if transferred to the private sector. During the next 3 years we will save $9 billion by shedding these unnecessary properties while fully protecting and preserving our national parks, forests, wilderness and scenic areas." Subsequently, Reagan established a Property Review Board to direct the inventory and prepare recommendations for properties that should be sold.

While this so-called privatization initiative seemed to confirm the [fears of] opponents of the Sagebrush Rebellion, reactions to it suggested a different interpretation. In addition to reaffirming support for the original Sagebrush Rebellion, for example, the Nevada Select Committee adopted another resolution opposing the privatization effort. This resolution is particularly interesting because it was endorsed by a wide array of interests, including the Nevada Cattleman's Association, the Nevada Miners and Prospectors Association, the Nevada Wildlife Federation, and the Nevada chapter of the Sierra Club. Moreover, the privatization issue did not sit well with some of the congressional rebels. James Santini, for instance, pulled no punches when he exclaimed: "I would like to put this Administration on notice once and for all that I will not stand idly by and see Nevada or the West put on the auction block." He went on to suggest: "Quite frankly, this is hardly the behavior I would expect from a 'Good Neighbor.' " . . .

Privatization

On the face of it, the Reagan administration's Federal Real Property Initiative (the so-called privatization initiative) contained several obvious problems. First, although presented as a debt reduction strategy, the scale of the proposal simply did not make sense. . . . The low revenue figures fed speculations that the initial proposal might be a prelude to a more ambitious sale planned by the administration. . . .

[And] It was not at all clear who might be interested in buying federal property. As Christopher Leman explained: "Western state and local governments went on record against the idea. Environmental, conservation, and recreation groups—including wilderness advocates, hunters, and off-road vehicle enthusiasts—achieved an unprecedented unity in opposition. Not a single major commodity sector supported privatization: livestock, mining, oil and gas, coal, or timber." In short, the privatization initiative appeared to be an ill-conceived proposal, lacking any identifiable political support. It is not at all surprising, therefore, that the scheme produced more rhetoric than revenue, and consequently, was quickly abandoned by the administration. . . .

Contrary to the view prevailing at the time, privatization was neither a goal of the Sagebrush Rebellion nor part of Interior Secretary James Watt's agenda. Instead, privatization advocates were attempting to use the controversies surrounding the Sagebrush Rebellion to advance their own political agenda. . . .

Privatization advocates represented a distinct faction within the natural resource policy arena. And though they appeared largely tangential to mainstream policy dialogue throughout the 1970s, they anticipated the themes that would dominate the nation's political agenda in the 1980s. It is not surprising, therefore, that privatization advocates would finally receive attention with the ascendancy of the New Right. Yet privatization advocates discovered, much to their chagrin, that recognition did not readily translate into policy success. Indeed, despite the intensity of their disagreements in other areas, neither environmentalists nor Sagebrush Rebels were ready to accept the radical changes implied by privatization. . . .

Even though the privatization proposal was ill-conceived, the controversy it generated redefined the terms of the argument. Recognizing the common threat posed by privatization, environmentalists and Sagebrush Rebels set aside their other disagreements in order to oppose it. Furthermore, the growing split within the Reagan administration led Watt to emphasize his role as spokesman for the New Right over his role as spokesman for the Sagebrush Rebellion. Although these moves succeeded in defeating the privatization effort, they left most of the issues surrounding the Sagebrush Rebellion unresolved. Thus, when the Nevada Sagebrush Rebels adopted their resolution calling for a return to their original conveyance proposal, it was clear that they had lost most of their earlier momentum. At the same time, there was little evidence that the defeat of the privatization effort had strengthened the hand of the environmental community. In short, the privatization episode appeared to have defused the controversy surrounding the Sagebrush Rebellion far more effectively than Watt's good neighbor policy. . . .

The Significance of the Sagebrush Rebellion

If we follow the dictates of traditional policy analysis, we would find little tangible evidence that the controversy spawned by the Sagebrush Rebellion produced any lasting consequences. The public lands remain in federal ownership and continue to be managed under the mandates adopted in the

1960s and 1970s. However, the argument advanced in this study is that the broader significance of the Sagebrush Rebellion lies within the less tangible context of political influence. In this context, there are several reasons to conclude that the Sagebrush Rebellion left an identifiable mark on the policy landscape.

At base, the Sagebrush Rebellion represented a protest against the growing influence of the environmental community. . . .

Although the Reagan administration did not effect a wholesale dismantling of environmental regulations, it did establish a policy tilt that paid renewed attention to the demands raised by the Sagebrush Rebels. . . .

Lacking sufficient support to eliminate objectionable environmental policies, the administration was able to slow the environmental movement's momentum. Conversely, the environmental community could not eliminate the threat posed by the administration, but it did block implementation of most of Reagan's environmental agenda. Whether or not this stalemate warrants classifying the Sagebrush Rebellion as a success, it does indicate that the relative influence of Sagebrush Rebels and environmentalists was approaching parity in the mid 1980s. . . .

The controversy spawned by the Sagebrush Rebellion introduced a new twist by bringing the traditional and the new definitions of conservation into direct conflict. Sagebrush Rebels, and more particularly James Watt, attempted to reclaim traditional conservation as a way to reopen negotiations about the relative balance between development and preservation in land use decisions. This move forced environmentalists to defend new conservation in order to protect the advances they had made during the 1970s. Although neither side prevailed, the argument offered a graphic reminder that conservation is a term with multiple, and not necessarily consistent, meanings. More important, it seems unlikely that future public land policy discussions will be able to assume that there is a widely accepted definition for conservation. In consequence, it also seems unlikely that either Sagebrush Rebels or environmentalists will be able to exert the dominant influence over the public land policy agenda they both once enjoyed.

The intervention of privatization and radical environmentalism illustrated the altered structure of the policy dialogue even more clearly than the argument over conservation. Indeed, the convention of portraying public land disputes as confrontations between development interests and preservation interests simply failed to capture the complexity of conflicts involving Sagebrush Rebels, privatization advocates, radical environmentalists, and the environmental establishment. And though privatization advocates retreated to academia after their brief stint in the Reagan administration, radical environmentalism remained a prominent feature in the policy arena. . . .

There were other signs that the arguments spawned by the Sagebrush Rebellion had not been resolved. . . . A national Multiple Use Strategy Conference was held in Reno, Nevada during August 1988. Sponsored by the Center for the Defense of Free Enterprise (CDFE), an organization founded by Alan Gottlieb, an active participant in the New Right movement, this conference gave birth to the Wise Use Movement. The conference participants were described as neither "single-minded preservationists" nor "single-minded apologists for industrial development," but rather "representatives of a new balance, of a middle way between extreme environmentalism and extreme industrialism." Yet the groups populating the Wise Use Movement fell into familiar categories: off-road-vehicle users, mining, grazing, timbering, and farming interests.

Ron Arnold, executive vice-president of CDFE and the driving force behind the Wise Use Movement, claims that the inspiration for the movement's name came from Gifford Pinchot's insistence that conservation meant the "wise use of resources." Arnold resists characterizations that portray the Wise Use Movement as the "Sagebrush Rebellion in a new suit of clothes," because in his view, the movement "is much broader and deeper than a temper tantrum over public lands thrown by a handful of Nevada cowboys." *The Wise Use Agenda,* which defines the unifying philosophy of the movement, outlines a far more diverse and sophisticated set of demands than the Sagebrush Rebels' call for conveyance of federal lands to the states.

Nevertheless, the parallels between the two movements are too obvious to be ignored. Arnold's invocation of Pinchot gives clear evidence that the Wise Use Movement is a continuation of the effort to reclaim traditional conservation. As mentioned above, the interests represented in the Wise Use Movement are virtually identical to those that populated the Sagebrush Rebellion. Finally, though the twenty-five goals identified by the Wise Use Movement are certainly more diverse than the call for conveyance, they nonetheless address most of the underlying issues raised by the Sagebrush Rebels. Thus, Arnold's protests notwithstanding, it seems safe to conclude that the Wise Use Movement is an extension of the effort begun by the Sagebrush Rebels. . . .

In one regard, all public land disputes evoke a sense of *déjà vu.* As we have seen, the Sagebrush Rebellion echoed the Stanfield and McCarran controversies. Moreover, the Sagebrush Rebellion has itself already become a recognized reference point for public land policy analysis. However, our study suggests the possibility for viewing the Sagebrush Rebellion as something more than just another episode in a long train of public land policy disputes.

The Sagebrush Rebellion marked the beginning of a period in which virtually every assumption about federal land policy underwent challenge and reconsideration. To be sure, the major assumptions—that public lands should remain in federal ownership and that they should be managed under the mandates enacted in the 1960s and 1970s—were reaffirmed by this process. But other assumptions did not fair so well. It is no longer possible, for example, to talk about conservation as if it possessed a widely accepted meaning. In a similar fashion, references to environmentalism must take into account both the moderate/radical distinction, and the differentiation among radical environmental postures. And since these shifts in the dialogue represent arguments that will not be resolved in the near future, there is reason to suspect that the controversy surrounding the Sagebrush Rebellion transformed the structure of the policy dialogue. . . .

Public Use and the Future of the Federal Lands

BRUCE BABBITT

The public lands of the American West are both a historical anomaly and a continuing political paradox. Given our individualistic culture, preference for private property, antipathy toward government, and recurrent movements to privatize anything public, one could reasonably assume that the public lands had long since been sold, auctioned off or given away simply to get government out of the land business. Yet in the twentieth century the public lands have remained largely intact, and the consensus for public ownership seems to grow with each generation.

If there is a solid consensus for public ownership, there is as yet no such agreement about how our Western lands should be used and administered. The century-old debate between the disciples of John Muir, preaching wilderness for its own sake, and the followers of Gifford Pinchot, advocating utilitarian doctrines of resource use, rages on unresolved and growing ever more intense as the once-empty spaces of the West begin to fill up. Likewise, there is still no settled consensus on where land-use decisions should be made—at the federal, state, or local level—or by whom—the public, elected officials, judges, or professional administrators. Given the unique history of public lands, proposals for reform require some discussion of what has happened in the past.

As the American frontier advanced from Atlantic shores across the Mississippi and onto the Great Plains, lands were routinely transferred into private ownership through land sales and the operation of the various preemption and homestead laws. As a result, public lands east of the Mississippi River have almost disappeared; they are now limited to a few small forests and parks and some larger tracts in New England and the Appalachians.

In the second half of the nineteenth century, as the line of settlement moved off the Great Plains into the front ranges of the Rocky Mountains and beyond, the historical process of privatization began to slow, eventually coming to a halt. As homesteaders, conditioned by their experience on the rich agricultural frontiers of Iowa and Nebraska, began trekking into the empty spaces of the West, they expected to plow the soil into a checkerboard extension of the Middle West. But for the most part it would not happen, for the climate was too cold in the high mountains and too hot in the desert bottoms, soils were often unproductive, and almost everywhere there was too little rainfall.

Out of the failure of the homestead experience, two opposing concepts of land tenure gradually emerged. One, rooted in the traditional urge to privatize, advocated that the public land be sold or given away in whatever quantities necessary to stimulate development. If small homestead grants

Bruce Babbitt, "Public Use and the Future of the Federal Lands," in *A Society to Match the Scenery: Personal Visions of the Future of the American West,* eds. Gary Holthaus, Limerick, Wilkinson, and Munson (Niwot, CO: University of Colorado Press, 1991), 163–170. Excerpted by permission of the University of Colorado Press.

were not a sufficient inducement to settlement, then large grants surely would be. In the nineteenth century Congress gave 58 million acres of land to Northern Pacific Railroad, just the first of many huge grants to railroad companies. As Congress enacted laws authorizing expanded mineral, timber and grazing grants, land monopolies began to develop as individuals and corporations manipulated and stepped over the edge of new land laws.

Even as Western lands were sold, granted, and otherwise concentrated into huge private landholdings, a new concept—that public lands should be retained in permanent ownership and managed for public purposes—gradually emerged. It began with a traditional concept—public parks—implemented on a grand scale. In 1872 Congress set aside 2 million acres in Yellowstone "as a public park or pleasuring ground for the benefit and enjoyment of the people." Yosemite National Park followed in 1890 after a long and acrimonious fight led by John Muir.

After parks came a less familiar concept—public forest reserves. In 1891 the Congress, in response to accelerating destruction of Western forests, authorized the President to "set apart and reserve, in any State or Territory having public land bearing forests, . . . any part of the public lands wholly or in part covered with timber or undergrowth, whether of commercial value or not, as public reservations." As Presidents Harrison, Cleveland, and then Theodore Roosevelt invoked this law to create a national forest system, Congress began backtracking, but by the time the executive authority was rescinded in 1907, the modern forest system was largely in place.

If one president gave shape to the public-land system that we enjoy today, it was Theodore Roosevelt. In seven years in the White House, he expanded the national forests fourfold to 172 million acres, established seventy-two wildlife refuges and eighteen national monuments, a new category of public reservations intended to preserve areas of scenic, scientific, and archaeological interest. He initiated the first mineral and reclamation withdrawals. Most importantly for the future of the public lands, it was T. R.'s enthusiastic evangelizing and instinctive love of the outdoors that once and for all established the concept of public lands as a permanent part of the American heritage.

After Theodore Roosevelt left office, the debate over public-land policy drifted off to the shadowy corners of American politics. Timber, oil, and mining companies, aided by the connivance or plain indifference of public officials, discovered they could exploit lands without bothering to own them. The Teapot Dome scandal came and went, yet in the easy atmosphere of the 1920s, the public seemed uninterested in demanding meaningful reforms.

The conservation movement revived with the coming of Franklin Roosevelt and the New Deal. Still, at heart, the New Dealers were social planners rather than environmentalists. To them, conservation meant building dams for flood control, public power, and reclamation; replanting forests to increase the timer harvest; and conserving soil to increase agricultural production.

The Tennessee Valley Authority became the model for Western lands; F. D. R. told the nation that TVA "leads logically to national planning for a complete river watershed involving many [States] and the future lives and welfare of millions." The Bureau of Reclamation was the Western TVA, and during the New Deal it geared up development programs that would eventually run amok, causing more environmental destruction than any other public-lands program.

If the New Deal emphasized the utilitarian aspects of conservation, implicitly exalting humans over nature everywhere in the West, it nonetheless clinched the idea of national ownership of Western lands as a permanent part of the national heritage. The Taylor Grazing Act effectively closed the public domain to homesteading and established federal management responsibility for the nonforest lands administered by the Bureau of Land Management. Public power legislation further strengthened the concept of public ownership of Western natural resources, even as it compromised environmental values.

The concept of public ownership is now so firmly established that it is no longer seriously in question, notwithstanding an occasional horse opera like the Sagebrush Rebellion. And in several Western states the Forest Service and, notably, the Bureau of Land Management have undertaken innovative land-exchange programs to consolidate inholdings and protect critical environmental areas. From this point forward, however, the public-land debate will shift to the task of reconciling the growing conflicts over the use of public lands.

Just as the struggle for public ownership began on Western forest lands in the last century, it was excessive timber cutting in this century that ignited the present use controversy. Congress reacted in 1960 by enacting the Multiple-Use Sustained-Yield Act, which formally introduced the concept of "multiple use," stating, "It is the policy of Congress that the national forests are established and shall be administered for outdoor recreation, range, timber, watershed, and wildlife and fish purposes."

For its time, multiple use was a forward-looking, progressive concept that at last awarded recreation, wildlife and watershed uses official parity with timber cutting. The act reflected the views of many, including the leadership of the Forest Service, that the agency was in danger of becoming little more than a government-owned timber company.

Whatever its original promise, multiple use is a concept that has proven unworkable in practice. Political pressure to increase timber cuts has caused the Forest Service to commit to doubling timber production from public lands. The service has accelerated road-building programs, increased clear-cutting, and put virgin old-growth forest to the saw. The federal courts have been largely unwilling to control forest abuse because the phrase "multiple use" is so vague that judges seem powerless to set priorities or otherwise limit the discretion of the Forest Service officials. Meanwhile, in Oregon, the heirs of John Muir are taking protest and civil disobedience directly into the old-growth forests.

The controversy persists; Congress, responding halfheartedly to public pressure, has enacted still more planning statutes, notably the National

Forest Management Act of 1976 (NFMA). Yet without congressionally set priorities, expanded multiple-use planning has resulted in little more than interminable hearings and administrative reviews, which do little to restrain an agency determined to elevate timber cutting above all other values.

A similar multiple-use controversy is unfolding on lands administered by the Bureau of Land Management. Just as the Organic Act of 1960 brought multiple use to the Forest Service, so the Federal Land Policy and Management Act of 1976 (FLPMA) established a similar mandate for the Bureau of Land Management. However, the bureau, lacking the professional esprit of the Forest Service, tainted by politics and incompetence in upper management and heavily influenced by mining and livestock constituencies, has been even slower to change.

No public-land policy can be complete without accounting for the waters that originate on and flow through the public lands, nourishing diverse communities of plants and wildlife. Unlike the land over which it flows, Western water has not remained under public stewardship. Beginning with the Desert Act of 1871, Congress ceded control over Western water to the states, which in turn allocated public waters to settlers on a first-come, first-served basis.

Given the scarcity of water and its essential role in development, it was perhaps inevitable that a large share of Western water would quickly be diverted into private use and ownership. But after yielding control of Western water in the nineteenth century, the federal government reentered the field in the twentieth century by means of a 1902 congressional enactment, the Newlands Act, which created the Bureau of Reclamation, and a 1908 court decision, *Winters v. United States,* which established the doctrine of federal reserved water rights.

In due course, the Bureau of Reclamation became the most formidable of all the federal agencies operating in the West. With a mandate to open desert lands to small farmers and with huge budgets financed by hydropower from federal dams, the bureau changed the course of western development. Its practices have been the most environmentally destructive of all the public land agencies, and to this day the bureau has been scarcely touched by the reform movements that have begun, however slowly, to change the Forest Service and the Bureau of Land Management.

The reform agenda for western land and water must start by recognizing the multiple-use planning has, for the most part, been a failure. Multiple use skirts the central reality that in the new urbanizing West, there is no longer enough space to accommodate every competing use on every section of the public domain. Commodity production, whether of timber, minerals, or livestock, is increasingly infringing on the broader public values of open space, wildlife, wilderness and recreation. Choices will have to be made, and those choices are too important to be left to district land managers imposing their own preferences camouflaged in the jargon of land-use planning.

To some degree, the environmental legislation of the last thirty years, notably the Wilderness Act, the Endangered Species Act, the National Environmental Protection Act, and the various clean-air and clean-water laws, has nudged the federal agencies toward administering their lands for public values. Wilderness classification represents a decision for wilderness and water and against mining and timber cutting, yet it applies to less than 5 percent of the public lands. And the listing of a threatened or endangered species can trigger strong measures against habitat destruction. Yet, as we are learning in the old-growth controversy in the Pacific Northwest, the presence of a threatened or endangered species such as the spotted owl is not an adequate substitute for an outright policy against cutting the remaining old-growth forests. And the fact remains that the vast majority of public lands are still administered free of the restraints imposed by generic environmental legislation.

The next step in the evolution of public land-use policy is to replace multiple-use management with a new concept—dominant public use—that gives priority to recreation, wildlife and watershed uses. Dominant public use would be a mandate to reconsider destructive resource exploitation that is of marginal economic importance.

Many areas of the West, especially in the southern Rocky Mountains, produce small amounts of timber whose harvest would not be economically justified without federal subsidies. In the Tongass and in Oregon and Washington the values of old-growth forest far outweigh the profits from exporting raw logs to Japan. The canyonlands of southern Utah, unique in the world, should be off-limits to prospectors. The introduction of heap-leach gold mining, a technique that allows on-site gold recovery by leaching with sulfuric acid, permits recovery of the microscopic amounts of gold present in the landscape all over the West. As one mountain ledge after another is blasted apart, crushed up and drenched in sulfuric acid, it is none too soon to ask why the mining of gold for monetary speculation, rings and necklaces, should be allowed everywhere on the public domain.

The battle for Western water reform will require changes in both the big land agencies and the Bureau of Reclamation. The Forest Service and the Bureau of Land Management still retain powers to protect streams and other riparian areas by asserting federal rights to instream flows. Federal agencies can also protect federal waters by petitioning for instream flow rights under state laws; yet with just an occasional exception they have failed to do so.

Court decisions and the hostility of the Reagan and Bush administrations to water protection have made the task all the more difficult. Conceivably, the Congress could step into the void by both asserting and creating reserved rights for wilderness and other public lands. Hamstrung by opposition from Western senators and representatives and the indifference of most others, it has so far refused to do so.

Now that streams and rivers are virtually exhausted, thirsty water users are flocking to the last water holes in the West, the huge groundwater reserves hidden beneath remote desert basins. While groundwater may be out of sight and of little direct use to humans or beasts, it does support the marshes, springs, and intermittent streams that maintain life in arid desert lands. Once the hydrologic connection is broken by pumping, the surface waters will disappear, altering desert ecosystems on an unprecedented scale.

The big test of federal resolve to protect the interconnected ground-water and surface waters on public lands will probably occur in Nevada, where the city of Las Vegas, asserting rights under state law, is preparing to pump groundwater from twenty thousand square miles of federal land in the remote desert basins of eastern Nevada. The project threatens the Pahranagat Wildlife Refuge in eastern Nevada, the Ash Meadows Wildlife Refuge and Devil's Hole National Monument in western Nevada, and even springwaters emerging across the state line in Death Valley National Monument.

The Fish and Wildlife Service, the National Park Service, and the Bureau of Land Management have filed protests before the Nevada State Water Engineer. The Secretary of the Interior and the Congress have remained silent. Ultimately, a federal groundwater-protection law may be the only way to avoid a repetition of the environmental tragedy of Owens Valley and Mono Lake from recurring in Nevada and throughout the West.

The Bureau of Reclamation presents a special challenge to public water reform. With its cultivated image as champion of the small farmer (although it is a longtime ally of corporate agriculture) and a long record of delivering water projects and public power to eager Western members of Congress, the bureau has never attracted the public scrutiny routinely accorded most other federal agencies. Even the great controversies of the past—Glen Canyon, Echo Park, Bridge Canyon, and Marble Canyon—and present—Glen Canyon again—do not seem to slow down the bureau juggernaut.

Remarkably, no member of Congress has, at least in modern times, ever come up with a comprehensive plan to reform the bureau. For non-Westerners, picking a quarrel with such a gargantuan bureaucracy is an all-consuming task of no interest to constituents. For a Westerner, taking on the bureau would amount to an assault on many venerable Western institutions, including the political power centers that have grown and intertwined around local reclamation projects.

In environmental terms, the case for taking on and reforming the bureau is simple. Growing Western cities must have more water, and they will either get that water from agriculture (which consumes more than 80 percent of the water used in the West) or they will continue to raid and destroy the remaining waters located on the public lands.

Meanwhile, the bureau remains locked in a tight embrace with the appa-ratchiks of Western agriculture, who are dedicated to protecting the politi-cal power of their organizations by blocking water transfers, even when individual farmers may want the option of selling their water. The reform task is to break the link between the bureau and the agricultural bureaucra-cies and redirect the bureau toward a policy of facilitating market water-transfers. Doing so will be about as easy as transitioning the Kremlin to a market economy.

One reform alternative is to abolish the bureau and transfer its river-management functions to interstate river-basin councils modeled on the Northwest Power Planning Council. A less drastic alternative is to abolish the bureau's construction budget and authority for new project starts, take hydropower revenues from the basin accounts that feed bureau projects, transfer them to the general fund, and enact a new reclamation law that eliminates all federal barriers to voluntary market water transfers.

Even a decade ago, talk of fundamental reclamation reform would have seemed utopian. Now a four-year drought in California is beginning to expose the institutional inadequacies of the present system. As California moves ever closer to crisis, there will be pressure to relax environmental standards in the Sacramento River delta, to dam more wild rivers in the Sierra Nevada, and to increase groundwater pumping in the Owens Valley and Mono Lake basins. None of these alternatives will be necessary in California or elsewhere if Congress will use the drought crisis as a spring-board to redesign the bureau from the ground up.

One hundred years ago Congress authorized the first forest reserves, putting a new concept of perpetual ownership of public lands on the path toward public acceptance and support. Now, at the start of the coming cen-tury, the American public and its leaders must accelerate and complete the step of dedicating public land and public waters unequivocally to the high-est and best public use.

Y F U R T H E R   R E A D I N G

Edward Abbey, "Even the Bad Guys Wear White Hats: Cowboys, Ranchers, and the Ruin of the West," *Harpers Magazine* 272 (January 1986), 51–55
———, *The Monkey Wrench Gang* (1975)
Larry Burt, "Western Tribes and Balance Sheets: Business Development Programs in the 1960s and 1970s," *Western Historical Quarterly* 23 (November 1992), 475–95
Wesley Calef, *Private Grazing and Public Lands* (1979)
David A. Clary, *Timber and the Forest Service* (1986)
James Coates, *Armed and Dangerous: The Rise of the Survivalist Right* (1987)
Richard Conniff, "Federal Lands: New Showdowns in the Old West," *National Geographic* 185 (February 1994)
William Deverell, "Fighting Words: The Significance of the American West in the History of the United States," *Western Historical Quarterly* 25 (Summer 1994), 185–206
Phillip O. Foss, *Politics and Grass: The Administration of Grazing on the Public Domain* (1960)
Al Gedicks, *The New Resource Wars: Native and Environmental Struggles Against Multinational Corporations* (1993)
Matthew Glass, *Citizens Against the MX: Public Languages in the Nuclear Age* (1993)
R. C. Gordon-McCutchan, *The Taos Indians and the Battle for Blue Lake* (1991)
William L. Graf, *Wilderness Preservation and the Sagebrush Rebellions* (1990)
E. Richard Hart, ed., *That Awesome Space: Human Interaction with the Intermountain Landscape* (1981)
Ronald J. Hrebenar and Clive S. Thomas, eds., *Interest Group Politics in the American West* (1986)
William Kittredge, *Owning It All* (1987)
———, *Who Owns the West* (1996)
Richard D. Lamm and Michael McCarthy, *The Angry West: A Vulnerable Land and Its Future* (1982)
Richard Lowitt, *Politics in the Postwar American West* (1995)

Michael P. Malone and F. Ross Peterson, "Politics and Protests," in *The Oxford History of the American West,* ed. Clyde A. Milner II, Carol A. O'Connor, and Martha A. Sandweiss (1994), 501–33

Thomas R. McGuire, William B. Lord, and Mary G. Wallace, eds., *Indian Water in the New West* (1993)

Clyde A. Milner II, "The View from Wisdom: Four Layers of History and Regional Identity," in *Under an Open Sky: Rethinking America's Western Past,* ed. William Cronon, George Miles, and Jay Gitlin (1992), 203–22

Paul A. Olson, ed., *The Struggle for the Land: Indigenous Insight and Industrial Empire in the Semi-Arid World* (1990)

Robert W. Righter, *Crucible for Conservation: The Creation of Grand Teton National Park* (1982)

Alfred Runte, *National Parks: The American Experience,* 2d ed. (1987)

C. Brant Short, *Ronald Reagan and the Public Lands: America's Conservation Debate, 1979–1984* (1989)

Wallace Stegner, *The Sound of Mountain Water: The Changing American West* (1969)

Clive S. Thomas, ed., *Politics and Public Policy in the Contemporary American West* (1991)

James A. Tober, *Who Owns the Wildlife? The Political Economy of Conservation in Nineteenth-Century America* (1981)

Eckard Toy, " 'Promised Land' or Armageddon? History, Survivalists, and the Aryan Nations in the Pacific Northwest," *Montana, The Magazine of Western History* 36 (Summer 1986), 80–82

Richard White, "The Current Weirdness in the West," *Western Historical Quarterly,* 28 (Spring 1997)

Charles F. Wilkinson, *Crossing the Next Meridian: Land, Water, and the Future of the West* (1992)

William K. Wyant, *Westward in Eden: The Public Lands and the Conservation Movement* (1982)

Samuel Zeveloff and Cyrus McKell, eds., *Wilderness Issues in the Arid Lands of the Western United States* (1992)

Imagining the West

Y

The West holds a powerful place in the American imagination. Vast numbers
of Americans can readily depict a favorite western place, event, or person. Very
often these specific images are the creation of popular culture sold to Americans
through many forms of entertainment. Nonetheless, personal identification
with the West is important to many people regardless of its fanciful origins.

The popularity of the West and all things western is not a recent phenomenon. Writers, artists, and poets began to use the West as a creative topic
from the earliest days of national expansion. Dime novels, lithographs, and
finally the wildly popular Buffalo Bill Cody Wild West shows distorted the
historical record, but they enjoyed adoration from the American public.
Although the day-to-day life of the nineteenth-century West changed, the fascination of the American public for the dramatic epic did not. In the twentieth century, new forms of entertainment, most especially the movie industry,
capitalized on the unending love affair of Americans for the West. Western
themes have become the regular stock of films, television, and music. Western
style has permeated American fashion, home decor, and advertising. Indeed,
the craze extends far beyond America's borders, and the West has become
one of our biggest international exports.

What remains most intriguing is the disparity between the attachment to
the West of the imagination and the reality of the West of the past. Why is it
that Americans willingly endorse an image of the West that marginalizes
Native Americans, Hispanics, Asians, and women, while it glorifies men in
their least attractive and most violent behavior? What personal sense of identity is it that Americans find in western forms? How do they extract the symbolism of the West and apply it to their own lives? How has it come about
that Americans perceive their national self almost exclusively through commercial venues? What future is there for a nation that defines itself by an
imaginary standard that never really existed?

Y D O C U M E N T S

Several years after his death, John Wayne remains the quintessential American
cowboy. Two documents here address his amazing status as a legend whose

public impact reached far beyond his screen portrayals. The decision to award Wayne a U.S. Congressional Gold Medal illustrates the way a movie performer came to embody the nation's western heritage. The eloquence of the obituary that announced his death captures the extent to which his persona had permeated American thinking. The two political cartoons that follow give a humorous spin to the objections westerners have about the modern "discovery" of the West. The West has become the commercial playground of those with the money to invest, and their "nouveau West" presence creates a certain irritation for long-time residents. Perhaps nothing illustrates this presence more than Ralph Lauren's commercial invasion of the West. A document that describes a visit to Lauren's Colorado ranch tells how the designer has marked off western space to suit his imagination. The next document shows that despite the resistance of western locals, "larger than life" movie stars want to be part of the "larger than life" West. The final document captures a central ingredient in why the West typifies the American spirit. It wasn't just that James Arness always got his man, it was that he and his cohorts represented our western family, people we knew, understood, and loved. Marshal Matt Dillon's Dodge City is more familiar than Robert Dykstra's cattle towns (see chapter six) and John Wayne's cowboy is far better known than Granville Stuart's cattleman (also chapter six). Will the historical West presented in primary documents and scholarly writing always pale beside the popular West of our imagination?

John Wayne Receives a Congressional Gold Medal, 1979

The consumer-affairs subcommittee of the House Banking, Finance and Urban Affairs Committee had no trouble yesterday getting an audience and television coverage of hearings on whether Congress should authorize a special gold medal in honor of John Wayne. A key witness was Maureen O'Hara, often Mr. Wayne's co-star, who tearily told the subcommittee: "John Wayne is not just an actor, John Wayne is the United States of America."

Miss O'Hara received a consoling pat on the back from Elizabeth Taylor. She said to the subcommittee chairman, Representative Frank Annunzio, Democrat of Illinois: "Please let us show him our appreciation and love. He is a hero, and there are so few left." Later the subcommittee approved the measure, calling for the medal to read—at Miss O'Hara's suggestion—"John Wayne, American."

Mr. Wayne, who is gravely ill with cancer, will be 72 years old on Saturday. President Carter supports legislation, already approved by the Senate, authorizing him to issue a gold medal in Mr. Wayne's honor. Similar legislation has been enacted 83 times for the striking of Congressional gold medals, given to Americans as diverse as George Washington, Charles A. Lindbergh, Robert Frost, the Wright Brothers, Dr. Jonas Salk and Bob Hope.

The Duke: "More Than Just a Hero," 1979

John Wayne was an American folk hero by reason of countless films in which he lived bigger, shot straighter and loomed larger than any man in real life ever could.

His death in Los Angeles on Monday at the age of 72 deprived the world of the last active survivor and exponent of the classic American action film. In the more than 200 features in which he appeared in a career that spanned half a century, "Duke" Wayne projected an image of rugged, sometimes muleheaded and always formidable masculinity.

His name was synonymous with the Western and, beyond that, with Hollywood and with what many Americans would like to believe about themselves and their country. He became a figure whose magnitude and emotional conviction took on an enduring symbolic importance.

Mr. Wayne's films earned about $700 million. For 25 consecutive years, he was listed among the top 10 box office attractions of American films. His only Academy Award came late in his career for his role as the cantankerous Marshal Rooster Cogburn in "True Grit" in 1969. The critic as well as the public thought it was well deserved.

Perhaps no Hollywood actor had a more distinctive appearance—a slightly tilted stance and a loping stride, an emphatic, syncopated way of speaking which delighted many a mimic, professional and amateur, and an awesome physical presence. His physicality was expressed most engagingly, perhaps, in a peerless ability to kick in locked doors.

In an interview in 1976, Mr. Wayne described the typical hero he portrayed:

"The man I played," he said slowly, "could be rough, he could be immoral, he could be cruel, tough or tender, but" his hand hit the table smartly—"he was never petty or small. Everyone in the audience wants to identify with that kind of character. He may be bad, but if he's bad, he's BAD. He's not just a petty little whiner."

Mr. Wayne died of cancer at 8:35 P.M. (Eastern time) at the UCLA Medical Center in Los Angeles. His death was announced three hours later by Dr. Bernard R. Strohm, the hospital administrator. The actor's seven children were at his bedside at the end.

The character Mr. Wayne played on the screen and the gallantry and stubbornness with which he fought repeated illnesses in recent years were evoked in the messages of sympathy that came from around the world.

In a statement issued by the White House, President Carter said that "in an age of few heroes" Mr. Wayne was "the genuine article."

"But he was more than just a hero," the president said. "He was a symbol of many of the most basic qualities that made America great. The ruggedness, the tough independence, the sense of personal conviction and courage—on and off the screen—reflected the best of our national character. It was because of what John Wayne said about what we are and what we can be that his great and deep love of America was returned in full measure." . . .

"The Duke: 'More Than Just a Hero'" by Gary Arnold and Kenneth Turan, *Washington Post,* June 13, 1979. Reprinted by permission of *Washington Post.*

Mr. Wayne starred in Hollywood action films beginning with a grandiose Western epic, "The Big Trail," and ending with "The Shootist" in 1976. Although he enjoyed success in many non-Western roles—at one time his identity as a movie soldier probably took precedence over his identity as a movie cowboy—Mr. Wayne's fame and appeal are likely to rest on such Westerns as John Ford's "Stagecoach," "She Wore a Yellow Ribbon," "Rio Grande," "The Searchers," and "The Man Who Shot Liberty Valance," Howard Hawks' "Red River" and "Rio Bravo," and Henry Hathaway's "North to Alaska" and "True Grit."

At once the most venerable and durable of Western stars, Mr. Wayne sustained this genre by the force and clarity of his personality years after other stars of his generation had abandoned it. Although some critics have felt that Mr. Wayne did little more than play himself in his movies, the image he projected was one he devised with considerable art. His walk and his manner of speaking, for example, were copied from his friend Yakima Canutt, the stunt man.

Film historian David Thomson wrote that "Wayne's sincere wrong-headedness may yet obliterate the fact he is a great screen actor. . . . It is a matter of some . . . importance that the student of film appreciate that Wayne is an actor of noble bearing. Good enough to survive innumerable bad films, he is a presence that makes meaning and appearance exactly congruent—one can ask for no more."

High Country News Spoofs Real Estate Development, 1994

Source: Greg Siple, High Country News.

I always had a dream of buying a little ranch out West—and selling if off piece by piece.

Ralph Lauren Builds His Ranch in Colorado, 1988

For most people, a huge duplex on Fifth Avenue with Central Park as a corral would be more than enough. Throw in a tropical estate on Montego Bay
in Jamaica, a one-hundred-odd-acre property in Pound Ridge, New York, a
beach house in Montauk on the tip of Long Island, a private jet to get around
in, and you might be able to stave off the onset of claustrophobia. Not, however, Ralph Lauren, designer of men's, women's, and children's clothes, and
of everyone's housewares, furniture, and sheets, not to mention perfume,
cologne, luggage, eyeglasses, purses, and shoes—in short, our material lives.

"I love land," he says emphatically. "I love land. I'm a land junkie. I
want the freedom. I want to feel the air."

Ralph Lauren, in fact, seems to be the archetypal American outdoors-
man: he could pass for a cowboy, pilot, wilderness outfitter, or lumberjack.
Since 1974 he has been his own best model; his face, which has appeared
frequently in ads for his merchandise, is rugged and perpetually tanned. In
spite of the appeal of his silver hair and gleaming blue eyes, his presence in
these photographs is oddly less compelling than in the flesh, where, though
slight of build, he projects an outsize drive and sex appeal.

Attired as usual in faded denim jacket and cowboy boots, he is now sitting in a scruffy old-fashioned swivel chair and gesticulating out the window
of his ranch manager's office at roughly 13,000 acres of southwestern-
Colorado ranchland, the bulk of which he acquired in 1982. It is a long way
from the Mosholu Parkway in the Bronx, where he grew up. Not accidentally, this office, like all the other buildings on the property, looks as if it has
been salvaged from the movies. When Lauren bought the land, there were
very few buildings on it, certainly none that met his standards, and he was
free to create his dream from scratch. This he did with a vengeance, using
local craftsmen to build the structures and a trusty design team from New
York to help decorate the interiors. Corrals were erected, and calving sheds
with medical facilities, cabins and stables and offices, his manager's house,
a guesthouse, a cookhouse, and his own house, plus a swimming pool. If he
wasn't satisfied with the construction—and from time to time he was not—
be it house or chimney, it was torn down and redone until every detail measured up to his idiosyncratic requirements.

What he wanted and what he got was an authentic, rustic, nineteenth-
century cattle ranch, no expense spared. Surrounding the whole is a ten-to-
fifteen-mile-long stretch of four-rail pine fence specially stained. That
fence is something of a local cause célèbre, but, as a neighbor says,
"Naturally, if you are a public figure, people are always jealous. And you
can hear stories. But in reality Lauren is a real godsend to Ouray County.
He set the tone for the new look of it—really beautiful, well-kept land. He
runs a first-rate ranch, absolutely. We call it designer ranching, which is
what it is. Everything there is done just first-class. . . .

Back at the ranch, a perfect example of this in miniature is the guesthouse known as the Little Brown Cabin. The oldest (1890s) building on the

Brooke Hayward, "A Visit with Ralph Lauren," Excerpted by permission of the author. The story originally appeared in *Vanity Fair* (February 1988), 108, 142–44.

property still extant, it probably served as a rough model for the more ambitious 1980s Cookhouse and Lodge. Lauren had it moved to a site a mile or so away from the main buildings. Then it was reframed and refurbished from the ground up. The exterior is classic log cabin and front porch overlooking, as far as the eye can see, a brook, cow pastures, woods, the San Juan Mountains, and Sneffles, one of the range star peaks. When you recover from the vista and go inside, you confront Lauren's home-furnishings ideal: fire blazing in stone fireplace, tan leather sofas strewn with Navaho rugs, wide-planked floors strewn with more Navaho rugs, walls upholstered in animal skins, wagon-wheel chandeliers overhead. Beyond, in the bedroom, flannel sheets on the antique iron-and-brass bed, leather slippers in *two* sizes neatly arranged bed-side, flannel bathrobes hanging from the hand-carved wood pegs that line the walls, red terry-cloth towels and facecloths of his design in the wood-siding-paneled bathroom, which also sports a small sauna and a washer and dryer. And to get back to the main body of the ranch, a battered Jeep, which may or may not start.

Ridgway is one of those unfortunate western towns of little distinction that were built in the twentieth century instead of the nineteenth; Lauren's aesthetic has led him to approach the town fathers with a proposal to redesign it, at his expense. "I've always had an ambition to be the sheriff," Lauren says teasingly. Perhaps the idea of the classic movie sheriff's black outfit and silver star tickles him.

More than that of any other designer, Lauren's work is directly influenced by personal experience. In 1977, for example, his love affair with things western was fired by a trip to Denver for the opening of his store there. To his chagrin, he could not locate a single authentic, western, snap-buttoned shirt anywhere. His fruitless search led to the creation of his Western Collection in 1978, which featured not only the aforementioned shirt but also cavalry shirts, prairie skirts, shearling jackets, cowboy boots, and stonewashed jeans. Several years later a trip to the Rancho Encantado in Santa Fe inspired his Santa Fe Collection, based on clothing and artifacts of the American Indian: hand-knit sweaters with Indian-blanket designs, suede skirts and shirts, tooled loafers and belts. . . .

Until the 1950s, the economy of Ouray County, Colorado, was predominantly based on silver mining and agriculture. The extraordinary thing about it, apart from the spectacular scenery, was that it was largely owned—some 70,000 acres of it—by a single feisty lady, Marie Scott, until she died in 1979.

"This land," as Lauren's neighbor puts it, "had been kept extremely clean and beautiful and off the market for thirty years. So when it was auctioned off, Ralph comes in and picks up a chunk and we come in and pick up a chunk . . . and that's the key to the county. Seventy-five percent of it is now in the hands of five big families, very strong hands. It could have gone another way; developers could have bought it, divided it up. Made it into another little Aspen. And although we've never talked about it, it's the completely understood rule: keep the land clean and clear."

The Double RL Ranch is named for Ralph and his wife, Ricky. They were married twenty-three years in December. Despite the pressures on both of them, particularly the demands on his time, it is clear that an important part of their lives is devoted to each other.

Slender, slight, graceful, with clear blue eyes and long golden hair, Ricky is the muse who originally inspired his clothes for women. Nobody wears them better. And yet she chooses not to be in the spotlight. In this era, when wives of mogul husbands tend to use the hubby's connections to build their own mini-empires, it's refreshing to encounter a quiet, unassuming woman more than content simply to share and contribute to her husband and family's life. . . .

Lauren is the quintessential family man. He makes no bones about it. This is what makes him comfortable, and it could be said that, more than most people, he is aware of what gives him comfort. And he sticks to it. All of his spare time is spent with Ricky and the children. Not incidentally, the children are attractive and unspoiled. Within the ever expanding boundaries of Lauren's vast domain—and despite his conspicuous role in maintaining it—he has also constructed a closely knit family unit that is truly insulated from public view. In this respect he is a throwback to another age, an age before mass communication and the media took over. If that seems contradictory, it's not. An icon, he is also an iconoclast. You will almost never see him in fashionable restaurants or at cocktail parties or openings. In fact, he says he doesn't like what's fashionable at all.

". . . Fashion always seemed fake. To me, the people who dressed well were not so much about fashion as they were about style. Cary Grant, Fred Astaire, the Duke of Windsor, Greta Garbo—that's what I related to: old movies, old pictures, people who had flair, elegance, who lived a certain kind of life that did not state 'Look at me.' People, things, clothes that get better with age. That's what I like about the West. It has an integrity, and so do its clothes—non-fashion, utility, rugged, staples, durable, wearable. Broken-in. A cowboy would never give up his saddle. Or his boots."

It is mud season at the Double RL. It is also calving season, and this is a serious operation. Larry Luke, the ranch manager, Bob Barnes, the foreman, and the four cowboys are all on around-the-clock duty. Luke, a large, canny, good-natured former investment adviser who gave up banking for ranching some years ago, runs the place like the business it is. For there is more to the Double RL than mere beauty; Lauren's master plan is to create quality beef under his own Double RL brand ("The first time I came out here I had a rotten steak. So I decided to develop a good one"). . . .

Not only can Luke come up with computer runs and genetic studies and consumer-test results, he can rope a steer or birth a calf, which is what he's doing right now. Between pushes and pulls and grunts, he discusses the traits he's looking for in the ideal brood cow . . . and also what he expects from the final result: "We've no intention of increasing the consumption of beef per capita; we'd like to offer a product that is tasty, juicy, flavorful—and in so doing obtain the goal of making this ranch a break-even proposition." And also the best ranch in the West.

An aura of glamour envelops the American cowboy, even when he's muddied and fatigued. In this regard, Lauren's crew is first-string. And, without exception, each has a face and demeanor that you'd swear you'd seen many times before, bigger than life, as big as the silver screen.

But nowadays a cowboy's life is not what it was in days of yore. Lauren's ranch hands are combination carpenters-mechanics-veterinarians-agriculturists. They are responsible for the total care of the cattle from birthing to surgery. In addition, they are expected to keep records, doctor, maintain fences, irrigate meadows, hay, drive machinery, bale, rake, fertilize, and produce the forage that the cattle will consume on the range as well as the forage they are fed six months of the year. Also, they have to know how to maintain equipment, take a tractor apart if necessary.

"Furthermore," continues Luke, "I expect them to keep a positive framework about this ranch, about their lives, about the work they do, to be proud of what they do and second to none."

A tall order, maybe, but not an impossible dream. None of Ralph Lauren's dreams seem to be. Except, perhaps, one.

"I always wanted to be a movie actor," he confides.

But maybe he's already been an actor on the grandest of scales. Whereas he may have once yearned to be like one of his screen heroes, now, not just in America but all over the world, he's creating the image that others are aspiring to. Taking off and putting on various personas is part of the Great American Tradition—we believe we're given not only the right but the ability to play comfortably many different roles in many times and places. Ralph Lauren, like that other Easterner who fell in love with the West and shaped our sense of what it was truly like—the original Rough Rider, Teddy Roosevelt—has reinterpreted the myth of the West for our times.

Dennis Quaid Dines Out in Montana, 1989

It's closing time. On this Tuesday at the Chico Inn in Pray, Montana, that means 9 P.M., and even then you're pushing it. If you really want something to eat this late at night, you have to drive 30 miles south to Gardiner and square off with the pizza at the K-Bar.

Chico's dining room is quiet now, its last customers paying up. Three waitresses are drifting toward one another to chat for a few moments before they start setting the tables for breakfast. Most of them have worked here on and off for years: Chico is the nice place to eat in Paradise Valley, and the regulars have learned not to wince when they have to shell out upwards of $25 per person for a fancy meal. The waitresses are laughing and telling tales about a regular who's one of their favorite pains in the neck.

"Do you remember the time he brought his own raw steak and told the kitchen to cook it?" says the first, rolling her eyes.

"Aww, he's getting better," says the second, laughing. "Do you remember when he would let only Rosemary make the Quaid martini?"

The Quaid martini?

Jan Hoffman, "The Devil and Dennis Quaid," *Premiere* (August 1989). Copyright © 1989 by Jan Hoffman.

The three recite in unison: "A shot of Stoli, a dash of Tabasco, a splash of dry vermouth, two anchovies, and three olives. Up."

"It says so on the Rolodex," offers the second waitress.

They set out coffee cups and bring out a mop and bucket. The hotel receptionist yells in from the front desk, "Somebody has to stay late—Dennis and Meg are coming in." The waitresses groan.

"I said, 'Dennis! Don't you have any groceries in your refrigerator?' " the receptionist explains. "But he didn't, of course."

She runs into the kitchen to sweet-talk the chef. This has happened many times before and no doubt will happen again. Dennis Quaid's place is just a few miles back on the old road; the Chico Inn might as well be his own dining room and the cowboy bars scattered throughout this valley his living room. Everybody, it seems, has seen him on one Saturday night or another getting up in the middle of some local band's gig and insisting on doing a couple of numbers with them. And while many privately suggest that maybe he should stick to his day job, they like him too much to say so to his face. "He's under so much pressure out there in Hollywood," says one waitress sympathetically. "Here it's wide open, so easy to let go. It's an Old West tradition that this is a great place to be an asshole."

It's almost ten o'clock, and there's a clatter in the front hall: two attractive young people, Dennis Quaid and Meg Ryan, slip into seats at a table, their grins, charmingly sheepish, putting out whatever embers of annoyance still smolder in the empty restaurant. Oh, that boy—he does test one's patience! A waitress smiles indulgently as she produces the wine list.

And what would have happened if the chef had already gone home? The hotel receptionist gives an exasperated shrug. "I would have called my mom and asked if she had any leftovers for Dennis."

Pat Bagley Lampoons the New Western Lifestyles, 1993

Source: Bagley 1993, *Salt Lake Tribune.*

Marshal Matt Dillon Has His Last Showdown, 1995

It was a 20-year shoot-out between wrong and right that began in 1955 and spanned three wildly diverse decades. There were 30 TV Westerns when the show expanded from 30 minutes to an hour in 1961, but when it was all over, on Sept. 1, 1975, *Gunsmoke* was the last one left standing. Naturally, it went tall and proud: *Gunsmoke,* starring 6'6" James Arness as the immensely good and unwaveringly fallible Marshal Matt Dillon, was the longest-running prime-time dramatic series the country had ever seen—and by golly, son, it still is.

For four of its years, the CBS series was the nation's No. 1 TV show; all told, it made the top 10 for 12 years. Like its hero, it was disarmingly simple: There was this town, Dodge City, out there on the Kansas plains in the year 1873, and Marshal Dillon was charged with maintaining law and order in it. He did, too, but the job was so tough and unpredictable that you never could be sure he'd succeed. Its regulars kept you off balance the way odd relatives do: Look, here's grumpy, all-healing Doc (Milburn Stone), who drinks a bit; here comes Matt's deputy, Chester (Dennis Weaver), gimpy, perplexed, heroic when you least expect; behind him there's shift-less-looking Festus (Ken Curtis), whom you'd trust with your life; and *look*—what will the neighbors think?—it's Miss Kitty (Amanda Blake)! A sly, buxom lady of palpable, ill-defined experience, she runs the saloon, is Matt's best friend, and more, we're sure, though we've never caught them kissing.

Contrary to TV lore, John Wayne was never seriously considered for the role of Marshal Dillon; instead, his protégé, 32-year-old Arness, whom the Duke had cast in four of his production company's films, got the job. Though he'd been in 20 films before *Gunsmoke,* Arness (big brother to Peter Graves) was pretty much unknown, the one exception being his role as the costume-engulfed monster in 1951's chilly *The Thing.* Making him Marshal Dillon was casting genius: Big of nose, steely of eye, wry of mouth, Arness could walk into a room under the watchful eye of millions of people and make them all trust him—and bad guys fear him.

In 1975, CBS brass bowed to changing times and demographics—Westerns' diminishing audiences were considered too old and too rural—and decided *Gunsmoke* had seen its last sunrise. Stone, Curtis, and Blake are gone from this world now. Arness, 72, lives in semi-retirement in L.A.; Weaver, 70, became *McCloud,* TV's urban-cowboy lawman, from 1970 to '77, lives in Ridgway, Colo., and takes occasional TV roles. *Gunsmoke* reruns still air in various parts of the country, and Arness and crew have made five *Gunsmoke* TV movies since '75, the last in 1994. "I think primarily the reason for *Gunsmoke*'s longevity . . . was the *Gunsmoke* family," says Weaver. "These people were very likable, very human, very believable."

Richard Lemon, "The Last Showdown," *Entertainment Weekly* (August 25, 1995), 126. Reprinted by permission.

Y *E S S A Y S*

In the first essay, Julian Crandall Hollick, a documentary producer for National Public Radio, explores the attraction that the American West had in the past and continues to have for Europeans. He shows that, like Americans, European writers invented a West that grabbed the imaginative spirit of several different national groups. Although these Europeans retain their own cultural distinctiveness, the American West appears to provide them with certain personal affirmations. Anne M. Butler teaches western history at Utah State University and is coeditor of the *Western Historical Quarterly*. Her essay examines the way in which the popular culture of the American West mushroomed in the twentieth century, inflated by a vast range of commercial ventures. Selling the West has become more important than knowing the West. Ultimately, popular culture and commercialism blended with political rhetoric. This blending of regional symbols with political values presents Americans with their greatest intellectual challenge in the preservation of devotion to the western epic. Is the West, as an export commodity, likely to dominate European markets, as it has American? Does the international affection for the West suggest a common meeting ground for Europeans and Americans? Or are the perceptions of America so erroneous as to only exacerbate misunderstanding? Do Americans themselves even comprehend the questionable veracity within their own national symbols?

The American West in the European Imagination

JULIAN CRANDALL HOLLICK

The "Wild West" is alive and well in Europe! But it is a Wild West that has very little to do with a reality called America. The Wild West for many Europeans has been, and always will be, a mythical place to stage their own adventures, fight their own battles, settle their own quarrels. If the Wild West had never existed, Europeans would have had to invent it.

Americans have been brought up on the notion of the frontier as something quintessentially American. It defines American character and America's self-images. But the frontier is also a European myth. After all, what else is America but Europe's own search for the last frontier? Seen in this context, the cowboy is very much a European invention—the white male adventurer who battles nature and heathen savages and tames the wilderness.

For more than five hundred years, European writers have invented an American West as a backdrop for stories that basically reflect Europe's quarrels and fantasies about itself, not about America. Remember Jonathan Swift's imaginary land and imaginary people—the Lilliputians—whom he

Julian Crandall Hollick, "The American West in the European Imagination," *Montana: The Magazine of Western History,* 42 (Spring 1992), 17–21. Excerpted by permission of the Montana Historical Society.

invented to better comment on his native England? Well, to a large extent that is the role the West fulfills in the European imagination.

Take Europeans and the Native American, or as every self-respecting European still calls him—the Red Indian. Since 1492 Europeans have been unable to make up their minds about him. Is he human or animal? Can you talk with him or should you hunt him?

Until the nineteenth century the Indian was the object of a great debate. If he was human, he could be converted to Christianity. This assumed great importance for Spain, which could then claim the New World for itself in the name of Rome. Imagine the prestige and legitimacy to be won by saving all those millions of unbelievers for God! Of course, if the Indian was animal, he could be exterminated and his land and property stolen with a clear conscience.

In eighteenth-century Europe, this ambivalence took on added significance in ideological debates. For liberals, the Red Indian was widely believed to be a throwback to a supposed Golden Age—a time of innocence—living in a society unblemished by all the vices and decadence a weary Europe called civilization. Rousseau, the philosopher and writer, called him a "Noble savage," free of laws and constraints on his behavior.

Paintings and sculptures of the period invariably show the Indian as a Roman or a Greek, who just happens to have copper-colored skin. The Red Indian, in other words, was the ideal to which liberal Europeans could aspire if only they could throw off the yoke of despotism and tyranny. Conservatives countered that Indians were half-naked savages, lacking all moral and social virtue. Moreover, their brains were smaller than those of the white man due, in large part, to the basic foulness of the American land. If the Red Indian proved anything, went this line of argument, it was that settling in the New World was dangerous and unwise and that so-called freedom was a mirage.

Europe's literary love affair with the Red Indian in the nineteenth century even accentuated this tendency to use the West as a self-reflecting mirror in which Europe could gaze at its own warts and worry lines. It is true that James Fenimore Cooper popularized the Indian. But the first frontier best-seller, the granddaddy of them all was *Atala,* written in 1800 by the French-Catholic writer Chateaubriand.

Atala inspired countless paintings and plays and tells the tragic story of the young Indian princess, Atala, who takes poison to protect her virginity rather than succumb to the ardent courtship of Chactas, a handsome Indian of the Natchez tribe, whose only crime was that he has not embraced Catholicism.

There were many other European writers of "Westerns" in the nineteenth century—Mayne Reid, Friedrick Gerstäcker, Gabriel Ferry. Most of their books are "boys-own" stories in which a young European, sowing his oats and looking for adventures in exotic climes, comes to America and absent-mindedly is plunged into the rescue of a damsel in distress. The locale is usually New Mexico or Arizona, which the author may or may not have ever visited.

In most of these European versions of the dime novel, Indians are savages and intrinsically evil, still viewed as obstacles to the great god of progress. This was by no means only confined to conservatives. Charles Dickens, for example, described the Native American as "a savage . . . and I call a savage something highly desirable to be civilized off the face of the earth."

But in Germany something totally different happened. The tragic fate of the American Indian only made him more attractive to a culture naturally inclined to romanticism. This convergence reaches its climax in the wonderful series of Winnetou and Old Shatterhand novels by the Saxon author Karl May, first published in Dresden one hundred years ago.

Ask any German today to name one American and he or she will instinctively say "Winnetou" or "Old Shatterhand," not Lincoln or Washington. In his dozen or so Winnetou novels, May created characters who have become living legends—for millions in German-speaking central Europe, an escapist reality that they still believe is a true representation of the real America.

Yet the astonishing facts are that Karl May never came to America until just four years before his death, that all his books were written on the basis of travel books and anthropological guides to the fauna and flora of the Southwest, and that his stories basically retell good old German myths about good versus evil, transported to Arizona and Colorado. "Richard Wagner for the masses," as one German filmmaker accurately describes the power of May's hold on the collective German imagination even today.

Winnetou is a good Apache who becomes the blood brother of Old Shatterhand, a German writer who can kill a man with a blow of his fist but who incarnates the virtues of a good Christian who prefers mercy to murder. They ride up and down the West righting wrongs and thwarting evil. Winnetou eventually is murdered by Yankees lusting for buried Indian gold.

May's basic message has little to do with the American West and everything to do with spreading the message of Christian brotherhood among all races. That and a severe case of wish fulfillment on the part of the diminutive and sickly May, who used to go around claiming to be Old Shatterhand in person, until he was sued. But the message of Christian love undoubtedly accounts for his continuing appeal.

According to May's maps, Winnetou is buried in the Grand Tetons. Many is the German who has made the pilgrimage to Wyoming in a vain search for the rock pile supposedly marking the burial mound where Winnetou is believed to sit astride his faithful steed Iltsche.

It is impossible to exaggerate the importance of May's western creations and their hold on the German mind. Even in an age when reading has taken a backseat to the VCR and the computer, Winnetou lives on in the person of French actor Pierre Brice, who for the past thirty years has played Winnetou in films and on stage, and who looks the way every European imagines a "Noble Savage" should look.

There are still plenty of contemporary Karl Mays churning out Westerns in Europe even today. I know of several in Poland and the former East

Germany. But my favorite is the Norwegian writer Kjell Hallbing, who has written more than eighty-five Westerns and sold maybe twenty-million books about his fictional creation, Morgan Kane.

In the beginning, Hallbing turned out a book a month. By the age of thirty-two he could afford to retire from his job in an Oslo bank. Like Karl May, he had never visited the United States. "I just faked it," he candidly admits. Since those early days, of course, he has traveled often to the United States. Interestingly, Kjell says he only found one serious factual error in those early books. He had his hero swim a river in Arizona that, when he actually got there, turned out to flow underground.

Hallbing insists his books are really not Westerns at all. They are a retelling of classic Norse myths in Western settings. His hero Morgan Kane bears an uncanny resemblance to any good introverted Norwegian boy.

Kjell Hallbing's hero, of course, is a cowboy, not an Indian. Much of Europe's fascination with the cowboy is due to one man—Buffalo Bill Cody—and his Wild West show that toured Europe for the better part of twenty years a century ago. Even today, many obscure provincial towns in Germany or Czechoslovakia proudly boast Buffalo Bill museums. People are still alive who can recall seeing the great man.

The Wild West show literally made dreams into reality for millions of young boys and girls. The flamboyant Buffalo Bill was Europe's idea of a contemporary knight. He was a character straight from the pages of novels by Sir Walter Scott. Cody probably did more than anyone before or since to give a face to the New World. Karl May, for example, took to dressing up like Buffalo Bill until he was sued for misrepresentation.

Cody's show popularized cowboys and Indians and spawned a host of contemporary western pursuits that once again tell us much more about Europe than about the Wild West.

Take, for example, the Czechoslovak passion for "tramping," except tramp in Czech does not quite mean what it means in English! Modern Czechoslovakia was founded in 1918, the direct consequence of Woodrow Wilson's policy of helping the former nations of the Austro-Hungarian empire acquire statehood. America and things American therefore have always enjoyed a special place in the hearts of ordinary Czechs.

Tramping is still an inexpensive way of expressing this new-found freedom on an individual level. Successive generations of girls and boys have learned to camp, canoe, hike, ride horses, all the while pretending to be Indians or cowboys. Country-and-western music has become a Czech art form, but the genre is not a pale imitation of Nashville. The Czechs have indigenized it, given it the rhythms of their country dances and polkas, turned it into yet another metaphor about freedom and the lack of it under Communism in their own country.

And there are even Czech cowboys! Hospadath, for example, is a wiry, unlined, sixty-five-year-old bachelor living in the mountains of Moravia, who should have been born in another country and another century. He has managed to eke out a living as a cowboy under Communism. Eight years ago, a former "Tramp" called Jindryk Bilek met Hospadath. Together they organized a re-creation of the Pony Express ride through Moravia to Bilek's hometown of Sochdul. On one level, it was a wonderful ride for man and horse. On another, it was a subtle statement that all could understand about freedom. The Communists could not ban the ride. But they could not ignore its popularity or its true significance.

Ironically, now that Communism is no more, the Pony Express is struggling to survive under capitalism. Under Communist rule everyone offered their services free. They were fighting a common enemy. Now, the enemy gone, they all want their cut, but commercial sponsorship is all but unknown in Czechoslovakia and how does one charge admission to a woman sitting in her garden watching the riders gallop through the woods?

All over former Communist Europe, it was the same story. Grown men and women spent every available moment of their free time dressing up as cowboys or Indians and learning to live—Friday through Sunday—as a cowhand or a Lakota Sioux. It was good fun. But it also made a political statement.

In western Europe there's a similar tradition of cowboy-and-Indian clubs. Thousands of Europeans take off their suits and ties every Friday evening, get in their cars, and drive to the club grounds in the forest to spend the weekend in a tepee or chuck wagon, eating, sleeping, living like cowboys or Red Indians.

Of course, this has nothing to do with Communism. But in its way it is also about freedom, a form of statement against an over-regimented society. (In Germany, for example, it is illegal to fire a rifle, ride a horse, or camp unless one belongs to a registered club and performs these activities on club premises.)

It is easy to poke fun at these weekend cowboys and Indians. But doing so is to ignore why they spend considerable money and risk such ridicule dressing up. If the American frontier is also Europe's frontier, it is legitimate and makes sense. Cowboy-and-Indian clubs, not to mention a small, cantankerous band of trappers, are a commentary about contemporary European concerns.

Many of the "Indians" I have met in Belgium and Germany, for instance, are attracted to their hobby out of a concern for ecology. They maintain that the Indian way of life and Indian values are statements against the rape of nature by man and machine in the name of a false god called progress. If this makes them romantics, so be it.

Escapism? Fantasy? Maybe. But these are intelligent men and women—computer programmers, truck drivers, interior decorators, for whom the American West offers another identity necessary for their mental stability, a means of going back into history to make sense of a world in which they often are alienated, another way for man to renew the search for identity and his relationship with nature.

Of course, many ordinary Europeans have now visited the West. They know full well their dream is about an America that no longer exists, and may never have existed. But they are content with the myth because it fulfills needs that are, have always been, and will doubtless remain profoundly

European in nature, owing only a passing acquaintance to a reality called America.

Selling the Popular Myth

ANNE M. BUTLER

Wall Drugstore, once a shabby soda fountain shop tucked deep into the South Dakota Badlands, exudes the rugged ambience of a popular culture that embraces the American West. An out-of-the-way pharmacy on the verge of collapse in 1936, . . . Wall Drugstore is both a geographic and a commercial entry point to the American West. . . . Over fifty years, the focus of the store shifted . . . [to] the mass marketing of the commercial baubles of western tourism. The customers browse through rooms of western gewgaws, souvenirs, they believe, of the "real" West. The success of Wall Drug—based on regional commercialism, national imagination, and mass marketing—mirrors much of the twentieth-century selling of the West. . . .

From the very earliest expansion, the nation built its epic lore. By the nineteenth century, almost three hundred years of exploration, settlement, and human exchanges had molded a popular culture that drew energy from song and story, event and myth, heroes and villains. Fact and fancy swirled and merged as a national population of increasing ethnic and cultural diversity struggled for identity. One nineteenth-century character, Davy Crockett, nicely illustrates this wedding of reality and fable, truth and legend. More than 150 years after his death at the Texas Alamo, Crockett maintains his status as an American folk hero. Crockett does so because his life—in both its real and its imagined events—captured important aspects of "Americanness." . . .

Crockett continues his hold on the national imagination, perhaps because he represents what some Americans want to believe about the West and about themselves. No historical revelation or scholarly analysis will shake Crockett from his pedestal, for his life provides the irrefutable evidence that the West of the popular imagination embraced an epic that belonged to white American males. His feats are tightly woven into the fabric of values that many Americans think they exhibit and cherish: independence, honesty, fair play, self-reliance, loyalty, courage, justice, love of freedom. . . .

White males controlled the central roles in America's popular West. They explored and settled a tough environment and battled its equally tough peoples. They handed over to the nation more than vast lands. On these champions, Americans hung their sense of winning and, perhaps even more important, their sense of adventure. Cowboys, miners, trappers, soldiers, outlaws, and even farmers seemed to prove to an adoring public that once life had held no tedium, no sense of entrapment. Rather, each day brought risks and challenges that enlivened the spirit and promoted American democratic principles. Whether a dashing cowboy or a raucous outlaw, these heroes—by their style, verve, and independence—"won" the West. . . . As the frontier era faded in the face of technology and change, twentieth-century Americans made no secret of their nostalgic longing for this grand era when gold was for the finding, land for the taking, and living for the bold.

Their imagined scenario depended on a regular cast of western characters against whom the hero figures regularly triumphed. An advancing white society drew Native American people into enough wars, economic clashes, and social destruction that a popular wisdom easily dismissed all tribes as inferior. Nonetheless, Native Americans, as supporting players in the western saga, were critically important props to document notions of the cultural superiority of white society. Without human adversaries for defeat, the conquering of the West remained incomplete. . . . Only with the suppression of those who truly called the West home could white society rest easy in its new surroundings. Few heroic tales of the West failed to include an obligatory cast of Indian people, either "noble" or "savage," foils who repeatedly reminded white America about the technological strength of its own culture.

Other indigenous populations fared badly too. Hispanic groups played a less central but no more dignified part in the tale of Anglo chauvinism. Cast as "colorful" standbys, Spanish-speaking people assumed rigidly defined roles in the popular vision of western history. Painted in the hues of docile peasants, ferocious bandits, or sensual fandango dancers, Mexican Americans provided the "humorous" proof of Anglo superiority. The internal contours of their world and their cultural responses as a community meant nothing in the construction of national myth.

African Americans also found their experiences distorted in the images of the American West. Indeed, the popular memory virtually expunged African American life from the written and oral records of the western movement, which emerged solely as a tale of white society. Although many black families looked to the West for opportunity after the Civil War, their homesteading and ranching lives never assumed a place in the popular discourse. The "buffalo soldiers" rode with the U.S. Cavalry, five thousand or more black cowboys herded cattle, and nineteenth-century African American communities sprang up in Colorado, Kansas, Texas, and Wyoming. Despite a well-documented involvement in the Far West, African Americans rarely saw public recognition given to their ancestors' presence in both the rural and the urban areas of the region.

If African Americans suffered from historical neglect, Asian Americans remained invisible in the popular perception of the West. White America vaguely connected Asian people to the 1860s effort to build railroads, but interest in the dynamics of their lives as a western minority group never materialized. . . .

Distortion and neglect characterized the presentation not only of these ethnic groups but also of western women. In the national imagination, nineteenth-century gender definitions intensified. Basic ideas about pioneer women sprang from a national conviction that frontier wives and mothers relentlessly followed a path dictated by courage, patience, and strength. In the American mind, these women, unquestioning of husbands' decisions, sustained families through any trauma of the pioneer West but contributed little of economic or political import. . . .

Furthermore, stereotypical versions of women's lives provided the basis for an unyielding attachment to racism, further enmeshing ethnic women in social bias and obscuring their historical past. Native, Mexican, African, and Asian American women struggled under the weight of gender constraints that have never evaporated. Within the popular language of the West, ethnic women rarely assumed any activist character but remained as shadow figures. Linguistic usage—generated from within the white community in academic texts, dime novels, and film—designated minority women as "dusky," "sensual," "earthy," "promiscuous," "exotic," "criminal," and "filthy." Within popular culture, ethnic women simply represented decorations that helped to reinforce the regional uniqueness of the West.

To some degree, this representation applied to all western women—they filled the background as decor. . . . Although the "good" women of the West—presumably white, married, middle-class pioneers—received a sort of obligatory nod in the western scenario, their status could be truly clarified only if they appeared in contrast to the "bad" women of the West. These, of course, included the prostitutes, dance-hall girls, and female outlaws. Within that framework, the mule skinner Calamity Jane, the bandit Belle Starr, and the sharpshooter Annie Oakley fit perfectly, for each could be dismissed as the quirky exception that affirmed the maleness of western society. The secondary players—women and minorities—got their parts only so that they could add greater glamour to the leading men of the West. . . .

However, these frontier characters were only one aspect of the modern popular attachment to the American West. The place itself took on great significance. . . .

But consumers did not need to leave home to see the West. Mass marketing brought images of the region to American households. Transformations in industrial production, especially improvements in the technology of printing, and expansion in communication media catapulted cultural images of an earlier age into the twentieth century. For example, after 1900, the production of western art, already a booming business of the nineteenth century, reached industrial proportions. A host of American illustrators took up pen and brush to depict the life and culture believed to be part of the western experience. These artists did so with a new dedication, for the advent of the twentieth century convinced Americans, once more, that rather than "capture" the West, they must "preserve" it. After all, only seven years earlier, the historian Frederick Jackson Turner, in his famous essay "The Significance of the Frontier in American History," had warned that the pioneer West and its democratic virtues had all but disappeared. The very essence of American social and political democracy appeared to be slipping through the nation's fingers.

Certain illustrators, even as they sought personal income, wanted to preserve within the American spirit this meaning of frontier life. . . . One of the most notable, William H. D. Koerner, exemplifies the impact of these artists on the American mind. During his career, Koerner turned out more than twenty-four hundred illustrations, approximately six hundred of which depicted western themes. . . .

Like Koerner, all the illustrators turned out appealing images of frontier people and heightened Americans' positive attitude toward western settlement. These artists presented westerners as individuals of character, refinement, and integrity. Perhaps more important, as the nation moved into a world that turned on mechanization and industrial growth, these illustrated western stories kept national frontier concepts at center stage for American readers. . . .

While illustrators advertised the West and its inhabitants through art forms of every style, other popular entertainments, some of which originated in the nineteenth century, also added to the West's specialized image. For the American public, nothing brought the West more directly into their lives than the Wild West shows. From among fifty or more traveling shows, the one to popularize the American West most successfully was Buffalo Bill's Wild West and Congress of Rough Riders. More than any other figure, Buffalo Bill Cody, himself a mixture of one part reality and two parts fiction, bridged the nineteenth- and twentieth-century evolution of western popular culture. Almost single-handedly he pushed frontier western notions into the modern scenario and made them accessible to a general audience.

Americans flocked to Cody's shows convinced he brought them the true West, for, as he promised, he gathered into his performing ranks "genuine characters"—Native Americans of several tribes. As these men, most in flowing headdress and carrying elegantly feathered coup sticks, rode bareback into the arena on stunning painted horses, who among the enthralled viewers questioned how well these appearances replicated tribal life on the Great Plains? In addition, Cody's ability, in 1885, to produce the most famous Indian of all, Sitting Bull, further underscored the reliability of his West.

The Indians themselves, still reeling from recent political and social events that had uprooted traditional economies, found needed employment with Buffalo Bill. Closed out of political decision making within white America, denied access to industrial training, and segregated from educational centers, Native American people accepted one of the few jobs they could easily secure—that of entertainment figures. This depressed economic track continued to haunt Indian endeavors throughout the twentieth century, leaving them with few options. Economic opportunities within the context of white America rarely broadened and typically centered on Native Americans' willingness to "play" at being Indians. America's entrepreneurs, such as Buffalo Bill, happily hired Indians who "stayed" native and, thus, furthered their own stereotyping. The Indians who galloped into Buffalo Bill's arena did much more than add a dash of color; they embodied the reality that the twentieth-century forces of commercial capitalism marginalized native peoples who found themselves in a fixed and ungenerous economic structure.

In addition to presenting Indian peoples as glamorous showstoppers completely divorced from their own environment and outside their economic milieu, Cody brought Americans the perfect frontierswoman in the person of Annie Oakley. Her remarkable skills at marksmanship set her apart from effete eastern women, but her genteel appearance and stylish costumes revealed her to be a "true" woman. In one more western paradox, Annie Oakley, born in the East, a child of Ohio, defined the nature of western women—capable and refined—for the country.

These images of Native Americans and white women slid easily into the national consciousness. . . . It was all right with his audiences if Buffalo Bill, transformed by fiction and fame into an elegant, patrician cowboy, became the national caretaker for western authenticity. . . .

The magnetism of the Buffalo Bill show could not draw audiences indefinitely. . . . But by the time that happened, Americans had discovered the rodeo as a western entertainment replacement. Predicated on work skills and frontier amusement formed in the earliest days of cattle raising, the rodeo proved a natural for promoters. The thundering action, the magnificent animals, the death-defying cowboys—all swirling around in a sweaty, dust-filled arena—added up to a certain crowd pleaser. For the price of admission, Americans saw, close up, examples of modern men who reflected western toughness, raw courage, and natural strength, living proof that the pioneer spirit of the West remained intact. Once an informal ranch sport that branched into local and regional competitions for seasonally unemployed cowboys, rodeos hit the national big time in the twentieth century. . . .

By 1936, both the Boston Garden and New York's Madison Square Garden hosted rodeos that ran for almost three weeks. In New York, audiences totaled nearly a quarter of a million, far surpassing the usual crowds of one hundred thousand associated with rodeos in Cheyenne, Wyoming. Once again, the "Wild West" had hit the eastern pocketbook.

Unlike several areas of western popularizing, the early rodeos made a place for women, who often competed in the same events as the men performers. . . . In the post–World War II years, however, rodeos generally barred women competitors, until only barrel-racing events remained for distaff performance.

As public interest continued to accelerate during the postwar 1940s and 1950s, rodeo officials considered ways to further exploit the growing popularity. . . . R. J. Reynolds Tobacco, Levi Strauss Clothing, Wrangler Jeans, Justin Boots, Frontier Airlines, Ford Motor, Coors Beer, Schlitz Brewery, Heublein Whiskey, Nestea Foods, and Hesston Farm Machinery all invested in underwriting various aspects of rodeo competition during the 1970s, 1980s, and 1990s. Although market indicators pointed to climbing profits for sponsors, companies insisted they endorsed rodeos because these events reinforced American family values.

In the midst of cow wrangling and bull goring, that rationale remained blurry, yet huge trophies and giant purses drew an ever-increasing number of contestants, many of whom had never worked as cowhands but had trained at rodeo schools to become professional riders. When the national finals, held each December, took up residence in Las Vegas, Nevada, the transformation of rodeo from local pastime to major sport industry was complete. Set in the tinsel mecca of the United States, the national finals now meant a massive influx of fans, costly seats, high-stakes gambling, rodeo stars, ersatz cowboys, and media hype. . . .

Local rodeos proved a popular sport for Native Americans and Mexican Americans as well as blacks. Within ethnic communities the rodeo served to strengthen the bonds of people who often lived great distances from each other. For example, the rodeo amplified earlier Indian social traditions. Building on the custom of tribal powwows, Indians added rodeos to their established social structure. However, within the context of mass marketing, the Indian rodeos, as well as the Mexican-American ones, have remained outside the commercial mainstream. Although ethnic groups have adopted some aspects of the "western" mode—clothing, jewelry, crafts, rodeos—they lack both internal capital and endorsement from big businesses and thus can point to only modest economic results.

Mexican Americans, however, were more successful in using their touring circuses as a source of ethnic support. Well into the 1950s, Mexican circuses brought regular ethnic entertainment to such southwestern cities as San Antonio and Tucson. The Escalante Circus, the Ortiz Brothers, and the Rivas Brothers—from the late nineteenth century—all enjoyed great popularity among Hispanic people. In the twentieth century, national entertainment agencies hired several of the performers from local Mexican circuses to tour on the vaudeville circuit throughout the United States. . . .

As American fans propelled rodeos—local and national—into a new status as western sport, they did so to a changing beat of music. . . . [M]ore and more musicians, often only as genuinely cowboy as the hats and boots they donned, invaded the national music scene—the Prairie Ramblers, the Monroe Brothers, the Blue Sky Boys, and Bob Wills and his western-swing band, the Texas Playboys. All benefited, at least peripherally, from the jingling spurs and simple melodies of the wildly popular and true westerner Gene Autry. Of equal importance to the western music scene was the easy sound of that unauthentic cowboy Roy Rogers, who began life as Leonard Slye from Duck Run, Ohio. . . .

Regardless of where these musicians lived or traveled, when the New York songwriters picked up on the distinctive beat and sound, it was not long until all Americans knew tunes for more than "Tumbling Tumble Weeds." Few noticed that easterners increasingly wrote the popular lyrics, managed the publicity, controlled the record distribution, and owned the radio stations that broadcast the new performers. That commercial day soon came when the public cared not who produced or sang western music. In fact, country music no longer required that the performers even offer the pretense of being western cowboys. . . .

From its heyday in the 1940s, commercial cowboy music took a substantial nosedive in the 1950s as competing styles within the genre struggled for commercial dominance. Then came the invasion of rock and roll and the eruption ten years later of a brash young group from England, the Beatles. Interestingly, it did not take rock and roll very long to turn to western themes, but these would veer away from the older cowboy lyrics of the nineteenth and early twentieth centuries. Instead, California as a sun-andsurf paradise emerged from the early music of the Beach Boys, only to be replaced in the mid-1970s by the more disillusioned Golden State vision of the Eagles. As groups proliferated and music escalated as a form of social comment, California and the West remained central to the themes, demonstrating once again the mythic power of western symbolism. No longer the Great Depression melancholy of Jimmie Rodgers's "California Blues," the musical message of the Pacific Coast now agonized over drugs, Haight-Ashbury, and America's failed revolution of the 1960s.

In this immense musical renovation, the guitar twangs of country-western music died away as listeners equated the sound with low-class, southern-white origins. American music, in songs like "If I Had a Hammer" and "Blowing in the Wind," took on more and more of the hues of a social protest—a protest that often placed the blame for America's ills in the heart of the South and in the homes of rural people. Country music, however, had not died. It merely waited for a changed climate of social impulses and a new generation of performers, all of whom would be handled by high-powered promoters. By the mid-1960s, as the nation absorbed the shock waves of political assassination, civil disorders, counterculture protests, and debilitating foreign entanglements, country-western music found its moment to go national, as never before. Although television altered production styles and personal costuming for performers, country music's original format—the radio—remained a powerful vehicle for selling the renovated sounds. No longer the music of the South and the West's rural whites, country music attracted the nation's yuppie commuters and blue-collar workers, who tuned their car and truck radios to those lyrics of heartbreak and loneliness, self-reliance and courage. An economic notch or two above the original country music crowd, these fans heaped their approval on a new generation of recording stars, such as Merle Haggard.

Haggard proved to be the perfect new champion of country music. Born to poor Oklahoma farmers, Haggard made the famous depression-style "Okie trek" to California, where he grew up in Bakersfield. After a troubled life that would one day be a press agent's dream, Haggard began to make a steady living with music. Haggard's 1969 hit "Okie from Muskogee," which celebrated people who did not smoke marijuana or burn a draft card, appealed to an entirely new national constituency of listeners: middle-class white Americans, who distrusted notions of social protest and increasingly endorsed conservative values and national conformity. That trend among Americans gained momentum until in the late 1980s and early 1990s two presidents, Ronald Reagan and George Bush, each attended star-studded performances at the Grand Ole Opry in Nashville, Tennessee, the eastern-based Vatican of country music. The importance of these visits—from presidents who pitched their political rhetoric in varying degrees of reactionary language targeted toward the white electorate of the South and the West—was not lost on the American public. Musical statement and political philosophy came together as never before.

Is it any surprise that many Americans longed to tour the West, to watch real cowboys leap into the saddle, to visit the haunting bluffs at the Little

Bighorn, to stand at the north rim of the Grand Canyon, to canoe down the magnificent Snake River, to squint out over barren Death Valley? . . . Although western tours had always attracted eastern and European visitors, the tourist industry, born in the late nineteenth century, gathered unprecedented steam in the first third of the twentieth century. . . .

The first influx of tourists guaranteed national publicity for the [dude ranch, a] new concept in western vacationing. . . . At the peak of popularity, over 350 dude ranches sprawled from Arizona to Montana. A far cry from the luxury resorts of the modern West, complete with swimming pools and gourmet dinners, the first dude ranches offered no softening amenities and totally immersed visitors in the physical and spiritual meaning of western living, as defined by the ranchers and their hands. . . . Indeed, the ranchers shifted from innkeepers to interpreters of the West with remarkable ease. Once merely the routines of a day-to-day existence, ranch schedules and daily chores transmuted into secular rituals for understanding the West.

The popularity of the dude ranches coincided with a growing attention to the spectacular scenery of the national parks. . . . As the general public expressed more interest in these remote regions, so did the corporate world. Inside Glacier National Park, the Great Northern Railway, like its southwestern counterpart the Atchison, Topeka, and Santa Fe at the Grand Canyon, built several hotels and oversaw the construction of trails to the interior. . . . By 1920, almost one million tourists a year visited the national parks. . . .

The commercial development of the interior reaches packaged a new western commodity for the American consumer—the wilderness. During the first four decades of the twentieth century, that wilderness remained largely the domain of the moneyed American. However, after World War II, accessibility to wilderness areas changed significantly. The expansion of the interstate highway system, along with a leap in the number of motel chains and campsites, gave American tourism a solid place in the West. A booming airline industry, the fad for oversized recreational vehicles, and the road appeal offered by snappy motorbikes and more gas-efficient cars put domestic travel within easy reach of most Americans. No longer did tourists need dude ranches as outposts from which to organize western sightseeing. Armed with a few guidebooks and a *Rand McNally Road Atlas,* Americans orchestrated their own getaways to the wilderness. . . .

In 1973, three million more people visited the national parks than in 1972. In the same year, almost four million people went to the Colorado Rockies for skiing. The economic complexities of environmentalism and wilderness preservation crystallized with stunning rapidity.

The national parks, always more closely wedded to economic interests than Americans wanted to realize, faced an avalanche of challenges. In the first place, local economic considerations had often outweighed aesthetic concerns when lands were set aside for the parks. In addition, nineteenth-century conservationists who wanted to preserve natural beauty understood little about ecosystems and biological integrity. As a result, the government often drew boundaries for national parks haphazardly, even before local logging and grazing companies complained about the borders and demanded further gerrymandering.

When millions of nature seekers added themselves to the equation in the post–World War II era, the full tangle of public land management, political pressure, and environmental issues hit the American West. . . . This massive human intrusion placed at risk the very wilderness the visitors believed they cherished. Into the 1980s and 1990s, problems of litter, sewage disposal, wildlife protection, and public safety multiplied at unprecedented speeds. . . . As the twentieth century came to a close, less and less of the West fit the description of true wilderness, but more and more Americans believed they needed a pilgrimage to that special environment. . . .

Vast numbers of people have experienced the West, through literature, art, entertainment, or tourism. Millions more may not have taken as active an interest in things western, but they, nonetheless, would know the singular icon whose image is emblematic for the region—the cowboy. Instantly and internationally recognizable, the cowboy is now a national symbol for America and not just for its western states. His glamour has drooped from time to time as foreign observers or Americans themselves followed other fads, but the cowboy as a beloved figure has demonstrated extraordinary staying power. . . .

The American cowboy, most often a youthful bachelor, rode into the hearts of Americans with a laconic but honorable manner. No great thinker, he was guided in life by a few simple principles: he was always willing to right a wrong, to save a damsel in distress, and to defend the underdog. With an ever-constant good disposition, the cowboy did not seek violence, but when confronted, he knew how to respond quickly and thoroughly. He was white America's mounted warrior, the defender of a national code of honor, the champion of the open range. He carried a gun and rode a horse, but he did not always herd cattle.

The cowboy became a multimedia figure. He graced the pages of Owen Wister's *The Virginian* (1902) and the later stories of Louis L'Amour's Sackett family. . . . As Hopalong Cassidy, he loaned his logo to the school lunch-box and the Hoppy thermos, making the sandwiches more appetizing and the milk more cooling. As the singing cowboy, Gene Autry, he crooned "Back in the Saddle Again" to listeners out in radio-land. . . . He kept the watch with Marshal Matt Dillon over Dodge City and the Long Branch Saloon.

Actually, Matt Dillon of *Gunsmoke* fame was just one television westerner from a string of shows that proliferated between 1947 and 1960. The western motif proved a successful formula for the burgeoning new world of television. . . . By 1959, Westerns captured the ratings as seven of the top-ten favorite shows on national television. Americans liked Matt Dillon and his cowboy friends so much that their televisions stayed tuned for *The Rifleman, Rawhide, Maverick, Wanted—Dead or Alive, Wagon Train, Have Gun, Will Travel, Lawman, Bat Masterson,* and *Bonanza.* . . .

In the 1960s and 1970s, changing viewer demands, as well as a shift in the demographics of audiences, sounded the death knell for the Westerns' exaggerated popularity. . . . Yet, the Western survived to make another resurgence. The introduction of cable television in the early 1980s brought the shoot-outs and cattle stampedes back into American living rooms. Reruns of television shows and movie classics offered an available, cheap commodity for network markets that ballooned almost overnight. The Westerns added to their rejuvenated popularity through an appeal to viewers' nostalgia. The introduction of the home videotape-player allowed television owners to accumulate a private film library, bringing the Westerns and their aging stars back to the attention of the American public. In this new age, the old "B" Westerns of the 1940s and 1950s lacked the sophistication of programming in the 1990s. However, they returned, much like long-lost friends, reminders of an earlier, simpler time. At least for the expanding population of elderly Americans, they provided an easy, inexpensive way to recapture the entertainment of youth, to delight in old stars made whole once more. . . .

Certainly this roller-coaster popularity of the film and television Western accounted for the cowboy careers of dozens of actors. . . . From William S. Hart to Kirk Douglas, from Joel McCrea to Michael Landon, from Randolph Scott to Jack Palance, from Hoot Gibson to Gary Cooper to Clint Eastwood—all had the western film to thank for major developments in their cinema success.

[In contrast,] women have fared poorly in Westerns. Their screen roles tended to copy the prevailing social attitudes toward womanhood. Accordingly, film heroines of the 1920s and 1930s smiled and simpered as the "gentle tamers," those who brought "civilization" and order to the West. By the 1940s, with American women generally cast into more active and productive economic endeavors to meet the war needs, Hollywood followed suit with films about strong-minded women, such as the 1941 *Gangs of Sonora,* in which a female newspaper editor in Wyoming took on and defeated a corrupt politician. As quickly as the gender trend of self-reliant, independent women lost vogue within American society, Hollywood also dropped scripts that showed females surviving on their own. Within the western genre, women became an environmental adornment. . . .

Jane Russell's sensuous portrayal in Howard Hughes's 1943 film *The Outlaw* presaged a changed tone and texture in women's roles in the Western. By the 1960s, western films assumed greater and greater sexual explicitness, with rape and torture as common themes. Although one might argue that this trend introduced fundamental realities to the Western, often criticized in an earlier era as too sanitary, a counterpoint suggests that filmmakers simply used women characters as the vehicle through which to exploit western violence and gender aggression in more horrifying terms.

This strategy dominated the portrayal of ethnic women. Native American women seldom emerged as personalities with identities and perspectives. Historically, Native American women of film appeared only as background "pack animals" to further document the "savagery" of the men or as victims in scenes of village slaughter by marauding army troops, as for example in the 1970 film *Soldier Blue.* Thus Native-American people continued to play their main role in the Western—that of subjects for cultural or political extermination.

In a further distortion in those rare scripts that called for an actual woman character, directors typically cast Anglo actresses as Native Americans. Thus, Debra Pagent, Jennifer Jones, and Virginia Mayo, in their Indian and mixed-blood roles, helped implant an inaccurate physical image of Native American women in the minds of moviegoers. In addition, the consistent refusal of the American film industry to hire appropriate ethnic females further codified the economic structures that unrelentingly kept Indian people from reaping personal or collective profits from western popular culture.

It appears Mexican American women also had little to applaud from the film industry. Along with Native Americans, Mexican Americans found only stereotyping and cavalier treatment of their culture. Scorned as docile and lazy, their speech patterns and language ridiculed, Mexican Americans forcefully held their place in the West despite abuse that dated to the earliest contacts with Anglo culture. The strength and diversity of the Mexican-American culture rarely gained acknowledgment in an entertainment medium that appeared content to create its own image of an entire community. The film characterizations of Mexican women ranged from the elegant Katy Jurado prostitute in the 1952 *High Noon* to the earthy Mexican prostitutes in the 1969 *The Wild Bunch* to the revolutionary Hispanic prostitute in the 1990 *Old Gringo*. In almost forty years of filmmaking, no appreciable refinement in the presentation of Mexican American or Native American women graced the American screen.

Despite these glaring weaknesses and offensive biases, the cowboy film continued to draw large audiences, and the intellectual analysis of the genre appealed to film critics, university professors, and cinema buffs. . . . Regardless of these sophisticated, often highly perceptive critiques, ordinary folk idolized screen cowboys for their bedrock devotion to American values and codes of behavior seemingly lost to the modern world. Scrubbed and polished in one era, rougher and dirtier in a more recent time, cowboys of film continued to suggest that within the confines of the rocky, barren West could be found valor, freedom, and, above all, justice.

Within that formula, American movie fans avidly followed the roles of their favorite stars and became conversant with Gary Cooper's angst in *High Noon* (1952), Lee Marvin's humor in *Cat Ballou* (1965), Marlon Brando's viciousness in *Missouri Breaks* (1976), or Kevin Costner's sensitivity in *Dances with Wolves* (1990). . . . But no one did more to perfect the cowboy figure than John Wayne. Indeed, he so absorbed the flint and fiber of the character that Americans forgot where the actor stopped and the role began. Wayne's screen credentials . . . among them *Stagecoach* (1939), *Tall in the Saddle* (1944), *Red River* (1948), *Fort Apache* (1948), *Rio Bravo* (1959), *The Man Who Shot Liberty Valance* (1962), *The Sons of Katie Elder* (1965), *El Dorado* (1967), and *Rio Lobo* (1970)—offered American viewers a straightforward, easily comprehended performance. Audiences knew what to expect in a John Wayne cowboy film: obvious heroes and villains whose final encounters affirmed that in the West, tough problems had clear-cut, honorable solutions. The Duke, as he was known, helped to cement that philosophy and its cowboy values of decency and honesty, valor and integrity, in living technicolor. . . .

His cowboy characters typically projected a solid wisdom, convinced that truth and justice would carry the day. As his physical body aged, Wayne's personal values—always very American, very masculine, and painfully simplistic—held constant. Once said to be the most recognized film star in the world, John Wayne personified the cinematic definition of cowboy life.

By the time he made his final appearance in *The Shootist,* a 1976 film about a dying gunfighter in a dying West, Wayne had won over even his critics. A brilliant opening sequence that used clips from a dozen of his earlier films reminded audiences that John Wayne had ridden hard on America's cinematic range for more than forty years; almost half of his nearly two hundred movies had been Westerns. At the end of *The Shootist,* as his character died on the barroom floor, Wayne, himself clearly losing a battle with cancer, seemed to say that the West *had* changed, but not the values he endorsed in those four decades of filmmaking. The American public worshiped this film and its dying cowboy hero, fictional and real. In its aftermath, many wept with the actress Maureen O'Hara, a longtime Wayne friend and costar, when she appeared before a congressional committee to plead that the dying John Wayne be honored with the highly coveted U.S. Medal of Freedom. It seemed fitting, for Wayne himself vigorously held to the conservative, masculine, chauvinistic values that so clearly shaped western films and came to dominate American political thinking in the 1980s. That this amazing career of film achievement had really explained very little about the historical realities of the nineteenth-century West mattered not at all to Wayne's fans, Maureen O'Hara, or the U.S. Congress.

Rather, the ultimate expression of Americans' confidence in John Wayne and the cowboy mentality occurred one year after the Duke's 1979 death, when an elderly ex-film star whose personal identity also seemed carefully woven into the many cowboy roles he played was elected president of the United States. Ronald Reagan stepped out of his job as host for television's *Death Valley Days* and into the White House without any visible transformation, even given an earlier tenure in the California governor's mansion. Though more often seen in a tuxedo than his ranch clothes, Reagan, in many aspects of his presidency, made clear his attachment to the basic western script formula that the "good guys wear white hats."

The Reagan conviction that the West defined the country and democracy revealed itself clearly in the administration's rapid-fire acquisition of numerous works of western art. By 1982, the White House permanent collection boasted forty new pieces—paintings, prints, and sculptures—with western themes. Additionally, almost 130 pieces of art on loan from around the country decorated the halls and offices of the White House. In the official West Wing and Oval office, Frederic Remington bronzes, Thomas Moran landscapes, and George Catlin Indians surrounded those privy to the inner circle. Upstairs, in their private quarters, Ronald and Nancy Reagan gazed on western landscapes painted by Thomas Moran and Thomas Hill.

The Reagans' choice for artistic decor well matched the general interests of the American public. During this same era, the craze for western design and culture reached new heights throughout the United States. Cowboys themselves, or many who claimed to be, led the charge. For example, the Cowboy Artists Association of America devoted itself to "preserving western tradition." . . .

After cowboy artists established their association, cowboy poets followed suit. By 1985, their organization set Elko, Nevada, as the site of its annual gathering. . . . In an event that quickly assumed commercial overtones, no one seemed ready with a definition of cowboy poetry or of the way of life to be preserved. Did poets or poems make cowboy poetry? Did one have to be a cowboy to write cowboy poetry? Was it necessary only to wear the appropriate attire to become a cowboy poet? Did cowboy poetry have any connection to nineteenth-century values, or did it focus on ranch humor? The answers to these questions remained blurry into the 1990s, but the popularity of and profits for the cowboy poets ballooned. . . .

Larger marketing schemes continued to sell western culture to the American consumer. In the mid-1970s, first-class eastern department stores sponsored annual trunk shows of silver and turquoise jewelry, complete with a Native American demonstrator. Leather boutiques that sold soft pouches, fringed jackets, and tooled vests dotted the nation's malls. On the clothing scene, the designer Ralph Lauren quickly dominated, setting a national style with his western line of stone-washed denim items, new clothes intended to look old, like the West itself. . . .

Between 1978 and 1988, Lauren's advertisements even more blatantly appealed to a distinctly white middle-class clientele that apparently wanted two things—stability and classiness. Sales exploded. Fashion-magazine advertisements sponsored by Lauren and other companies such as Dan Post Boots, Jacques Carcanques Jewelry, and Butterick Patterns framed lean, long-haired young women resting against sun-dappled rocks, old-time saloon fronts, and horse stalls. In various wordings, the advertisements mentioned the "pure America," where clothes in "pretty pioneer styles" had a "sense of adventure" and a "respect for tradition." Among these businesses, the West not only represented the best of the nation's history but also offered solid values, made a fashion statement, and defined style. . . .

The West had galloped onto Madison Avenue. The country rushed into an era that, perhaps more than any earlier time of western adoration, cared little for the artistic renderings of the individual and only for the image that could be purchased. As a 1982 *Mademoiselle* spread entitled "Colors of the Earth" recommended, fashionable products appeared in "earth shades reminiscent of desert horizons, sun-drenched canyons, and mesas." . . . Ubiquitous cowboys in Marlboro cigarette advertisements peppered urban billboards and every kind of national publication. Automobile companies set the sleekest new car model, along with an alluring woman, atop a high red-rock butte. Florists recommended a masculine cactus dish-garden for

that recently promoted company executive. Architects advocated underground structures for residential and commercial needs, drawing on the
frontier sod house for inspiration and design. . . . Amid a clamor of western
music, old and new, in 1978, the rusty voice of Willie Nelson rose above all
others, urging, "Mommas, Don't Let Your Babies Grow Up to Be
Cowboys."

In 1991, Billy Crystal, a stand-up comic from the Catskills, ignored
Nelson's advice and tried his hand at cow-punching stardom. In his film
City Slickers, Crystal teamed with old-time western star Jack Palance to
warn young American males that unless they literally plunged back into a
nineteenth-century cattle drive and learned "to be men," modern society
threatened to emasculate them. In technology and sophistication, the nation
had surpassed that nineteenth-century West, but American men needed to
cherish the skills, the simplicity, the honesty, and the bravery—the maleness of its day. The grandeur of the scenery, the swelling music, the cowboy
plot complete with self-reliance, heroism, and honesty, and the gentle,
unchallenging women convinced viewers that two weeks in the West
rearranged the values of these overpampered New York executives. *City
Slickers* broke records at the box office, and Jack Palance won an Oscar for
his role as the tough cowboy who snarled, "We are a dying breed."

In all these ventures, from the nineteenth through the twentieth century,
the West meant something special to American consumers. From wilderness
tales to splashy television productions, a substantial group of Americans
derived national meaning from western expansion, and the experience
touched the country's collective spirit. Although the fadlike aspects of western commercialism ebbed from time to time, the affection these Americans
harbored for the West never totally died. In general, many Americans displayed remarkable consistency in their willingness to buy into the western
myth in almost any form. Clearly, through mass marketing and commercial
exploitation, powerful elements in western popular culture escaped the confines of region and embraced the nation. Yet, nagging problems linger about
this bonding of national myth with commercial enterprise. Elements—some
of them not especially edifying—lurk in the background of this apparent
success story.

Essentially, across the span of the nation, many Americans—young and
old, men and women—indulged their western fantasies so completely that
they tolerated and encouraged misrepresentations of history. As a result,
America saddled itself with a popular culture organized around problematic
expressions of race, class, and gender. Yet, western popular culture persists
in its suggestion that Americans shared a commonality of experience.

Profound contradictions mark the popular culture of the West, but there
is no reason to assume that these cultural markers are permanently defined.
Smug assumptions that the West is an easy place to understand have been
proven wrong before. Revisionist thinking will continue, since the changing
configurations of western history beckon to each new generation. Not just
white Americans but also the sons and daughters of many cultures will have
the opportunity, should they choose, to recast the symbols of the legacy of
the West. After all, the images of the West belong to everyone, despite

efforts, in both the past and the present, to kidnap them for only a select audience. If anything, the West gave all people a historical arena in which to imagine the opportunity and justice that define America's most positive national values. Although the formula for the popular story of the West often fell short of accuracy, the essentials empower those who demand a reinterpretation of the people and events. Those people, and there are many around the world, feel a sense of kinship with the place and purpose of the West. They can still reclaim its justice, its opportunity, its identity, and its spirit and rework western popular culture into larger, more attractive, more generous patterns. The American West deserves the effort, and who is to say that such a transformation will not happen?

Y *FURTHER READING*

Robert G. Athearn, *The Mythic West in Twentieth-Century America* (1986)

Susan Armitage, "Women and Men in Western History: A Stereoptical Vision," *Western Historical Quarterly,* 16 (1985), 381–95

Gretchen M. Bataille and Charles L.P. Silet, eds., *The Pretend Indians: Images of Native Americans in the Movies* (1980)

Ray Allen Billington, *Land of Savagery, Land of Promises: The European Image of the American Frontier* (1981)

Patricia Janis Broder, *The American West: The Modern Vision* (1984)

Jenni Calder, *There Must Be a Lone Ranger: The American West in Film and in Reality* (1975)

John G. Cawelti, *The Six-Gun Mystique* (1984)

Ronald L. Davis, *John Ford: Hollywood's Old Master* (1995)

Richard Etulain, *The Popular Western: Essays toward a Definition* (1974)

Ann Fabian, "History for the Masses: Commercializing the Western Past" in *Under an Open Sky: Rethinking America's Western Past,* eds., William Cronon, George Miles, and Jay Gitlin (1992)

Philip French, *Westerns: Aspects of a Movie Genre* (1974)

Edwin Fussell, *Frontier American Literature and the American West* (1965)

Dawn Glanz, *How the West Was Drawn: American Art and the Settling of the Frontier* (1982)

William H. Goetzmann and William N. Goetzmann, *The West of the Imagination* (1986)

Peter B. Hales, *William Henry Jackson and the Transformation of the American Landscape* (1988)

Paul Andrew Hutton, "Correct in Every Detail: General Custer in Hollywood," *Montana: The Magazine of Western History,* 41 (Winter 1991), 29–57

———, "Showdown at the Hollywood Corral: Wyatt Earp and the Movies," *Montana: The Magazine of Western History,* 45 (Summer 1995), 2–31

Anne Farrar Hyde, *An American Vision: Far Western Landscape and National Culture, 1820–1920* (1990)

Michael L. Johnson, *New Westers: The West in Contemporary American Culture* (1996)

Daryl Jones, *The Dime Novel Western* (1978)

Annette Kolodny, *The Land Before Her: Fantasy and Experience of the American Frontiers, 1630–1860* (1984)

John H. Lenihan, *Showdown: Confronting Modern America in the Western Film* (1980)

Michael A. Lofaro and Joe Cummings, *Crockett at Two Hundred: New Perspectives on the Man and the Myth* (1989)

Thomas J. Lyon, et al., eds., *A Literary History of the American West* (1987)

John R. Milton, *The Novel of the American West* (1980)

Rita Parks, *The Western Hero in Film and Television: Mass Media Mythology* (1982)

Earl Pomeroy, *In Search of the Golden West: The Tourist in Western America* (1957)

Jules Prown, et al., *Discovered Lands, Invented Pasts: Transforming Visions of the American West* (1992)

Cecil Robinson, *Mexico and the Hispanic Southwest in American Literature* (1977)

Don Russell, *The Lives and Lessons of Buffalo Bill* (1988)

Paul Seydor, *Peckinpah: The Western Films* (1980)

Henry Nash Smith, *Virgin Land: The American West as Symbol and Myth* (1950)

C. L. Sonnichsen, *From Hopalong to Hud: Thoughts on Western Fiction* (1978)

Kent Ladd Steckmesser, *The Western Hero in History and Legend* (1965)

William H. Truettner, ed., *The West as America: Reinterpreting Images of the Frontier, 1820–1920* (1991)

David J. Weber, *Myth and the History of the Hispanic Southwest* (1988)

G. Edward White, *The Eastern Establishment and the Western Experience: The West of Frederick Remington, Theodore Roosevelt, and Owen Wister* (1969)

Will Wright, *Six-guns and Society: A Structural Study of the Western* (1975)